To dear Alan, I thank you for your ... Nas Kak ☺ 8/6/2015

AMERICA'S SACRIFICES IN MYTHOLOGICAL AFGHANISTAN

Not only for America, but the world as well,
to understand not what things look like in my native land,
but what they really are.

NASRAT KAKAR

America's Sacrifices in Mythological Afghanistan

For information about this title or to order other books and/or electronic media, contact the publisher:
www.nasratkakar.com
naskakar@nasratkakar.com

Library of Congress Control Number: 2015901934

ISBN: 978-0-9862636-8-2 (Print)
          978-0-9862636-6-8 (eBook)

Printed in the United States of America

Cover and Interior design: 1106 Design

Acknowledgements

S INCERE APPRECIATION, not only to each and every one of the brave men and women of the United States military with whom I had the honor to serve as a civilian in Afghanistan, my native land, but to those who have served our great nation throughout America's history, not only to protect us, but to be a force of goodness for the world's well-being. Words in books will never be enough to describe what our brave men and women go through during deployment, especially those in combat who fight the enemy on the frontline. My special heartfelt appreciation goes out as well to all of the ODA (Special Forces) team members in the Ghazni Province of Afghanistan, as well as to those infantry soldiers in Yahya Khel and Sarkari Bagh who tirelessly fought the "bad guys" without fear.

A special thank you to Anita and Leo Scott, whose help throughout the process of my writing this book was invaluable. And, last but not least, for being in the right place at the right time by running into dear friends and neighbors who recommended and introduced me to Sharon Young, my copyeditor, who I not only trusted throughout this entire project but, most especially, for her ability to understand me, thus making it possible to tell my story and better enable my readers to also understand not only the sacrifices of our soldiers, but the truth about my native land.

Contents

Dedication

*To my beloved wife, Laila, and
my two beautiful children,
Omar and Sabrina…
thank you all for your love, encouragement, and support.*

Introduction

As a proud American, not only do I owe my fellow Americans the truth about Afghanistan and the sacrifice America has made in my native land, most importantly I want to let the Afghan people, and the world in general, know what it really means to be an Afghan or a native of the country called Afghanistan.

My deployment to Afghanistan from the spring of 2009 to the winter of 2012 was like no other experience I have ever had, especially since I survived and came out of it alive to tell you all not to make the same mistakes others have made in Afghanistan in the past. Working with the brave men and women of the United States military of my 33 months in the war on terror have made me a stronger person, thus enabling me to tell you what I experienced and witnessed, but also heard from both the American military personnel on the frontline, as well as the local Afghan villagers whose homes we raided.

I had a firsthand look at every aspect discussed in this book and am honored to have been able to serve with every branch of the United States military, as well as the civilian agencies of the State Department, CIA, and FBI. Unless I wasn't fit for it physically or seriously disagreed with their personal behavior, I enjoyed working with every single unit to which I was assigned.

I enjoyed going on dismounted missions, whether they involved combat, humanitarianism, Afghan government compounds, or simply foot patrolling the villages so we could pinpoint the enemy's locations. These missions provided me with the only way to stay in contact with the local villagers with whom I not only wanted to talk, understand, and help, but to do the same with most of my military buddies. In addition to more than hundreds of missions, I had also been involved in more than 350 interrogations of Pashton detainees (the only natives we ever interrogated), which gave me a broader sense of perspective to understand my native tribes. Most importantly, these missions provided me with what I needed to do for 18 months during my deployment to not only Kandahar and the Arghandab District, the most dangerous section in all of Afghanistan, but also to experience the miracle of going on a mission to my adoptive parents' home 40 years later.

My wide-range of experience and eyewitness events included not only working with the military personnel of the Special Forces on the front line, covering the Provinces of Ghazni, Logar, Wardak, Paktia, Urozgan, Dehkondi, and Zabul, but also the detention center in Kowst Province, dismounted missions with infantry soldiers in Paktika Province, volunteering with the Marines in Helmand Province, the battlefield surveillance brigade in Kandahar Province, Navy Cyber on the P3 Aircraft over the entirety of the Afghan airspace, and my final 3x5 cubical assignment at the AROCC at Bagram Airfield, Parwan Province, but also working with personal of ANA (Afghan National Army), ANP (Afghan National Police), NDS (National Defense Service), governors, Sub-governors, prosecutors, local linguists, and day laborers who worked for the Americans.

My wife, Laila, a Tajik from Kabul, and I have been married for more than 30 years. As a Pashton, living in America for over 35 years has helped me to equally understand both of my adopted cultures (American and Tajik), as well as to speak, understand, read, and write all three languages (Pastho, English, and Farsi). Having left Afghanistan at the age of 16, and then going back as an American 30 years later, even I, a native of Afghanistan, had found myself blindsided that *there really is no Afghanistan*.

I am writing this book not only for America and the world to recognize the sacrifices made by our brave men and women of the United States military in Afghanistan but also to give the Afghan people an opportunity to have freedom and prosperity, and for the West to understand the people of Afghanistan who don't even understand themselves why they are being called as Afghans. For security reasons, the names of all U.S. military personnel have been changed.

About the Author

My name is Nasrat Kakar. I am a native Afghan—more specifically, Pashton. Being a victim of circumstance from birth until that horrible Tuesday, September 11, 2001, I am sharing a tiny bit of history regarding my personal life, which is similar to the history of my native land and its people. I finally found an identity for myself, which enables me not only to respect and understand myself better, but also those around me. I have lived in the U.S. since January 1979. The details of my birth are unclear but according to my biological mother, I was born during the winter season in Kandahar City, Afghanistan, which is all she could remember to tell me the last time I asked. Since there were no birth records kept in Afghanistan, I will never know the actual date of my birth. Since my biological parents had failed to do so, I never thought I'd have to be the one who would be responsible for creating my own birthdate. According to my own estimate, I determined that I was born during the winter of 1963–64.

Like many other wealthy people in Afghanistan, my grandfather had 14 children—my father was the eighth of 11 boys. Since my wealthy grandfather provided for his children, they didn't have to work for the government. Between the late 1950s and 1970s, my father and most of my uncles immigrated to either England or the United States. Those of my family members, including my father, that moved to the West while I was growing up, did so to get away from being sent to the then-Afghan National Army in which none of the wealthy ever had to serve. I never saw my father around to care for my mother and their three children, including me. I was the middle child who was adopted at the age of six months by one of my father's cousins who lived in the Arghandab District, located west of Kandahar City. I spent the first six years of my life with my dear adoptive parents. I did not realize what real love, caring, and nurturing was until I returned to the city at the age of six to my biological family's abuse and neglect.

Upon my arrival in the city from the village, I learned that my biological father had already left Afghanistan for the United States, leaving us behind for others to take care of; I believe that who and what I am today is the result of the loving care of my adoptive parents.

Since I was only six years old at the time, returning to Kandahar City from a very conservative, rural Arghandab District to live with my biological family was an absolute nightmare. My adoptive mom was never supportive of my adoptive dad taking me back to the city to my biological family, but he did it for one reason and one reason only: so that I could be enrolled in school in the city, since there was no reliable school in the village where we lived. My adoptive dad was a part-time teacher. As such, he was very much involved in the building of a school in his village. Since there was no government funding available, he used his own money to fund the project because of his passion for teaching others.

During that same period of time, the Afghan government built Sarkari Bagh (government orchard), a getaway resort, in our backyard, on top of the hill overlooking the Arghandab River. There were lush green pomegranate orchards on both sides of the river, where Afghan government officials visited during the summer at the expense of the hard-working people in the village, like my dad.

For the next 10 years I lived the life of a slave to my biological family while also attending school in Kandahar City.

My adoptive dad raised me to be a good human being; he cared for me when I needed it the most, and because education was very important to him, he desperately wanted me to be educated. For the 10 years I lived in the city attending school, my dad requested my biological family to allow me to visit him and my adoptive mom during the summer recess. But, instead of the whole summer, my biological family would only let me visit them for a month each year. Still, for me, a month was better than nothing. In that 10-year period when I visited my adoptive parents, never once did I want to go back to my biological family. At the beginning, it was difficult to try to assimilate myself to my biological, "new" family. However, as time passed, I learned to cope with the reality by taking the advice of my adoptive parents to do everything I was told to do in order to avoid physical abuse from my biological family. But, despite my best efforts, no matter what I did to try to please them, it was never enough or right for them, and so the physical abuse continued.

From six to 16 years of age, the 11 months that I spent with my biological family every year were the times that I never wish for any other child to have to endure. I was stuck between the proverbial rock and a hard place. I survived it only because of the single month's visit to my adoptive parents' home in Arghandab. They would guide me by telling me not to disrespect any members of my biological family—no matter what they did to me—even if I was physically abused, which is commonplace in Afghanistan. It's not just that I was used like a slave by my biological family, but I was also bullied and made fun of by classmates at school and around the neighborhood for being, as they would call me, *Saraye,* which in Pashto translates to "indigenous." Or perhaps those who lived in the city labeled me as a person of the dirt and trees. In fact, I agree with them because that's all there was in the village. Regardless, I could tell as a young boy, that life in the village was a more honest place to make a living than it was in the city.

To make matters worse, even the school teachers in the city made fun of me in front of the whole class. Not knowing that I was raised in conservative Arghandab, they called me *Da Kafer zoy* (the son of an infidel). Everyone in the school knew that my biological father had left the Islamic country of Afghanistan for an infidel country—America. Although people in the city were much more secular than those in the rural districts, in conservative Kandahar the common attitude was that anyone who went to America was considered an infidel.

My adoptive parents had a dream for me: to be an educated man one day. They always taught me the value of hard work and how to make an honest living by earning through my own labor and endeavors—a philosophy I have carried with me throughout my life. They also taught me the most important and valuable lessons of my life.

Starting at the age of seven, Dad taught me the lesson of hard work by taking me to his orchard from sunrise to sunset and helping me learn how to pick fruit from the trees. Once a year, he would *ejara* (lease) his entire orchard of about 200 trees of apricots to a wholesaler in the city, who would then bring his day laborers to pick all the fruit from the trees within a seven- or 10-day period of time. Once the wholesaler was done picking all the fruit, Dad would give me a long wooden stick, pick me up, and then carry me on his shoulders to each tree, one by one, to pick the scattered apricots that the wholesaler and his day laborers had left behind. On each tree, I would find an average of 10 to 15 apricots (and sometimes even more) within my reach. As I grew older, I learned how to climb the trees so that Dad didn't have to carry me on his shoulders anymore. And, so it was that at the young age of seven or eight, Dad taught me one of life's most important lessons: what hard work and its rewards were all about.

I recalled one summer, on a very hot July day, when I was given permission by my dad to go to the orchards with my cousin Zahir Shah to pick the apricots on our own. Upon our arrival, I noticed that at one end of the orchard there were about 10 to 15 trees that had not been touched by the wholesaler. My cousin and I went to the fully-loaded trees and picked a bucketful of apricots within a very short period of time, and then went home with big smiles on our faces, fully expecting that when my dad saw us he would be happy that we had picked so many apricots in one day.

Well, from the look on his face—and at my young age, not really knowing right from wrong—I was taught two lessons, both of which have stayed with me to this day. First, the lesson of hard work; second, the lesson of honesty. I learned that Dad had an orchard keeper, Haji Gran, who had a percentage share in the orchard fruit that was sold each year. Since my dad sold his share of the fruit to a wholesaler for one fixed price, Haji Gran sold his share of the 10 to 15 trees by himself, on a daily basis, by taking the fruit to the city and selling it on the street corner for more profit. This made sense if you only had 10 to 15 trees and only one month to sell the fruit before the season ended.

So, after walking into the house with a full bucket of apricots, Dad was not particularly happy to see me because he knew that it was not possible for me to pick a bucketful of apricots in a single day. His facial expression was somewhat angry, but his voice was soft when he asked me where I had gotten all of the apricots. I told him that they had come from the orchard. "From which trees?" he asked. "The trees that were full of apricots," I told him. At that moment, I knew I had done something wrong, and even when I was walking back from the orchard, I was thinking to myself: *Why would there still be trees full of apricots if the wholesaler had already been gone for quite some time already?* My dad got up and told me to pick up the bucket. While holding me by my right ear with a gentle twist, Dad then walked me over three houses behind our house to where Haji Gran lived. (By the way, this gentle twist of the ear is the only physical "abuse" I can remember ever getting from him.) On the way to Haji Gran's house, Dad was telling me that the apricots that I had picked belonged to Haji Gran, and that I was going to return them and tell him that I was sorry for stealing apricots from his trees.

As a young boy, it was difficult for me to say that I had stolen the apricots from Haji Gran without knowing what stealing really meant. I didn't know they were his trees. What I did know is that it was easier for me to go to the trees that were full of apricots than having to climb to the top in order to pick the scattered apricots, which added to the risk of falling down.

No matter what I thought with my young mind, Dad thought I had done the wrong thing by taking other people's property, and so that I learned and understood right from wrong, he wanted me to admit and apologize to Haji Gran for the wrong I had done. Of course, I did exactly what I was told to do. Now I regret that I will never have the chance to thank him for the lessons he taught me. But there will always be other ways to thank him, such as doing things in his honor, raising my own children through what he had done for me, and remembering when he told me, "Don't take it if you didn't earn it, and educate yourself so you can help others."

I worked at the orchard every summer and gave the apricots I picked to Haji Gran, who would then help me sell them for me at the street corner in the city with the request of my dad. Every year, I earned around 400 to 500 Afghanis (which, at the time equaled $12), which would be my personal money for the upcoming school year when I was in the city.

My adoptive mom always told me that since I didn't like going back to my biological family's house because of the way they treated me, I should always do everything they asked of me so that I would not be physically abused. As a woman and loving mom to me and her biological daughter, who is five years older than I, Mom would also always tell me not to bring children into this world (like my biological father had done) if I was not man enough to be there for them when they needed me.

In January of 1979, when I was 16 and halfway into the 10th grade in high school, my biological father (whom I had never met) suddenly arrived from America to take my younger brother and me to the United States. At first, hearing the news that he had arrived was bittersweet. Bitter because I never had the chance to say goodbye to my adoptive parents that I knew I would never see again; and, sweet because I was finally escaping the 10 years of misery living in Kandahar City, not only with my biological family, but everyone in school and around the neighborhood, who had nothing but abuse for me. Because of my biological father's fear of persecution by the Afghan government for leaving Afghanistan, he was not able to come to Kandahar himself, so—with the help of our two uncles—my brother and I traveled to Quetta, a city in southwestern Pakistan, to meet our biological father.

The journey to the United States only added more misery to my life than that I had already experienced living with my biological family for 10 years. For those 10 years in Kandahar City, besides my biological family, I had been bullied and physically abused by people in the city because I was considered a *Saraye* from Arghandab. Now I was in America at the age of 16, being abused by my own biological father, but in a different way—not physically, but financially. Even in America with all of its laws and rules of protection, physical abuse still existed for me—not from my father but from the kids in school and those who often robbed me on the subway while I was living in New York City. I was so eager to go back to my homeland—not to Kandahar—but to the people in Arghandab who had loved me the most.

The Soviets invaded Afghanistan a year after my arrival in America. Within six months, I received the heartbreaking news that my adoptive dad had been taken from his home in a raid by the Soviet-backed communist regime of Babrak Karmal. It was the summer of 1980, and hundreds of other village intellects (like my dad) around the remote villages in Kandahar Province and throughout Afghanistan, had been taken away from their families and never heard from again. God only knows how they had been tortured and killed. According to my adoptive cousin, whom I visited while on deployment to Afghanistan with the U.S military, the Soviets took Dad and one other person from our village in the Arghandab District, because they were both intellects respected by the people in Arghandab. My Dad was conservative in the village. Leaving him there was a threat to the Soviets.

Meanwhile, as this was happening, 7,000 miles away in New York City where I was living at the time, I was dealing with another of my own difficulties: making the transition from my native Kandahar culture, especially those in the Arghandab District, where people still lived in the 14th-century, mud-hut homes lifestyle, to an entirely different and new world of the 20th century in New York City. Things were different and much more difficult to adjust to culturally. In America, I needed to learn a lot more at the age of 16 than I had to in Kandahar at the age of six.

Prior to coming to America, I didn't know anything about Americans, their history, or their language. We were taught nothing in school about America. The only things I knew about the country were: my biological father (again, who I had never met) had lived in America for 11 years prior to my brother's and my arrival; I was called the son of an infidel in my native homeland because my father lived in America; and, in the mid-1970s, I had received a pair of Lee's jeans from my father that had been made in the U.S.A.

Upon our arrival in America, my father told me that he had borrowed $2,000 from one of my uncles for our travel expenses from Afghanistan to America, and I needed to pay my uncle back. In order to help do so, he took me to a donut shop where I worked for the next two years to pay for me and my younger brother's travel expenses. Then he took both of us to a middle school where we were enrolled with absolutely no knowledge of the English language. I left Afghanistan in the middle of the 10th grade and was enrolled in America in junior high in the middle of the eighth grade.

Since the donut shop was owned by one of our neighbors from Kandahar who had immigrated to the United States at approximately the same time my father did, English was not required. From January 1979 until the summer of 1983, all I did was attend school from seven in the morning to three in the afternoon. Then, right after school, I went to work until midnight six days a week to support a family of four with food, utilities, rent, furniture, and clothing, because all the money I earned went to my father.

Work was the only thing I realized my father was very sensitive about; for example, every time I got home from work, I would find him watching two of his favorite TV shows—"Tom and Jerry" and "The Jeffersons." Back in those days, TV didn't have remotes, so, sometimes my father would either call me or my younger brother from the other room just to come into the living room to change the TV channel; and, since there was no cable or an outside antenna to get a clear signal, he would ask me to stay by the TV to move the indoor antenna around the living room until the signal met with his approval. Since I only got six hours of sleep a night, it was very difficult for me to wake up in the morning for school, and even more difficult to get my homework done.

I arrived in America with 16 Afghanis (42 American cents). By the summer of 1983, when I had left home and was on my own, for the four years I lived with my biological father, I earned $200 a week, which ultimately amounted to thousands of dollars over that period of time. But because of my father's abuse and manipulation, I still only had 16 Afghanis, despite my four years of hard work.

By now, I had lived in America for more than four years, had one more year of high school to finish, and had no money in my pocket. Because I was working to support others, school was very difficult for me, so I went to my classes tired, sleeping as much as I could in the classrooms since I had no other time to sleep. I was young and didn't like to go to school, especially since I wasn't getting support from anyone. I wanted to learn, but couldn't because I was bullied most of the time. Since everyone in school knew that I was working full-time, they always asked me for money. To avoid the bullying, I would "pay them off" just to get them off my back. But even after paying them, they would still ask for more. Except for one time, I never stood up to the bullies, in either Kandahar City or New York City. In Kandahar, I took the physical abuse because my mom told me not to disrespect my biological family. In Afghanistan, if your family physically abuses you, it means they love you, and in return you show your respect for them by simply taking the abuse. Outside of my biological home, I was physically abused because I had no father or older brother to protect me, so people took advantage. On the other hand, while in school in New York City, I was bullied for not being able to speak or understand English. During one instance during a lunch break, one of the kids snuck up behind me and poured milk over my head. I got up and punched him in the face. Before I knew what was happening, I was shoved to the floor by more than five other kids. Once beaten, I was taken by cafeteria personnel to Mr. Hirsch's (Dean of Discipline) office. Since I couldn't speak or understand English so I could tell him my side of the story, I was blamed for the fight and given a week's suspension. I can still remember how Mr. Hirsch wagged his finger in my face in an effort to make me understand that I shouldn't hit people, which reminded me of how my adoptive mother told me to listen to my biological family, without the finger wagging, in order for me to avoid not getting hurt physically. Well, there I was, with Mr. Hirsch telling me the same thing. But, since I wasn't able to explain myself, I knew he didn't know the truth about the fight. So, when given the option, I took the physical abuse rather than being suspended from school.

Things seemed to be the same for me, whether moving from Arghandab to Kandahar City, or Kandahar City to New York City. All I wanted to do was go back to my native land, but that wasn't possible; first, because my adoptive dad had been taken away by the Soviets; second, because my biological father in New York was holding my passport; and third, since I had given all of my paychecks to my father, even if I had my passport, I didn't have any money.

It was that same year that I moved out of my father's house and, as noted earlier, met my future wife, a Tajik, whom I fell in love with and wanted to marry. Despite being poor with no money in the bank—and not being able to communicate in Farsi, her native language—I was brave enough (and somehow able) to propose to her. She accepted, but with a couple of conditions: First, we would get married in London, England, where her family had recently moved from Kabul, Afghanistan; and, second, I had to buy a car. So, there we were—a Pashton who couldn't speak the language of his future wife, and a Tajik who couldn't speak the language of her future husband, not to mention how both of our families would react to our decision to try to build a future together. Since I had never received support of any kind from my biological family, I had no one to talk with about marrying a Tajik. Therefore, the burden fell on her to convince her family that she wanted to marry a Pashton.

After our engagement became official, for the next three years until our marriage I had to work even harder to support myself, buy a car, and find my own place to live. Additionally, I had to consider the expenses to go to London for our wedding ceremony. Starting from ground zero, within three years I worked as many hours as I could and saved enough money to buy the car, rent an apartment, buy furniture, and travel to London to get married—all because I loved Laila and wanted to have a family I could take care of and protect—something I never had growing up after the age of six.

We were married at the London central mosque where my father-in-law had made the arrangements. All of the religious marriage procedures were performed by the Imam (Head Mullah of the mosque) in Arabic, which none of us spoke or understood. After the Imam translated the ceremony from Arabic to English, he congratulated us and then said, "As it is the duty of every Muslim, have a lot of children so they can do *jihad* (a word used for people who are fighting the enemy of their religion; in this case, Muslims fighting the infidels) in Afghanistan." As a young man, I wasn't really interested in what the Imam had said to us—whether it was said in Arabic or English—because I had no interest in either language at the time. However, I *was* very much focused on learning Farsi as fluently as I could. But, by watching the homemade video of my wedding many years later, I realize that the Imam's comment meant to have a lot of children so they could fight *jihad* in Afghanistan. I can't help but wonder if the Imam asked every couple who got married to have a lot of children to fight *jihad*, or if he only asked those of Afghan descent.

Now that I was married, life was more challenging than ever before. I wanted to be a good husband and father to my future children, whom I couldn't wait to have and protect. Since the memories of my homeland were more in the back of my mind, I was more focused on starting a family of my own. During the worst period of my life (i.e., from age six to 16) when I was with my biological family and attending school in Kandahar City, I still needed to learn English, although Farsi—my wife's language—was a top priority to me.

After seven years of living in America, my relationship with my father was nonexistent. I was busy getting to know my in-laws, and still didn't know anything about America. However, I was very much focused on getting to know my wife's family more than I was on learning about America. The only thing everyone in the Afghan community knew or thought about America was that it was just another infidel country and had a culture that we Afghans should distance ourselves from and not be part of. My father-in-law, and every other Afghan elder I knew who had children my age, would always tell their children, "We Afghans should work very hard on our American-born children to make sure that they are not persuaded by anyone outside of our Afghan culture to become Americanized." Since I have been involved with both my native Pashton culture and my wife's Tajik culture, I have learned that they're equally in conflict with each other, just as much as they both are with the Western culture. Almost every single time I visited my in-laws' house, my father-in-law would criticize me because I allowed my American-born children to speak to me in English. Oftentimes, my son Omar would hesitate to visit his grandparents because he was criticized for not being able to speak either Pashto or Farsi. In fact, on one occasion, when my son was seven or eight years old, we visited my father's house; when he started to speak Pashto, my son told him, "I don't speak Spanish."

Shortly after my marriage, my in-laws all moved to America from England, not because they liked America, according to my father-in-law, but because their children lived in America. Once they arrived, they always complained about the U.S. and its culture. Whether I visited them or they visited us, they (especially my father-in-law, in his native Farsi) would always say things like, *"Imroz Rossa az Afganistan baraya, saba ma merom."* ("As soon as Afghanistan is free from Soviet occupation, I will leave this country the very next day.")

Well, as of 2013, the Soviets left Afghanistan as of 1989, and all the Afghans who claim to love their country so much are still in America. Despite everything that America has given me, from the very first day of walking into the U.S. consulate's office in Karachi, Pakistan, to get my American passport and receive the goodbye and good luck hug from Elizabeth Bowen (American Consul), until the Tuesday morning of 9/11, it never crossed my mind to take the necessary time to educate myself about the Americans and their history.

I was so preoccupied by the Afghan culture through my own family, my in-laws, and many others in the Afghan community, I was prevented from learning more about the country of which I had chosen to be a citizen. Why would it take 9/11 for me to know more about the America that I had lived in for 22 years prior to that date? Well, before 9/11, all I really knew was that I had lived in America by choice, whether that choice was made for me by my biological father (who brought me into America for his own personal financial gain), or whether it was my own choice to stay in America after leaving his house. Rather than loving the country, I know that falling in love with Laila was the main reason for my decision to stay in America.

Since I and everyone else that I have known—both in my own family and those in the Afghan community in America, who consider themselves to be Afghans—there was no need or reason for me to know what America and its value really were. Even if I had known and understood that I should be an American first (and I can only speak for myself), I could not have done so prior to 9/11 because of my personal ideological thinking of being an Afghan, especially being surrounded by all the others in the Afghan community who think and act like I do.

Yes, I lived in America, but never "found the American" in me until 9/11 changed everything within me. I wish I could say the same for most of the others in the Afghan communities throughout America. I was confused as to why 19 Arabs would fly airplanes into buildings to kill innocent people. I might have been preoccupied by my Afghan culture through the Afghan community, but that didn't prevent me from seeing evil people doing evil things to innocent people. It only made me start to think for myself and realize that I needed to learn more about the U.S. I have traveled to 37 states and have read extensively about the history and culture of America. The more I have seen of this beautiful country, met its people, and read about its history, the more I had fallen in love with America's values and been willing to die, if necessary, in order to defend and protect them.

Thus, this book is written to reveal a series of events that I experienced, especially during my deployment to Afghanistan with the U.S. military between 2009 and 2012. I think it would be fair to say that my belief in God and my equal love for both America and my family helped and directed me in all aspects of my decision making. Otherwise, there are no adequate words to describe or characterize my belief in God.

It never crossed my mind that I would author a book. My inspiration for doing so has been granted through encounters with every branch of the military as well as the civilians (most of whom strongly recommended that I write this book) that I met during my 33 month deployment to Afghanistan. I have nothing but deep respect for each and every man and woman wearing the uniform of the U.S. military, as well as those of our allies, who assist the Afghan people on their path to democracy and prosperity, more than any other human beings I have known in my lifetime. My decision to write this book received strong encouragement, especially in late 2010, from two members of the Australian Federal Police at Kandahar Airfield, which was a very intense time for the massive troop movement to the Arghandab District for the push to liberate Kandahar from the Taliban's oppression. I am proud to say, as an American by choice, that it was an extreme honor for me to have been a part of their team and the mission granted by our blessed nation. Just as I have personally been a victim of circumstances throughout my life, after my deployment to Afghanistan and witnessing everything I saw and heard from all the locals, I have come to the conclusion that approximately two-thirds of the population in Afghanistan are simply victims of circumstance who cannot change situations that are beyond their control, which I can relate to and understand. For two-thirds of the Afghans who have gone through the same hardship for centuries, they, too, need to find their own identities— not only to protect their families but their country as well. But more than anything else, for that to happen, they first need a national identity and long-term help from the international community, which will be beneficial not only for the sake of any nationalism they may choose, but also for the well-being of a safer and more secure society.

In closing this section of my book, I merely want to say that: *A man without the courage to protect his country or family deserves neither.*

PART I

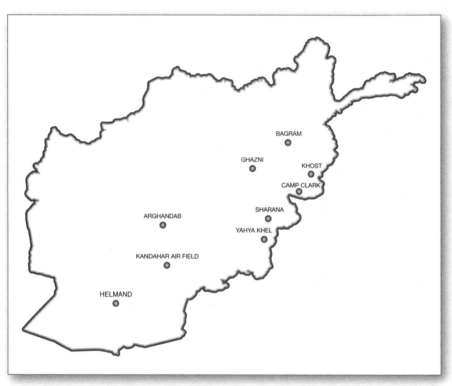

My deployment to Mythological Afghanistan

CHAPTER ONE

Why did it take 9/11 for America to become so strongly inborn in me?

I COULDN'T BELIEVE WHAT I WAS SEEING for the first time in my life. I wasn't sure whether Bravo and Oscar had ever seen such a thing either, as we walked from our location to another to get to the mud hut. We were literally walking through a field of body parts, and in some cases several bodies were still intact. I saw severed heads and limbs everywhere and started taking pictures. This was a good (bad) Hollywood movie scene, but not really one in real life. We walked through the area and found that the mud hut wasn't there any longer. Instead, it was now the remains of the Taliban's body parts covered with a blanket of clay-powder dust from the mud hut. Oscar and I started using our bottles of water to wash the faces of the dead that we would need for mug shots and then fingerprints that we needed in able to accumulate as much evidence as we possibly could to identify the bodies, which will never be erased from my mind. At the same time, I knew one thing for certain: All who were dead were not only the enemies of Afghanistan and America, but of society as well.

I was lying in my daughter Sabrina's bed, just like I did on every other school day morning, when I would walk into her room to wake her up at 6:00 AM for school. I would usually fall back to sleep in her bed while she went to get ready for school. Sabrina would ultimately return to awaken me by asking, "Dad, can you get out of my room now?" (which she usually did every morning when I fell asleep in her bed). However, on Tuesday, 9/11, she didn't do so. Instead, I heard Laila's frightened voice, saying in Farsi, *"Nasrat, Thu bekhey bebey key e padarnalata chey kada. Chey ahl ast da thalvezon!"* ("Nasrat, wake up! Go to the television to see what those bastards did!") While I had no idea what she was talking about, I sensed the fear in her voice as I opened my eyes and looked at her red, sweaty face, her eyes seemingly popping out of their sockets. As I ran downstairs to turn on the television in the family room, Laila had returned to the treadmill in the garage, where she continued to watch everything on her small TV. I sat on the edge of the couch, shocked and confused to see what was happening to the World Trade Center towers, which were burning like two giant cigarettes side by side. I cried when they tumbled down to the ground as the mushroom clouds flowed into the clear skies of lower Manhattan with people screaming and running for their lives. After the collapse of the towers, I felt emptiness inside me. While the morning of 9/11 took the symbol of the towers from me, at the same time, it gave me an opportunity to think for myself about what America really was about.

It all started with a postcard in my mailbox that had originally been addressed to Omar. The postcard was a marketing tool recruiting linguists for a job requiring the ability to speak, read, write, and understand all three languages (English, Pashto, and Farsi) that are spoken in Afghanistan. It also required the willingness to deploy to Afghanistan and be able to obtain a security clearance through the U.S. government.

I am not sure how the company knew where to send their marketing materials to recruit linguists, but I give credit to their marketing strategy for their ability to find the appropriate people. In a country of more than 300 million people, of which the Afghan community is small, I recognize the difficulty involved with recruiting linguists like myself.

The postcard was addressed to Omar, who was not capable of speaking, reading, or writing two of the languages required (Pashto and Farsi). I knew that he was not the appropriate candidate for the job. On his behalf, I took advantage of the opportunity and called the number on the postcard to apply for the job. At the time, I did not know if I was making the right decision or not. My physical capability to perform the job was not my main concern, which was being away from my family for a long period of time—something I had never done before. I knew I was obligated and responsible for the well-being of my beloved family. While I was equally concerned about being away from each one of them, the thought of me being away from Sabrina was unbearable because she is my youngest child. At the time of my deployment, she was only 15 years old and a freshman in high school. The most difficult part for me being deployed to Afghanistan meant that I would not be able to drop her off before or pick her up after school. Since I had been dropping her off at school since she was in kindergarten, it was difficult for me to let go of that, knowing that I wouldn't be there for her.

When compared with the kids her age, I knew that Sabrina was more mature and wise from a very young age, which gave me comfort when we were apart. I have always taught Omar and Sabrina that their education was my main concern. At the same time, I was focused on them being morally upright and honest. The manner in which they were raised was of great importance to me. I have always told them that a person with morals and values is more valuable than a person with education alone; therefore, a person with both values and an education is even better for society as a whole.

Just like most other service members of the United States Armed Forces who have served and are still serving, because of my love for the U.S., at that particular time, I knew that America needed me more than my family did because I knew they were living in one of the greatest nations in the history of the world. With that being said, I was on my way to protect my adoptive nation.

Regardless, Afghanistan is still the birthplace of my ancestors. What better time would there have been to go than this? When else could I go to Afghanistan as a proud American who also had the ability to speak, read, write, and understand all three languages and cultures? I believe that if I had not made the decision to go as a linguist, it would have been a disservice not only to Afghanistan and America, but to society as well, for which I would have carried the burden of moral guilt for the rest of my life.

Omar was in his first year of college studying architecture. I was proud and confident of his ability to succeed in school and life in general because he has always been a responsible young man. I was worried the most about Sabrina because of her age at the time of my deployment. Just like Omar, I trusted her with all my heart and soul and had no doubt that she would succeed in school. Like most parents with moral values, I have also made morality the first brick of their foundation, and education the second. To quote Theodore Roosevelt: *"To educate a man in mind and not morals is to educate a menace to society."*

I am proud to say that I do not make decisions that are not beneficial to society. There were times when I was willing to give my life to save the lives of others, and I can say without a doubt that the same applies to most of the U.S. military because I was a witness to it happening a countless number of times during my tenure in Afghanistan. Regardless of the setbacks, I do not regret my decision. When I responded to the ad on the postcard, Bryan Spencer, the man who I initially talked with, was extremely helpful in the process from day one. He started by taking my Social Security number for a quick background check while at the same time setting up an appointment for me to take the Pashto, Farsi, and English verbal tests over the telephone. Bryan told me that someone would call me within three to four days for that test, which actually took place the very next day. The person who took the verbal test on the phone was very brief. He only asked me three to four questions in Pashto.

I was never asked about the other two languages mentioned on the postcard. I then realized that Pashto was the primary language and, thus, was far more important for one to know in order to qualify for the job.

Despite the oral exam, I know that I did not have any issues with speaking English or Farsi as well. I can speak all three languages fluently. Once I passed the verbal phone test, I was signed up for the writing test in all three languages. I remember going to the location where the test was being given. I was asked for my driver's license and Social Security card, and was not allowed to leave the premises for any reason, other than to use the men's restroom. I was able to complete the test within the ninety minute timeframe. I was told by the examiner that I would be notified of the results by Mr. Spencer, my recruiter. Before I left the facility, I asked the woman who had given me the test, how long it would take for me to get the results. She told me that they were only monitoring the test; once the test was taken, it would then be sent to the company that would be my future employer.

My main concern with passing the test was the Farsi portion. However, I did not have a doubt in my mind regarding the results since all of my schooling in Afghanistan was in the Pashto language, and two-thirds of the population of Afghanistan speak Pashto.

Upon my arrival in America, I knew only my native language. I did not know more than three to five percent of my adoptive languages (English and Farsi). As I still struggled to learn English from Americans, and Farsi from Laila, I strongly believed that if I wanted to be an American, then I should speak the language of the land. Similarly, if I wanted to spend the rest of my life with Laila, then I should speak her language because I chose to be with her just like I wanted to be an American.

Two days after taking the test, I received a call from Mr. Spencer, who told me that there were some problems with my American citizenship, which I never considered would be an issue. My biological father always told me that having an American passport alone was good enough for proof of American citizenship. Therefore, that was the only document I had.

Living in the U.S. for 30 years, since I had never been asked if I had a Naturalization Certificate, I never thought about it one way or the other. When I applied for the linguist job, I had to have the actual Certificate of Citizenship, which I thought would not be an issue; unfortunately, that was not the case.

Since I was under the age of 18 and lived abroad in Afghanistan at the time of becoming an American citizen, because of my father, I was not required to have a Certificate of Naturalization since I was living outside the United States. Instead, I was issued an American passport but only so I could travel to the U.S. Upon our arrival in America, my father should have applied for my Certificate, as he was told to do by the U.S. Embassy in Karachi, according to the Immigration officials when I went to apply for the Certificate before my deployment. Unfortunately, like most other things in my life, this was not a high priority on my father's to-do list.

The issue that Mr. Spencer had was not that I wasn't a citizen, but that I did not have a Certificate of Naturalization. In order for me to have my secret clearance and be deployed to Afghanistan, I was going to have to apply for the hard copy of my Certificate of Naturalization. In May 2008, this would cost me $460 to the USDHS (United States Department of Homeland Security), for which I was issued a receipt.

Although I never received the Certificate, I was allowed to deploy to Afghanistan with a little white receipt indicating that I had paid the fee for my Certificate to the USDHS. Apparently, since the USDHS's system showed that I was a citizen of the United States, all I needed to do was pay the fee to get the Certificate. Not actually having the Certificate itself was no longer an issue.

While I'm not sure if I was the only one carrying a cash register receipt as a document of citizenship to obtain my clearance from the U.S. government, I think there's a distinct possibility that I might have been. In any event, I was finally given the green light from Mr. Spencer to travel to Baltimore, Maryland, for my medical and clearance process before deployment.

One thing has always been very clear to me since I was in high school: I always had a passion for the U.S. military and wanted to serve. In fact, on my 18th birthday the first thing I did was register with Selective Services. I remember going to one of the U.S. Army recruiting offices in Manhattan, New York, but that was as far as I went with the military at that time. The reason I decided against signing up for the Army was that I was given a choice by Laila: either I stay with her or join the military. At the time, I was young and convinced that I was going to lose her if I joined the military, so I stayed with her instead of going into the Army; 28 years later I was faced with the same decision, whether I should stay with Laila or go to Afghanistan and be part of the U.S. mission.

When I was in high school, I really didn't know the meaning of *true* love, whether that love was for Laila or America. All I knew was that I wanted to be in the military regardless of whether I was doing it out of love for America at the time or if I just wanted to be in the military. Now I know that my true love was equal for both America and Laila. In my heart, the more I stay married to Laila, the more I want to be with her, just like any other married couple who truly loves one another. We both have different opinions on certain things, but that does not prevent me from loving her any less as a person. I'm proud to say the same about America.

Baltimore, Maryland: January 15, 2009

I arrived at the Baltimore International Airport and was informed by the company handling the testing, etc., for my ultimate deployment that I was to wait for the shuttle bus, which was my transportation to the hotel where I would be staying for the next two weeks for the training and clearance process. Being away from the east coast for two decades made it difficult to predict how cold it would be, so as it turned out, I was not dressed appropriately. Coming from southern California in mid-January, where the temperatures are usually around 60 degrees, walking out of the terminal—with icy winds and the temperature in the mid-teens—to catch the shuttle was very challenging. Although the wait for the bus was not that long, the freezing winds and snow made the wait extremely unpleasant. The bus finally arrived and after a 20-minute ride, we reached the hotel.

Thinking that I was the only linguist applying for the job was a huge mistake, so walking into the hotel lobby was a bit of a shock. While making my way to the reception desk, I had to walk through a crowd of a number of other linguists, all standing in the lobby staring at me. At first, I thought perhaps what I was seeing was a typical Afghan wedding or a concert where most Afghans usually hang out in the hotel lobby. However, I later realized that was not the case and they were all there for the same reason I was. In fact, some of the linguists had checked into the hotel weeks and months prior to my arrival.

After finally being able to check in, I was told by the desk clerk to report to the meeting room upstairs for my check-in with the company staff for which I would be working. After checking all required documents, the staff gave the four new arrivals, including me, our schedule for the next 14 days. The whole presentation took less than an hour. We were then told to be back the next morning for our writing exam: Pashto to English, Farsi to English, and English to both Pashto and Farsi.

We all showed up the next morning at the same room for the test. On the white board at the front of the room, written with a black marker, in plain English, was the fact that the first part of the test was translating English into Pashto and that we had 90 minutes to finish the test. While reading the test that had to be translated into Pashto, I noticed that the person to my right was constantly coughing. At first, since the weather was very cold, I thought that he had probably caught a cold. I ultimately realized that his coughing was not related to Mother Nature in any way but it was that of a man who was coughing in an effort to get my attention. When I looked at him, he smiled at me and whispered something I could not understand. I continued with the exam, but he continued to interrupt me repeatedly by whispering. Then, I understood that he was trying to ask me if I would move over to the edge of the desk to my right so that he could see my answers. Not only did I refuse to do so, but I moved to my left instead so he would not be able to cheat by looking at my answers.

The next day, the four of us (including the cheater), were on our way to the dentist's office for check-ups. While waiting for our ride, I noticed that the cheater was trying to start a conversation with me. I did everything I could to avoid making eye contact with him, but he was staring at me the entire time we were waiting for the shuttle ride to the dentist's office. It was one of those moments where time felt frozen in place, where 10 minutes went by as if it were forever. Our ride finally arrived, and we all hurried into the shuttle because of the cold.

Choosing to be last, once I got on the shuttle I saw the cheater sitting by a window toward the back. He was waving to me, indicating that he wanted me to sit next to him. I ignored him and moved on to three seats behind him. I continued to try to ignore him, but he just would *not* leave me alone. Confronting me while we were waiting at the dentist's office, he told me that he knew I was a Kandahari (native of Kandahar) as well as an Afghan. I couldn't help but wonder how he knew that I was a native of Kandahar; then I realized that he knew on the first day when we went to the presentation, because all of our names were listed on the board at the front of the room. Since my last name was a common Pashton tribe name, almost everyone from Kandahar is familiar with it, which is why he probably wanted to be close to me in an effort to get all the help he could.

When I asked him what being Kandahari and an Afghan had to do with anything, he said that since we were both Kandahari, we should always stick together and help each other in any way possible. I was confused for a second and then asked him what he meant by us sticking together and helping each other. He responded with, "What kind of Kandahari are you who wouldn't even help his fellow Kandahari with his Pashto exam?" I wasn't prepared for his nonsense and ignorance, but I wanted to tell him why I was not willing to help him cheat on the exam.

I explained that I was not there to help him cheat; it did not matter to me whether he was a Kandahari, New Yorker, or Floridian; and, that I would never allow anyone to cheat from me on any exam. I also told him that I was neither Kandahari nor Afghan, and reminded him that we were both American citizens. The expression on his face was not very pleasant, and the tone of his voice was very angry when he said, "That is impossible!" For a split second, I thought if I had been in Afghanistan at that moment, he would have probably killed me just because I said we were Americans. He continued to repeat himself over and over again that it wasn't possible for me to consider myself an American. I didn't blame my fellow linguist for his ignorance by not understanding the difference between my ethnicity and nationality. Unlike those in America—or any other Western nation who consider themselves as Afghan national—everyone in Afghanistan associates themselves with their tribes rather than with their actual nationalism.

"I could *not* be an American because I am a Kandahari Afghan," he continued, pointing out that I was never going to be able to change that. Just so you know, sometimes I go through a lot to be an American amongst the Afghans, and you will read similar stories—one of them going to the extent that they threatened my life during my deployment. What I said to the cheater was not important to him because, in his mind, I was just like him: Kandahari first and Afghan second, and I, as a fellow Kandahari, was obligated to help him cheat on the exam.

This was just the beginning of my battle with almost every other Afghan I met. The majority would not accept me as an American. However, while I was still in America, I wanted to deal with this one person who had offended my allegiance to the United States. I wanted him to understand the difference between right and wrong, not whether I was an American or Afghan. I knew who I was and told him what I needed to tell him, but was I able to change his way of thinking? I doubt it, but I knew it was the right thing to do: to stand up for what I believed was right.

During our training process, we were given an assortment of pages, one asking for the Province we preferred to be located in once we arrived in Afghanistan. At that time, I had some knowledge about the military and their main objective in Afghanistan, including removing the threats of terrorism not only from Afghanistan but also in defense of America and her allies. Additionally, I was very well-informed about the war on terror around the world in which America was involved, including OEF (Operation Enduring Freedom) in Afghanistan. While I was not certain whether I was prepared for it, that was not my major concern. All I really wanted was to be with those brave Americans who were fighting on the frontline. My main goal was to be with Special Forces, who were fighting the Taliban. Since 90 percent of the Taliban who are Pashton were in the south and east of Afghanistan, I wanted to be part of that fight where I could be of greater assistance. Not only did I want to be a part of the Special Forces to help fight the enemy, I knew that my knowledge of the Pashton culture and language qualified me for the job in the Pashton tribal areas of Afghanistan. I wanted to be where my expertise and abilities could be of the greatest benefit, not only to the military, but also to the Afghan people, which is why I wrote on that page that my first choice was the Special Forces in Kandahar.

Most other linguists—Pashton, Tajik, and Hazara alike—filling out that form requested Kabul, the capital, as their first choice, because there weren't many combat missions there; and Bagram, Afghanistan, their second choice, which was the largest U.S. military airbase, mostly used for logistic and civilian contractors. They chose those two locations to avoid dismounted missions so that their lives would not be threatened. Whereas, I was willing to die for my country, if necessary.

By the end of our two weeks of training in Baltimore, Maryland, those of us who were most qualified for deployment to Afghanistan would be going to Columbus, Georgia, for our gear and other military training. The list of linguists had grown to approximately 16 people. Since we were all recruited from different parts of the U.S., we were given one more chance to return to our homes for a final goodbye to our families and take care of our finances and other personal obligations, or we could just go to Georgia and then be deployed to Afghanistan a week later, after receiving our military gear and training.

I chose to go home with a couple of other linguists while the others went to Georgia. I had a week to be home so I could spend time with my family. In the course of that week, I prepared all of the legal documents required for Laila to use during my absence, and then a week later, I was deployed.

On the day of my departure, I dropped Sabrina off at school that morning and knew that I would not be there for her when she got out of school that afternoon. Laila dropped me off at the airport, and I couldn't help but wonder if I would ever see her and my children again. Was it difficult leaving my family behind for the first time, ever? Yes, it sure was, but the reward of what I would be doing in my native land, my love for America, and my passion for the military was a greater cause than the sadness of being away from my family. I strongly believed that America needed me more than my family did at that particular time; and, knowing what America had given me, my family, and the world—the freedom and liberty that no one else had ever given us—I was ready to go and protect that same American value, no matter the price. Needless to say, it was very difficult to my loved ones, especially when I knew that I had done it once before at a very young age, when I was also much weaker physically and mentally when I was separated from my adoptive mother at the age of six; therefore, I knew I could do it this time as well. Back then, it was the darkest day of my life being taken away from the only person I knew and loved. But this time was different; I was 40 years older than the first time, and was willingly saying goodbye to the family I loved.

Columbus, Georgia: February 9, 2009

I arrived at the CRC (Conus Replacement Center) at the Fort Banning military base for training and to be issued my military gear. Unlike Baltimore, Maryland, this was an Army facility for deployment of soldiers and civilians to either Iraq or Afghanistan. Everyone lived in the base barracks. It was a week-long process, and once finished, we were deployed to Afghanistan via Qatar, which is also in the Middle East. After going through all of our training, vaccinations, first-aid training, and receiving our gear, we were taken off base to a hotel and put on a first-come-first-served waiting list in order to be deployed.

Staying at the hotel was supposed to be a two- to three-day process before our flight to Qatar. But, instead, for some of us it ended up being nine weeks of waiting—and maybe longer for others. When I arrived on February 16, 2009, the hotel had approximately 30 linguists staying there, which grew to be more than 100 by the time I left on April 17, 2009. The reason for the backlog of linguists was because the military didn't need them at that particular time. We were only deployed as required. Those of us who had made it to Columbus, Georgia, were the most likely to be deployed, unless there were issues with their clearances or a linguist changed their mind. The man who had wanted to cheat off me back in Maryland made it to Georgia, but was sent home a week later. I don't know why, but I had to face other linguists whose thoughts were similar in that they never considered themselves Americans nor did they appreciate or value the American way of life. To avoid confrontation, I simply kept my distance from them as much as I could.

Since we were all required to be at the hotel until we were chosen for deployment, we were also required to check-in with the company staff twice a day: once at 9:00 AM and then, for accountability purposes, again at 5:00 PM, Monday through Friday; we were free on the weekends. Additionally, we were all paid a base salary, our hotel rooms were paid for, as were three meals a day. Many of the linguists would not only have breakfast in the lobby where it was served, but they would also take more of it with them to their rooms so they could have it for lunch and/or dinner later.

Of course, this practice didn't please the hotel staff because they would run out of breakfast for their other guests. Despite the safety hazards, some linguists were also cooking in their rooms, which were not designed for home cooking. There wasn't a single morning of briefing from our company staff where there wasn't a linguist who did not do something out of the ordinary. It was more like dealing with kindergarteners than with people undergoing military training.

Every morning, the company's instructor would come in to tell us how to behave (e.g., such issues as: linguists who were drunk the night before and could not show up for the morning briefings, or the site manager bringing in a half-burned towel because of the cooking taking place in a room the night before). In a couple of cases, the police would show up to take a linguist into custody for fighting with the hotel staff or amongst themselves. There were constant complaints. I watched most of these linguists and asked myself why they were acting like children in preschool. Then I realized that most of them had issues with their morals from the start.

I always stayed away from the morning breakfast in the hotel lobby. The only time I was there was when I was required to attend the morning and evening briefings, or obtain any other news of the day that the company representative passed on to us. Since the company paid us for it, I went out for breakfast, lunch, and dinner every day.

On Friday, since we were free for the weekend and there was no briefing again until Monday morning, I would leave the hotel right after the 5:00 PM briefing and walk over to the local car rental place to rent a car for the two-day weekend. From February 23 until April 17, I rented a car from that same place for nine consecutive weeks. With their southern hospitality, the people at the car rental place were extremely nice and helpful; and, when they found out which hotel I was walking from (which was about a mile and a half each way), the manager arranged for me to be picked up and dropped off at the hotel each time I rented a car. To top it off, he even gave me the last weekend of my rental at no charge. When I insisted otherwise, he told me that I earned it by renting from him for eight consecutive weeks. I cannot explain how nice the people in Georgia were to me, especially since I was once told by someone back in the early '80s, when I have lived in New York City, that people in the south were very racist. Well, based on the way I was treated, they were very wrong.

Most of the other linguists complained about everything they encountered from the hotel staff to the company staff, and even the hotel shuttle drivers who were simply driving us from point A to point B. In fact, the hotel was providing shuttle service to the nearest Wal-Mart at no charge. It ran every hour from 8:00 AM to 8:00 PM. The hotel had a sign on the front counter which clearly read that in order to receive free shuttle service to Wal-Mart, the front desk had to be informed an hour prior to departure time.

One night at around 9:00 PM, I came down by elevator to meet the delivery man for a pizza I had ordered. There were two other linguists in their mid-20s who also came down on the elevator with me because, according to their conversation in the elevator, they wanted to go to Wal-Mart to buy more beer. They also talked about calling for a taxi from the front desk. Once we reached the lobby, not only were they drunk, but they were asking the hotel clerk to get them the free shuttle to Wal-Mart around 9:00 PM in the evening. The hotel clerk was attempting to explain the free shuttle service to Wal-Mart to them, even though it was already an hour after the service stopped for the day. While I was waiting for my pizza to arrive, these two linguists were shouting at the clerk, complaining about how racist he was, and how bad the people in Georgia were for not providing them with free shuttle service.

I watched the clerk as he frantically looked for ways to try and help the two linguists by arranging alternative transportation, such as a taxi. But the linguists continued their nonstop shouting and cursing at him in Farsi, *"Shuma, Amrikaya-e-khusmadar-e-beh ghayrat"* ("All you Americans are coward motherfuckers.") I didn't know if they knew the meaning of the words they were shouting at the clerk, but I knew that he had no idea what they were saying. For instance, let's start with the word "coward." I'm reasonably certain that the hotel clerk was not a coward. In fact, he was anything but. In this instance, I would say that a coward is a person who will say things in a language that another person can't possibly understand. The two linguists not only cursed at the clerk but me as well because I considered myself to be an American.

I wondered why one would act in such a way to humiliate another person by calling us American cowards. I decided it was because of moral issues; I had to take a stand against their behavior towards the clerk and me by walking toward the linguist who was doing most of the cursing and simply telling him in English, "So he could understand, if you were man enough, you would've talked with the clerk in English, not in your native Farsi. I understand what you said, which makes *you* the coward."

He told me in Farsi that he was only cursing the American, not the Afghan. When I asked him why he didn't think of me as an American, he said he did so because I was an Afghan and, as such, he didn't understand why I was offended when he cursed the desk clerk. I told him that he was dead wrong in my case and that he should watch his mouth next time he said things about Americans around me. Both linguists left the lobby without further conflict while I continued to wait for my pizza to be delivered.

When he was certain they were gone, the clerk came over to me and asked what I had told the argumentative linguist. I explained that the linguist who did most of the shouting was not man enough to talk with the clerk in English and that, despite his drunken behavior, he was only trying to arrange for some kind of transportation to Wal-Mart but was too inebriated to do so politely. The clerk never asked what the linguist had said but merely explained that he was trying to arrange some kind of transportation for them, but was unable to do so. Since I had been watching and listening to everything that took place, I assured him that I knew he had done everything he could and was not to blame in any way for the linguists' rude and totally unacceptable behavior.

When I ask myself why most Afghans don't consider themselves to be Americans, I remind myself that it starts at home when their parents tell them that no matter what they do or where they go, they will always be Afghans, even though their parents don't really know the definition of what being Afghan is. How can one succeed in a society they reject? Why would one leave a society that they dearly love to adopt a totally different society of their own choice, and then hate everything about it? I, too, was once ignorant about America, and was in the same situation as most other

Afghans still are. Their ethnicity is more important than their nationality, and if you were to disagree with that, you would be labeled a traitor.

While I was in Georgia waiting for my deployment, I read much about America. What a beautiful country! The nine weeks I spent in Columbus, Georgia, gave me an opportunity to see much of the country as I drove through 13 states and the District of Columbia. I drove 12,431 miles and visited 67 cities: from the northeast to Annapolis, Maryland; to the south to Key West, Florida; to the west to San Antonio, Texas; north to Louisville, Kentucky; and everywhere in between—at a cost of only about $3,600, which included the car rental, hotel, food, gas, and a myriad of souvenirs along the way. Not only did I see the America that I had come to love, but I also contributed to the local economy for a price I could never have afforded if I'd lived on the east or west coasts where the cost of living is far more expensive. I was grateful for that opportunity, and thanked God again that I was fortunate enough to be an American.

While staying at the hotel waiting for our deployment, time moved very slowly. New linguists were added to the already long list of people waiting to leave. Some would be sent home from time to time, either for medical reasons, disciplinary actions, or simply because they were too afraid to go to the war zone after all. Slowly but surely, my name was on the list of seven linguists who would ultimately be deployed on April 17, 2009.

Doha, Qatar: April 18, 2009

After a 15-hour flight from Washington, D.C., we arrived at the Doha International Airport around 10:00 PM local time. I had never been in any of the Arab countries. Needless to say, everything felt much different than it did in America. You could sense it just by going through Customs that people were not very happy, despite all the oil wealth that existed in that part of the world. But then, I believe it's not money that makes people happy, but rather one's own personal behavior. We were met with stares and stone-faced greetings. All the Customs officers did was stamp our passports and then we were out of there. I had personally received more friendly greetings from the homeless people in Georgia, Alabama, Mississippi, and Louisiana than I did from the Customs officers in Doha, Qatar.

As soon as we had gone through Customs, we waited to be picked up by my company's representative. We were told to stay in a group so that it would be easy for the representative to find us easily. While waiting, I

needed to use the restroom, When I found it, I didn't see even one uri-
nal. Not only that, but I was greeted with every toilet being unflushed or
clogged, and after trying to flush a couple of them, I wasn't able to unclog
them. Obviously, they were either broken or the water had been shut off
so, because of the odor, I left as quickly as I could.

Our ride finally arrived, and we were en route to our final destination
before being deployed to Afghanistan. After going through a couple of
military checkpoints, we arrived at the United States Air Force base. We
were promptly given a tour of the base by the company's representative.
To familiarize ourselves and use them while we were there, we were also
given a sheet of paper listing all the rules of the facility. We were then
dropped off at the transition tent where we would be staying until we were
deployed to Afghanistan.

The worst part of my deployment to Afghanistan was staying in the
transition tents with 80 other linguists, none of whom appreciated America
and all of whom broke most of the rules that were posted in the tent. It was
apparent to me that most of the linguists thought that the rules didn't apply
to them. Fortunately, my time in Qatar was brief. We were there for only five
days before being deployed on a C130 military cargo plane to Afghanistan.

This base was in the middle of nowhere and it was hot with temperatures well above 100 degrees at the end of April. I did not feel good
immediately after eating my first breakfast; my stomach rejected everything
that I ate that morning. I was always worried about getting sick from the
food, and I wasn't even in Afghanistan yet. I heard a lot of stories from other
linguists about getting sick once they arrived in Afghanistan. But here in
Qatar, I was already getting sick. Concerned about becoming dehydrated
in the searing heat, I drank all the water I could. For the first four days,
I was nauseated and, therefore, worried about arriving ill in Afghanistan.
Luckily, as it turned out, nothing to that extent happened to me, which
provided me with relief for two reasons: First, not knowing the condition
and bacteria level if it happened to me in Afghanistan, it could have had
a much worse effect on my system; and, second, in Qatar, I was on a U.S.
military Air Force base, so medical treatment wasn't going to be a problem
in case my symptoms worsened.

On this leg of my journey, all the other linguists who traveled with
me to Qatar were more moderate and understanding, unlike most of the
linguists who were very extreme in their views regarding America and its

values. Most of them who were with me never criticized America, whether it was out of their own passion for the country or because they knew me from my prior confrontations with other linguists; and, they were simply keeping their opinions to themselves.

In order for anyone to be an American, or any other nationality (perhaps an Afghan, in this case), they must act as either an American or an Afghan (again, in this case) to be regarded as such. It's not important where one is born, and ethnicity should not be associated with nationality. But most Afghans who live in the United States or any other Western country are not allowing themselves to accept and practice being a citizen of that country. Most of them have immigrated to America for the same reasons I did, and they accepted the citizenship by choice for the value that comes with it. I often wonder what would differentiate them from those who still live in Afghanistan and consider themselves as Pashtons, Tajiks, Hazaras, and Uzbeks? Are they, who have lived all their lives in Afghanistan, not considering themselves as what they profess to be? If that's the case, then what would happen to those people who had risked everything that they had to leave Afghanistan to immigrate and live in the West?

Two-thirds of the Afghans who live in Afghanistan—those I consider to be victims of circumstance—speak the language, but most of all, they act like Afghans. For one to be either an Afghan or an American, I believe they should have all of the following: citizenship, the ability to speak the language, be a resident of that country, and most of all, act like one. One without the other will not make them a good citizen.

Early one morning, our company representative notified us that we should be ready for an 11:00 PM pick up to the airfield for our military flight to Afghanistan. Since we lived on the base, the airfield was within walking distance from our tent, but only if we didn't have three duffel bags and our personal belongings. In this case, because we each had three duffel bags filled with military gear that was issued to us at the CRC in Columbus, Georgia, our company representative provided us with a ride to the airfield. I was excited about going to Afghanistan for three reasons: (1) to be with Special Forces; (2) because I knew that I could speak, read, write, and understand English, Pashto, and Farsi; and (3) to be in my native land so I could be part of the bridge that could culturally connect the two countries.

From the very first day when the postcard was received in the mail until I left Afghanistan, 33 months later, my objective was always the same: to help the military defeat the common enemy that America, Afghanistan, and the world faced, by signing up to be with Special Forces; to help my fellow Americans understand the Afghan culture; and to try to volunteer for every mission that America asked of me.

While sitting at the terminal waiting for the C130 military cargo flight to Afghanistan, I realized that in approximately six to seven hours, we'd be in the war zone. Every linguist in our group was talking about and hoping that they were not going to be assigned to combat dismounted missions once we arrived in Afghanistan. If they were, they would simply refuse or resign and return to the States. I understood their fears about going to the war zone, especially those who hadn't even considered ever going on a combat mission. No one wants to go on dangerous missions, including me. But someone has to do it; that someone was going to be me—and I was prepared for the worst.

There were 13 of us on that flight, none of whom wanted to go on missions, except me, which made it obvious that none of the others were willing to die for a cause greater than themselves, which is why God created the U.S. military—all of whom are willing to die for freedom. I was honored to be a part of that calling for our country and the world, in general. And for that, I thank every single member of the U.S. Armed Forces for their bravery, courage, compassion, and sacrifice.

Some linguists refused missions for a number of different reasons; the majority, to avoid the danger that was involved. I signed up for Special Forces in Kandahar because they were always on a mission, which none of the others linguists knew. And none of these linguists knew that I had already signed up to be with Special Forces in Kandahar. They wanted to stay at either Bagram Airfield—the main base for American military operations, and the safest place in Afghanistan to be when compared with other military bases—or they wanted to be in Kabul, which is considered to be the second safest place. Kabul and Bagram are approximately 25 miles apart in the northeast part of the country. Both are the least dangerous of the provinces because of the mass NATO troop presence in both locations. The most dangerous provinces are in the deep south in Kandahar and Helmand; and, in the east and northeast in Paktika, Khost, Ghazni, and Konar.

Kandahar is (and always has been) one of the most dangerous provinces of Afghanistan for foreign invaders. Most linguists were so afraid of Kandahar, that if they were assigned to be there, they would simply resign. I could understand that reasoning for those who weren't natives of Kandahar and would face rejection by the people of Kandahar once they were on the ground as linguists working with the U.S. military. Even the linguists who were natives of Kandahar didn't want to go there because of the danger that came with the territory. But that wasn't the case for me. I *wanted* to be in Kandahar from day one. Because I was a native and knew the culture and language fluently, I was ready, without fear, to help the people of Kandahar.

Around 2:00 AM, our flight departed the American military base in Doha, Qatar, for Bagram, Afghanistan. With approximately 60 passengers, 13 of them being civilians and linguists and the rest American soldiers. The aircraft was unlike any other I had ever flown on before (or since). Most of the aircraft was loaded with cargo and didn't have real seats on which to sit. Not only were the seats missing, but there was no real bathroom, either. We were told to hold the urge to go to the bathroom for the next five hours of the flight.

Just before takeoff, because of the noise, we were all given earplugs. Besides having no real bathroom, there was no covering over the sides of the aircraft, which gave it the appearance of an unfinished house without drywall, leaving interior walls exposed.

Not only was the aircraft noisy, but most of us had our body armor and helmets on for the duration of the flight, which made us even more uncomfortable. Oddly enough, being on this aircraft for the first time, headed to a war zone that happened to be my native land, was very exciting for me. I really couldn't tell whether my excitement was because I was on this particular military aircraft as an American, or if it was that I couldn't wait to be in my native land to help my fellow American soldiers understand my fellow natives. I ultimately determined that it was both.

My arrival on C130 from Doha Qatar. Bagram airfield, Parwan province. April 23, 2009.

CHAPTER TWO

April 23, 2009: Bagram Airfield, Afghanistan

WE ARRIVED AT 7:00 AM LOCAL TIME, and once the backside of the aircraft had been opened, we could all feel the cold (45 degrees) and crisp breeze but could also see that the sun was coming up behind the mountains to the east. Since we were all supposed to come out from the rear of the aircraft, we had to wait until the cargo was unloaded first in order to clear the way for us to disembark. Once we were informed by a crewmember to exit the aircraft, I was looking for someone who could take a picture of my arrival in Afghanistan. At first, I was hesitant to ask anyone. In my lifetime, I have always wanted things more than I have feared them, which is why I can say with great certainty that anyone can have what they want, if they can only overcome their fears. The process of being received in Bagram, Afghanistan, by a company representative was similar to the one we experienced in Doha, Qatar. But, unlike our arrival in Doha, Qatar, at the civilian airport, here we were already on a U.S. military airbase. A visa was not required and there was no Customs to go through. However, the process of accountability was similar, except it was done by U.S. Air Force personnel.

After being checked in by the military, we were briefed right inside the terminal by our company's movement manager ("V"), a straightforward and down-to-earth kinda guy. He introduced himself by saying, "Good morning, ladies and gentlemen. My name is V. Welcome to Afghanistan." He informed us that he was the person in charge of all our movements while we were at Bagram Airfield. To me, his briefing was very informative.

Before he read the rules to us, I could tell that he had read them often and could relate to how he felt and why he got straight to the point by saying, "The rules are very simple to follow, but only if you listen while I'm reading them to you." At first, I thought he was talking to an elementary school audience, but then I realized that most linguists were worse than children of that age, which V undoubtedly knew from experience. I give the company and its staff a lot of credit for their patience with most of the linguists who needed to be babysat rather than taught.

After V read all of the rules to us, we were taken outside to collect our bags. As noted earlier, we all had three military duffle bags packed full of gear, each of which weighed approximately 70 pounds. In addition to that, most of us had personal luggage as well for our civilian clothes. Everything was loaded onto a large truck that was provided by the company, and it was delivered to the transition tent where we all stayed until we were assigned to our military units. Before we were dropped off at the transition tent, V was nice enough to take us all to breakfast before the DFAC (dining facility) closed at 9:00 AM. There are some things in life that you will see or hear and never forget. On this occasion, there were two things that I will always remember when we entered the DFAC: Coming from a civilian life to be with the military was very different, to say the least (e.g., seeing more than 200 soldiers, all with pistols and machineguns was understandably "out of the ordinary" for me. One of the linguists in our group, who was always mocking me for being an American, was also quite impressed. In fact, upon seeing the facility, almost every linguist's jaw dropped because none of us, me included, ever expected that such a facility existed, especially in Afghanistan.

In fact, based on my 30-year-old memories of Afghanistan—to see how it was designed and how much food was available was stunning to all of us. Of course, at the time, we didn't realize that although we were in Afghanistan, we were on a U.S. Air Force base, which meant it was technically like being in America.

The cafeteria had a vast assortment of fruit, pastries, juices, and cereals, plus made-to-order breakfasts by the chefs at the grills. It was like one of those all-you-can-eat buffets on a cruise ship or at any of the casinos in Vegas—except the American taxpayers were paying for a cafeteria located in the middle of a dusty desert within a U.S. Air Force Base surrounded by high-peaked mountains somewhere in Bagram, Afghanistan.

We all went through the facility just to check it out, and I knew beforehand that everything must have come from somewhere other than Afghanistan. Most of the workers at the facility were locals who were just trying to keep everything in order by cleaning tabletops, floors, refilling the fridges, and all the other things that needed to be done. And there I was, holding a tray piled high with fruits and vegetables, looking for the rest of my group. I ultimately noticed they were already sitting at a table next to the buffet, so I walked over and joined them.

We were all happy about everything we had seen during the first couple of hours at Bagram. Despite everything being so Americanized, everyone was pleased. Nonetheless, they all found something negative to complain about, primarily the physical appearance of the local, male Afghans who worked at the facility, most of whom wore their hair long and had long (three- to six-inch) beards, which is normal in the Afghan culture. As native Afghans who had just arrived from the U.S., we were not happy with the way our fellow native Afghans looked physically, and couldn't help but wonder why they were working at the cafeteria in the first place. My point here is, why do the so-called Afghans who live in America, or any of the other Western nations, consider themselves to be Afghans; but, when it comes to the reality of being in Afghanistan, they distance themselves from that same culture.

When I joined them, one of the linguists pointed to my tray (because, as a morning person, I had it loaded with fruit [e.g., pineapple, kiwi, banana, and watermelon) and asked in his native Farsi, *"Agha-E-kakar, deh deh mehway-E-Afghanistan ra?"* ("Mr. Kakar, do you see the quality of the fruits here in Afghanistan?") He was trying to imply that Afghanistan wasn't as bad as people thought it was because, just like any other place, it had a variety of quality fruit. This particular linguist was so ignorant about Afghanistan's agriculture production that he didn't have any knowledge of what farmers in Afghanistan grow and in which seasons. It's just a cultural thing amongst most Afghans who have immigrated to the West to make such a comment, especially when it comes to fruit and seasons, because every Afghan will tell you that Afghanistan has the best. Since I had mostly pineapple and kiwi on my tray, I knew that his claim was based on nothing. I am not a person who is very passive toward other people's baseless statements. I know for a fact that Afghanistan never had fruit such as kiwi and pineapple. I looked him in the eye and asked, "What makes you think that this fruit is grown in Afghanistan?" I thought I knew what his response would be, but his answer was even worse than I had expected when he said, "Well, obviously this fruit is Afghan grown since we're in Afghanistan." At that point, I just wanted to eat my fruit and not say anything further, but I could only do so for 10 to 15 minutes when one of the local Afghan workers who was cleaning the tabletops next to us got involved in a conversation with one of the other linguists. The person cleaning the tabletops had a roll of paper towels in one hand and an empty tray in the other hand, so that when he cleaned the tabletops, he could hold the tray against the edge of the table and then wipe crumbs, etc., from the tabletops onto the tray. In this worker's case, however, I noticed that he wasn't doing it as he was instructed. Instead, he wiped whatever crumbs were on each tabletop onto the floor, holding the tray in his left hand behind his back while talking with one of my fellow linguists.

One member of our group started asking the local Afghan worker about his job at the DFAC. He wanted to know how long he had worked there, and so forth. The worker said that he had worked there four years as of the month before. I heard another linguist ask the worker how he was being treated by the Americans and how much he was paid. The worker said in his native Farsi, *"Amrikayaye-E-khosmadari bay ghayrat, pisay-E-kam metha, magar kar zeyad makhayan."* ("The coward American fuckers make us work hard for less money.") This was not just a statement made by this one local worker about Americans and how they treat Afghans. In the Afghan culture, the word "coward" is used just as much as the word "tea" has been used when offering the beverage to others. Let me clarify what I mean.

Whether you're in Afghanistan or involved in an Afghan community anywhere outside Afghanistan; or, you're visiting someone in their home, office, or just have a chance encounter with them on a street corner, a bus, in the park, or anywhere in between, if you don't offer them tea, you're considered a *bay ghayrat* (coward). I know this is harsh because it goes both ways in that you're a coward if you don't offer and a coward if you accept the offer. So, as we Americans would say, "You're damned if you do, and damned if you don't." Is it because the word coward is used improperly, more often than it should be, and has therefore lost its meaning? Or is it that the word coward might be misinterpreted? I'll let you be the judge of that. I can only say this: If one word can be so complicated in the Afghan culture, imagine the complications involved for Western society to understand the four main ethnic groups (Pashton, Tajik, Hazara, and Uzbek) combined into one group called Afghans, who for the most part don't even understand one another, which is why they're always in conflict even if no one is invading their country. As a native Pashton, I can honestly say that from my experience of being married to a Tajik for 30 years, we still have issues from time to time when it comes to understanding my native Afghans, or vice versa. So, anytime you run into an Afghan, don't forget to offer tea, even if you don't mean it; and, make sure you don't accept it!

It doesn't matter how much the Americans, or the world for that matter, have done and can do for most Afghans who work for the Americans because it will never be enough. Now, before I said anything to the local regarding the Americans' treatment of the Afghans, I questioned the cafeteria worker first to make a point to my other fellow linguists regarding the argument over the fruit issue I had with the one specific fellow linguist. Again, knowing where the fruit was coming from, I specifically asked the local worker, "Which part of Afghanistan does all of the fruit and vegetables at the cafeteria come from?" Of course, the linguist who had raised this issue listened closely to the worker's response.

With a smirk on his face, as if I was out of my mind to ask such a question, the worker responded, "You know, if Afghanistan already has quality fruit like this, why would they import it from America?" The local Afghan had answered my question perfectly, especially since the linguist who had lived in America for close to 30 years still didn't know what the farmers in his beloved Afghanistan were growing or in which season.

I tried to make eye contact with the linguist after the local worker's response to see if he wanted to say anything else, but he avoided eye contact with me, simply ignoring being part of the conversation any longer. And, even if the linguist responded in any way, my response to the linguist would've been, "The only quality product that Afghanistan is known for is the opium poppy and the Taliban, which are both destructive to society." I had one down and one more point to make to the cafeteria worker regarding what he had said about how the Americans treated the Afghans.

I asked the worker what his job required. He described the process I described earlier about holding the tray at the edge of the table and wiping any crumbs, etc., from the tabletop onto the tray, which is when I pointed out that he was only doing half his job. He said that he didn't care, he just wanted to keep the tables clean however he chose to do so. I asked him if he thought it was fair getting paid for something he didn't do correctly. In a more confrontational tone of voice, he pointed out that he thought I was much too protective of the Americans, reiterated that his job was merely to clean the tables, and he wasn't worried about wiping crumbs onto the floor because cleaning the floor was someone else's job. Well, here is a person who already doesn't like me, and I am about to tell him something else, in which case he won't like me even more. Since I wasn't there to be liked by him, I simply told him the same thing I told the linguist in the hotel lobby back in Columbus, Georgia. First, I asked him if he had ever told his boss what he told us about the Americans not treating him right by making him work harder than he deemed he should.

Rather than answering my question, he sidetracked it by saying, "Every Afghan feels the same way," which I assumed was the approach he was going to use to support his argument. "Just because other people think or say things about the Americans doesn't make it right for him not to do the job he was hired to do correctly," I said. "What did you and your fellow Afghans working at the DFAC do for a living when the Taliban were running your country?" Again, he wouldn't respond to my questions and, in fact, ignored me by walking away. I called out, "If it weren't for America, you wouldn't be here working at the base and getting paid, no matter how little, so you should be thankful to the Americans for giving you a job so you can provide for your family!"

I had pissed off two people in less than an hour since my arrival in Afghanistan—first, a fellow linguist from the U.S. who was a native of Afghanistan; and, the second, a young Afghan who felt justified in doing his job *his* way, specifically knowing that he was doing so incorrectly.

After eating, we returned to the van and were on our way to the transition tent where we would all be staying until given our assignments, which took four weeks. During that four-week period of time, I lived with (and diligently tried to tolerate) a minimum of 80 linguists in the tent at one time, so there were 80 different mindsets, all of which apparently didn't understand the rules that were clearly described to us.

In my mind, I determined it wasn't because they didn't understand the rules—it was that they were not accustomed to having to do so, which is why, however unfortunate, the physical presence of a rules enforcer is required in Afghanistan.

Before we were dropped off at the tent, we were told that we had until the next morning to relax and that we should show up at the company office at 1:00 PM the next day for further briefing. As I was walking to the transition tent, I looked for a place that was as far away from the doorway as possible so that I didn't have to put up with the noise from the flow of traffic that was coming and going out of the tent 24/7. In my diligent search for a desirable location, I saw linguists of various ages (i.e., 19 to 85). They were all American citizens: 70 percent Tajiks, 20 percent Pashtons, and a 10 percent mix of Hazaras and Uzbeks. I finally found an acceptable spot in the middle of the tent, away from both of the two entryways at either side of the tent. I also found a clean cot on which to sleep. I put my three duffle bags, which were each about two-and-a-half feet long, in an upright position alongside the cot to make a wall between it and the one to the right of me.

The person to my right was a young linguist who, at first, I thought seemed to sleep a lot; but I was wrong. Over the next two days, I realized that he slept as much as he could during the day in order to stay awake at night. Most linguists, and especially the young ones, had no regard for others. All they wanted to do was have fun, gossip, and curse about everyone else who wasn't around as much as they were. I simply could *not* sleep at all in this tent. Not only was their constant movement and noise—which included watching movies and listening to music without using their headphones—unbearable, but the tent just happened to be located directly under the runway where F-16s were constantly taking off and landing.

One night around midnight (when I again couldn't sleep because of all the noise), I got up and walked around the tent, turning off all of the lights. Everyone saw me doing this, but no one had the guts to say anything. When all was dark and I had returned to my cot, they started talking in their native Farsi by saying such things as, *"Che qadar yak adam-e-beh nezakat bood!"* ("What a disrespectful man!") Some chose to call me names, while others whispered, "What an asshole." I wasn't afraid to talk back to them, but preferred not to. Since the tent had four fluorescent lights throughout, I got up and turned on the one that was the closest to my cot so they could see me. At that point, all was quiet with everyone just looking at me, wondering what I was going to say or do next. I made it simple by merely saying what I needed to say in Pashto or my adoptive language of Farsi, and then made certain to say it all again loud and clear, in English as I pointed to the sign posted inside the tent for everyone to see.

"It's after midnight, and everyone knows that the quiet hours require lights out with *no* noise from 10:00 PM to 6:00 AM. These rules are clearly posted in this tent. Now, anyone who can't read English, shouldn't be here as a linguist in the first place. But, all of you who can read it but are not obeying it, are assholes for disrespecting the rules of the tent, which have been put in place for everyone to follow and likewise protect for all others who transition through here."

My point was well taken by some in the group. In fact, after I turned off the light, one spoke out in my defense. "It's about time someone with logic took a stand." He, too, was apparently sick and tired of all the noise and the lights being on throughout the night. As it turned out, I had a couple of other linguists come up to me the following day, supporting what I had said in the tent the night before. However, no matter how much I tried to talk to them, the rules were never followed. Since we were in a transition tent, with people coming and going on a daily basis, it wasn't easy (or possible) for me to lecture them when they weren't willing to do anything for others.

As noted earlier, being in this tent for four weeks was the worst part of my deployment to Afghanistan. Don't get me wrong—we all got paid for the hardship by American taxpayers, and I was not complaining about the hardship per se, just that I was not happy being with people who had no regard for the rules or anyone else—and most especially those who were constantly complaining about everything and everyone.

Some of my fellow Americans may not agree with me, but being a native of Afghanistan, knowing the culture of both countries, gave me an advantage over the "native" American or the Western culture's knowledge and understanding of the truth about the Afghans, who are very secretive by nature, even within their own society, from one tribe to another.

For the four weeks that I stayed in the tent at Bagram, I met more than 1,000 Afghan linguists transitioning through the tent—some on more than one occasion. In all that time, I never met one who was happy about anything. For them, it was all about the money, even if that meant getting maximum pay for a minimal amount of work. Unfortunately, the problem in Afghanistan is not an easy task to fix until we know and separate those who *claim* to be Afghans from those who really *are* Afghans.

Just like in Columbus, Georgia, we had to account for our presence to our company representative every day at 9:00 AM and then again at 5:00 PM in front of the tent to make sure that everyone was not only accounted for but were apprised of the information being received from the company's main office. Bagram was the main hub, not only for the U.S. military, but for the linguists as well. Every linguist came through Bagram and was ultimately returned to the States through Bagram. According to one of the managers at the main DFAC, at the peak of the war (May 2009 until the end of 2011), the population of Bagram was 20,000 at any given time.

Most linguists who were older than 50 and had left Afghanistan in the 1980s were very patriotic and proud to be an Afghan, without actually knowing what it meant to be one. In fact, one was with me throughout the entire process: from Baltimore, Maryland; to Bagram, Afghanistan. He loved Afghanistan very much, to the extent that there was not a day that passed where he would not tell me about one of his good memories from the old days when he lived in Afghanistan. I remember him telling me on many occasion when we were in Columbus, Georgia, that he missed Afghanistan so much, once he arrived there, the first thing he would do was kiss the ground. Well, he didn't actually do that; instead, he bent over and touched the ground in the parking lot in front of the tent with four fingers and then kissed those fingers as a gesture of showing his love for Afghanistan. I don't believe that one can be a patriot by simply kissing the ground or the flag of his or her native land. In my mind, they can only be patriotic by contributing to the land and the flag by serving to defend it at all times when the country needs that patriotism the most, something this particular linguist had never done for Afghanistan. Instead, he left the country in the early 1980s in order to avoid defending it from the Soviet's invasion.

During our morning accountability meeting on May 12, 2009, my name was called, and I was asked to go to the office sometime that day so I could receive my assignment. *Yes! I am finally out of this place!* I thought to myself, obviously referring to the tent and everyone who had occupied it with me.

After the meeting, I got on the shuttle bus that went around the base, in this case to the west side where our company's headquarters were located. Walking up the stairs to meet the person who was in charge of our assignments was very exciting for me. Just like Mr. V, Roni was a down-to-earth guy who was in charge of all. He showed me to his office and, once we were seated, told me he got me the assignment I had requested with Special Forces. I smiled and thanked him for his efforts in doing so on my behalf. I was then given the assignment letter to read, which Roni explained to me in depth. The letter contained five rules and other distinct pieces of information: (1) my name, gender, and level of clearance, which was Cat II at the time; (2) my primary language, which was Pashto; (3) my blood type, which was A+; (4) the unit that I was assigned to, which was CJSOTF-A (Combined Joint Special Operation Task Force Afghanistan), the location where the unit was located, which was the Province of Ghazni; and, (5) my POC's (point of contact) name and contact information.

I believed that (2) as noted above was the most important of the five because it stated that "The linguist assigned to this contract must have the ability to write and speak in a clear and concise grammar and pronunciation of the specific contract required language." The second important one was (4) that stated: "Duration of assignment not guaranteed. Assignment may change at any time based on the needs of the military." It also stated that "...the refusal of assignment could result in termination of employment." Before I left Roni's office, he shook my hand and told me how happy he was that I got the assignment I wanted. I smiled and looked him in the eye, thanking him for assigning me to Special Forces. Then Roni told me two things that I really took to heart. First, he said that I should always do the right things and never try to play "Rambo." Second, he said that every Special Forces team has an asshole or two, so I should make it a point to limit my contact with those people, making sure that I stayed close to all the other good ones on the team. He also told me that once I arrived at the Special Forces unit, I should ask them who the asshole(s) on their team are so that I could stay away from them. Roni added that whoever I asked would get a big laugh out of the question, primarily because it was coming from a civilian linguist.

The rules were explained to us again (the first time during the two-week training period in Baltimore, Maryland) before we signed our assignment orders. Some of the linguists refused the assignment in Bagram by not even agreeing to go to their assigned units; others simply took the assignment, went to the unit to which they were assigned, and waited it out for as long as they could. But, whenever the unit they were assigned to went on a dismounted mission, the linguist would refuse to go and would be sent back to the company's main office at Bagram, regardless of where in Afghanistan the assigned military unit might have been. This process of linguists going from the main American military base at Bagram Airfield and then being returned to the same airfield would normally take a month, or even longer in some cases, depending on the location of the unit where the linguist had been assigned.

Those of you who are familiar with the military process know exactly what I am talking about, especially those of you who have served in Afghanistan. As they say in the military, 80 percent of the time is used for preparation and traveling; the remaining 20 percent is used for the actual mission itself. Unlike most of the military personal who would usually talk about how to help the local Afghans and kill the bad guys when they went on a mission, the linguists always talked about how to find ways to avoid having to participate in the missions and instead mocked America, the company they worked for, and the locals who they claimed to be helping.

I am proud to say that I never refused an assignment or mission. Once I was given the assignment to be with the unit that I was assigned to, I would volunteer to go on dismounted missions. Throughout my 33-month deployment to Afghanistan, I had been assigned to eight different units in the military; if I was to be pulled out of one unit and put into another, it was either because of the urgency of the mission or my ability of knowing both the Afghan and American cultures, plus all three required languages.

I'm also proud to say that every unit I was assigned to never wanted to let me go when I was pulled out of that unit and sent to another. The commanding officers would try to keep me on their teams, but since the missions always changed, I would be sent where I was needed the most. Sometimes the mission was too dangerous for other linguists to carry, so I would volunteer to go instead. Even though I preferred units that went on dismounted missions, on numerous occasions we "stayed down" for weeks, not doing anything.

Mr. G, the Director of Operations for the company I worked for, reminded me that on one occasion, when I was pulled out of one unit to be assigned to another, when I showed up at his office at Bagram, he had complimented me, by saying, "Man, you're the only linguist who shows up for reassignment as soon as you're at Bagram!" The linguists who were pulled out of other units, or were kicked out for either refusing to go on dismounted missions, would be sent back for reassignment or the linguist would resign and be sent home. In either case, they would not go to Mr. G's office willingly, so they would be sent to the transition tent, where they would stay for as long as possible to avoid being reassigned or sent home.

There are three reasons why linguists would do such a thing: (1) whether they worked or not, as a courtesy of American taxpayers, they got paid just for being in Afghanistan; (2) the longer they stayed in the tent, the more they could avoid being with a military unit and going on missions; and (3) linguists loved to be in the tent with the other linguists that were all "peas in a pod"—willing to get paid without being willing to work.

It's not really that difficult to understand how they got away with not being sent to an assigned unit, because every time they went to the company office for their assignment, once it was given to them, they had to go to the company's ground movement crew who would ask to see the assignment order so they could catch their flight to wherever the military unit was. The ground movement crew would then arrange everything for them. It all depended on which Province was assigned. The ground movement crew's job was to get them from the transition tent to the Airfield which, in most cases, was by military aircraft.

Our company had offices at all of the major military bases in Afghanistan. Unless the unit was somewhere at a remote COP, the company would still arrange the movement to the nearest FOB where the assigned military unit was operating. The movement crew was always very busy at Bagram, because part of what they had to deal with was the mass number of people moving in and out of Bagram—whether they're newly hired, going home for PTO (paid time-off), leaving for medical emergencies, or other reasons. The movement crew used an efficient in-and-out process through the Airfield; however, because they were moving so many people in and out, it's understanding how they could very well lose track of linguists in a normal situation, let alone those who tried to avoid going on a mission by hiding from them.

The movement of soldiers, civilians, and equipment was a 24/7 operation. Once the linguists received their assignment orders, the movement crew arranged for their flight with the military and notified them of what time they were leaving. Everyone had to show up four hours prior to flight departure. Chances were 50/50 whether we'd be able to get on the aircraft or not, and if the latter, we'd make our way back to the tent. When the company movement crew received our assignment, they would make a note of our phone number and call us once they had arranged our flights. Sometimes we could get a flight to the FOB that we were assigned to on the same day, but other times it could take longer than a day or two, and maybe even as long as a week. It all depended on where the military flights were required. For example, if I was scheduled to go to Ghazni where my unit was, I was to show up at the Airfield every day to see if there was a flight available to Ghazni. Whether I made that flight or not depended on whether or not there was room left for a civilian. Understandably, the military always had priority over civilians. We could all be sitting on the aircraft waiting for takeoff, but there could be a last-minute military change to use that same aircraft for a more important mission. Consequently, in this example, the flight to Ghazni would have been cancelled.

In addition to the four-hour timeframe required to be at the Airfield before departure, there was one hour for linguists to be ready at the tent for pick up by our company's movement crew, who (I believe) had the hardest job at the Airfield by having to pick up and drop off linguists day after day. For example, when the movement crew called us to be ready for pick up at 1:00 PM, the linguists who did not want to go to their assignment tried to leave the tent so that when the movement crew showed up, they would not be there; and the movement crew would not wait for them—they would take only the people who there, ready to be picked up. The linguists who avoided going on a mission would keep doing so as long as they possibly could, always blaming their behavior on the ground movement crew for not calling them to be ready for pick up.

On the flight to Ghazni on my first assignment, I had to show up three times at the Airfield before I could get on the flight. The fourth time, I was picked up at the tent at 5:00 AM for arrival at the Airfield at 6:00 AM, with the departure time to Ghazni scheduled to take place at 10:00 AM. The arrival time in Ghazni was never disclosed to us because the aircraft had five other stops, and it was also difficult to predict the arrival time in a war zone, because chances were we might not arrive at our destination at all.

I was very excited when I boarded the military helicopter (a Chinook H-47) that was taking us to Ghazni. Once I got on this particular aircraft, it was kind of scary to see all of the soldiers and civilians onboard who would be flying over a war zone. I had only seen things like this in films, but now I was actually involved with others who were doing the real thing.

After boarding the aircraft, once the crew was ready for departure, the propeller was turned on (and it was noisy as hell), which, when flying over Afghanistan, meant we weren't that far away from hell. Even scarier is that the whole aircraft was shaking, and the whole experience became a lot scarier when the helicopter (with the backside wide open) lifted off the ground. At the time, I was not experienced enough to know that getting on and off of this aircraft while anywhere in Afghanistan (other than Bagram or Kandahar Airfields) was a huge hassle. Nonetheless, while in Afghanistan, I had ultimately been on a Chinook more than a dozen times and regardless of the hassle, I still volunteered for missions where this aircraft was used for our transportation. I always looked at it from the perspective of helping other human beings, so I didn't consider it to be a hassle when using this aircraft, even though it was. Rather, I considered it a reward for me to get on this aircraft by volunteering for each of the missions made available to me. Oftentimes, it's painful doing good things in life, but once you go through the pain, the reward quickly follows the feeling of doing good—a reward that brings you great happiness and, thus, stays with you forever.

I am aware from firsthand knowledge that people who do good things in life are happier. I saw more happy people in the military in Afghanistan than I had seen anywhere else. I also witnessed their goodness, which is why they were probably happier, despite being away from their loved ones. I got so accustomed to getting on and off the Chinook that I ended up flying on it 53 times throughout my deployment, the majority of them on combat missions.

The twin-engine tandem rotors, heavy-lift CH-47 Chinook helicopter is mostly used for transportation of troops, cargo, and other combat or rescue missions throughout Afghanistan. It's used like a bus that leaves Bagram Airfield with troops and cargo needed at different FOBs and COPs to pick up other troops and cargo from those to be brought back to Bagram. Unlike the normal helicopter that we have seen locally here in the U.S., the Chinook is much larger in size and carries more weight than do the regular-size helicopters. Its overall length is about 99 feet with a height of approximately 19 feet. It weighs close to 20,000 pounds when empty. It can carry up to 44 people, cargo and fuel, up to approximately another 20,000 pounds—for a total weight obviously approximating 40,000 pounds at any given time, and it can travel at a speed of 144 MPH, maximum.

While preparing for takeoff, I held onto my seat firmly and watched the five crewmembers prepare for takeoff. The first two crewmembers were in the cockpit going through their checklist while crewmembers three and four were positioned, one on each side of the aircraft, at the window behind the cockpit. They were loading their mini guns with ammunition, turning them toward the outside of the windows. The fifth crewmember was at the tail end of the aircraft that had no door. Instead, it had a loading dock that was lowered to the ground after landing so passengers could exit and the cargo could be unloaded. All the passengers, mostly soldiers and a few civilians (approximately 15 to 20 on each side), sat with their backs against the walls, facing each other. The middle of the aircraft was filled with cargo (e.g., anything from military duffle bags and suitcases that belonged to the people on the aircraft, or any other military equipment that needed to be dropped off at any of the FOBs where the Chinook would be stopping.

For a minute, I thought I was the only one who was holding onto my seat, but as I looked around I realized that wasn't the case because other people who holding onto theirs as well, while others—mostly soldiers—just sat quietly, their headphones in place while they listened to music, leaving no doubt in any of the rest of our minds who was accustomed to the noise.

When the aircraft finally took off, eventually reaching a level of 10-thousand to 15-thousand feet, the noise level got louder and louder, which eventually didn't matter to us because we were able to see everything on the ground below from the huge opening at the rear of the aircraft. Five minutes into the flight, I saw the fifth crewmember sitting at the edge with his legs hanging out through the opening of the loading dock below. I thought it was amazing to see someone who had no fear of falling if turbulence occurred. Meanwhile, there I was, well inside the aircraft surrounded by soldiers, other civilians, and tons of cargo, trying to hold on so as to avoid being sucked out of the aircraft. This soldier's action gave me confidence. His bravery, ability to serve our great nation, and risk-taking attitude helped me in achieving our country's mission in Afghanistan. Comparing this crewmember's position to mine made me comfortable enough to stop clinging to my seat. Instead, I used my hand to pull out my camera to take pictures of this brave and fearless man.

Remember when I said that getting on and off the Chinook was a hassle? Well, it was even more so because the Chinook had to make five stops before it got to Ghazni, my final destination. Since these aircraft are so large and they fly very low, it's very easy to be shot down by the enemy, and especially at remote COPs without landing zones, making it necessary for the pilot to land the aircraft wherever they could find open fields. For security reasons, the challenging part was to get on and off in the least amount of time possible so that the enemy would not have the time they needed to shoot at the aircraft. It had to land, drop us off, and then quickly leave.

Before we boarded, we were told the number of stops this aircraft would be making, and where. Since the only way to get on and off was through the rear of the aircraft, those who boarded last got off first because they sat to the rear and could disembark as soon as the aircraft landed. Once it did, we were all required to load and unload our own belongings in the order of where we were sitting. Of course, this never really worked the way it was supposed to so everything got mixed up after the first or second stop.

Needless to say, had we were been sitting in an orderly fashion, it would have worked accordingly to plan, as long as no one else got on the helicopter. However, almost every stop that we made brought more people with their belonging onto the aircraft to be taken back to Bagram, which would be the last stop for the additional people who got on the aircraft, but they were sitting and blocking the way for the people who were trying to get off at the each stop. After the second stop, everything became chaotic, primarily because of all the military duffle bags, which were essentially identical, making them more difficult for each of us to identify. Nonetheless, we all worked together, especially the military who helped the civilians find their own duffle bags. They wanted to help us get our own bags so that we could get the hell out of that area before we got attacked.

The four stops we made before reaching my destination were small COPs in the remote areas of eastern Afghanistan along the Pakistani border. Even though most of the COPs had American names, it wasn't easy for me recognize them or their cities or provinces. Nonetheless, I considered myself to be quite informed about the geography of Afghanistan, and knew for certain that every stop we made was somewhere in the mountains; and, once we got out of the mountains, I immediately recognized that we were on our way to Ghazni.

Ghazni is an old historic city located at the foot of the mountains on the main highway between Kabul, the capital to the north, and Kandahar, the second largest city to the south. Growing up in Kandahar back in the 1970s, I had traveled with my family between Kandahar and Kabul on this same highway, which was now visible once the Chinook had passed the mountains en route to Ghazni. Returning 30 years later was a miracle to me because I never imagined that I would ever be able to do so again. I was returning as an American, with American soldiers. I couldn't wait to be on the ground so I could see the *real*, authentic Afghan people. This was a dream come true for me, not only to be in my homeland to help the Afghan people, but also to soon be serving with the Army's Special Forces.

Looking at the brave American soldier, on the Chinook from Bagram airfield to Ghazni, May 15, 2009.

On the Chinook waiting for take off at Bagram air base.

CHAPTER THREE

May 16, 2009: FOB, Ghazni, Special Forces (ODA Team-1)

U NLIKE THE PREVIOUS FOUR STOPS that we had made since leaving Bagram, the one in Ghazni was different, primarily because we (two other civilians and I) didn't have to be rushed off the aircraft. We actually landed on a field inside the base in a well-protected area. I couldn't help but notice that Ghazni, when compared to the prior four bases I had seen while en route, looked far better developed.

We removed our bags from the aircraft and sat them on the tarmac. Since this was my first time traveling by Chinook in a war zone, I had no idea how things worked (i.e., where we would be going or who would be picking us up), so while I waited by the aircraft, the other two civilians started moving their belongings closer to the airfield's exit that was about 100 feet beyond the landing zone, which is where one of the crewmembers ordered me to move my bags. Ever mindful of the fact that I could be knocked to the ground by the force of the wind from the aircraft's rotors, I started to move my bags from the tarmac one by one, until I was able to move them far enough away so that the aircraft could take off; however, before doing so, it moved to the opposite side of where we stood for refueling.

We waited at the Airfield to be picked up, all confused by who would be doing so. Since I had no idea how to contact the Special Forces unit or my company representative who was supposed to be picking me up at the Airfield once I had arrived, I asked one of them if he knew who would be picking us up. Since he didn't, he said he would walk to the compound, which was about a mile away from the Airfield, to find out if he could get a vehicle large enough to hold us and our gear, etc.; so, the other civilian and I waited at the Airfield for him to return.

After waiting for about half an hour, the civilian who went to the compound to get a vehicle returned in a white Toyota pickup truck with another person. When they reached us, they exited the truck and started to load baggage and gear into the back of the truck. The man driving the truck asked me if I needed to be dropped off anywhere else on the base.

Even though I still didn't know where I was going and who was meeting me, I told him that I did but didn't know where the Special Forces' compound was, which is where I was supposed to be. He smiled and told me he knew exactly where it was because he was a Special Forces' team member, too.

I started to load my duffle bags and personal belongings into the back of the pickup truck. The Special Forces' team member, whose name was Delta, was very polite and helped me load my belongings in the truck. We were then on our way to the compound where I would be staying for the next seven to eight months.

While driving though the base, all I saw were the Polish military personnel and tanks that looked like they were left over from the Soviet war era when they occupied Afghanistan back in the 1980s. The Special Forces' compound was located on the opposite side of the Airfield.

I was thrilled knowing that a Special Forces soldier had picked me up from the Airfield and taken me into the compound, where I could see and be with the rest of the team. As we drove through the base, into our private compound, I also got to see all of the military vehicles, including the HMMWV (High Mobility Multipurpose Wheeled Vehicle, better known as Humvees), which I had only seen on TV or in the movies. But here I was in the middle of it all, up close and personal, in real life. I looked forward to when I would actually be inside one of the Humvees with other members of the Special Forces.

For me, seeing Special Forces soldiers in real life was a dream come true. Once Delta had stopped the truck inside the compound, we got out and were greeted by the other team members: Bravo, Mitch, and Charlie.

Once the introductions were made, as usual, I had to explain my name. Ever since leaving Afghanistan in the late '70s and growing up in America, people have had a problem pronouncing my name. It wasn't that they didn't know how to pronounce it, but primarily because my biological father had misspelled it when we came to the U.S. Subsequently, throughout my deployment, I used my name with the correct spelling, shortening it from Nasrat to Nas.

After explaining my name, I couldn't wait to ask the magic question Roni had told me to ask: "So, who is the asshole of the team?" Since we had just met and talked for only about 10 minutes, I didn't know if this was the right moment, but since I wanted to get it over with, I simply asked the question, hoping that it would make them laugh. So, since I had spent more time with him than the others, I decided to ask Delta. Once the question had been posed, by looking at the serious look on Bravo's face, I sensed that he wasn't the kind of guy who would laugh at my stupid question. On the other hand, Charlie, who was more than six feet tall, looked around and said it wasn't him. Delta laughed and pointed his finger at Mitch, the shortest of the three, and said, "That would be him," at which point they all laughed, especially since the question was asked by a linguist who has just joined their team.

They helped me take my bags out of the truck, while Bravo helped the other two civilians, who had come with me on the flight from Bagram, to their rooms. Meanwhile, I waited with my bags in front of the office for Bravo to return so he could assign me to the room where I would be staying. While waiting, Delta, Charlie, and Mitch questioned me about why I chose to be with Special Forces, where I lived in the States, and myriad other questions so they could get to know me better.

When Bravo finally returned to take me to my room, before doing so, he took me into the office where our team members would be meeting for mission briefings and where we could find out about any other information that we would need to know when it was passed on by the team leaders.

What I saw didn't look like a "typical" office, since it was for the ODA team members only. There was a lock on the front door that required a code in order to gain access. Obviously, Bravo had the code and punched it so we could get inside. Walking into the office was like walking into an electronic repair shop where you can see dusty TVs, VCRs, and camcorders scattered about waiting to be fixed. However, this office was quite the opposite because all I could see were heavy machineguns, grenade launchers, and ammunition—you name it, it was there. Now I felt as though I was finally in a war zone, which sort of freaked me out for a split second as I briefly wondered what I had gotten myself into. Reality is extremely different from imagining the unknown, which really hit me in the gut as we walked to the back of the room. Well, after seeing all of these weapons in one place, I didn't really have time to think about whether I had made the right decision to be where I was or not.

As I followed Bravo to the back of the office, I saw two other team members sitting at their desks, working on their computers. Bravo turned to face me as he introduced me as the new Cat II terp (Category II Linguist with a top-secret clearance) to the first person, Captain Alfa; and then the second, Ray, the Chief. Both stood to shake my hand and welcome me to the team. I thanked them both, telling them how glad I was to be able to join them. Bravo and I then left the office so he could take me to my room.

Before being shown to my room, Bravo took me on a tour of the compound, showing me where the kitchen, bathroom, gym, and so forth were located. Our compound was within the FOB, but kept separate from everything else. Once the tour was over, Bravo helped me carry my bags to my room, which, except for the dust and a bed, was empty. Apparently, no one had lived in it for quite some time. Bravo told me that the bed had been custom built by a local Afghan carpenter. It was approximately four to five feet high so that team members could store their duffel bags and other possessions under the bed in order to save space for other things. Bravo told me that Charlie would make the necessary arrangements for the rest of the furniture I needed.

I couldn't help but notice how tired Bravo looked or how red his eyes were—much like the other team members I had previously met—because they had gone on a combat mission the night before, which is undoubtedly why all the weapons in the office looked so dusty.

Before Bravo left my room, he told me that later that night we would have some Afghan food for dinner in the kitchen; otherwise, if I wanted to, I could go to the DFAC. Since I didn't knew where the main DFAC was and didn't want to eat any Afghan food for fear of getting sick, Bravo asked one of the other civilians—who was probably working for the CIA or the State Department, since he never wore a military uniform—who had been with me on the flight from Bagram to show me around those parts of the base that I had not yet seen. The civilian said that since he had been to FOB Ghazni once before, he knew where everything was located; Bravo gave him the key to one of the team's vehicles so he could show his linguist and me around the base—including the DFAC—as well as the outside of the compound.

Later that day, while I was trying to dust, Dan, the company's site manager, came to my room. He introduced himself and then asked me if I had yet had a chance to meet my POC (Point of Contact). When I told him I had not and asked who he was, Dan explained that Echo was the person responsible for my point of contact if I ever needed anything while there. Since FOB Ghazni was an 80 percent Polish base, our company didn't have an office on the FOB, so my site manager was at another American base about 50 miles east.

Shortly before dinnertime, Dan asked me if he could show me around the base, but when I told him I had already done so, he insisted that we do it again. I appreciated him taking the time to show me around one more time while at the same time explaining how things worked with linguists from the States who were working with Special Forces. Since it was my first time being in Afghanistan as a linguist, I knew that I could use all the advice I could get. I remember Dan telling me to stay away from the local Afghan linguists (a.k.a.: Cat I Local Terps without a clearance) and not to act as though I was their boss or order them around, which is what most of the other linguists from the States did. Most Afghan linguists, who went there from the States, always used their Americanism as an advantage not to help their fellow, local Afghans. Instead, they would dictate and humiliate them as much as they possibly could. In order for one to have a clearance, they had to be a citizen of the United States. So, when Dan asked me to limit my contact with the local Cat I linguists, I told him I would follow his advice, and then we returned to the compound for dinner.

As Dan and I were walking from the front gate of the compound towards the kitchen, we ran into my POC, who was walking out of the MWR (Morale Welfare Recreation, a family room where soldiers can socialize on their down time). Since I had not yet met him, Dan introduced me to Echo, the individual in charge of all linguists assigned to the team. Almost immediately after being introduced, before welcoming me to the team, Echo told me to never discuss my salary with any of the Cat I linguists, which I already knew I shouldn't do.

We talked a little longer and then went to the kitchen for dinner. The kitchen/dining room area was large and, as such, accommodated the guys who liked to play foosball from time to time. Dan accompanied me around the room, introducing me to everyone on the team, including many whom I had met earlier that day. It was interesting for me to be in a room that was filled with military guys who kill the enemy for a living. I also realized that I had never in my life heard the word *fuck* as much as I did on this one night alone. They, of course, were using the word mixed with laughter versus the way I had always heard it used, mostly when someone was really angry. Under the circumstances, these guys appeared to me to be very happy. I wasn't expecting this type of upbeat attitude or outlook from guys who were on the frontline in Afghanistan, engaged in a war on terror. I didn't sense fear in any of them. Simply put, I was confused and didn't know how to react to their behavior as they discussed their mission from the night before.

Our compound had a front gate. No one from the outside was allowed entry. Those of us who could enter walked on gravel—used primarily because the soil turned into mud when it rained and, by using gravel, the dust was kept to a minimum when it was windy—to our rooms.

For the next week or so, I was starting to get accustomed to things that were new to me, meeting new people and trying to remember all 18 of the team members' names. We also had nine other linguists—local Afghan nationals—who lived on the compound, but not where the Americans were. Instead, they lived in a separate area of the compound. Additionally, there were 32 ANP (Afghan National Police) officers, an integral part of our team, who lived on the compound close to the local linguists. We also had three other local Afghans who came to the compound during the daytime to clean and take care of other issues like plumbing, electricity, and carpentry repairs. It wasn't that we needed these three on a daily basis, but they were required just in case we needed their services.

The following day, Bravo introduced me to the local linguists. One in particular, Jabar, had been with Special Forces for seven years. Since he had seniority over the other eight local linguists, he told me how every linguist followed his orders because he was the manager of all the Afghans on the base, including me. According to Jabar, he was a "big deal," not only in the compound, but also on the entire base. He knew all of the Polish military commanders on the base as well as every local Afghan who had worked on FOB Ghazni. The local Afghans who were hired—whether by the Polish or American military—were hired by Jabar. On FOB Ghazni, we also had a small market area where the local

Afghan merchants brought an assortment of Afghan crafts, clothing, and electronics to sell to the troops. Jabar told me that he owned a couple of electronic stores on the base. If anyone needed any kind of repairs, whether they were part of the American or Polish military, Jabar would provide them with the services required by bringing locals in from the outside. Obviously, Jabar wasn't only a linguist to Special Forces, he was also a maintenance manager, which is why he didn't want other linguists to advance to his position. He made it very clear that anyone who didn't follow his orders wasn't going to be permitted to stay at the base for very long because he knew how to get rid of them.

There was another Afghan local on the base, Qasim, who was initially hired through Jabar as a cook by Captain Alfa. In addition to cooking, Qasim also cleaned the kitchen every morning when he showed up for work. Rice was the only thing he could cook. I introduced myself to him and greeted him with respect. Besides being a fellow Pashton, I could see by his reaction to my greeting that he knew I respected him. Most people in Afghanistan don't respect others for who they are; they only show respect if they are superior to them. I saw Qasim for who he was, not for what he was—a cook—who are the least respected human beings in the Afghan society—who was working for us. If I am going to respect myself, which I do, then I will respect others who have been created by *my* Creator.

I made it clear to Qasim that I was an American and a native of Kandahar who spoke to and respected everyone, regardless of whether they spoke Pashto, Farsi, or English, and I was in Afghanistan to be part of the ODA team who were here to help and protect the Afghan people. He was shocked when I said this. As I looked at him, I knew he didn't like what I had just told him. I turned and walked away as I said in his native Pashto: *"The khudie pa aman, shapah de pa khayer."* ("Goodnight and may God be with you.")

The following morning, I ran into "someone" who attacked me and was even ruder to me than Qasim was the night before. Ultimately, Jimbo—a German Shepard—became my best friend and loved me unconditionally for the rest of my stay in Ghazni. Jimbo was six months old and understood both English and Farsi. Charlie, one of my buddies who stayed across the walkway, came out of his room to save me from Jimbo and calm the dog down. Once that had been accomplished, Charlie and I walked to the kitchen to see if we could get something for breakfast. When we entered the kitchen, we saw Jabar and Qasim, who were drinking tea and eating fresh, flat Afghan bread. Since Qasim and the other three local Afghans who worked on our compound lived off base, they came to work at 8:00 in the morning. While en route, Qasim would stop at a bakery so he could bring fresh baked Afghan bread to his boss, Jabar.

When he saw Charlie and me, Jabar offered us some of the bread. Charlie declined, and I still wasn't ready to take the risk of eating food from the outside. As noted earlier, I'm more of a fruit and vegetable kind of guy, at breakfast and throughout the day. I am very cautious about my cholesterol, which was in the 250 to 280 range when I arrived in Afghanistan. Charlie showed me the boxes filled with dry, fresh, and uncooked food, including fruit and vegetables. I was amazed that most members of the team didn't eat either, most of which was shipped to Ghazni from America. On my tour of the kitchen with Charlie, I especially enjoyed seeing the fruit and vegetable walk-in refrigerator, which didn't hold just any kind of fruit and vegetables, but rather the top of the line, quality products—everything from avocados, strawberries, pineapples, kiwis, and Washington red and green apples, which would last at least a month—all available to us because of the American taxpayers. There were actually three different Connexes (a 20 ft. long x 8 ft. wide container used by the military for almost everything [e.g., refrigeration, bathrooms, living rooms, storage facilities, and everything else they could think of]): one was a refrigerator for fruit and vegetables, one was a freezer for all the meat and other frozen food plus one for all the dry goods. Charlie then took me to another Connex that was full of unassembled furniture for our rooms. He told me that he would ask Jabar to provide me with the furniture I needed for my room.

We returned to the kitchen, and when Charlie asked Jabar to help me with whatever I needed for my room, Jabar's quick response was, "Sure, no problem." Then he looked at me and said in Pashto, *"Sama dah, mazey jagh kawa."* ("Absolutely, just ask.") Except for a bed, since I had no other furniture in my room, it didn't take long for me to tell Jabar what I needed; a desk, chair, refrigerator, and wardrobe. I also wanted to know if he would ask the carpenter to lower my bed, which was about five feet high with no stepladder to climb up to it. Since I had lower back problems, I wanted the carpenter to lower the bed by cutting off its legs at least a couple of feet. Jabar assured Charlie and me that he would take care of everything.

By now, I had met all the members of our team, including the verbally rude Jimbo. Other than Jabar, however, I had not yet met any of the other local Cat I linguists or ANP officers. I was excited to go outside our compound, which was not far from the main highway that connected Afghanistan's two major cities—Kandahar and Kabul.

Until any dismounted missions happened, one morning after breakfast, I didn't have anything to do, so I took a book with me and went to the top of one of the Connexes, in which we lived, and sat watching the traffic on the main highway. I understand why you might ask, "What was there for me to see while sitting on top of the roof just to watch the people and traffic on the road below?" Well, being reunited with the country and the people where I was born, sitting on the roof made it possible for me to remember a myriad of old memories from prior years. So, I just sat there and watched the people doing their thing—some with pushcarts filled with vegetables; others riding in a carriage, which was either pulled by a skinny donkey or a skinny person; watching buses filled with people, the tops overloaded with all kinds of items, from fire logs to sacks of wheat rice, to barrels of gasoline and, in some cases, even cars. I saw people, donkeys,

Unimaginable Afghan way of transporting people and cargo on the bus.

cars, bicycles, motorcycles, trucks, buses, and dogs sharing this same road just as I had 30 years prior, but now it's 10 times more jammed than it used to be. I cried when I saw that nothing, except me, had changed in the past 30 years. I cried tears of joy, not because I was sorry to see that nothing had changed in my homeland, but because I was so filled with gratitude for being an American returning to my homeland in order to help Special Forces. I couldn't help but wonder why nothing had changed in the past 30 years while I was away. Perhaps I might be returning from America, a country well into the 21st century, while my homeland is still in the 13th century. Upon further reflection, I realized that perhaps the Afghans didn't want anything to change.

I took my assignment with Special Forces as seriously as each of the other members did, even if I had to make the ultimate sacrifice. Simply put, I have lived my life as described in the following: Whoever you are and whatever you do, be good at both.

I knew how important my job was. I made sure that anything and everything I did was done correctly. I also knew that any incorrect translations could lead to another human being's sufferings, or perhaps even their death.

By the end of my first week, I had met everyone at the compound, doing as I was told: to stay away from the local linguists as much as I could. However, this wasn't always easy to do because the locals would do anything they could to try to start a conversation with me. I didn't mind if I could have had an informative conversation with them, but that was never the case because their conversations were always one-sided, ultimately turning into a confrontation of some sort, especially if you were younger than they, which wasn't the case with me since I was the oldest among the linguists.

As an example of what I meant by the conversation turning into a confrontation can best be described by my first conversation with one of the linguists, who never used his real name, or at least I didn't know what it was. Everyone called him Haji Saheb (which refers to a Muslim who has been to Mecca for his once-in-a-lifetime pilgrimage). Since this particular linguist was very young and had never been to Mecca, the free title of Haji Saheb had been bestowed upon him to make him happy. He started calling me Haji Saheb as well, out of respect, not only to make me happy but also because I was older than he was.

I can say this with total certainty that if you call any Afghan something with a title attached to their name, or just the title alone, they will respect you more than if you were to call them by their given name. Knowing Afghans, I believe Afghanistan is a country that has close to 50 percent of its population preferring to be called by titled names rather than their given names. The remaining 50 percent was younger than the first half, so they couldn't be called by a titled name because most of the older generation in Afghanistan don't respect those who are younger. Besides religious titles like Haji Saheb, there are other professional titles that Afghans; especially those in the cities, like to use instead of their given names including: *dactar-Saheb* (dear doctor), *engenyar-Saheb* (dear engineer), *profysar-Saheb* (dear professor), *mahandes-Saheb* (dear architect), and *ustad* (mentor). One can find more people with the titles of doctors, engineers, professors, architects, and mentors in Afghanistan than any other place in the world (even though 90 percent of them aren't any of these titles by trade).

In addition to the traditional religious title of Haji Saheb, other titles include, *Mawlawai Saheb, Qari Saheb, Mullah Saheb, Akhundzada Saheb,* and *Mulana Saheb.* When you go to suburban villages where people are more conservative and holier, the use of these titles is more appropriate.

My conversation with Haji Saheb (which means "Dear Haji" in English) was meant for us to get to know each other. Well, I called him Haji Saheb as well so as to make him even happier and out of respect because, even though he was younger, he was the first to call me Haji Saheb instead of my given name.

Since I was older, Haji Saheb allowed me to ask the first questions, so I asked him how long he had been working with Special Forces and how he liked working with the team. His response was positive because he was happy to be working with the current team. I asked his age, his marital status, and also asked him which part of Afghanistan he was from (which, in Afghanistan, is an important topic to bring up because of the pride involved, especially if both people talking are from the same part or the same tribes of Afghanistan). I knew he was a Pashton, but didn't know which tribe or location, except that he wasn't from Kandahar or anywhere from the south. He responded to my questions by telling me that he was 28 years old; was from the city of Jalalabad, which is in eastern Afghanistan, bordering Pakistan on the east; was married with two children; and they all lived with his parents in Kabul.

He asked me similar questions but included a few more than I had asked him. For example, he wanted to know how long I had been away from Afghanistan. I, of course, told him more than 30 years. While he was also very much interested in knowing about the living conditions and life in general in America, there was one question that struck me the most when he asked why I chose to be in Afghanistan and why with Special Forces. He said that most linguists who came from America never wanted to be with Special Forces, or for that matter any other units that went on dismounted combat missions, because of their fear of dying.

I told the young man that as an American, just like everyone else on the ODA team, plain and simple, I was here to help defeat the enemy and help the Afghan people succeed—always the same explanation I told others who asked. But, unlike Qasim, the look on Haji's face was far from the same. In fact, he had his own thoughts and opinions of me and why I wanted to be on the Special Forces team, to the extent that he said what I had just told him wasn't true. When I asked him why, he gave me a two-part answer: First, that I could never be an American; second, that I wasn't really in Afghanistan to help the Afghan people but rather, just like all the other linguists who had come before me, I was only there for the paycheck. I agreed that most of the linguists who work for the Afghan government are primarily concerned about the paycheck. It's natural that money is essential to every human being's way of life, and I would be lying if I wasn't concerned about mine, too. But more importantly, I was concerned about our country's mission just as much as all other Americans in the military. Since most of the Afghans, local or otherwise, were more concerned about their paychecks, they always assumed everyone else felt the same way.

Haji Saheb continued to argue with me, saying that if I really wanted to help the Afghan people, I should've stayed in Afghanistan 30 years ago and fought the Soviets just like his father did. Instead, I left for America like every other linguist from the States, and now I had returned as a linguist just for the money. For the most part, I believed he was right, especially since most of the Afghans *did* leave Afghanistan in the early '80s so as to avoid fighting the Soviets, while others left because of the civil war of the '90s. Those who remained fell under the Taliban's power. To make matters worse, Haji Saheb pointed out that most of the linguists who had come to Afghanistan from America didn't even speak Pashto. I couldn't argue with him about that; in fact, I really didn't want to argue with him at all, because, even though I had explained, he really didn't want to know why I wanted to be with Special Forces in Afghanistan and I wanted to do what I had been told by Dan and Echo—keep my contact with the local Afghans to an absolute minimum, which is what I ultimately did with Haji Saheb. I didn't really care what other people thought of me or what opinion they had pre-formed. I knew who I was, which was all that really mattered to me. I wasn't there to argue with linguists like Haji or any of the other linguists I met. My goal was to protect and defend America, while at the same time helping the Afghans. I was simply mission driven, even if that mission included face-to-face combat.

As time passed, I got to know the team members on a more personal level, but I was still curious and anxious to find out who the team's asshole was. Everyone was so nice and friendly and very appreciative that I was a member of their team. During my first week of time with them, I hadn't yet worked as a linguist; I was just getting acquainted with everyone on the compound, whether they were members of Special Forces or otherwise.

One morning after breakfast, I was sitting and reading at the kitchen table as Qasim started mopping the kitchen floor. Bravo walk in and joined me. When he asked what I was reading, I closed the book and showed him the title on the front: *Benjamin Franklin, an American Life* by Walter Isaacson. When Bravo asked what I thought about the book, I told him that I thought America was a great country because of people like Benjamin Franklin and the other founding fathers who took a stand by doing the right thing, so that America could be the country it is today. Bravo agreed, but since he really wasn't there to discuss books with me, he got to the point by telling me about the morning briefing, which I had never attended since my arrival at the compound—however, he told me that I could start attending the briefings now, which were held every morning at 9:00 AM at the OPS (our main office where the team could pass on information) center. He also explained that the white board on the front door of the OPS center was used to post any messages that the commander wanted to pass on to the other team members. Since the OPS center was right in the middle of the compound, the door with the white board was facing our rooms, so any team member could see it by just stepping outside.

Bravo asked me if I wanted to go on a mission sometime after midnight that night. Naturally, I gave him an enthusiastic affirmative reply, adding that I was indeed ready and couldn't wait to get started. When he asked how long it would take me to be ready if the mission was at 2:00 AM, I told him I could be ready and set to go in 15 minutes. He smiled at my eagerness and told me he'd wake me up around 1:30 AM. He said to make sure that I was wearing my uniform. Since I had not yet been able to wear my military uniform, I asked Bravo if he would mind helping me assemble my gear (body armor). Bravo suggested I ask Charlie to do so since that was his area of expertise. Well, after knocking on his door and looking for Charlie everywhere, unfortunately, he was nowhere to be found. In order for me to be ready for the mission, I needed help from someone on the compound, and immediately thought of Echo. At first, I thought I'd just ask if he knew where I could find Charlie; if not, I was going to ask for his help in assembling my gear. So I went and knocked on Echo's door.

When he opened the door, he was smiling and I noticed that one of his front teeth was missing. He asked me why I needed to find Charlie, and I told him I needed help putting my body armor together. Echo offered to help me later that night. After talking with him, I ran into Bravo again, who told me to get some sleep before getting ready to go on the late-night mission. I noticed throughout the day that each one of the team members was sleeping at some point during the day, which I ultimately learned was the reason I couldn't find Charlie.

I went to the main DFAC for dinner at 7:00 that night and was back at the compound by 8:00 to see everyone moving around, doing their tasks to get ready for the mission later that night. I went to Echo's room just to remind him about my body armor, but he was busy preparing himself for the mission. However, he said he would come to my room when he was finished. Echo had a unique way of preparing for missions. He always had the music playing loud enough in his room that everyone on our compound could hear it, too. I thought his music was a little too loud and crazy, but as time passed, I got accustomed to it.

I went to my room and waited for Echo to show up. When he finally did, since I didn't have the rest of my furniture yet, we sat on the floor and opened all three of my military duffel bags that were full of gear. In order to put the body armor together, there were a lot of pieces involved; and, I didn't know which bag contained the various pieces. Therefore, I dumped the contents of all three bags on the floor so that when Echo asked me for the piece he needed, I could hand it to him. During the process, Echo and I were having a friendly conversation. Sometimes he would ask me a question, which I would answer; then I would ask a question or two of him, and he, too, would answer. I mention this because it was normal for me not to expect anyone to be nice or kind to me, particularly since they were all in the business of killing bad people for a living. During our conversation, I primarily wanted to question him about his experience and the missions he had been on in the past so I could get an idea of what to expect and how to prepare.

We talked and assembled my body armor for about an hour. Once done, Echo said to me, "There you go; it's all ready, so be sure you wear it tonight with the hope that it will save your life." I didn't recall what I was thinking at that moment—perhaps our conversation and, particularly, his answers to my questions that frightened me, especially when he truthfully told me about his experiences in combat. As though sensing what I was thinking, Echo asked me if I was scared. When I confirmed that I was, he told me that my fear was normal and that I should be scared, because we were going out on missions to kill "the real motherfuckers." I appreciated that Echo told me the truth and that it was normal for me to be scared. But when he said we were going out on missions to kill the real motherfuckers, I was no longer fearful. I'd rather be frightened by something a truthful person tells me than one who lies to me. So, I not only trusted Echo, but everyone else on the team on every mission we ultimately went on together.

The next morning when I woke up, I didn't see anyone to ask about the mission. Bravo had not come by my room to wake me so that I could go with the rest of the team. Therefore, I started my normal routine when I had nothing else to do: breakfast first and then reading a book. Needless to say, I was getting bored with all of the idle time I had on my hands. I wanted something—anything—to fill my time while I waited to go on my first mission.

When Bravo joined me, I asked him about what happened last night and why I wasn't awakened so I could go on the mission. He explained that there wasn't room for me because every seat had been taken. He filled me in on what had happened on the mission: None of our team members got hurt, but a couple of the ANP guys were wounded, as well as one of the high-ranking members of the Taliban (Baqi, who was the brother of one the detainees captured during last night's mission), who Oscar, our team interrogator, and I were going to be interrogating after lunch.

Following lunch, Oscar knocked on my door, introduced himself, and then asked me if Bravo talked with me about the interrogation. When I told him Bravo had done so, Oscar proceeded by briefly going over the interrogation procedures and the prisoners' backgrounds. When done, I accompanied Oscar to the holding cell where a detainee was being held. We blindfolded and then took him into the interrogation room, where another team member, Damon, sat waiting outside the interrogation room's door, just in case a bunch of shit happened. All I can remember about this particular detainee was that he was around 45 and crying, which continued for the remaining three days that we interrogated him.

There were two other detainees that Oscar and I interrogated, which I liked doing very much. For me, it was rewarding that I could sit in a room between two other human beings—an American from my adoptive land and an Afghan from my native land, who had no cultural bonds whatsoever—and watch them connect and understand each other's languages and cultures so that they could help each other bridge the gap between the two. Having never been with an interrogator before—and having only seen them on television or in the movies (both of which are *very* different than they are in real life—now here I was, sitting between Oscar and the detainee to make an effort to help them understand each other. In the movies, you can do it over and over again until you get it right. But in real life, you don't have the luxury of doing it over and over again because if I made the mistake of misinterpreting, especially in cultures that are so far apart from one another, not to mention being in a war zone, someone could die.

As a human with feelings, I am embarrassed to admit that sometimes during our interrogations, I couldn't hold myself together, no matter how hard I tried. Tears would fall from my eyes and run down my cheeks. Knowing both cultures very well, I saw how Oscar would treat the detainee with dignity and all the respect that a human being deserves. Oscar never mistreated or disrespected them in any way; but, God forbid, had any of the detainees that we were interrogating been on the opposite side of the table, they would have treated Oscar quite differently.

One day before our next mission, most of the guys on the team were sitting and talking in front of the OPS center. The weather in Ghazni was mild at the end of May, the week of the Memorial Day weekend in 2009. There were six or seven of us sitting around, making fun of Jimbo, who was running around catching the tennis ball that we took turns throwing to the other end of the compound because Jimbo loved catching and bringing it back so he could choose who to give it to next. Believe me, even Jimbo knew who the asshole of the team was, with whom his contact was kept to a minimum. As a matter of fact, Jimbo was the only entertainment that most of the other team members and I had.

One day, as we sat in front of the OPS center, some of the guys started talking about their past missions. Delta joined in and started cracking jokes. He was not only friendly to everyone, but he also had a great sense of humor. As I wrote at the beginning of this chapter, there are some things in life that you will hear or see that will stay with you forever, never to be forgotten, which is why I will never forget one thing Delta said at this gathering. The guys were talking about the mission they had been on four days earlier. As the banter went back and forth, I specifically remember when Delta suddenly disagreed with a couple of the other team members when he said, "Wait a minute, guys! As human beings, I know we're all fucked up; but, as Americans, we are about this much (he held his hand up in front of his face with his index finger almost touching his thumb) less fucked up than everyone else in the world." When Delta said this and held his hand up in front of his face, as an American, I thought to myself that it was very selfless and honest of him to tell the truth about human nature, no matter what it was—American or otherwise.

This was another reason why I loved America and the guys on my team, because the U.S. produces the guys who sacrifice their lives day in and day out for other human beings—guys like Captain Alfa, Chief Ray, Sergeant Bravo, Echo, Delta, Fox, Damon, Oscar, Charlie, Mitch, Jim, Jack, Rick, Paul, Marx, Ricardo, Kent, and Ross—all selflessly contributing to society so as to make America the country that it is. I am deeply honored—and will continue to be until the day I die—to have been a part of their team.

As the days passed, I was getting more and more acquainted with everyone on the team and the more I got to know them, the more I wanted to continue to be a part of the team (even as the oldest person in the group!). The only other person who was close to my age was my buddy, Echo, who was 44, soon to be 45. Everyone else was in their late 20s to late 30s.

Bravo always made sure I got what I needed, including the furniture for my room. He had once asked me if I was ever trained on the use of weapons before coming to Special Forces. When I said I hadn't been trained, much less actually touching any kind of weapon, he was concerned that I was on the team and especially concerned about me going out on combat missions without a weapon. When he asked me if I wanted to be trained on weapons, before saying yes, I first glanced at Charlie and Echo's faces to see what their reactions were to Bravo's offer; both were positive. Needless to say, at that point I was thinking to myself, *Well, hell yeah, that's what I'm talking about! Now I'm going to be just like them!* Bravo said that he had to ask Captain Alfa first to make sure he'd approve me carrying a weapon. Before the Captain would give approval, he asked me if I was certain that I was willing to get the weapon training I needed to so that I could carry a gun on our missions. My answer was a resounding *yes*, said with a smile.

Since it had been recommended and approved that I carry a weapon on our missions, we were now on our way to find Ricardo—who was in charge of all the weapons on our compound—so he could issue me an AK47. Ricardo and I went into one of the Connexes where he had a variety of weapons for me to choose from; I picked the one I liked the most, which was a black, Russian-made automatic that used the longer magazine that carried 39 bullets. (By the way, all of these weapons were confiscated from the bad guys on the battlefield. Almost every one of the linguists and the ANP officers who were part of our team carried one of these weapons. They weren't all Russian-made but included several different kinds: from Pakistani to Egyptian to Chinese.)

After picking up the weapon, we were on our way to the next Connex to pick up empty magazines, an ammunition belt, and a box of ammunition. So far, since my arrival, this was the most exciting part of being with Special Forces.

Ricardo and I walked over to my room so he could teach me the basics of the weapon—everything from taking it apart when it's time to be cleaned to reassembling it once the cleaning had been completed. Ricardo also taught me how to adjust the weapon on its target and how to load the magazines, which were very basic. He then showed me how to put my ammunition belt into my body armor, which turned out to be a no-brainer for me. When I said this to Ricardo, he reminded me of how stupid the local linguists were while he was trying to teach them how to attach their ammunition belt to their body armor. When I asked him if I looked like Jabar, one of the local linguists, he smiled as he said, "Fucking yeah! Aren't you a fucking terp just like all the others?" I thought he was stepping over the line with his assumption that all terps were the same, especially when he went on to say that they were are fucking cowards. They never want to go on missions, but when they're taken anyway, they're fucking hiding behind trees. All I could think of at the time was that Ricardo was just another one of those young ignorant soldiers who said things out of ignorance, which is why I then thought to myself that Ricardo was probably the asshole of the group—the guy I should stay away from and avoid.

At this point, I wanted to stop him, but he continued by saying, "What makes you think that you're any different from all the rest of them?" My answer to him was, "As an American, I see most of the local linguists the very same way you do, which is why I think I'm different from them." I realized that unless Ricardo was asked by our team leaders to do something, he wasn't the kind of guy who would give a fuck about any of the other people in the compound. In his mid-20s, he was in his own little world and much more immature than the rest of the team members. He was notorious for walking around the base half naked, with his shorts hanging over the crack of his butt, which definitely did not mesh with the rest of the team.

After a brief training on the weapon, I attached my ammunition belt into my body armor and filled up the three magazines with ammunition, and then Ricardo and I went to the shooting range. Ricardo wore his protective earplugs and put up a target poster for my first practice lesson. Having never actually held a weapon before, as Ricardo taught me how to hold and shoot it, I was more focused and worried about the consequences of missing the target. Unfortunately, I missed the target with every shot. I was embarrassed that I hadn't hit the target even once with the first magazine of ammunition; with the second, I was just able to hit the poster but not the circle in the middle. However, by the third magazine, I was able to hit the circle around the target—a thrilling experience for me!

Done for the day, I was already feeling the pain and bruise in my right shoulder where the rifle had jerked back, hitting my shoulder each time I pulled the trigger. But, all in all, I thought to myself, *Not bad for a 47-year-old civilian who has never held a gun before!* I was willing to take all the training I could get in order to be prepared for the worst. And while Ricardo might have been the asshole of the team, he knew his job and did it well.

As I was starting to leave the range, Paul was entering. When he saw me, he immediately offered to help train me on how to shoot with his pistol. I gladly accepted. First, he showed me how to hold the pistol. Needless to say, holding the pistol in my hand was much easier than holding the AK47, but then I found that shooting a pistol was much more difficult than shooting the rifle, primarily because the weight of the pistol was so much lighter. Second, when you shoot a pistol, your arm jerks up versus the rifle reflecting back against your shoulder. This had been a good day for me—not only because I had my first training on an AK47, but a pistol as well—while also finding out who the asshole of the team was.

The following day, Echo came to my room to see if I wanted to go to the range for some more shooting practice. "Of course!" I enthusiastically said. Since our team had four ATVs (All-Terrain Vehicles)—all parked in front of the OPS center—that were used by everyone on the team for things that needed to be done around the base, Echo got on one and told me to get on the front. At first, I didn't know what he was talking about until he tapped the area in front of him. Well, that area had enough room where you could put some cargo or equipment that you might want to transport, but I didn't see that there'd be enough room for another passenger. Although it was a tight squeeze, I sat there nonetheless and we were on our way to the shooting range—not the one on the compound, but the main range on the other side of the base where the Polish and American soldiers practiced. This time, however, I was going to get my first lesson using a mini gun that used more powerful and long-range bullets. Since Echo wasn't going to stay, he dropped me off to join the others—including Ricardo, Jack, and Rick, each training other people who were already there practicing.

As was not the case with Ricardo, this time Jack gave me a set of headphones to use as earplugs and told me he was going to train me on the sniper rifle, which was a lot more difficult to use than a pistol and the AK47. The difference between the AK47 and the sniper rifle was that the latter was equipped with a monocular, which was used to look through so you could see the target poster. Once I had located my target through the monocular, it was not easy to miss because it appeared to be closer than it actually was. Nonetheless, I missed most of the shots, but managed to make a couple that actually hit the target, much different than the sniper rifle that required you to lay face down on the ground, with it held firmly against your shoulder to prevent it from moving. Despite holding the rifle against my shoulder and laying on the ground, the impact of the shot still pushed me backward every time I pulled the trigger, so I had a very sore shoulder for more than a week after only two days of training.

I had come to agree with Bravo, Alfa, and everyone else on the team that recommended I be trained on all weapons. While out on combat missions, it made sense that I should carry a weapon so I'd be able to defend myself and others, if necessary.

My training of sniper rifle by our team member Jack.

After our shooting practice on the range in our compound. Left to right: Charlie, Ross, myself, and Alfa. Compound in Ghazni city Afghanistan. June 2009.

One morning, Charlie, whose room was located directly across from mine and who knew that I really wanted to go on a mission, told me after breakfast that the team was going on a mission to downtown Ghazni within the next hour and if I wanted to go, I should be ready by 11:00 AM. I told him I'd be ready and, in fact, was, complete with military uniform and gear—15 minutes after Charlie told me about the mission. Leaving my room, I saw Charlie, Echo, and Damon standing in front of Echo's room, looking at me as I left my room with a big smile plastered across my face. Charlie and Echo were both laughing at how I looked in my brand new uniform. Once the other team members had their uniforms and gear on, Charlie told me I'd look like a sore thumb standing next to them. I didn't understand what Charlie was talking about, so I asked him.

Charlie explained that most of the teams' uniforms were more mixed and matched with military camouflage. The body armor was their own personal gear that each had purchased themselves, which made it look different from the uniform I was wearing. Since he had helped me put it together, Echo also asked me if everything was okay with my body armor. Since I'd never worn it before, I responded, "Yeah, it's great." All I really knew at that moment was that I was very excited to be going out on a mission.

As the three of them continued to stand in front of Echo's room, I went back to my room and grabbed my camera so Charlie could take a picture of me with Echo and Damon.

Since it was getting closer to 11:00 AM, I saw a lot of movement throughout the compound as everyone got ready to go. A number of team members, and the local interpreters were still putting on the last of their gear. The ANP guys were preparing their green Ford Ranger pickup trucks with Ghazni Police logos. As I walked around excitedly while waiting to go out on my first mission, I couldn't help but notice that most of the local interpreters and the ANP were staring at me. Since staring is a norm in the Afghan culture, all I could do was ignore them.

While I was busy looking for the vehicle I should be in, Bravo approached me to ask if I knew which one it was. When I said that I had no idea, he told me which vehicle number was applicable to me. Since I had no clue where the numbers were located on the vehicles, I started examining each other, but still couldn't locate them. Seeing Charlie in one of the Humvees, I walked over to ask him for that information, which

12th century historic minaret in Ghazni City, Afghanistan. From left to right: my buddies with Special Forces, Ross, Mitch, myself, Charlie, and Marx.

he showed me was directly above the taillight on the driver's side of the vehicle. He then told me that the numbers on the larger vehicles—called RGs (Royal Guards)—were located on their front doors.

Three RGs, two Humvees, and three green Ford Rangers with ANP officers were lined up for the mission. The RG leading the convoy had mine rollers (used to detect mines on the road) attached to the front of it. Bravo was in the vehicle that Rick was driving, along with Mitch and one of the local interpreters. Fox was driving the Humvee behind Bravo's; Charlie, the gunner, was standing in the middle of the vehicle; the lower half of his body was inside, the upper half sticking out of the vehicle so he could monitor the mini gun, which is capable of being rotated 360 degrees by the gunner. Captain Alfa was a passenger in the backseat.

Our Humvee was driven by Fox, the only one in our team that had an open back, which allowed room for cargo and three other people, one sitting on each side and the third standing to monitor the second heavy machinegun that was mounted in the back opening where I sat, directly behind Captain Alfa in case he needed me to translate anything.

After Ricardo checked all of the weapons, Echo checked the radios, and Bravo took a head count, we drove out of the compound to the main road. Once on the road, we were then given the okay by the Polish military—who were in charge of the base's main exit and entry—to proceed. Since we were simply meeting with the Afghan government officials' (the Afghan NDS [National Defense Services]) Chief in his office in Ghazni City—this might not have been considered by others to be a "true" combat mission, but in an Afghanistan war zone, every trip of this nature was considered a combat mission.

Driving on the same road I was watching from the rooftop a week earlier gave me goose-bumps because, for me, this was a dream come true. I had my camera out and was taking pictures of almost everything I saw, including such incredible poverty just during the first 10 minutes of the mission. It was so overwhelming just on the small patch of road we had traveled—a dumpsite close to our base where the poor locals dug and looked through the American military's trash with the hope of finding something—anything—of value.

Our convoy seemed to be moving more like a Saint Patrick's Day parade on Fifth Avenue in New York City, with poor, homeless spectators lined up on both sides of the road to watch our huge vehicles passing by. I saw more trash in the first five miles from the compound than I've ever had the misfortune to see before in my life. The closer we got to the center of the city, even more trash could be seen—and the smell from the open sewers was literally overwhelming.

Back in the 1970s when I traveled on this same stretch of road between Kabul and Kandahar, I hardly saw anyone or anything. The population of Afghanistan at that time was around 12 to 13 million (although I'm not really sure who came up with that number). And, even if that was indeed correct at that time, seeing the masses now at 10 times that number made the concept of there now being more than 100 million was overwhelming. My point here is not to argue about what the population of Afghanistan was then or is today, but to wonder why statistics regarding Afghanistan are so wrong from a Western point of view.

Driving through downtown Ghazni was like driving through 12 hundred years of history. I couldn't help but see from the reactions on the faces of the local Afghans lined on both sides of the road, that we looked like aliens from outer space who had landed to take over their town.

We finally reached the NDS headquarters and were allowed by the Afghan police to drive into the compound. Seeing the compound from the outside, it looked like a maximum-security prison with triple layers of barbed wire surrounding it. Once inside the compound, it still looked like a prison, but there no prisoners in sight while we were there. While Captain Alfa and a few of the team members entered the building for the meeting with the NDS Chief, Charlie and I remained in our Humvee in the courtyard, watching the local Afghans perform their normal routines throughout the afternoon.

As we were sitting in our vehicle and monitoring the movement of the local Afghans, Echo came out of the building and ran toward the main exit where we had entered the compound earlier. Within a few minutes, Bravo did the same thing. I obviously didn't know what was happening, but the way Echo and Bravo were running for the exit gave us the feeling that something bad had happened or was about to. Later, I learned that the ANP officers had been fighting amongst themselves.

Internal fights are common within the Afghan culture more than in any other, which is undoubtedly why no foreign power in history, from Alexander the Great to Americans, will ever succeed until we spend enough time understanding what causes it. The ANP officers, who were part of our team, were also from the NDS compound. The fight broke out when one of our NDS officers was trying to get into the compound, but the guard at the front gate would not allow him access. It was all about one thinking he was more superior than the other and wanting to prove who had the most power. Since the NDS officers who chose to work for the Americans considered themselves to be far more superior than those who worked for the Afghan government, in his mind, the officer at the front gate was merely trying to demonstrate how he thought he had the power to deny access to the NDS officers working for the Americans—thus, the resulting confrontation.

Team members, both inside and out, had to remain ever vigilant while our commander was inside meeting with the Afghan officials; therefore, we were unable to even try to stop the fight, which was getting out of hand, so they had to call Echo and Bravo in for help. Unfortunately, as noted earlier, fighting amongst themselves is really the only thing most Afghans are good at, and their neighbor countries know and take advantage of it. I can't but blame the Afghans for allowing it, not knowing whether to choose between nationalism or their own ethnicity and personal greed.

Fortunately, no one was killed and our team members were finally able to leave the building and then ultimately the compound. Captain Alfa decided to drive through the center of the village so we could talk with some of the local Afghans regarding the security situation in their city. Because of fear of retribution by the Taliban, not many would talk with us. As Fox and I were standing in the middle of a busy intersection so we could start a conversation with anyone who might be interested, what appeared to be a young man around 19 years old approached Fox and started to speak broken English.

We were both surprised that this young man could speak English at all. When I asked the man where he had learned English, he ignored me and responded directly to Fox. We then asked him why he didn't want to speak Pashto or Farsi with me, to which he responded, "If I spoke either of those two languages, I might get in trouble for what I am about to say, because all the locals around us can understand either the two local languages, but none know any English." While he was apparently very intelligent, he continued speaking in broken English, which was difficult for Fox to understand, but I knew exactly what he was saying. He wanted to tell us that the people of Ghazni did *not* welcome American support for the local Afghan government. Although he acknowledged that the Americans were trying to build schools and medical facilities for the Afghan people, they didn't have teachers to teach or doctors to care for the ill. He said he would like to return to school one day, but he complained about the city's schools. When Fox asked him who and/or what was preventing him from going to school, the young man said there were primarily three reasons: (1) there were no teachers to teach, (2) lack of security, and (3) the threats of persecution from the Taliban. In addition to the education problem, he also mentioned the problems with medical care for the citizens of Ghazni, because there were no doctors at the medical facility to care for the people who were ill. "What good are school and medical facilities," he asked, "if there are no teachers or doctors to work in the buildings that remain empty?"

During our conversation with this young man, we were all standing on the main road, with a center divider, which had recently been in the process of being rebuilt but had apparently been abandoned by the contractor because it was only half finished and would hopefully someday be wide enough that the locals could use it as a park where they could hang out. Noticing our attention to the half-completed construction, the young man pointed out that the construction on the road had started to be paid for by Americans through the Afghan government contractors three or four years ago, but the specific contactor involved had abandoned the half-finished project once he got paid (or perhaps because he was related to the governor or some other government official who might have been transferred out of the city). Needless to say, Fox and I were quite impressed with the young man's knowledge and involvement regarding what was going on in and around the city.

Seeing and hearing things from other locals disappointed us even more as we wondered how the Afghan government officials would do things simply for their own personal gains and greed, while at the same time bragging about their Afghan patriotism, while they were actually robbing the ordinary Afghans—like the young one with whom we were talking—who only wanted to have a chance to educate themselves and were willing to risk their lives by telling us the truth regarding what was going on in the city.

We couldn't spend too much time in one place (because the longer we stayed in one place, the more people we would attract, which stood the chance of leading to any number of dangerous situations such as being attacked by the bad guys). Nevertheless, despite the danger (e.g., getting out of vehicles and talking with the local population face-to-face), we continued to seek the opinions of the ordinary Afghans because that's where we could really find out what they needed. Since our team was really committed to helping the local Afghans by listening to their concerns and ideas, that was but another reason why I loved being part of Special Forces.

Since it was located on the main highway en route to our base, Captain Alfa and one of the team members decided to make a quick stop at the ANA (Afghan National Army) compound. As we made the turn into the compound, which was located approximately 500 feet on a dirt road off the main highway, we were stopped by the guards at the front gate who would not allow us to enter the compound. Our convoy was backed up to the main road, blocking the flow of traffic, which we really didn't want to do because (1) of the security concerns that we might get attacked while lined up in the middle of the road and (2) we didn't want to create a bad image in the minds of the local Afghans because, besides blocking the flow of travel on the main highway, our convoy of eight vehicles on a narrow road was making it difficult for other vehicles to pass.

Captain Alfa asked me to go over to the front gate and ask the guards to let us in so we could meet with the compound's ANA commander. One of them told me that his commander wasn't on the compound. Therefore, the guard wasn't authorized to allow us entrance.

I returned to Captain Alfa and told him what the guard had said. We obviously needed to move to prevent attacks. In order for us to make a U-turn and exit, we needed enter the compound to turn around. However, the guards would not allow us to even do that; rather, they expected us to simply back out to the main road, which the dumbass guard knew was impossible, especially since traffic on the main road was backed up for more than a mile. Simply put, this was yet another one of those instances where the ANAs were merely trying to show us their power over the Americans— the same Americans who were paying to build their compound, provide electricity, water, food, clothes, a salary, and ammunition.

Alfa was mad as hell when I told him the guards wanted us to back out to the main highway rather than driving into the compound to make a U-turn. Wanting to take matters into his own hands, we walked to the guard shack, where he told me to ask the asshole guards if they didn't see that the traffic on the main road was backed up, and told me that I was to tell them to open the fucking gate before we blew their fucking heads off. The frightening looks on the guards' faces after hearing what Alfa had asked me to say (since they didn't understand English), clearly indicated that they now got the message loud and clear, and they opened the gate immediately and so we could make the necessary U-turn.

On the way out of the compound, the ANA officers were both saying, "Tell the American fuckers not to come here again." Before I could even tell Alfa what the ANA guards had said, I responded to them. "The two of you are fucking assholes, especially since the Americans are paying for your food and salary." Of course, the guards did not expect me to take a stand for America and/or Americans because they thought I should be on their side since they considered me to be a fellow Afghan; therefore, they asked me, *"Tho ham taraf darey amrekaya ra maykoni?"* ("You're also taking sides with the Americans?") I responded that not only was I taking sides with the Americans, I was one of them. Since all of our conversation was in Farsi, once we returned to our own compound, Alfa wanted to know what the argument between the guards and me was all about before we left. I told him exactly what the ANA guards had asked and were saying about the Americans.

Obviously, Alfa wasn't very pleased by what they had said about the Americans, but had I not told him I would have failed to do my job as an interpreter. Also, if I had told Alfa while we were there, we would undoubtedly have had a fight between us and the ANA guards. Either way would not have changed my decision about waiting to tell Captain Alfa when we reached our base. By just looking at his face and body language, I could tell that he was pissed enough to have blown their heads off if he'd had the opportunity to do so.

"Nas, you should've told me while we were there so I could have taught the bastards a lesson," Captain Alfa said.

"Sir, I don't believe we can change Afghanistan by teaching a couple of ANA thugs a lesson."

"I'm not here to change Afghanistan, Nas," he said, "but I could've changed at least those two guards, one at a time or both at the same time, if necessary."

Of course, he was absolutely right, which is why I still regret—and always will—not telling him before returning to our compound. It was a difficult lesson to learn. Life is an everyday learning process; this one was an important and difficult lesson to learn, and I will always be grateful to Captain Alfa for teaching it to me.

It had been two weeks since going with the team to Ghazni. By now, I had gotten accustomed to the guys on the team; the local Afghans, who I had daily contact with, and, of course, Jimbo, our four-legged friend. Since everyone on the team loved Jimbo, he got spoiled every time any of us had a chance. I could go on and on about Jimbo, but will keep it short for now by simply adding that he was not only the cutest German Shepherd I had ever seen, but he was incredibly smart as well. However, unlike the Americans, the local linguists and ANPs hated him to the extent that some of them would go out of their way to physically abuse him from time to time—when the Americans weren't watching, of course. Following my arrival in Ghazni, since most of the locals considered me as one of their fellow Afghans, I would see them physically abuse Jimbo because 80 percent of the Afghan population, especially those in the big cities like Kabul and Kandahar, hate dogs. In fact, 50 percent of those who hated dogs would not even touch one because they considered them to be filthy animals, but will go out of their way to physically abuse them which is why most of my fellow Americans who have been to Afghanistan have seen that most of the dogs on the streets are either blind in one eye or have missing limbs, ears, or tails. Jimbo knew that abuse very well, which was why he would always walk the other way when he saw a local Afghan coming his way.

As usual, every morning after breakfast I would go to the kitchen where the phone was located so I could call Laila in the States, usually between 8:30 and 9:00; because of the 12½ hour difference in time, it would not be too late for her. One might ask why it is that Afghanistan has only a half-hour time difference with a couple of other countries in the region (which involves politics, even in their own time zone) than it does with the rest of the world.

Since Jimbo usually hung out with me, one day when I was on the phone talking with Laila, he was laying on the floor next to me. Qasim, who was cleaning the kitchen and mopping the floor, came over to where I was sitting. He was not aware that Jimbo was lying next to the stool on which I was sitting. As soon as he saw Jimbo, Qasim opened the kitchen door and yelled at him in his native Pashto, "*JAMBU, THE KHOSEY ZOW, WAZA!*" ("Jimbo, get out, motherfucker!") while pointing at the open door. Jimbo, of course, didn't leave. Instead, he looked up at me, supposedly to see if I was either going to translate what Qasim had said or perhaps he was simply asking me for permission to stay. Since I was still on the phone, Jimbo (who did not like Qasim even a little) continued to lay on the floor, uncertain of what he should do. Meanwhile, Qasim came over and kicked Jimbo in the stomach, all the while shouting at him in Pashto in an effort to get him out of the kitchen. Since I was still on the phone talking with Laila, I signaled Qasim to stop kicking Jimbo and to leave him alone because he didn't want to leave. But, instead of stopping, Qasim was hurting Jimbo by pulling him by one of his ears, trying to throw him out of the kitchen. Unable to watch this abuse any longer, I put the phone on hold and instead of lecturing Qasim, I asked Jimbo to go outside, at least for the time being. Jimbo left within seconds, at which point Qasim looked at me and smiled as he said in Pashto, *"DHA JAMBU THE KHOSEY ZOY ZAMA PA KHULA NA KAWEY."* ("Jimbo motherfucker doesn't listen to me.") I wanted to explain why but decided to continue my conversation with my wife instead. Once we were done talking, I would then talk with Qasim regarding Jimbo's behavior. Because of the lesson I learned from Alfa, I decided I was no longer going to be passive about things I saw, even if it meant changing Afghanistan one person at a time, which for now meant Qasim, who really didn't know any better about how to treat others—humans and animals alike.

When I had finished talking with my wife, I talked with Qasim about Jimbo. Qasim was still "pouting" about Jimbo's behavior. However, before I could say anything to Qasim, he had something he wanted to say first: Because Jimbo was afraid of them both, whenever he or Jabar were in the kitchen, Jimbo would never come in, let alone act the way he was acting since I had arrived. This was not uncommon because most Afghans feel the same way: Those who fear you also respect you. Thus, in Qasim's mind, Jimbo disrespected him. Qasim added that Jimbo only came into the kitchen when Americans were present.

I couldn't wait to respond to Qasim's comments, during which he never called me by my given name ("Nas," like everyone else on the team did), which I had insisted he do on more than one occasion, to which his response was always the same: that, out of respect for the fact that I was older, even though I wasn't an engineer by trade, he preferred calling me *"Ingenyer Saheb"* ("Dear Engineer") from the very first day we had met. He seemingly never understood or respected that I wanted him to call me by my given name and, in fact, he even called me Ustad (which, in English, translates to mean either a mentor or teacher) from time to time. I was well aware that if I continued trying to convince him to call me by my given name, I would be disrespecting *his* wishes. In other words, in Afghanistan, for me to respect Qasim, I had to allow him to call me by whatever name he wished. Since Qasim did not speak or understand English, because he had asked me a couple of days earlier to teach him the language (which I agreed to do), I opted to only allow him to call me Ustad, which he agreed to do. New to the American culture, Qasim had just joined the team a week prior to my arrival in Ghazni. A native Pashton from the Province of Logar, Qasim was hired as a cook by Jabar (also a native Pashton, but from the Province of Paktia), who was born and raised in Pakistan during the Soviets' occupation of Afghanistan.

I opened the conversation with Qasim regarding the physical abuse of Jimbo and other animals as well. Being familiar with Afghan culture, I knew beforehand that I would not be able to convince him to agree with me as to why he physically abused Jimbo. I just wanted to point out that there were other ways to do things without the necessity of physically abusing any creature, whether human or animal.

In Afghanistan, almost every conversation either starts or ends with God's name in it; the most common is *"Insahllah"* ("God willing"). So, I started by asking him who his creator was. Obviously, with a smile on his face, his answer was "God." I then asked him if he knew who my creator was. Again, with an even bigger smile on his face, his answer was "God." My third question was going to be as simple as the first two: "Who is Jimbo's creator?" As expected, he again answered, "God." At this point, I could tell that Qasim was listening very carefully. Needless to say, I was pleased that I had been able to get and hold on to his full attention. Although he was confused as to why I was asking him such obvious questions, I could actually see the interest in his eyes. Having learned throughout my life that if I wanted someone to understand me, I had to start with the basics, making the initial conversation rational and as simple as possible in order to get them interested and involved.

Most people tend to take obvious questions for granted. Since Qasim agreed with me that the three of us were created by the same God, I took my conversation to the next level by asking, "Do you respect our creator—yours, mine, and Jimbo's?" He responded that indeed he did. I then asked him,

"Then why would you disrespect God, our creator, by physically abusing His creation, in this case, Jimbo?" He said Jimbo didn't listen, which is why he kicked him. Since Qasim didn't speak or understand English, and wanting desperately for him to understand, I asked him what he would do if one of the Americans came to the kitchen and asked him in English to do something for them. "Let's assume you don't do it, not because you don't want to, but because you didn't understand. Would it be fair to you to be physically abused by the American who asked you to do something in a language other than the one that you can understand?"

Smiling, in an effort to justify his reason for physically abusing Jimbo, he responded, "Well, Jimbo is an animal." Even though I knew in my heart that he believed he was wrong for abusing Jimbo, no matter how hard I tried, I couldn't convince him to admit to his wrongdoings, which as noted earlier continues to be a major problem in the Afghan society. I tried to convince him with logic and reasoning that abusing Jimbo disrespected our Creator. I sensed that Qasim understood me, but he would not admit it, which I expected would be the case. I didn't anticipate that I could change Qasim's mind, but I, at the very least, wanted to plant a reasonable doubt in his mind, so I could feel that I had done my moral duty to society.

On mission to old historic Ghazni city where above ground raw sewer is visible.

Typical Afghan medical clinic in Qarabagh district. The sign reads, "Dr. Abdul Khaliq Zaland. Pediatrician and Dermatology specialist (graduate of Jalalabda's school of medicine)."

On Sunday, May 30, 2009, a day before Memorial Day, we had a mission briefing—my first—in the OPS center around 9:00 in the morning. The OPS center was packed and included Captain Ansari, the ANP commander, and four of his squad leaders. Not that all missions aren't important, but this one sounded much more dangerous than the others. Since I had never been on a dangerous combat mission since my arrival, I really didn't know the unfamiliar military terms that the team members were using or what everyone was talking about in terms of executing the mission. I was told that all I needed to do was translate to the members of the ANP.

With the same scenario, preparation for the mission started immediately after the briefing: Bravo would make the list of people who should be in which RGs or Humvees; Echo was in charge of all the radios and other necessary sources of communication; Ricardo and Charlie were putting up the big guns that needed to be mounted to the tops of the armored vehicles. Ross (our JTAC [Joint Tactical Air Controller] from the United States Air Force) was always in the same vehicle with Alfa, Charlie, Fox, and me. Ross and I were always at the back of the vehicle along with an ANP officer, who usually positioned himself at the big gun that was mounted there. The mission was originally planned for 11:00 that morning, but it was pushed back to 2:00 in the afternoon and then later in the day, it was pushed back yet again to around 5:00 in the afternoon.

I could not believe how great the team operated. There were cheers and laughter throughout the day because the guys were looking forward to the mission. I saw no fear whatsoever. In fact, it felt more like we were going to a Memorial Day picnic. I heard loud music coming from Echo's room, and saw Delta, Charlie, Mitch, and Jack standing in front of Echo's room as Delta tried to entertain them, as usual. Then Fox and Damon joined the group. I saw Alfa came out of the OPS center and go to his room. A short time later, Bravo came out of the OPS center and walked over to me to confirm that I would be in the same Humvee with Alfa again, which would be the same for all future missions.

We lined up with our armored vehicles facing the compound's exit as Bravo walked to every vehicle to do a head count while Alfa checked radio communications. We were then on our way, out of our compound, and on the main road on the base to get an all-clear signal from the Polish military so we could depart. For some reason, there was an unusual delay before we could leave the base. While parked on the road inside the base waiting for the signal that we could move out, because of the hot summer-like temperature inside the vehicles, almost everyone—except Charlie and me because of our vehicle's open end—stepped out of them in an effort to somehow stay cooler. Delta walked over to the back of our vehicle and started dancing the moonwalk in an effort to entertain us while we continued to wait. He was hilarious and took our minds off the mission (and how the Taliban might greet us), if for only a short period of time. I looked around at the other courageous team members—all of whom had no fear that we were going on this mission; again, I was honored to be a member of this team.

After Delta's short but very entertaining dance, we finally received permission from the Polish military to leave the base. Our vehicle was second behind Bravo's. Looking behind, I saw that Delta—who was laughing and singing as he drove—was behind us. Sitting in our Humvee with the open back had its disadvantages, too, because the open back made for an easy entrance of the clay dust coming from Bravo's RG. The dust was so thick, within only a matter of a few minutes, our faces were unrecognizable. If dust had any value, Afghanistan would be the wealthiest country in the world.

Once off base, we were on the main highway going south, in stop-and-go traffic, toward Kandahar until we finally arrived at the District of Qarabagh, about 25 miles south of downtown Ghazni.

Qarabagh is a village on the east side of the main highway. On both sides of the main road, there's a little bazaar with a convenience store and other small shops, as well as a rest area for those who are making the long journey between Kabul and Kandahar. We stopped our vehicles in front of one of the roadside cafés. As usual, we attracted the local Afghans as spectators. We got their attention this time because most of the guys had boxes of candy in their vehicles, which they threw out to all of the kids who usually gathered or chased after us.

When our convoy pulled over to the side of the road, although I saw them leave the base with us, I didn't see any of the ANP guys who were supposed to be with us on this mission. I remember having seen them leave the base with us. I asked my buddy Charlie if he knew what in the hell happened to the ANP guys. Charlie told me that they were already on the mission. They had taken a detour on one of the dirt roads alongside the main road before we reached the rest area in Qarabagh.

The plan for us was to wait for the ANPs to carry out their part of the mission and then signal us if anything went wrong or they ran into something they couldn't handle; if so, we would then go to help them. Meanwhile, we remained parked alongside the road, our engines running, and all of us staring to the east, waiting for some kind of message from the ANPs.

It was now early evening, and the sun was still out, when I suddenly saw a bright orange ball of light, golf ball size, shoot up into the air; then it disappeared. I wasn't immediately sure what it was until all of the team members jumped into their vehicles and headed toward the area where the bright orange ball of light had been seen. I knew something was wrong, but I wasn't sure what it was or what was going to happen. Fox was driving our Humvee as fast as he could right behind Bravo's. I stood and looked out to the front to see what the hell was going on but, in this case, it wasn't possible for me to see anything because of the thick dust raised from the RG in front of us. Not only could I not see anything because of the dust, but the rough part of the countryside desert on which we were riding bounced me up and down, causing pain in my lower back. I felt like I was on a rollercoaster, but in this case, the ride wasn't fun.

At first, we started to drive in a single line, following each other, convoy style; however, the closer we got to the mud huts where we had seen the bright orange light, the more we spread out, with all of our armored vehicles now driving side by side as fast as they could. The closer we got to the mud huts, the more intense were the sounds of gunfire between the ANPs and the Taliban, who appeared to be in one or perhaps two of the mud huts on the side of the road. The scene before us reminded me of an article I had once read and a statement it contained, which I now offered as a prayer: "You know death is a possibility going in…you focus on the mission at hand, take care of each other, and cheat death every chance you get. However, it's destiny or fate when it's your time to go."

Although I couldn't see him, I could hear Alfa talking nonstop, but didn't know whether he was talking with Charlie, Fox, Ross, or someone else on the radio. He was asking where the gunshots were coming from and where everyone should be positioned in order to avoid casualties.

Once we got close to one of the mud huts, I could see Bravo's RG stopped at the south side of the hut. I also saw the second RG, which was stopped next to Bravo's. Alfa told Fox, our driver, to drive another 100 feet north of the last mud hut, where I saw an ANP officer who had been shot in the leg; he was lying on the ground and couldn't move. A second ANP officer was trying to flag us down by waving his rifle in the air with his right hand while pointing to the wounded ANP officer with his left hand in order to tell us that he had a man down. I looked around the field and saw the ANP officer on the ground, his weapon pointed toward one of the mud huts, which was on the north side of the first mud hut, where Bravo, Mitch, and Delta were also pointing their weapons. As soon as we stopped next to the last hut, I saw one of the ANP unmarked, civilian-type vehicles parked in the middle of the road directly in front of the mud hut on the far north side of the village. All of the vehicle's doors were open. It appeared to have been abandoned by the ANPs when the Taliban had confronted them following their arrival in the village. Since we had come through the farmland from the backside of the mud hut, we couldn't see what was going on in front of it, so Alfa told Fox to drive past the last mud hut and park on the dirt road so we could have a better vantage point.

Once Fox had parked the Humvee about 50 feet away from the mud hut, almost every ANP officer called to ask me to tell Alfa that all of the bad guys were in the first mud hut where we were parked. I tried to communicate with Alfa about what the ANPs had told me but couldn't see him because he was busy in the Humvee, talking on the radio with other team members. So, all I could do was scream and yell in an effort to get his attention. Since I didn't get a response from Alfa, Charlie asked me what I needed him for. Pointing to the mud hut directly behind us, I told Charlie that the ANPs told me that all the bad guys were in there. Meanwhile, in the midst of all this chaos—with the *pop, pop, pop, pop* sound of guns going on nonstop—I did a crazy thing by pulling out my camera so I could take a picture or two, but only had a chance to take one shot of the mud hut where all of the ANP officers were pointing their rifles.

Needless to say, being in an open-back vehicle 50 feet away from a mud hut full of bad guys, shooting at me as I tried to keep my head up to take pictures, was rather challenging. I gave up on my efforts and focused instead on trying to avoid getting hit by a bullet as I ducked down in the Humvee as much as I could. All I could see were the sparks of the bullets coming from behind the mud hut like fireworks. Although we could still see daylight to the west, the sun had set where we were. Unless I was very angry or frightened, unlike the guys in the military, as a civilian, I didn't use the four-letter word very often. However, this situation definitely was appropriate, so, mumbling aloud to myself, I asked, "What the fuck is going on?" I was scared and freaking out as bullets continued to fly like fireworks above my head as I continued to lay in the back of the Humvee. Nonetheless, I wanted to see where the bullets were coming from.

Suddenly, I heard someone call from behind the Humvee, "Oh crap, I got shot!" I immediately got up, looked toward the mud hut, and saw one of our guys run out, falling to the ground before he could reach our Humvee. The shooting was getting more and more intense. I was frustrated as I stood in the back of the Humvee, with bullets flying all around, making it impossible for me to do anything for the guy who had just been shot. Undecided about what I could do, I suddenly saw Fox running over to wounded man lying on the ground. Then I saw Damon run over to help Fox with the downed soldier.

I could see that Fox was busy doing something to the lower part of the wounded man's body while Damon was doing something to his arm. Needless to say, I was very concerned about the three of them being out in the open while the gunfire continued. Fox and Damon were desperately trying to save the person on the ground under an intense situation, yet another example of the bravery of our soldiers who are all committed to give their lives, if necessary, to save the life of a fellow comrade. I wanted to help but didn't know how.

One of the ANP officers came over to our Humvee to request that I ask Alfa if he could bring one of their wounded guys (who had been shot in the leg) over to our Humvee. Alfa, of course, said, "Hell yes! Fuck, we have another officer down besides Delta," which is when I realized he was the wounded man Damon and Fox were trying to help. Meanwhile, the ANP guys had carried their wounded officer to the back of our Humvee. Charlie and I helped him as much as we could by laying him down in the back of the Humvee, putting pressure on the wound in an effort to slow the bleeding. It was very difficult for him to tell me that he was thirsty in his native Farsi but he managed to get a couple of words out nonetheless: *"Tushna, Aow."* ("Thirsty, water."). He was very weak and couldn't say anything else because of all the blood he had lost. I tried to talk with him as much as I could to keep him awake, but he was complaining of his pain by repeating over and over again, *"Dard, dard!"* ("Pain, pain!") I was experiencing a much different kind of pain because I wasn't able to help him except to ask that he continue to put pressure on his wound to stop the bleeding. Knowing that he would bleed out if help didn't arrive soon, I felt so helpless and was desperate to do something—anything—to help him.

While talking with the wounded ANP officer, since the situation was so chaotic, I was also listening to Alfa, just in case he needed me for any reason. I saw him opening the back door of the Humvee as he talked on the radio with our command center, apprising them that two of his men were down, an American and one of the Afghan's ANP officers. I realized that Alfa had opened the Humvee's door in an effort to get a clearer signal so he could relay his message while he continued to move the antenna around as he repeated himself over and over again to know if the person on the other end of the line could hear him.

Alfa continued his radio communication with our team members on the battlefield, as well as with the main command center, asking for help in arranging for a medical evacuation for Delta and the wounded ANP officer. Meanwhile, Charlie tried to talk with Alfa at the same time.

"Yes, Charlie, what do you need?" Alfa asked.

"Sir, the gunfire is coming from directly behind us. May I use the big one?" he asked, referring to the 300PX-M-32 grenade launcher.

After Alfa gave him the okay to use whatever he had, Charlie asked me to hand him the grenade launcher, which was in its cover next to my seat. After I handed him the heavy weapon, Charlie suggested that I cover my ears before he fired it. I did so but the grenade launcher was so powerful that no matter how hard I covered my ears, I could still hear not only the sound but feel the Humvee shaking every time Charlie fired it. This whole thing started around 5:00 or 6:00, shortly before sundown, and two hours later the shooting continued. At one point, the gunfire was so intense almost everyone I saw was just shooting toward that one mud hut that was surrounded by our guys and the ANP officers, where the bullets were flying above their heads earlier. I saw that Fox, Damon, and Delta weren't in the open anymore, while at the same time Charlie was moving around from one weapon to the next to see which of them had ammunition left so he could continue shooting at the mud hut. At one point, I heard Charlie asking me to pass him a box of ammunition next to my seat that was used for the mini gun mounted to the top of the Humvee. Sometimes I'd drop down to the floor of the Humvee to make sure I was out of Charlie's way while he was trying to shoot at the mud hut. Since Charlie was always the gunner on our Humvee, he was always right above our heads where he could make 360-degree turns. In this situation, since our Humvee had backed in as close as it could to the mud hut, had I stood in the open backside of the Humvee, which I did most of the time, it obviously would have been a bad idea. Since 99.9 percent of the team members had never been in a similar situation, it's impossible for them to understand how crucial it would be that someone could be shot accidentally by one of their own men. My concern was not for our American team members shooting one of our own; I was more concerned about the ANP officers, who, like me, were all terrible at aiming and shooting straight.

I could still see Alfa's body, half inside the vehicle and half outside, trying to get good signals while talking on different radios to various people at the same time. Meanwhile, I was still trying to help the bleeding man in our Humvee, and the process was even worse now that it had gotten dark. I didn't have night goggles and even if did, I knew I wouldn't be able to see anything anyhow. Afghanistan is a very dark place at night, especially when the moon isn't out; so, without night goggles I couldn't see anything, especially in Qarabagh where the *only* light that can be used is the sun and the moon. "Hey, Nas," Alfa called. I answered, "Yes, Sir." The next word out of his mouth was "fuck," which I'd rarely heard him use. But tonight was an exception because Alfa was mad and frustrated when he told me to "bring your fucking ass down here and start driving this fucking vehicle." I felt just like Jimbo when he had been told during one of our briefings to "get the fuck out" of the OPS center. Jimbo was lucky to have been asked to leave the OPS center during one of our briefings, while I on the other hand was being called in to go into the front seat of the Humvee where I would be closer to Alfa.

Despite being shaken up by the way I was asked to come down, at the same time I was happy that I could help in any way possible. Alfa needed me to drive the Humvee because Fox, our driver, was busy trying to save Delta from bleeding to death, and because Alfa either needed someone to move the Humvee around because he wasn't getting a radio signal, or maybe because he felt he was too close to the mud hut where all the shooting was taking place. Whatever the reason, I got in the driver's seat, which I had never occupied before. Now, I was asking myself, *What should I do?* The Humvee didn't have any dashboard lights or headlights, so, since I didn't have any night goggles either, I was surrounded by total darkness—it was pitch black.

Since Charlie was still busy shooting his gun and the ANP officer was still in the back of the vehicle bleeding to death, Alfa continued to try to talk to more than one person at the same time while also waiting for me to move the vehicle around. I was sitting in the driver's seat of the Humvee with absolutely *no* fucking idea how to operate the vehicle. I knew it wasn't rocket science, but it had more to do with the circumstances that I was involved in that made a simple task mentally more difficult to handle. It was dark as hell and bullets were still flying all over the place, which added even more to my misery.

While still sitting behind the steering wheel, not knowing what to do much less being able to see where I was going, I was ready for another ass chewing, verbal confrontation with Alfa, who seemed to be not only frustrated because of the poor radio reception but frustrated as hell because the person (a.k.a.: me) in the front seat didn't know shit about how to drive and/or handle the vehicle.

"Nas, where the fuck are you?" Alfa hissed. I am still sitting in the front seat, behind the steering wheel, all the while trying to get Alfa's attention. Most of the time I didn't know who Alfa was talking to, whether on the radio or Charlie, who was still on the mini gun, shooting toward the mud hut, or me. I heard Charlie telling Alfa that I was already in the driver's seat but needed to be instructed on how to operate the vehicle. Once I heard Charlie tell Alfa that, I knew I was in for another Alfa ass-chewing for not being trained or knowing how to drive the Humvee. Sometimes I could just read people's minds, and this time, I was exactly right when Alfa said more aggressively than usual, "So, you don't even know how to drive this fucking vehicle?" Before answering, I thought to myself, *Why am I here if I can't even drive this vehicle?* and then answered Alfa's question. "Well, Sir, first, I have never been presented with an opportunity to drive this thing before now, and second, even if I had, I can't see anything because I don't have night goggles."

I didn't even know how to start the vehicle, nor did I know that it was never turned off in the first place but was kept running the whole time it was used on a mission. All I had to do was put it in gear and drive. Alfa really needed me to drive the Humvee—the sooner the better—to get us out of there, away from the gunfire that obviously wasn't going to stop any time soon. We had to do something fast or, God forbid, he would lose the wounded soldiers who were both losing a significant amount of blood. Alfa deserved a lot of credit for all of his efforts to keep the line of communication open with all of our team members in the battlefield.

Anyhow, here I was sitting in the front seat of the Humvee, using my flashlight in an effort to find the gear so I could put the damn thing in drive. As it ultimately turned out, I had to ask Charlie what to do. Since he was the only man on our team who could operate all the weapons, serve as our main source of protection, and watch our backs, I knew that he wouldn't be able to come down to help me. Alfa was still busy on the radio, and then I heard him ask me, "Nas, what the fuck are you trying to do? Are you going to move this thing out of here anytime soon, or what?"

"Sir, I can't see anything." This time, within seconds, Alfa handed over his night goggles and asked me to put them on so I could move this fucking thing. This time, I sensed that he was trying a more gentle approach and yelling at me much less than usual.

Since Alfa had calmed down significantly, I became more confused than usual. At first, I was looking for the gear so I could put the vehicle into drive and start moving, but now I was worried about the night goggles. Everyone on ODA had night goggles attached to their helmets, but my helmet didn't have the goggle mount so that I could simply attach the goggles to it. Instead, I had to hold the night goggles with my right hand so that I could start to look for the gears with my left. Unlike civilian vehicles, the Humvee's ignition switch and gears were located in the same place on the dashboard. Once I finally managed to get them on, they made me feel like I imagined a blind person, one whose vision had been restored, would feel. In this situation, however, since I didn't know what the fuck I was doing, I felt completely useless. (As an aside, night goggles are well worth wearing, if for no other reason than the fact that they can instantly turn pitch-black darkness into daylight—but another one of God's miracles for creating people who can provide such things so they can save many lives on the battlefield.)

From the driver's seat, I could still hear Alfa talking on two separate radio frequencies—one internal between the team members in order to control the fight, the other to the command center in an effort to coordinate a safe location for the medic helicopters to be dispatched and land. I had no idea how the wounded ANP officer was doing in the back of our Humvee, but feared that he might not make it because of all the blood he was losing. I felt distraught and incredibly guilty that I couldn't help him, and guilty because I didn't know how to drive this damned vehicle. In combat, every second is crucial, especially in the situation in which we now found ourselves. I knew that if any of our guys died because of me or my lack of knowledge, I would never forgive myself.

After seemingly taking me forever, I *finally* found the gear! When you're in an area that is pitch black, even if you know where things are, you'd still have a difficult time finding them. Well, for me, night goggles were the light at the end of the tunnel. I was finally able to put the damn thing into drive and stepped on the gas pedal before even looking to make sure everyone was in the vehicle. Still trying to find a better signal, Alfa had one leg inside the vehicle and the other out. When I pushed on the gas pedal—at first, not realizing I was doing so because of the weight of the military boots I was wearing—the Humvee jumped, jerked, and ultimately moved forward more smoothly, which unfortunately caused the door to hit Alfa in the face, fall to the ground, and create even more static in the radio signal he had found. Needless to say, the next thing from Alfa's mouth started with my name followed by a resounding "FUCK!," which only tended to make me feel much, *much* worse. Obviously, I knew that Alfa was very angry with me, which I understood because I was very angry with me, too, for not being trained on vehicles at the compound during my free time when I thought I didn't have anything else to do. Had I done so, we would not have been in this situation.

Well, after all the chaos with not being able to do shit, Charlie came to my rescue by shouting at Alfa. "Sir, that's not Nas's job! You need to give him a chance." While they argued about me, I couldn't help but wonder if it was even remotely possible in the military to raise your voice to your superior. At the same time, I couldn't help but wonder why I was even here in the first place. Being a civilian in the middle of a situation where guys who had spent most of their adult lives being soldiers, fighting terrorists to protect America and Afghanistan, was an honor for me—so much so that I was never offended by a single, harsh word that came out of Alfa's mouth. Granted, his verbal "abuse," if you will, added even more to my already existing nervousness, but at the same time, I also understood where Charlie was coming from to protect me as a civilian. Additionally, Alfa's leadership and the way he took control of a situation, under intense pressure in the middle of combat, also amazed me. One simple mistake on his part could've resulted in life or death for any member of our team.

When their arguing had come to an end, except for the continuing gunfire, things had quieted down a bit, especially since they were no longer cursing and shouting at each other. While I drove slowly through the freshly plowed farmland, it was inevitable that I would hit my head against the door or the rooftop because of the shallow ditches and water streams I had to drive through to get the hell out of the red zone as quickly as possible.

Since he had the GPS and I had no fucking clue where I was going, to this day I can still hear Alfa's voice as he directed me on which way to go.

I noticed, too, that Alfa was now [somewhat] comfortably talking on the radio with the medic evacuation team, providing them with the necessary grids they needed to pinpoint our location so that they could land the medevac helicopters without being shot down by the enemy. Since I had no idea where I was headed, I drove slowly about (5–10 mph) while Alfa gave me such directions as, "Nas, ass right," to which I merely responded, "Yes, Sir." However, several seconds later, he again told me, "Nas, I said ass right!" As I made another right turn, he told me to stop the vehicle. Until this day, I still don't know what "Ass right" means, and wonder why Alfa kept saying it rather than simply saying, "Right." Since there was "no harm, no foul" involved, I didn't care to ask, but wondered if Alfa perhaps meant to say, "Asshole, right," and I just never heard the "hole" part.

Now approximately 500 feet away from the mud hut where Delta had been shot, we were waiting for the medevac to land so that Delta and the wounded ANP officer could be evacuated. Within 10 more minutes, the helicopter landed within 50 feet of our vehicle. Within another minute, the medevac helicopter crew took both of the wounded soldiers away to the Bagram Airfield where the American military hospital is located. Fox, our driver as well as a medic, had gone with Delta on the medevac to keep him and the ANP officer alive, which meant that our vehicle would not have a permanent driver to take us back to the compound.

Once Delta and the wounded ANP officer were removed from the battlefield, the gunfire resumed, albeit not as intensely. I noticed that Charlie had almost emptied all of the ammunition boxes that we had loaded in the back of the Humvee. At around 9:00 PM, I overheard Alfa calling for air support to bomb the hut containing members of the Taliban. He then walked over to the RG where Echo was standing by. Since I didn't have an internal radio, I was unable to listen to what they were talking about, so didn't know what was going to happen next until Charlie told me.

He said that I should *not*, under any circumstances, look in the direction of the hut and recommended that I stay inside the vehicle when the bomb was dropped. I was scared and excited at the same time—scared because of the possibility that they could make a mistake and miss their target, thus missing the correct location and bombing the wrong place, which I knew happened in war zones—and excited because after seeing two of our guys wounded, I knew the Taliban would soon be dead once the bombs were dropped on the hut.

Suddenly, we all heard the huge sound of an explosion that shook the ground like a major earthquake. The bombs had to have been dropped from a very high altitude because none of us heard the aircraft overhead before the bombs were dropped. We waited for a short period of time after the bombing had taken place. Since I had returned the night goggles to Alfa, I couldn't see a thing. However, I could hear Alfa talking directly with Ross (the JTAC), who was in contact with the Air Force as he coordinated the dropping of the bombs. Alfa was ordering a second round of bombs to be dropped on the mud hut, which would turn the mud hut into a pile of dust with more bad guys on their way to get their just rewards.

We waited about 20 minutes for the dust to settle, and then slowly drove back toward the huge sinkhole where the mud hut had once been. Alfa asked me to help Bravo, who was waiting for me at his RG about 50 feet to our right. As I walked toward Bravo, I was reminded by Captain Alfa asking me where my fucking rifle was. I told him that it was somewhere in the back of the Humvee where I have left it after becoming the driver. He told me that I was crazy to be walking around without it. I went to the Humvee to get it and then went to the RG to see Bravo. He wanted to know how I was doing after all the chaos. When I told him that I was doing okay, he wanted to know if I'd join Oscar (the interrogator), him, and three ANP officers to hold security positions so we could walk through the still-standing mud huts to see what was there.

My instinct was to find Ansari, but on second thought, since everyone was scattered throughout the field and it was so dark that you couldn't see anything, I decided against doing that. So, I returned to our Humvee where I knew there were three ANP rangers with six to seven blindfolded detainees who had been captured in the battlefield. I asked one of them to call Ansari on his radio to ask him for three ANP officers to go with me to hold security positions while Bravo, Oscar, and I searched the other mud huts. When the officer reached Ansari to find out where he was, Ansari told him he was already with the rest of his officers by the other mud huts, which didn't surprise me. I went back to the RG to report what I had learned. Bravo, Oscar, and I started walking toward the other mud huts amidst a sea of body parts, some (by the grace of God) unidentifiable because of the darkness. When one of the ANP officers accompanying us suddenly came up behind me and tapped me on the shoulder, he scared the living shit out of me until he whispered, "Ustad, Ansari needs you." I told the officer to tell Ansari that we were on our way to meet him.

Before I could reach the mud huts, while Bravo and Oscar went ahead, Ansari stopped me to ask, "Ustad, can you ask the boy what he was trying to say? I can't understand him." Since I didn't have night goggles, I followed Ansari to where he had left the boy in one of the huts. Being of average height, I felt a lot taller because I had to duck my head in order to be able to enter the hut through its small door opening. The hut was a version of a street-corner convenience store that sold anything from housewares to shoes, gasoline, flour, fruit, vegetables (dried and fresh), candy, condoms (which were not being used as intended, but rather for kids to buy and play with, like balloons), toys, cigarettes, and prepaid phone cards, to name but a few. Much of the fruit and vegetables were from last season. If it wasn't sold then, when it was fresh, it was being sold as dried fruit and vegetables the following season.

Once inside the store, I was finally able to find Bravo, who was shining his flashlight on an eight- or nine-year-old boy's face. The boy was in a corner in a fetal position, fearfully looking at me once I was able to make eye contact with him. In that 10 to 15 seconds, the smells surrounding me in that room almost made me puke. I stood, speechless, not immediately able to speak to this frightened and very unfortunate boy who was still alive, with no scratches in sight, after the hut next door had been bombed and turned to dust.

Glancing at Bravo, I could see that he was signaling me to hurry the fuck up so we could get the hell out of there, pronto. Bravo told me to ask the boy some questions, like who he was, what he was doing there, and where he lived.

Glancing again at the boy, the look on his face clearly reflected that he was even more afraid than before; he was also shaking as though he was in the freezing cold, which wasn't the case. In fact, it was very warm that night with almost summer-like temperatures. Finally able to speak, I asked the boy, *"Halaka czouk yeh, dalta czha she khaway?"* ("Hey, youngster, who are you and what are you doing here?") Finally able to hear someone speak to him in a language he understood, the boy suddenly jumped up, the fear on his face disappearing as a smile emerged. He responded in Pashto, *"Mama, Mama, sta khu Pashto zda dah!"* ("Uncle, Uncle, you can speak Pashto!") I simply responded, *"Wo, wo."* ("Yes, yes.") Before the boy could tell me anything more, Bravo wanted to know what he had said thus far. I told him, explaining the boy's surprise that I could speak in Pashto to him. Bravo suggested that I tell the boy that he was lucky to be alive. I was proud to have been able to witness the U.S. Air Force and Captain Alfa's joint coordination to hit its target so precisely. It was truly a miracle that this boy—and an Afghan shopkeeper directly next door—were still alive!

Glancing back at the boy, I noticed that he was still shaking but appeared to be somewhat more comfortable and was willing to talk with me. I also noticed the spot where we found him was wet, as was his "Partog" (the bottom half of his traditional Afghan clothing). From the smell, I guessed that he had also lost his bowels—something anyone, including me, would have done under the same circumstances. When asked, the boy, in a shaky voice, said that his father left the store earlier that evening when the shooting started, but never came back to get him. He was too frightened to leave the store on his own. He said he wanted me to tell the infidels—referring to Bravo and Oscar—that if they wanted to search the store, they'd be welcome to do so, but only if they didn't kill him. "The Hazaras (referring to the ANPs) were here earlier," he continued. "I couldn't understand them. They beat me up and took some of our things."

I asked the boy where he lived. He merely responded with an "over there," while pointing his right hand toward the exit door to a village in that direction. After telling this to Bravo, he asked me to tell the boy not to go anywhere until morning. Then, just to forewarn him, he also asked me tell the boy before we left that he would hear another loud explosion within the next 20 minutes. As soon as I told the boy what to expect, he was frightened again and started to shake, clearly distressed to know that we were leaving and he had to stay by himself until morning. "Uncle," he asked, "are the infidels going to drop a bomb on *me?*" I assured him that a bomb wasn't going to be dropped on him and prayed to myself that I was correct.

As we walked away, I considered that the boy's father was either one of the Taliban who left his son behind or was either dead or captured by the ANPs before he escaped. I was saddened that in this case, the boy was simply a victim of circumstance, not only from the actions of his own native Afghans, but by his father who had left him behind,

As we left the mud hut to return to our vehicles, I wondered why Bravo wanted me to tell the boy he would hear another loud explosion within 20 minutes. When I asked, he told me that Charlie had discovered some explosives in the motorcycle shop next door. Since they belonged to the Taliban, they were going to be destroyed in the open field, and that's exactly what happened 20 minutes later.

By then, it was 11:00 PM, and the six hours that had passed since the time of our arrival felt like six minutes to me. Since we were preparing for our departure back to the compound, I started to worry and wonder who was going to drive our Humvee to the base, especially since Fox wasn't with us and I sucked at driving. By the time we reached our Humvee, I saw that Captain Alfa had already found my replacement—Rick—who drove us back to the base safe and sound—without any yelling or cursing from Captain Alfa.

During our drive, I couldn't help but think about everything that had taken place during the past six hours, what I saw and heard—throughout it all, coming out uninjured and alive, yet another miracle from God. This mission of life or death was a lesson well learned for me, one that cannot be erased from my memory and then, at that time in my life, challenged me to be prepared for future missions with Special Forces (and think about whether I wanted to stay with the team or simply pack my bags the next day and get the fuck out of there).

As I continued to think about what had happened on this mission, I recognized that Delta was a prime example of the bravery I had seen as he entered the mud hut where he was greeted by the Taliban, while Fox and Damon ran to save lives without any fear for their own lives—a perfect example of bravery, courage, and selflessness. I couldn't help but wonder how others could be like them and the rest of our team members. I still haven't come up with an answer of my own but if anyone wants to know why they do what they do, I recommend they ask anyone serving in the U.S. Armed Forces; and, most especially, members of the Special Forces. I can only speak for myself as to why I wanted to be a member of the Special Forces team, which, simply put is: *My love for America*, the same thing I witnessed in all the guys with whom I worked.

Most of our guys who fought and got killed while I was there, did so—not because they were in combat 24/7—but simply because they were in Afghanistan. Categorically speaking, there are two reasons for this: (1) There were the "known" missions (where everyone could basically anticipate what was going to take place), and (2) there were the more dangerous missions (primarily because the team had no idea where they were going or why). At least when we were on the (1) missions noted above, we knew where the enemy might be and were prepared for it. However, driving outside the base to get to where we were going, or perhaps even when we were returning after a mission, was oftentimes more challenging than the mission itself because of the unexpected IEDs on the road or being trapped in an ambush by the bad guys who knew that we were either leaving or returning to our base.

When we arrived back at the base, we had 11 to 12 detainees that we had captured on the battlefield and needed to be processed—everything from getting their fingerprints, taking their mug shots, followed by medical examinations. Then we had to interrogate each and every one of them. The first phase took a couple of hours; and, once we were done, we put the detainees in their cells to be interrogated within the next 72 hours. Interrogations were never predictable. Depending on a detainee's cooperation, sometimes they took longer than expected. Even though we were aware that these detainees might have been the same people who were shooting at us the night before, the detainees were all treated with the respect they deserved as human beings.

As an aside, knowing the Afghan culture as I do, as I was then, and still am aware now, most people in Afghanistan can't afford to go to a doctor, even if one had been available, which was probably the reason there aren't any doctors to begin with, especially in the villages. This thought occurred to me because it was quite evident that this group of detainees had never seen a doctor or a medic, nor had they ever been treated and/or screened for any illness they may have had thus far in their lifetimes. Except for drawing blood, we gave them a complete physical. Had it been up to me, I would've given all of them a prostate exam, if for no other reason (except for the boy) than to have them suffer the discomfort and pain for the runaround they had put us through the night before. But Damon and the medic treated them with respect as each one asked me why we were doing this to them. They were well aware that seeing a doctor was out of their reach, which understandably caused them great confusion by the generosity of the American people, as demonstrated by our medic. Remembering they might have been the very same people who had shot Delta and the

ANP officer the day before, they were astounded that we were providing them with free medical care (which most Americans, including me, have to pay for out of our own pockets when we visit our doctors back home. The detainees were given a complete physical examination and screening to check to make sure they were healthy and fit to be interrogated. They were examined before the interrogation and afterwards to ensure that the interrogator had not physically abused them. For as long as they were in our custody, they were treated far better than any American would have been had the situation been reversed.

During both processes (medical and interrogation), being an interpreter can oftentimes be very challenging. It's difficult to ask questions of local Afghan detainees that are not "appropriate" because of cultural barriers. However, if a local Afghan had to answer a question necessary to help the interrogators or the medic understand their medical conditions, I would not hesitate to do so.

As mentioned earlier, medical care (or medical terminology, for that matter) is very limited or, in most cases, nonexistent in Afghanistan. One question that I came across often from our American medic who was treating a patient, that was particularly difficult for me to ask the local Afghans, was: "Are you aware if you have ever had any sexually-transmitted diseases (a term that does not exist in the Pashto language, so it presented a huge problem since all of the detainees we brought in for interrogation were Pashtons)?" Therefore, I had to pose the question as professionally as possible so the detainee somehow could understand. Since most of the local Afghans had never seen a doctor before, and the whole procedure was confusing enough for them, how could I make them also understand why we were questioning them about their sexuality? However, I ultimately figured out how to ask the question, in Pashto, as simply as possible: "Do you know if you have any disease from having sex?" If the detainee was really young, I usually got laughed at, while those who were older merely refused to talk about it.

Culturally, they thought that I was disrespecting or making fun of them, or that I might perhaps be offering them some kind of "sexually-related service" along with the medical examination. One of the detainees asked me in return, *"Dah hum sawal dey che tay kawai?"* ("What kind of a question is that?") Then he told me that, so far, he had never heard that anyone could get a disease from having sex—a perfect example that demonstrates how sensitive a cultural divide can make things worse during the medical checkup and the interrogation processes, because such a question often results in the detainee shutting down, thus lessening his willingness to cooperate.

I once suggested to the medic that this question not be asked, but my advice was ignored, which only tended to add additional humiliation to the detainee's physiological state of mind. Certainly, I could understand both sides of the issue, but at the same time, as a linguist/cultural adviser, I also wanted to do my job by trying not to ask questions that were really not beneficial to the task at hand.

After three long days of interrogation, Oscar and I were both exhausted. Interrogating 12 people who had nothing in common with Oscar culturally was very challenging for me to translate. Had Oscar interrogated a detainee back in the States, he would've undoubtedly known what, which, and how to ask the necessary questions so he could make the appropriate decision of what to do with the detainees. But here, in Afghanistan, it was a very different situation, which required that I be ultra-careful translating his words to the detainee and vice versa. While not an easy task, I completely understood why I was an integral part of the interrogation process. It was equally important that I understand both the interrogator and the detainee in order for me to do my job adequately. While listening to Oscar's words in English, I was also translating the words into Pashto in my head, while also watching Oscar's facial expressions so that the words coming out of my mouth were appropriate and accurate.

During an interrogation, because most detainees cried while answering the questions, as an interpreter, I had to make sure I didn't cry as well while translating a detainee's words from Pashto to English. From a cultural standpoint, detainees would cry just to get out of a particular conversation or avoid answering a particular question. Needless to say, like all of us, I have done my share of crying, not because of anything bad that had happened to anyone, but because of the goodness of the people involved. For instance, although I was certainly saddened by it, I didn't cry when Delta got shot on the night of our last mission, but did because of the goodness, courage, and bravery demonstrated by Fox and Damon as they ran through the bullets that were flying all around us to save Delta's life. I didn't cry as I walked through the field of dead bodies because I knew they were the bad guys that members of the team had eliminated for the sake of America and Afghanistan. What also made me emotional was when the American medic helicopter crew risked their lives to save the lives of others by landing in a hot zone, next to our Humvee, and then running to pick up Delta and the wounded ANP officer, the latter of whom wasn't even an American. All of the above are examples of the type of actions that make me cry—when other people risk their own lives to save the lives of others.

On the other hand, the detainees' reasons to cry were childish. They were merely trying to get what they wanted from us by crying, but soon learned that their tears were worthless; they needed to tell us the truth—a quality that was difficult to get out of most of them, especially if the interpreter happened to be from a different tribe than the detainee. Knowing the Afghan culture, torture—which I do *not* promote or believe in—was usually the only option that could be used to get the truth out of them; but because we showed them respect as human beings, they told us the truth and torture was not necessary. While we technically called them detainees, in reality, they knew that instead of their mud huts, they were better off in our custody—where they had air-conditioning during the summer and heat during the winter, not to mention three meals a day, courtesy of the American taxpayers. Frankly, instead of being called detainees, they should have been called our guests since our detention centers were much, much better than the normal lives they led.

Since our holding cells in the compound were for temporary use only, after three days of interrogation, our team made the decision where next to send the really bad guys, which was usually the main detention center in Bagram, while the "not so bad guys" would be turned over to the local Afghan authorities—usually the NDS—in Ghazni.

Since everyone on the team knew this was my first time being with the military and I had just experienced my first combat mission, they were all very supportive of me, thanking me for being part of their team every chance they got. For the first three days following the mission, Oscar and I were both busy interrogating the detainees, so I never had an opportunity to ask anyone how Delta was doing or how badly he'd been hit. At this point, since I had only been with the team for about three weeks, except for Delta, I didn't really know anyone else on a personal level, except for my observations of each one of them. After the last mission—seeing how they were willing to make the ultimate sacrifice for their comrades—I also knew that I could trust them all.

I felt a bond with Delta because we first met when he picked me from the airfield when I arrived in Ghazni. Additionally, upon his return from Bagram, where he had gone for his physical, he had come over to my room to say hello, give me a hug, and ask how I was doing. And now, three weeks later, I found myself not even knowing how he was doing.

The next day, we had another debriefing at the OPS center so that we could be prepared for our next mission. During the debriefings, everyone shared their thoughts and ideas regarding the prior mission. Since all missions are unpredictable and seldom, if ever, similar, Alfa usually led the conversation by addressing how the last one went and what needed to be done differently on the next one, especially since it was impossible to be prepared for how things turned out based on the need for second-by-second decisions.

In my mind, Alfa made all the right decisions on our last mission, including the "your fucking ass and drive the fucking vehicle" part (a statement I will *never* forget, by the way)—a point that was raised (by Alfa, of course). As Alfa recounts that statement, I saw him (a man for whom I have the utmost respect) looking me in the eye, visually asking me to forgive him for saying that during the mission. Since I was not offended by his words, I didn't want Alfa to be sorry or apologetic. I realized that because of Alfa's precise coordinates, the Air Force was able to drop the bomb precisely where it was meant to be dropped, which saved an innocent boy's life.

As the debriefing continued, Alfa said that I needed to be trained on everything in the compound that was used on our missions, including being able to drive the armored vehicles.

Since I was standing next to Fox, who had been in contact with the medical staff in charge of Delta's medical care, I leaned toward him and whispered, "How is Delta doing?" Instead of quietly responding, he said out loud for the whole team to hear, "Delta was transported from Bagram Airfield, Afghanistan, to Germany, and he's responding to the medical staff there very well. The primary concern right now is his high fever." Fox also assured the team that Delta would make it and would be Stateside within days.

Fox had brought Delta's body armor—which saved his life—to the debriefing, which clearly showed that two bullets had hit him in the chest. One of the other two bullets seared his pelvis, just below his body armor; the fourth bullet shattered his left forearm, causing him to drop his weapon. According to Fox, that's when Delta ran toward our Humvee and fell to the ground before he could reach us. Hearing the news about Delta's condition was very comforting to us all, and I was relieved to know that the person who shot him was dead.

Ray then informed us that the Chief of NDS from Ghazni Province was invited to our compound for lunch and would be at the base within the next couple of days. The Chief's primary visit was to discuss the mission (the one I missed during my first week with the team) that the team carried out when Baqi, the Taliban's leader, was killed and his brother was captured. On the day of his arrival, Qasim, our so called "chef" cooked rice for about 50 people, which included all of our team members and most of the ANP officers who were part of our team.

It was on a hot summer day in mid-June 2009. We all gathered together to stand on the gravel in the middle of the compound for a ceremonial picture to honor the ANP officers who were on the mission and killed Baqi. Three other ANP officers, who were also wounded during that combat mission, were recognized for their bravery. Following the presentation of the awards, Ray asked me to translate a few words of encouragement that he wanted to share with the group concerning the mission, including the overall performance of those who were wounded. Since this was the first such gathering ceremony of its kind since my arrival in Afghanistan, I was impressed by the professionalism displayed by Alfa and Ray, our team leaders, in recognition of the ANP officers. While Ray spoke in English, I translated his every word in Farsi, since every ANP officer was a native of the Farsi language, as was the NDS Chief of Ghazni. For 20 minutes, Ray and Alfa spoke words of encouragement to each and every one of the ANP officers attending the ceremony.

Before Alfa could present the ANP officers with their gifts and certificates of recognition as a token of appreciation from the American Special Forces, Alfa requested that I ask the NDS Chief if he had anything he wanted to say to his officers. Translating the question to the Chief, he smiled and told me to tell Alfa in Farsi that since Alfa had talked for such a long period of time (adding, "...but don't tell him that"), tell that because of the heat, he wanted to go inside so we could eat. In the way of an explanation as to why the NDS Chief said what he did, in the Afghan government or its culture, most people are incapable of acknowledging others for their achievements or even offering a simple word of encouragement. Most high-ranking government officers never compliment anyone under their command, primarily because they don't want those with lower rankings to think that they're capable of doing their jobs. So, as in this particular case with the NDS Chief, he could've said a couple of encouraging words when Alfa asked him to do so but had to refuse because he didn't want to tell his officers that they had done a good job by encouraging them; therefore, they would do an even better job in the future. Not encouraging them is also all about money. If the NDS Chief had recognized his officers for a job well done, he would then have had to reward them; but, if he kept criticizing them (despite their excellent performances), he didn't have to reward them in any way.

In most cultures, recognition and promotions usually are accompanied by some kind of monetary reward, which is not the case with most Afghans in the Afghan culture, especially if family members are involved. The Chief didn't even bother recognizing the officers' hard work—another cultural thing that will never be changed overnight. In the Afghan culture, most of the natives will not directly recognize others for their hard work and/ or achievements because it's not culturally appropriate. As they would say in Pashton,*"Tarif ya makawa, bya kona zindy wrokezhy,"* or in Farsi, *"Pashey royish tarifa sha na ko, key baz khoda gom maykonad."* ("Don't say anything encouraging; s/he might think they're a big deal.")

Since Afghanistan is one of the poorest countries in the world, most people are not fortunate enough to eat three meals a day; therefore, food becomes more of a luxury than that of necessity, which is why most Afghans weigh far less than they should because of the lack of nutrition. There are a very limited number of people who are obese. Unlike Americans, the only people who are obese in Afghanistan are the top 1 percent who are wealthy or have access to food, just like the NDS Chief—because of his status in the Afghan society—did in this case because his primary focus, rather than anything else, was to get as much food as he could.

When the NDS Chief asked me not to translate the first part of his answer to Alfa's question (when he said Alfa had talked for such a long time) since I wasn't there to be selective about what I did or did not translate, but chose to do what was required of me (i.e., to do an accurate job translating), I repeated the Chief's entire answer, because it wasn't about me and what I wanted—it was about the two people who needed to understand and help each other as much as they could. Alfa didn't comment about the first half of the Chief's answer. Instead, he said, "Our Special Forces team members would like to present your officers with gifts and certificates of merit as a small token of our appreciation for a job well done," which we then proceeded to do, shaking their hands, patting them on their backs, and congratulating each accordingly. Watching this take place, I became emotional, again because of the respect and kindness I was witnessing by my fellow Americans toward the Afghan ANP officers. I thought it a shame that the NDS Chief could not have done this himself.

While the presentations were taking place, the NDS Chief approached me and started to ask me personal questions, such as where in Afghanistan was I born and why and when had I immigrated to the United States. I responded to his questions, but not satisfied with my answers, he then asked, "Why did you leave Afghanistan in the late seventies; and, if you were born in Kandahar, where did you learn to speak Farsi so well?" He then went on to tell me that he understood Pashto, too, but couldn't speak it—which was common for Tajiks to say whenever they confronted me and learned that I was a native Pashton, just to make me feel good—another plus in the Afghan culture, in general, to make one feel good rather than tell them the truth. Being married to a Tajik, I have met my share of them, all telling me that they understood Pashto but couldn't speak it, which was really never the case. I had answered the NDS Chief's questions honestly, which can oftentimes be very offensive to the opposite side, especially in Afghanistan. Being in Afghanistan and answering the Chief's questions honestly was even more crucial (and sometimes dangerous) for me. Nonetheless, no matter who I was talking with, I always spoke my mind, so I went on to tell him that the reason I chose to leave Afghanistan for America was because of family ties to the U.S., where, at the time, my biological father was a citizen. I told him that

I chose to speak and understand Farsi because my wife is a Tajik from Kabul. Needless to say, when I said I was American, the Chief was not pleased. In fact, most other Afghans—and even members of my own family, who have lived in the United States for more than 30 years—are more often than not offended that I admit to being an American. In the Afghan culture, if you say aloud that you're an American, you're committing a crime and labeled a traitor.

What most people don't know about me is that my life had been very difficult since the age of six. However, no matter where I went, I was never prevented from choosing my own destiny or who I would become. It was not easy to be an American in a foreign country, and, most especially, being a native Afghan in Afghanistan oftentimes made it even worse in the Afghan community itself or even amongst members of your own family.

The NDS Chief told me that I was the only linguist to speak to him in Farsi rather than Pashto, the language used by most other linguists before me. In other words, the Chief appreciated the manner in which he had been treated by other linguists he had been in contact with, even though he didn't like the fact that I spoke to him in Farsi as an American. Since he was older than me by about 15 to 20 years, he wanted me to listen to him "because he had more gray hair than I did." I ultimately asked him what he wanted from me. His response was, "No matter what you do, you can *never* be an American."

According to the Chief, I was disrespecting him by not admitting that I am an Afghan but rather had convinced myself that I was an American—his interpretation and belief. Frankly, adding one more item of disrespect to my already existing tally for being an American (including the awards/recognition ceremony for the ANP officers) wasn't really going to hurt me. The ANP officers who worked with our team were ethnic Hazaras. Despite the fact that they all worked under the NDS Chief's command, who was an ethnic Tajik, since he wouldn't take the time to do it himself, he did not appreciate seeing them being recognized by our commander.

In preparation for a mission in our compound in Ghazni City Afghanistan.

The mud hut full of bad guys where Delta and the ANP officer got shot. Picture taken from the back of our Humvee two minutes before the shooting started. Qarabagh district.

At 7:00 AM, I left my room and walked towards the bathroom to wash-up and saw the message on the white board in front of the office: "Briefing at 9:00 AM"—a briefing that was being held to discuss the upcoming mission later in the day. Shortly before 9:00, I was the third person to show up for the briefing just before Jimbo arrived.

Everyone but Bravo had arrived by 9:00, so Alfa started the briefings and then everyone else on the team shared their expertise, followed by Alfa or Ray bringing the briefings to a close. Before Alfa could end the briefing, he asked if I had had the time to familiarize myself with the radio and all of the other equipment in the armored vehicles. I told him that I hadn't yet been able to do so but assured him that I was ready to take whatever lessons were necessary when anyone had the time. He reiterated that the more I knew, the better it would be for me and the team. I agreed, wondering who I could ask to teach me before going on the mission later that morning. Ultimately, I asked Ross, the JTAC who happened to be exceptionally knowledgeable about such things. Fortunately, he was willing to show me around and teach me what I needed to know. As I followed him to the vehicles, he told me that I wouldn't have time to learn everything the professional way, but he would teach me enough so that I had the general knowledge I needed as to how everything (e.g., guns and other items considered to be tactical in military vehicles) operated, just in case I needed to know any of it while on missions. Then he said something that I will remember for as long as I live: *"It's good for you to know how to use them; but don't worry—all eighteen of us have to die first before you do."*

Despite Ross's assurance, I still had a 10 percent fear in the back of my mind about being in combat with Special Forces. Sometimes the other 90 percent wants something badly—for example, my wanting to be a part of a Special Forces team—even though "what ifs" continue to linger, creating doubts that form fears. Such thinking can prevent you from doing what you want to do most. Well, that's where my mind was until Ross said what he said so that all of my fears were quickly blown away. I knew all along the kind of people with whom I was working—Americans…people who would sacrifice their lives so others (in this case, Afghans) could live and prosper.

We were on our way to this mission, which happened to be humanitarian in nature, in the District of Dayak in the eastern portion of the Ghazni Province—the same village where the team had gone two weeks prior, killing Baqi, one of the Taliban's leaders. On the road to the village,

I had my camera out and was taking as many pictures as I could. Having been away from my homeland for more than 30 years and now having the opportunity to return and actually be riding in a U.S. military Humvee was very exciting for me when we went out on dismounted missions. I also had a box of chocolate energy bars that had been sent to our team in care packages that were sent from the States. The box had been sitting in the kitchen, but since nobody wanted to eat them, with Alfa's permission, I brought the box with me and was throwing the bars out to kids lining both sides of the road. I soon realized my mistake because the kids started fighting over them. Since I didn't want them to get too close to our vehicles where the drivers might not see and run over them, I stopped throwing them to the kids on the road, waiting to hand them out when we arrived at the village. We also had two of the ANP's pickup trucks full of humanitarian goods (e.g., flour, sugar, oil, school supplies, and blankets) to distribute amongst the villagers.

Upon arrival, the first thing we did was have all of the ANP officers hold a security position by blocking the exit and the entrance of the only road going through the village. Almost all the villages in Afghanistan are connected by one narrow dirt road that runs through the village to go to the next village and beyond. There are no villages in Afghanistan with any of the services (e.g., running water, electricity, a medical facility, etc.) that most people in the city are fortunate enough to have. Very few villages have schools, and even if they did, it was a challenge to operate them because of the lack of teachers and school supplies. The village we entered was one of those that didn't have a school of its own.

Once everything in the village had been secured, Charlie (the gunner of our Humvee) told me I should meet with Alfa and Ray, who were both walking through the village talking with people, because they needed my help translating. Before I went to join Alfa and Ray, I lingered with Charlie in the Humvee for a few minutes while he told me stories about this village and its people who had been providing sanctuary to the Taliban. According to things I had heard from other members of the team, this village was not only friendly to the Taliban but it was also kids-oriented, which is why the team had named it "Toddlers Town."

When I found Alfa and Ray standing next to the main paved road, Alfa asked me again where my fucking rifle was. I told him I had left it in the Humvee and went back to get it. I wasn't accustomed to carrying a rifle, but—because of the ongoing danger that existed due to our location, I could understand his point when he yelled at me every time he saw me without it. When I returned to them, Alfa and Ray asked me to follow them, as closely as possible, as they walked to the other end of the village.

Having been told by Charlie that this was a Taliban-friendly village not only made it more scary for me to walk through the middle of it, but it made it scary for the locals, too, all of whom were staring at us. But it was scarier for us, especially since we didn't know which of the villagers were enemies likely to start shooting at us, or which were friends, if there were any. As I walked close to Alfa and Ray, I stayed alert, constantly looking from side to side from the corners of my eyes. I couldn't help but wonder if someone was going to start shooting at us but figured if they did, they would certainly have the home-court advantage. I had every confidence in my team, knowing that if the bad guys started anything crazy or stupid by attacking us in the light of day, they would be destroyed. But those were split-second thoughts running through my mind as we crossed the enemies' village.

Walking some distance into the heart of the village, away from everyone else on our team, I noticed Alfa and Ray as they suddenly stopped. Looking to my right, I saw a wide-open space, across which were some trees at the other end; in fact, they were the only trees I could see in the village. For security reasons, Alfa had to make sure that no one was hiding behind them to attack us. Still looking to my right, just before the beginning of the open space, I saw a blue, seven-to-eight-foot-tall, double-entry door in which there was a smaller three-to-four-foot door used by people to get in and out of the compound that was surrounded by a 10-to-15-foot-tall wall. One needed to duck their head in order to get into the house through the smaller door within the bigger door. I knew it was common for villagers with farming equipment like tractors to have such large doors. It's also common that the only person in the village who had the largest house would have the money to have farming equipment the size of a tractor.

The house belonged to either Baqi, the Taliban leader who was killed on the nightly raid by the ANP officers, or the detainee who was in our custody. Alfa told me to knock on the door. In less than a minute, someone I thought I had seen somewhere before opened the door and stepped outside. Then it occurred to me that I hadn't seen *this* person but rather his twin brother who had been in our custody. After identifying ourselves, shaking hands, and saying our hellos, Alfa—who was holding a clear, zip-line, plastic bag containing a cell phone and other personal items confiscated from the man's twin on the night we had captured him—handed him the bag, asking if he could identify the contents as those belonging to his brother, who was still in one of our holding cells. He nodded his head and said in Pashto, "Yes, that's my brother's stuff, but my brother is innocent, so please release him back to his family."

While Alfa didn't believe his story (nor did I), he made his point when he told the brother that we knew Baqi had been at the house with his brother when the ANP raided the village and killed the Taliban leader, because he refused to surrender; therefore, his brother was lucky to still be alive. Alfa asked me to tell the twin that because of his brother's association with Baqi, if he didn't help the Afghan government he might not be able to see his family for a very long time, if ever. The brother argued with Alfa that his twin was the wealthiest man in the entire village; he pointed out that there were some people working for the Afghan government who were after the farmland and the money it would bring if sold, which is why his brother had been taken away for a second time. He explained that his brother had been taken away once before but, after paying a bribe, was eventually released. Alfa, Ray, and the rest of our team didn't really have the time to be standing in one spot talking with this villager for so long. When the brother offered us tea, I didn't like the idea of entering the house, especially in this neighborhood. Fortunately, neither did Alfa. So we politely declined, offering him and his family something instead by asking him to join us at the west end of the village so that they could receive an assortment of humanitarian supplies that our team had brought for the villagers.

While en route, Alfa told me to inform every villager we met about the humanitarian aid the ANP would be distributing at the west end of the village. It was quite an experience for me to not only be walking around with Alfa and Ray, talking with the local villagers, who could understand me but were also confused about why we were giving out food and school supplies, as well as houseware items and blankets, because in the Afghan culture, if you gave someone something, it was expected that you were asking for something in return. I was asked repeatedly why the Americans were doing this. I explained they were gifts from the American people, but it was still difficult for them to understand. In retrospect, the ANPs were disbursing humanitarian aid to the villagers to make them look good so the villagers would respect them; a good concept, but since the villagers knew the aid was not coming from the Afghan government, the locals were suspicious.

As we started to distribute the items, having not been in Afghanistan for so long, I was promptly reminded that the Afghan people were not disciplined enough to stay in line when asked to do so because, despite their suspicions, they all wanted to get as much as they could for their families. Vying to be first in line, they started jumping on one another, taking things on their own by either snatching them from the hands of the ANPs or out of the hands of others, taking the items home, and then coming back a second, and in some cases, a third time for more. Damon and I watched a couple of guys fighting over a sack of rice; they were gripping it at each end and, as predicted, the bag ripped open and the rice covered the ground around them.

On the trip back to our base, I noticed that the ANP officer who was assigned to the heavy, automatic machinegun mounted to the back of our Humvee was trying to get my attention. He was speaking and wanted to tell me something, but I couldn't hear him over all the noise coming from the convoy. So I stood and got closer, asking him in his native language what he was trying to say. He responded, *"Balay"* ("Yes"), and then explained by asking if I had seen the large area surrounded by a wall on all four sides that we had just driven by. When I told him that I had, he told me that the Americans wanted to build a soccer stadium for the people of Ghazni, but Baqi wouldn't allow it to happen, which is why it was half finished and no one wanted to finish building the other half because they were too afraid to do so.

Upon hearing this, I really couldn't think of how to respond to what he had told me other than to encourage him to do all he could to protect the people of Afghanistan so the Taliban couldn't harass them during their efforts to rebuild their country with the help of the Americans, who were trying to do everything they could to help the Afghans build the infrastructure they needed—but we couldn't build it for them, if they weren't willing to do it themselves.

Having passed the half-built stadium, we saw a single grave/shrine alongside the road that was covered with more than 100 small green pieces of cloth, which (according to the ANP officer) represented a symbol of the Islamic flag that were customarily attached by the locals, showing their support—which, in this case, was dedicated to the person who was at one time in charge of building the stadium but had been murdered by Mullah Baqi.

The world witnessed the Taliban's cruelty when they were in charge of the government in Afghanistan. Building the stadium in Kabul—or stadiums anywhere else, for that matter—had been abandoned so it could be used for punishment or public executions for the approximately five-year period of time the Taliban were in power.

Most of the ANP officers in our team didn't know me personally, nor I them; the only person who knew me through Jabar was Ansari, their Captain whom I had met on numerous occasions while translating for team members whenever Jabar wasn't available. Since the team had nine other local interpreters on the compound, if the members wanted to talk with the ANPs or other locals, they would usually call upon a local interpreter since I was considered as more of an internal interpreter. Most of the ANP officers were young men in their 20s, except for Ansari, who was around 40 but looked closer to 70. Afzali—another officer in his mid-40s who also worked under Ansari's command—and I had met on only a couple of occasions. Of all the ANP officers, I respected him the most.

The ANPs were a unique group of guys who were, for the most part, related to each other. Ansari had four daughters who were all married to ANP officers under Ansari's command—a perfect example of how to keep it all in the family. Added to the mix was that all four of Ansari's sons-in-law either had a brother or brother-in-law who was also on the ANP team—all working under Ansari's command. Additionally, as the squad leader, Afzali had a couple of his sons-in-law working directly under his command in his squad. As Hazaras, they were united, but as a team, they were somehow divided from squad to squad, each doing their own thing, especially when on a mission.

Out of respect, Ansari and his officers also called me Ustad. Here again, I insisted on numerous occasions that they call me by my given name, but they refused to do so. In Afghanistan, you can never have things your own way; you must do whatever they offer you. If you refused to accept the offer, you would be disrespecting your host. For example, if someone invites you to their home, you lose all of your rights—you sit where you are asked to sit, you eat what they put on your plate (whether you like it or not), and you sleep when and wherever they tell you to—which is usually in their (your host's) own personal bed. Make sure to return the favor when they visit you. If you make the mistake of disagreeing with any of the rules, you would be called *baynezakat* (disrespectful). So, in order to keep the peace, so to speak, and in order to *not* disrespect your host, do as they say, not as you wish. Or my father-in-law would say, since I have spent most of my adult life with Tajiks in Farsi: *amdan-et-ba pie-e-khodet, ekhtyar, et, ba desti ma* (If you come to our home with your free will, you will not be allowed to use your free will until you leave our home).

In addition to the ANP officers, besides me, Jabar, and Haji Saheb, there were seven other local linguists on our compound, five were Pashtons from the city of Jalalabad in the east of Afghanistan, and the other two were Norm, who was a Tajik from Kabul, and Mike, who was a Hazara native from Ghazni.

The ANP always wanted to use Mike as their translator if they needed anything from the Americans, because they were more comfortable using someone from the same tribe. I found Mike to be intelligent and an open-minded, bright young man. He spoke and understood English very well and even had taken an American name for himself, just like Norm, the only Tajik linguist from Kabul, had done. Norm was usually never available to translate for the ANP (or anyone else for that matter), but when it came time to translate for the team, he was able to do so, even though his English was not as good as Mike's. All the other interpreters (Haji Saheb, Ingenyar Saheb, Assad, Najib, Atal, and, of course, Jabar, plus one other that I never got a chance to meet in person) were Pashtons and very weak in both English and Farsi. Haji Saheb could speak Pashto and Farsi fluently, but only some English.

Since most of our missions were to the villages where most of the locals spoke Pashto, it was more convenient to use the Pashto-speaking linguists. Mike was used more by the ANPs to translate Farsi to English and vice versa, while Norm was used more for speaking to Afghan government officials, who were mostly Tajiks. In other words, none of the Americans knew which local linguist spoke which language fluently. When Norm or Mike went home for their vacations, I was the only linguist the team had who could be used for all of their translation requirements, whether it was to talk with the ANPs, the detainees, other linguists, high-ranking government officials like the governor and the NDS Chief from Ghazni, or any of the district's sub-governors.

Since I lived on the compound 24/7 and most of the other local linguists went home once a month on a rotational basis, I was understandably more accessible to the team. A majority of the local linguists were notorious for trying to stall, especially when they knew there was going to be a dismounted combat mission within a few days. Although they didn't like going on these missions (primarily because they didn't like to do the dirty work involved with going after the bad guys), they were getting paid extra, nonetheless, and were provided with better living conditions because they were assigned to Special Forces. Linguists from the States who were U.S. citizens got paid the same whether they worked their asses off or sat on them all day long, the latter of which was what most of the linguists did, including me, but only during down times.

During the reviews I conducted every six months, every local linguist assigned to our team was in it solely for their own self-interests, which required they stay with the team (or any other military unit) for five years, which would then enable them to get their visas so they could go to the United States. Certainly, I couldn't blame them for risking their lives just so they could get their visas to the U.S., all the while getting paid more than the other local Afghans. Because of the men and women in the United States military who are making sacrifices to protect our values, freedom, and liberties (which are taken for granted by most Americans), how fortunate we are to live in such a great country.

On the other hand, I can comfortably say that the linguists I met would also risk their lives to get to America. One thing I will never understand is why most of the local linguists want to get out of Afghanistan, a place they profess to love so much, and yet they still labeled me as a traitor when I said I was an American. No matter the answer, I see the Americans, who are willing to risk their lives to *protect* their country, while the Afghans are also willing to risk their lives to get *out* of their country.

In Jabar's case—a linguist who had worked seven years risking his life as a part of Special Forces just so he could obtain a visa to leave Afghanistan for America—according to Damon and another of our team members, he (Jabar) failed the polygraph test five times. In addition to serving for at least five years, every six months linguists were required to have a positive review from the team with which they worked.

At this point, I had been in Ghazni for close to a month but still hadn't received the furniture for my room. So, I went and asked Charlie to see if

Jabar was going to get me the furniture or not. Charlie was surprised when I asked, telling me it usually only takes a day. I told Charlie that I had asked Jabar more than three times, but he kept telling me he didn't have any available. Charlie and I both knew that one of the Connexes was full of unassembled furniture so that all the carpenter needed to do was assemble and bring it all to my room. So we went to the Connex again to check for ourselves. Seeing that there was plenty of unassembled furniture, we asked the carpenter directly to assemble a desk and wardrobe for my room. Since the carpenter works and gets paid by the team, he said he had to get Jabar's permission first. Knowing that the furniture belonged to the Americans and not Jabar, Charlie asked me to tell the carpenter that he doesn't need permission from anyone to assemble a desk and wardrobe. Once we convinced him that the furniture belonged to the Americans, he agreed to do it.

I usually go to the main DFAC at the opposite end of the base from our compound for breakfast, lunch, and dinner, although I rarely ate lunch or dinner in our compound because Qasim really hadn't as yet mastered the art of cooking. According to his own admission to me, he had never cooked anything in his life until coming to the compound. Every time Alfa asked him to cook Afghan food, Qasim would simply put some rice and a one-pound brick of butter into a pressure cooker with some water, let it cook the appropriate length of time, dump it into a large bowl, and then serve it as Afghan rice, which most of our team members loved and would eat without complaint—at least for a while, primarily because the guys on our team didn't know what real Afghan rice was supposed to taste like.

Unfortunately, everyone on the team eventually got sick and tired of eating the so-called Afghan dish known as "butter rice," what the Afghans called *shola,* which, in the Afghan culture, was rice boiled in water until it became the consistency of mashed potatoes, which is then usually given to the very young or elderly (especially those without teeth) because it's easy to digest.

One day Alfa called me to the OPS Center and asked me to tell Qasim to cook some other kind of Afghan food besides the fucking rice he cooked over and over again. I went to the kitchen to give Qasim Alfa's message. After hearing Alfa's request, Qasim looked worried, and asked me in Pashto, "But I was hired on as a dishwasher! I'm not a cook, so what do you suggest?" Except for suggesting that he talk with Jabar, his boss, to see if he could help him cook something else, I had no other answer for him. When I shared the conversation with Alfa, he got mad and told me to go back to the kitchen to tell Qasim that he *had* to cook something else; and if he didn't know how to do that, then he should read a fucking book and start learning. He added that we didn't need a fucking dishwasher, we needed someone who could cook.

I returned to the kitchen again with Alfa's message. Now, Qasim looked more frightened than before as he asked me what I thought he should cook that the Americans would like. I told him that it didn't matter at this point, especially since he didn't know how to cook in the first place. He then asked if I knew how to cook and, if so, could I teach him? I knew how to cook but at that moment, I didn't have time to teach him, so I again suggested that he find Jabar to help him. A couple of hours later, I saw them with three local Afghans, who usually came every morning to clean the compound and whatever other chores (like electrical, plumbing, and carpentry) needed to be done. At this point, they were all busy cleaning a lamb they had just slaughtered for Alfa's dinner. (As an aside, when Alfa got mad, everyone, including me, jumped to do whatever was necessary to calm him down.) None of the Afghans wanted to get fired from their jobs. When Alfa needed someone to cook dinner or wanted anything to be done, it was done in a timely matter, primarily because Alfa was a man of his word and everyone under his command knew that.

Of the three locals who were going to help cook the lamb, only one in his 40s knew how to [sorta] cook, but had been hired to clean, not cook. It was obvious that Qasim should've been the cleaning guy, while the cleaning guy should have been hired to cook. Apparently, however, when Americans need a local Afghan for any kind of work, Jabar went out and grabbed anyone off the street. According to Qasim, ever since his father had passed away, he had always worked as a day laborer to support his family. He saw being hired as a dishwasher as a great opportunity for him to work for the Americans. Despite the fact that he wasn't a cook, he was very happy to be working for us and didn't want to get fired. He said he was more than willing to learn—cooking and English—in order to not only keep his job, but also be an interpreter one day.

While observing the five guys trying to come up with some kind of Afghan cuisine to please the Captain so they wouldn't get fired, since one was usually unable to get ahold of Jabar (who considered himself a true

Muslim while labeling me an American infidel), because he hung out during the night drinking and smoking hash, sleeping during the day, I found another opportunity to confront him and the carpenter (who were luckily both in the same room at the same time) about the furniture for my room. According to other linguists, Jabar was usually nowhere to be found on the compound because he also typically hung out at the bazaar on the base where he owned a couple of electronics shops. Undoubtedly, the carpenter had already mentioned the subject to him, because Jabar brought up the subject first by saying that the last set of furniture they had had been given to a local interpreter. Before I said anything to him, I turned to the carpenter and reminded him that when Charlie and I talked with him a week ago, he said he was going to assemble a set of furniture for my room because, according to him at that time, there was "tons" of unassembled furniture in the Connex that would enable him to take care of my request. I then turned back to Jabar, asking why he was telling me that the last set of furniture had been given it to another linguist, especially when he knew that Charlie and I had already talked with the carpenter.

At this point, whether the furniture had been given to the local inter-preter—who was not qualified to get it in the first place—intentionally or erroneously, was no longer the point. The carpenter told me that Jabar had instructed him to give it to the other linguist. Knowing where and how the other linguists lived, I reminded Jabar and the carpenter that the other linguist didn't even have the space in his room in which to fit the furniture; in fact, he wasn't allowed to have the furniture in the first place. I didn't blame the carpenter; he was simply a victim of circumstance. Instead, without saying a word, I looked Jabar in the eye, just to let him know that I knew who was really preventing me to get the furniture I needed. Then I simply turned and left the kitchen.

When I saw Charlie the following day, I told him what Jabar had done regarding my request for furniture. Charlie told me that the furniture was intended for the Americans only. Obviously, Jabar just didn't want me to have it. I believe the carpenter really didn't have anything to do with it; Jabar was simply trying to tuck it away from the Americans by giving it to one of his buddies who wasn't even an American or a taxpayer. None of the local linguists, ANP officers, or the local Afghan workers (carpenters, electricians, plumber, or cleaning people, including Qasim) on our base paid any taxes to either government. And don't get me wrong about Afghanistan's tax collecting system. They do have one, and it's called *Reshwat* (bribe) in both the Pashto and Farsi languages. It is usually paid from one person to another instead of an institution or a treasury.

So, because I had a purpose and a mission to accomplish while in Afghanistan, I came up with a plan. Not only did I want to be with Special Forces and guys like Alfa and his team to defeat the enemy of both American and Afghanistan, I was also there to help contribute to the education of young Afghans who desperately needed our assistance so they could succeed intellectually. I strongly believed then, as I do now, that the only way Afghanistan can pull itself up out of poverty and towards prosperity is by allowing us to provide their young generation with the tools of education necessary for them to succeed. With that plan in mind, one day when Alfa and I were both in the kitchen having breakfast—mine, the usual: a plate full of fruit; Alfa, scrambled eggs and sausage—I told him what I had wanted to say when I had first arrived in Ghazni, but, until now, there had never been an opportunity to do so. Now, finally having the chance, I told him what my intentions were by coming to Afghanistan and being with Special Forces, in particular. While in the States, I had heard what the Special Forces were doing (beside killing the bad guys), including the humanitarian missions in which they helped with the building infrastructure (i.e., construction of schools, medical clinics, governmental institutions, and the training of the Afghan Security Forces)—not to mention all of the combat missions they went on to kill or capture the bad guys. I told Alfa that I loved both aspects of what the Special Forces did. Then, since I had been with the team for a little over a month, we had gone on both combat and humanitarian missions, and I was now ready to offer my financial help to the Afghan people, particularly—if one wants Afghanistan to succeed—the children who needed it most. In addition to my own personal funding, I told Alfa about my intention to offer additional aid by either helping to build or refurbish an existing school in the area of Ghazni City, where we could manage and monitor the work taking place.

Having been away from my native land since the age of 16, I had no knowledge of how things worked regarding the building and/or refurbishing of a school, especially since I didn't know anyone in the area anymore. I asked Alfa if he had any suggestions who I could talk with or otherwise get started. Since Alfa had been in Afghanistan for the past six months and, thus, outside the base on many occasions, I thought that he was my only option, which is why I asked for his opinion and assistance on how to start my project. Obviously, we all had our own different perspectives and mindsets before arriving in Afghanistan. Once on the ground and in contact with the locals, opinions were totally different from those we—even a native like me—had before arriving.

When Alfa asked for more specifics about what I wanted to accomplish, I told him that, unlike all the other rebuilding projects by the international community, I didn't want my project or my funding to be handled by the Afghan government. I wanted to do it on my own, for two reasons. First, I wanted to build the school where it was needed the most, not where it was politically needed by the Afghan government officials or their affiliates merely for the profit it could bring to them personally. Second, I wanted my money to be spent locally, in the city of Ghazni, by hiring local contractors and buying materials from the local business owners, which would put my hard-earned cash into the hands of the dedicated and hard-working locals who needed it the most. I knew my project would provide work for a minimum of 15 to 20 people for at least a four- to six-month period of time. I realized that my personal funding ($50,000) wasn't really much when compared with the costs involved in the States, but it was important for me to conduct the project according to my plans by keeping it as far away as possible from the culture of the very corrupt Afghan government.

From a very young age, I have always worked very hard for every penny earned—which is why I didn't just want to "give it away," in this instance—and I know the value of hard work and can spot a hardworking person when I see one. I have seen people who value the fruits of their labor; when Fox and I walked through Ghazni City and talked with the locals, I could see that the city was full of local, hard-working Afghans. I knew then and now how to spend my money (and it definitely wasn't going to be through a corrupt cousin contractor of an Afghan government official). Afghans in large cities like Kabul and Kandahar might be living in million-dollar homes, enjoying their lavish Western life, while the local villagers still lived under the same poverty standards as they did when I was growing up in my adoptive Arghandab District.

I knew it would cost a lot less if I purchased everything from local businesses rather than just writing a check to the Afghan government so they could hire the people I needed on my behalf to build the school. If this were to be allowed, I was certain that my project would never happen, just like all the other contracts and projects that had been funded by international donors through the Afghan government. If anything could be built to benefit the local Afghans, it had to be done *without* the Afghan government's involvement.

Since Afghanistan's living standards are among the lowest in the world, the country is very dependent on foreign aid. According to the CIA's world facts book, during the period 2003–2010, Afghanistan was given $67 billion in funding for redevelopment projects. However, most of that money was taken out of Afghanistan by the so-called Afghan government officials and sent to either Dubai, where it was invested, or the funds were transferred back to the West for personal investments.

Until the Afghan government overcomes a number of challenges (which I hope and pray they do), including the collection of revenue— that is, while revenue might not be low, the money does not go into the national treasury but, rather, directly into the pockets of those government officials who initially receive it—I will not trust them. Most importantly, Afghanistan needs to correct a strong government capacity at all levels of corruption, which leads to a poor public infrastructure. As mentioned earlier, no one in the government pays any income or sales taxes, while 65 percent (two-thirds) of the Afghan population is not only taxed to the max via *reshwat* but goes to bed hungry.

Since I believed that anyone *besides* the Afghan government would do a far better job of rebuilding Afghanistan, I also knew that I could spend every dime of my funding to hire local Afghans who would finish building the school on time—much the same as the Afghanistan government officials had done to build their million-dollar mansions. As an example of how much a day laborer would cost me if I were to hire local Afghans off the street: Qasim, our so-called cook, was getting paid $300 a month, which is six times more than the normal rate for local Afghans. The average *annual income* for local Afghans is somewhere between $400 to $500. Frankly, I wouldn't be surprised if Qasim paid a percentage of his paycheck to either Jabar, or whoever introduced the two, for getting him a job with the Americans. If Jabar didn't get a cut out of everything he controlled, then how was he able to purchase a penthouse in Dubai with the money he earned as a local linguist? He also had a family of six, including his parents, who were living quite lavishly in Kabul.

Local Afghan civilians pay *reshwat* directly to anyone who works for the Afghan government, but in the form of gifts so it doesn't go to the Afghan government's treasury, but only to the individuals who are at the receiving end. Afghan civilians cannot have anything done in the Afghan government until money changes hands. *Reshwat* is even more common between the government officials themselves to get promotions—the higher the ranking, the more you would pay. And at the end, everything has been passed on and paid by the ordinary, poverty-stricken Afghans who are already struggling to survive. To make my point even clearer, if I had involved the Afghan officials in my project of building or refurbishing an existing school, I would undoubtedly have had to pay most of my money toward the *reshwat* before I would have been able to have anything done. Not only that, none of the people who really needed the work would have gotten the job.

Alfa understood my point but couldn't see how I would be able to coordinate such a project alone, especially since I would not be able to leave the base to monitor the progress at the construction site without involving the Afghan government. Alfa recommended I talk with the PRT (Provincial Reconstruction Team) unit located within our base, since all they do is work on the redevelopment of Afghan infrastructure projects. I went to their office to get some information, but learned that their projects were through the Afghan government as well; so, since I was not part of their team, I would have no way of monitoring their progress once I had given my money to them. The PRT representative gave me the same advice Alfa had a week earlier: They both suggested that I write checks to the charities of my choice, or to the PRT since they were already involved in rebuilding Afghanistan's infrastructure.

After my conversation with Alfa and the PRT, I sadly realized that my plan and dream of building or refurbishing a school was not going to be possible—at least not the way I wanted it to be done—although the other option of simply giving the money to a charity or charities of my choice was still a possibility for me. At that time, not knowing how charitable funds were distributed, I wasn't particularly thrilled about donating my money just yet.

I now completely understood Alfa's point of view that things were not as easy as I thought, but at least I had tried and was determined to continue trying—when opportunities presented themselves to me—for as long as I was in Afghanistan

As we finished our breakfasts, Alfa thanked me for what I had in mind as my way to help the Afghan people succeed. I knew that Alfa and I shared the same compassion for the Afghan people. As he stood, he turned and looked at Qasim. "Nas is a good man," he said before leaving the kitchen. Since the only words Qasim understood in English were "good morning," "goodnight," "very good," and "thank you," he didn't understand what Alfa had just said, but he smiled and nodded his head nonetheless. When I then briefly reviewed with Qasim the proposal I had discussed with Alfa, he shook his head and told me he didn't like my idea of building a school in the city of Ghazni because he thought I'd be spending an excessive amount of money for just one school.

As soon as Alfa left the kitchen, I made my morning call back to the States to talk with Laila and ask how things were going for Omar, Sabrina, and members of our extended family. She assured me that everything was just fine with everyone. When I called her, I was always keenly aware and kept in mind that she was going through a multitude of emotions being alone (without me by her side), while she cared for her mother, who was undergoing chemo for her cancer. Being 9,000 miles away—somewhere in a war zone where she didn't want me to be in the first place—was taking its toll on her. For her to know that I was with Special Forces and was going on combat missions was unbearable, just like it is for all other women married to men who either enlisted in the military or provided civilian assistance in order to support our country's mission. Since I could/would not lie just to make her feel more secure and safe, I called her every morning to say hello, ask about our family, and tell her that, so far, everything was okay with me. Before hanging up the phone, I told her that I'd talk with her the next day.

Having returned to the kitchen while I was on the phone, Alfa couldn't help but hear my closing statement to my wife; so, as soon as I hung up the phone, he asked, "How do you know you're going to be able to call your wife tomorrow? How can you be sure of that? That's fucking bullshit!" Recognizing from the tone of his voice that he was quite serious, I was suddenly confused as to why he would say such a thing, most especially when he did so by using profanity. It was one of those rare moments where I couldn't think of anything to say. Not waiting for my answer, Alfa explained that he had stopped telling his wife that he'd call her again the next day because he really didn't know if he'd be able to do so. He then asked, "What if we leave on a mission tonight and don't come back for two or three days? Would you be able to call your wife tomorrow?" Now, I was finally getting Alfa's point and imagined how Laila would be concerned and frightened. I knew she'd have nightmares wondering what had happened to me, her misery caused because I would not have been able to call her as promised.

Every time I came in contact with the captain, my respect for Alfa's leadership and his concern for our wellbeing grew more and more each day. Qasim, who doesn't even speak or understand Alfa's language, would tell me in Pashto, *"Kep tan Alfa dear zabardasta sarrey dey"* ("Alfa is a very confident man"), to which I would respond, *"Woa"* ("Yes"). Then he added (which I thought was very funny), *"Da Jimbo la da kep tan Alfa pa khula kawey"* ("Even Jimbo listens to Captain Alfa"). At this point, I'm sure you can understand why I respected the people I was working with—and most especially, Captain Alfa—more and more.

When I see Americans like Alfa and the other team members, I can't help but wonder why everyone couldn't fall in love with America. But again, not everyone was as privileged as I was to have served with people like members of the special forces. Personally, I believe there are three kinds of people in the world: (1) those on the ODA team, where each and every one of them are willing to die, not only for America but the world in general; (2) those at the opposite end of the spectrum, who are doing everything they can to destroy the value that Americans love, protect, and enjoy; and (3) the majority of the people in the middle, which is sad because they would see the battle between (1) [force of goodness] and (2) [force of evil] and do nothing to stop it to avoid criticism or they would simply look the other way, thinking it wouldn't affect them. Sadly, this is the kind of world we are [still] living in today, where almost 90 percent of the people reside in their own personal bubble and don't even have a clue that there are other people who are willing to die to protect the world from those who are evil enough to destroy it. I am a very strong believer in the following 16th-century philosophical quote made by Maimonides:

> *"Every human being at any time should always view himself and the world as a balance scale. One act tips the scale."*

So, just as much as one's good acts benefit society, it's also important to realize that it takes only one bad act to destroy it. Or, perhaps to make my point even clearer, it was Napoleon who once said, *"The world suffers a lot, not because of the violence of bad people, but because of the silence of good people."* It is quotes such as these by which I try to live my life.

Once Qasim told me he didn't think it was a good idea to build a school in the city of Ghazni, where it was needed the most, he explained that in order for me to build a school there, I was going to have to hire the Hazaras as day laborers; so, once the school was built, everyone who attended would either be Hazaras or Tajiks; it would not be attended by the Pashtons or the Uzbeks because it's a simple fact of life that the word *Afghan* does not really exist in my native land. Qasim had totally forgotten my stance regarding ethnicity. Before I could remind him, yet again, he had a recommendation of his own. Since his hometown was in Logar Province, about 50 miles south of Kabul, he tried to convince me to build the school there. I reminded him that since it wasn't possible for me to build a school in Ghazni, which was only five miles from our compound, there would be no way for me to do so 60 miles to the east in Logar. As a Pashton, Qasim persistently told me that he would help me build the school in Logar Province, reiterating that was where it was needed the most.

I will admit to being shocked that Qasim, a day laborer with no formal education, was trying to convince me to put my money for the school in Logar because, according to him, not only did Logar need a school the most, as a Pashton he would not waste other Pashton's (referring to me) *"halal"* ("honestly earned") money on a school that was going to undoubtedly be built by Pashtons (who I assumed would be all of his cousins). Then, once construction was completed, it would also be attended by Pashton children. Qasim didn't like the idea of my money going to the city of Ghazni, where the majority of the population were Hazara. Instead, he wanted my money to go where the majority of the people were Pashtons (obviously, the only thing on Qasim's mind was anything that was even minutely Pashton-related).

I reminded Qasim again that I wasn't building the school because I was a Pashton, Tajik, Hazara, or Uzbek; as an American, I reiterated that I simply wanted to help build a school for the children of Afghanistan who needed it the most. When I explained why it wasn't even possible for me to build it anyway, and gave him the reasons why, he didn't want to discuss it anymore, especially if I continued to refuse to build it in his hometown. I couldn't help but wonder if he was really focused on helping me build the school or if he only wanted to rip me off so he could get my money.

My offer to build a school in Ghazni City quickly spread throughout the compound and much of Ghazni itself. The ANP officers approached me, asking if I needed any help with day laborers, electricians, carpenters, plumbers, and the like. Since most of the day laborers and ANP officers were Hazaras, I understood why they asked me if I needed help. To most of the local Afghans, it seemed strange, and they simply couldn't understand why I was doing something of such magnitude, especially with my own money, which equaled about 25 million Afghanis (Afghan currency).

In Afghanistan, people don't usually do things like this, especially someone (me) who isn't even from the same tribe as the people for whom I wanted to build the school. In fact, most people, not only in Afghanistan but around the world, would try to help each other by sticking to their own culture. However, on this issue, the Afghan and American cultures were totally on opposite ends of the spectrum. As an example, every time a manmade or a natural disaster occurs anywhere in the world, Americans are the first on the scene to help, regardless of race, religion, or nationality. However, Afghanistan is the direct opposite because Afghans are more focused on helping their own tribes first, then their main tribes, and their countrymen last. It's not that they didn't want to help but that being extremely poor, to the point where they couldn't even help themselves, made it impossible for them to help others. Most of the local Afghans who were offering to help me build the school weren't actually interested in building it. They were more interested in their own personal gain they could derive from the project. All of the local Afghans who had worked with us on the base—whether linguists, the ANP, ANA, or NDS—knew it was impossible for me to leave the base so I could monitor how the construction was progressing. Sure, they could help me monitor the project, but only by having the contractors cheat us just like they did on every other project in Afghanistan contracted out through the Afghan government.

I began to notice that some of the officers' attitudes toward and treatment of me changed more into how they treated other team members who were Americans. I knew that most of the officers respected our team members a lot more than they did their own NDS Chief, who treated them like trash. All of the officers who worked for our team on the compound were paid more than the officers who had worked under the command of their NDS Chief in Ghazni, and, out of all the local Afghan workers on our compound, the Hazaras were the hardest working.

I was always given an unwelcome look from several of the officers who lived on our compound who didn't really know me personally. In the Afghan culture, you're labeled for what you are, not who you are. Once they got to know me, they became much more friendly. That didn't happen with most of the local linguists, who were also mostly Pashtons. I knew why they didn't like me; the reason was obvious: I chose to be an American. I could not change who I was just because they didn't like it. Frankly, I was quite proud of who I was.

CHAPTER FOUR

Real death threat, or just a scary tactic?

ONE NIGHT, SHORTLY AFTER MIDNIGHT, someone knocked on my door. I thought it might be Bravo coming to tell me there was a mission that we needed to get ready for, but when I turned on the light and opened the door, it was Jabar, who stormed into my room without even asking for permission. Raising his voice, he said he wanted to talk with me...*now!* I asked him what was so important that he had to wake me instead of waiting for morning; I also wanted to know why he was raising his voice. I was surprised by his vehement response: "Don't fucking act like an American in *my* compound! You think you can put up your fucking American flag on the wall in your room and act like you're a fucking American? I don't think you will ever become a fucking American, you motherfucker. I'm so pissed I want to kill you." He shouted this quickly, in one nonstop sentence. On more than one occasion, I had been insulted before and screamed at and yelled at for simply being an American. I wasn't frightened by Jabar or his insults; I was just sort of confused about why he felt the need to storm into my room at midnight and start cursing at me just for being an American and putting up an American flag.

Although he'd been acting respectful toward the other team members (who were also Americans with American flags hanging in their rooms), I realized that he was either acting this way out of jealousy for his own personal gains—the normal thing to do in the Afghan culture—or he was frustrated that I was an American citizen while he had tried several times to get the necessary visa required to go to the United States. Or perhaps intimidating me was somehow a way of bringing him comfort.

Jabar had applied for a visa to go to the U.S. for more than seven years, longer than any other linguist had tried. So, was he faking that he loved America by failing the polygraph on numerous attempts, and now coming to my room in the middle of the night to prove it to me? Or was he frustrated just because I was already a citizen of the United States? I would say *yes* to both, because 99.9 percent of his rage was directed toward my American citizenship.

When I realized that he was blocking the way for me to leave the room, if necessary, I told him to get the fuck out. Instead of leaving, he intimidated me further by showing me that he was carrying a pistol, which I saw sticking out of his shirt, above the waistline of his trousers.

"I said get the fuck out of my room," I repeated, more loudly this time, but he still wouldn't move out of the doorway. Instead, he continued to try to intimidate me by placing both of his hands on his waist, drawing closer attention to the pistol poking out of his shirt, to make it clear that he thought he was completely in control of the situation, especially if he decided to shoot me. He continued to curse and threaten to kill me if I didn't stop acting like an American. When he noticed that he wasn't intimidating me and I wasn't buying any of his shit, he became even more frustrated. Being American comes with a price and all the consequences that go with it, especially if you're a native of Afghanistan who chose to be an American and had the guts to tell your native Afghans.

I couldn't understand why he was offended by my allegiance to the flag of the United States of America, while he desperately wanted the same for himself. With the exception of Jabar, everyone else on the team treated me like one of their own They also requested me more as their translator than Jabar, which is why he and the other linguists didn't like me, because I wasn't one of them.

As Jabar continued to block the door and intimidate me by acting like he was going to shoot me, I grabbed my AK47 off the wall to my right; it was fully loaded with a magazine containing 39 rounds. Pointing the rifle at him, I said, "Listen to me, and listen very carefully. You have forced yourself into my room in the middle of the night, cursing me and my country, and trying to intimidate me with the gun sticking out of your shirt. Well, as I'm sure you've noticed, I am holding a weapon much more powerful than yours. It's also a lot bigger, but know that I am not afraid of using it if I have to. So, I am asking you one more time to get the fuck out of my room, *now!*" Unfortunately, he wouldn't shut up but continued shouting and yelling with even more fervor and frustration in his voice than before. Since his insults weren't disturbing me as much as he had wanted, he shifted his verbal assault away from me being an American to me being a Kandahari. Despite the fact that we were fellow Pashtons, he was now mocking me for being a Kandahari just to see if that would anger me. Well, that didn't work either, even though he was now cursing about how fucked up all the Kandaharis were and then became even more frustrated when I didn't react or respond to those insults and his verbal abuse, except to remind him that I was an American, not a Kandahari.

Before I asked him for the last time to leave my room, he had calmed down considerably and seemed to be getting my message as I simply pushed him away, to the side of the doorway, and left the room, which angered him, so he started yelling and threatening to kill me again. By this time, I had had enough and wanted him out of my room! "If you're man enough to kill me, go ahead and do it already! I'm sick of listening to your fucking bullshit and want you out of here! Get out, damnit," this time waving my gun to show him I meant business.

Apparently, he believed that I might shoot him, so as he left my room. We saw one of our team members, Jack, whose room was next door to mine, so he had undoubtedly heard the argument going on in my room and came out to see what all the noise was about. Jabar and I had noticed that Jack had walked by my room twice in an effort to find out what was going on, at which point Jabar would not say a word and then after Jack had walked by, out of hearing range, Jabar would start arguing, yelling, and saying fuck as often as he could. Once, when he had stopped to take a break, I asked him why he used fuck to the point where it didn't have meaning or impact anymore. He said, with a sneer on his face, that he had learned it from my fucking American buddies (referring to our team members). He was probably right about that because he always hung out with Ricardo, who had a bad habit of starting and ending every sentence with the word fuck.

Fed up with his shouting and yelling, I told him one last time to shut up and tell me what he wanted from me. He was so riled up, he couldn't speak coherently, and I made the decision to wake up Alfa to see if he could do something about Jabar's behavior—and get him out of there! When I told Jabar that I was going to call the captain, he sneered, asking me why I was going to bring Alfa into this because the whole compound belonged to him (Jabar) and neither Alfa or I had any right whatsoever to tell him what to do. "Why the team even brought you here when there was no need for your services as a linguist is beyond me." Jabar was notorious for intimidating linguists from the States, so he was apparently on a mission to get rid of me so that the compound would return to being under his control. Little did he know that he had picked the wrong American to intimidate, because I planned to stay with Special Forces as long as I was in Afghanistan.

I mentioned again that I was going to call Alfa. When I did, he turned and quickly left the front of my room and walked away, still cursing loudly. As Jabar's voice and curses faded, I went back to bed, making a mental note to bring up what had just happened tomorrow morning during our daily briefing with Alfa and the rest of the team.

It was the normal morning briefing, where Bravo and Alfa would update us with what was going on and then, before the meeting ask if we had any questions or concerns regarding our daily routines, which—in addition to going out on combat missions—varied from day to day (e.g., training the ANP, ANA, or NDS officers, or meeting with any of the other Afghan government officials). At the end of Bravo's review of the list of things that the team needed to perform that day, he asked if anyone had anything to add or change to anything he had said. Rather than all 18 members immediately starting to talk at the same time, this part of the meeting was handled in a very professional manner. Without saying anything, Bravo simply pointed an index finger at each member. If that member had anything to say, then he would proceed on to someone else, and Bravo would then listen, dealing with the comment/question then or telling them he would get back to them at a later time. I usually didn't have anything to say when Bravo pointed to me but such was not the case at this morning's meeting.

Since I had never spoken at these briefings before, Bravo raised his eyebrows in surprise, and said, "Yes, Nas." Before I could speak, I couldn't help but notice that all eyes in the room were staring at me. Since Bravo always stood by the door while Alfa sat at his desk where his computer was, I made it a point to make eye contact with them both "Sir, I want to bring to your attention that shortly after midnight last night, to my surprise, I had an unexpected visit by Jabar, who entered my room, cursing and yelling, for what reasons I don't know. He was not only threatening to kill me, but he was cursing at me and everyone else on the team, referring to us as fucking Americans. He was also cursing the American flag hanging on the wall in my room."

Before I could continue, Alfa looked at Bravo and asked, "What's going on with all this Jabar shit again?" Before Bravo could respond, Charlie confirmed what I had just told them. Charlie also told them that Jabar was drunk last night and had apparently initially come to my room because he was angry about a comment I made one day to Ricardo about the local linguists. At that point, I could see that Alfa was no longer interested in hearing anything further about my encounter with Jabar the night before because he obviously had more important things to worry about. Nonetheless, Bravo agreed with Charlie about Jabar being drunk and how mean and vile he could become when he had consumed too much booze. Bravo assured me and Alfa that he would talk with Jabar after the debriefing.

After the meeting, everyone else left the OPS center, while Bravo, Alfa, Ray, and I stayed behind so Bravo could talk with me about what had happened the night before, which I did. Before Alfa could speak, Bravo asked me, "Why do you think he came to *your* room in the middle of the night and tried to intimidate you?" I told Bravo why I thought Jabar had done so. After listening to my side of the story, Alfa, Ray, and, I were all anxious to hear what Bravo had to say, which basically was that Jabar was ticked off because a couple of weeks earlier, when Ricardo was trying to show me how to clean and load my weapon, during that lesson, Ricardo asked me if I knew how to load a magazine, to which I promptly responded in what I thought was a joking way. "What? Do you think I'm one of the local interpreters?" Well, Ricardo didn't take it humorously and told Jabar what I had said, which obviously offended Jabar considerably.

Alfa, Ray, and Bravo wanted to know what my thoughts were about all of this, and most especially if I knew why Jabar would behave so vehemently about linguists from the States. I explained my thoughts on the subject. Based on Jabar's behavior, when they then asked me whether I was planning to quit the team and my assignment because I was afraid of Jabar, I assured them that I was *not* going to leave the team. It was suggested that perhaps the team should get rid of Jabar (or as Alfa put it, "Let's just fire his ass!").

"Sir, certainly I am not in a position to make that decision. I am not afraid of him and am *not* leaving the team," I reiterated. "I asked him repeatedly last night what his problem was, but he wouldn't listen, so I got no answers from him in that regard whatsoever." Glancing at Bravo, I added, "Please tell Jabar not to *ever* come to my room again, for as long as I am a team member." It was determined that Bravo would talk with Jabar once he knew he was awake. (Jabar and Ricardo were notorious for staying up all night and sleeping until midafternoon.)

When the briefing session was concluded, I walked over to the kitchen to make my morning phone call to Laila. About halfway into my conversation, Bravo walk in and crossed the room to stand by the fridge. He didn't say anything or even look at me directly, but I suspected that he was waiting for me to get off the phone so he could talk to me about Jabar. I tried to cut my conversation short so Bravo could talk with me, but by the time I managed to end the conversation and turned around, he had already left the kitchen. So, I walked back to the OPS center to see if he was there. He wasn't, so I went to his room. After my initial knock, Bravo opened the door and told me he would be right out to talk to me about Jabar.

When he finally came out, we went to my room. Bravo's first question was whether Jabar had ever talked to me before last night's confrontation. I told him that Jabar and I had never talked regarding anything or anyone. Bravo said he had talked with Jabar after the debriefing and clearly and specifically told him *never* to come to my room and harass me again. He confirmed that Jabar had acted the way he did because he was indeed very drunk but, more specifically, he always tried to intimidate linguists from the States who were given a room amidst the ODA team—something Jabar desperately wanted because he had worked for the team the longest and felt, therefore, that linguists who came from the States should not be entitled to a room. Bravo confirmed what I already knew—that Jabar simply didn't understand the difference between being an American linguist and the local linguists working for Americans. Jabar was frustrated that things didn't work out the way he wanted them to; he thought the longer a linguist had worked with the team, the bigger priority they should have to get a room. Bottom line: Bravo told Jabar that if he ever harassed the Americans one more time, he would be off the team, a risk Bravo didn't think Jabar would ever want to risk.

It only took a couple of days before everyone in the compound, including Qasim (who was misled because Jabar told him that when Bravo talked with him, he supposedly told Jabar that if he wanted me to be fired from the team, Bravo would do so), heard about my confrontation.

According to Qasim, Jabar told Bravo that it was okay for me to stay with the team, but only because he wanted to give me one more chance to do so. From what Qasim was telling me, it sounded more like Jabar was in charge of the compound, which is what he continued to imply during our argument. It was the norm for local Afghans to talk about things that I really didn't care to hear, and, in this case, I really didn't want in any way to be a part of their gossiping. The only time I interfered with any of the locals is if they talked unkindly behind peoples' backs who were not there to defend themselves.

Later that same day, I saw Norm, who also wanted to share some thoughts about Jabar's behavior. He confirmed that Jabar had tried the same intimidation tactics on him a couple of years earlier, and Norm had also taken a stand against Jabar. Since then, Norm simply tried to avoid him, which was the only way he knew to not go through Jabar's intimidation tactics again, which is probably the reason why I never saw Norm—a Tajik from Kabul—as often as I did the other Pashton linguists. According to Norm, Jabar was always up to no good and was dishonest with everyone on the base, whether they were American or Polish. He not only ripped off everyone on the base, but he also had a lot of enemies off base as well, which is why he never left the compound or went on missions. Truthfully, I could really care less about Jabar or anyone else who wanted to distract me. My focus was to be with the team and contribute to their success, whatever success that might be (e.g., dismounted humanitarian and combat missions or any of the training that the team provided to the ANP, ANA, and NDS) which is what I shared with Norm—that I had a set of rules that I respected and followed rigidly, whether they were about me or others. So that Norm would understand my respect, I told him that if I wanted to say something to anyone, I was man enough to tell them to their face, rather than talk about them behind their back—which, in turn, is what I expected from others. Norm understood.

Since the confrontation had gone to ANP as well, Ansari—who also had a close relationship with Jabar—asked me about the now "infamous confrontation," with him, and I told him that whatever he had heard from anyone else was pretty much what happened, with the exception of any added embellishment. When I told Ansari that I wasn't interested in talking about the past, that I just wanted to move on, he pretended to be siding with me as he tried to convince me to say something about Jabar, so he could talk with him about it. I really didn't have time for all of this nonsense and told Ansari that I don't talk behind people's backs, most especially if they're not on-hand to defend themselves. I made sure that Ansari understood how I treated people, even if they were badmouthing me behind my back. Ansari didn't like my response, and in order for him to change the subject, he just kind of stepped away from me, pulled out a pack of cigarettes, and extended his arm to offer me one as he asked, "What else is going on with you, Ustad? I hope you're not homesick." I told him that I didn't smoke, was doing okay, and [of course] I missed my family. I had come to learn that Ansari's sweet talks carried little to no substance. Ansari referred to himself as a 40-year-old Hazara, who had been through a lot of harsh times from a very young age, since the days of the Soviet invasion of Afghanistan until the present. He said he had oftentimes switched sides and worked for every government that had ever controlled Afghanistan for the past 30 years. He never left the country but always stayed in his native Ghazni. I wasn't sure if that was a good or bad thing but could understand that when you're in Afghanistan, you keep switching sides if you want to stay alive. However, on the other hand, you would lose your identity by not knowing who you really were or what you were really trying to defend if you didn't believe in yourself.

As summer was fast approaching, the daytime temperatures were reaching into the 90s by the end of June. In one of our morning briefings, Alfa announced our next, upcoming, humanitarian mission, carried out by the Ghazni PRT unit, which would be to the District of Dayak again. This Taliban-friendly village (or perhaps they were being intimidated by them); thus, the PRT team was going to attempt to provide humanitarian aid to the local villagers by building a medical clinic so they would have access to the medical care provided by the PRT medical staff to capture the hearts and minds of the locals. Our team wasn't going to be working on humanitarian aid this time; rather, we were going to be in charge of security for the PRT while they were doing whatever was necessary. The PRT team had been to this village on four other occasions but had been attacked by the Taliban and prevented from doing their humanitarian missions. However, this time around wasn't going to be like any other where the PRT would even attempt to do it on their own. Our team would join them to hold the security perimeter around the village to protect the PRT from any attacks, while the PRT provided medical care to the local Afghans.

Since the village was only about 15 miles east of our base, we had left the compound around 2:00 AM and arrived at the village of Dayak about an hour and a half later. We didn't use the main road because of the IED dangers, but chose the off-the-road drive, with all of the bumps and ditches, to the village.

Immediately following our arrival, our team held a security position by surrounding the village from all sides before sunrise. Within half an hour following our arrival, I could see the scatter of orange clouds, where only a couple of hours later the sun was up in full force. By 6:00 AM, it felt like it was noon, probably because Ghazni is at an elevation of approximately 9,000 feet above sea level, which made the sun rise earlier.

For the next four hours, we were told to sit back and wait for the PRT team to arrive around 8:00 AM to set up their medical tent so they could start giving medical care to the villagers. Four hours of being in one spot was not only a very long time, but a dangerous time as well, especially in a "Taliban-friendly neighborhood." I wasn't worried about whatever shit might happen, but I was anxious to get out of the vehicle so I could walk around the village and talk with the locals. While that wasn't a decision I could make on my own, I was never reluctant to ask if it was alright for me to do it nonetheless.

When I asked Alfa for permission do so, he asked, "Nas, where the hell do you think we can go to find people to talk with at this time of the day?" Since I always sat in the open back of the Humvee, upon our arrival at the village, I heard the morning *"Azan"* ("Calling to prayer") echoing from a distance, which I knew would bring out many locals to the mosque. "If we can find it, there will be people in the village mosque."

From when I was a young boy, I remember that I would once in a while go to the early morning prayers with my adoptive dad on a special occasion where the adults brought their children so they could play in the mosque's courtyard while the adults prayed. Most of the men in the village went to the morning prayers before sunrise, and once they were done, several would hang out in front of the mosque for social conversation so they could stay updated and informed about what was happening in and around the village.

After explaining my reasoning to Alfa, he agreed with the plan, if we asked Ansari to accompany us with a members of his squad to hold a security position while we talked to the villagers and elders, especially since most of our team and all of Ansari's officers were scattered throughout the village. I was apprehensive about trying to find Ansari and asking him for a squad of his officers because he could be sleeping somewhere in any one of his many pickup trucks—especially on night missions—or waking him up to help us hold a security position (which the ANP never liked doing in the first place), especially in an area where the Taliban had a strong presence. Well, to add to the already bad image of me in the ANPs' minds—like going through the villages talking with people, which they didn't like doing, either, added to an even worse image that I already had in their minds. Even though I realized this, I really didn't care. I was all for the challenge of finding Ansari and asking him to go with us to the village, especially since that was his job. This was yet another one of the reasons most of the local linguists and ANP officers didn't like me to go on a mission with them, just because of things like this where Alfa and I were going to walk through the villages, or stopping the ANPs from doing things they weren't supposed to be doing, especially to the innocent locals.

Ansari (and several of his men), Alfa, and I walked toward the center of the village to find the mosque, which turned out to be very challenging because we didn't see one anywhere. Since this was considered to be a very large village—with more than 40 homes—most this size usually had more than one mosque. Needless to say, since that appeared *not* to be the case with this village, I was beginning to worry as I noticed many of the villagers staring at us, wondering why we were walking around so early in the morning. I couldn't help but wonder if we were going to get ambushed or any number of other things, and then worried if I'd be blamed for anything that could possibly go wrong or (God forbid) if any of us got hurt or even died.

When we saw in the distance a long pole on one of the rooftops with four bullhorns attached to the very top—one pointed in each of four directions—we knew we had found the mosque. As we got closer, it appeared to be large enough to serve all of the villagers. The battery-operated bullhorns were large enough for everyone in the village to hear when the *Azan* was played, no matter how far the houses were located from the mosque. Since every Muslim is required to pray five times a day, in order for individuals to know what time of the day they should pray, in every mosque the *mullah* (leader of the mosque) read a particular set of verses from the *Quran* (religious book) through the loudspeakers so that everyone could then report to the mosque within 10 minutes to start praying.

Afghanistan, for the most part, is a very quiet country, especially when it comes to the level of any kind of noise, including traffic. The exception, of course, is in the remote villages where the deafening noise of guns and bullets has become the norm in Afghanistan for more than three decades.

We arrived at the mosque just as everyone was about to leave following their morning prayers. Before Alfa and I got to the front of the mosque, Alfa told me to tell Ansari to make sure his guys were all awake, alert, and blocking the alleyways on both sides of the village so no one could get in or out of the area without search until we were done speaking with the elders. For some reason, Ansari, other ANPs, and local linguists always stayed behind whenever Alfa and I walked through any of the villages because they wanted to be protected in case the bad guys started shooting so they would not be hit first.

I turned around and told Ansari what Alfa wanted him to tell his officers, which Ansari did on his radio immediately by contacting Afzali, his squad leader. Meanwhile, Alfa and I had stopped in front of the mosque with the hope that we could talk with some of the villagers who had gathered there. Other men of all ages were coming out of the mosque, none of whom wanted to talk with us. Alfa told me to ask them for the name of their village elder and where we could find him. As I made the effort to do so with the hope that someone would stop to talk with us or, at the very least, provide us with the name of their village elder, those who had been standing in front of the mosque and the rest who were still coming out ignored my questions and simply walked by us as though we weren't even there.

Ansari quickly jumped in front of us and started demanding that the villagers respond to the questions I was asking. Around 20 to 30 people slowed down and grouped together to talk with Ansari, many leaning against the mud wall of the mosque. As one of them started answering Ansari's questions, others stood or sat. When several villagers eventually joined in and started talking louder and louder so as to be overheard over the din of the others, arguments began while confusion took over. Because of the angry tone of the villagers' voices as they talked with Ansari, Alfa looked at me with concern as he asked me what they were saying. After listening to the entire conversation between Ansari and the villager who was apparently chosen to speak for the gathering, the villager wanted to know why we were in the village so early in the morning. He said that no one knew who the village elder was and even if they did, they wouldn't tell us. Since it's the norm in Afghanistan for one person to talk for an entire group, another villager took over as the lead speaker. He was obviously talking with us out of fear for his life, knowing the Taliban could be any one of the other 20 to 30 people who had gathered. He told us that all he knew was that every time the Americans—PRT soldiers who risked their lives being attacked by the Taliban—came to the village, the Taliban arrived the next day to take all of the humanitarian aid the soldiers had left for the villagers. The villager went on to say that the Taliban took the food items for themselves. Anything else would be burned in the center of the village for all the villagers to see. Those who had accepted the items from the American infidels would be punished, which is why no one was willing to be the village's elder.

Once the second villager was done talking, someone else started, which inspired other villagers sitting against the wall to suddenly start talking over each other, some agreeing with the first villager's point of view while others vehemently disagreed. Some asked for American support; others asked us to leave. With everyone talking at the same time, Alfa was understandably confused. "Nas, what the fuck are they saying? Why are they arguing with each other?" I explained to him that although it might appear and sound as though they were arguing with each other, the scene taking place around us was actually the normal way Afghans talk amongst themselves—in a confrontational way so that, from the Western point of view, it looked and sounded like they were fighting. Since Afghanistan is known for conflict, even a normal conversation between its people sounds like verbal conflict; and, in the Afghan society in general, because of their lack of education, people are more accustomed to raising their voices to have their point across.

After explaining all of this to Alfa so far, I saw that Ansari was still talking with the villagers in an effort to find the village elder. I heard him tell them to just choose an elder amongst themselves and tell the Americans who he was. At that point, an older man of the group stepped forward and said he was the village elder. Alfa and I didn't believe him, and once he professed to being the village elder, almost half of the villagers denied his claim, professing that he was *not* the village elder. Since we were in a village that supported the Taliban, we surmised that this person's claim meant that he was probably supporting the Taliban directly by attempting to find out what the Americans were trying to do so he could report it back to his high-ranking leaders.

I thought it irresponsible on Ansari's part to tell the villagers to "create" an elder just to find out what Alfa had to say to him, especially when Ansari knew that a village elder did not exist and didn't really care because he didn't want the Americans to help the villagers. Ansari obviously wanted to make this mission as short as possible so we could leave the village much sooner rather than later. In Afghan society, rules are made and broken in the same conversation. And as if this weren't enough, Ansari was in all actuality telling the villages that it was okay to lie.

Alfa asked me to tell everyone to stop talking and listen to what he wanted to say. When he had their attention, he turned to me and said, "Nas, don't get fucking excited. I want you to talk to these villagers and tell them exactly what our intentions are and what we are expecting from them in return for our commitment to the village's security and well-being. I do *not* want you to be talking directly with one person only. I want you to talk with everyone as a group because we need their combined support in our efforts to help them." Since I knew what this mission was all about, I was ready to talk to those gathered in order to explain what our objectives were for the people of the village.

After Alfa introduced himself, he again asked that everyone be quiet so they could listen very carefully to what he had to say. He wanted them to know that his offer was only intended to benefit the villagers. He told them how he had left his family behind—thousands of miles away in America—and traveled to Afghanistan so he could help the Afghan people. He further explained that in order for him to do that, he needed all of the villagers' help and cooperation. "But before I can help you," he said, "I need *your* help in finding the 'real' village elder. For example, we will start by resuming construction on the building that will house the clinic that has already been started by the PRT. If we don't find the village elder, we can't make the decision ourselves to build anything else, especially since a number of people in the village continue their efforts to destroy what the PRT has already accomplished."

As I translated Alfa's words, I added, "The reason the Americans and ANP are here is very simple. Alfa, Ansari, and I want to help you. In order to do that, all of you have to help us first." I repeated this simple fact over and over again with the hope of getting my point across. Of course, none of them understood that my point, simply put, was: "Help us to help you." Rather, all I got in return to this statement were looks of concern on everyone's faces, with one in the crowd asking, "How is it possible for us to help you, when you guys are the ones with all the money. You said you were going to help us." In their minds, money was the only thing that would help them. In order for me to enable the villagers to understand the fundamentals of "Help us to help you," I reiterated that we were in their village now in an effort to help this village and PRT, who on several other occasions had attempted to complete their work only to be attacked by the same people they were trying to help. "As you well know, the PRT has already started to build a clinic for your village but, because of security concerns, it remains only half finished. Every time they try to come in to help you, you start shooting at them. Please understand that we're here to help you build a school for your children; and clinics for your elders, women, and children, so that your sick can have medical care and your kids can be educated at school, but each and every time we try to do either, you attack us," which met with immediate disagreement. By pointing at one of the villagers, I responded with, "I'm not saying that *you* personally attacked us; I am merely saying that we have been attacked by this village, not once, but several times that we have been here; and don't tell me that people from this village have never attacked us, because if it's not people from your village, who else could it be? How could we possibly know who is attacking us? After all, it's *your* village, and if you've lived in this village all your lives and don't know who is attacking us, then how would we know what you, yourselves, claim not to know?" After a brief pause, I added, "So, in order for us to help you, you are going to have to tell us who's attacking us. The sooner we know, the sooner we can capture them and help you. But we need your help in finding those who are responsible."

Despite my explanation, we didn't see any signs of people willing to help. For me, besides not making my point clear to them, it was like talking to a group of people not interested in our help, nor were they willing to help us in any way. However, before I could turn back to tell Alfa what I had just told the villagers, the man claiming to be the village elder posed a question of his own directly to me.

"What would you do if you were in our shoes? You guys are all armed with rifles, but none of us have anything with which to defend ourselves. You guys come here once a year, but those guys who attack you are here every night, asking us for money and food, so what can we do about them? Anyone in our situation would listen to them. If they found out that any one of us had even talked to you guys, they might cut our throats. You guys coming here is *not* helping us, which hurts us even more."

Alfa wanted to give it one more try. "I have everything back home and don't need anything from you, but I came here to Afghanistan none-theless in order to help you to have what I have in America: opportunity, prosperity, and security. To that end, here is my offer to you. My partners (PRT) will be here around 8:00 AM to give medical care to your villagers, including your women and children. I have two female medical doctors who are ready to take care of the women in your village. In addition to everything I just said, I will still give you my offer of helping your village in the long-term. I have cash with me to build that clinic at the other end of the village, which remains half built by the PRT—not only destroyed by the Taliban before, but also by us being prevented by the Taliban to rebuild. There is also a school that has been closed for a while, and once we're done with the clinic, we can work on the school. Once security in the village improves, and that security is in your own hands, we can also start working on the electricity. For instance, in America each of us protects our own individual homes, and we also have villages in America just like yours here in Afghanistan. Together, all of us protect our village just like we do our homes. I can't protect your village for you, because I don't know your people. Only you know your villagers—those who are bad and those who are good. If you tell me who the bad guys are in your village that are preventing us from helping you build it, then I can guarantee you that they will no longer be threatening or stopping us from helping you build your village for the future of you children and grandchildren."

Knowing the culture, I also knew that what Alfa had said was well beyond the capability of the villagers to understand, but he couldn't have said it any better than he already had. Looking around at the villagers' faces, I didn't see any convincing or hopeful signs that they wanted to help us help them. They all stood stone-faced and stoic, definitely not ready to take Alfa's offer to help us help them build the clinic and the school because they'd have to tell us who the bad guys were in order to make that happen.

Before leaving the village around 8:00 AM, I heard through Alfa's radio that the PRT team was on its way to meet us in the middle of the village to give medical care to the villagers who needed it. On our way to meet them, Alfa told me that he had to ask them one last time for their help to see if it would work. Using himself as an example, he told them: "If someone came to my village and told me they were trying to help me so that my children and grandchildren could have a better future, I would do everything possible to help them, because I love my family and my children. And now, I am that someone offering that help to you and your children, but you're simply rejecting it by not telling me who the bad guys are, and obviously not loving your family and children as much as I do." After saying this, the villagers still had blank expressions on their faces because they did not understand what we were trying to tell them. It was not easy to convince a many-centuries old culture what we trying to explain to them.

As we started to walk back through the village, Alfa suddenly stopped so he could point something out to the villagers. In the alleyway by the mosque, where we were standing earlier, was a ditch right in the middle of the alleyway that had raw sewage coming from all the homes in the village. Every village and major city in Afghanistan had similar above-ground ditches for such purposes—some narrow in size and others more shallow and wide, depending on the village or city's size. In another last attempt, Captain Alfa asked the villagers, "Do you see this?" he asked, pointing to the sewer in the alleyway, "In addition to the school and clinic that I promise to build for your village, I can also put this sewer underground so your children and grandchildren will not get sick from being exposed to it, and you won't have to sit next to it or look at it all day. All you have to do is tell us who the bad guys are."

No matter what Alfa and I said or did, we could not convince the villagers to accept our offer. As we were leaving, one of the villagers asked me with a most insulting tone in his voice, "Hey, interpreter, ask this guy (pointing to Alfa) what difference it would make if the sewer is underground or aboveground. My father and grandfather lived and died here while the sewer was aboveground. How would it benefit me or my children if the sewer went underground?" (By the way, this village in the northeast of the Ghazni Province happened to speak Farsi—mostly the Tajiks and Hazaras—therefore, they preferred speaking to Ansari rather than me.

Alfa and I looked at each other, both thinking the same thing: "Fuck, why are we even here to help people who don't want to help themselves?" We were both speechless and, frankly, disappointed that we couldn't change their minds, but at least we had tried by risking our lives to help them. This was the very first time for me to be out with the team, talking with villagers who had made no sense whatsoever. Yet, I understood their point of view, which is why my job became extremely important. I tried everything possible to be the bridge between the two cultures so they could somehow make a connection, but realized that the bridge that I tried so hard to build went in only one direction, especially in this village.

As the crowd grew larger and larger, we continued to look around the village, walking from house to house for about three hours in an effort to find the village elder. Some villagers would tell us where the village elder lived, but once we got there and knocked on the door, the man of the house would at first agree that he was indeed the village elder, but changed his mind when he saw a bunch of American soldiers surrounding his house. So, we finally had to admit that it was time for us to leave the village, because we had been in one place for far too long with people who were anything but friendly.

Since we couldn't get any information from the villagers, we went to meet the PRT team to coordinate the security so they could set up their tent and start their medical treatment of the villagers. Since none of the people by the mosque wanted to take any responsibility for telling us who the real village elder was, Alfa and our team were going to leave the village for our vehicles so we could hold security positions outside the village perimeter. After Alfa met with the PRT captain to inform him of the situation regarding our talks with the villagers, the PRT captain decided to do his own walk throughout the village to see if he could find out who the village elder was, even if him doing so meant more of a security risk.

Before Alfa could leave the village, the PRT captain asked him if I could stay to be his interpreter. "It's up to Nas if he wants to stay or not," Alfa responded. I was happy to stay behind and help the PRT captain any way I could, even though I knew the risks involved.

The PRT captain took a different approach, however. While Alfa was a combat captain with Special Forces, the PRT captain was noticeably much mellower when talking with the villagers. Being with the military for only a little more than a month, I didn't know who was better at this part of their job. Even though I knew Alfa more than the PRT captain, I was also unable to make any judgment calls about their performance as soldiers. All I could say with certainty is that they were both brave and courageous Americans, and, having seen him in combat and how he handled things, I knew I was safer being around Alfa if we were ever under attack.

As we left the village for our vehicles, we tried to talk with more villagers,but, remembering what the villager in front of the mosque had told us, if they did talk with us, someone would die the next day. It was a very hot and dusty day in late June or early July in the deserts of Ghazni. By the time we were safely inside our vehicles and en route back to the base, part of our team was still holding security positions around the village so that the PRT team could leave safely. Before we could all leave, however, the moment we were anticipating arrived.

The first rocket hit 20 feet away from one of the PRT vehicles, which were still traveling in the wide-open desert where they could be easily seen, even from the village rooftops, not too long before the second rocket hit one of the PRT vehicles, which is when the situation got even more intense. Suddenly, Alfa, Fox, Damon, and one other civilian American government official—either from the State Department or the CIA, who was also riding with us in our vehicle—made a U-turn and headed back toward the village where the rockets were being fired. Well, we couldn't see anything. As we got closer to the village, everyone heard small arms being fired seemingly from our right where I saw one of the ANP vehicles. One of the officers was shouting at me and pointing toward the village in an effort to let me know that we were indeed being attacked from the village. When Alfa asked me, "Who the fuck was shooting," wanting to know if it was one of the ANP guys, I responded in the affirmative. Since Captain Alfa was in contact with all of our ODA members on an internal radio, he already knew that none of our guys were taking part in the shooting. When he asked me to "open the fucking door and ask the ANP guys to stop shooting," doing as instructed, I opened the door and shouted at the ANPs in Farsi, *"Oh bacha haa, chea ra mazanin."* ("Hey, guys, what are you shooting at?") One of them shouted back to me, *"Yaki azi mordagawa da sari bam may dawed"* ("One of the motherfuckers was running on a rooftop"), referring to the bad guys—information that I quickly related to Alfa.

As the shooting started to intensify, I saw the unknown civilian who was riding in our vehicle start video recording what was happening. I didn't had a video recorder but pulled out my camera to take some pictures. Being out in the open, things were starting to get more and more intense in our vehicle as we continued to look in all directions to see if we could pinpoint where the attack was coming from; unfortunately, while we couldn't see the bad guys, they could see us (a.k.a.: the home-court advantage for the bad guys).

While taking pictures from inside the vehicle, I saw a man shooting at the ANP vehicles and immediately shouted at Alfa, who was sitting in the front passenger seat of the vehicle. "Sir, Sir…there!" I yelled, pointing at the man I had seen shooting at the ANP vehicle. "Where? Where is he, Nas?" he asked. "There, there," I shouted, pointing to the right. "What the fuck are you talking about; I can't see anyone. What fucking right side are you talking about?" I suddenly realized that I was fucking things up yet again, just like I did on the last combat mission when I couldn't move the Humvee. But this time, Damon came to my rescue by standing up above the mini gun before he turned around and asked me, "Nas, where did you see the guy?" I pointed to my right, Damon saw the guy and yelled to Alfa that the person I saw was shooting from two o'clock on Alfa's right. At first, I didn't understand what Damon was saying, but then realized what he meant, since it was the first time I heard someone use "o'clock times" as locational directions. Since I was sitting in the back of the vehicle and Alfa was in front facing the same way, his right side was my right side, but he couldn't see which way I was facing when I said, "On the right side." So, when he said "two o'clock," it suddenly made more sense to me, and it certainly made it possible for everyone in the vehicle to understand, even if they weren't actually looking at you. This was yet another one of those "on-the-job training" experiences with Special Forces, under intense pressure, that I will never forget. By nature, I consider myself a fast learner, but learning the things I was learning during combat missions with Special Forces, I wanted to learn quickly while still being able to stay alive.

After seeing the bad guys running out of one house with a red door and going into another with a blue door, I passed on the message, this time to Damon because he was in charge of the big gun that shot grenades every time he pulled the trigger. Before I knew it, the large blue door had five huge holes in it, and I could actually see through the hole inside the compound where the bad guy (who wore white) had entered. We were well aware that this village was Taliban-friendly—the prior times when the PRT was attacked, and now as our Special Forces were likewise being attacked. However, this time not only the bad guys were going to pay the price, but the villagers as well for supporting them.

The remaining members of the PRT team—a couple of whom were wounded during the rocket attack earlier—were now on their way out of the village following yet another attempt to give medical care to the villagers. The PRT would arrive, the bad guys would attack, and the PRT would retreat so they could return to the base. However, this time was different for the Taliban because we didn't just pack up and go. Alfa was coordinating with Ansari and the rest of our team that we were going back into the village so we could find the motherfuckers who had attacked us.

I knew the villagers were going to have to pay the price for this. We had spent more than six hours in the village talking with all of the villagers we could find, trying to help them by risking our own lives; but, in the end, although they knew who and where the bad guys were, they never attempted to help us find them, attacking us like the cowards they were as we were leaving the village. I do not call this bravery on the part of the Talibans; instead, I call it cowardice because only cowards attack you from behind.

Our guys were compassionate enough to give the villagers free medical care while risking their own lives and brave enough to walk into their village to do it, while the Taliban looked on and were not brave enough to attack us while we were in the middle of the village earlier in the day. I can only assume that everyone has a different definition for the words *brave* and *coward*, but based on my experience thus far, Americans are brave enough to walk around the Taliban village for more than six hours while the Taliban looked on, not attacking until we were on our way out. When I told Captain Alfa earlier that morning that I wanted to go into the village to talk with the villagers, or when I volunteered with the PRT Captain, who wanted to look for the village elders while walking around the village, knowing full well that this was a Taliban-friendly village, I was criticized not only by Ansari from the ANP, but all the other local linguists who accompanied us on this mission because they didn't understand why I would risk knowing that I would end up getting shot at. Most of the officers, including Ansari and all of the other linguists—whether they were local linguists or the one from the States—never wanted to be on any of the team's missions, and even if they went, they would do their very best to hide. If you asked what nationality they were, they would not only respond with, "Afghan, of course," but would criticize you for having doubts about their nationality.

> *"To avoid criticism, do nothing, say nothing, and be nothing."*
> — AUTHOR

I never wanted to avoid criticism of any kind, because I didn't want to "be nothing." I can take criticism, even at the expense of my life. While I didn't avoid or stop people from criticizing me when I was in Afghanistan, I did tell them that how they felt and what they said about Afghanistan only mattered to them; it all came down to what they did to Afghanistan that mattered the most, and the majority of them had never done anything that Afghanistan could benefit from. Instead, they had taken everything Afghanistan had been given by the international community. Since I personally live my life by the quotes that appear throughout this book, they motivate me more and more to act upon them.

> *"What you feel or say only matters to you; it's what you do to the people you say you love, that matters and counts the most."*
> — AUTHOR

Every time I read the quote above, it helps me to continue to attempt to encourage the local Afghans to understand me versus other Afghans I meet who just look me in the eyes and do as they wish to keep themselves happy and feel good.

○═◆═○

The hunt for the Taliban in this village was going to be very challenging because everyone dressed in *Kamis, Partog, Lungota,* in native Pashto, and *Peran, Tomban,* and *Longey* in native Farsi (both meaning "traditional Afghan clothing"), which made it difficult for us to identify them. Identifying the difference between a civilian and a Taliban, and fighting an enemy who has no uniform, is essentially like fighting a ghost. We had searched the entire village, almost house to house with no sign or leads on the bad guys. It's not that there were no bad guys, it's just primarily because we couldn't tell them apart. The bad guys don't have to do much to get away from us. All they do is hide their rifle or any other weapons they may have. They could've been in the village the whole time we were searching or they were probably following us without us even knowing it. It took us the whole day with no success. We had vacated the village by sundown, trying to provide the local Afghans with their basic medical treatments, but all we got were a couple of our guys critically injured by the rocket attack. This is the price Americans pay for trying to help people with whom we have nothing in common. The Afghans do not have the capability to understand the Americans' standpoint, and vice versa. It's all a misconception for which no one can truly be blamed. For as long as Americans are not being told the truth, two-thirds of the Afghan population will always be living as victims, much like the people in this village.

It was a normal routine for our team members to go to the range, practice shooting, and clean up our wide-range of weapons, especially after a run to a dusty village. In addition to our own practice, everyone in the ANP would be given ammunition to practice as well. Every time we asked them to be at the range for practice, most would not show up, and, the ones who did usually said that they didn't really need to practice because they have lived all their lives fighting in Afghanistan; therefore, they already knew how to shoot. Nonetheless, it was required of them if they wanted to continue working with our team.

Out of all 30 officers, there were only two that were actually willingly to listen to us and follow instructions on how things would be taught to them by the Special Forces. I believed that Officers Afzali and Ramazan were the only patriotic police officers out of the group that Afghanistan could be proud of, because both would always show up on time, ready for the mission or other tasks that needed to be done. They not only showed up on time, but they always asked questions if they didn't understand what the Americans were trying to teach them. Unlike Afzali and Ramazan, however, other officers would come up with something of their own they felt had to be taught—which they would not say to the Special Forces guys directly, but in a way where they would not do as they were told but would rather do it as they wished (e.g., for example, if our guys told the ANP officers how to stand while shooting their weapons or how to hold their weapons while pulling the trigger). Since the ANP preferred to do things their own way, one had once told me in Farsi, "Ustad, ask the Americans what difference it makes how I stand or how I hold the weapon, as long as I can shoot the motherfuckers, right?" This was not only our situation with the ANP officers on the shooting range but throughout our daily training of everything we tried to teach all of the locals on the compound. How is it possible to train people who, in their minds, know more than the people who are there to teach them?

When we went on missions, they were never ready by the time we told them to be. Not only that, but everyone on our team was frustrated with their behavior, but even two of their own officers, Afzali and Ramazan, always complained about how the rest of the ANP officers never took their job very seriously, including Ansari. Well, I knew that Ansari wasn't interested in his duties as much as he was in the salary he was getting.

It was the beginning of July when the first ODA that I had started working with was ready to break away one by one and make room for the new ODA2 soon to arrive as their replacement unit. The guys of the first ODA were an awesome bunch of dudes. I was honored to know and work with them, so hearing the news of their departure from Ghazni was heartbreaking for me. It took me a while to get to know them, and I wasn't sure if the next team would be as good as the one on its way out of Afghanistan. Since each ODA spends six months on each deployment to Afghanistan, I couldn't blame them for being excited to get the fuck out so they could go home to their families. When I learned the current ODA would be staying later than usual, I asked Charlie why they were still here if their deployment was supposed to be for only six months at a time. Charlie said they had to stay a little while longer because the team that was supposed to take over was on their way, but would not arrive until the end of July. Unless you're the one on deployment, it's beyond one's imagination to realize how slowly time passes. I knew it was difficult for everyone on the team, as well as their families back home, to learn that they had to stay an extra month.

It was the summer of 2009, the busiest deployment time in the war on terror. President Obama had ordered 30,000 troops to be deployed to Afghanistan. Things were somehow behind for most new units to arrive as replacements for outgoing units. Although new to military deployment procedures, I didn't know how things worked, but was never reluctant to ask. The team members I was in contact with the most were, of course, Alfa, Echo, Charlie, Damon, and Ross, the latter of whom trained me on all of the various vehicle equipment, including the weapons, whenever we went on missions, and also informed me of anything else I needed to know. Charlie was not only my buddy because we both spent a lot of time together in the same Humvee, but, since he liked to cook, he was also my kitchen buddy, which meant we spent whatever free time we could get (besides going on missions) to go to the kitchen to join Qasim's crew to help prepare meals. Charlie was as passionate as I was when it came to cooking. Since most of the guys on the team knew that I had once owned an Italian fast food pasta and pizza restaurant in Queens, New York, and Costa Mesa, California, I offered to cook for them. Besides cooking Italian food, I knew how to cook Afghan food as well.

One night, everyone (including Alfa) asked if I could make them pizza for dinner. Besides being able to make the dough, knowing that making a decent pizza was going to take more than we had in the kitchen (e.g., not only the necessary ingredients but a large enough oven in which to bake it), Alfa said he was willing to provide me with the ingredients but wanted to know how I was going to be able to make the dough and then bake the pizza. While I pondered the oven problem, Alfa asked me to make a list of the pizza ingredients I would need and then told Charlie to ask Jabar, our so-called compound manager, to see if he could get them for me from Kabul. Well, whether he understood them or not, since Jabar never said no to anyone else on the team, he simply told us, "Sure. No problem." Knowing Jabar as I did, I knew in my heart that he would, in fact, *not* be getting me any of the pizza ingredients requested, so there was no pizza that night or perhaps in the near future.

Every night after dinner, I went to the kitchen to make myself some green tea; I always offered a cup to Qasim as well. One night he wasn't there, so I didn't leave him the cup of tea that he usually accepted. After making my own, I returned to my room to watch a movie when someone knocked on my door. When I opened it, I was surprised to find Qasim standing there, empty cup in hand. I invited him inside and once he was seated, I poured tea into his cup. Since I had often invited him to my room, he had never accepted—until now. As we sat enjoying our tea, for the first 10 to 15 minutes Qasim proceeded to tell me about his personal life, how his father was killed during the Soviet invasion, and how this happened when Qasim was only in his early teens, so he had to quit school to work as a day laborer in order to support his mother and three siblings. He told me about his dream to go to school, but he was not able to do so because of the circumstances at that time, and now there was a desperate need for a school in his native village where everyone is Pashton, "like you and me." As I was also aware, and for as long as he could remember, he told me how the Pashtons were all being neglected and abused, just like everyone else in Afghanistan. It was then that I realized again that Qasim was still after my money to spend on his own personal agenda. He was not particularly bright in the mental department, so he never completely understood how some things play out; even if he did, he would not be able to accept the fact that a Pashton (in this case, me) could possibly say no to him, especially when considering what he was telling me.

When Qasim had [finally] finished, I told him that his village wasn't the only one in need of a school—with few exceptions, almost every village in Afghanistan needed one. Since I had talked with him once before about his concern for his fellow Pashtons, I knew he wasn't going to understand me this time, either. Before I could pour him another cup of tea, I saw that he hadn't yet finished the first cup.

He abruptly stood and thanked me for the tea. Before leaving my room, he wanted to know what the word "ingredients" meant. When I asked why he needed to know, he said Jabar had asked him to ask me. Obviously, as soon as he mentioned Jabar's name, I knew the question had to be about the pizza and asked him if that was the case. At that point, his face lit up with a big smile when he said, "Yes! Pizza…that's what it's called. What are the ingredients that you need for this thing called pizza?" As I explained what a pizza was and then told him what ingredients were needed to make one, I realized that neither had a clue about what I was talking about.

With that realization in mind, I explained to Qasim that the word ingredient referred to a combination of products that are mixed together to make something, in this case, a pizza. Hoping I had defined the word adequately, Qasim thanked me and left my room. Since he didn't drink it, I wasn't sure that night if he really wanted to have tea with me or not. Instead, he had come to my room (1) because of Jabar's question and (2) Qasim's own curiosity as to whether I'd agree to be financially committed to building a school in his village—a perfect example of how not even one person I'd met thus far was committed, including the Afghan government, to something, anything, bigger than themselves. It was the Afghan civilians who were the victims of both the Taliban's oppression and the Afghan government's brutality.

At the end of one of our early morning briefings at the OPS center, Alfa closed with his usual: "Let's not terrify the villagers. We'll go in and get the bad guys and then get out, without the villagers even knowing the next morning that we were there," which I would then translate to the ANP officers, as I had on many previous occasions.

Our mission that night was to a village in central Ghazni Province. We always had our ANPs with us, so this mission was no different from any other. I always followed them whenever we raided a home. We arrived at the target village around midnight and parked our vehicles about half a mile away so that the noise made by our armored vehicles would not awaken the villagers. During our briefing that morning, we were shown a map of the village. In order for us to reach it, we had to enter it in a straight line, no matter what crossed our path. Because we oftentimes had to face the challenges of walking through farmland; crossing rivers, creeks, or other bodies of water; and climbing walls as high as six to seven feet tall, it was always difficult for me to walk in a straight line.

Wearing boots that weighed five pounds and became even heavier with mud because the farmland had been watered earlier that evening, we started toward our objective. Despite the fact that my boots were getting heavier—which significantly added to my 162-pound body, not to mention the 50 pounds of body armor, a rifle, seven magazines of ammunition holding 39 rounds each, plus food and water—as we walked over the farmland, crossing through various pools of water, to say that I felt weighted down would be putting it lightly (no pun intended). My main challenge wasn't the walk, because after seeing the map of the village at the briefing, I was more concerned about climbing the six-to-seven-foot tall wall we had to get over. At the age of 47, the oldest member on the team, combined with the condition of my lower back (posterior disc bulge, according to the MRI done prior to my deployment), I was apprehensive about making it over the wall. Alfa and Ray—who were both six foot tall and weighed in excess of 200 pounds each—were in front of me. I had no doubt but that they would both be able to scale the wall without a problem.

As we neared the wall, they both said, almost in unison, "Oh fuck, this thing is tall!" Just as Afghanistan's people are unpredictable, so, too, is it unpredictable geographically. As I watched, I could barely see how Alfa had managed to climb the wall to the other side, but once he did it, I heard him telling Ray that the wall was even taller on the other side where the ground was even higher just outside an orchard we were then going to face. Needless to say, hearing Alfa say that made me even more apprehensive. Suddenly realizing that everyone else had been able to make it over the wall, as the only one left it was time for me to make the decision whether I could do it or not. When we left the base, I was naïve to think that every mission would be similar to the one when Delta was shot. While I didn't want to be a burden to any of my team members by asking them to help me climb the wall, I had no choice but to ask Ray (who was still sitting on top of the wall) if he would mind lending me a hand so I could get over to the other side. Before I had even finished asking, Ray offered me a helping hand by pulling me up to the top of the wall. Not knowing how much of a jump it was going to be to the ground below, I sat on top of the wall waiting for Ray to get down. Once he did, he reached for my feet so he could catch me and I could then slide (rather than jump) down to the ground beside him.

At that point, everything was going smoothly, but my worries weren't over yet because I was already thinking of the return trip to our vehicles when we'd have to climb the wall again—if we all made it back alive, of course. Walking through the farmland, crossing the bodies of water, and climbing the wall were the physical, challenging parts of the mission—not to mention the unknowns about the mission itself, which were the biggest psychological challenge.

We walked very slowly as we followed Alfa and Ray. Suddenly, we could hear the creaking of a door being opened and our guys screaming and yelling, "Get down, get down!" while women and children were also screaming and yelling. After a minute or so, I could still hear our guys talking but heard no shots fired, which gave me comfort. The next thing I heard was Alfa calling my name. When I reached him, he said, "Fox needs you inside the house." Well, since it was very dark, I unfortunately couldn't see the house because there was no moon to provide even a sliver of light. When I asked, "Sir, where and which house do you want me to go to?" Alfa told me, "The house right in front of us." Well, since I couldn't see the house at all (I still didn't have night goggles), Ray moved toward me and said, "Let's go; just follow me."

As I started to enter the house, I saw Mitch, Echo, and two ANP officers, holding security positions right outside the front door. Upon entering the room, I saw two additional ANP officers, one holding his rifle to the head of a woman—her four young children, ages three to about seven nearby—while the second ANP officer was ransacking the house, searching for possible weapons, explosives, or anything else that they could find to remove from the premises. Since most of the ANP officers didn't know our team members by name, in Farsi I asked the officer holding his rifle to the woman's head, *"Amrekayi kuja ast?"* ("Where are the Americans?"). He responded by pointing his rifle across the room, toward the other side of the courtyard. I immediately left the room and looked over my shoulder to the right, across the way, where I saw flashes of light moving around, which is where I thought Fox was. Not seeing many entrances to the house's various rooms, I walked into another, which happened to be the kitchen that was connected to the so-called master bedroom, where I found Fox, Damon, and our explosives expert. Beside them, I then saw an elderly Afghan man and two young boys, one around the age of 10; the other, 12. I saw the elderly man being tested for explosives by our expert. As it turned out, Fox and Damon had been waiting for me to arrive so we could interrogate the adults of the house. While I could not make a judgment call as to what these people had been through or what they may have, according to Fox, our intelligence report indicated that all of the IED attacks on the main road five miles east of the village—that had killed many Afghan civilians—were coming from the people in this particular house.

While our explosives expert was doing his thing on the elderly Afghan man by swiping his hands, clothes, and even his beard to see if there were any signs of explosives, Fox was asking him questions like who he was, what he did for a living, what everyone's relation in the house was to him, and what else he and the other male adults in the room had done during the past few days, weeks, and months so he could determine if their stories matched and if their patterns of activity were the same so we could decide if they were, in fact, members of the same family.

I did everything I could not to break down emotionally as I listened to the manner in which the elderly man was responding to our questions. For numerous reasons, there were so many things going through my mind in the short period of time we had been in this poor man's house. He was probably in his 60s, so I had no clue why all six of his children were under the age of 14. But I'm not going there now because doing so would create a whole different story and another book about the Afghan culture.

Fox would ask his questions in a very respectful manner, and every answer the man gave in response was, I believed, truthful. Not only did he answer truthfully, but every time he did so, he would also add to his answer in Pashto, *"Tasi wali walar yast, tah da tah wawaya, chea ksheyni, zaba chai dar pakhay kam, pa qarari ba majlas sara wakro."* ("Why are you guys standing? Can you tell him [referring to Fox] to sit down so I can make you some tea and we can talk more in detail?") As I listened for a few minutes, I couldn't tell where these two men were going with their questions and the answers they were receiving. As for me, at the moment, all I was trying to do was keep my lips from quivering and my eyes from shedding tears. Here we were with a compassionate American soldier, trying to understand another compassionate and hospitable fellow human being, halfway around the world, in a dark room somewhere in Afghanistan, who offered us tea in the middle of the night after we had broken into his home—all of which was very emotional for me. As noted earlier, it's not the bad who make me cry, only the goodness and kindness of others, from their hearts—this was definitely one of those situations.

While our interrogation of the elderly Afghan continued, two of the ANP officers marched into the room with their rifles and flashlights, trying to search the room for explosives or anything else they might find. As they were going through the room moving things around, I heard our explosives expert tell Fox that there were no signs of explosives on any of the people he had just questioned and searched—referring, of course, to the elderly man and his sons. Meanwhile, I watched one of the ANP officers trying to break the lock on one of two aluminum suitcases. Growing up in my adoptive village, I knew aluminum suitcases were very common possessions for Afghan people to safeguard their valuables. It's their only "safe deposit box" that's usually kept locked and in the room where the man of the house sleeps. Since the first room I entered was where the woman and her children were, this room was apparently where the man of this house and his older sons slept. The ANP approach was routine every time we raided a home: some held security positions while others searched the homes for weapons, explosives, and other harmful things (e.g., bomb-making components and materials).

As I continued to watch the ANP officer busily working on the suitcase in an effort to break the lock and see what was inside, I noticed the elderly man turn around to see what was going on behind him. When he noticed the ANP officer attempting to break the lock on the suitcase, he told him in Pashto (not knowing that none of them spoke or understand it), "Please don't break it; my wife has the key, so please get it from her so you can open it." Not surprisingly, the officer ignored the old man's request and did what he had to do to break the lock so he could find out what was in the suitcase. While that ANP officer was busy turning the suitcase upside down, another was looking under the rug and the homemade mattress that the old man and his sons were undoubtedly sleeping on before we broke into their home. As the two officers did their damage, a third ANP officer entered the room holding two "C" batteries, telling me to tell Fox that he had found them on a the shelf on the wall just outside the room in which we were standing.

During the interrogation, the elderly man answered the questions honestly, at least that's what our explosives expert, Fox, Damon, and I thought. However, the batteries found by the ANP officer raised a red flag in the minds of all the ANP officers, because they thought they were probably used for the detonation of the IEDs. Since there was no sign of anything electrical in the house, we had no choice but to wonder what the batteries were used for, so we asked the man to explain why they were there. He leaned against the wall where there was a 2x2-foot shelf carved within the wall. He then reached for a dark square, cover-type cloth about the size of a small mini-pillow, pulled it out, and tried to hand it to Fox. At first, since most people in Afghanistan wrap the holy book of Quran and keep it up above their heads in the wall, I thought he was reaching for it so he could swear on the book that he was innocent. However, since Fox refused to take it from him, the elderly man—whose hands were shaking, from either being nervous or cold—started to open the cloth cover, layer by layer, which is when we realized that it was a battery operated AM radio from the 1950s or '60s, which again brought back many of my own old memories, like when my adoptive dad owned the same, exact radio that we used to listen to. According to the elder, the radio was given to him by his father when he was in his teens. He said he only used the radio when he could find batteries for it. Since he couldn't afford to buy them, he said he was once told by someone that if he pulled the batteries out of the radio and left them in the sun long enough, they would be recharged and work for a day or two. But, of course, that never happened, no matter how long he left them in the sun. We found his story to be very interesting, but we were especially impressed by how long he had been able to keep the radio for more than five decades, like a holy book.

By now, the four of us were convinced that this man and his family were innocent and simply and unfortunately, a phrase you are now very familiar with, victims of circumstance—in other words, they were in the wrong place at the wrong time. At one point during the interrogation process, our explosives expert and I wanted to take the man's fingerprints to see if he was in our tracking system, but when we tried to fingerprint him, none of his fingers had any marks that the computer could read in order to try to find them in the database. His hands were shaking the entire time we interrogated him. At one point, I tried to help him hold his fingers (one at a time) straight so that he could put them in the fingerprint slot so the machine could read them, but when I touched his hand, the roughness felt like someone had handed me a pinecone. I wondered how hard this man could have worked for so little that he couldn't even afford a couple of batteries for his radio. Meanwhile, the fingerprint machine kept responding "unreadable" on every single finger that we tried to register on it. Every time I tried to help the old man, our explosives expert found my efforts to be very amusing and looked at Fox to say, "This guy has no marks left on his fingers that the computer can even read." According to the old man, he had worked on the farm as a day laborer for other people during the peak spring and early summer months of farming, and was as hard-working as any poor man could be. Not only was he hard-working and poor—surprisingly, he liked Americans as well.

Before we left the house, Fox had me ask the man what his two sons did during the day. He answered that he would get a job as a day laborer and he and his two sons went to the job to finish the work. Fox then wanted to know if his sons ever wanted to join the Taliban. Without any hesitation, the old man quickly responded with, *"Ka docy dasi kar wakrcy, hagha wraz ba no da doey da jawand akheyri wraz wey"* ("If my sons ever did such a thing, that would be the last day of their lives"). He said that he had condemned the Taliban and would *never* allow his sons to join. We all furtively glanced at each other, wondering what the man was saying and whether it was actually true or not, until he said, "Listen, dear interpreter, can you ask them (referring to all of the Americans present in the room) to sit down so I can make you guys some tea?" Fox looked at our explosives expert and said, "Incredible! This man would like to make us tea, despite the fact that we have broken into his home and interrogated him in the middle of the night!" We all refused the man's offer but thanked him for his kind hospitality nonetheless.

Before leaving the room, Fox apologized for being at the elder's house in the middle of the night, awakening him and his family. But he refused to let us go as he kept insisting that we have tea with him. When we still refused, before leaving his house, he told us that he would've been very happy if we had accepted his tea offer. He added, "If you guys (Americans) can build a paved road for us, the least I can do for you is make you guys some tea." We still refused but thanked him again for his gracious offer.

Leaving his house, as we walked through the courtyard, thinking that the old man might be walking out with us, when his wife heard us leaving she yelled at her husband not to forget to get the key to the suitcase back from us. Before we left the room, we told the man and his sons not to leave his room until the morning. I will never forget this man, who was so poor he couldn't even afford to buy two "C" batteries for his old radio, and yet there he was offering us tea and thanking us for the road we were building. Unfortunately, in return, the ANP officers, who represent the Afghan government, broke into one of the family's suitcases, not because they were looking for explosives or weapons, but because they just wanted to break the poor man's suitcase, while they were being given the key to the suitcase by the woman of the house. In this particular incident, this is what we called rivalry between the different Afghan tribes—in this case, between the Hazaras ANP and dirt-poor Pashtons. Since I, too, on many occasions in my life, had been a victim of circumstance—whether physical, financial, or psychological abuse—by my biological family as well as others—I would've been most appreciative if someone had come to my rescue.

Whenever possible, going to the gym was a regular routine for me. One day, a couple of hours after breakfast, I went there for my normal, daily cardio exercise on the elliptical. Ten minutes into my workout, I saw Echo walk in and over, directly to where I was working out. The look on his face concerned me. All he said was, "Hey, Nas, get ready; we're leaving in half an hour." Working with Special Forces for the past couple of months, by then, I really felt that I was one of them. When informed by any of the team members that we were going on a mission, I would first get ready and then ask questions later. I wasn't a rookie anymore. Now, I was even more proudly one of them, and when asked to get ready, I made sure I was.

Within 10 minutes, I was ready. In my room, I pulled out my body armor and rifle and took it to the Humvee to which I was assigned. Every time we went on a mission, our whole compound looked and felt like a department store on Christmas Eve with shoppers trying to buy last-minute gifts before the stores closed. For this mission, there were more than 30 ANP officers, five to six local linguists, and 18 of our team members moving around the compound at the same time, gathering everything that was needed. This was apparently one of those missions where we had to hurry up and wait—and the wait time went from the 30 minutes Echo said to four hours, during which I had plenty of time to ask questions about the mission. Since Echo was the one who told me to get ready, I went to him to find out what the mission was all about. He told me that the PRT team had gone to a village to give humanitarian aid to the villagers, but before they could even get there, one of their vehicles was hit by an IED and the PRT team was ambushed soon after—so we needed to rescue them. To be able to do that, it took four hours before we could leave the compound so that everything could be coordinated so we wouldn't be attacked.

We left the base around 3:00 PM and headed south on the main highway toward Kandahar. For me, excitement was the main factor every time I went on a mission, but it was even more exciting when our missions took us south toward Kandahar, despite the danger.

This was probably the closest I would get to Kandahar in more than 30 years.

We arrived at a village east of the objective village where the PRT team had been attacked. Driving through this adjacent village was challenging and dangerous because of the narrow alleyways and unsafe culvert over which we had to drive. Along the way, we stopped to search people on motorcycles or any parked vehicles that we passed along the way. Around 6:00 PM, our convoy left the tail-end of the village and entered the very tight alleyways between the orchards on both our left and right. Our convoy consisted of five armored vehicles and three to four ANP pickup trucks carrying 30 ANP officers. On most of our missions, Bravo's vehicle—which was equipped with mine-detecting rollers—was in front of our Humvee. About 200 yards into the narrow alleyway, the mine-detecting rollers ran over an IED, which detonated a massive explosion that knocked me and everyone else who was standing in our vehicle to the ground. We didn't know what had just happened; the explosion was so loud and powerful that the ground shook, and we weren't able to tell if it had occurred in the front of us or behind until the dust settled. The explosion was so powerful and the dust so thick that none of us could see anything for about 30 seconds. I could hear Alfa asking if everyone was okay, and in response heard Charlie saying, "Yes, but I think the vehicle in front of us got hit." No one in our vehicle knew what had just happened. The mine-detecting rollers, which weighed more than 500 pounds, had been disengaged and knocked by the power of the explosion into the orchard. There were a total of six rollers, three in front of each front wheel. We were able to recover the three that flew into the orchard and couldn't locate the other three that had rolled over the IED. At that point, we found ourselves stuck in a very narrow alleyway with orchards on both side, and none of us knew what would happen next. We couldn't move the vehicles until we had cleared the debris that was blocking the front of the vehicle that had been blown up by the IED.

About 200 yards in front of us was an opening between the walls, which is where Charlie, Echo, and Rick were running so they could take up security positions. Alfa called out to me to call Ansari. Unfortunately, I didn't have a clue where Ansari was at that moment. Noticing an ANP vehicle behind us, I walked back and asked one of the officers to call Ansari on his radio and tell him to get his ass over here as soon as possible. (We were all aware that Ansari always took his time to get where he needed to be, especially during combat or when we were being attacked.) Except for the gunners on each of the vehicles, Alfa asked me to tell Ansari to tell all of his guys to come over to the open area to hold security positions so no one else would be able to pass through. Most of Ansari's officers were just like him, sort of like father, like son—very slow in responding during an attack—very different from our guys who only had to be told once what they needed to do when we were attacked. Ansari and his officers were notorious for always doing things their own way. I had once seen three of them standing in one spot, taking cover for themselves, while there was a wide open area that needed to be secured.

Once Ansari had finally been able to coordinate all of his guys to take their positions, Alfa and I walked to the front of the two wide openings on each side of the alleyway. To my right was a wide-open field where Rick was holding his security position; Charlie, Ansari, and a couple of his officers were to my left with Najib, one of the local interpreters—all were holding security positions behind a three-foot-tall mud wall. Alfa had called Paul, our explosives dog handler, to bring Sami over to check for other IEDs that might be in the alleyway ahead of us so we would then be able to clear away the debris and move our vehicles out of the tight spot in which we were trapped at the moment and could easily be ambushed.

Alfa asked me to stay behind while he, Paul, and Sami moved forward to check the rest of the alley way. Standing next to Charlie and Najib, I noticed that Charlie had already captured one young man whose face was unrecognizable because it was encrusted with the dust that had blown all over the place when the IED exploded. His hands were tied behind his back, and he was sitting on the ground. I could see that Najib was already interrogating the young man by holding him by his hair with one hand, while his other hand was slapping the young man across the face. Najib screamed and yelled as he asked why he had put the IED in the alleyway and then was running in an effort to get away. After seeing the first two slaps that Najib inflicted to the young man's face, I looked at Charlie who didn't seem to be even slightly interested in what Najib was doing to the young man; for that matter, neither did Ansari, who was also standing next to Najib and the detainee. When Najib noticed that no one said or did anything to stop him from what he was doing, he punched the detainee on the right side of his face, which caused the young man to fall to the ground. I ran over to where they were sitting and held Najib's hand before he could throw another punch, especially since the young man had been knocked to the ground and his hands were tied behind his back. Looking Najib in the eyes, I asked why he was hitting the detainee. Instead of looking at me to answer my question, Najib looked to his right to see if Charlie was going to say anything or defend him against me. Although Charlie had heard and seen everything that was going on, he still didn't react or say anything so I asked Najib again why he was hitting the young man. This time he did not ignore my question, answering it in Pashto. *"Kho da bam ishey woa."* ("Because he had put the bomb [in the alleyway.]") "How do you know that he was the one responsible for the bomb?" I asked. "Because once he saw us after the dust had settled, I saw him running away in the opposite direction, so I captured him." I had no other questions to ask Najib nor did I really have the time to do so. However, I felt strongly compelled to remind him that his job was not to interrogate the detainees nor was he allowed to hit them. When Najib again looked toward Charlie to see if he was going to say anything to defend him, Charlie merely said, "Najib, don't hit him." For some reason, Najib was somehow calmer now than before, because he was no longer screaming and yelling at the detainee. Before I walked away from Najib, I heard the detainee ask me to give him the small plastic bag that was lying on the ground in front of my feet, almost falling into the stream of water. Although I didn't know what was in the bag, I picked it up so it wouldn't fall into the water, and left it on top of the wall in front of the young man.

Alfa returned and told me to tell Ansari to ask one of his officers to take the detainee to their vehicle. Ansari turned to one of his officers standing next to him, holding a security position. "Hey you, take this motherfucker (pointing his rifle at the detainee) to our vehicle. Before the detainee was pulled into a standing position, he asked me again for his plastic bag. Not knowing what the plastic bag contained, I asked Alfa if I was allowed to give it to the detainee. Alfa told me to keep the bag for now; before the detainee was taken away by the ANP officer, I assured the young man that I would keep his plastic bag for the time being and then give it to him once he was cleared and free to go.

Meanwhile, Paul had taken Sami to sniff around the alleyway to see if there were any other IEDs. Sami ultimately discovered three others, all within 50 feet of each other. Obviously, without Sami's help, they would have blown up in our faces. Once the IEDs had been discovered by Sami, Alfa called to request that the EOD (Explosive Ordinance Disposal) team be flown to our location. Within 15 minutes, I heard two helicopters flying over to drop off an EOD team to help pull out the IEDs, which were then taken out to the open field and detonated.

Once we had secured the area and everything was calmer, Alfa asked me to go toward the village where my buddy, Oscar, the interrogator, and Echo were both standing amidst a crowd of 15 or 20 villagers that had gathered so I could translate what the villagers were trying to tell Oscar and Echo. For security reasons, with the help of a couple of ANP officers, when I reached Oscar and Echo, I could hear the villagers complaining to the two Americans that one of their fellow villagers had been beaten by an ANP officer for no apparent reason. I was asked to tell the villagers that this time they had attacked us. "But remember this," said Echo, "we'll be back to find the fuckers responsible for what happened today." Before we walked away, a villager came quietly up to me and whispered that we should come back to the village and search every house because he could guarantee that we would find a lot of stuff hidden that shouldn't be in the village. Echo wanted to know what kind of stuff the villager was talking about and who had it. The villager responded that he really couldn't tell us what kind of stuff we'd find or in which house it was located—he just wanted us to return one day so we could search all the houses in the village.

Echo, Oscar, and I walked over to the ANP vehicle where the detainee was being held. Oscar told me that he wanted to ask the detainee a few questions to see if his answers might possibly lead us to the individuals who were responsible for planting the IEDs in the alleyway. We talked to the young man for 10 or 15 fifteen minutes but couldn't get anything out of him that would either lead us to believe he was involved or that he knew anyone else who might have been responsible. Since our questions had been asked and answered to our satisfaction, Oscar and I were convinced that the detainee's testimony was the truth—that he was in the wrong place at the wrong time, and he was very lucky to be alive.

After my initial contact with the detainee, I realized that the young man's concern wasn't about the IED explosion or Najib beating him up. Rather, his main concern was about the plastic bag that he asked for over and over again. He also begged us to let him go home because he had to take the medication in the plastic bag to his father, who was very ill. The young man explained that he had gone to the pharmacy in the bazaar—which was a half-day's walk from his village—to get the medication for his father.

Thinking that I was the person in charge of his captivity, the young man asked me repeatedly to let him go. I told him I wasn't the guy who could either keep him or let him go, but I assured him that I would talk to the officer in charge of making such decisions as to what would happen to him from this point forward and whether he would further be interrogated or not.

As soon as the young man heard there was still a chance that he might be interrogated again, he pleaded, "Dear uncle, my father is very ill. Our house is right behind the orchard; can I please take the medication to him? One of your soldiers can come with me so he can bring me back to you." I could see that he obviously wasn't concerned for himself as much as he was for his sick father. Since I couldn't stand the pain he was going through, I went to Alfa so I could relate the young man's story. Alfa told me to let him go. However, when I returned to the truck where he was being detained, the ANP guys would not release him. I told them that Alfa gave me permission to release the young man, but they didn't trust me and said they had to hear it directly from Alfa. Before I went back to Alfa, I asked the ANP officers what difference it made if Alfa told them or not—they didn't speak English so wouldn't understand what Alfa was saying one way or another. Since they still refused to release the young man, I had no choice but to go back to Alfa again to tell him what the ANP officers had said. I knew that if I had bribed these officers with $5 each, they would've released the detainee without further argument, and blamed me for it if ever questioned. "Just go and let the young man go and tell the ANPs that I said so," Alfa insisted. Yet another example of the norm in the Afghan culture where this young man was detained, not because he was guilty of a crime, but because he was unfortunately in the wrong place at the wrong time.

Najib wanted to continue to detain him for his personal gain by showing the Americans how aggressive he was at capturing the bad guys and beating the hell out of them. I learned that the young man's misery was far from over because not only did Najib beat him, the ANP officers did he same while detaining and keeping him captive in their pickup truck. The ANPs were beating the young man simply because he was Pashton. Since the Hazaras were now in power, the ANP officers took out their revenge on the young detainee.

Before I released the young man's hands from bondage, he continued to beg me to give him the medication for his father. I pulled the bag out of my pocket and gave it to him as he cried and thanked me profusely for untying his hands, not for his sake but for that of his ailing father. Again, as was the norm in the Afghan society, his face was badly bruised and his nose was bloody from all the beatings he had received from Najib and the ANPs. As he walked away, I couldn't help but notice that the bottom half of the *partog* (trousers) were soaking wet, undoubtedly because the young man had relieved himself—whether from fear when the IED exploded, or because of the beatings he had received. Personally, I feel that anyone who is taking revenge by beating someone whose hands are tied behind his back is a coward.

Before leaving the village, I had a brief conversation with Najib, asking him again why he had beaten up the young detainee. Najib kept looking down at the ground, not making eye contact with me. When I gently tapped him on the shoulder and asked him to look at me and explain why he had done what he did to the young man, he still wouldn't answer me. Instead, I saw tears running down his cheeks. I didn't press him any further, deciding to leave him alone instead. However, before doing so, I had to point something out to him so he would, hopefully, remember not to do what he had done, ever again. "What if you were that young detainee, I was you, Najib, and I had your hands tied behind your back, beating you, whether I knew for certain if you had committed a crime or not? How would you feel if what you did to that young man happened to you?" Still no answer, but by the look on his face and the tears still running down his face, I knew he was getting the message, so I turned and walked away.

Since it was getting dark, in order for us to leave the village the same way we had entered it earlier in the day, most of us were going to leave on foot so the vehicles could follow us. None of our vehicles had mine rollers and the only one that was equipped that way had been destroyed by the IED. Now, our only detection to find an IED again was Paul and Sami's sniffing. Since we had been stuck at one end of the village for close to six hours, the bad guys could very well have planted more IEDs for us to find as we left the village. With that possibility in mind, we all lined up as close as possible on each side of the alleyway while Paul and Sami did their thing so we could leave the village.

At one point, we noticed that we were approaching an intersection where another alleyway crossed the one on which we were walking—in other words, a four-way intersection. We stopped and held our positions. EOD radioed Alfa that he had heard noise coming from his left side that sounded like someone was digging in the ground. Wanting to check it out, he turned left when we got closer to the middle of the intersection. Mike, the local interpreter, was supposed to follow him, but instead he stopped because he would no longer have the wall for protection and was afraid he might be shot. Alfa, Paul, Sami, and I turned left so we could follow EOD who was now about 200 feet ahead of us. I heard Alfa asking Mike (who was still holding back, behind the wall for cover), "What the fuck are you doing, Mike? Are you scared of being in your own fucking country enough that you want us to die for you?" Mike did not respond.

We walked on; before getting to the end of the alleyway, Alfa told me that EOD needed someone to translate while EOD questioned two of the locals he had stopped while they were digging a hole in the ground. I ran over to EOD, with Alfa close behind me. The two locals were facing the wall, their shovels there as well. EOD asked me to ask them what the fuck they were doing out this late at night, digging a hole in the ground. While asking them EOD's question, I learned that one of the two was the father of the other; they were digging the hole in order to divert a little stream of water to their farmland. When asked why they were doing it in the middle of the night, the father explained that the *Malak* (Village Elder) of his village was selling them the water, which he said was a God-given right to every villager. Continuing, he said, "Today you Americans were here in our village, and there was a lot of noise from bombs and the aircraft flying overhead. Therefore, I thought that since the Malak was probably not going to come out of his home, my son and I would seize the opportunity to steal some water for our farmland, which is what we were doing when this man (pointing to EOD) came along." Alfa interjected with, "By being here, in the middle of the night, you motherfuckers almost got killed!" When I finished translating what Alfa has said, the old man laughed and responded in Pashto, *"Bas no czha darta Wawa yam, khodie la marga khlas kro, oawka mrasawey ham why no par ghla bandi mra keydo, aow da ba czhona nam bade why."* ("Well, what can I say; God saved us, and if we had been killed, it would probably be a very shameful death for us for stealing water.")

We finally managed to leave the village without further incident. The father and son could very well have been dead victims of circumstance if any of our guys had simply blindly shot at them in the dark. Luckily, for all concerned, that did not happen.

The front of our armor vehicle After hitting the IED.

Recovering our mine rollers from the IED blast. Unlike the Soviets who left all their garbage behind after leaving Afghanistan, Americans made sure to leave Afghanistan better than we found it.

As Charlie took security position, most other ANP officers also gathered around Americans for protections, while Najib physically abused the local sitting on the ground facing him, as Ansari stood behind to look on.

Before we could leave the narrow alleyway. With Sami's help, three other IEDs were found within fifteen yards, which the EOD were flown in to detonate before we could leave the village.

A couple of days later, Echo came to my room to tell me that we were planning to go back to the village (where the IED explosion had occurred) so we could do a house-to-house search. I was just as pleased by the news as Echo was. However, two days later we learned that it wouldn't be possible to go back to that village after all, because we didn't have sufficient manpower to search all of it. Sometimes our guys who are on the ground in the war zone, as well as those who are on the frontline, see and hear things that they try to fix but can't because such decisions have to be made by the people in higher positions. We knew that this particular village was full of bad guys (like the Malak being up to no good), which was why one of the villagers told me we should do a complete sweep of the village to find out how really bad it was.

Afghanistan has a very complicated society for the West to understand. In this village alone, some villagers are telling us that there are bad guys, while others aren't saying anything about the four IEDs that were plotted for us. At the same time, there were still others who would risk their lives just to steal water in the middle of the night because the villagers thought he owned the water rights just as much as the village Malak did. Since it's very complex how they work, one must be a villager to completely understand the rules, with which I was very familiar.

A few nights later, there was yet another nightly knock on my door; this time it was Najib. When I opened the door, he asked if he could come in so we could talk. Since Jabar's last confrontation with me, I didn't allow any of the locals to enter my room without my permission, so I jokingly asked him, "Are you here to tell me what Jabar did, that you hate America and want to kill me because I am an American?" Najib laughed and extended his right hand. Naturally, I thought he wanted to shake hands with me; but, instead, he held my right hand in his as he tried to bend over to kiss it, primarily out of respect since I was twice his age (another cultural thing in the Afghan society, a way to show respect). I pulled my hand away before he could do that; instead, I hugged him. When Najib continued to insist he be allowed to kiss my hand, I again declined, telling him that I don't even allow my own children to do that. Besides, I wasn't a big fan of kissing hands as a way of getting out of telling the truth, and I told him so. Eventually, I learned that Najib had come to my room to apologize for what he had done to the young detainee on our last mission. I told him that he didn't have to apologize because he really didn't do anything wrong to me. "But I want to thank you for being like an uncle to me and for giving me the advice I needed," he said. In response, I told him, "I'm glad you had the wisdom to understand my point of view and what I was trying to tell you." Najib felt the need to explain that all of the other linguists who went on missions with the Americans would do the same exact thing to the detainee that he had done. "Why?" I asked. He explained that when he first started working for the Americans, a fellow linguist told him that the more aggressive he acted in front of the Americans, the more they would respect him, and the more the Americans respected you, they'd give you a better review, and the better your review, the more chances you had of getting that all-important green card to the United States. As mentioned earlier, everything in Afghanistan leads to getting a green card or perhaps even citizenship in the U.S., which is why they go out of their way to victimize their fellow Afghans.

When I told Najib that the young man he had beaten up wasn't even a member of the Taliban, he said, "Well, all I wanted to do was look aggressive to the Americans, just like all the other linguists do." I responded, "You can't justify your bad behavior by pointing to other linguists' bad behaviors. I didn't understand why people, such as the local Afghans, always say bad things about our beloved United States, especially when those same people would do bad things to their own people just to get to the very country they condemn."

During one of our missions on the main highway going towards a village in the southern Ghazni Province to look for the missing American soldier, our convoy ran into a shootout between the ASF (Afghan Security Forces) and the local militia from one of the villages alongside the main highway. We supported both groups of the ASF, especially those who are officially within the Afghan government fighting the Taliban under the banners of the ANA, ANP, NDS, and the local militias that were independent groups of thugs protecting their own villages and interests. When it came to trust, the local militia groups—who were much like the Taliban—were far worse than the ANA, ANP, and NDS. Anytime circumstances changed, not only would they switch sides in a split second, but they also wouldn't wear a uniform so they couldn't be easily identified.

Even though we now found ourselves trapped in the ANP and local militia's firefight, we were well prepared to defend ourselves with our own fighting power. However, Alfa decided it was best for us not to be part of their internal fight and told us we would wait it out behind a couple of small hills that were the only protection we could find to accommodate all of our team members.

So, we stopped our convoy on the main road behind the protection of the hills. As I always sat in the back of the open Humvee, I could see that one of the ANP officers involved in the fight was running toward our Humvee asking me if I would ask the Americans to help them or, at the very least, give them some ammunition. I relayed the officer's request to Alfa who immediately responded that he would *not* give out any of our ammunition. I was to also ask Charlie to shoot several warning shots behind the hills, toward the village, to see if the local militia or perhaps even the Taliban stopped shooting toward us. Once Charlie fired his mini gun from the top of the Humvee, everything went quiet immediately. The mini gun was loud and scary, so you could instantly understand why everyone disappeared after Charlie fired his. In this case, everything was getting quiet because all of the shooting had stopped.

When the situation had become calmer, the same ANP officer returned to ask me for a case of water that we usually loaded in our trucks for emergencies. It was a hot day, but not knowing what our situation was, I couldn't make the decision of whether to give any of our water to the ANP without asking for Alfa's permission to do so. When I asked Alfa, he told me that it was up to me and the other team members, especially if we were certain that we had enough for ourselves that we could spare a case (12 bottles) of water to the ANP. Well, I couldn't help but wonder how in the hell we would know if we had enough water for ourselves before giving the ANP officer any. No one could predict, not even Alfa, how long we were going to be on this mission. So, before giving him the whole case, I asked the ANP officer how much water he needed. He held his right hand up, his five fingers indicating the number of bottles he needed. I gave them to him so that we could continue on our way to our mission's objective.

The village that we were going to was like most of the other villages in Afghanistan, located in the middle of nowhere. Not only was this village in the middle of nowhere but it was also in an open desert area not surrounded by anything, which meant that any of the villagers could probably see us from their rooftops 10 miles away while we were driving through the countryside toward their village. Our convoy was progressing toward the village on one straight line, which had created a huge wall of dust in the air. As soon as we got closer to the village, our team split up into two groups so we could enter the village from both sides, thus hoping that no bad guys could escape.

Most of the other villages had at least some kind of river stream or canal going through their village. Luckily, however, this village didn't have any such waterways—or at least none that we could see while en route—which made our drive much easier. As usual, we drove into the village through very narrow alleyways, so our vehicles would oftentimes have a difficult time making the turns, sometimes knocking down part of the walls along the way.

When we had finally reached the main house of the village, which was our target, it was easy to see that it was the largest house of all the others in the village. Not only was it a house, but it also had a two-story shop attached on one side, facing the main intersection of the village, seemingly a place for the villagers to gather and socialize during the day.

Once most of the team were out of their vehicles so we could break into the house, Alfa, Charlie, and I stayed in our Humvee waiting for Fox and Marx, who would break into the house followed by the ANP officers who would also go in, as usual, to hold security positions as well as search for explosives, or perhaps make their own personal searches for whatever valuables they might be able to find to claim as their own.

I was taking pictures of what was happening when Captain Alfa told me Fox needed to see me inside the house. I jumped out the back of the Humvee and was headed toward the house when Alfa asked me, "Where the fuck's your rifle, Nas?" I didn't have a clue why I always forgot to take my rifle. I assumed that I did so, first, because I wasn't accustomed or trained as a soldier to carry one, and second, I was so excited to be in

Afghanistan helping my team, that I just simply forgot to take it. I was always thankful for Alfa, who always protected and looked out for me.

When I entered the house, I saw Fox and Marx standing next to a young man in his mid-teens and three women who were all sitting down on the floor, their heads covered by a *porany* in Pashto, or a *chadar* in Farsi (a shawl to cover their head). With one eye, the women were all peeking at us through a small whole in their head covers, while tightly holding 13 young children ranging in age from six months to about 12 years. The male owner of the house, who was about 70 years of age and appeared to be quite wealthy, had been taken outside. We always separated the adult males from the women and children during our questioning; then, once we were done interrogating them separately, we would determine if their stories matched.

The young man we had questioned first told us that all of the young children were his brothers and sisters; the elderly man outside was his father. The young man also said that he had a couple of older brothers who were living somewhere in the Arab world, but he didn't know exactly which country. The only thing that was confusing to Fox, Marx, and me was that six out of the 13 younger children were from age three to six years. When I asked the oldest of the women how she could have six children so young, pointing to the young man we had just interrogated, she said, "He is my son; all the other kids are my stepchildren, who belong to my husband's second and third wives." So, the old man had three wives at the same time and most of his children were from the two youngest wives, who were either in their late teens or early 20s!

Divided into three different sections, the house was huge. One part was the two-story shop area facing the main village square, the second was at the back of the house and had a back door leading directly out to the farmland and livestock, while the middle part, where we were standing, was used as the living area. Of all the villages we had visited, this was by far one of the wealthiest villagers I had seen thus far. Most of the stuff in his shop consisted of cooking oil, flour, rice, candy, gasoline, and other household supplies.

While we were interrogating the young man and his family, the ANP guys continued their search of the house, breaking things as they looked for explosives or anything else used for making IEDs.

Once I had finished translating for Fox, he said that Alfa needed me outside where he was standing with the elderly man who, we learned, was also the village elder. As Alfa was being straightforward in his questioning, he told me to ask the elder why he was supporting the Taliban, who visited with him last night. Without the slightest hesitation, the old man told me that it was his duty as a Muslim to give the Taliban food and shelter when required, because they were the helpers (caregivers) of their village's mosque, their house of Allah (God). Alfa told the elder that those same members of the Taliban—who were supported by their village elders—were not only killing innocent Afghans but were also putting IEDs on the main highway to kill the Coalition Forces who had come to the country to help the Afghan civilians. The old man responded by saying that most of what was going on, on the main road, could also be the work of the ASF, who had planted most of the bombs but always blamed someone else. Since this old man was apparently not afraid of us, he went on to mention that two of the Taliban leaders had been at his house two nights prior for dinner. Frankly, we didn't know what else to say to someone like this elder who was telling us that he supported the Taliban.

Since it was getting dark as we left the village, we were going to spend the night somewhere in the desert until morning. This would be one of those nights when everyone had to sleep with one eye open until sunrise. Most of the linguists and ANP officers slept on the ground next to the Humvees while all the Americans stayed awake, holding security positions. The next morning, before the sun had completely risen, we were on our way back to the base.

Now into mid-July, because of the new team members who arrived one by one, our compound was getting pretty crowded. One of our first missions together with the new team was by air, during which Chinook helicopters were used to drop us all down to the objective village in search of the missing American soldier, and then come back for us once we were done with our mission. On this particular occasion, it was around 2:00 PM when we were dropped off, away from the village in an open wheat field. From there, we walked to the village and started searching the houses one by one. Once finished, we walked down a narrow dirt road through an open area to reach the next village when a rocket hit the ground within 50 feet to the south of where we were walking. The sound of the explosion was tremendous. We had no idea where it came from but all knew that we had to run in opposite directions from where the rocket had landed. Some of our guys ran west to the next village to take cover behind the houses, while others went back to the village we had just left in order to get away and out of the open space where the rocket had hit. I was the only one who ran in the opposite direction, to the open field. Within seconds, I realized my dumbed ass mistake. All team members in the immediate area were shouting at me. "Hey, you fucking asshole, where are you going? Get back here, you motherfucker." Now that everyone had confirmed how fucking stupid I felt, I immediately dropped on the ground, flat on my stomach. However, the yelling and cursing continued nonstop. I was going to have to make the decision on which way to run, and I had to do it fast before I was hit by another rocket. Meanwhile, the guys were still yelling, "Get the fuck out of the open field, you asshole!" Unlike all the other attacks we had encountered by the bad guys, this one happened to be a single-rocket attack. Once the first rocket had hit, not a single shot had yet been fired. My obvious concern was the thought that the bad guys were waiting for me to get up so they could shoot me. To make sure that no one was waiting somewhere to do just that, I decided that I should at least face the opposite way so I could see where all of my team members were.

While still flat on my stomach on the ground, I turned my head to the south in an effort to determine in which direction I should run. Once I had made the clockwise turn from my 12 o'clock north to the six o'clock south, I checked out the three o'clock and nine o'clock directions to see which way would be the shortest distance for me to run. Seeing that my nine o'clock was the shortest distance, I got up and ran as fast as I could to get out of the open field. Once I got back where Alfa, Charlie, and Bravo2 (the new replacement for the first Bravo on our previous team) were standing, Bravo2 immediately asked, "Nas, what the fuck were you thinking, running into an open field?" I told him I wasn't really thinking of running into the open field; I was thinking more about running away from the area where the rocket had hit and instead of running for cover, I followed my initial instinct to run in the opposite direction. Since I had never been in a situation like this before, how was I supposed to know? I had come to realize that every combat situation was different. However, surviving it was not, so I felt truly blessed that I had survived this one and been given another chance not to be dumb again. Since I was not a trained soldier, I realized that each and every one of my reactions in combat was impulsive.

We later learned that the single rocket was fired from the rooftop of a mosque in the village we had just searched and were about to leave. Obviously, our plans had now changed. We had to stay in this village and look for the bad guys. First, after we were all retrieved, we went to the first village from where we had been attacked and searched every house again. Still, we could find nothing out of the ordinary, and (as usual) no one in the village would tell us anything. Although it was getting darker, everyone on our team had scattered themselves throughout the village searching homes. Alfa and our new ODA Captain Alfa2, who had just joined us on this mission, were both standing around the open area in the center of the village to coordinate plans for our dinner, which would be dropped off by helicopter. Since no one could predict how long or when we would be done with this mission, it sounded like we were going to be in this village for the long haul.

Alfa2 requested me to ask the ANP officers what kind of MRE (Meal Ready to Eat) they would like for dinner. MRE came in four different varieties: pork, beef, veggie, and pasta. Well, obviously, since the ANPs were all Muslims, I anticipated that they wouldn't want the pork, but when I asked them if they wanted the other three choices, they declined. To them, since the MREs were made by the infidels, it was considered not *Halal* (anything the Muslims eat should be considered holy); therefore, the ANPs declined Alfa2's offer for the MREs.

While everyone else on our team were still in the village searching from house to house, I was with Alfa and Alfa2 discussing a plan regarding our mission for the rest of the night. One of the ANP officers came over and tapped me on the shoulder, asking me if I could go with him. Since I didn't know what he wanted to tell me or where he wanted or take me, as dark as it was, I wanted to know. "What's going on?" I asked. "Just come with me for a minute, okay?" he responded. When I thought, *Well, how bad can it be?*, I went with him. He just took me around the corner, where all I could see were seven dark, human shadows sitting on the ground, leaning against the wall. Ansari invited me to join them; since his was the only voice I recognized, I did.

Prior to my arrival, it was apparent that they had already broken into one of the village shops and stolen watermelons (which they were eating with great gusto) and cigarettes, both of which they offered when I was asked to join them. Curious as to whether they would tell me the truth or not, I asked where they got the watermelon and cigarettes. When they answered, it was quite clear that they weren't ashamed of what they had done. In fact, they seemed to be quite proud of their "accomplishment" because they "got them from the shop that belonged to the Taliban motherfuckers." Still curious, I asked, "How did you guys know this shop belonged to the Taliban?" One of them told me, "Ustad, this whole village belongs to the Taliban." I wanted to tell them that what they had done was wrong, but it was not my job to do so, and I knew that even if it were, I would never be able to change their mindset. Although the urge was strong, I didn't want to talk to them by myself, especially since I didn't know what the consequences of my actions would be or what would happen with these seven thugs sitting and leaning against a wall, eating something that they had stolen, while our guys were still scattered throughout the village look-ing for the bad guys. All seven of them considered themselves Muslims by declining our MRE offer because it was not *Halal*, but nothing thought of going out of their way to steal from the poor shopkeeper.

Since I was so undecided, I went to Alfa and Alfa2 and informed them of what the ANP had done. (As an aside, by the ANPs own disclo-sure to me that everyone in this village was associated with the Taliban, they didn't have the courage to do anything about it. Nonetheless, they felt brave and proud enough to steal watermelons and cigarettes from a local store. They believed that stealing from a store that belonged to the Taliban was their way of defeating the enemy. When I told Alfa what the ANPs were up to, he said, "Fuck, are you kidding me, Nas?" I responded, "Sir, I kid you not. Come with me so you can see for yourself." So, Alfa, Alfa2, and I walked around the corner to see the seven men still sitting, eating watermelons and smoking cigarettes. Alfa wanted to know where Ansari was. Curious, because before I went to get Alfa, Ansari had been there, eating watermelon with the rest of the ANPs, but when I came back with both commanders, he was gone. So I asked the officers where Ansari went, but they wouldn't answer me.

Suddenly, there he was and asked suspiciously, "Ustad, is everything okay?" When Alfa saw that Ansari had returned, his first question for him was, "Ask him whose watermelon they're eating." Ansari said it was theirs, nodding his head to include the seven men leaning against the wall. When Alfa said he didn't see anyone carrying watermelon with them when we left the base, rather than translate this to Ansari, I told Alfa, "Sir, they have just told me that they broke into this shop and took the watermelons and cigarettes." Alfa sighed, "Okay, Nas, I get the picture now. Ask Ansari if he and his men aren't supposed to be protecting the Afghan civilians rather than stealing from them." Ansari's response was: "Ustad, ask Alfa how in the hell he can possibly expect me to be running after all of these guys in the dark so I can monitor what they're doing?" Alfa explained to Ansari that he didn't need to run after them to know what they were doing because, as an officer, he just needed to have the leadership required to watch over them. "Am I running after my guys everywhere they go?" Alfa asked. When Ansari didn't respond, Alfa continued with, "I want you guys to return what's left of your pilferage back to the shop; as for whatever you've eaten or smoked, leave the money for them in the shop where it can easily be found in the morning by the owner." I knew that it was just wishful thinking on Alfa's part that Ansari and his men would simply do as Alfa had ordered—that just was *not* going to happen.

Alfa and Alfa2 returned to where they were standing by the open field, while I stayed where I was, waiting to see what Ansari and his men would do, which is what is expected—however, they merely continued to eat the stolen watermelon. When their stomachs were full, they stood and left the alleyway with their pockets full of cigarettes. I couldn't help but wonder what the villagers and shopkeeper would say in the morning when the shopkeeper saw the broken door to his shop, that he'd been robbed, and immediately thought that the Americans had looted his shop. Certainly, the villagers knew we were not responsible but were bound to blame us for bringing the ANPs into their village because, otherwise, they are not permitted (brave enough) to enter any of the villages on their own.

While waiting with Alfa and Alfa2, Alfa told me that I was needed for translation at one of the houses in the village up the hill. Our guys were sending a couple of ANP officers down the hill to get me. When they arrived, I went with them to the house, where our guys had discovered an antiaircraft missile launcher in the garage, mounted to the bed of a Toyota pickup truck, which appeared to have been parked in the garage for quite some time—perhaps as far back as the Soviet invasion in the early 1980s.

This house also had three different parts to it: a guesthouse in the front, the garage at the other end of the house, and a large four- to five-bedroom living space in the middle. A number of men were being detained by our guys in every corner of the courtyard. People who lived in the guesthouse didn't know who the middle of the house belonged to, nor did the man who had been living there with his family. They all lived in a house that didn't belong to anyone? Welcome to Afghanistan! The man who lived in the middle section with his family said they had moved into the house a long time ago, when it was empty; he never saw anyone so he could ask who the owner was. I suspect there is probably some truth to that; most people who left their homes during the Soviet invasion never returned to claim them.

Since our chief concern was trying to start the pickup truck in the garage, we tried, to no avail. The only alternative left was to destroy the garage and the truck inside, which had probably been parked there for more than 20 years. I didn't agree with that decision, especially since a number of people lived in the same house and another house was attached to the garage.

Since it wasn't their house in the first place, at some point, we were going to ask the people in the middle to leave. Once they were gone, our guys were going to detonate and destroy the garage and the pickup truck. Well, as it turned out—and thanks to Alfa's leadership—he saved the poor Afghan family who were going to be evicted because while it wasn't their house technically, making them homeless wasn't the right thing to do morally. Therefore, Alfa would not allow our team members to destroy the vehicle in the garage. Instead, he suggested that they take one of our ATVs and hook its towing cable to the pickup truck so it could be pulled out of the garage and towed to the open field so it could later be destroyed by the Chinook around midnight when it returned to pick us up. We were then told that there would be no dinner drop-off after all; instead, we would be picked up by the Chinook within half an hour, which would be the end of this mission.

A little more than half an hour later, we heard the welcoming sound—
TaTaTaTaTaTaTa—of the Chinook, from a distance. We all moved away
from the huts, closer to the open field. There were more than 80 of us,
divided into two groups, each of which formed a line for pick up, one
group at a time. My group was first. I don't think it was easy task for any
of us to get on the Chinook, not only in the dark of night but in any of
the dusty villages of Afghanistan, either. Since landing space was limited,
this particular pickup by the Chinook was the more frightening I had
experienced since my arrival.

Upon landing, the helicopter lost balance and got closer to us than
normal. All we could see and hear were the sparks and sounds of the
Chinook's blades. The more than 100 mile per hour wind with its temperature of 100 degrees didn't help matters, either, because they were
obviously so strong, some of us were being knocked to the ground, while
others willingly dropped to the ground which saved us all from being
beheaded or even slightly hurt by the blades of the Chinook. Since the
helicopter couldn't land in the space between the mud huts and the
pickup truck we had moved to the open field, we had to find another
location where the Chinook could land and pick us up, a task that took
us 20 minutes to walk to in order for the helicopter to be able to make
a safe landing.

Finally, we were all out of there, en route to the compound!

Everyone on the old team was packing to go home while the new
team was settling in and getting acquainted with all of the local linguists
and ANP officers at the compound. While the local linguists and ANP
officers were introduced to the new team, Alfa was updating Alfa2 with
their resumes.

One morning after breakfast, during the transfer of responsibility of
the compound to the new team, Echo asked me to talk with Zuhair, one
of the squad leaders, regarding the ammunition/rocket shells/grenades that
he had in his possession, which were given to all squad leaders before every
mission; if it wasn't used on that mission, they were required to return it
to Echo. So he wanted me to ask Zuhair what had happened to the eight
rocket shells that his squad had received but never used or returned to

the team. When I questioned Zuhair about the rocket shells, he said his brother, who was on his squad, was supposed to have turned them in, but his brother had not done so. When we went to Zuhair's brother and asked him about the rocket shells, he told us he had given them to Ansari. (Yet another normal ANP scenario where one would always say that someone else had whatever was missing and was supposed to have returned it; therefore, the individual being questioned obviously had no clue where the missing item(s) were.)

I was reasonably positive that Echo didn't have time to take any bullshit from Zuhair or his brother. Since Echo had given Zuhair the rockets, he went directly to him, reminding Zuhair that, as a squad leader, he had given the rockets to him, and he wanted them back no later than day's end or Echo would not only fire Zuhair's ass but his squad of eight ANP officers as well. Since the last thing Zuhair wanted was to get fired, his brother miraculously found the missing rocket shells and returned them later that day—again, the norm for the ANP. Zuhair happened to be one of the ring leaders and knew how to take advantage of any situation of this nature, not only by stealing ammunition but by also abusing the new police vehicle that he had just received, which was, of course, paid for by the American taxpayers. Zuhair had been caught twice before: once for taking one of the brand new police trucks to downtown Ghazni City so he could sell its brand new tires and bring the truck back to the compound with bald tires; and the second time, taking the truck with a full tank of gasoline, only to return it with an empty tank.

Throughout my deployment with Special Forces, I have experienced a number of very scary moments—situations like bullets flying all around our heads, frightening moments when we all thought our heads might be chopped off by the Chinook, and those times when I felt I might lose some of the team—or even myself—in just a matter of seconds. But, while one particular situation is not only frightening and unimaginable (i.e., "Now you see him, now you don't."), there was the time when Captain Alfa was lost in just a matter of seconds, even though I was following him very closely in the dark.

Once again, during one of our missions to northern Ghazni Province to look for the missing American soldier, the Chinook, as usual, had dropped us off about a mile away from the objective compound so the bad guys wouldn't hear us coming. As we were walking on an unpredictable, plowed farmland towards the compound (where, by the way, walking could be very challenging when trying to keep up with six-foot-tall soldiers who could walk twice as fast as me), I always followed Alfa very closely, not only because it was dark and I didn't want to lose him, but also to be very close, just in case he needed me for translation or if unexpected shit happened to be protected.

As we continued to walk, from time-to-time I would glance down to my feet to make sure there were no ditches or streams of water that I might fall into. Obviously, Alfa and everyone else on the team could walk much faster than I because they could see things much more clearly than I did, especially since I still didn't have night goggles nor did I ever. Anyhow, by constantly looking up and down, I did everything I could to catch up to Alfa, without falling into a ditch or losing sight of his shadow. Then came the moment when I looked up to where the dark shadow had been for the past 10 minutes, only to find that Alfa was no longer in front of me. I didn't know what had happened to him. I looked around but couldn't see anything except two ANP officers directly behind me. (This is the perfect example of why I didn't like night missions, because I couldn't see anything.) Besides, being a native Pashton—which most Taliban are—I had one other thing in common with them: They hated nightly missions as much as I did, because they couldn't escape, not knowing where the fuck they were going—something our guys loved, by the way.

As the ANP officers and I looked for Alfa, I suddenly saw a flashing light coming out of the ground to my left. When I tried to get closer to it, I saw a dark, deep sinkhole that Captain Alfa had fallen into, which is why he was trying to get our attention with his flashlight. At first, I had no idea how he could have missed such a large and deep open-ing in the ground. Second, while I desperately wanted to pull him out of the hole, I had no clue how to make that happen. It was definitely one of those situations where I didn't know what to do or who to call for help—besides that, as dark as it was, I didn't know if anyone could hear me yelling anyhow. I was stuck with the two ANP officers who were unable to provide me with help of any kind. To complicate matters even more, every time we went on nightly missions, we were supposed to whisper our communications on an internal radio so as not to alert the enemy. But this was really freaky because I had absolutely no idea what to do but to start screaming so someone might hear me and come to Alfa's rescue.

The hole was so deep, there was no possible way for Alfa to come out of it on his own. Even though I knew that bad guys would be awakened, I started screaming for help, not worrying whether doing so would be helping the cause by someone coming to help us, or hurting the cause by waking up the bad guys. At the moment, my focus was more on Alfa's safety than anything else. After all of my screaming and yelling, I saw Echo2 had returned after he had left to see if he could find something with which to pull Alfa out of the sinkhole. At first, I thought my screaming and yelling was the reason for Echo2's return; however, I soon learned that wasn't the case. Alfa had communicated through his radio to all of the team members that he had fallen into a sinkhole and needed help. Whatever the reason, I was delighted to see Echo2. I knew that the ANP officers and I weren't capable of rescuing Alfa by ourselves and I also knew I was lucky that I hadn't fallen into the hole on top of Alfa!

Although Echo2 and I attempted to pull Alfa out, there was no way we could reach him. Echo2 called for more help from our other team members. Since Delta2 was the closest person on one of our ATVs, he soon joined us. And thank God he did because, otherwise, we wouldn't have been able to do anything.

In order for us to pull Alfa out, Delta2 dropped the long towing cable from the front of the ATV into the hole so that Alfa could grab and hold on to it. When Alfa was finally pulled out of the hole, we regrouped and were back on our way to the objective. I knew that the 20-foot fall into the sinkhole had hurt Alfa because I could see that he was walking with a limp. Before arriving at our objective, Alfa, the two ANP officers, and I stopped and waited for our guys to breach into the compound. Soon after the first explosion of a door being blown away, Alfa told me that we were ready to enter the compound. As we walked in, although we had not yet met, I saw Jay, one of ODA2's team members who had taken over for Fox. He was busy separating three adult males in the house, one of whom was an elderly man who was blind in one eye and couldn't see out of his other eye very well, either. While I helped Jay hold the blind man against the wall for interrogation, I heard Scott, another new team member, calling me over to where he was holding the other two young men, both in their mid-teens, for interrogation at the other end of the courtyard. When Jay asked me to stay with him and started to ask the blind man questions, I told Scott I'd be over to help him as soon as I could. The blind man told us that the house wasn't his; it belonged to someone who was currently living in France. He was just a house-sitter living there with two teenage sons and other members of his family.

While we were interrogating the male adults of the house, the ANPs were busy doing their own things (e.g., ransacking the house and generally just destroying as many items as they could find). Every house that we raided was assumed to belong to the Taliban; thus, the ANPs treated them as such. In Afghanistan, while almost every Afghan in every village looks like they belong to the Taliban—which is just the nature of the species—by the same token, that doesn't make every Afghan a Taliban. It was sad for me to notice how almost every ANP officer and local linguist became interrogators and prosecutors at the same time by coming up with a 100% guilty verdict for every man in every house we raided.

After we had finished searching the house and interrogating the three men, almost three hours had passed. It was early dawn and the sun was about to come up. The three detainees were now sitting in separate corners of the courtyard, their hands tied behind their backs with an AK47 held to their heads by three ANP officers, one of whom came to tell me that the blind man wanted to talk with me since none of the ANP officers understood Pashto. When I reached the old man, he said, in Pashto, "Dear interpreter, my elder son has his finals today. His school is an hour away, can you please let him go?" I went to ask Jay if it was possible to let one of the boys go to school because of his finals. Since Jay didn't want to release any of the detainees, he suggested I talk with Alfa. When I told Alfa, he not only let the boy go, but was happy to do so because of the fact that there was a school in the area. However, before Alfa released the boy, Scott reported that the results of the explosive test were negative for both boys. With that news, Alfa told Scott and Jay to release all three males and to allow the one who needed to go to school to leave the house. Jay and I both unlocked the handcuffs and told the elder man to return to his family, but cautioned him not to leave the house until we had left the village. He said he didn't have anywhere to go, then added, "The whole night I wanted to make you guys some tea, but my hands were tied. I asked the police officer if I could make you some tea, but he didn't understand me nor I him. Now that my hands are free, may I now make the tea for all of you?" He didn't offer the tea because he had to, but because he wanted to—another norm and kind gesture by many of the villagers. Despite my knowledge and expertise of Afghanistan's culture, I was astounded by what this poor man was trying to do for us, especially after what we had just put his family and him through.

Feeling very emotional by it all, I told Alfa what the blind man had offered. Alfa returned to the house with me and told the blind man the exact same thing I had on my mind and would've told him, had I the authority to do so. "We broke into your house in the middle of the night and handcuffed you and your sons and, despite that, you still want to offer us tea?" The blind man responded, "None of this is your fault or mine; it's the Taliban causing you trouble and making us crazy. My God curses them!" Alfa accepted the man's offer to make us tea.

It was around 8:00 o'clock in the morning and the sun was now up. When I saw Fox taking pictures from the rooftop of the house we had just searched, I joined him. It was a very large and well-built house located at the outskirts of the village, away from all the mud huts. No wonder the owner was in France! The view from the rooftop was spectacular—certainly not as good as the views in the south of France, but more beautiful here because of the countryside. Everywhere I looked, there were no signs of development of any kind. It was all pure and natural beauty with rocky mountains in the distance, surrounded by parcels of green- and khaki-colored farmland, divided by tall tree lines with scattered orchards. The house had four guard towers, each taller than 20 feet at each corner of the compound, each with four "French" windows, one facing in each direction. Behind the house was an apricot orchard with direct access from the backdoor of the house. Others had joined Fox and me—either ANP officers or the local linguists, all sleeping instead of holding their security positions—another norm.

As I walked around the roof while taking pictures of the surrounding mountains and valley, I noticed a couple of ANP officers picking apricots in the orchard behind the house. As soon as one of them saw me, he offered to throw some up to me. I refused and, instead, asked him if he had gotten permission from anyone to pick the apricots. He denied having permission and then, with a smile on his face, said, "Ustad, in Afghanistan no one asks for permission. If I throw some up to you, just eat and enjoy them." "No, but thank you anyhow; you just enjoy them yourself." I wondered if I was being too harsh or rude by trying to stop the other officer and him from doing something that is supposedly only normal in their minds. But I really didn't care because I was simply trying to protect the poor man's property by not allowing them to steal apricots from an orchard that didn't belong to them.

Morally, I was strong and willing enough to protect those who were victims of circumstance, just like I was when I lived in Kandahar City or New York City without protection of any kind. So I couldn't allow them to continue to steal from the poor man's orchard by simply pointing out that what they were doing was wrong.

As I was going back and forth with the ANP officer, one of the linguists woke up and said, "You worry too much. No one in Afghanistan asks anyone for permission to do anything," he said, repeating what the other officer had just told me. Now I had a bigger challenge to deal with; since some of the linguists were more intelligent than most of the ANP officers, I simply asked the linguist if that's how things work in Afghanistan, then how would anyone know what belonged to them or someone else? To make my point more understandable for the linguist, I asked, "Is that why this house has walls 20-feet high and guard towers on each corner to make sure people don't come and take what belongs to the owner?" This linguist, who was no longer thinking rationally (if he even was before) responded in Farsi, *"Pash amad, khosh amad,"* ("What is in front of you is yours, even if it belongs to someone else"). I could've gone back and forth with him as well, but I knew it would be fruitless to do so, no matter how much I tried to reason with him.

I took a few pictures from the rooftop to the ground when a loud explosion suddenly shook the whole house. I thought that an IED had just exploded and hoped everyone outside the house wasn't hurt. Since I was not completely down from the rooftop when the explosion occurred, I scurried back up to see where it had occurred. The huge mushroom cloud of dust from the explosion was coming down so thick I could hardly see in front of me much less try to determine where the explosion had occurred. I waited for the cloud of dust to dissipate so I could more clearly see what was going on around me. Approximately 200 feet to the west of the compound was a small mud hut, one wall missing and smoke billowing outside from inside the hut. As all of us standing on rooftops watched the mud hut for a few more minutes, another explosion occurred in the same hut, but this time there was metal debris flying everywhere, which made us all run for cover—at least as much as those of us standing on rooftops could do under the circumstances.

We still didn't know what the hell was going on or what to make of all of this. I couldn't help but notice that all of the Americans on our team didn't react in any way that would signal that anything bad was happening—only the ANP officers and local linguist were freaking out. I went to the ground to find Alfa, who told me it was a control detonation, which was carried out by Charlie. The small mud hut west of the compound was one of the Taliban's garages where they would come in the night to store all their ammunition and other bomb-making materials. As it turned out, the explosion was actually a good thing for our team, because most of the stuff that was detonated in that one small mud hut were explosives stored by the Taliban. We had experienced similar situations in most of our other missions where we would go into a village, not finding anything in the houses that we raided, but finding dangerous materials in places one would never expect, like mud huts or garages located away from the homes, which no one in the village knew about (or at least that's what they told us).

Since he didn't have enough cups to serve us all at the same time, the blind man brought out a second round of tea for those who didn't get any the first time. I noticed the young ANP officer who had offered me apricots from the orchard walking towards me. Since he didn't speak Pashto, Afzali brought the young officer to me so I could ask the blind man if it was okay for the officer to pick some apricots from the orchard. When I asked the old man, he said, "Go ahead; eat as much as you can." Not only was the blind elder compassionate toward the ANP officers—who had been holding AK47s to their heads all night long—but he was also compassionate toward us because of his kind act of decency making us tea but also allowing the ANP to have as many apricots as they wanted.

We were about to leave the village to be picked up sometime within the next hour in an open area where the Chinook could make a safe landing, which Alfa was looking for now. As I was leaving the compound, in front, I met the same ANP officer waiting for me so he could offer the apricots again.

I smiled, thanked him, still hesitating to take them, but he insisted. "Ustad, here, have some; you know we have been granted permission to pick them." Before I took the apricots from him, I smiled to let him know that I knew he had understood what I said to him from the rooftop; he smiled back in an apologetic way. To show my appreciation that he had done the right thing, I placed my right hand on his left shoulder while extending my left hand so he could give me the apricots. "See? Now you feel good about yourself, and I am willing to take some apricots from you because we have permission to do so. But most of all, you have made God happy."

As I turned to walk away so I could catch up with Alfa and Jag, our new JTAC replacement for Ross, I thanked the ANP officer for the apricots. In response, he said, "No, Ustad, you don't need to thank me because I am the one who's thanking you." It's good to know in my heart that this young officer will remember what I had told him for the rest of his life about taking other people's property without their permission. I will always remember, now some 40 years later, at the early age of about seven or eight, when my adoptive dad told me that I shouldn't take what wasn't mine. If I can remember my own apricot story for as long as I live and pass it on to others, I have no doubt that this particular officer will also remember it as well, just by having admitted his own wrongdoing of offering me apricots that he had had no right to pick.

Alfa, Jag, and I were walking away from the village toward the mountain area where we had been dropped off the night before. Jag, who was on his first mission with us, was already complaining to me about why we were walking so far away from the village when there were plenty of wheat fields on which the Chinook could land easily when it picked us up. Well, since that decision wasn't ours to make, Alfa had to determine where the Chinook should land. Unlike Ross, our previous JTAC, Jag was somewhat lazy and frightened to go on missions, so he wanted to get out of there as soon as possible. As I watched Alfa move forward to find the proper place away from the farmland where the Chinook could land, I was glad that Jag wasn't the decision-maker in this regard. By the way, Jag's ass has been chewed just like mine by Alfa on one of our missions in the past when Jag couldn't operate the RG.

It was around 2:00 in the afternoon, and it was hot. Since I always followed Alfa closely, I heard one of our team members call him on his radio, asking where we were headed, to which Alfa responded, "Well, I'm looking for a spot where we won't ruin the poor Afghan farmer's crops."

Despite the temperature and humidity, we had been walking for quite a while (uphill). Once Alfa found the proper place for us to be picked up, he radioed our guys to meet us at the top of the hill, which was located far enough away to protect the farmland. During missions, most of my time was always spent with Alfa. Whether he was communicating on the radio with other team members or I was translating for him with the local Afghans or ANPs, I learned that Alfa did not once do or say things that would either harm any of our team members or any of the local Afghans. Rather, in most cases, he went out of his way to make sure no one got hurt and that no damage to the local Afghans was caused by our actions. It was because of his superb leadership that all of our team members worked so well together—and I was happy, proud, and honored to be part of his team.

The next couple weeks involved the "changing of the guard," one moving out and another coming in. As Alfa and his team turned over the responsibility and inventory of our compound, plus also introducing the new team to the Governor of Ghazni Province and all of the other Afghan officials that the old team would have to work with in a variety of issues from social, political, redevelopment, and most importantly, the training of the new Afghan Security Forces.

Echo2 of the new team had the same duty as the first Echo from the previous team did, which was handling the bookkeeping of our compound as far as inventory and logistics were concerned. While Echo2 was making sure that the log sheet matched the inventory on the compound, he came across one major discrepancy during his initial walkthrough. Our team had four Toyota pickup trucks that were used by team members on the base; according to Damon, they were leased from the local linguists, which he shared with me when we used one of the trucks to go to the DFAC on the opposite side of the base. On the log sheet given to ODA2, it was indicated that the departing team was in possession of four gray Toyota pickup trucks; however, Echo2 had only counted three, plus a very old, non-functioning Ford pickup. When Echo2 asked the first Echo who was in charge of the inventory while part of the previous team and about the discrepancy regarding the fourth truck, Echo said that one of the linguists had probably taken it somewhere for his own personal use (which most linguists would do, despite the fact that the pickups were leased to the team).

A couple days passed and still the linguists knew nothing about where the fourth truck was. Since Echo2 couldn't count the fourth truck as part of his inventory, he went to ask Alfa to sign for the missing truck, which would cost Alfa's team $6,000. Meanwhile, Alfa had recalled that Ansari had once asked for Jabar's permission to use the missing truck for a couple of days for his own personal use. Since he claimed to be in command of our compound, Jabar had given Ansari permission to do so. Alfa asked me to tell Ansari to meet him in the kitchen so they could talk about the truck. He also wanted Echo and Charlie—the only member of Alfa's team still in Afghanistan—to attend as well.

When we all met in the kitchen later that day, through my translation, Alfa asked Ansari where the truck was. Ansari explained, "Well, Ustad, what happened was that one day I drove to Mazar (a city in northern Afghanistan) in that vehicle. Someone saw it, liked it, and I sold it to him." When Alfa asked why he had done that, Ansari told him, "When I asked Jabar Ustad for the vehicle, he told me that Delta had given him permission for me to take the vehicle." "How much did you sell it for?" Alpha pressed. "I sold it for three hundred thousand Kaldar," Ansari said, referring to Pakistani currency. Alfa turned to me. "Nas, how much is three hundred thousand fucking Kaldar in dollars?" After a quick calculation, I told him that it was around $3,400, which angered Alfa so much he slammed the kitchen counter with his fist and shouted, "Fucking shit! I didn't expect this from you Ansari! You're a fucking team leader, man!" I had never seen Alfa so angry and was glad that I hadn't been the one to do something wrong. By the look on Ansari's face, I could tell he was worried about how Alfa was reacting, as were Echo and Charlie. Ansari said nothing more as he just stood there looking down at his shoes.

Alfa remained by the kitchen counter for a few more minutes and then turned to walk out of the kitchen. Before doing so, he got very close to Ansari, looked him in the eye, and told him, "Today is Tuesday; I want that truck back here by Friday or *you* will come up with six thousand dollars, do you understand me?" Alfa then started to leave the room again, the rage still evident on his face and by his body language—not just because of what Ansari had done with the truck for because of what he had done to the team as a whole. As Alfa left, he opened the kitchen door all the way and slammed it as hard as he could. It was obvious that Ansari had been scared shitless when Alfa slammed his fist on the kitchen counter; however, when Alfa slammed the door as hard as he did, he really got his message across to Ansari to think twice before even trying to fuck with Alfa's property, which I believe was the only way to deal with Afghan officials.

Ansari, Echo, and Charlie then left the kitchen. As I was about to leave, our buddy, Qasim, who was on the other side of the kitchen, couldn't help but overhear some, if not most, of the conversation between Alfa and Ansari. Qasim, who was notorious when it came to giving his opinion—solicited or not—always had something to offer, especially when a Hazara or Tajik was being humiliated. So I wasn't surprised when he approached me to offer his opinion, not even knowing for sure what Ansari had done. "Well, Ustad, Alfa is a very tough guy, it's good that he had scared the crap out of the Hazara (referring to Ansari)." I knew it was typical of Qasim to say such a thing once in a while, especially when he seemed to forget that I did not like his discriminatory comments; therefore, he either wanted to piss me off with his remarks or he was inevitably prejudiced and couldn't hold back from making such remarks.

It was that same day, Tuesday, around 4:00 PM, when Ansari returned the fourth Toyota pickup to the compound. We knew that there was absolutely no way for him to get back to Mazar—more than 300 miles each way—to get the truck back so quickly from the person he claimed to have sold it to. Yet another perfect example of Ansari and Jabar trying to rip-off the new team they thought would never notice. Jabar and Ansari had planned this rip-off well by blaming the whole thing on Delta—a good choice since he was no longer around to defend himself or to say that he had not given the truck to Ansari in the first place, much less given him permission to sell it.

As a good example of how the ANP view themselves, their government, and the local Afghans is when we were on a mission and Ansari insisted that I ride with them in their police pickup truck, which I really didn't want to do, primarily because of the way they drove, coupled with the other myriad risks involved. Nonetheless, after getting permission from my new commander, Alfa2, I decided to ride with them. Zuhair drove and Ansari sat in the front passenger seat, while I sat with one of the other ANP officers in the backseat. Because of the way Zuhair drove on the narrow dirt alleyways through the village, I thought for sure that he would either run over a local villager or a donkey, or the truck would flip over into the creek next to us.

Needless to say, it was nerve-wracking for us in the backseat. I couldn't take it anymore and knew I had to say something to either Zuhair or ask Ansari to tell him to slow down and stop driving so erratically. I decided to start with Zuhair, asking him to slow down so he wouldn't kill anyone, or, because of the way he was driving the pickup through the ditches and the roughest part of the road, the truck could break down at any minute. Furthermore, villagers saw them as Afghan police officers, there to protect them, not run them over. At the rate of speed Zuhair was driving, every time a villager saw us coming, they would run for safety to avoid getting hit by the truck.

I was blindsided by what Zuhair and Ansari said to me after what I had just told Zuhair. Being the more macho of the two, Zuhair said in his native Farsi, *"Usatd, kodam Awghanistana maygey, Awghanistan go ish baramadagey ast, imroz e Amrikaya az enja baraya, baz bebe chea maysha"* ("Ustad, which Afghanistan are you talking about? It does not exist. Afghanistan is all fucked up. As soon as the Americans leave, you will see nothing but chaos"). "Can I ask you something?" I said. He responded, "Ustad, just don't ask me for money, other than that, ask me for anything else you wish." "Aren't you an Afghan?" I asked. "And if you are, how can you say that Afghanistan is fucked up?" His response to my question was, "Ustad, it's not only me who is saying Afghanistan is fucked up, everyone is saying that; you can ask Ansari if you don't believe me." So I looked at Ansari and asked as politely as I could, "Mr. Ansari, what is Zuhair saying? Is he insane, or what?" Ansari's answer surprised me. "Well, Ustad, the boy is right. Afghanistan does *not* exist. Which one of us is the Afghan? There are no Afghans. The Pashtons fight for Islam, the Tajiks and Uzbeks fight for money, and all that's left are the Hazaras, and whatever other minorities are fighting to be the breadwinners for their wives and children. Now, where do *you* see Afghanistan in all of this?" I could not believe what I was hearing. Certainly, while I sensed the division between the various ethnic groups, there were still doubts in my mind that the Afghan history was probably manipulated. But, now, here in the villages of Afghanistan, I could see it with my eyes and hear it with my own ears after talking with Ansari, Zuhair, and many of the other local Afghans I had met so far. Ansari may not have been the brightest person in Afghanistan, but he certainly made his point by removing all my doubts about the deep-rooted division amongst the Afghans.

My next question to the ANP officers, including Ansari, was, "What do you all consider yourselves to be?" Ansari took the lead by answering, "The three of us will die as Hazaras. Today, the Americans are here and have given us jobs. When they leave tomorrow, we will do the same," which prompted me to ask, "Where do you think you'll go?" to which Ansari responded, "Where else can we go besides Iran?" *Are the Hazaras victims of circumstance, despite the way they treat local Pashtons, which I have witnessed every time we raided Pashton homes?* I asked myself. Then I answered my own question: *Yes, they've been victimized for centuries, not only by the Pashtons and Tajiks, but by the Pakistanis and Persians as well.*

I had a great time working with Alfa and his team. Each and every one of them were America's heroes, and I deeply respected them for representing the U.S. and its values by respecting my native people and their culture. I remember how Alfa would always say at our briefings, "Listen up, guys—we'll go in and out of the village in such a way that the villagers won't even know we'd been there the night before." It was that final day when I woke up and walked out of my room towards the bathroom when I saw the writing on the white board in front of the OPS Center. I was sure that it was either Alfa, Echo, or Charlie's writing, with a welcoming message to the new team that read, "Welcome to Ghazni ODA ****. I expect you guys to do good things for the Afghan people. Good luck from ODA ****. (Note: The asterisks represent team numbers, which I am not authorized to publish.)

First Special Forces team. Left to right, knee down: Damon, Mitch, Jack, Rick, EOD, Bravo, Lucky. Middle, standing: Ron, Fox, Ray, Sami, Paul, Echo, Charlie, Alfa, Max, myself. Back row: Ross and Ricardo.

CHAPTER FIVE

August 1, 2009: Special Forces (ODA Team-2)

EVERYONE ON ODA2 TEAM were informed by members of the previous ODA about the behaviors of the ANPs, local linguists, and Afghans who had worked on our compound. The new team had rules of its own. Most of my time with them was spent working with Echo2, training the ANP, ANA, and NDS officers. Helping Oscar with the interrogations and Delta2, the medic, was still top priority. Theft was a common practice with most of the locals who were working with us—whether they were the ANP, linguists, or others who visited our compound from time to time. They would try to steal as much as they could, including (but not limited to) anything from big-ticket items (e.g., vehicles, ammunition, and furniture) to everything in between.

The most important thing I wanted to stop the ANPs from stealing was gasoline, which was getting out of control. I came up with an idea that needed to be approved by Echo2 and Bravo2, who were both in charge of logistics, even though I knew that I would probably be hated even more by the locals—including all of the ANP officers—for doing the right thing. So, I suggested to Echo2 and Bravo2 that I make a log sheet, with current mileage, for the ANP's pickup trucks. Since we had to keep track of it, we would not have the problem of ANP filling up the tank with the gasoline going to downtown Ghazni to be sold and then bringing the truck come back on empty. Our team members didn't have the time to monitor the behaviors of the more than 50 locals who had worked with us on the compound, which is why the locals seized every opportunity they could to take everything they could while our team members were busy doing their other tasks. Echo2 and Bravo2 considered my suggestion and agreed with me, so I went ahead and made a log sheet by numbering each ANP vehicle as well as logging its miles. Anyone in charge of a truck who wanted to fill up with gasoline had to come to me. I would then accompany them while they filled up the tank and then enter the new mileage on the log sheet. The ANPs and locals didn't like the new plan; they never liked me before but hated me even more now because of the rules they had to follow. Since I had to protect the American taxpayers as much as I possibly could, even one dollar at a time, I knew that saving a couple gallons of gasoline, compared to what our government was spending in Afghanistan, didn't really amount too much, but my main point wasn't to save the money they wasted—it was the principal of teaching the ANPs and local linguists the lesson about the difference between right and wrong. I wasn't in Afghanistan to cut our government spending and wouldn't have been able to do so anyhow, especially while my life was being threatened by people like Jabar. Alfa's words became stuck in my mind forever when he told me, "Nas, I am not here in Afghanistan to change the whole country, but if I can change one person at a time, then my time is worth being here." I took that advice from him, and carried it with me every day of my deployment in Afghanistan.

Delta2, the medic for the new team, approached me one day, asking if he could talk with me when I had the time. I invited him to my room that night, any time after 8:00, and told him I would make him some tea if he wanted. I wasn't sure if he would want to have tea with me or not, because—except for Echo and Damon—most of the guys on the previous ODA team would not drink tea at nighttime. As it turned out, Delta2 didn't mind drinking tea at night. While drinking it, we got acquainted with questions like where we lived in the States, what kind of work we did, how many kids, and so forth. It turned out that we had three very important things in common: Delta2 loved his country and his family, he loved representing his country by helping others, and he wanted a good education for his children. We then got down to the reason for his visit. "Sorry for taking up your time, Nas, but the reason that I wanted to talk with you tonight was because I would like to learn more about the Afghan culture. I think I can help them more if I know about them." When Delta2 said that, I knew he wasn't in Afghanistan just because he was sent here, but rather because he really did *want* to be here. We talked for almost two hours before he left my room confused to find out so much that he never knew. During that time, I told him I was in Afghanistan for the same reasons he was and was willing to help him with anything I could so he'd be able to accomplish his mission as well as that of our country. He thanked me, and before leaving my room, said, "Thanks for the tea, Nas. I enjoyed it and would like to come by for more sometime." I assured him that he was welcome to do so anytime. (By the way, Delta2 was a former Marine sniper, a professional photographer, *and* a civilian shooting instructor.)

A few days later, Delta2 asked me to help him with the medical examination of a couple of detainees who had been brought in for interrogation. We went to the holding cell to get the detainees so we could take them to the medical shack. While he gave the detainees a full medical exam, he would ask medical questions that I would then translate in Pashto to the detainees. During their exams, one of the detainees started to cry. When asked why, he said that his two little girls were left at home alone, while he sat in jail.

His comment was another part of the culture. The detainee didn't mean that his little girls were literally left at home alone; what he meant was they didn't have their father at home to provide for them. Since women have no right to make decisions about their household, especially in the villages, it was the men who worried about what would happen if they weren't in the house. When Delta2 asked the detainee how old his daughters were, the man told him they were very young and couldn't live without their father. "I also have two very young daughters," Delta2 said, "both of whom I love dearly, and they're more than seven thousand miles away from here. But if you can help us by telling the truth, then we can both go home to our daughters."

"But I am innocent," the detainee argued. "You guys have brought me here—we didn't bring you; you came on your own. I didn't choose to be in jail away from my daughters, but *you*, on the other hand, chose to be in Afghanistan away from your daughters."

"It's not my job to determine whether you're innocent or guilty; I'm here to make sure you're healthy," Delta2 explained. But, the detainee really wasn't interested in hearing what Delta2 had to say; he just kept crying and saying that he wanted to go home to his daughters. I knew that the detainee was trying to pull his usual emotional tricks on us because it's normal in the Afghan culture for an adult male to cry just to get attention. Fortunately, Delta2 wasn't going to buy it, so in an effort to calm the sobbing man, he asked, "What do you want your daughters to be when they grow up?"

"I have no control over that," the detainee wept. "It's all up to God. Right now I don't even know what I'm going to be doing, let alone knowing anything about their future." Delta2 nodded his head to acknowledge that he had heard what he said and then continued with the detainee's complete medical checkup to ensure that he was fit for interrogation. At one point during the exam, I told Delta2 that he was giving these guys a physical that I never once got from my doctor in the States, whom I had been paying out of my own pocket. Delta2 laughed and told me to change doctors. He smiled at me while the detainee looked on grimly, wondering what we infidels were saying. "I'm not joking. Seriously, you're giving these guys a thorough physical checkup that they don't have to pay for and, if the situation was reversed, we can only imagine what they would do to us if we were in their custody." Delta2 glanced sideways at me and said, "Nas, I don't see things the way they do. I will treat them like the human beings they are, no matter what they think or would possibly do to me if I were to ever be in their custody." Well, that was Delta2, a guy who did what was right—something the detainee would never understand. But, then, only I sensed the truth about what both sides were thinking.

A few days later Oscar told me that we'd both be very busy for the next couple of weeks, screening all the ANP officers and every local who now worked on the compound. It was one of our normal routines: once every six months, besides screening all the locals on the compound, we hired additional ANP officers, all of whom were, for the most part, referred to us by either Ansari or other ANP officers who were already working for us. During our screening process, there were forms that had to be filled out by the new hires. Since all forms were in English, I would fill out the forms for them by posing each question to the ANP officer with Oscar typing their responses directly into the computer data base rather than leaving a paper trail, which made the process much easier. Once we were done putting all their information into the system, we took their picture and fingerprints, which were then attached to their online applications.

Sometimes when Oscar asked a simple question from the application, it would be a struggle for me to get any kind of answer from the local Afghans or ANP officers because we couldn't ask an Afghan a question the way you could an American. For example: A generic question Oscar would ask would be, "In case of an emergency, who would you like us to notify?" The ANPs would typically ask me what that meant, and I would explain it to them in more detail than was really required, primarily because there was no such thing as "in case of an emergency," not to mention that just being in Afghanistan was a *huge* case of emergency in and of itself. The ANP officers not only wouldn't answer the question, but they would say, "Ustad, can you tell him (referring to Oscar) to not let my parents know if anything happens to me, because I never told them that I was working with you guys," which were the kinds of cultural things difficult for Oscar and other American team members to understand.

If you're not from the Afghan culture, it's a challenge to understand why it would be such a big deal for his parents to know if something happened to him. In general, Afghans are very secretive about their daily activities; they don't want anyone to know what they're up to, even if those people happen to be their parents or their own children. We asked them numerous questions during our interview process; for example, why they wanted to work for the Americans.

Throughout all of my screening time while in Ghazni, I only came across two ANP officers who gave me straight answers: first, they wanted to serve their country, and second, they were being paid by the Americans. All of the other ANP officers I interviewed were simply in it for the paycheck and could care less about their country, which they didn't claim as their own anyhow. Most of the new hires brought in by other ANP officers who were already working for us never wanted to work with their own police department in Ghazni City, first, because they were paid more working with us, and second, they were paid on time. In addition to all of the other questions, the last one on the application was asked simply to find out what their mindset was.

The question wanted to know who they thought the enemies of Afghanistan were. Responses were 50/50. Half said Afghanistan's enemy was Pakistan, while the other half said the enemy was the Taliban. There was one officer who answered the question in Farsi, *"Wala, Ustad, shoma bayhtar may fahmen, kho ba nazari ma ami Pshtonnai kosmadar doshmani Awghanistan astan."* ("Well, Ustad, you probably know better than me but, in my opinion, the Pashton motherfuckers are the enemy of Afghanistan.") I couldn't help but laugh uncontrollably. Oscar wanted to know what was so funny. When I was finally able to catch my breath I told him exactly what the man had said. Oscar was curious if the officer knew that I was a native Pashton. In response, I told him that I didn't think he knew; if he did, I was reasonably certain that he wouldn't have said what he had. I assured Oscar that I didn't really care what the officer had said, which Oscar already knew from working with me. He told me that unlike all the other interpreters he'd worked with, I was the one who always treated the local Afghans with dignity and respect, despite their tribal or language differences. We were still laughing while the ANP officer sat before us looking very confused because he didn't know what so funny.

Once we were done screening the ANP officers, we recognized the similarity that the majority of the officers we interviewed had lived most of their childhood in Iran and were simply in Afghanistan now to work for the Americans. They also told us that when we Americans left Afghanistan, they would return to Iran. Captain Ansari—who had never left Afghanistan before but had always worked with every government that came into power—was also considering going to Iran this time, once the American forces were out of Afghanistan. After Oscar and I were done screening the new hires, Echo2 took the ANP officers for further testing to check their physical abilities: running, weapon training, and climbing.

My next task was to help Delta2 with his request to introduce himself, not only to the ANP officers, but also all of the locals who worked at the compound as part of the cleaning crew. Most of our meetings with the locals were in the kitchen, and this morning was no exception. When everyone had taken a seat, Delta2 introduced himself and asked each for their name. After those introductions were completed, Delta2 told everyone on the cleaning crew how to clean from that point forward and then told them that whoever completed their job per his requirements would be rewarded at the end of the month. He then asked them to follow him into the bathroom.

Once in the bathroom, Delta2 put on a pair of yellow rubber gloves, picked up a green scouring pad and was about to start demonstrating when he realized that two of the three cleaning guys had not followed us into the bathroom. I found them outside sitting in the shade against the wall. When I asked them to get up and go into the bathroom, one of them told me that cleaning bathrooms wasn't their job—it was the job of whoever was already inside. After much bickering, I finally convinced them to go into the bathroom so Delta2 could show them how they should clean the bathroom every day. Needless to say, the cleaning crew was shocked as they watched an American Special Forces guy stick his hand into a dirty toilet, amazed that an American would ever do such a thing.

The one who had told me that cleaning a bathroom wasn't his job, now said, "Ustad, tell him (referring to Delta2) that cleaning bathrooms is *not* our job." But Delta2 could have cared less whose job they thought it was. "All three of you need to rotate your cleaning duties, either on a daily or weekly basis," Delta2 told them. "In case one of you doesn't show up for work, I want you guys to take turns so you all know how to properly clean every part of our compound, not just one specific area. We operate better as a team, not as individuals."

After we were done with the cleaning crew, Delta2 asked me to find Ansari and bring him to the kitchen. When we returned to the kitchen, since Ansari had been caught stealing a pickup truck from the previous team, his attitude and voice were much softer now. As we settled around a table, Delta2 told Ansari, "This is what I want you to do: I want all of your officers to come over here to the kitchen so I can personally introduce myself to them, while at the same time helping them to learn a number of lifesaving techniques that will be beneficial to them during our combat missions. Please have them all here after lunch, say around 1:00 o'clock." Ansari agreed to do so, and Delta2 and I left to have lunch at the main DFAC. We used one of the pickup trucks. Usually there's a long line at the DFAC around lunchtime, oftentimes wrapped completely around the building, but today there was no line, at least none that we could see from the outside.

Once the truck was parked and we got out to walk the approximate 200 feet to the entrance, I saw two Polish soldiers walking in the same direction. Somehow, over time, it had become a race to see who could get to the DFAC first—typically, the local Afghans and Polish soldiers always beat me. Once we got closer to the entrance, I noticed that Delta2 had started to walk a bit faster, trying to beat the Polish soldiers, who had also started to walk faster in an effort to beat us. When Delta2 beat them, I wasn't sure why he had left me behind while he raced to the door ahead of me. I had often experienced such behavior from the Polish soldiers and local Afghans, but never expected it from my fellow Americans. Since he didn't seem the type, I couldn't help but wonder why Delta2 would even want to race anyone just so he could be first in line. I was relieved to find out I was right—he didn't race to the door to beat the Polish; he was simply doing it out of courtesy so he could hold the door open for all of us.

Following lunch, Delta2 and I stayed in the kitchen for the meeting at 1:00 PM. Two ANP officers showed up: Afzali, one of the squad leaders, and Ramazan, one of Afzali's officers, who hung out together and were known for always showing up on time. We waited until around 1:45 for others to show up, but no one did. Delta2 thanked Afzali and Ramazan for coming and asked them to tell Ansari and the rest of his team to be here in the kitchen by 9:00 AM tomorrow morning—no exceptions. "Nas, is that how they do things when you ask them to be here? They just don't show up?" Delta2 asked me. "Yep. Welcome to Afghanistan!" I responded. Since Delta2 never had dealt with the Afghans before, he asked, "Wow, even soldiers and police?" I nodded. "Yea, unfortunately," I told him. "Since time is the only thing Afghans have plenty of, they could care less."

The following morning most, but not all, of the ANP officers showed up by 9:30. Delta2 introduced himself and thanked them for coming. He told me to ask Ansari why his guys hadn't shown yesterday afternoon, and Ansari told me, "Well, Ustad, the guys took a nap after lunch, which is why they couldn't make it," a response Delta2 wasn't expecting, so he simply said, "No shit!"

To make a point, Delta2 told them that if any one of them would one day ask him to meet them somewhere at a certain time, out of respect, he'd be there precisely at the allotted time, as requested. He told them that they were like brothers to him, because there weren't too many people who'd do what they were doing, being police officers and protecting their country and its people, something he wanted to help them achieve. (Frankly, I strongly believe that the only way we can make the Afghan Security Forces and even the Afghan government officials to be more productive by showing up for work would be if they were paid by the hour for time worked only versus just paying them a monthly salary.)

After the brief introductions and his conversation with the group, Delta2 started teaching them the basic first-aid, life-saving techniques so they would be able to help their buddies during combat if anyone got wounded. He started by demonstrating how to stop someone from bleeding to death by applying the combat tourniquet to the body. Just like everything else we had tried to teach them in the past, it was apparent that the ANP officers weren't even remotely interested in learning this life-saving technique. While Delta2 was demonstrating how to apply the tourniquet, it wasn't long before Zuhair, one of the squad leaders, asked me, "Ustad, ask Delta2 how one can be risking his own life to save someone else's during combat." When I translated this to Delta2, his jaw dropped. "Wow, Nas," he said, "are you shitin' me? What the fuck is this guy talking about?" Since I couldn't explain this to him within a short period of time, it was going to have to be discussed during another tea visit to my room one night soon so I could tell him how and why most Afghans say such things. To make a point to Zuhair and his officers, I reminded them what Fox and Damon had done during one of our missions—the one when Delta got shot. Obviously, since Delta2 hadn't been on that mission with us, so didn't know anything about Delta's situation, he asked me what everyone was talking about. While I told him what had happened to Delta on one of our missions, Zuhair argued, "Ustad, are you comparing Americans with Afghans when you know that as soon as Afghans hear the sound of shooting, they all disappear?" I translated this to Delta2, adding that I couldn't agree more with what Zuhair had just asked, especially since he was at least being honest enough to say what he believed to be true.

Around 8:00 that night, there was a knock on my door. At first I thought it was Delta2 stopping by to ask for help with the translation during the morning meeting. But when I opened the door, I was surprised to see Afzali and Ramazan, guys I considered the only real patriots in the Afghan government. I invited them in and offered them tea, which they both rejected. Getting down to the purpose of their visit, Afzali said, "Ustad, we're here to ask you something. We'd like to talk with the team leader, in charge of the ANPs, about issues that we have, and Ramazan and I want you to be our interpreter." When I told them I'd be more than happy to do so, I said I'd talk with Bravo2 the next morning to see if he had time to talk with them and would then let them know his answer. Before they left, Afzali requested that this be kept amongst the three of us because he didn't want anyone else to know—I assured him I wouldn't tell anyone else.

The following morning I went to the OPS Center, saw Bravo2, and told him that Afzali and Ramazan wanted to talk with him. Bravo2 asked, "Nas, what the fuck do they want; do you know?" In response, I said, "All they told me was that they would like to talk to someone who is in charge of the ANPs, and they want me to be their interpreter. That's all I know for now." Bravo2 was the kind of person who did not like talking with people if he didn't know what they wanted to talk about, especially if they had issues that had to be resolved. Nonetheless, he told me to tell them that he would be available that night around 7:30, after our team meeting. Unlike the previous team who had their meetings at 9:00 AM, Bravo2 conducted the team meetings at 7:00 PM. I told Afzali to be at the MWR, where our meetings were held, at around 7:15. Once the meeting was over, I saw Afazali, Ramazan, Zuhair, and one other squad member I didn't know by name standing outside by the front door of the MWR.

While the other team members had already left the MWR immediately following the conclusion of our briefings, Bravo2 stayed at the MWR to talk with the ANP squad leaders. As soon as all four walked in, there were no words of greeting or introduction from Bravo2. He simply went straight to the point. "How can I help you?" Afzali started talking first. "We have been working here for a number of years now and are here to tell you that we don't want Ansari to be our Team Captain. If he remains as our captain, then we will not work here any longer." I could see immediately that Bravo2 was confused and looking at me like he wanted to say, *Nas, help me out here! What the fuck do they want?*

After gathering his thoughts, Bravo2 said to the four, "Wait a minute, guys. What's going on? What's this really all about?" After translating Bravo2's question, Afzali responded, "First, Ansari is not very useful.

Second, he cannot read or write. Third, he is not giving us our rations, which are sent to us from our station in Ghazni every month." Bravo2 assured them that he would take care of everything once things settled down a little. Since his team had just arrived in Afghanistan, they were currently preparing for an important combat mission.

When the ANP officers left, Bravo2 asked me if the ANP squad leaders had ever told the other team about the problems they were having with Ansari. I shook my head. "Not that I know of." Bravo2 frowned. "Well, I don't want the fuckers to quit on me." With that, I didn't know what else to say to Bravo2, and even if I did, he wouldn't take it into consideration anyhow because he was the kind of person who knew a lot that really wasn't so. Therefore, I merely walked out of the MWR and to my room.

Within 15 minutes, someone knocked on my door. When I opened it, Afzali and Ramazan were standing there again, asking me if they could come inside. After I let them in, and before I could offer them tea, Afzali said, "Ustad, thank you for helping us, but we need more of your help. Every time we ask the other interpreters to help us talk with the Americans, they never translate for us the way you do; in fact, they never even allow us to actually talk with the Americans." When I assured them they were welcome to ask me to translate for them any time they needed me, Ramazan interjected by saying, "Ustad, we undoubtedly know that you are going to help us, but tonight we are also here to apologize to you." Needless to say, that caught me off-guard. "Why? What are you apologizing for?" Afzali explained that, "Several days ago, during our screening, when you asked us questions, one of our officers who cursed all Pashtons didn't realize you were one. When he realized this, he was too ashamed to come here to apologize to you in person, which is why we're here to apologize on his behalf." I thanked them both but assured them that they really didn't have to apologize for anything or anyone and confirmed I was indeed a native Pashton, born in Kandahar. While I would never be able to change my ethnicity, I was now an American. When I said that, the expression on their faces made it clear that they didn't believe or accept that I was an American, and they weren't the only ones.

Afzali and Ramazan always talked at the same time, while looking at each other for confirmation that what they were telling me was the truth. "Usatd, you can call yourself an American, but we still consider you to be an Afghan." I knew that there was no way for me to convince them that they would change their way of thinking of me, but I still wanted to try to make one last point to them. It is very difficult for most Afghans to understand the difference between a person's nationality and ethnicity. It didn't matter how often I defined or clarified the difference between being a native of Afghanistan, while being an American as well, which is probably the main and only reason the so-called Afghans would never be able to find or understand their own nationality rather than their ethnicity. So I told them, "Listen, you two. I am not here to change your way of thinking, but I do want to tell you one thing. If I had reacted the way other Afghans or Pashtons did, then I would have handled things differently when the officer cursed all Pashtons. As an Afghan and Pashton, I would've punched him in the face first and then fired him before we even offered him a job, don't you agree?" Afzali quickly agreed, which indicated that they were both finally getting my point. "I didn't do what an Afghan or Pashton would've done to that officer, or what the Pashtons have done to the Hazaras and vice versa throughout history. I was merely there, talking to them, and asking them questions as a human being who just so happens to be an American native of Pashton. What he told me was the truth, because ninety percent of the Taliban are Pashtons, which is why he felt that the problem in his country was indeed caused by the Pashtons."

Afzali and Ramazan looked confused, not in a way that indicated they didn't understand my point, but in a way that clearly said they didn't felt comfortable agreeing with me at that moment, but I knew that I hit the proverbial nail on the head as I looked at the expressions on their faces. Before leaving my room, Afzali shook my hand, putting his other on top, continuing to shake my hand with an unusually firm squeeze as his way of telling me that this gesture meant he supported me for treating everyone as human beings, not as Pashtons, Tajiks, Hazaras, or Uzbeks. Suddenly, he started to cry. "Dear Ustad, ever since you Americans have come here, you guys have respected the Hazaras more than anyone else. And another very important thing that I have learned is to never allow my soldiers to pick apricots without permission," he smiled through his tears.

As Afzali continued holding my hand, I was now emotional myself. It's not that I enjoy holding hands with another man, it was simply a cultural thing in Afghanistan. When someone respects you, while talking with you they hold your hand for as long as they have good things to say about you.

Before I share what else Afzali had to say, I want to clarify something about my deployment to Afghanistan. I was initially very disappointed during the early days of my deployment because of how many things were going wrong. But the words out of Afzali and Ramazan's mouths, but more importantly from their hearts and minds, were well worth the 33-month hardship just to hear Afzali say, "Dear Ustad, believe me when I say this, during my entire life, I never learned so many morals or humanity from my own biological father as I have from you in the past three months." I was not only speechless by his comment, but I was also embarrassed, so that all I could say was, *"Tashakor aghai, Afzali, wa Ramazan shoma mara kheyjalat may thin."* ("Thank you, dear Afzali and Ramazan, but stop because you're embarrassing me.") Before leaving my room, while still holding my hand, Afzali said, *"Kashkey, misley shoma yak chand ta tarjumani dega ham my bood."* ("I wish there were more interpreters like you.") Again, I was speechless. As they both were leaving my room, about 20 feet from the door Afzali's right hand moved from the left side of his chest to the right side of his forehead—a gesture and normal etiquette in the Afghan culture—thanking me from his heart while saluting me to say goodbye as he gradually walked away into the night.

During my time with the ODA2, one morning I got an email from my site manager of the company that I worked for, asking me to be in Bagram to take my polygraph test for upgrading from a Category II level clearance to Category III. In order for me to be able to go to the main U.S. military base, which, in our case, was in Bagram. I asked Jag, the JTAC, to put me on the next available flight to Bagram, which I learned would be in two days.

Before I arrived at the airfield for my flight to Bagram, I stopped by the OPS Center—where I saw Jag, Alfa2, Bravo2, and Delta2—to make sure the flight had not been cancelled. Jag told me that my flight, which was around noon, was on time. Since I would only be gone a couple of days, I didn't have too much to carry.

As I started to leave the OPS Center and was saying goodbye to everyone, Alfa2 and Bravo2 asked if I'd be back in time for the upcoming major combat mission for which our team was preparing. I told them that, according to my site manager, I was only going to be gone a couple of days and foresaw no reason why I shouldn't be back on time.

As I was walking out the door, Delta2 called out, "Hey, Nas, is anyone giving you a ride to the airfield?" I told him, "Nope, I can walk. It's not that far." Delta2 shook his head. "No, you're not going to walk. Let's get on the ATV so you can be dropped off." Naturally, I accepted Delta2's offer and got on the front of the ATV as he drove me to the airfield. When he dropped me off, he asked me to call him when I got back so he could pick me up. At first, I told him I could walk back to the compound, but when he continued to insist, I told him I'd call him once I had returned.

We shook hands, hugged, and then Delta2 left the airfield while I waited for my flight to Bagram, which was nonstop since the Chinook had made all the rest of its stops en route to Ghazni. Upon my arrival, as a part of the normal routine, our company's movement crew in Bagram picked us up and then took us to the company's office to check in, and then to the dreaded transition tent. Our company's security officers had confirmed my appointment for the polygraph for the following morning. It was a crazy night at the tent—the same old stuff where the majority of the linguists never followed any rules, so falling asleep was extremely challenging.

My polygraph test was given the following morning, and I was scheduled to go back to Ghazni when that had been completed. However, I was stuck in Bagram for a whole week because of the number of limited flights back to FOB in Ghazni. During my time in the tent, one night two linguists started a conversation about their experiences in Afghanistan (as linguists). Linguist A had been in Afghanistan for a while; Linguist B has just arrived in Bagram from the States and been assigned to a military unit in Kandahar, which he didn't like, and made it quite clear that he did *not* want to be there. When Linguist A asked B why he didn't want to be at Kandahar, B said, "First, I don't understand Pashto; second, all the Taliban motherfuckers are in Kandahar." A said to B, "Listen to me—most linguists who have gone to Kandahar can't speak Pashto either. Once they get there, they can speak Farsi to the locals because all the Pashton fuckers can understand Farsi. The good thing is, the Americans won't know the difference what language you're using to speak with them." Linguist B responded, "The language part I can manage, but what about the danger?" Since the conversation started between A and B, there were now others linguists joining to give their professional advice how to fake it. I was fed up with their nonsense and constant flipping back and forth from side to side so I had to do something to somehow take my mind off their conversation. Well, I couldn't do it, which meant that I just had to say something to all of these cowards. "You guys are cowards. If you don't speak the language, then why did you come to Afghanistan?" Fortunately, I heard nothing further from any of them until the next morning. While waiting for my flight back to my unit, to avoid further nonsense from other linguists in the tent every time I came to Bagram, I spent most of my time during the day in the library, but at night, when all I wanted to do was sleep, I had no choice but to take a stand against the foolishness that was happening all around me.

One day before I went back to my unit in Ghazni, I came out of the library to go to lunch, when I ran into one of the PRT soldiers from Ghazni who I had been on missions with on a couple of occasions. Knowing that I liked going on missions, he told me that my team in Ghazni went on a mission a couple of days ago. The mission turned out to be a deadly; one of our team members had been shot in the head. Hearing the news, I felt like someone had just punched me in the guts. No doubt the soldier could tell how I had reacted badly to the news, but he went on to tell me that the wounded team member had been taken to Bagram Hospital's ICU and suggested that if I wanted to visit him I should do so before he was sent to Germany for surgery. I asked the soldier if he knew the name of the man who had been shot. "Hey, Nas, I'm really sorry to be the one to tell you, but it's your buddy Delta2; I've heard they don't think he'll make it." He then told me that one of the ANP officers was also hit by a rocket and had been killed on the spot. Needless to say, this news didn't sound good at all. After hearing what the soldier had just told me, my guts felt like they were on fire, primarily because my buddy Delta2 was in critical condition.

Just like the morning of 9/11 when Laila told me about the first airplane hitting the World Trade Center, since I knew Delta2 personally and considered him to be my friend, him being shot was another one of those moments in life that will never be erased from my memory. Instead of going to the DFAC for lunch, I hurried to the hospital, which was within walking distance from the DFAC. As I entered the hospital, all I could remember was Delta2's first name; I had no idea what his last name was. I asked the young female soldier at the front desk if Delta2 was still in ICU. She asked me what had happened to Delta2 and if I knew what his injuries were. All I could tell her was what the soldier had told me and add what unit he was with. She asked me to wait while she went to check. She returned within minutes to tell me that Delta2 had been flown to Germany for surgery early that morning.

The following day I arrived in Ghazni after a long day and many stops along the way, as usual. Once I arrived at the Airfield in Ghazni, it was emotional because I couldn't help but remember that exactly one week earlier, Delta2 had dropped me off here and said he'd pick me up when I returned. I remembered how he shook my hand, hugged me, and said goodbye, so coming back and not seeing him was difficult for me to accept. I walked from the airfield to the compound, straight to the OPS Center. The only person there was Bravo2, who was watching CNN, as usual. I said hello to him first before asking about Delta2. "Well, Nas, there's no easy way for me to tell you this, but Delta2 was shot in the head; he's only been kept alive so that his family can visit him in Germany to say their goodbyes." I suddenly felt chilled and sick to my stomach. The loss of not only my dear friend, but a brave, compassionate soldier whose life was taken by the very people he treated with dignity and respect was not only a loss for America, but his family and me as well. I would really miss translating his words to the Afghans he loved and wanted to help succeed. I was so distraught over the loss of Delta2 that I didn't even think to ask Bravo2 about the ANP officer who had been killed.

As I walked through the compound to ask the ANP guys where I could find Ansari so I could find out what had happened, the atmosphere in the compound—and the looks on the guys' faces, both American and ANP—were not the same as they had been before I went to Bagram. When I found Ansari, he told me, "Ustad, what more can I tell you? It was a *very* bad day, just like the day you were with us when Delta got shot." He took me to one of the Humvees parked at the corner of the compound, covered with a blue tarp.

When I lifted the tarp to see the damage from the impact on the right side of the Humvee, I also saw splashes of blood on the shattered windshield. One side of the vehicle, where the rocket had hit, was destroyed beyond anything I could have imagined. Seeing the damage to the Humvee, I knew that no one could have survived the rocket used in the attack, "Who got killed in this vehicle ?" I asked. "Ustad," Ansari said gently, "Afzali was the one who got martyred, and Ramazan's face has been wounded badly; he is currently in the hospital. He will probably be okay, because he doesn't have anyone to worry about him, but Afzali left behind a wife and three young children, now without a father, and the oldest child is only nine."

This was way too much tragedy for me to bear on one single day. The loss of any human life is too precious in the first place, but losing someone that I not only knew personally but considered a friend, was difficult for me to handle. It was even more painful for me to know that I had lost two people who I appreciated and admired.

Ansari and a number of his officers who had witnessed the tragedy told me that as Afzali was standing by the door of the Humvee, the rocket hit him; upon impact, his body was cut in half—without a doubt, a most painful and gruesome way to watch a comrade die. The sadness and mourning was evident on everyone's faces throughout the compound because of the loss of our dear friends—soldiers, patriots, and decent human beings, everyone—who had made the ultimate sacrifice for their countries.

The following week was very busy preparing for the upcoming Afghan national election, which would be held on August 20, 2009. On that day, every one of our team members left the compound, including the ANP officers and local interpreters. The only people who were left behind were the two American civilians; one other person who had also been working with the team; our four-legged friend, Jimbo; and me. For the next two days we, with the help of Jimbo, were the compound's watchdogs while the rest of the team had gone to downtown Ghazni, mainly to protect the governor's compound and also the polling locations throughout the city. Thanks to the tight security provided, all went smoothly with the election.

Our compound was now more crowded than it had been with the previous ODA. In addition to the ODA2 team itself, we also had a team of PSYOPS (Psychological Operations) join our team that I helped on a daily basis with their in-compound radio station by reading segments of the news in Pashto and Farsi. In addition to the PSYOPS, we trained groups of 15 to 20 officers of the ANP, NDS, and ANA at a time. Our interrogations of the prisoners we brought in from all the missions we carried out almost every day were also getting underway. Additionally, we had the civilians of other law enforcement agencies (e.g., the FBI and State Department) living on the compound, who also occasionally accompanied us on our missions.

On one of my missions with ODA2, we went to Dayak districts again where the Taliban had a strong presence, this time not to the village but to the district center. The mission was in response to a complaint from the sub-governor of that particular District to the governor of Ghazni Province. Because of the Taliban harassment to the sub-governor of that District, the Governor of Ghazni called the American Special Forces to protect the District. Since the Afghan government officials are only good at taking financial support from the Americans (and totally incapable of defending themselves), they were unable to face their country's real enemy, so our team was used by the Afghan government as a " 911" call for their first emergency responder whenever Afghan officials felt threatened by the Taliban.

We arrived at the District Center—between the Taliban control village to the south which we had been to and attacked at, and the police station to the north—on a narrow dirt road atop the hills, about 500 feet directly behind the sub-governor's compound. Alfa2, Bravo2, Jay, and I were going into the police compound while the rest of our guys were holding security positions. Once reaching the top of the hill at the front gate of the police station, we were all escorted by one of the guards to the room where we'd meet the police chief and his captain.

The room was on the east side of the compound where you could see the main highway below and the entire village across the desert. We sat on Afghan-made mattresses and leaned against the wall, waiting for the police chief and his captain to show up. Of course, they took their time like we were the ones who needed their help. When they finally entered the room, they, too, sat on one of the mattresses at the opposite end of the room. Soon after the greetings were exchanged, one of the chief's officers brought us green tea with sugar cubes—a normal Afghan ritual. At first, I was surprised to see brown sugar cubes, but later realized that wasn't really the case—the cubes were brown from sitting, collecting dust in the open—for how long, God only knew.

At Alfa2's request, I introduced our team members to the Afghan officials. When the introductions were completed, Jay (who was third in command) always insisted on taking the lead, so he was the first to question the chief. Frankly, in the military this would only happen when a low-ranking soldier like Jay jumped into the conversation without his captain's approval, primarily because of the lack of leadership on the team's part. Jay got straight to the point with the aggressive and dictatorial tone in his voice by asking the chief, "What seems to be the problem in your District?" I'm guessing that the police chief was not expecting Jay's questioning approach, especially since it undoubtedly made him feel as though he was being interrogated instead of merely being questioned.

Nonetheless, the chief started to answer by saying, "I don't know where to start because we have many problems. First, as you can see, we don't have any desks or chairs to sit on; second, our facility doesn't have heating and air-conditioning; third, we don't have any gasoline for our vehicles; and, fourth, our officers don't have anything to eat. Just because of issues like these, the sub-governor has left, and if we don't get what we need, we might have no other choice but to do the same thing."

Was I surprised and shocked by how the Afghan police chief answered with a softer and more gentle Western-style manner to Jay's question? Not really. Usually, it's the other way around, where the Afghan would be behaving in a dictatorial manner, since they're not only the host country, but also know the Americans, who are more cooperative by not offending them, while at the same time being a great listener to anything and everything the Afghan officials requested. Since the police Chief started by asking for everything for his own personal reasons, he had to start out gently. But, no matter how gentle he asked for whatever he needed, Jay really didn't want to hear what the chief had to say, so he rephrased his question. "We're here to help you defeat the enemy and bring security and stability to your district, so what do we need to do to help you in that regard?" In my opinion, this was the right tone of questioning for Jay to set from the start—but only during the initial meeting with the Afghans and until he understood them better. The police chief's response to Jay's question was, "We can see the Taliban with our own eyes going back and forth from our compound; therefore, we can't leave our office."

I couldn't help but notice that our conversation with the Afghan officials wasn't going anywhere. It seemed their minds were more fixated on their own personal needs and wants rather than helping us to help them defeat the bad guys. Our guys were not there to provide logistic needs for the Afghan officials here, but to focus more on how to bring security and stability to their district. It was truly mindboggling for me to hear the Afghan police chief tell us that the Taliban were cruising back and forth in his district, but he couldn't do anything about it. I also couldn't help but notice that the conversation between Jay and the police chief was based more on a personal "wants and needs" list between the two. Unlike most other members of the ODA2, or perhaps almost every member of the previous ODA, Jay was not in a position to be negotiating between his team and the Afghan police chief. Because of the lack of communication, the meeting between the Americans and the Afghan officials was concluded on a sour note and, during my time with the team, we never went to that police compound again.

In my mind, the memories of Delta2's compassion toward the Afghan people is still so fresh, even to me today, that I must wonder why Jay, a fellow American, never cared about anything or anyone besides himself and his own personal ego. On the other hand, Delta2 really touched my heart in many ways within the four short weeks that I had known him, yet I felt as though I had known him all my life—that's the kind of person he was. Unlike Jay, Delta2 had approached others with respect and decency, and if he didn't know anything about the Afghan culture, he would always ask me questions beforehand to keep himself informed of important issues, whether they were people who had worked for us, had concerns, or needed help, including the ANA, ANP, NDS, or any other Afghan officials we trained.

Being a father of two children myself, I want to protect them and want them to be educated so they aren't only contributors to society, but successful in life financially, rather than being burdens on society. Knowing Delta2 as I did, he had the same mindset to do for his children exactly what I wanted to do for mine. *Well*, I thought to myself, *while I am still alive and able to do what I am capable of accomplishing for my wife and children, Delta2 will not be able to do the same for his family or his country that he loved so dearly and wanted to protect.*

Therefore, as a fellow American, I decided that I wanted to do something for Delta2's daughters and chose to do so financially with their college funds. Not knowing how to proceed, I went to the OPS Center and asked Alfa2 and Bravo2 if they could provide me with the information I needed to donate to a college fund for Delta2's daughters. When Alfa2 said he would help me get the information I needed, I called my wife to send me a check and told her why. I then told Alfa2 and Bravo2, who were appreciative of what I wanted to do for Delta2's daughters. I explained to them that I would do the same for their kids if, God forbid, anything happened to them or anyone else on our team—even Jay, who mistreated people for his own personal gain. Besides, in the whole scheme of things, the college fund I was starting for Delta2's daughters was minute when compared to what Delta2 had sacrificed and given to his country. The check from Laila arrived in Ghazni two weeks later, which I, in turn, then sent directly to Delta2's family in the States.

I also knew that Afzali was the father of three young children. When I asked Alfa2 if anything had been done for Afzali's family, either by members of our team or anyone else, he told me that our team had helped the family financially but he wasn't sure of the amount. Just as I had helped Delta2's children for their father's sacrifice for America, I wanted to help Afzali's children for his sacrifice for my native land. To that end, I asked Alfa2 if it would be possible for Afzali's family to visit our compound so I could help them directly rather than involving the Afghan government officials unless absolutely necessary. Since the only person in the Afghan government I had trusted the most was Afzali, in order for me to meet his family, I needed Alfa2's permission to invite Afzali's family to the compound via Ansari, who was the only contact we had to the family.

When Alfa2 gave me permission to invite them to the compound, I went to talk with Ansari, asking him first about Afzali family's financial situation so I had an idea of exactly how much help they needed. "Well, my dear Ustad," Ansari explained, "Afzali doesn't have anyone on his side of the family who can help. The only person who can take care of Afzali's wife and children is his brother-in-law." As I questioned Ansari further about Afzali's financial situation, he told me that the American Special Forces had given Afzali's family $1,100, plus the Afghan government gave them an additional 80,000 Afghanis ($1,700). The family, in turn, took the money and purchased a parcel of land from the government in Ghazni, for which they still needed additional funds in order to build a two- or three-bedroom house on the land they purchased. "How much would it cost to build a three-bedroom house?" I asked. "Well, Ustad, it all depends on the contractor, but I'd guess building one room would cost anywhere from 20 to 30 thousand Afghanis," which I calculated meant that for approximately 100,000 Afghanis, the Afzalis could build a home and still have money left over. Well, I am definitely not Warren Buffet or Bill Gates, but I thought, *if I can put a roof over the heads of Afzali's children and their mother, I'm going to do so.* Once I had made my decision to help the family and asked Ansari if he could arrange for the Afzalis to meet with me at the compound, he immediately insisted that he would like to help by taking the money to the family so I wouldn't have to bother meeting with them. Sure…like I was going to pay a character like Ansari 100,000 Afghanis that I felt reasonably certain the Afzalis would never see, so I rejected his offer, telling him I would prefer to see Afzali's family in person, which Alfa2 had already approved.

Since Afghanistan is a place where cash is the only trusted currency, I didn't carry much of it on me while there, so I told Ansari to wait a couple of weeks—until I got some cash from the States—before he notified the Afzalis. I called Laila again and asked her to send me some more money, which I received within 10 days after making the call. Thinking it wiser for me not to hand the Afzalis cash in dollars, I asked Ali—an electrician, plumber, and member of one of our cleaning crews—who lived in downtown Ghazni City, if he could get U.S. dollars converted to Afghanis. He responded in Farsi, *"Ustad, imroz dollar narkhish besayar payeen amada."* ("Ustad, the dollar dropped in value today.") Welcome to Afghanistan! As soon as you open your mouth with the word "dollar" spoken, it miraculously drops in value. Why would Ali say such a thing if it weren't true? He wasn't a money exchange dealer nor had he ever been asked by anyone in our compound to exchange dollars to Afghanis. I knew immediately that he said what he said so he could get less Afghanis for more dollars and make a buck or two for himself. While I had planned to pay Ali for his trouble, the cleverness of his immediate reaction was very disappointing because it followed the norm of how everyone who worked for us was always trying to rip us off, even the most innocent looking Ali.

Since there was no other way for me to convert my currency, I gave Ali twenty $100 dollar bills, or the equivalent of 100,000 Afghanis at the then normal market exchange rate: $1 = 50 Afghanis, the amount required to build the house for Afzali's family. Although Ali left and came back shortly thereafter with the required Afghanis, he also wanted an additional $200 because, as he had mentioned earlier, the dollar had dropped in value that day. Since I had no way of knowing what Ali was doing with my other $200, and chose not to argue, I gave it to him—a perfect example of why the local Afghans ripped Americans off every chance they got is because we allowed them to do so.

Afghanistan is not a country where the dollar can lose its value, especially for the amount Ali—who worked for $30 a month—was charging me. Rather, Afghanistan is the only country where the dollar can be more valuable than the Afghan currency on almost every street corner.

As I was counting the money in the kitchen to make sure I wasn't shortchanged on top of the $200 it cost me just to convert the $2,000, I noticed Qasim watching me from the corners of his eyes. After I had finished counting the money, Qasim asked me why I hadn't asked him to exchange the money for me. I told him that I hadn't expected it to be such a big deal to convert the dollars to Afghanis (of course, I didn't mention what it cost me to do so!). Remaining true to his attacks on the Hazaras, Qasim shared with me that Ali was the #1 thief on the whole compound, and if I would've asked Ali, he would with no doubt have said the same thing about Qasim. And how did Qasim know that? Well, in Afghanistan the locals always tell you that everyone else is the biggest thief and, therefore, should not be trusted. All I knew was that Qasim didn't like anyone but the Pashtons, and Ali was a Hazara. I've heard that money makes the world go 'round, but not to the extent that anyone should want to lose their dignity because of it or, in most cases, be willing to give their lives for it.

I had the money, which was all I needed for right now to take care of the Afzalis. I again asked Ansari to make the necessary arrangements for the Afzalis to come to the compound. He made the call to Afzali's brother-in-law, and the meeting was set for the following morning at around 9:00. I informed Alfa2 of the meeting and time should he want to be with me to meet the family. As he looked forward to meeting them as well, he agreed to be there.

The next morning, Ansari came to my room to tell me that Afzali's brother-in-law and eldest, nine-year-old son were at the front gate and needed to be escorted to our compound by an American. Ansari and I drove to the front gate, where I had to show my military ID to the Polish guards before they would allow the man and his nephew into the compound.

While introductions were made, the guards issued them visitors' passes, which got them into our pickup truck for the drive to the compound.

Upon our arrival at the compound, I invited them inside the MWR and then sent word to Alfa2 that they had arrived. Knowing Afghan kids and their culture of being very shy when talking with adults, I could sense that Afzali's son was a bit more mature for his age. I asked him, in Farsi, conversational questions, which—although he didn't speak a word of English—he answered without hesitation.

After getting somewhat acquainted, I told the brother-in-law and boy that I wanted to help Afzali's family, which is why I had invited them to the compound. Before I even had a chance to tell them what kind of help I was planning to give them, the boy's uncle took the lead in thanking me. I knew Ansari probably told them what my plans were well before they even arrived. I told the boy's uncle that I hoped the boy, his siblings, and their mother would not be cheated out of what I was planning to give them. The boy's uncle promised me that no one would betray or try to cheat Afzali's family out of anything. "Dear Ustad," he continued, "I give you my word."

I wanted to ask the boy and his uncle a few additional questions so I could determine if their information matched what Ansari had told me. For example, I wanted to know what other help or money they had received from the Americans as well as the Afghan government. The boy's uncle took the lead by telling me the boy had received 80,000 Afghanis from the Afghan government and an unspecified amount from the Americans—and everything had then been given back to the Afghan government officials in Ghazni in exchange for a parcel of land outside the city. I was satisfied because they had confirmed that there was land they could build a three-bedroom house on, which, for confirmation, I then asked how much it would cost to do so. Their answer was the same as what Ansari had told me, so Ansari had undoubtedly prepared them with what to say, or the price for building a house in Ghazni was fixed and what they were telling me was the truth.

Before I pulled the cash out of my pocket, I asked Alfa2—who had entered the room a few minutes prior and taken a seat next to me—for his opinion regarding what he thought of the boy's uncle and if he thought we should trust him. Alfa2's reply was simple: "Hey, Nas, it's your call—whatever you want to do, it's your money. You can either give it to them or, if you don't feel comfortable, then give it to one of your favorite charities. Depending on what you ultimately decide, you will have no control over how they decide to spend it. Besides, it's your thoughtfulness that counts, not what happens to the money."

My next move was to put my hand into the pocket of my jacket to pull out the cash, which was in two separate bundles of 50,000 Afghanis each. I placed the money on the table, but before handing it to the uncle or the boy, I couldn't shake the lingering thoughts in my head that I shouldn't be doing this—after all, what if the boy's uncle took the money for himself? Thinking of what Alfa2 had just said, I knew he was 100 percent correct: I would have no control over the money once it left my hands. But before I gave it to either of them, I told the boy, "Your father was not only a brave Afghan patriot who loved his country and sacrificed his life, but he was also a decent human being. I hope you will one day turn out to be like your father so that you, too, will do whatever you can to protect your homeland." The boy got emotional and said shakily, "My dear uncle, I also want to be an officer one day, so I can destroy the Taliban in Afghanistan." Originally, I had planned to give the money to the uncle but having heard what the boy just said, I had more confidence in his ability to handle it. So, I handed him one of the bundles and asked if he knew how to count it. To demonstrate that he could, he picked up the bundle, held it sideways in his left hand and used his right thumb to tilt the bundle to the right so he could flip through the bills with his index finger, counting all the 50s like an Afghan banker I remembered when I was young and living in Afghanistan. After counting the money, the boy smiled and told me, "Dear uncle, this is fifty thousand Afghanis." I returned his smile and asked where he had learned to count money at such a young age. His only response was, *Namay fahmum*, (don't know). Then I handed him the second bundle and told him it was also 50,000 Afghanis, and that he didn't have to count unless he wanted to. He got up from his chair and tried to fit the money into his pockets, but since he couldn't do so, he handed it to his uncle. Once he had filled his pockets, he and the boy stood. I shook the uncle's hand to say goodbye, and leaned over in an effort to hug the boy while his uncle whispered in his ear, *Destayesha machko* ("Kiss his hand"), which in the Afghan culture is a common practice, especially if you give them money. While I continued to try to hug him, he tried diligently to grab my hands so he could kiss one of them. Once those formalities had come to a satisfactory conclusion, we left the room as Ansari was waiting outside to give them a ride back to the front gate.

Our team was getting ready for one of the biggest missions we'd ever had—a mission we'd been planning for well over a month. This one wasn't going to be like any of those "normal missions" our team and the ANPs went on because this time, it was all of us, an additional ODA team from another province, and about 40 of their ANA officers. Between the two ODAs, the ANA, the ANP, and all the linguists, there would be approximately 120 people combined. It was also a by-air, nightly mission, which meant we would be dropped off and picked up by Chinooks. Our flight would depart Ghazni Airfield around 11:00 PM. In preparation for this mission, we had all of the other soldiers coming to our compound, which really only had room for 50 to 60 people max. In order for our team to accommodate for the additional soldiers at our compound for a week, we had to put up a very large tent for all the ANA officers who were coming with the other ODAs. While most of the visiting ANA used the tent for their living quarters, the other ODA guys split themselves up between our gym and the MWR as their sleeping quarters. Because everyone just left everything everywhere for more than a week, our compound looked more like a refugee camp.

Before our mission, I was informed by Bravo2 that this was going to be a 72-hour mission, if not longer. I needed to make sure I had enough of everything I would need to take for the three days we'd be somewhere in the mountains of central Afghanistan. We were going to an area that the Afghan government had no control over, which automatically meant it was a Taliban-friendly district (according to the briefing we had in the OPS Center). The location, a remote district at an elevation of about 9,000 feet above sea level, was somewhere between three provinces: Dehkondi on the north, Ghazni on the south, and the Urozgan Province on the west. Aside from all of the Americans and Afghans, we also had a team of the Polish Special Forces with us. Our flight took off from Ghazni Airfield around 11:00 PM.

The mission was to sweep clean the whole District of Ajristan, and, in order to do that, half of us were going to be dropped off at the east end of the district, and the other half at the west end; we would then walk through the whole valley of the Ajristan District until both teams met at the center to make sure that none of the bad guys escaped. Flying to the north of Afghanistan over the dark mountains at night was scary, especially when I saw any of the other Chinooks—with all the sparks coming out of their blades—flying directly adjacent to us. I couldn't help but wonder how the pilots saw where they were going. I kept thinking of scenes in movies where helicopters flew into mountains or had some other horrible kind of accident. It was just me reacting to my fear of flying on nightly missions. While I'm thinking all this about helicopter accidents, etc., at the same time, I realized that there weren't that many people who were fortunate enough to have been in my position to be on such a mission with Special Forces, America's best-trained guys who not only were brave, but also fun to be around.

Movie scenes aside, flying between the high peaks of the mountains in the dark of night I realized that I was sitting right next to real people doing real stuff, unlike the "Hollywood guys" who are only actors doing what they do best because of their love for money, while all of these guys were doing it because of their love for their country.

Our 20-minute flight from takeoff to drop-off felt more like forever. As we were dropped off in an open farmland, and in order for us to be at the first objective on time, we had to walk a straight line for about half a mile before we could get to where we had to be. I was again walking blindly in the pitch black of night until dawn. I was not sure whether to follow Alfa2 closely or stay some distance behind him to make sure that the same incident with Alfa falling into a 20-foot deep sinkhole wouldn't happen again to the new captain on this mission. Unlike that particular mission with Alfa, which was in July, this mission was taking place in October, which made it much colder because we were in the mountains. Before we could get to the village, we were stopped by a fast-moving river that we had to cross; since no one had a clue how deep and muddy it was, someone had to jump in first to find out—and that lucky someone was me.

I asked Alfa2 to hold me through my body armor, which had a handle on the top of my shoulder. As he held me, I slowly slid into the river. At first step, the water was cold and knee deep at the edge of the river, but as I moved a couple of steps further into the river, not only was the mud now stopping me from moving forward, but the water was up to my hips.

I retreated back to see if there was any other narrower crossing nearby, but I couldn't go too far out to look since most of the guys were just jumping into the water in an effort to cross over to the other side. Well, if I didn't want to be left behind, I needed to think quickly and find another crossing one that was not necessarily less shallow. There was a huge tree on the other side of the river with branches I could simply grab onto for protection from drowning, not by the fast-moving water but because of the mud. I was most worried about my AK47, which I wanted to keep dry since it was the only protection I had in the bad-guy territory. As I played monkey from one branch of the tree to the next as I was trained when picking apricots as a young kid, I finally managed to get to the other side.

The team split: the Polish guys going to the village market, our guys going to the village itself. Alfa2 and I would stay behind to secure the area. Because we were on a three-day mission, each of our guys had large backpacks, which they left with us until they returned.

Ten minutes later, they had all left us in an open field behind the village. First, we heard dogs barking, then *pop, pop, pop*—small arms' fire. I thought someone had just been shot, but prayed to God that every one of our guys was okay. Shortly afterwards, we could hear the shouting and yelling in Pashton, *"Lasona porta kah, lasona shah ta ka!"* ("Hands up! Hands behind your back!") coming from the village. We could also hear the nonstop breaking in of doors as well as all the other various noises coming from the village as our guys went from house to house.

Within two minutes from when the first shots were fired, we heard another *pop, pop, pop*. Alfa2 was trying to contact our guys on their radios to ask why all the shots were being fired. They had responded back, saying no shots had been fired from our team's side. The three of us waited for about 10 or 15 fifteen minutes, while the cold that had frozen my feet was now spreading to my ass. My boots were full of water, my pants were soaked through (and through), and the temperature was in the mid-40s. There was no way my body temperature could warm my feet, especially since my boots were still full of muddy water. As for the freezing pain in my ass from the cold, that just came with the territory of being a part of Special Forces. I was definitely not complaining; I was merely considering unlacing my boots in an effort to dump the water out and take off my socks so I could squeeze the water out of them as much as I could when Alfa2 called me, "Hey, Nas, Jay and Scott need your help with the interrogations at the house in the village." I asked him, "How can I get to the house when I don't even have night goggles to see where I'm going?" Alfa2 responded, "Hold on a sec. Let me ask if they can send a couple of ANP officers so they can take you to the house."

While Alfa2 was communicating with our guys at the house, I thought to myself, *Am I ready to walk with two ANP officers in the middle of the night, especially since they don't even like me?* Well, I wasn't there to be flaking out, and was ready to walk over to the house with the ANP officers once they came to get me. I made sure that both hands were on the trigger just like Alfa always told me, "Nas, put your fucking camera away and put your hand on the weapon." Since Alfa wasn't here to remind me of this, his advice was always with me. While the two ANP officers walked in front of me as I followed them to the house, I was holding onto my rifle very firmly.

Before I knew it, it was time to cross the river to the other side again. I was confused; it didn't make any sense for us to cross the river again, since we had already crossed it to be on this side where the village was located. I asked the officers, "Hey, guys, why are you going back to the other side of the river?" to which I got the following explanation: "Ustad, we had to cross the river twice before we got to the village." I couldn't help but think to myself that this was probably the luckiest village in the whole of Afghanistan, which had two rivers located approximately 200 feet apart. Well, I guess I needed to cross one more river one more time, but that wasn't the end of my worries. While my feet were getting warmer because of the walk, I knew that it was going to be cold when I jumped into the water again. However, once I took the plunge, I found that it wasn't as difficult as the last time because my feet were already cold and numb.

As we crossed the river to the other side while walking towards the village, I heard one of the officers asking another, *"Oh bacha, az kodam rah amadim, azi rah ya azo rah."* ("Hey, you, which way did we come from, this way or that way?" At that moment, I couldn't help but think to myself, *Oh great, these fuckers don't even know where we're headed !* I also thought, especially after hearing those shots earlier, *What if someone is waiting for us, and we don't even know where the fuck we're going!* Both of these guys were talking very loud in Farsi, which would make it even worse for us, especially if this was a Taliban-friendly neighborhood.

I asked both of the ANP officers to be quiet and suggested we not go anywhere for the moment. I also asked them to wait for a couple of minutes to make sure we remembered where the fuck the house was before we moved any farther into the village. I'd experienced a lot of scary moments so far by being in Afghanistan, and this happened to be one of them where my feet and ass were literally melting from being frozen, when you're scared, your body temperature rises. As I waited for them to decide which way they were planning to go, I could see that they were both much more frightened than I was. Finally, one of them said, "We came from that side (pointing to the left). Do you remember [asking his buddy] whether we passed by that shop?" As they discussed the possibilities, I followed them, praying and hoping we wouldn't run into the bad guys in the middle of the night when I couldn't see anything farther than 15 to 20 feet ahead of us.

We finally got to the house in one piece with our heads still attached to our bodies. As I entered the house, I saw three adult males being detained, two where Jay was standing, the other one where Scott was sitting. Jay wanted me to help him first, while Scott wanted me to go to him first as well. But, if I had to choose between the two, I'd rather be translating for Scott, who was more human than Jay, who was sorta on the insane side of the spectrum.

The biggest difference between Scott and Jay was the manner in which they treated the detainees. Scott, as did others on the current and previous ODA, treated detainees under the age-old philosophy that they were innocent until proven guilty. Jay, however, saw and treated everyone in Afghanistan as though they were all Taliban until proven innocent, and he made this "judgment call" based solely by the clothes and beards they wore. Since everyone in Afghanistan stares—and Jay didn't like people to stare at him—his second "judgment call" had him considering them to be Taliban as well, no matter how many times I told him otherwise.

After arriving at the house, and before I even started the interrogation, I told Scott I had to remove my boots so I could dump out the water, and then my socks so I could squeeze the water out of them. Scott was fine with it but reminded me that we had to leave this place as quickly as possible. "I understand," I said, "and will walk out of here barefoot if I have to." I removed the boots and socks, which I placed on top of the boots after squeezing as much water out of them as possible. Once that was done, I noticed an older detainee nudging his head toward the corner opposite Scott as though he was trying to communicate that he wanted to tell me something. Since he had no way of knowing if I could speak his language, he didn't say a word; he just kept nudging his head toward the opposite side of the courtyard where there was a room with a wide opening. Noticing what was going on, Scott told me to ask him what he wanted. Since every house we had raided so far had been the Pashtons' houses, I knew that had to be the language he spoke, too. When I asked him what he wanted to say, he smiled immediately and said, "Oh, thank God you are Pashton!" I gave him an encouraging smile so that he felt comfortable enough to proceed with what he had to tell me. "I thought you might speak Farsi," he said, "which I don't know how to speak." After a short pause, he continued by telling me there was a fire-pit in one of the other corners of the room (and he nudged his head toward the one he meant) in front of which I could place my socks to dry. Scott nodded his head in approval, so I walked over to the fire-pit, where I didn't see much of a fire but felt some heat coming from it nonetheless. Almost every house in the village had one of these wood-burning fire-pits so the villagers could stay warm during the winter months.

With this done, Scott and I were finally able to start questioning the detainee. Other detainees we had questioned told us from the very start that we were in the wrong village, assuring us that their village was in no way Taliban friendly. This older detainee told us he had lived in this house since birth, as had his father and grandfather. The two other detainees, one in each corner of the courtyard, were his sons. He said he also owned the mills behind the house and knew everyone else who lived in his village. As Scott and I asked the detainee questions, I suddenly realized that Jay was standing directly behind me, and anytime the detainee said he had nothing to do with the Taliban, or that there were no Taliban in his village, Jay would argue, "That's a fucking lie; he *is* a fucking Taliban." Ignoring Jay, Scott went on to ask the detainee, "If you know everyone in the village is not Taliban, then why are the Taliban coming to your village?" Pondering the question, the detainee responded, "The Taliban come during the fall season to collect *Hajhur* (a 10 percent Islamic tax collected by the Taliban from landowners and farmers on the crops they sold). The money is normally used for the poor and needy during peacetime, but during a *jihad* the money is used to fight the Taliban's cause of defeating the infidels. The Taliban had been in the village a couple of days ago to collect their Hajhur."

Since Scott didn't have any further questions, I went to Jay so I could help him interrogate the sons. After hearing our interrogation of their father, Jay was already pissed off because we couldn't find the Taliban in this house. He asked one of the young men, "Where the fuck is the Taliban? You know where they are, so tell us," he shouted. The boy insisted that he had no idea where any Taliban were. He had been working with his father in the mills all day long. Jay went back and forth between the two young men, but couldn't get anything out of them. Finally Scott said that it was time for us to leave the house, and he radioed Alfa2 that we were coming out. Before leaving, I went to get my socks from the fire-pit when the father approached and told me that if we wanted to go back to the other side of the river, when we left his house, we could turn to the right to avoid the river entirely. Once we passed his mills behind the house, we would see a bridge behind the mills that we could cross to the other side. I was going to tell the others so we could take his advice, but since Jay didn't want to listen to what the elder had said, he told us all that we would not go the way the villager had directed us. Giving Jay the benefit of the doubt, since he didn't know these people culturally, I could understand his point of view, thinking the father was setting us up for an ambush by the villagers. Despite my opinion and assurances that was not going to be the case, unfortunately, Jay didn't trust anyone but himself, so we went back the same way we had come, walking through the water, where my once-warm socks became soaked and freezing again.

We returned to where Alfa2 and the PRT commander were so we could collect our backpacks and the rest of our gear. So far, we'd crossed the river three times and were yet to cross it again so we could get to the other side of the village where the shooting was heard earlier. Once we had crossed the river for the fourth time, Alfa2, Major Mark (the first major we had with us on a dismounted mission), and I had an uphill walk ahead of us. After about 10- to 15-minutes, we reached the top of the hill where the village shops lined both side of the narrow dirt road.

As we passed the shops, we could see that the Polish soldiers had already broken into them on the right side of the road, looking for anything suspicious. There were four mud hut structures without doors on the left side of the road; one of them had barrels of gasoline stacked in front of it. It was then that we realized what the shooting was all about—the Polish had shot at the locks so they could more easily break into the shops, not to steal water melons and cigarettes like the ANP, but to see what was inside.

As Major Mark, Alfa2, the JTAC, and I walked further up the hill, one of the Polish Special Forces' guys came over to Alfa2 to tell him in broken English that bad guys had run away from this location when they saw the Polish soldiers arrive earlier in the night. Mark and Alfa2 already knew that air support had already been monitoring our movement and had thus followed the bad guys and killed them.

Major Mark decided that some of us should identify the bodies of the bad guys who had been killed. By then, it was around 2:30 in the morning, and in order for us to get to the location where the bodies were, we had to walk about seven kilometers up the mountains to get there. Before we took off, Alfa2 gave me the choice of either going or staying behind with 40 to 50 other guys who would be staying behind to hold onto our strong point. Despite the fact that we had to walk seven kilometers each way (not to mention we had to cross the river again, plus only God knew what else) being the adventurous type, I chose to join the guys going uphill, despite the fact that Jay was joining us as well.

When we started our walk toward the mountains, there were about 18 of us: 10 Americans, seven Afghan ANP officers, and one local interpreter. I was hoping we wouldn't really have to cross the water again, but then realized that we were on a dirt road, not farmland, so we should be okay—except for the uphill climb. It was the physical exercise that kept me warm, despite my again wet socks and water-filled boots.

The higher we climbed, the colder it got. We walked for more than three hours and reached our destination before sunrise, only to find that the bodies were on the opposite side of the river. Alfa2 asked my buddy Oscar, a couple of other team members, and me to stay behind to keep the roadblock secure. It was early morning. Instead of it getting warmer, the temperature dropped, making it even colder by the minute, until the sun finally came out. We waited there for close to two hours before we were radioed by Alfa2 and asked to start heading back down the mountain to join the others.

Walking back in the light of day, our surroundings didn't look quite as spooky as they had during the night. After an hour's descent, we were back with our guys who were still on the other side of the river, hoping they could find a crossing. Unfortunately, that didn't happen, so they obviously had to cross the water so they could return to the other side. The area looked as though it had never been visited by other human beings, except the Taliban.

All we saw were cave after cave in this rugged mountain area of central Afghanistan, that others probably didn't know even existed. Occasionally, we had to take a break—not because we wanted to, but because the ANP guys were complaining of being tired from walking all night. Most of them didn't even know that we were going to be here for two more nights chasing more bad guys.

Around noon, we ultimately met the rest of our guys, including the Polish, by the shops we had seen the night before. I couldn't believe what I saw in this little market area. All of the ANP officers were sleeping in the shade alongside the dirt road, so I can only guess that you already know who was holding the security positions on the rooftops—yeah, you guessed correctly—it was indeed the Americans.

Since every spot on the road where one could lie down and relax/sleep in the shade was taken by the ANPs, our group who had just returned from a 10-hour (14-kilometer) walk, had to find a place where we, too, could relax, We decided to do so behind the shops, which was mostly an area where the Taliban or other villagers would literally take a crap. No joke intended, I actually recorded most of my experiences by discovering the Midvale Society of Afghanistan that still existed while the rest of the world was well into the 21st century. I recorded the lives of the Afghans living in these remote villages—not because I wanted to humiliate them, but to show my children or any of my other fellow Americans—who had no idea how people in other parts of the world—still live and are so far less fortunate than we are.

Alfa2 chose a place for us to rest, not the most desirable, but the only one he had, because it was the lone spot where we could take cover if anything happened as far as safety and security issues were concerned. Unfortunately, it also consisted of hard rocks and a lot of gravel that we not only needed to sit on but perhaps sleep on as well if anyone wanted to take a quick nap after the weariness following 14 hours of walking.

It had only been a half-hour break for the JTAC and me before Alfa2 told me that he needed us to accompany him to rescue four of our guys who were stuck in the same spot as the night before: the wide-open field where the Chinook had dropped them off. From our location on top of the hill, we could see the entire valley below. Overlooking the route from above, where we had crossed the river four times the night before, I could see a bridge crossing the water that was directly behind the mill, just as the old man had told us. Our guys were stuck because they were all riding on ATVs fully loaded with water as well as other heavy weapons and ammunition. Before we started walking down to the village to find the open field on our search-and-rescue mission, Alfa2 asked me to choose a couple of ANP officers—who had rested the night before—to take with us.

Ultimately, Alfa2, the JTAC, two ANP officers, and I walked toward the village. While en route, the first thing one of the ANP officers asked me was, "Ustad, since you know Pashto, why don't you take the lead, and we will follow you." (They asked this because they will never be able to take the lead.) It's not that the ANP necessarily wanted me to take the lead—it was mainly because I spoke Pashto and they were too afraid of getting shot if they were in the front.

I took the lead and all four of them: two Afghan officers, Alfa2, and the JTAC, followed me. Before we reached the village, Alfa2 asked me if we could walk by the area in the open field, where we had been waiting with all of our backpacks and weapons the night before. Since I didn't understand why he wanted to go back there, I asked him for his reason. He told me that one of our rocket launchers was missing, and he thought we might have left it in that area last night.

In order for me to cross over to the other side to check if the rocket launcher was there, I had to make anther round-trip across the river. The parcels of land we were walking across were divided by dense, tall tree lines. We couldn't see anything once on the opposite side. Despite the fact that I didn't know what I'd be walking into once I reached the other side, I crossed over the river but couldn't find the rocket launchers, which concerned me because they might end up in the bad guys' hands—or maybe they might already had them and were aiming them at me.

Once I crossed the river again, for what I hoped would be the last time, we continued on our way to the middle of the valley. It was around 1:00 PM, which made it 14 hours that the others had been in a wide-open field, the perfect place for an easy ambush from all directions. The one saving grace was knowing that this was not a Taliban-friendly village; if it had been, they would undoubtedly have attacked us by now.

The weather was sunny and warm. Despite my reluctance, it would've been a lot easier for us to just cross the river again to get to our guys, but we needed to find a way because we had to drive the ATVs out of there as well. The only way we could do that was by walking through the entire village. Even though we could never be sure, we were reasonably positive that this wasn't a Taliban village. Obviously, no one was particularly happy with my suggestion to walk through the middle of the village. I reminded them that if we wanted to get the ATVs out, there was no other way but to walk through the village to get to our guys.

While still walking through the farmland—just before we reached the village—I saw a couple of adult males at one corner of the field, close to the village. I asked Alfa2 to keep an eye on me while I went to ask the men if they would give us directions on how to go through the village into the open field where our guys had been trapped. Alfa2 gave me permission, so I crossed to the corner of the field where they were standing and asked them who the owners of the land were.

I greeted them in Pashton, *"Salamalykom Kako."* ("Greetings, respectful elders.") They both responded, *"Walaykom they salam."* ("Greetings to you as well.") To be expected, they were surprised to see someone in an American military uniform, wearing dark glasses, suddenly appearing and speaking to them in Pashto—not just any Pashto, but a dialogue very similar to their own. I asked them how to get to the open field, without having to cross the river, to the west of where we were standing. One of them asked if I meant "over there, where your guys are?" I was surprised and asked him how he knew they were there. The other elder answered, "Well, we heard the birds that came last night and saw your guys sitting over there at the farm this morning." I was more comfortable now, especially since they knew exactly where our guys were.

Pointing to the west, they said that we could walk straight, through the first tree line, and by passing the second tree line, we would find our guys waiting. Well, it sounded very easy—in fact, too easy—because I knew and had experienced Afghanistan as having one of the most rugged terrains on earth, so I knew we'd have to overcome challenges along the way. But, I took the elders' advice and asked Alfa2, the JTAC, and the two ANP officers to follow me. Of course, I couldn't help but see the startled looks on Alfa2 and the JTAC's faces (i.e., their silent question: *Are you fucking sure you know where we're going?*). The two ANP officers looked even more frightened than the rest of us. Only Afghans are frightened by their own native if not from the same tribe or ethnic group.

As we walked, the more I talked with the locals the more I was convinced that there were no bad guys in this village—that, in and of itself, greatly alleviated my worries about being attacked. When we reached the outskirts of the village, we confronted several other villagers, some of whom looked at us like we were aliens from another planet. Meanwhile, my "followers" took turns asking me if I really knew where we were going. I assured them that I did but also told them I wasn't sure we'd find our guys before nightfall.

I was comforted that the villagers that we had confronted along the way weren't bad people; here, too, they were simply victims of circumstance, harassed by the Taliban. Their primary reason for staring at us was because their village was so remotely located, other human beings were foreign to them, especially in their village where they only knew one other. These were the most ancient and simple down-to-earth people, who not only grew their own crops in the mud, but they lived in huts made from the same mud, and relieved themselves in the same mud and eventually died and were buried under the same mud. All of these people lived their entire lives within this farming community just as I did growing up in Arghandab.

We left the village safe and sound, and I thanked God that we didn't have to cross the river again—although, quite frankly, it really wouldn't have mattered anymore because I had become accustomed to it. It was 3:00 PM. The walk was made shorter because we'd been able to cross a narrow and shallow creek alongside each of the tree lines we passed, coupled with the fact that the village turned out to be safer than we originally anticipated. We always avoid walking or driving the same route as much as possible for security reasons, so as to avoid attacks, and in this particular situation, because the narrow creek we had jumped was too shallow for the ATVs.

One thing that I had learned by talking with the villagers was that I could trust them. When I spoke to them in Pashto, I could sense the myriad welcome signs from the villagers. Through the way they responded to me, I could also sense that they thought they were talking to someone who was a Pashton native.

Whether they were Pashtons, Tajiks, or Hazaras (and, here, I'm necessarily excluding the Uzbeks because I'd never met them), they would listen to me when I talked with them because, as an American, I treated them with respect. I didn't look down on them with disdain like other Afghans did, whether they were local interpreters, ANAs, ANPs, NDs, or linguists from the States.

Most of the local villagers feared these groups more than they feared the Americans. Of course, the villagers didn't necessarily like Americans, but did appreciate the way we treated them and didn't steal from them, whereas the others would not only steal from them but enjoyed intimidating and physically abusing them. It's normal in the Afghan culture that people who worked for the government always used their power and authority to oppress the poor villagers, so it was no surprise to learn why the villagers never liked the Afghan Security Forces or any of the Afghan government officials, including the linguists. On many occasions, I asked the ANP officers not to terrorize women and children by pointing AK47s to their heads, but they did it anyway, for purposes of revenge and just to plain terrify them.

We finally reached the location where the two Americans and two Polish Special Forces guys were waiting alongside their ATVs loaded with supplies of water, food, and ammunition. Damon2 and one other team member, along with the Polish soldiers, were telling us that they had tried everything they could to get out of this place last night but couldn't because of the rough terrain. Since the four of them didn't know that the village wasn't Taliban friendly, they thought it would be a bad idea to be stuck in the middle of an open field once the sun came up because they knew they could be easily ambushed. Thank God nothing had happened before we reached them.

While Alfa2, the JTAC, and the two ANP officers took a break from the long walk coming here, I started looking for a way to get out of there before dark. Looking around, I could see that we would have to go in the opposite direction (south). I looked around and saw two farmers and a young boy sitting in the sun, watching us from a distance. I walked over, introduced myself, and asked if they could tell us how to go back to the village on top of the hill. One of the men told me that in order for us to do that, we had to go to the end of the tree line (where he was pointing), which was about a mile long. I thanked them, fully aware that I was going to follow their instructions just as I had earlier from the other two villagers.

We all started to move alongside the tree line to the end, where we found that the creek we had jumped over coming here was much flatter at this end. When Alfa2 asked me again if I knew where I was going, I assured him that I did—sorta. I explained that in order for us to get to the other side of the creek, we needed to get out of the farmland first, then go through the village so we could cross the only bridge there was so our ATVs could cross over the river. Needless to say, it turned out to be much more challenging than we thought it would be.

We really needed to get out of this slope-shaped farmland, which was a giant step-by-step process with each parcel being on top of another and a five- to six-foot slope between them. Just to get out of the first parcel was a challenge because our ATVs were overloaded with all of our supplies. In order for our ATVs to move over the muddy slope, we took everything off one of them and pushed it up the slope to the top parcel of land and then used it to pull the other three up—a process that had to be repeated until we got to the end of the tree line so that we could cross over the not so shallow part of the creek. Needless to say, I was greatly relieved that the farmer had given us the right directions.

Shallow creek aside, we still needed some kind of support for the ATVs to be able to cross over it. Thank God no shortage of rocks, we all rolled up our sleeves and got busy picking up all of the basketball-sized rocks and dropping them in the creek to make a crossing bridge so our ATVs could be driven over it. As we all—Americans and Polish alike—got busy with that task, the two Afghan ANP officers just stood there—with their hands behind their backs—watching us like it was solely our problem alone; it had nothing to do with them. I got pissed and had no choice but to ask for their help. They still didn't move. Angry, I told one of the officers, "If that's how you are going to do things, by doing nothing, you will never succeed in life." Instead of doing the right thing to help us, one of the offices told me, *"Ustad, banish key ya bokona"* ("Ustad, let them do it"), referring, of course, to the Americans.

Once we filled the creek with rocks, our ATVs crossed over to the other side. Then we obviously had to remove every rock from the creek to allow the water to flow again so we wouldn't damage the poor farmers' only source of irrigation. So, we started to remove the rocks again. As anticipated, the ANP officers didn't want to help us with this task, either, but said instead, "Ustad, tell them to leave the rocks so *we* can leave." Hearing their constant badgering, Damon2 asked me, "Nas, what are those fuckers saying?" When I told him they were insisting that we leave immediately, he said to ask the fuckers how they'd feel if someone came to their village and did something like this, leaving all the rocks in the creek so that the next day when they came to their farm and saw that the water was blocked by a group of assholes, what would they say then? When I told the officers exactly what Damon2 had said, one of them responded, "Ustad, tell the American this is *not* our village; it's the village of the motherfucking Taliban." Damon2 and I had the same thought in mind when I was told by Damon2 to tell the damn officers, "Don't you realize that this is *your* fucking country? Do both of you only care about *your* fucking village?" Shaking their heads, one told me, "This is not our country. Our country is Malistan (a 100 percent Hazara District in the Western Ghazni Province). If we stayed here for even one more day, these people would probably eat us alive." This is how things work in Afghanistan; except for our brave men and women in the U.S. military, no one really cares about these poor villagers.

As we were pulling the last rocks out of the creek, Alfa2 asked if I knew how to get back. I told him I did—we were directly behind the village on the opposite side of the shops, and in order for us to get back, we would have to go through the village and cross the bridge by the mills.

Of course, not really certain of where I was going, I didn't want to just walk into the village; therefore, I looked around to see if I could find someone who could give me more precise directions. I saw two young boys in their early teens walking toward the village. I called out to them to ask if they could come over to where we were. At first, they were understandably hesitant and stayed where they were, looking at me like I was talking to them in a language they didn't understand, which wasn't the case. As usual they were either confused by someone in an American military uniform talking to them in Pashto or were simply afraid of us, which is why they were hesitant to come closer. Instead of asking them again to come over to where we were, I called out to ask if they knew where the bridge was. Sensing that we weren't going to hurt them, they slowly moved toward us. When they got closer, the older of the two asked me in Pashto, "What do you want?" I again asked if they could show us the way to the crossing bridge. They knew how to get to the shops and were willing to walk with me through the village to the bridge. I tried to keep my conversation with the boys as friendly as possible in an effort to ensure they felt comfortable with me—simple things like their names and ages. When they told me they didn't know how old they were, I asked them if they were going to school. When one wanted to know what "school" meant, I was shocked. Certainly, I was aware that very few children went to school in the remote villages of Afghanistan, but to not even know the meaning of the word was totally mindboggling to me.

When our guys were finally done with removing all of the rocks from the creek, Alfa2 again asked if I knew where the bridge was. I told him that one of the teenage boys was going to be our tour guide to get us there. While Alfa2 didn't like that we had to go through the village, he also knew it was the only way to get to the bridge.

Before we entered the village, I pulled out my video recorder and started recording so that if we were attacked, I would have the attacker(s) on camera. Midway into the village, it got more and more crowded as the villagers followed and stared at us. The boy who was supposed to help take us through the village to the bridge was now gone and nowhere to be found. The deeper we went into the village, the more villagers crowded around us. I started to talk with them by saying, in Pashto "Greetings, how're you guys doing?" just to see their reactions. Not only that, but I spoke to them with their local vernacular from the Province of Uruzgan, which was similar to the Kandahari vernacular. Every time I said *"Salamalykom"* ("Greetings to you"), the villagers would say with a surprised smile, *"Stakho Pashto ham zadada"* ("You can speak Pashto!").

While walking through the village, not knowing where the fuck I was headed, since I lost my tour guide, I noticed Damon2 behind me, asking, "Hey, Nas, aren't you fucking scared? What if you get shot?" I shrugged my shoulders and told him, "Nope, I'm not scared; these are people of the dirt and tree just like me, not bad people—they're simply victims of circumstance—the people I consider to be true Afghans." "Why don't you at least put your hand on your rifle?" Damon2 suggested, which I did. "Hey," I told him, "don't worry, okay? I'm in front of you so if someone started shooting at us, I'd be the first to get hit. And do you know what that would mean to me?" Damon2 shook his head. "No, what?" I paused and then said, "If I got shot right here and died, it would be an honor for me to die in my native land as an American so that my casket could be draped with the American flag that I love so much." Damon2 shook his head again. "Nas, you are one crazy dude."

After a long walk, with many *Salamalykom*s along the way, we were finally out of the village and on our way to crossing the bridge to safety. Fortunately, we hadn't been confronted by any of the bad guys, which is what usually happened on most of our other missions. And, after talking with the man the night before who offered me the fire pit to dry my wet socks, I was convinced the village we were leaving weren't supporters of the Taliban, in fact victims of the Taliban.

It was about 6:00 in the evening, an hour before it got dark. After almost 20 hours, this had been the longest nonstop mission, but I still wasn't tired. What gave me joy instead of fatigue was bringing those four guys who were stuck in the open field for more than 14 hours back to safety, and taking all eight of them (including two Polish soldiers and two ANP officers) through the village without harm. The accomplishment made me happy, and I knew I'd do it again, in a heartbeat.

Upon our arrival back to the top of the hill, I went back to my spot behind the shops (with all the human feces) so I could lay down and wait for our ride later that night in order for us to continue the second part of our mission. The Chinook was scheduled to pick us up around 11:00. I tried to get some sleep, but after several efforts, knew that wasn't going to happen. Alfa2 called to help him translate with some of the local villagers who were protesting against our raids of their homes the night before. Many of the villagers had reached the roadblocks we had set up at the bottom of the hill so they wouldn't be able to use this particular road blocked off for reasons of security. One of the local villagers, who didn't know my name, asked the ANP officer at the roadblock to get him the interpreter with the wet boots and socks who was at his house the night before. Well, since all of us had crossed the river more than once and had wet boots and socks, no one knew to whom the villager was referring. So the ANP officer sent one of the other interpreters, who worked for the Polish, to talk with the villagers. Since the villager didn't get the interpreter he wanted, he rejected the Polish interpreter (who was also a native Pashton from Konar Province). The villager insisted that he needed to talk with the interpreter who was a fellow *watandar* (countryman).

Since Afghanistan is one of the most isolated societies in the world, the locals were only comfortable talking with people from their own sub-tribes who could speak their own specific language dialogue. Alfa2 and I walked down the hill to meet the villager who had been so kind to me the night before. We learned that he came to ask me if the Americans would pay for the damage that had been done to his front door when our guys broke into his house. On most of our nightly raids, we had to blow the doors away so we could enter the homes. I asked Alfa2 if we could compensate the villager for the damage we had caused to his front door. "Nas, ask him how much it would cost to fix the door," Alfa2 said. When I asked the villager, he said it had cost him 10,000 Afghanis when he had to replace it not too long ago. Before Alfa2 could say what he'd be willing to pay for the door, I asked one of the ANP officers in Farsi so the villager wouldn't understand since none had spoken or understood anything but Pashto, what it would cost to replace a similar door as long as he knew we weren't being ripped off. The ANP officer said it would cost about 12,000 Afghanis for such a door. When I then told Alfa2 that the villager had paid 10,000 Afghanis to install the door, I pointed out that we hadn't really damaged the door itself. Our guys had only damaged the one side of the door when they blew the door open so they could enter the house.

Alfa2 reached into his pocket and pulled out all of his cash, which turned out to be 7,000 Afghanis. He told me to tell the villager that was all he had. Before I told the villager what the captain had said, I told Alfa2 that 7,000 Afghanis was still too much to offer for a couple of broken hinges; after all, it wasn't like the whole door had been damaged. On that basis, Alfa2 asked me to negotiate with the villager in an effort to keep him happy. When I told the villager that the door itself wasn't broken, but that it was just the two hinges that were blown away by the detonation, the villager looked at me with the smile and said, "Okay then, listen—can I get at least five thousand Afghanis from him?" (referring, of course, to Alfa2). I told the villager, "Hmm, well, hold on a second; let me ask." Since I knew that Alfa2 was offering all the cash he had on him, I explained that the villager wanted to settle for 5,000 Afghanis. Not too surprisingly, Alfa2 was generous when he said, "I'll give him the seven thousand Afghanis for his trouble. What do you think, Nas?" When I told him it was his decision, he handed me the money, requesting that I tell the villager that he wanted him to take the 7,000 Afghanis. He also asked me to apologize by telling him, "Here, take all seven thousand. We're sorry for breaking your door and waking you and your family in the middle of the night." The villager smiled with appreciation, saying, "Please tell him not to worry about the door. Meanwhile, I hope you can stop the Taliban from coming here." Since many of the villagers were standing around and listening to our conversation, Alfa2 told them, "By not supporting them, all of you can get together and stop the Taliban from coming here."

This was the same exact conversation that we would have with 80 percent of the villagers whose homes we had broken into. We would tell them time and time again to unite against the Taliban by not supporting them. Unfortunately, their doing so would not change because the fact that our guys only go to the remote villages probably once every other year or so, breaking through their doors, differed to the degree that the Taliban was going there more often not to break their doors, but to demand the collection of taxes, which the villagers are willing to do because they see it as a religious duty. So with whom should the villagers be more cooperative? The Taliban, of course—not only because they are fellow countrymen, but because, according to every villager, they are also doing God's work—or because the infidels, in every villager's mind, support the Afghan government for simply coming to their villages to break their doors and steal from them. The villager added that: first, they couldn't do anything barehanded, and second, everyone in the village was afraid to do anything about it.

Are they better off with the Taliban being in charge of their village or the Afghan government? Meeting these victims of circumstance throughout Ghazni and the surrounding provinces, I personally believe that they're confused as to who they should side with; the villagers are frustrated because it was either the Afghan government who stole from them or the Taliban who would behead them if they didn't meet their demands. I also sensed that most villagers were more afraid of the ANP, ANA and NDS officials than they were the Taliban, who they feared because of their religious beliefs; in other words, if they didn't believe them, they might go to hell. Their fear of the Afghan government officials was more personal because of the government's thievery and the excessive corruption and physical abuse that the locals had to endure.

⚜

It was getting dark as I went back behind the shops to try and get some sleep again. But no luck: it wasn't possible to sleep on gravel, not to mention the smell of feces. Plus, it was also getting very cold, which helped to keep the smell of feces at a minimum but kept me awake nonetheless. Then, of course, I couldn't help but remember all the things we had accomplished throughout the day—of the hard labor involved putting in and then removing the basketball-size rocks from the creek. I was even prouder and more honored to be part of a country where its soldiers did good for the world's overall well-being. Their thoughtfulness about the rocks was just another example of how they thought it was their responsibility by simply doing the right thing. I couldn't help but be amazed by their kindness and consideration. It was around 10:30 in the evening as we prepared to walk away from the shop area into the open field to be picked up by the Chinook for our next mission. Not knowing we were going on our next mission, the ANP officers kept asking me how soon we were going to go back to the base. When I told them that we were not going to the base for two more nights, needless to say, they were not pleased with the news.

Because of the experience from the last pickup in the dark, when I heard the *TaTaTaTa* sound of the Chinook getting closer and closer, I fell flat on my stomach until the aircraft had landed safely. We were picked up and dropped off 20 miles west of the location we had just left and needed to do this whole thing all over again for another 24 hours, except in a different village. We followed the same exact scenario: a house-to-house search, holding detainees for interrogation, and paying for broken doors. Unlike the last one, this was more of a desert village, with little to no farming or river, creek, and ditch crossings. As before, our strongest point was the village's main market area—basically in the middle of nowhere on a narrow dirt road—where there were four empty mud huts where we could stay. After all the house-to-house searches and interrogations, we were done by 3:00 in the morning, so everyone was retrieved from the village to the four empty mud huts so we could rest, and hopefully sleep. Fortunately, I slept for about four to five hours sitting against the wall inside one of the mud huts next to all of the ANP officers. I could not believe how easily the ANP officers could fall asleep on the gravel-covered ground.

Awakening to a brisk sunny morning was very refreshing. I walked down the hill to the river to freshen up. The water was ice cold. I drank enough for the day, but now I was hungry. All I had brought were three cinnamon-flavored energy bars, which I usually carried with me, especially on long missions. I had one of them for breakfast, leaving the remaining two for lunch and dinner.

The other two teams of soldiers who had been dropped off at the other end of the Ajristan District the night before, joined us around noon. The area where we spent the night looked like one of those Wild Wild West John Wayne movie scenes where one can only see a couple of rundown buildings where the bad guys are usually hiding so they can attack passersby. Since the four mud huts we had used were empty and full of human waste, we named them the Motel Taliban. In the light of day, we noticed that there were two other shops about 100 feet to our north, which were probably owned by the villagers. The two other teams joined us; obviously, all were exhausted from their long trek in the dark. They had also brought some detainees with them, so Oscar and I started to interrogate them behind the Motel Taliban to see if they had any valuable information or if we should just let them go. Eventually, we determined that we needed we continue holding a few for interrogation and let the others go. The whole day was spent at the Motel Taliban; as usual, our next mission was going to start around 11:00 that night.

The temperature dropped rapidly close to nightfall. The JTAC, our medic, and I got on top of the roof of the Motel Taliban, looking around through sniper rifle binoculars to see if there was anything suspicious going on in the area. I heard the breaking of a door noise below. When I looked down to my left, there were two shops about 100 feet to our north, where I saw several ANA officers breaking into one of the two shops. I called down to them, "Hey, what are you guys doing?" Their reply: "What the fuck do you think we're doing?" Not wanting to yell back and forth with them, especially while standing on a rooftop, I went down and walked toward the shop, where I could more clearly see them taking out everything they could get their hands on, including firewood and gasoline. I couldn't help but stand in front of the shop, thinking to myself, *Do I really want to interfere with these thugs who are stealing a poor villager's property?*

I'm not the kind of guy who could just stand there and do nothing. Laila and Sabrina could confirm this in a heartbeat! In fact, Laila's worst fear while I was in Afghanistan was that I might get hurt or perhaps even killed by one of the locals that I might argue with or try to stop from doing wrong. Laila's own words, every time we spoke on the phone while

I was in Afghanistan, were, "Nasrat, we both know that the Afghans would never admit their wrongdoings. so what's the point in talking with them?" Obviously, just like everyone else, she had given up on the Afghan society as well.

Well, despite what Laila told me, not too surprisingly, I asked them why they were stealing from a villager's shop, to which one of the ANA officers replied in a confrontational tone of voice, "If this isn't your store, then it's none of your business!" I countered with, "If it's none of *my* business because it's not *my* store, then why is it *your* business if it's not *your* store? Instead, you as an ANA officer are stealing from a poor person." While I am neither a police officer nor a soldier, I was simply trying to do the right thing by protecting the poor villager's property. Well, as anticipated, the officer would not answer as he reentered the shop to help his cohorts pull out even more firewood. As Laila would say: "You can't teach them."

The whole platoon of ANA had now joined the first two, coming and going, taking whatever they could. I just couldn't stand there and talk with everyone who walked in and out of the shop, nor was I physically able to stop them. Instead, I went to Alfa2 to inform him about what the ANAs were doing. Alfa2 then talked with Major Mark (who happened to be in charge of this particular mission), who said he couldn't do anything about it—or perhaps he just didn't want to do anything about it.

Knowing that no one could do anything about it, I sat there hopelessly and watched the cowardly ANA officers loot the whole store, down to the bare walls. As I sat and looked around me, I could see several small bonfires with three to four ANA and ANP officers gathered to keep themselves warm at the poor shopkeeper's expense, since they had taken all of his wood, which was undoubtedly the firewood he had in inventory for the upcoming winter season. How sad to see it all go up in smoke in just one night because of the Afghan Security Forces, who were supposed to be protecting shopkeepers, not stealing their property. I asked Alfa2 why no one was doing anything about it. "Nas, we can't tell the ANA what to do; it's their country." I gave up and walked away from the scene, with my heart aching knowing that the shopkeeper, whenever he found out, would blame the Americans for the theft, despite all the ANA and ANP officers who were there with us—but, then, the villagers don't see that and know that the ANA or ANP would not be in their villages if it weren't for the Americans. So, why would the villagers support us when the ANP and

ANA were breaking into their stores and stealing from them when it was the Americans who brought them to their villages?

Since 120 of us were here and the third mission was going to be around 11:00 at night as usual, I learned that all of us wouldn't be required to go on this mission. Those who were not going—which included Oscar and me—would return to the base. I was not too surprised by the news, especially since I couldn't keep my mouth shut about what the ANA and ANP officers were doing by stealing from the poor villagers. Or perhaps they just wanted me to take it easy and get some rest, which would surprise me, especially since I was the only linguist who was much better doing his job than any of the others.

Bravo2 explained that we were only getting two Chinooks that night to take the first group of our guys to their mission, which was only 20 miles to the north of us. Once they had been dropped off at the objective village, the Chinooks would come back around 11:30 and take those of who remained back to the base waiting for our flight.

I returned to the Motel Taliban, which was already full of sleeping ANA and ANP officers. I found enough space to squeeze between a couple of the ANP officers in one corner of the mud hut, so that I could lay my head against the wall for support, with the hope of ultimately falling asleep. A very small mud hut full of about 15 to 16 ANA and ANP guys—who usually don't take showers—added an even fouler odor to the place, which already smelled bad. Despite the stench, in the midst of all the others, it was warm enough to fall asleep.

I was awakened by the sound of the Chinook landing right behind the mud hut. I looked around me to find that the place was empty, except for an officer still sleeping in a corner on the other side of the hut. I stood, grabbed my rifle, and kicked the ANP officer so he'd wake up. I knew we didn't have time to waste. We had to get to the Chinook quickly; otherwise, we'd both be fucked by being left behind. The officer was still lying on the ground, half asleep. I screamed at him as loud as I could. Then I realized that if this crazy fucker could sleep through the sounds of the Chinook only 100 yards away, how would it be possible for me to scream loud enough to wake him up? Since time was of the essence (we had 90 seconds before the Chinook took off without us), I only had two options: either kick him again, harder this time, in the ass with my boot, or leave him behind. I decided on the kick in the ass. When I did, he was fully awake and running toward the Chinook even faster than I was.

When we got to the line to board the Chinook, Oscar has already taken head count and was already at the end of the line, ready to have everyone board the aircraft, when the two of us showed up behind him. Noticing we were late, he asked me where the hell we'd been. When I told him we had been sleeping in the mud hut, Oscar said that Bravo2 never told him that I was supposed to be going back to the base with Oscar and his group. In fact, he thought I had left earlier on the mission with Bravo2 and the other group of guys on the Chinook's first pick-up. Since it was too noisy to discuss this any further, at that point I just wanted to get on the Chinook and then talk with Oscar and Bravo2 once we were all back on base.

Finally allowed to board the Chinook, as we flew over the dark mountains, I mulled over the fact that Bravo from the previous ODA would have informed Oscar that the ANP officer and I were going to be on the flight back to the base. To ensure that we were all present and accounted for, Bravo on the previous ODA did things responsibly by personally doing a head count three times before we left the compound, and three times when we departed a village after our mission had been completed—each time by either touching us on the head or on one of our shoulders while calling our names.

The next day, when I asked Bravo2 why he hadn't informed Oscar that I would be on the flight returning to the base, his response was, "Hell, sorry, bro. I thought I told Oscar that you were going back to the base with them." Not one to normally place blame, rather than faulting Bravo2, I *had* briefly considered blaming myself for not waking up so I could have reached the Chinook sooner (the thought of being left behind still makes me shudder!). In the end, it came down to not *blaming* anyone—I am merely pointing out the lack of leadership on Bravo2s part for not communicating relevant information to Oscar.

After the long missions, all of the other ODA members and their ANA officers had returned to their own base, but not until the ANA officers left our compound in a state of total "tornado-like" destruction by breaking everything in sight. All toilets and sinks were either broken or damaged by the visiting ANA, primarily because they didn't use toilets the way they were intended to be used. For instance, in this case, the ANA and ANP guys got on top of the toilets, with both feet on the rims, so their bodies would not come into direct contact with the toilets themselves. The same destruction applied to the sinks, in which they washed their feet—not to mention that since most of them didn't know the purpose of the showers, they washed in the rivers. To make matters worse, they used the shower pans as urinals.

During our interrogation of some of the detainees we brought back with us from the last village, Abdul Bari—whose name will always stay in my mind for the rest of my life—presented himself fearlessly when he unhesitatingly admitted to being a bad guy. Frankly, I really didn't know what to make of him: Was he a committed Pashton or a terrorist who didn't care about anything or anyone other than himself? As soon as I started to speak with him in Pashto, he gave me the title of coward and spit on me, figuratively speaking, because it's a cultural thing in Afghanistan that one who disowns others spits either downward toward their feet or anywhere in front of the disowned individual to suggest that they are not only not one of them, but they are also disgraced from sharing their common values. In my case, the detainees thought I was a fellow Pashton; therefore, if I was working with the Americans, they disowned me or, in other words, considered me to be a traitor and a coward.

Spitting in the Afghan culture can be *the* most humiliating thing one can do to another, which I never took seriously, which ticked them off even more. Only your parents, who might want to disown you, would spit directly in your face. I was physically spit on by my biological mother once, either because I was no longer her Pashton son for marrying a Tajik or I was taking what she considered to be a stand to protect my Tajik wife against her. Either way, in my mother's mind it was the clash between the Tajiks and the Pashtons.

Oscar knew the detainee was upset, but didn't know why he got upset so quickly. I explained to him what was on the detainee's mind: since I'm a Pashton working for the Americans, he didn't consider me either Pashton or Muslim, but did think that I was a coward. Since the detainee admitted that he was a Taliban commander and had 60 other low-ranking Taliban soldiers working under his command—a fact of which he was very proud—we didn't spend too much time with him, primarily because he didn't want to answer our questions but rather chose to tell us about how he, his children, his grandchildren, and his great-grandchildren were going to fight the *jihad* to defeat the infidels, at which point Oscar and I left the room, telling Jay, our intelligence gathering officer that he was welcome to listen, if he was so inclined, to what Abdul Bari was saying.

Since Jay agreed to enter the room to "do his thing," Oscar and I returned to listen to Jay as he started to question Abdul. I understood the reason Oscar didn't want to ask the detainee any further questions because Abdul Bari had already admitted that he was a Taliban commander; therefore, Oscar had no case to make out of Abdul Bari's testimony, so there was absolutely no need for further interrogation. Most of Oscar's work required that he interrogate and see if detainees—that we were interrogating under normal circumstances—could be linked to any terrorist activities. Since Abdul Bari admitted to being a Taliban commander, he was, in essence, turned over to Jay for further interrogation.

I confess to being amused to find myself translating for a detainee who was much more in control of asking Jay questions rather than vice versa. Whether on our dismounted missions or otherwise, it was well known that Jay always immediately labelled local villagers to be Taliban—despite the fact that at least 80 percent of them were ordinary Afghans. So, we had Abdul Bari telling us that he was a Taliban commander, but rather than Jay doing anything about it, Abdul Bari appeared to be in charge because he was the one asking Jay questions! At one point, I was told by Abdul Bari to be sure to tell Jay that what he was about to tell him should be passed on to his superior. When I told Jay what Abdul Bari expected, Jay's response was, "Well, then tell him to start fucking talking."

With that, Abdul Bari said, "I want you guys to know that I will fight you until the day I die. Then my sons and their sons will fight you after that, and on and on until we take back our homeland. We took our country back from the Tajiks in five years (he was referring to the Taliban regime of 1996–2001), sending them all to the mountains. You Americans came over here and gave Kabul back to them. You guys are not going to stay here forever, and the day after you leave, we will send the Tajiks back to the mountains again and the Hazaras back to their holes. Now, if you want to kill me or do anything else with me, go ahead and do it."

Jay didn't understand what Abdul Bari was talking about when he mentioned taking their country back from the Tajiks in five years. Well, I obviously couldn't fault Jay for not understanding what that meant, especially since he didn't know anything about the Pashtons, Tajiks, Hazaras, and perhaps even Afghans in general. As noted earlier, Jay believed that anyone/everyone who wore traditional Afghan clothes with stares and a beard on their face were Taliban. There was no time for me to give Jay a lesson regarding Afghan culture while he, Oscar, Abdul Bari, and I were sitting in the interrogation room. Jay wasn't even slightly interested in knowing what our mission in Afghanistan was all about—for the sake of his own personal ego, he had his own mission of rounding up as many Afghans as he possibly could so he could label them as Taliban; therefore, one person admitting that he was Taliban was of no benefit to him. He really wanted to make innocent people Taliban so he could get the credit for being an aggressive soldier. Jay was more focused on the quantity of his work than the quality; that, in and of itself, was causing more problems than he could solve. While Jay wanted to ask Abdul Bari more questions, Abdul Bari was no longer willing to talk and, as a matter of fact, said, *"Za stasi sara noori khabari na laram"* ("I don't have anything to say to you guys"), which was the official end of our conversation with him, so the three of us left the interrogation room.

Wanting to point something out to Jay—not to piss him off, but just so he would understand the Afghan culture a bit better—I told him, "Now you know what and how a real and committed Taliban would say and act. Abdul Bari is not only the enemy of Afghanistan, but he's also an enemy of society in general, willing to die for his cause. But you couldn't push him around because he wasn't innocent and actually admitted to you that he was a Taliban commander. You couldn't treat him the way you treat other innocent detainees who are not Taliban, but I'm curious as to why you didn't treat him as such, especially since he admitted that he was a Taliban. Instead, you simply walked away." Jay's response was, "Whatever, Nas."

One day I received another email from my site manager, asking me to pack up my gear and go back to Bagram, because my Cat III status was being finalized and I needed to read and sign the official paperwork designating me as a Cat III linguist. Since my site manager didn't know who my POC with new the ODA was, I asked Alfa2 for this information. When he told me that Damon2 was the person I needed to talk with, I went to Damon2 with a request that he contact my site manager regarding my departure from the team. When he did, later asking, "Hey, Nas, are you leaving us?" Not knowing my own status, all I could say was, "Nope, why would I do that? It's the site manager who wants me to go to Bagram," to which Damon2 responded, "Well, it's sad to lose you, brother." When he said that, it definitely sounded as though I was being transferred from the team.

I packed all my gear and emptied my room for my flight to Bagram, which would be around 1:00 in the afternoon. This time I needed a ride to the airfield because of the number of bags and amount of gear I'd have with me. Damon2 offered to help and pulled one of the pickup trucks outside my room so he could help me load all of my gear and then we'd be on our way to the airfield. Before he started driving in that direction, I told him what had happened to two of our other team members who were both shot by the Taliban: Delta, who had picked me up from the airfield when I first arrived in Ghazni; and Delta2, who dropped me off at the airfield the last time. Delta survived his wounds; Delta2 didn't. On that basis, I asked Damon2 if he was sure he still wanted to give me a ride to the airfield, especially after hearing what had happened to our other two brothers who had given me a ride from and to the airfield. "God forbid that this is the trend that takes place for anyone who gives me a ride to the airfield. If it were, I would much rather Abdul Bari gave me a ride since he had told us during our interrogation that he was ready to die. Not knowing the situation with Abdul Bari, Delta2 asked, "Who the fuck is Abdul Bari?" I told Damon2 that Abdul Bari was one of the detainees we had just interrogated, who admitted to being a Taliban commander and being sent to Bagram, where the maximum security prison is located. Damon2 laughed when he asked, "Hey, Nas, how do you come up so quickly with shit that make so much sense?" I smiled and answered, "I really don't know. It all just comes naturally to me, and if I can save you from getting shot, then I'm all for it." We both laughed as Damon2 dropped me off at the airfield; we said our goodbyes and then I was on my way to the lovely transition tent in Bagram—yet again—for how long, only God knew.

The following morning, I showed up at the office at 11:45 and was escorted by a security officer to the applicable building. Everything was done within an hour, which made me officially a Cat III linguist. There was an increased demand for Cat III linguists, which would require mostly working inside the base rather than going on dismounted missions. I didn't like that I'd be sitting behind a desk, which is not why I came to Afghanistan. I had a behind-the-desk job in the States and didn't care for it as much, either. I'm more of an adventurous, hands-on person who prefers being physically active rather than sedentary, meeting people face-to-face in order to understand and help them better.

Once I became a Cat III, my company sent me to a unit called AROCC (Afghanistan Remote Operation Cryptologic Center) where Cat III linguists were needed the most. In order for me to be qualified to work there, I had to take a Pashto/English language efficiency exam, which was administered by the AROCC. I did not want to be working in an office if I didn't have to, not because of the work, but because of the other 90 linguists—some I knew personally—would do nothing but bash America for being infidels and because of its values, which to them were inferior. Why would most native Afghans view America the way they did, yet still want to be citizens? Because of the benefits and protection of being an American.

The only way to get out of working at the AROCC unit was by intentionally failing the exam, which is exactly what I intended to do. Why? Certainly, being around 90 other linguists wasn't my only concern: a couple of others included the fact that as mentioned earlier, there were a lot of other linguists who were doing everything they could *not* to be assigned to units that went on dismounted missions, and the other linguists did everything they could to be at the AROCC—reasons enough for me not to want to be there if I really didn't have to be. I wanted to go on dismounted missions, which, to me, meant that I would be filling a much more purposeful demand. If I stayed at the AROCC, there would no doubt be a linguist in the field who didn't want to be there, and there would be a linguist (me) who didn't want to be at the AROCC. If the right linguist is in the right place, I think that, within itself, is an accomplished mission, which was my main goal for being in Afghanistan—to accomplish our country's mission, not to be involved in the political aspects, but rather the physical, military aspects. Once getting the news that I failed the exam, since there was no other unit in Bagram that could use a Cat III linguist at that time, I was on my way back to Ghazni.

Of course, I had the same crazy situation of going back and forth from the tent to the airfield, but I was finally out of Bagram and in Ghazni. The flight was similar: long and bumpy, especially when having to carry all of my gear, and traveling by Chinook that made many stops on the way. Since no one had been informed that I was returning to Ghazni, no one was there to pick me up at the airfield. However, upon my arrival Alfa2 was coincidently at the airfield dropping off someone else to catch the same flight I had just come in on; when he saw me, needless to say, he was completely surprised. "Welcome back, Nas. I'm happy that you've returned." He helped me load my stuff into the truck. As we drove toward the compound, he told me that my room had been assigned to someone else already, but there was another room that I could use. He also informed me about the upcoming nighttime air mission within the next couple of days. Unlike our others, this one sounded more like an in and out mission.

During our 20-minute flying time, I was sandwiched between Echo2 and Jay, and since this was a single Chinook flight, I happened to be the only linguist. As we neared the village, we were given the five-minute warning signal to be ready for landing, which meant having all of our gear ready and at hand, ready to disembark the Chinook as quickly as possible once it landed. When we heard the one-minute call signal, everyone stood, waiting for the aircraft to touch the ground. Once landed, we started jumping out, usually hitting the ground running. Well, as it turned out, tonight wasn't like any other night because right after the one-minute call, everyone got up, except me. Not that I didn't want to get up, but because assuming the strap on my rifle was stuck to one of the hooks on the floor, I couldn't get it loose. It was dark, I couldn't see what the strap was stuck to, but when I bent over to check I noticed that Echo2 was standing on it. Before I could push Echo2's foot away, there was a loud thump; everyone who was standing, fell to the floor.

Soon we learned that the crew was attempting to land the Chinook in a very tight spot between two orchards. During the process, the back wheels hit a mud wall, knocking it down. Thank God it was an Afghan mud wall; otherwise, the aircraft could have very easily lost its balance and crashed onto the ground, possibly killing everyone on board.

We were literally pushed out of the aircraft by the crew so they could take off as quickly as possible from where the aircraft had landed in the middle of the village. As I followed Echo2, I could tell that he was hurt; he had fallen to the floor on both of his knees. Not only was he hurt, but since Echo2 was about six feet tall and weighed more than 200 pounds, he also carried about 70 pounds of gear, ammo, and usually the biggest gun I'd ever seen. Falling suddenly to his knees must have been quite painful because he was limping noticeably while walking to the objective, but never said anything and still executed the mission as planned.

There were several houses that we had to search for a high-ranking Taliban commander. The first house was totally empty. The second, which was attached to the first, was occupied by an elderly man, his son and his wife, and their three small children. The first thing Jay and I did was take the son outside and tie his hands behind his back, making him sit facing the wall. While the ANP ran around doing their usual, Jay and I went back and got the elderly man, who couldn't see and had a difficult time walking. Jay wanted to look around the house a bit more to see what else he could find; at one point, he asked me to remove the woman and children from the room. He also wanted me to tell a couple of the ANP officers to go into the basement to find out what was there. While Jay and the ANPs were searching the rooms and basement, I asked the woman to come outside with her children, to which she responded, "My dear brother, my kids can't go outside in this cold temperature (which was about 40 degrees Fahrenheit); one is still in the cradle." Looking at the two small children standing beside their mother while she held on to one side of the cradle where the baby was, I knew it wasn't right for me to take them outside.

Instead, I told them to sit down, that they didn't need to go outside. Since Jay wasn't aware of the children's ages, I went to find him. "Hey, Jay, I don't think it's a good decision for the woman and children to be outside in the cold." As anticipated, Jay didn't like what I had just told him. "Nas, I want everyone out of this fucking house *right now*," to which I countered, "You don't need to fucking yell at me, Jay. I asked the woman to leave already and take her children with her, but she refused to go out-side because of the cold. And, she's right because the kids are much too young to be outside in these freezing temperatures." As though he had not heard me, Jay repeated, louder than the first time, *"I want everyone out of this fucking room right now!"* I turned, walked away from him, and went outside to join Echo2 and the three ANP officers, who were about to go on to the third house so they asked me to join them.

Before proceeding, however, I asked Echo2 if he could come inside the second house to see the woman and her children so he could determine if they should be pulled outside into the cold, as Jay had ordered. I knew Echo2 was a decent man and would never agree with what Jay wanted to do. When Echo2 asked the ages of the children, I told him one was a baby still in a cradle, while the other two were about two or three years old. Echo2 told me to tell the mother that she and her children didn't have to come outside. He then asked me and five ANP officers to join him, and to also let Jay know that we were en route to the third house. I went to where Jay and the ANP officers were and asked the ANP officers to come with me. Jay stopped me and asked where we were going. "Echo2 told me to get five ANP officers so we can move on to the next house."

Once we got to the third house, Echo2, the five ANP officers, and I broke into it. Jay had soon joined us. Once inside, Echo2 asked me, "Nas, I want you to tell three of the officers to get on top of the roof and the other two to come with us." After passing on Echo2's request, he then told me to tell the two officers to go into the rooms across the courtyard and search them thoroughly.

Neither wanted to go. When I asked them again, one of them told me, "Ustad, the light on my rifle doesn't work, and it's dark over there. We won't be able to see anything." When I passed this information on to Echo2, he got mad and said to the officers, "Did I not ask each and every one of you, before we left the compound, to tell me if you guys needed anything?" to which one of the ANP officer replied, "It was working then; I don't know what's happened to it since then."

Echo2 asked Jay and me to check out the rooms instead. He also asked me to tell the ANP fuckers to watch the front door to ensure that no one entered or escaped. Echo2 tried to open the door for us, but it was apparently locked from the inside; therefore, in order for us to go in, he had to shoot off the hinges while Jay opened the second door that was located approximately 20 feet to our right. Once both doors had been opened, their entrances lead us to a 50-foot tunnel that lead us to a room where we could see the proverbial light at the end of the tunnel. When we reached the end, we found another young family (husband, wife, and two children) who were all in a fetal position, screaming in Pashto, *"Ma waley, ma waley, moge bay guna you hitzh mo nadey kary."* ("Don't shoot, don't shoot; we're innocent, we didn't do anything.") Unlike Jay, Echo2 wasn't using all the four-letter words he could think of; instead, he treated the woman and her children with respect, requesting that they stay in the room for the rest of the night. He then asked the male of the house to join us outside. Jay took the lead by tying the man's hands behind his back as he took him to the dark alleyway where other blindfolded detainees were sitting against the wall.

Before I returned to the house, I was asked by the elder detainee who had been taken from the second house, "Dear interpreter, I am very cold. Would you ask my wife to send me a blanket?" I knew beforehand if I told Jay what the detainee wanted, he would not allow me to do it. However, I asked him anyhow and was not surprised when he adamantly said, *"No, he can't have it."* After searching both houses, we were done and taking two of the detainees with us to the base for further interrogation, while letting the older man return to his family.

The following day, Oscar and I interrogated the two detainees—brothers, working at the same school—we had taken with us from the mission the night before for further interrogation. The older brother detained from the second house was the principal of the school. The younger brother captured in the third house was a math teacher who also spoke limited English. After the initial medical exams, the older brother was pleased with the treatment he had received from our medic. As Oscar and I started to interrogate him, he was very polite and cooperative and answered every question we asked. Before returning him to his cell, he asked me very politely, "Listen, my dear brother, can you tell Oscar that I'm okay with whatever you Americans want me to do, but please don't turn me over to the Afghan NDS torturers." Once translated to Oscar, he asked the detainee why he would not be happy being turned over to the NDS officials and questioned his use of the word "torturers." The detainee explained by saying, "This is my third time being captured and brought in here—first, by the Polish, who then turned me into the NDS; second, by the NDS officials; and now, this time, by you guys. I was not treated as humanely the first two times I was captured as you Americans are treating me now." With curiosity, Oscar asked, "Don't you see something wrong, either with you or something in your house?

Otherwise, why would the Polish, NDS, *and* Americans go to *your* village and then to *your* house, in particular, to pick you up, rather than go to the thousands of other villages and houses in Afghanistan?" The detainee responded that, "The owner of the house next to us is a high-ranking Taliban official. He currently lives in Pakistan but visits once in a while during the night so no one can see him." "Then why," Oscar asked, "were you brought in the other two times by the Polish and the NDS?" The detainee told him that he was still as innocent this time as he had been the first two times. "The first time," he explained, "I had to sell my land to bribe myself out of Polish capture. The second time I had to put up my house in lieu of cash to get myself out of the NDS situation. Now, if you guys turn me into the NDS, I don't have anything left to use to bribe myself out."

Observing Oscar's interrogation for the past six months, I noticed that he listened to the detainees first and then reasoned with them. Oscar sensed and kind of understood how the Afghan society worked, especially in this detainee's case. I understood even more—most villagers were innocent. They were not only victims of the Taliban, but they were also victims of their own government.

Why was the man captured three times in the past five years, but never convicted? The answer was simple: He was attacked by his own Afghan officials for financial gain, while American soldiers risked dying in the process by picking up innocent people 80 percent of the time, which further proved the nature of the Afghan government, where human lives are not as valuable as money they take from their "victims." They not only get money from the Americans by reporting on innocent people but, once in their custody, they take bribes from those same innocent people. In other words, it's a win-win situation for the Afghan government.

Unlike his older brother, the younger brother/math teacher had never been in custody before. He was frightened and more aggressive during his interrogation and didn't like being in our custody. Despite the fact that Oscar and I knew the younger brother's occupation, we asked him what he did for a living. He responded that his brother had given him a position as a math teacher at the school. He also said that he loved learning English. When Oscar asked him why he wanted to learn English, the detainee told him, "I want to learn English so I can be an interpreter for the Americans."

At the end of our interrogation process, we asked the detainees for their opinions and thoughts regarding the Taliban and the Afghan government. The older brother told us that he could care less about either of them. He added that the Taliban would bring security but wipe out the education system. He wasn't sure about the Afghan government except that, so far, his land and house had been taken away by the its corrupt officials.

As we asked the younger brother what he had in mind for himself and his children's future, he answered, "God willing, if I get enough money to leave this country, just like you did," he said, nodding his head at me, "that would be great." I couldn't help but think about what our guys went through just to pick up an innocent principal and math teacher of a school, the latter doing everything he could to get out of Afghanistan. I thought that only the local interpreters who worked for the Americans were doing so just so they could get out of Afghanistan. But, then I saw this young detainee (a.k.a.: math teacher) trying to learn English to be an interpreter so he could save enough money to get out of his country like everyone else was either doing or trying to accomplish.

One day Echo2 asked me to help him translate while he was weapons training the newly hired ANP officers, because he thought the local linguists were misinterpreting his message to the ANP. We all went to the range for shooting practice. Every time Echo2 tried to demonstrate to the ANP officers how to stand while shooting or how to hold their weapons so they could better shoot at the target, the officers missed 80 percent of their shots. On numerous occasions, Echo2 would personally walk over to each and every one to teach them how to stand and hold their weapons while shooting. I thought Echo2 was not only being very patient, but he was also a great trainer because he worked with every officer on a personal level so they could learn to shoot accurately. Most of the ANP officers never took anything seriously. If most in the Afghan society would step back and actually listen to those who were there to teach them, they would not only be more productive as a country but as individuals as well. And if the Afghans truly believed in their hearts and minds that they were capable of doing everything, and that they know it all (besides fighting to destroy each other), then why would Afghanistan be where it is today—where it absolutely *cannot* stand on its own to survive?

I didn't need to tell Echo2 what every ANP officer said, even if we'd had the time. I was there to take Echo2's words and translate them so the ANPs understood them. As a matter of fact, the very next day I actually told that same ANP officer who was complaining about Echo2's demonstration on how to shoot (which, according to them, they already knew how to do) that if the ANP were ready to defend their country, then why couldn't they go out and defend their country without the international community's help? Their answer was always the same, "Let *them* do it."

One of the safest mission approaches was when we didn't fly or drive. We got there safer because we walked in a dry riverbed from our base directly to the village, which eliminated the IED threat if we drove, as well as the threat of being shot down or avoiding a crash landing like on our last mission simply to pick up a principal and math teacher of school. Round trip, it was only about five miles' walking distance from our base, which we left at midnight. Most of us walked except for the four guys who brought the ATVs with the medical supply kits and stretchers, just in case any of us got wounded on the mission and needed to be transported back to the base.

Despite being the safest route to walk, it also felt like the longest and most difficult because we had to walk in sand more than a foot deep while carrying close to 70 pounds in addition to our own weight. Furthermore, our only GPS was an Afghan source who didn't even know where the fuck the target house was because, according to him, he had never gone to the village via the dry riverbed. We wandered around the village for a couple of hours while wild dogs barked and chased us. We had absolutely no luck finding the house we were looking for because our Afghan GPS source was now afraid of wandering around the village for too long.

We were going from the village back to the base when we heard a very loud and powerful explosion that shook the village from one side to the other. It frightened me and Damon2, one of our medics, who was directly in front of me. While I had seen and heard an IED explosion in front of me on other missions, this one happened to be ten times louder and much more powerful. I hoped and prayed to God that none of our guys had stepped on or driven the ATV over it. Since he had an internal radio so he could communicate with the rest of our team members, I asked Damon2 what it was. He told me it was a control detonation set off by one of our guys, but he was surprised it was so powerful. I didn't know what he meant by control detonation since we didn't even search any of the houses for explosives, but asked if everyone was okay. I was relieved when he assured me that everyone was fine.

Major Mark was present during our debriefings the following night. I noticed that some of the guys were smiling and making fun of someone or something while others had looks of concern on their faces. I noticed, too, that Charlie2, one of the bravest American soldiers I have ever met—who also happened to be our team expert on explosives—was also laughing and smiling at everyone with whom he made eye contact. At one point during the meeting, Jay joined Charlie2 and congratulated him for some kind of a great accomplishment about which I had no clue.

When it was time for team members to share their thoughts or concerns with Major Mark, and it was Charlie2's turn to speak, all he had to say was, "That was fucking awesome; the whole fucking village shook and everyone was probably awakened by the penetration of the bomb." Charlie2 was referring to one of the bombs that he made the day before, which—at the time—he couldn't wait to use on the door of the house we were going to in order to get the bad guys. Since we couldn't find the house, Charlie2 was stuck with his explosive, so he decided to use it on something else, primarily because he liked blowing things up by experimenting with his knowledge of making, as he put it, "The most awesome fucking bombs *ever!*"

Instead of keeping the bomb for our next mission, before we left the village, Charlie2 and Jay attached the bomb to one of the orchard's 4-foot-thick mud walls and detonated it to prove to everyone how powerful Charlie2's bomb was. This was simply Charlie2 and Jay's way of doing things so they could have something to talk about around the dinner table. If this had been Alfa's mission, none of his guys would have gotten away with doing such things. There was little to no—or perhaps I should say, not as strong—leadership with this ODA2 as there had been with the previous ODA, especially with Bravo2's overall mission coordination.

Members of the team (e.g., like Charlie2 and Jay) would do things they felt good about personally, not things that our missions required. After Charlie2's comment to Major Mark during the debriefing, Mark asked, "Hey, Charlie2, from now on make your bombs, but give them to us so we know when to use them, okay?" Obviously, Major Mark had actually just told Charlie2 not to do such a fucking crazy thing like that again, albeit in a more polite way. I noticed that Charlie2 wasn't smiling anymore; neither were Bravo2 or Jay, who had been smiling earlier during the debriefing because they liked what Charlie2 had done the night before.

After the meeting, I walked over to Charlie2 and told him, "What you did last night was totally un-American. What if you were one of the villagers and someone did what you did at 2:00 in the morning; how would you feel about that?" The fucker's smartass response was: *"GOOD TIMES!"* I really didn't know what he meant, which is probably just as well, but it aggravated me enough to tell him that, "This mission isn't about you and me personally; it's about our country—*our country*! We should represent America for what it is! You should be ashamed of yourself for misrepresenting our country." To that, all Charlie2 did was smile and walk away as he repeated, *"GOOD TIMES!"*

However, I can say one thing for certain about Charlie2 and Jay: They were both brave and courageous soldiers but, because of the lack of leadership from our team leaders, especially Bravo2, they more often than not behaved like anything but.

In the past six months, I had been on every mission except the first following my arrival or unless I wasn't in Ghazni. When it came time to go out on a mission, I was usually the first one to have my body armor and rifle in the vehicle to which I was assigned.

Just before we were about to leave on a dismounted mission, Bravo2 asked, "Nas, I'm sorry, but you'll have to give your seat to Tyson (an FBI agent who had joined our team). I'll send you out on our next mission." I knew from our briefing that Tyson was assigned to a different vehicle, but now he was brought over by Bravo2 to our vehicle to replace me? *Why?*

I wondered. Well, obviously I couldn't say no to Bravo2 or even Tyson, for that matter. Besides, how could one choose to fuck with an FBI agent if he wanted your seat? Exactly—if you're smart, you can't. For the past six months, I had always been assigned to the same vehicle where the commander—whether Alfa or Alfa2—was.

Alfa2 had just recently returned to the States to accompany the body of his brother-in-law who had been killed while flying in the Chinook on a mission in western Afghanistan. Therefore, I had no one to complain to for being bumped off the mission, so I went to my room for the rest of the night. I would much rather have been going on the mission than going to my room for what I knew would be a restless and sleepless night.

At our briefing the next day, Bravo2 gave me a new assignment conducting classes a couple hours a day to teach English to the ANP officers. I tried everything I could to teach them not only English, but elevate their morals as well. Given a week to do so, it didn't take long for me to realize (not surprisingly) that the officers weren't even remotely interested in learning anything, much less English. They were only interested in getting paid, and, in fact, at one point during that one-week class, one of the ANP officers had the nerve to ask me if the Special Forces team would pay them extra money for their time coming to a class to learn English. I was so aggravated, I didn't even answer his question. Besides, I had enough on my plate already and didn't want to be part of something that had no positive outcome by being in a room full of ANP officers who never took anything serious, except for what they were being paid. Not only for them, in the Afghan culture in general everything was turned into a joke. Ninety percent of these guys didn't even know how to read or write Farsi, their native language. I would much rather have been able to spend my time achieving something, like working with Oscar on interrogations, Echo2 to train the ANP, and Kyle and Tim on the compound's PSYOPS local radio station.

I liked helping the PSYOPS with their news announcements—in both Pashto and Farsi—between every segment of music they played. As with everything else involved with the Special Forces, nothing was more joyful to me than doing something that other people couldn't or wouldn't do—mostly dismounted missions, of course.

While Alfa2 was gone, I wasn't assigned to even one dismounted mission. Instead, my work was limited to various tasks within the compound. By the time Alfa2 had returned from the States, I had already missed four missions. Since he had no control over Charlie2 and Jay's behavior, I was convinced that Bravo2 didn't like me going on dismounted missions.

In one of our mission briefings, Bravo2 assigned me to be in the same vehicle with Alfa2, which is where I usually was anyhow. This time, however, Bravo2 assigned my seat to a local linguist. Alfa2 didn't say anything, and I had nothing to say to Bravo2, so I simply took my stuff and changed vehicles. I was frustrated and wanted to get a second opinion on what I should do regarding how I had been treated lately (all without Alfa2's knowledge), so I asked Tim, my buddy from the radio station for his opinion. Since we hang out together, I wanted to see what he thought about why Bravo2 was not taking me on dismounted missions.

Tim thought Bravo2's lack of leadership always allowed Jay and Charlie2 to be in control whenever they wanted. Tim also told me that he thought I was acting crazy for being so mad for being bumped off of dismounted missions. I told Tim that I wasn't in Ghazni or Afghanistan, away from my family, just to be sitting in my room with nothing to do. Had I wanted to do that, I could've just stayed in Bagram and not come back here to Ghazni to be with Special Forces. I respected Tim's opinion but wasn't satisfied with his answer.

So, I asked Alfa2 why the team was excluding me on dismounted missions. Not knowing I'd been bumped four times during his absence, he said he thought it was probably because there weren't enough seats in the vehicles. When I told him I had been excluded from a total of five missions so far, a look of surprise and concern crossed his face, and he assured me that he would talk with Bravo2 and make sure I was included on the next one.

Unfortunately, as it turned out, I missed the sixth mission as well. During our briefing, Bravo2 told everyone what vehicle they were assigned to; I was in the same vehicle with Alfa2. To say it frustrated me would be putting it mildly when Bravo2 told me a few hours later, just before we were about to leave, "Hey, Nas; sorry, bro, but I need to have him (another local linguist) go on this mission instead."

The next day, Echo2 asked me, "What happened, brother? You don't like going on missions anymore? I miss having you with us." I told him that, "It's not up to me. Ask Bravo2 why he's not letting me go on the missions, or perhaps you should ask either Jay or Charlie2, since they appear to be the guys running the team these days."

During this period of time, a couple of the local linguists had come to my room, not because they wanted to know if I was feeling okay like they claimed, but to find out why I wasn't going on missions anymore. If I wasn't assigned to a dismounted mission, one of the locals had to fill in for me, which they didn't like doing. Everyone knew that I liked going on these missions. Every time I met and talked with the local villagers, the more I wanted to help them. Just like Michel de Montaigne had once said, "*I prefer the company of peasants because they have not been educated sufficiently to reason incorrectly.*"

Since I couldn't get any help from Alfa2, I wasn't sure what to do next, until I decided to ask my site manager if she could assign me to another unit. After contacting her, she told me I could not be transferred from one unit to another until my current unit released me from their team. Well, ODA2 wasn't going to merely release me, especially if they didn't find me doing anything wrong. In fact, I had received a performance evaluation from ODA2 a couple weeks prior to my talk with the site manager, on which Damon2, our team evaluator, had checked "Outstanding" in every category. As time passed, I became more and more frustrated because I still didn't have a clue why Bravo2 continued to exclude me from dismounted missions.

Ultimately, I had no choice but to go to the source directly. So, one night after dinner, I knocked on the door of Bravo2's room. Surprised to see me, he asked, "Yes, Nas, what can I do for you?" I asked if I could go inside so we could talk about something that was bothering me. Knowing Bravo2 was far from being a problem solver, good or otherwise, I also was aware that he always did his best to avoid talking with anyone who came to him for help. But this time he didn't have a chance to ignore me by simply walking away rather than solving the problem I had come to discuss with him.

When he reluctantly allowed me to enter his room, I got straight to the point by asking why I had been bumped off every single dismounted mission for the past few weeks. In order for Bravo2 to make me think he was doing me a favor by not taking me on dismounted missions, he responded with a bit too much bravado, "Hey, brother, you do know, right, that all the other linguists don't want to go on dismounted missions, but when I don't send you out there, you're complaining about it?" I told Bravo2 that, "I don't care what the other linguists want to say or do. All I know is that I'm here to go out on as many dismounted missions as possible, but if you can't do that, then give me one good reason why you schedule me to go out on a mission during our briefings, only to bump me just before we're about to leave—not once but six times in a row now. If you don't want me on the mission, why do you assign me to one only to tell me later that someone else is taking over for me? If your intention is for me to not be on dismounted missions, than don't schedule me to be on one in the first place, and if you really feel I shouldn't be a part of your team, then you should tell me so my company can assign me to another unit."

In an effort to convince Bravo2 to either fire me or take me on the missions, I added, "As often as the ODA goes out on dismounted missions, that's how much our success is measured as a team. And the more I was out there, the more I contributed to the team's success. But the more you keep me in the compound, the less I can do my job by helping you on the missions." To make sure I had made my point clear, I told him again, "With that being said, you either take me on dismounted missions or simply fire me so I can be assigned to another unit." Having finished what I had come to say, I noticed that Bravo2's demeanor had changed a bit, but he merely smiled and said, "Nas, you're crazy. Why would you want me to fire you?" I wouldn't let him off so easily. "There's a reason why you won't send me on missions," I said, "and it's not because you really think I'm crazy. I need to know why you're doing this to me." Bravo2 avoided answering my questions or providing me with any information at all by simply saying, "Okay, Nas; I'll think about it." Not clear about what he meant, I asked, "Thinking about firing me, or thinking about putting me back out on dismounted missions?" Smiling, as he escorted me to the door so he could obviously get rid of me, he merely responded that he'd let me know.

Meanwhile, I kept in touch with my site manager in an effort to be assigned elsewhere. Since Bravo2 had not yet answered my questions, I again knocked on his door a week later. After opening the door, as with the first time, he again asked what he could do for me. When I asked if I could go inside so we could talk, his demeanor was more welcoming as he opened the door so I could enter his room. I got straight to the point again by telling him that I felt something was wrong, and he wasn't telling me what it was. "You know I haven't done anything wrong, which is probably why you can't tell me but also aren't willing to fire me. Since you won't answer my questions, here's what I think's going on, and if I'm correct, you'll fire me. On the other hand, if I'm correct, you'll put me back on dismounted missions. It's because of your inability and lack of leadership that you can't make the decision whether you should fire or keep me." With a puzzled look on his face, Bravo2 asked, "Nas, what the fuck are you talking about?" to which I responded, "You know exactly what I'm talking about, but in case you actually missed the point of what I just said, let me say it one more time. It's your lack of leadership that prevents you from making decisions not only in my case but in every other case since you've arrived here." He stood quietly as I turned and left his room.

Within half an hour, there was a knock on my door. Before even opening the door, I knew it was Bravo2, and he was mad as hell. "Nas, you can pack your shit and get the fuck out of here on the next flight," which proved and supported my claim about his poor leadership.

I emailed my site manager the next morning to update her about my situation, and also to coordinate what I should do once I was back in Bagram. She emailed me back by saying that I wasn't going anywhere until she got a word from CJSOTF-A (Combined Joint Special Operation Task Force-Afghanistan), which is our team's command center that requests linguists for every ODA throughout Afghanistan. According to my site manager, Bravo2 wasn't allowed to simply tell me to pack my shit and get the fuck out of there.

In order for the ODA to send me back to the company, CJSOTF-A had to provide our company with the reason(s) for my termination. Because of Bravo2's lack of leadership, he didn't even knew the procedures of how to handle my situation. He just thought telling me verbally was how things worked.

At the advice of my site manager, I went back to the OPS Center and told Bravo2 that I would not leave the team until he officially fired me. Angered further, he responded "Shit, Nas, why can't you just leave on the next flight to Bagram?" to which I said, "Well, Sir, it's not as simple as you just verbally asking me to leave. You either have to talk with my site manager directly, or email my company a written termination so it's official for me to leave. I don't make the rules, I simply follow them." Now even more frustrated, Bravo2 then asked, "Why the fuck do I have to do that?" I was getting sick and tired of our constant badgering back and forth. "Sir, don't ask me because I don't know. As my site manager has advised, I will continue to stay here until she is advised by one of your team members that I am fired and no longer needed here. Until that occurs, I will not leave until my site manager tells me it's okay to do so." Fed up with the whole thing, Bravo2 told me to get Damon2, who was supposedly my POC, and bring him back to the OPS Center.

I went to Damon2's room and asked him to come over to the OPS Center because Bravo2 wanted to talk with him. When we got there, Bravo2 asked Damon2 if he had my site manager's contact information. Damon2 told him he didn't, primarily because he joined our team after Delta2 was gone (Killed in Action). Since leadership never really took control of the situation to inform Damon2 of his responsibilities regarding all of the linguists, he didn't know anything about my company or my site manager, so he asked me to provide him with that information, which I did. Before Damon2 contacted my site manager, he asked Bravo2 why he needed to contact her. Before Bravo2 could answer, he asked me to leave the OPS Center. I'm guessing that Bravo2 didn't want me to know—even at the last minute—what he was going to tell Damon2, including why Bravo2 was firing me. Personally, I thought I should have been allowed to stay so I could hear what Bravo2 was going to tell Damon2 and defend myself accordingly. But since I really wasn't worried about it, I left the OPS Center and went to my room.

Half an hour later, Damon2 knocked on my door. When I opened it, the first thing he asked me was, "Hey, brother, what in the hell happened between you and Bravo2?" to which I responded, "Why didn't you ask Bravo2 that question?" I sensed that, whatever he was doing, Damon2 knew that Bravo2 was doing the wrong thing but didn't say anything other than, "I hate to lose you." I told him that I hated to leave but thought it was time for me to move on. "I'll get you on tomorrow's flight and let your site manager know that you're coming." I thanked him and once he had left my room, I started to pack my stuff so I could go to Bagram.

The next morning, I went to say goodbye to every member of the team, including Jay, Charlie2, and Bravo2. Having already heard about my departure, Echo2 asked me why was I leaving. I told him the same thing I told Damon2, "I think you should ask Bravo2 for an answer to that question." When Echo2 asked me if another linguist was coming to replace me, I told him I wasn't sure, but suggested that Damon2 and/or Bravo2 would probably know.

As concerned as I was about the team's leadership—especially since I wouldn't be in Ghazni any longer, I wanted to not only say goodbye to my team members, but to Jay and Charlie2 as well so that I could tell them what had to be said before I left. Never being one to keep something that needed to be said to myself, I went to Jay's room first. "You're like a brother to me," I told him, "just like Delta2 was for what he sacrificed to protect America. If I had to give my blood to save your life, I would do so, not only for you but every member of our team, including Bravo2 and Charlie2. I am here to ask you not to misrepresent America by treating every villager as if they were part of the Taliban. Everyone in Afghanistan looks like Taliban, but that doesn't make them one." Jay's response was simply, "Whatever, Nas," at which point I ended our conversation, saying, "Goodbye, good luck, and thank you for your service to our country, Jay."

Then I went two rooms down the walkway and knocked on Charlie2's door. He wasn't there, so I went to the kitchen but he wasn't there, either. I finally caught up with him in the bathroom. The first thing he said was his usual, "GOOD TIMES!" I told him what I told Jay who, like Charlie2, was a young Special Forces soldier, probably in his mid-20s. Since it was their first time in Afghanistan, they were both ignorant about the Afghan culture, which was part of the reason they behaved like they did. Unlike Jay, Charlie2 didn't really have anything personal against anyone. "You're a very brave man," I told him. "I observed every single move you made on every single dismounted mission in which we've participated. If I had to, I would've taken a bullet for you." Charlie2 smiled when he responded, "Oh yeah? Well, thank you, bro." And then he hugged me. But I wasn't finished with him yet. "I'm not saying you don't love America, but I believe I love the country more because I chose to be an American while you were simply given the gift of America at birth, which is why I believe I understand its value more than you do. It's okay that the leadership on this team is not as strong as it should be. I see other fellow team members taking advantage of that poor leadership by not doing what's right, like Jay, Bravo2, and you are doing—something I consider and believe to be totally un-American.

I don't want you to misrepresent America as your personal ego because the U.S. is much more important than that." With that, I wished Charlie2 the best of luck before leaving the bathroom.

The following day Damon2 gave me a ride with all my gear back to the airfield for my flight to Bagram. Upon my arrival there, I was asked by my company to simply write a brief two-page summary of what happened in Ghazni and why I was back in Bagram. After writing the report and meeting with the director of the company (who was very helpful, just like everyone else who worked for the company), I was then referred to the company's deputy director of operations in Afghanistan, who asked me what I wanted to do. I told him exactly what I wanted to do by asking him, "Are you just asking me or are you really going to offer me what I really want to do?" My question surprised him. "Nasrat," he said, "what is it that you're going to ask for?" I didn't waste any time responding. "Since the very first day of my arrival, I've been telling the company that I want to join Special Forces in Kandahar. Can you send me there?" My question to go to Kandahar clearly shocked him. He looked around the office until his eyes rested on the only other two people sitting at their desks across from him. "Why don't we get more linguists like Nasrat?" They shrugged their shoulders as he continued by telling me what he wanted me to do, which wasn't what I requested. "I want you to go on this assignment to Khost (a Province in eastern Afghanistan bordering Pakistan). The unit that I am assigning you to is going on a dismounted mission, which I know you like. Within the next couple of weeks, they need someone like you for those kinds of missions. You'll like it there, Nasrat; but if for any reason you don't, come back and I'll send you to Kandahar for sure." Knowing now that it wasn't up to me, whether I liked it there or not, once I was assigned to a unit I couldn't just walk away from it. So for him to say I could come back if I didn't like it, in which case he'd send me to Kandahar, made me very happy. So I was on my way to Khost.

One of the old abandoned Soviet era's school with the only single text book in Farsi language I found. Dayak district, Ghazni province. August, 2009.

Down time spent with Jimbo who loved to be entertained.

The discovery of an anti aircraft machine gun mounted to the bed of a pickup truck from the time of the Soviet invasion of Afghanistan in the 1980s.

Myself on the ATV, Delta2 directly behind me leaving the
compound we had raided the night before.

Boarding the Chinook. The decency of Capt. Alfa made us all walk toward the
mountain to find a landing zone that would not destroy the poor farmer's crops.

The 14 hours of walk to rescue our soldiers from being left
behind in a open field for easy ambush by the bad guys.

My arrival at the open field to take the two American and
two Polish Special Forces soldiers back to safety.

Standing at the entrance of Motel Taliban, where me and one of the
ANP officer were almost left behind by our team leader.

Taking the famous Abdul Bari to his before-praying wash.

CHAPTER SIX

November 24, 2009: Bravo Company, 425th Brigade Special Troops Battalion, 4th Brigade Combat Team (Airborne), 25th Infantry Division, Camp Clark, Eastern Afghanistan

I T WAS MY SECOND TIME on a C130, flying from Bagram to FOB Salerno, Khost Province, arriving around 3:00 in the morning. I waited at the airfield in the pitch dark for someone to pick me up, but no one did. I called the site manager for FOB Salerno, who knew nothing about my arrival. He gave me the number for the movement person who would pick me up and then take me to what I assumed would be my transition tent. I called and woke him up as well. He ultimately arrived and took me to a large, real concrete barracks, the first I'd seen since my arrival in Afghanistan. The large room was divided into six separate living quarters. Each section was partitioned with plywood about six feet high. While you couldn't see anyone or anything except the light showing at the top of the partition, you could hear everything going on in each of the five other areas.

The barracks looked nothing like a transition facility; it resembled permanent living quarters for linguists from the States. At the time of my arrival, there were only two other linguists, both in their 70s. One introduced himself to me (primarily to complain and criticize his fellow linguist who lived next to him, which is the norm in Afghan culture), while the other shied away for a day or two.

It was common practice for linguists to approach, complain, and criticize other linguists, especially if they were from different ethnic groups. Everyone wanted to buddy-up with others in their own groups. Despite their ethnic background difference—one being Hazara and the other Pashton—they had one thing in common: They listened to a local Afghan radio station in the same room, one in Pashto, the second in Farsi. Being in their 70s, listening to Pashto and Farsi news on an AM radio, with weak frequencies and mostly static, was annoying not only to me but to them as well. Not knowing their situation for a couple of days following my arrival, I couldn't help but wonder if this was how it was going to be from now on—stuck in a room with two 70-year-olds who not only listened to static all day but constantly complained to me about one another, not to mention both of their nightstands covered with a variety of prescription drugs just to keep them alive.

Two days after my arrival, my site manager called, asking me to meet him in his office the next morning at 9:00. He told me I was going to meet my POC, Platoon Sergeant, who looked forward to meeting me. The site manager also told me that my POC would arrange for my transportation to the COP (Command Outpost), which was located approximately 50 miles from FOB Salerno. Despite the difficulty involved with moving around from place to place, I was glad to find this out—staying with two 70-year-old linguists who not only couldn't speak much English, but also tried to stay alive by taking all the prescription medication they could—was only a temporary stop for me.

When I arrived at my site manager's office to meet my POC, I noticed another linguist also assigned to the same unit I was. At 9:00 on the dot, our POC arrived. Once our site manager introduced us to him, the first words out of his mouth were, "So, which one of you is coming to us from Special Forces?" Before I could respond, my site manager pointed at me. "It's Mr. Kakar." The sergeant shook my hand and said, "I was told that you like Special Forces and their tactical dismounted missions." I smiled and told the Sergeant, "Yes, Sir, I do."

My fellow linguist, who happened to be new to his job, was quite nervous, just like I was on the first day I arrived at the Special Forces compound in Ghazni. Being an ethnic Hazara, he looked frightened about being assigned to Khost Province, especially to a unit that was about to go on a dismounted mission in a Pashton-dominated region.

After our introduction to the Platoon Sergeant, he told us he would make the necessary transportation arrangements—he didn't specify if we were flying or riding in a convoy—to our unit at Camp Clark, not too far from the Pakistani border. I thought that since we both had more than six duffel bags of gear, it would be impossible for us to go with a convoy, so I was relieved when we boarded an early morning flight to Camp Clark the following day.

Flying from FOB Salerno to Camp Clark provided an incredible view of the terrain, the most beautiful that I had flown over since my arrival in Afghanistan. Unlike Ghazni, which was mostly rocky mountains and sandy deserts, Khost was much greener. The weather in December was mild just like it was in my hometown in southern California.

As we approached Camp Clark for landing, the base was incomparable to any other I had seen since arriving in the country. Everything below looked beautiful and brand new—like we were flying over a small town somewhere in America.

After landing at the base, my fellow linguist and I waited for someone to pick us up from the airfield. Besides us, there was also a soldier on our flight who was returning from his R&R. Within 10 minutes, a huge military cargo truck arrived. The captain in the truck was picking up the other soldier but asked if we were the linguists assigned to the LLVI (Lower Level Voice Interception) team. When we responded in the affirmative, he offered us a ride to our compound, and then both soldiers helped us load our bags into the truck and drove us through the base.

As we drove from the airfield to the compound on the other side of the base, the soldier driving the truck introduced himself as the captain of the unit to which the LLVI team was attached. While en route, I couldn't help but notice that the road was new, as were all of the buildings, and a parking lot full of new Ford trucks, military vehicles, and heavy-duty equipment, all painted tan with the ANA logo and Afghan flag (black, red, and green), which were also new. It was so amazing and very difficult for me to believe that such a well-built and equipped military base existed in Afghanistan! When I made a comment to the captain about how beautiful the base was, he agreed, adding, "It's a good example of the American taxpayers' money hard at work. But unfortunately, it's only for the ANA to live in; the compound for Americans is outside the base, and most of us live in tents. For some of us, if we're lucky enough, maybe a B-hut (barracks-hut), which is a construction of plywood, divided up into two, four, six, or eight separate rooms with a common walkway down the center or on the left. A typical B-hut usually has two entrances and two or three fluorescent lights in the ceiling." I was surprised and told him, "Well, that's not fair for our soldiers to have to live in tents or B huts while the ANA soldiers get to live in the concrete buildings." The captain agreed but pointed out that there was nothing he or I could do about it.

Coming from Special Forces where everyone had their own private room with cable TV, Internet, refrigerator, dresser, desk, and a chair, was like going from the Ritz Carlton of the military to a Motel 6. There were 16 of us in this one room: three linguists, two LLVI soldiers, and a whole squad of soldiers between the ages of 19 to 23. Camp Clark served as a staging base for the LLVI unit when they were not on dismounted missions. My assigned COP was a remote base called "Deysie" where we would be leaving on dismounted missions within the next couple of days. It was now the beginning of December 2009, and snow was predicted for the next couple of weeks. Our mission was originally planned for December 4 but was postponed for five days because we all needed to stay put for the time being. In addition to the other new linguist and me, there was one other linguist already with the team who was due to leave on PTO (Paid Time Off).

Besides me, this was the first time I was with a unit that had two other linguists from the States of which—in a 100 percent Pashton-dominated province and district—spoke or understood absolutely *no* Pashto whatsoever. There really wasn't any work for all three of us linguists to do at this time of the year, especially in the mountainous region of Afghanistan.

As we sat and waited for the mission to happen, I got easily bored with nothing to do. I asked the sergeant of the LLVI team if, during this downtime while we all waited, he could find me other jobs to do besides translation. Unfortunately, his response was, "Nas, you're going to have to wait until we go on the dismounted mission." On December 10, we were told that our upcoming mission would be on the 12th, which was also the day I was supposed to leave Camp Clark for my upcoming PTO (December 19) to fly to the States from Bagram.

Moving around from place to place in Afghanistan does not provide sufficient time for someone to leave on a set date, at an exact time. It would take at least a week (and, in some cases, even longer) for me to get from Camp Clark to FOB Salerno and then to Bagram. In my case, so my gear would not get lost or left behind, I had to take it all back with me to FOB Salerno just in case the LLVI team left to go somewhere else. Of course, I was asked by my site manager to bring all of my gear with me to FOB Salerno before I left Camp Clark. As anticipated, I was put back on a flight by my POC in Camp Clark for the return to FOB Salerno. Upon my arrival there, I had to wait four days before I could get a flight out.

Coming back from my PTO, upon arrival in Bagram I was immediately ordered to return to the LLVI team to which I had originally been assigned while at Camp Clark. I arrived back at Camp Clark on January 17 only to find out that the LLVI team was going to be called back to FOB Salerno at month's end. As it turned out, the LLVI team to which I had been assigned, and was prepared for, never went out on a mission. It was almost the end of January, and we linguists had not done anything but eat, sleep, and watch movies for the entire six- to seven-week period of time we'd been in Camp Clark. Of course, my fellow linguists loved it that we hadn't gone on any dismounted missions. The first mission had been called off because of the weather, and the current brigade that the LLVI unit was part of was leaving Afghanistan and preparing to change its responsibilities over to its successor unit, the 3rd BCT (Brigade Combat Team), 101st Airborne Division.

In order for the two Brigades to change responsibility, everyone in the outgoing brigade had to return to the main base (Salerno) from all the COPs throughout the province. Since the weather had prevented us from going on dismounted missions, we could have left Camp Clark even earlier than January 31.

Once we were back at FOB Salerno, we (the two other linguists and I) were given rooms at the barracks amongst the military personal, rather than being taken to the transition tent. Unlike my fellow linguists, I loved to be around military personnel because almost every one of them followed the rules of the barracks, and also loved America and was as willing to die for it as I was.

Our outgoing POC introduced us to his replacement, Sergeant Wilder, who would be in charge of the new LLVI unit. Wilder told us that it would be at least three to four weeks before we could start doing missions or any other kind of work, so we should just kick back and relax. As soon as another LLVI team was put in place, we would be advised where our team would be going. Knowing there wouldn't be any missions for the next few weeks, I could sense the joy and happiness in the other linguists' faces and could tell that they were definitely ready to party after hearing the good news! The experienced linguist repeated the good news to the new linguist, "There will not be anything for the next couple of months, so just kick back!" However, just like everything else in the military, the more experienced linguists knew everything about how the military worked. If they said there would be no missions or work for the next three to four weeks, more than likely it was going to be much longer than that. As my buddy Echo in Ghazni used to say: "In the military there's a saying: 'Hurry up and wait,'" which, since we had no choice, is exactly what we were doing. During the first 10-day waiting period, my schedule was:

10:00 PM to 6:00 AM:	Sleep
6:00 AM to 7:00 AM:	Shower and get ready for the day
7:00 AM to 8:00 AM:	Breakfast
8:00 AM to 9:00 AM:	Call Laila in the States
9:00 AM to Noon:	Go to the library
Noon to 1:00 PM:	Lunch
1:00 PM to 2:00 PM:	Kick back and do nothing
2:00 PM to 5:00 PM:	Workout at the gym
5:00 PM to 6:00 PM:	Shower and get cleaned up
6:00 PM to 7:00 PM:	Dinner
7:00 PM to 10:00 PM:	Watch a movie or two
10:00 PM	Go to bed

While I hated the mission delay, since Khost was a lot warmer than any other part of Afghanistan in January, I will admit that my daily routine made me feel like I was in an all-inclusive resort. I can still remember that feeling. On the other hand, the only things the other two linguists did that were different than my own "resort schedule" were skipping the gym and the library; instead, they added extra time to sleep and socialize with the local linguists on the base. Ninety percent of other linguists' conversations primarily included bragging about having jobs doing nothing while earning a paycheck. All of the local linguists were notorious for this kind of conversation because in their minds, getting paid for doing nothing was the best job one could ever hope to have.

Fortunately, I didn't see it that way. It was not fair or right to be sitting, doing nothing, while getting paid to do so by the U.S. With that thought in mind, I went to Sergeant Wilder and asked him if he knew of anyone on the base who might have need for my help as a translator. Wilder asked me for my cellphone number and told me if he came across anyone, he'd let me know. Needless to say, I was disappointed when I didn't hear anything from him. However, my faith in God grew ever stronger the next morning when I checked my emails because it contained one I felt was sent from Heaven above, answering my prayers to get me out of here so I would have something to do.

It was, in fact, a general email from our company to all linguists, in essence stating that the Marines in Helmand Province in southern Afghanistan needed linguists for an upcoming mission: the Marines' most important dismounted mission to Marjah District on February 15, 2010, to remove the Taliban from their stronghold in an area where the Afghan government had no control. More specifically, the email stated that the Marines needed a Cat II linguist to volunteer for the 45-day combat mission. After reading the email, I realized that I might not be qualified for the mission since it specifically called for a Cat II linguist. Nonetheless, I didn't want to waste time sitting at the computer, reading other emails, while someone else might beat me to this opportunity. So, I immediately closed my email and hurried to my site manager's office to tell him that I was ready to go to Helmand where the Marines needed help

"But, Mr. Kakar," he said, "you're a Cat III. I don't know if they will take a Cat III, but I will certainly call our headquarters in Bagram and ask." I waited as patiently as I could while he called the Bagram office and spoke with the person in charge of the reassignment, telling him that I wanted to volunteer for the Marines in Helmand. I was relieved when my site manager was given the okay for me to go as soon as possible. He added that in order for me to volunteer there, I had to get permission from my current POC, Sergeant Wilder, since I was officially assigned to his unit.

When my site manager said he'd go with me to talk with Wilder, I gratefully accepted his offer. As we entered Wilder's office, we saw my previous Platoon Sergeant and my POC from LLVI, Camp Clark, who were getting ready to go home. My site manager explained that I was willing to volunteer for the Marines in Helmand for the next 45 days, and asked for permission for me to do so. Everyone in the room looked at me while my previous platoon sergeant said with obvious admiration, "That's so awesome for you to do." Wilder told my site manager, "Yes, he can do that. I don't think we'll have anything going on by April, anyhow." To say I was elated would be an understatement!

After saying goodbye to everyone in the room, my manager and I returned to his office so I could have my new assignment/movement orders signed for me to be moved to Helmand Province. I learned that in order for me to go to Helmand, I was probably going to make at least four stops before I got there. In other words, I would have to go to Bagram first, and then fly to Kandahar. From Kandahar, I'd fly to Camp Leatherneck in Helmand. Once in Helmand, the Marines would then decide where and when I would be going. Well, even though I knew how much of a hassle it was to move from one base to another, I wasn't thinking of that or any other problems I might confront along the way. I was more focused on how I could be of use and contribute to the Marines' mission in Helmand. Since Helmand was similar to my hometown of Kandahar, I knew the language and culture more than I did any other parts of Afghanistan. By comparison, there isn't much difference in the Pashto dialect between Helmand and Kandahar versus that between the English used in New York and New Jersey.

My site manager told me not to take any of my gear because the Marines would provide me with one of their own uniforms once I got there, to which I told him that, "I was planning *not* to return to Khost unless I absolutely had to; I wanted to take all of my belongings with me so I didn't have to come back if the Marines wanted me to stay with them in Helmand for good." My site manager reminded me that I was already assigned to the Brigade in Khost and was only going on a TDY (temporary duty) assignment, which was not to exceed 45 days after my arrival at Camp Leatherneck. Despite my site manager's suggestion, I insisted on taking my gear with me—just in case—despite all of the hassle I would encounter when going through the four transition tents. Knowing that I was going to take my belongings, despite his advice, he told me to pack my stuff and be ready for tonight's flight to Bagram, if there was space for me. I knew this was going to be a tiring trip but, as an American, I felt obligated to the U.S., not only because I was getting paid, but primarily because I was going to be able to do something for my country and my native land.

As I was packing my bags, my two fellow linguists came to my room, initially under the guise of discouraging me from going to Helmand. When they realized they weren't going to be able to talk me out of going, they offered to help me pack. I thanked them but declined their offer. Before leaving my room, one of the two linguists said, "Kakar Saheb, I think you're doing something very dangerous. You know the Marines always go on dismounted missions to fight, especially in Helmand where most of the Taliban are. You could've stayed here and relaxed and got paid for doing so." I ignored him as I continued to pack my bags. When he realized that I wasn't going to respond, they turned to leave me room as I said goodbye and wished them well.

On my second attempt, I was able to leave Khost to the airfield on my way to Bagram. Upon my arrival there, I was picked up by the movement manager and signed up immediately for the next leg of my flight to Kandahar, which was later that same day, I was able to avoid staying at the transition tent. I wandered around the terminal for about 15 hours until my 2:00 AM flight. Upon my arrival at Kandahar Airfield around 3:00 AM, I found it much more crowded and disorganized compared to Bagram. Besides that, waiting for more than two hours while I smelled the stench of raw sewage until sunrise was almost unbearable. Since no one had ever provided me with any information regarding my movement from Kandahar to Helmand, I couldn't leave the terminal to find out if anyone might be picking me up.

Unlike most of the other bases in Afghanistan, where you could access entry with your U.S. military card, Kandahar was controlled by NATO. In order to leave the terminal, where you had access to everything on the base (e.g., like the DFAC and gym) one needed an access card, which was issued upon arrival by the ISAF (International Security Assistance Force). The card was only issued in the event that someone from my company or the unit—if I had been assigned to one in Kandahar—would come to the terminal to help me get the card. Traveling for 48 hours without sleep, smelling the stench, and not knowing if anyone would come to pick me up, was making me even more aggravated and nervous. When I called the main office in Bagram to see if anyone would be picking me up, I talked with one person who connected me to another, etc., and so on, No one knew who I was, why I was in Kandahar, or why was I calling Bagram at all.

After a myriad of calls and arguments with everyone on the other end of the line, I finally was connected with someone who agreed to pick me up. Not only was I hungry, but as we drove toward the transition tent, my weariness and headache worsened. The sandy dust from the desert and the bright sun from the east were hitting me squarely in the face, and the smell of the stench was also getting even stronger. Since I was not assigned to a military unit in Kandahar, but simply transitioning to Helmand, ISAF only issued me a temporary transition pass.

Since I hadn't been issued a card to the DFAC, one of the movement people gave me a temporary pass so I could access the DFAC for breakfast. The variety of the food served at the DFAC in Kandahar was much different from that at the DFACs in Bagram, Ghazni, and Khost. None of the employees were local Afghans—or perhaps I should say Kandahari. They were either from Nepal, the Philippines, or India. Perhaps the people in Kandahar didn't want to work for the foreigners because of the strong Taliban existence in the area, or because NATO was probably not interested in hiring the local Kandahari by going through the hassle of screening people coming in and going out of the base.

Anyhow, as it turned out, a single day's transition through Kandahar turned into five days of misery and confusion. Getting out of the Kandahar Airfield to go to Helmand was just as difficult and hellish as trying to get in.

CHAPTER SEVEN

February 17, 2010: Camp Leatherneck, 2nd Marine Expeditionary Brigade, 3rd Radio Battalion Detachment, Helmand Province, Afghanistan

I ARRIVED AT CAMP LEATHERNECK with two other linguists and after a long wait, I wondered if it might have been easier to have requested being picked up by the movement people. I finally decided to call the site manager to find out if he could make arrangements to pick us up at the airfield.

As I introduced myself over the phone, he obviously already knew who I was, but told me I was supposed be in Helmand five days ago. Even though I explained my situation in Kandahar, he told me that I was supposed to have been coming in direct from Bagram to Camp Leatherneck, but someone somehow made the mistake of sending me to Helmand via Kandahar. Although it was one huge misunderstanding by everyone from the company I worked for, I had to pay the price by being assigned to a transition tent in Kandahar for longer than necessary.

We were finally picked up and taken to the company offices, which were located in one single Connex, where three company employees, each with their own desk and a chair, were cramped into an 8x19-foot Connex space, with room for only one other person to stand. However, so as to stay out of the cold and dusty wind, we all three managed to squeeze into the Connex's limited space as everyone tried to be taken care of first. One of the other two linguists was in his mid-60s, the other a young woman in her mid-20s. While we waited, after introducing himself, the site manager called out, "Which one of you is the volunteer from Khost?" Before I could say anything, the other linguists turned around and looked at me, with expressions on their faces reflecting that they clearly thought there was something wrong with me for volunteering for the Marines. Nonetheless, I raised my hand and, while smiling at the other two, said, "That would be me." The manager looked at me with his own smile and said, "Have you heard of a place called Marjah?" I told him that I had not only heard of it, but I had been there when I was in my early teens while living in Afghanistan back in the mid-'70s. "I also know why the Marines are going there," I said, "to liberate the people of Marjah from the Taliban oppression." Shaking his head, the site manager then asked, "Knowing all of this—that the Marines are going on this combat mission to fight, you still volunteered anyhow?"

Obviously, the site manager wasn't there to encourage and thank me for volunteering; instead he was attempting to discourage me from what he knew I was getting myself into. When I told him that I couldn't wait to get there, the other linguists looked at me as though they, too, thought I was crazy for volunteering for a mission that could possibly turn out to be deadly. Seeing that I was serious, the site manager suggested we meet my Marine POC, who was looking forward to meeting me. Before we left the tiny Connex, he sarcastically asked me so the other two linguists could clearly hear, "By the way, can you leave us a vial of blood so we can inject it in most of the other linguists, who always refuse to go on *any* dismounted missions, so they can turn out to be just like you?" I wisely did not respond.

We walked out of the offices to a pickup truck that was parked in front of the Connex. I was introduced to Captain Carter, who was in charge of receiving all the linguists for the Marines' operation at Camp Leatherneck. After the introductions were made, the first question the captain asked me was the same question posed by my site manager a few minutes earlier. Not knowing why I was here in Helmand in the first place, the captain probably wanted to know if I was willing to go on dismounted missions, since most of the other linguists refused to do so. "Do you know anything about Marjeh and why the Marines are going there?" asked the captain.

"Yes, Sir, I do. The Marines are going there to kill the fucking Taliban." Smiling at my site manager, the captain also chuckled aloud. "This is what I'm talking about! Get me more linguists like him," he said as he pointed at me. "Well," the site manager responded, "we didn't just assign him to the Marines; he volunteered for this mission." Smiling again, the captain said, "Knowing that Nas volunteered is even better because it tells me that he won't quit on us after he goes on his first dismounted mission."

Captain Carter helped me load my gear in his truck and then drove me to the first row of linguist tents to see if he could find me a bed. Having been deployed to Helmand Province, it was a very busy time for the Marines, so every tent and every bed was occupied, but the Captain continued to diligently try to find me a vacant bed. As we went from tent to tent, he told me that since I got to Helmand late by a couple of days, the dismounted mission I was supposed go on had already left, so Captain Carter had to send another linguist—who wasn't happy that he had to go—in my place, so that was the only bed available for me to use. Before the captain left my tent, he assured me that he would get me to Marjeh with the next unit being sent there within the next week or so.

Linguists were constantly moved in and out of the tent I was in almost on a daily basis—primarily because the linguists who were taken on dismounted missions by the Marines did not last long. Most of them either quit after the first mission or got fired. Camp Leatherneck was just like most of the other bases I had been to. Except for Bagram and Kanadahar, Camp Leatherneck was very dark at night, too. In order for anyone to get around the base, they had to use their own, handheld flashlight. In addition to the darkness, everything from bathrooms to DFACs, sleeping quarters to where we worked, and everything else in between, was operated from tents.

Mid-February was cold and windy, which created dust storms practically every other day. On occasion, the desert wind would be so strong, so much sand hit you in the face that you couldn't even open your eyes. Or, if you took a shower in the shower tent, by the time you got back to your sleeping tent, you needed another shower.

While waiting to be sent to Marjeh with the next platoon of Marines, I told the captain that if he ever needed help with other translations in the meantime, I'd be happy to do so. As it turned out, the following day Captain Carter came to my tent and asked me if I could help him in his office, translating Pashto to English. Of course, I went with him and worked the whole day there. Unlike most other linguists, every one of the Marines in the office liked the way I performed and complimented me personally for working so tirelessly without any complaints or bitching. I told them I was simply there to help the Marines to understand the Afghan culture in any way I could to accomplish our goal. There were six or seven other linguists who had worked in this office with the Marines for a couple of years, but their work performance was inferior to mine.

The military office operated 24/7 with three eight-hour shifts: 00:00, 08:00, and 16:00. Since I had willingly volunteered for his unit, Captain Carter offered me whatever shift I wanted. When he told me that, I responded that he could give me the shift that other linguists didn't want, which surprised him. "Why are you so easy to work with?" he asked. Jokingly, I responded "That's not what my wife tells me," which made him laugh. I didn't know if I was just easy for the captain to work with or whether the other linguists, by comparison, were more difficult.

The Captain told me that I could pick whichever station I wanted. I worked there for about a week. At the end of that week, I asked him what had happened to the dismounted Marjeh mission I was supposed to go on. He told me, "Knowing that you're a Cat III, I would really like to use your expertise in the office, if I may. I know you came all the way here to go on dismounted missions, but your expertise in Pashto and English translations is far more valuable to the success of our mission if you would stay with us here at the base because your presence would be greatly beneficial to accomplishing our overall mission." I told him that I'd be happy to do so until the first of April, so he could use me any way he wanted so that I could help the mission to succeed. Relieved, he said, "Thank you, Nas, not only for volunteering but for understanding our needs." I said to him he really didn't have to thank me because I was honored to be helping the Marines in any way I could.

Since the Captain had given me the option, I chose the midnight 00:00 to 08:00 shifts, which the other linguists avoided, and started working them immediately. A week later, a master sergeant came over to advise me that Captain Carter had told him all about me as far as my passion for dismounted combat missions was concerned. He said that he was sending a unit out for a three-week dismounted mission going to the District of Bakwa which was either in the northwestern part of Helmand Province or perhaps in Farah Province west of Helmand, and asked if I wanted to go. Of course, I told him I'd be more than happy to join the unit.

At the beginning of March 2010, it was my third week at Camp Leatherneck. Once realizing that the mission would take place sometime toward the latter part of the month, I asked Captain Carter to be sure to let the master sergeant know that my assignment with the Marines was only temporary, until the first of April. If I went on this mission, I couldn't help but be curious what would happen to my assignment with the brigade in Khost. Even if other linguists understood the locals, most would treat them just like my fellow linguist, Najib, had in Ghazni Province when we worked with Special Forces. No matter where I went or who I worked with, it was always a win-win situation for all of us: the Marines; the local Afghans, if I went on dismounted missions; and me, for being so happy that I could help the American military and local Afghans or, even better, both.

Nothing was more important to me than my ability to translate something that could lead to life-saving situations, whatever nationalities were involved, whether they be American, Afghan, or any of the other coalition forces who were involved in the freedom and prosperity of my native people—all were equally important.

Since Captain Carter worked during the day and I worked the midnight shift, we didn't see each other in person. So, one day I found a note on my desk from him requesting that I meet with him at 9:00 AM before I went to bed after my work shift. Since I never went to bed right after getting off of work anyway (instead, I went straight to the gym until 11:00 AM), right after breakfast before going to the gym I went see the captain as requested. He thanked me for coming and then asked, "What would it take for me to keep you here with the Marines permanently for as long as you like? Everyone is so impressed with your performance and knowledge of both the Pashto and English languages." I was obviously amazed and quite pleased by the Captain's comments. "Two things I must first request, Sir. First, for my permanent transfer from my assigned unit in Khost. Second, although the posted sign in the tent specifically reads: 'Quiet, no lights, 24-hour sleeping tent,' it is nonetheless very noisy during the day, and none of the linguists have any regard for the sign or respect for others who work the night shift and, therefore, must try to sleep during the day." Needless to say, I was delighted when Captain Carter said, "Once I receive approval to keep you here, I can provide you with a room." With that, I told him, "Then, I'm all yours; as a matter of fact, when I left Khost, since I was only coming here for a TDY as a 45-day volunteer, despite my site manager's request not to take all of my gear, I brought it anyway, just in case of an opportunity like this. So, fortunately, I not only don't have to go through retrieving my gear, but I can also save time going back and forth." Captain Carter smiled when he said, "Well, be assured that I'll do everything in my power to keep you here; and, if I'm not able to do that, I'll get my major involved to do everything possible *she* can to ensure that you stay with our unit." I couldn't ask for anything more!

As time went by, as I walked around the base, I liked the Marines more and more. In an effort to coordinate my transfer as quickly as possible, Captain Carter repeatedly was in touch with everyone in my company for me to stay with the Marines—sadly, to no avail because I had already been assigned to a brigade in Khost, and they wanted me back just as much as the Marines wanted me to stay in Helmand.

I only had a little more than two weeks left to be with the Marines, when I suddenly got very ill with intense, nonstop coughing. I was admitted to the Marine medical facility where the doctors ordered chest X-rays. Diagnosis: upper respiratory infection. Not only was I prescribed antibiotics, but I was also isolated with orders not to go anywhere or be in contact with anyone else until I had finished taking all of the antibiotics. The doctor told me to report back if my symptoms didn't improve within two days, in which case they would fly me to an advanced medical facility in Bagram.

In addition to everything else that was operated out of the tent, so was the Marines' medical facility. My illness was probably caused by a combination of lack of sleep (because of the constant noise made by the other linguists) and the nonstop dust storms with temperatures between 35 to 45 degrees Fahrenheit. Despite the hardships involved with being with the Marines, the experience was rewarding because I knew they were so appreciative of my work.

I worked with three other permanent Cat III linguists on the midnight shift, all of whom were assigned to a separate tent for Cat III linguists only, since they weren't sent on dismounted missions. While I was originally brought in to go out on dismounted missions, I was put into the Cat II tent where most of the linguists were in their early 20s and could care less whether others got any sleep or not. They just wanted to have fun socializing and listening to their native Afghan music as loud as they possibly could. While I tried to sleep, a linguist on another side of the tent would ask another on a different side of the tent to turn up the volume so everyone could hear the music at the same time. It was a nightmare!

Despite sleep deprivation, when I was feeling better after my bout with the upper respiratory infection, I had no choice but to confront the young man who always played his music too loud. I also did so based on the assumption that his buddy at the other side of the tent would hear me as well. I asked the man to either shut off his music or use his headphones so I and others who worked the graveyard shift would not be disturbed. Not only did the young man say he would *not* stop but he was offended that I had asked him to do so. In order for him to justify his actions, he told me that in the year he had lived in the tent no one else had *ever* complained about his native music but, in fact, loved the variety of songs he played.

From the way he responded to me, I could sense that he didn't like me being there in the first place and was certain of it when he sneered, "Why would the Marines even bring you here? This is a Cat II linguists tent only." As I had on the other numerous occasions I had the distinct displeasure of staying in tents like this, I argued that, "It doesn't matter what your level of clearance is—Cat II or III—it's the rules of the tent that need to be followed," pointing at the sign the Marines has posted on the inside of the door that read: "24-hour sleeping tent, no lights or noise." The linguist shrugged his shoulders and scoffed. "The Marines didn't put that sign on the door; we did," he said, looking around the room at the other linguists. Needless to say, even in my current state of mind, him telling me that he and the other linguists had put the sign up—a sign that they themselves didn't even obey—made me laugh aloud. "What the hell are you talking about? Are you fucking crazy? You're telling me that all of you (waving my arm around the room) put a sign up with rules that none of you even fucking follow? What? Do the rules on the sign only apply to me? That when you all go to sleep, if you ever do, I'm not allowed to make noise or turn on the lights, is that it?" He stared at me silently, mumbled something to himself, and then turned and walked away.

Only people without a rational argument would walk way. When he was out of my sight, I turned off all the lights and attempted to sleep. The music stopped playing, but in order for them to have their revenge—which in the Afghan society, where both sides can't win (in other words, it was either them or me), is the cultural thing for them to get back at me in other ways. To make sure I stayed awake, three of the linguists took a football outside and started playing in the narrow, 10-foot space between the rows of tents. Their purpose, of course, was simply to irritate me even more by hitting the tent with the football. To add salt to the wound, every time they walked in and out of the tent, they slammed the door as hard as they could to ensure that I wouldn't be able to go to sleep.

Since one cannot argue with ignorance, I left the tent and headed to the office to find the master sergeant so I could tell him know what was happening in the tent. He was nice enough to ask one of the three Marine corporals, who were guarding the front entrance to the office, to accompany me back to the tent to help me move my gear to the Cat III tent.

The next night when I went to work, I was approached by one of the linguists in his late 70s, who never came to work on time. Not only was he always late by at least 30 to 45 minutes, but he would also leave work early by the same amount of time. To make matters worse, he took 30-minute breaks every two hours while he was supposed to be working (even though he couldn't speak or understood Pashto or English). Therefore, during his "eight-hour shift," he only worked four hours, and he spent those four hours mostly talking with the other linguists or young Marines in the office who, out of respect for his age, called him "uncle."

One night, "uncle" approached me to tell me that because he was the oldest linguist, which made him believe that he was a big deal in our office, he needed to be respected as such. As an Afghan, of course, his definition of respect was that he always had to have the last word. Like Jabar, by using his age to take advantage of others, he wanted to dictate the "rules." According to him, he was also the first linguist who started working with the Marines when they arrived in Helmand two years ago.

During this conversation with me, since his English was very weak and he had no knowledge of Pashto whatsoever, he asked me in Farsi, "Mr. Kakar, in the minds of the Marines, in the past month you have lowered our standard of work significantly. Because you work more, the Marines now expect the same from us. Not only did you create a problem for yourself, but you created one for us as well." From what he had just said, it was obvious that he had spoken for the other linguists in the office without their consent, although it was also apparent from the number of heads being nodded as the old man spoke, that most of the linguists agreed with him. Because he chose to stand behind me while he talked, I turned to face him. "So, if I understand correctly, you want me to do what you're doing? Just come here and not only waste my own day, but disrupt everyone else who wants to work?" He laughed. "Do you believe that all linguists in Afghanistan really want to translate?" In response, I told him that I could only speak for myself because I didn't really know anything about him or the other linguists, or why they were in Afghanistan. "If I was like you and most of the other linguists," I added, "then why would I volunteer to be with the Marines in Helmand? I could've just stayed in Khost, eating and sleeping all day long." Although he wanted to continue the conversation, I told him that even if he didn't have anything to do, I did and, to make my point, turned my back to him so I could go back to work.

Not to be silenced, "uncle" said with great pride that, "Even back in the old days, when I worked in an office in Kabul, all we did was socialize with each other. There was no one to tell me what to do. I'm not worried about anyone here, either—in fact, I could care less about this job." This is how things worked in Afghanistan in the past, then, and still today. Most linguists—or perhaps I should say, most Afghan government workers—don't want to work for anything except the money, because that's how they were trained. I was simply labeled as being disrespectful for arguing in a rational way by trying to reason with him, while most other linguists avoided saying anything because if they did, in the Afghan culture, they would be considered disrespectful by talking back to an elder.

According to one of the other linguists, who was also sick and tired of the older man's behavior, he had never had the courage to tell the elder that he had never had a real job in all his life and, therefore, didn't know what real work was. The elder had immigrated to the United States after the Soviet invasion of Afghanistan, where he worked at a flea market on Saturdays and Sundays for 30 years until he got the job as a linguist. According to one of the younger linguists, he was also being pushed around by the elder and taken advantage of simply because he was younger. According to what the elder had told one of the younger linguists, when he went to work, all he and the other Afghan vendors at the flea market did was socialize all day (and they called that work!). The older man's work habits reminded me of my own father-in-law, who had once said to me, "Dear Nasrat, you guys are working much too hard, which is the American way, and that isn't good. Since our work in Kabul was mostly socializing and drinking tea, the day would go by before we knew it." Unless they decide to work for themselves and believe strongly, Afghanistan will never be a productive society. No matter what the international community tries to do to help them succeed, it will never happen.

My time with the Marines sped by too quickly. Just as much as I wanted to stay in Helmand, they tried diligently to keep me there. As I have felt throughout my deployment, circumstances can sometimes prevent people who are trying to contribute, not be able to do so. In my opinion, there are often times when decisions should be made at the battalion or company levels. Since soldiers on the frontline are sent to fight and, therefore, only be able to assess the situation on the ground firsthand, those same people should be able to make those kinds of decisions in a place like Afghanistan, a very difficult place to culturally understand by the West.

Before I left the Marines to return to my permanent assignment in Khost, Captain Carter, who was also on the last leg of his deployment to Afghanistan, would also be leaving soon. One day, he came to my desk to present me with a Certificate of Appreciation from the USMC. Accepting it with much pride and appreciation, I told him, "Sir, I was here for one thing and one thing only—our country's mission—not for the recognition, but I appreciate it very much nonetheless." The captain nodded his understanding. "Everyone in this office that has known and worked with you," he said, "knows exactly why you were here, and they have appreciated your dedication to duty, which is why they would like to present you with this certificate."

Volunteering with the Marines, and at the age of 47, I had no clue whether I would have survived on their dismounted combat missions. I only volunteered knowing if I could do it with Special Forces at the same age, then I saw no reason for me not to try it with the Marines as well, especially since I wanted it so strongly. Before coming to Helmand, the only former Marine I had ever known was my dear true friend and fellow American, Delta2, who had made the ultimate sacrifice for our country. By simply knowing him, I had every reason to believe if I had had the chance to tell him that I wanted to be with the Marines rather than being in the luxury of Khost, doing absolutely nothing for a couple of months, he would have urged me to do so. Although I didn't get to go on dismounted missions with the Marines, if Captain Carter and his team were happy that I was working with them, that was more than rewarding for me.

I strongly agree that the United States Marines should be the 911 emergency call response team for the problems of the world. Aside from knowing Delta2, an ex-Marine, one of my favorite presidents, Ronald Reagan, once said something about the Marines, which I will always remember because it played an integral part in why I decided that I wanted to volunteer for, and stay with them. Reagan said, *"Some people live an entire lifetime and wonder if they have made a difference in the world. Marines don't have that problem."* You were absolutely correct then, Mr. President, and what you said remains so today. I know it for a fact because I saw it in my dear friend, Delta2, and all of the Marines I had the pleasure of meeting and working with in Helmand.

Capt. Carter from the United States Marine Expeditionary Brigade presented me certificate of appreciation for volunteering to the Marines in Camp Leatherneck, Helmand province, Afghanistan. March, 2010.

CHAPTER EIGHT

April 4, 2010: TF RAKKASANS 3/187 BDT, FOB, Salerno, Khost Province, Afghanistan

AFTER A DIRECT, NONSTOP STOP FLIGHT from Helmand to Bagram, with a couple days' layover at the transition tent without any glitches, I was back in FOB Salerno, Khost Province. The LLVI team that I had once been assigned to was no longer there, so I was reassigned by my site manager to the new Brigade Combat Team—in other words, I was going to be working for the brigade directly, wherever and whenever an individual unit needed me. I was given back my room and again told by Sergeant Wilder to sit back and relax. They would let me know when they needed me.

This is precisely what frustrated me the most: Why would they do such a thing as bring me back all the way here from Helmand just to tell me to sit back and relax while the Marines in Helmand were in desperate need of linguists like me? Upon my return to Khost, I suddenly realized one thing that might have resulted in my return. As I had left Khost to volunteer for the Marines, the LLVI unit I was assigned to before I left for Helmand was also leaving Khost. My POC with the LLVI team had left a Letter of Continuity—a recommendation for the incoming brigade regarding my knowledge of the Pashton culture and language. A copy of the letter was also given to my company site manager, which was to be given to me upon my return to Khost.

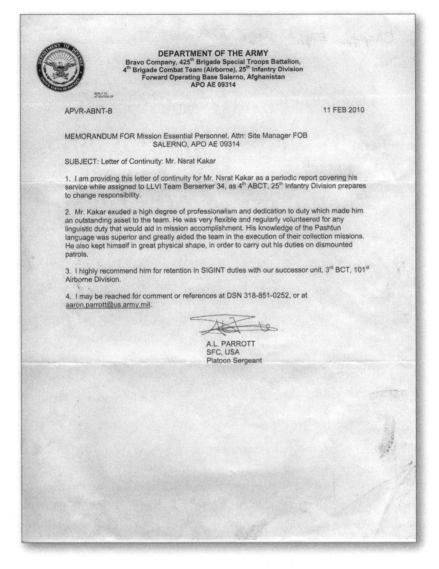

DEPARTMENT OF THE ARMY
Bravo Company, 425th Brigade Special Troops Battalion,
4th Brigade Combat Team (Airborne), 25th Infantry Division
Forward Operating Base Salerno, Afghanistan
APO AE 09314

REPLY TO
ATTENTION OF

APVR-ABNT-B   11 FEB 2010

MEMORANDUM FOR Mission Essential Personnel, Attn: Site Manager FOB
SALERNO, APO AE 09314

SUBJECT: Letter of Continuity: Mr. Nsrat Kakar

1. I am providing this letter of continuity for Mr. Nsrat Kakar as a periodic report covering his service while assigned to LLVI Team Berserker 34, as 4th ABCT, 25th Infantry Division prepares to change responsibility.

2. Mr. Kakar exuded a high degree of professionalism and dedication to duty which made him an outstanding asset to the team. He was very flexible and regularly volunteered for any linguistic duty that would aid in mission accomplishment. His knowledge of the Pashtun language was superior and greatly aided the team in the execution of their collection missions. He also kept himself in great physical shape, in order to carry out his duties on dismounted patrols.

3. I highly recommend him for retention in SIGINT duties with our successor unit, 3rd BCT, 101st Airborne Division.

4. I may be reached for comment or references at DSN 318-851-0252, or at aaron.parrott@us.army.mil.

A.L. PARROTT
SFC, USA
Platoon Sergeant

After my site manager handed me the letter so I could read it, he said, "So, you thought you could stay with the Marines in Helmand, but you didn't realize no one would like having to give you up so easily. This letter from the old team was probably the reason why this new unit didn't want to lose you, just like the Marines in Helmand wanted to keep you." I responded, "Well, since this unit in Khost didn't have anything for me to do, all I wanted was to do something helpful. I don't like sitting around doing nothing while there are tremendous needs for linguists in other places in Afghanistan."

I personally thought it was very kind of the POC to recognize my work by providing a letter of recommendation not only to the brigade, but also sending one to the company I worked for—which only motivated me more to help the military in order for them, in turn, to help my native people succeed.

The following morning after breakfast, as I walked toward the library, I ran into one of my fellow linguists from the States I had known in Columbus, Georgia, when we were waiting to be deployed to Afghanistan. He was sitting in front of the coffee shop as I passed by and called out to me. "Greetings, Nasrat! Come over here and tell me what you did in Helmand." I walked over to his table, shook his hand, and sat in a chair across from him. When he offered me coffee, I thanked him for the offer but told him I just had a cup with my breakfast. He started questioning me about the Marines, the linguists who worked with the Marines, their living conditions, etc., and so on. It seemed to be important for him to point out to me how poorly the tent conditions were for the linguists in Helmand. Everyone already knew how poorly the Marines and their linguists' living conditions were in comparison to what they were here in Khost.

When it came to living conditions, FOB Salerno was one of the best in all of Afghanistan. The linguist continued by saying, "You went all the way over there, for what? The dust storms and tent living conditions? Otherwise, what else did you achieve?" In other words, his real question was the same as many others had asked me: "Why is it that you always volunteer for all of these dangerous missions?" In order for me to make my point to this particular linguist—who was sitting across from me, smoking—I turned the question around. "Well, let me ask you this about the cigarette you're smoking. First, you give your money to buy them; second, you inhale the smoke into your body; and third, knowing that it will harm you, what are the benefits of you doing that?" He missed my point entirely. "What does my cigarette smoking have to do with you going to the Marines in Helmand, putting your life in danger, and not even getting paid extra for doing so?" I countered with, "Until you can tell me the benefits of smoking, I will not be able to make you understand the benefits of volunteering." The linguist shrugged his shoulders. "Well," he said, "I enjoy smoking." I responded with, "I am just like you in that I enjoy what I do by putting myself in danger so others can be helped or perhaps even saved." He still didn't get my point, and I no longer had the time to try and make him understand. As I stood to walk away, he insisted I stay a little longer and continued the argument by saying, "If you think what you're doing is making people feel good, then why aren't billions of people in the world doing it, like smoking cigarettes?" I sat quietly for a few seconds, looked him in the eyes, and (out of respect) told him goodbye and that I hoped he had a nice day. As I walked away, I could still hear him mumbling, "No matter how many Marines they bring, they will never be able to fix the problems in Afghanistan. All Afghans know this."

Not only was it boring sitting around doing nothing, it was also an immense waste of time. I went back to my POC's office and, as was my usual custom, told him if anyone needed any help with linguistic work, I'd be more than happy to do it. He thanked me and said he'd let me know. The very next day when I saw Wilder at the DFAC, he told me to see him in his office after lunch. When I did, he said that the chief in charge of the detention center on FOB Salerno could use my help interrogating detainees. He escorted me to the brigade's headquarters where I was introduced to the chief, who asked me a few questions regarding my interrogation skills and also wanted to know how many detainees I had interrogated in the past. I told him I had done more than 200 interrogations during the seven-month period I'd been working with Special Forces in Ghazni. This obviously pleased the Chief because upon hearing my answer, he said, "No more questions! Let's go to the detention center to introduce you to Staff Sergeant Karr, who is in charge of interrogations."

On the way to the detention center, the chief asked me about my experience with Special Forces and also said that Sergeant Wilder had mentioned that I had just returned from volunteering for the Marines in Helmand. He was shocked to hear how, at my age, I was able to do all of the Special Forces' physical work involved with dismounted missions, especially since I'd had no former military training or experience. I told him, growing up in the village as child in the terrain of my native land not only prepared me for the physical work, but always wanted to be a part of Special Forces, but now I'd ended up in Khost with nothing to do. Upon reaching the detention center, I was introduced to Staff Sergeant Karr who, after hearing all of the chief's compliments regarding my interrogation experience with Special Forces, asked the chief if I was going to be working at the detention center permanently. The chief told him that I was a Cat III linguist assigned to the brigade, and wanted to volunteer because I was bored sitting around doing nothing. So, if the brigade needed me anywhere at any time for translation duty, I wanted them to take me back and put me where I would be needed the most. Sergeant Karr said he definitely needed someone like me, as often as possible, who had gone through the experience of more than 200 interrogations with Special Forces. It was music to my ears when the chief told the sergeant, "Okay. Good. Go ahead, he's all yours." I was immediately given a work schedule of 8:00 AM to 2:00 PM the following day.

The next morning when I went to the detention center, I was introduced to the three interrogators with whom I would be working: Tyron, a male interrogator, and Regina and Laila, two female interrogators. Knowing the Afghan culture as I did, I wasn't sure female interrogators were a good idea since a male-dominated society, which was thought to be superior, rejects women to be of the same caliber.

My very first interrogation was with Sergeant Karr. I could sense that he had vast experience in the field and thought he probably wanted to try me first himself to see what interrogation skills I had. I would soon learn that because of the cultural differences, his interrogation skills were more "Stateside" in nature versus those that were used and could be greatly different in Afghanistan, technically and intellectually. With that said, I will admit that Karr was one of the best interrogators with whom I'd ever worked. Why would there be differences in the interrogation technique? Well, frankly, because there's only one country called Afghanistan, which makes its people more different than any other in the world. In other words, as any native of the country will tell you—you *must* be a native of Afghanistan to understand the Afghans.

As we were walking out of the room following our first interrogation, Karr's first words were that he had never before worked with a linguist who could be a linguist and an interrogator at the same time. I told him that I had learned a lot from my buddy, Oscar, with Special Forces. Some aspects of the interrogation with Special Forces were noticeably different from those used here at the detention center—not because of the interrogation tactics used by Special Forces but because of the circumstances under which we operated as far as timing and the number of detainees involved. When I was with Special Forces, very rarely did we have more than four to five detainees in our cells at one time. In fact, most of our interrogations were in the field during combat missions. The detention center here in Khost was operated more like a fully-staffed motel—20 rooms filled with the Taliban, and sometimes there were no vacancies, especially during the peak season from May to October, which was the "fighting season" for the bad guys. In addition to me, linguists were all Cat II, each limited to three interrogations per day. I didn't care because I could've done them nonstop, 24/7, as long as I could get in a couple hours of gym time between interrogations.

The facility was literally operated like a five-star motel regarding Taliban's treatment while in our custody. Moreover, it was an all-inclusive courtesy of the American taxpayers where the detainees not only didn't pay a dime for their stay or the amenities—which included three meals a day; all the religious freedom they required because we provided all the necessary tools for them to practice their daily rituals, including a copy of the Quran for each detainee; as well as medical treatment before and after their interrogation.

On my second day on the job, all of the other interrogators wanted me to be the linguist of their choice. Well, I knew it wasn't possible for me to be in four different rooms with four different interrogators, all at the same time. I wasn't in a position of choosing who I wanted to be with, and was also simply there to be part of anyone's team Sergeant Karr chose for me. Karr had selected me to be with whichever of the other interrogators had a high-value target detainee for interrogation. Two-thirds of the time, translating for an interrogator can be very difficult in order to ensure the effectiveness of the interrogation, especially when working with an inexperienced interrogator.

In addition to women interrogators, we also had two women linguists, which made it even more difficult for the interrogation to be productive. How can it be fair for women to perform interrogations when 100 percent of the detainees were Pashton males who would reject them just for simply being women, but an Afghan native woman, was a big "NO." The two female linguists, a native Pashton in her 30s, saw the detainees as fellow Pashtons rather than being able to see them as either innocent or criminal. The second female linguist was a Tajik in her 60s who had no knowledge of Pashto while working at the detention center where 100 percent of the detainees were Pashton. Not only didn't she speak or understand the language, she always assumed that every detainee was a terrorist simply because they were Pashton.

In addition to the two females, there was a young Tajik male linguist in his early 20s and an elderly Hazara in his late 70s, in fact that same person whom I met at the barrack who always listened to the static Afghan radio station all day long. The young Tajik, who was brought up in America, didn't know much about the Pashton language and culture, let alone how to interrogate elder detainees who rejected him because of his youthful appearance, as well as the fact that he was Tajik. On the other hand, the ethnic Hazara linguist could speak and understand perfect Pashto because he'd been raised in southeast Afghanistan where Pashto is the primary language.

Every interrogator wanted me to be their linguist for the interrogations because I was an American who treated the detainees with respect and dignity. While the other linguists tried to score points with one another because of their ethnic differences, (i.e., like the Pashton female linguist, who only saw the detainees as her fellow Pashtons; or the young Tajik male and female linguists who not only not spoke enough Pashto to understand the detainees, but considered them as terrorists before they were even interrogated; or the native Hazara, who always told the detainees they were crazy Taliban bastards) each considered themselves as Afghans, but none acted other than what they actually were: Pashton, Tajik, and Hazara.

Therefore, my question would again be: In order to be productive, could these interrogators perform their jobs, and why were they all willing to use me as their linguist? None of the American interrogators knew if the linguists were asking the actual questions to which they wanted answers. I knew for a fact—after hearing it every time the linguists got together—that they would always talk about their translations and how they made things up during the interrogations by not asking the detainees the right questions and vice versa as far as what they told the interrogators regarding their answers. According to the linguists, they did that for two reasons: (1) to make the interrogation shorter because they wanted to get out of the room as soon as possible or, in the case of the Tajik linguists, they couldn't speak enough Pashto, and/or (2) in the case of the Pashton linguists, they were sympathizing with the detainees because they were Pashtons.

During our break in front of the detention center, where all of us linguists would sit and wait for the next round of interrogations, we challenged each other about who was capable of killing more flies. I failed to kill any flies every time my fellow linguists challenged me, which seemed to bring them great joy. So, one day during our fly killing competition, as we were chatting, I casually asked why they weren't translating what the interrogator was asking of the detainees, and vice versa. Their combined answer was, *"Shoma ba khyalim har chezey key interrogator porsan kard tarjoma my konin?"* ("You really translate everything the interrogator asks?"). My thought to their response was, *If these linguists don't want to translate, how could the interrogators and the detainees communicate so they could understand each other? Is that why we can't succeed in Afghanistan, because we don't understand the people that we're trying to help?* Probably. Seeing other linguists either not doing their job correctly or not being able to speak the language made me work even harder by putting in longer hours and volunteering every time I had nothing else to do.

One day, while working from 8:00 AM until 11:00 PM, my head was exploding from all of the translating I had been doing. I was so tired I couldn't hold my head up any longer and needed to rest, so I went to my room where I fell asleep immediately. Suddenly, I thought I was dreaming when I heard someone calling my name. As the voice grew louder and closer, I woke up to realize I wasn't dreaming. Tyron was calling me from outside, through the open window, trying to wake me up. As I got out of bed and opened the door, Tyron asked me, "Hey Nas, we just got a high value target detainee. Karr sent me here to ask if you can come over right now to help us with the interrogation, because you're the only one we can use for this one." Since I was so tired, I asked Tyron, "Since they haven't done any other interrogations today, why can't the other two linguists be asked?" Shrugging his shoulders, Tyron said, "Nas, I'm just the messenger. Karr asked me to come, so I did. You're the best linguist, which is why we can't use anyone else for this particular detainee." Therefore, tired or not, I told him, "No problem, Tyron. Tell Karr I'll be there in ten minutes." It's not that I didn't want to go, I was just really exhausted and was concerned that I wouldn't perform as well as I should.

It was around 1:30 in the morning when I arrived at the detention center. Karr not only thanked me for coming, but was very apologetic for waking me up so late in the middle of the night. I assured him it was not a problem. We were done with the interrogation of the high-level detainee by 3:00 in the morning. Before I left to return to my room, Karr told me

I could come to work tomorrow at 2:00 PM instead of 8:00 AM. Since breakfast is the most important meal of the day for me, I told Karr that I'd be awake at 6:00 AM anyway, so could report for work at 8:00 as usual. Whichever time I chose was alright with him.

When I went to work the next morning, as had become the norm, every interrogator wanted to use me as their linguist, while the other four linguists merely looked on to see who would get me. This kind of treatment also made me more vulnerable amongst the other linguists, who already made it perfectly clear that they didn't like me for being who I was. Since every interrogator wanted me and it wasn't possible for me to help them all at the same time, Karr assigned me to one of the young and inexperienced interrogators who needed someone like me to help during the interrogation. While this particular interrogator had been on interrogations with other linguists, she didn't like any of them to be in the interrogation rooms with her. After our first interrogation, she told Karr that she needed me to be her linguist on every interrogation. Not only did she like my style of translating, as well as the fact that I was a Cat III, I was also able to help her analyze more detailed information on any particular case she chose.

One day before we started our daily interrogations of the detainees, Karr, Regina, Tyron, Laila, and Aron, who were all ready to start the day, would usually check the schedule sheet on the front door of our office to find out which interrogators were going to work with which linguists and in what room with each detainee. Oddly, today there was no schedule on the front door. Just before my assigned interrogator and I were about to leave the room, Tyron looked at Karr and asked, probably jokingly to get his point across, "Why does she (referring to Laila) have to have Nas on every interrogation? Aren't the rest of us able to use him as well?" Karr responded, "Why, do you need him?" Argumentatively, Tyron responded, "Well, I'd like to use him for one of my detainees that I can't get anything out of by using any of the other linguists." Laila interjected, "So, then, you want me to use the other linguists who are unable to translate for you so you can get something out of your detainee? If that's the case, then how can I possibly get what I need from my detainee with those same linguists?"

As it eventually turned out, I ended up going with Tyron on this one interrogation, which made him very happy. After our interrogation,

Tyron said he couldn't help but notice that the detainee was more open and willing to talk than he had been with any of the other linguists he had used in the past with this particular detainee. Unlike the other linguists who always did the same thing—simply translating what they personally thought was important—as an American, I treated the detainees just like every interrogator had treated them before they were accused of being criminals. I was gentle but could be harsh, if necessary. I was angry when they lied to me just as I smiled when they told me the truth, which is why most of the detainees would rather be in an American's custody than their own Afghan security forces, where they would lose not only everything financially, but their dignity as well.

Despite the fact that the detainee and linguist alike came in contact with the infidel Americans, they were nonetheless shocked by how humanly we treated them. In fact, they would occasionally ask me why the Americans not only smiled at them, but treated them medically before and after each interrogation, which most of them loved. Afghanistan is culturally and completely the opposite of the West, because the Afghan government officials treat their civilians not only in a disrespectful way, but also abuse them physically. Most Afghans in general would love our way of treating them, but their suspicion that all Americans were infidels will always exist there for as long as Afghans are influenced by others, even if those others happen to be within their own country or perhaps, in some cases, even within their own tribes and family members.

Afghans only treat you nice if they want something from you. So, again, Americans are between a rock and a hard place when it comes to how we should treat them. As much as I loved working at the detention center with the other interrogators, my time with them turned out to be very short when Sergeant Wilder called me to his office and asked me if I would be willing to go on a dismounted mission to the Paktika Province where one of the LLVI teams needed a linguist. With no questions asked, I agreed to go. Within 20 minutes from the time we spoke, I was packing to go as soon as possible.

As I started to pack I couldn't help but think, *I've only been here in FOB Salerno for a little more than a week, and here I am packing my bags, moving out again, and headed God knows where or for how long—yet another hassle of moving from place to place. I like working at the detention center, despite every interrogator using me to the max, while most other linguists sit on their asses all day, doing nothing.*

As we drove toward the airfield so I could catch the flight, I remembered that I had forgotten to say goodbye to Karr. I asked Wilder before he dropped me off at the airfield if it was possible to stop by the detention center so I could say goodbye to everyone, but because Wilder didn't want me to miss the flight, he said he'd take care of it for me. Before dropping me off at the airfield, Wilder told me there would be someone waiting for me upon my arrival at FOB Sharana.

Flying over the high-peaked, green luscious mountains of Paktia Province, we approached a new airfield with a runway long enough for a C17 to land and takeoff. Sharana is the capital city of Paktika Province in eastern Afghanistan, which borders Pakistan to the east and Kandahar Province to the south.

I arrived in Sharana around 1:00 PM local time on a Chinook filled with soldiers. By 3:00 PM, everyone else had been picked up by their unit. I was the only one left, and there was no one in sight who appeared to be there to pick me up. When I called Wilder to inform him of my situation, he told me to wait at the airfield; someone would come to pick me up. At around 4:00, I saw a white Toyota pickup truck coming toward me and then pulling over, stopping next to me. Two young, six-foot tall soldiers got out of the truck. One of them asked, "Since you're the only one here, are we correct in assuming that you're Mr. Kakar?" Acknowledging that I was indeed Mr. Kakar, they introduced themselves, "Hi," one said. "I'm Specialist Thunder, and this is my buddy, Private First Class Hero." As we shook hands, they apologized for the confusion of being so late in picking me up. They then helped me load my gear in the back of the truck and we were on our way toward the barracks where I would be staying for the night.

As we were driving through the base, it reminded me somewhat of Camp Clark except this place was at least ten times bigger. There was a lot of construction taking place, from the building of runways to the construction of various structures and paved roads. I had never seen so many earthmoving vehicles like this anywhere in Afghanistan before. It looked exactly like ground zero or perhaps, better put, an entirely new city.

I sat in the backseat. Hero (who was in his early 20s) drove, and Thunder (in his mid-20s) was in the front passenger seat. They both questioned me regarding my abilities to carryout dismounted missions. They were probably thinking to themselves, *not another one of these fifty-year-old linguists who hates to go on missions*!

The first question Thunder asked me was, "Are you afraid of going on dismounted missions?" I told him, "Nope, not at all. In fact, I actually like going on dismounted missions." Thunder immediately looked toward Hero and said to him with a big smile on his face, "Now that's what I'm talking about," nodding his head toward me in the backseat. "We have someone who is actually *willing* to go on missions! Outstanding!"

I told Thunder that not only did I like going on missions, but I had been on 53 dismounted combat missions with Special Forces in less than eight months. Thunder was thrilled because his unit had a difficult time finding linguists willing to go on dismounted combat missions. I told them that they would *not* have any issues with me in that regard. Thunder said he was glad to hear it because the three linguists prior to me were either afraid of going or they didn't understand the language once his unit arrived at its destination. Even those who spoke the language would say that they didn't, just so they could be bumped off the mission.

I wasn't sure whether Thunder was trying to prepare me for the worst or if he was simply trying to test me by telling me that his unit had lost three linguists in the past two weeks because of all the fighting in the District of Yahya Khel, to which we were assigned. When I asked where in the hell this scary place called Yahya Khel was, Thunder told me it was about 35 miles southeast of FOB Sharana. According to Thunder, the first linguist had simply quit because he was afraid to go on dismounted missions. The second linguist was in his late 60s; his inability to communicate with the team resulted in the death of the platoon's medic. The third linguist, who I knew personally from FOB Salerno, had also been sent to FOB Sharana. However, a week prior, as soon as Thunder told him that the unit was going to be fighting almost every other day, he quit while he was still at the airfield being picked up.

Not only did the third linguist quit before even going to Yahya Khel, according to Thunder, the linguist told them both that they could go to Yahya Khel to die if they wanted, but because he wasn't ready to die, he refused the assignment so he could return to FOB Salerno, where all he had to do was, eat, sleep, and smoke (and not necessarily in that order). Most linguists at the major FOB didn't do much; it was mostly politics, as usual. Most of the heavy work and combat missions were carried out by the brave soldiers of the U.S. military at small outposts just like the one that we were going to in Yahya Khel. Thunder was telling me all of this because he wanted to make sure I was prepared for the Yahya Khel District mission—not only to save me the hassle, but to also save them from the huge hassle of going to FOB Sharana to pick up and drop off linguists who weren't even going to put in the necessary effort to do their jobs.

Thunder told me he knew as soon as I told him I had worked with Special Forces that I wasn't going to quit like all the other linguists had done in the past. He also said that he wanted to tell me the truth about where we were going, and what I was getting myself into. Besides all the life and death stories they told me in the short amount of time since my arrival, Thunder warned me beforehand that there would not be any real food at the COP in Yahya Khel. Because of all the fighting in the district, our only limited supplies of food were MREs, canned food, and frozen stuff, which were air dropped from a helicopter once a week—but only if security permitted.

Since we were driving from FOB Sharana to the Yahya Khel District by convoy, I was asked by Thunder to pack some drinks and items of food like chips, cookies, and power bars while we were in FOB Sharana. They would come in handy, especially when we wouldn't get any helicopter drop offs because of the fighting going on at our combat destination. After hearing all of this, I was somewhat confused about whether Thunder was simply pulling my leg or if he was actually serious. Thinking to myself, my main concern was whether we were going to starve or if Thunder was just joking to scare me.

I soon learned that Thunder wasn't joking when I saw all the other soldiers going to Yahya Khel packing up with all the food items they could fit in their vehicles before we departed FOB Sharana. I was also warned to make sure that I had my seatbelt fastened securely at all times while we were in armored vehicles. The road we would travel was one of the heaviest bombed roads, which is why it had been given the name "IED Alley." In many places, physical scars were visible throughout the 35 or so mile stretch.

The first five miles of the road were newly paved. However, as soon as we drove away from FOB Sharana toward the Yahya Khel District, the same road that had been in the process of being repaired and repaved had been abandoned, either by the contactors (because of security threats from the Taliban) or perhaps they got paid and could have cared less if the remaining 30 miles were completed or not.

It took us more than two hours to get to Yahya Khel on the 35-mile stretch of road. Oftentimes, for security purposes (e.g., not wanting to get hit by an IED), we drove off the road into the countryside until we got stuck in the sand, and then we would return to the road.

After many twists and turns, our bumpy ride was finally over when we arrived at the center of the Yahya Khel District, one of the poorest places I had ever seen. I was shocked; I never imagined that there was poverty to this degree in Yahya Khel. Since the phrase "Stone Ages" didn't really apply, I can say instead that the people I saw were still living in the "Mud Ages," primarily because everything was made out of mud and tree branches. I couldn't help but ask myself, *Why are our guys even here to begin with? What is it that we want to build here or protect?* Well, according to everyone on the compound—from the local linguists to the ANA officers—the center of this district had been taken by the Taliban in December 2009, which resulted in the killing of the sub-governor. Everyone else who worked for the Afghan government and survived the attack had run away. The Taliban had virtually taken over the entire district in only a couple of days. At the request of the Afghan government, we were to recapture the district from the bad guys.

Upon my arrival, I learned that the platoon, with the help of the LLVI team who were sent to this District to fight the Taliban, had taken the district center back from the bad guys. The Americans had now turned the district center into an ANA compound. In addition, our guys were also in the process of building an ANP compound adjacent to the old district center. There were about 50 Americans and 20 ANA officers cramped into this six-room compound with windows half covered with sandbags for protection from the bullets. There was no running water or bathroom. In fact, our "bathroom" was a 20x40-foot deep hole in the ground where all the garbage and human waste went. The good thing (if you can call it that) is if we didn't have much to eat, we didn't have much human waste or garbage to contribute to the "bathroom." However, from time to time we somehow managed to create waste, which was burned every morning. We also had no shower or any other area in which to wash; the only water we could use to clean ourselves was water from the wells, which the ANA didn't have any problem using for drinking and cooking as well.

Because of the shortage of delivering supplies, we were provided with limited bottled water for drinking. The only other thing that we could use was mostly baby wipes for hygiene and other cleaning purposes that were sent to us in the care packages we received. As mentioned earlier, as for our supply of food, we had a single refrigerator Connex in which to store a one-week supply of frozen and canned food that was dropped off to us from a helicopter when it was safe to do so. But the Connex would get empty within the first couple of days because the ANA guys would steal the food every time they got the chance to do so. For breakfast, we got frozen scrambled eggs, which were ready to eat. All we needed to do was take some of the well water, boil it, then drop the bag of frozen scrambled eggs into the hot water until they melted. Once they were melted, we'd pull the bag out of the water and dump the eggs on a ready-to-serve tray. Everyone lined up for breakfast and loved it. Well, frankly, I'm not sure they "loved it," but they really didn't have any other choice. Because of my high cholesterol, I couldn't have the scrambled eggs anyhow.

I always found other things for breakfast, like green tea from the market outside the compound. I asked one of the local interpreters if he could get me some green tea from the market, which he was kind enough to do for me. As I tried to pull money out of my pocket to pay him for the tea, he refused to take it but merely walked away, only to return an hour later with a half-pound of loose green tea. Before taking it, I again offered to pay him, but he was hesitant to take my money and said it was alright with him if I didn't pay him for it, which is the normal thing to do in the Afghan culture. Just as him not taking the money was a noble thing to do by Afghan standards, it would have been equally wrong of me not to pay him for it. Confusing, eh? Well, it's Afghanistan; so, when in Afghanistan, do as the Afghans do.

Who would have guessed that half a pound of loose green tea mixed with gravel, sand, dust, donkey manure, and everything and anything else one could find in Yahya Khel would cost me 10 American dollars? At least the donkey manure was probably the least harmful since it all came from the same vegetation. After going back and forth, the linguist finally decided to tell me that it cost him 10 American dollars That's how much I was asked to pay by the local linguists and how they made their fortunes by charging us ten times more than what they had to pay when they went to the market for us.

I wasn't worried about the price of the tea because I wanted it and was able to get it. What irritated me was why someone would argue with me and not take my money in the first place, but then suddenly turn around and charge me ten times more than he had to pay for it, which is known as *"Da darwagho sala" or "Sala-E-Dorogh"* ("A fake offer you're not supposed to accept," both in Pashto and Farsi). Why do they do that? Simply put, because it comes with the territory in the Afghan culture.

The district center where we lived had three separate rooms for the Americans to share amongst the 50 of us. They were adjacent to each other; each room was of a different size. The room where our squad was staying (25x30 feet) was the smallest of the three. Our room's windows faced the main road that connected the marketplace with the village of Yahya Khel. The windows were blocked to their two-third height by sandbags strategically placed for our protection from small arm fire or grenades that the bad guys might throw into our rooms from the outside. There were about 18 of us in this small, cramped room with no ventilation whatsoever, except for the three uncovered windows, which not only didn't allow fresh air to enter the room, but did manage access for more dust and the stenches of human waste from the dumpsite along the roadside.

The bunk beds were made by the same soldiers who occupied them. Upon my arrival, there was hardly room left for anything else. The only vacant bed available was a top bunk located directly across from one of the windows. This particular bed would undoubtedly be a death trap for anyone who slept on it during battle. Scars of bullet holes were visible around the top bunk from the last fight. Of course, no one would be sleeping anyway if there were any shootings. As small and dark as the room was for 18 soldiers plus interpreters, the stench was overwhelming. Also to be considered was that the 18 soldiers and one interpreter hadn't showered for only God knew how long, which only added to the already, ever-increasing smelly surroundings.

Of interest to me is that most human beings, even those in the military (especially infantry solders like in this platoon), who have never been sent to the frontline, have no idea what these guys go through simply by the way they live, let alone fighting those who want to kill us. This was one hell of a "stench-filled" mission our young infantry soldiers were going through, on top of everything else they needed to do just to stay alive in the face of an enemy who loves to die.

When our guys went out on dismounted missions in this particular district, they would walk from one end of the district to the other, just to tempt the bad guys to attack us (if they were brave enough) while we were walking out in the open. This district contained more Taliban-friendly villages than I had ever seen since first arriving in Afghanistan. Very rarely would the Taliban attack us while we were on foot patrol because they knew if they did, that would be their last day on earth. Of course, there were some who were crazy enough to do just that—not because they were brave, but because they believed if they died killing the infidels, they would go straight to heaven. I witnessed sending my share of those who were willing to die for that reason, especially during my time with Special Forces. They all had their own reasons to die—some simply wanted to kill the infidels, while others were trying to meet the 72 virgins they had been promised.

While this platoon also provided training to the ANA and ANP, they did everything else on the compound. The first squad of soldiers would go on a dismounted patrol mission, the second squad would take guard duty in the tower to protect us from attacks, while the third had eight hours of down time. Every squad rotated every eight hours so we would have a 24/7 dismounted patrol and guard duty combined. While the ANA soldiers in our compound would hang out around the compound smoking, playing cards or volleyball, and drinking green tea laced with an extra shot of donkey manure, while the Americans did all the dirty work. Personally, I was honored to be with all of these young infantry soldiers who loved what they did—not only serving our country, but providing security for the Afghan villagers who don't have anything in common with these young American soldiers. I admired each and every one of them for their bravery, courage, and compassion toward the Afghan people, even under very harsh and hazardous living conditions.

Imagine, if you can, living life for a couple of days with no real food, no running water, no shower (hot or cold), and no heat or air-conditioning—not to mention having to wear the same uniform day in and day out in order to try to give others the chance to have the freedom we do. I felt fortunate that I was able to witness and live that experience, and see what our soldiers go through. What made it more amazing and heartwarming for me was that most of the soldiers in this platoon were between 19 and 23 years of age, which made me twice their age.

Within a week, I got accustomed to the smell, obviously not because it ever went away (and never will) but because I had the wisdom to overcome that particular obstacle that initially was almost intolerable. A favorite quote of mine comes to mind about wisdom...

*"God, grant me the serenity to accept the things I cannot change, the courage
to change the things I can, and the wisdom to know the difference."*
— St. Francis of Assisi

I felt someone pulling on my leg, while calling to me, "Nas, wake up!
Nas, *wake up!*" As I looked down from my upper bunk, I saw Sergeant
Patrick telling me to, "Get down from that fucking bed!" Not knowing
what the hell was going on, I jumped down to the floor while Patrick was
telling me that we were being attacked by the bad guys.

As Patrick, Thunder, Hero, and I worked as the LLVI team as an
attachment to the infantry platoon, Patrick was busy organizing our team
in the dark. At first, I didn't know what it meant by "being attacked," or
what the hell was going on with all of the shooting and yelling I heard
going on around the district center. After a barrage of intense shooting,
I immediately knew that some serious shit was going on. In fact, at one
point, it was so intense and shaky that I thought I wasn't going to make
it out alive. The bad guys were attacking us within a very close range of
our compound. I looked for my video recorder but, because it was so dark,
I wasn't able to locate where it was stored. Then, I tried to locate my flashlight but the rocket that hit the ground within 20 feet behind the wall of
our compound stopped me. It was at that moment that it finally sunk in
and I realized this was the real thing—this was not the time for me to sit
in this room without my body armor and helmet, so I pulled them out from
under the bunk beds and put them on. I also got Patrick's because he was
busy at the radio communicating with the platoon leader and monitoring
what was taking place.

The noise from the guns from the top of our roof was so loud and
intense, I couldn't hear what Patrick was trying to tell me. Every two
to three minutes, a grenade would hit the walls of our building, which
happened to be the only one in the whole district that was built from
concrete, with 12-inch thick walls, which were the only protection unless
grenades were thrown into our room through one of the windows. Our
building had rooftop access from one of the hallways next to our room.
As I heard and felt the panic emanating from every soldier who was
headed for the rooftop, I asked Patrick if I could go to the top of the

roof, too. "Are you fucking crazy?" he shouted. Needless to say, I took that as a resounding *no*.

The nonstop fighting, shooting, and yelling went on for more than 30 minutes. By now, I was deafened by the sound of bullets, I couldn't hear anything, even though Patrick was screaming and yelling, asking if I was doing okay. I nodded that I was while thinking, *If I die, because of our location, this is where it will be.*

The bad guys needed to get lucky by hitting our room directly; if they succeeded, since we were the only two people in the room to monitor the radio, Patrick and I would be killed. Everyone else had either gone outside the compound or were shooting from the rooftop. The intense shooting was finally over after 45 minutes. Unlike most other combat that I had been involved in, this was a totally different and more terrifying experience. The fact that we were stuck in a room—and a very small one at that—unable to see anyone, made it difficult and frustrating for me to handle. This was truly a very near-death experience. At one point during the shooting, when one of the rockets hit very close, I thought we were dead for sure.

I have learned many things from being in combat, but one in particular to which I'm sure others who have been in combat can also relate: On my very first combat mission with ODA, when Delta and the ANP officer got shot, it was frightening (to say the least) because it was not only my first time in combat, but also my first time seeing someone (in this case, Fox and Damon) trying to save Delta's life. Bullets flying from all directions made it even scarier for me to see. I kept thinking, *God forbid, what if one of the two gets shot?* That thought alone intensified my fear. But, at least on that mission, I was in the back of a Humvee and could see everything that was going on around me. Here, in the Yahya Khel District, I had no way of knowing how close our enemies were to us or when/if the rocket would be launched into the room. Once you see and hear so much of the shootings, in a way your mind becomes desensitized, and you're not as scared as you used to be. At least that's how I felt.

Being the only civilian, and the oldest of them all, surviving the attack was a milestone for me. On the morning following the attack, almost everyone in our squad was asking me how I liked Yahya Khel so far. Since they had been in situations like this before, but didn't know that I had been in combat with Special Forces before coming here, they thought I didn't react the way other civilians would who had never been in combat. I told them that it was not the bullets that were scaring me, it was the uncertainty of where those bullets were coming from. Almost everyone thought I would quit and go back home just like all the other linguists had done prior to my arrival in Yahya Khel. My issue was being scared during the attack, which would never have been the time for me to quit, even if I had wanted to do so. For me, once the shooting stopped, it was like nothing had happened, which was probably the reason why I never quit, despite all the combat that I had encountered up to that point.

Breakfast, and where I ate it, was the same every morning: an eight-ounce can of cranberry juice, a pot of green tea, energy candy bars, and a book. To get away from the smell of the dark room in which I slept, and so as not to interfere with those soldiers who were on guard duty the night before and slept during the day, I would climb on top of the roof. I constructed a small area at one corner of the roof where I had put up some sandbags high enough that they would cover me from any sniper attacks or from any shooting that might occur while I was having my breakfast and reading.

It was mid-April; on most days, the weather in Yahya Khel was very pleasant. All the trees were green and in full bloom, giving the whole valley a beautiful landscape. The usual high winds and dust would unexpectedly slap us in the face from time to time, but it wasn't the slap of the wind that bothered me the most—it was the smell of human waste not only from the side of the road but from the local market that would use our space as their outdoor "relieve center."

On days when we had no missions, I liked to sit on top of the roof and look toward the entrance of the compound to see who was coming and going. Every time I saw a squad of our soldiers leaving the compound on their daily patrol of the village (which, by the way, was the same village from which we were attacked in the middle of the night), I couldn't help but hope they would all come back alive. When I looked over to the roof of the building across from ours, where the ANA were staying, I would see ANA soldiers and their captain sitting, having their morning tea, smoking cigarettes, and talking on their cellphones in the heart of Yahya Khel where the locals struggled to provide even a single meal a day in order for their families to survive. Remember, too, that those people on cellphones were the very same people of the Afghan government who lived at the expense of the American taxpayers and the poor villagers of Yahya Khel, the same people from whom they were stealing and were supposed to be protecting.

There was another building—occupied by the ANP—to the east of our compound that was still under construction. The ANP officers sat on their roof to watch a group of local militia soldiers playing volleyball in the sandy courtyard below. While all of these restful activities were going on for the ANA and ANP soldiers, our brave American soldiers were changing shifts from their all-night guard duty to dismounted foot patrols for the next eight hours—not only to protect the Afghan civilians, but to be shot at every time they left the compound.

Besides watching the ANA and ANP on rooftops, getting paid for doing their recreational activities, I noticed another most important aspect of life in Afghanistan—people from all walks of life—walking on the dirt road below me that connected the village to the bazaar. There were elderly men with canes, who could hardly walk, women under their *boghra* (full body cover), young boys with no shoes on their feet, and skinny dogs with a missing limb, ear, eye, or tail. Some rode in their donkey carriages, while others took their livestock for their daily feeding, which always reminded me of my own childhood memories from Arghandab. But there were still others who were wealthy enough, by Afghan standards, to ride bicycles, and in some cases, motorcycles. Not only was this narrow, dirt road traveled by humans and animals alike, it was also used as a site for everyone to relieve themselves whenever necessary. Fortunately for them, it was quite a simple process because all they had to do was squat, alongside the road, do their business, and then just move on. Sitting on top of the roof watching poor people go back and forth in their struggle of everyday life just to survive, was probably the unhappiest thing I have ever had to witnessed. I did not see even one happy face.

As I was leaving the rooftop, one of the ANP officers shouted from his roof where they were watching volleyball, asking me in Farsi, *"Tarjuman sahab, dena shab Janga key board?"* ("Dear interpreter, who won the fight last night?"). Obviously, he wasn't asking about a boxing match on TV the night before. He was, of course, referring to the shootout between the Americans and the bad guys. I couldn't help but ask, "Who did you think should've won?" His answer: "Don't know. We never went outside." His last words speak for themselves because they indicated that he and his ANP buddies were hiding in their hole. Although the U.S., ANA, and ANP soldiers were attacked in two side-by-side compounds, the only people who fought back were the Americans.

Returning to my barracks, I saw that Private Eric was being punished by Sergeant Gayle, the squad leader. Eric was 19 years old—the only private in our squad who always fucked things up and got punished repeatedly, not only by Gayle, but everyone else in the squad. Unlimited pushups were Gayle's favorite punishment. Being a civilian, my problem with Gayle's form of punishment was seeing a soldier being punished by his commander to the extent that the soldier was pushed to tears. Eric would also sweat so profusely that, after having been out on foot patrol for eight hours, the double stench of sweat made the barracks all the more unbearable.

Young soldiers like Eric and his comrades go through hellish conditions to protect us *and* our country. I could feel Eric's pain by not only watching him do the seemingly unending pushups but especially from the fear he felt when going out on dismounted missions to get shot at and maybe even killed.

One of the main reasons for this platoon's dismounted missions was to go out to patrol the village 24/7 in an effort to pinpoint the enemy. On the other hand, the cowardly Taliban would only attack us when we weren't looking, when our guys were sleeping, or by hiding IEDs on the road to blow us up. Watching our brave soldiers going on dismounted missions every day, I couldn't resist going with them, despite the danger. So, one day I asked Patrick, my POC, if it was possible for me to go out on a dismounted mission with our squad. Since I was technically assigned to the LLVI team, not to the platoon itself, Patrick could not allow me to go without Thunder, Hero, or perhaps even himself.

Since I knew that Thunder and Hero liked going out on dismounted missions, I asked Thunder first if he would like to go out with the squad on the next mission. He told me that he liked the idea of going out because it was part of his job as LLVI to go on missions with the squad every time they went on patrol. In the past, the primary reason they didn't go most of the time was because they never found a linguist who wanted to go with them. When I told Thunder I would like to join Hero and him on dismounted missions, he told Patrick about my offer. He was elated and said he couldn't wait to send us out on a mission as soon as possible. However, in order for him to be able to do that, he had to ask the lieutenant, the platoon's commanding officer for our compound.

As it turned out, the lieutenant welcomed the news of me volunteering to go on a mission and came in person to thank me. Around 4:00 the very next morning, the lieutenant ordered two of the three squads to go out with three of us, so Thunder, Hero, and I joined the squads on their dismounted foot patrol mission to see if we'd get attacked by the bad guys. As with most of the other villages in Afghanistan, Yahya Khel was a valley of mostly flat parcels of farmland separated by tall tree lines surrounded by mountains.

We left the compound by walking through the farmland, which, unlike most other villages, didn't have any natural bodies of water. I couldn't help but wonder how all of the farms could be so green without visible signs of water sources.

Once we arrived deep into the farmland, we found several scattered, 10x15 mud huts. Not knowing their purpose, we peeked into one; we found gasoline-run water pumps were being installed inside the hut for pulling water from underground wells for farming purposes. Almost every parcel of land had its own mud hut, which was well covered. In fact, most of the mud huts were also used by the Taliban for their hideouts and sleepovers.

As we started to scatter throughout the farmland to take up security positions, the local farmers began showing up to work on their farms. Rather than being out in the open, for protection purposes Thunder asked me to go with him to put most of our heavy equipment on top of one of the mud huts that we'd use as our strong point for cover until our replacement squad showed up. The mud hut he had in mind was not only devoid of water (i.e., it had no water pump), but based on the trash that had been left behind, it was also obviously being used as a rest area for the Taliban. Once we were set up, everything was quiet until about noon, when there was the sudden *pop, pop, pop* sound of shooting in the distance. While they were walking to our location to replace us, our guys were being attacked by the Taliban—luckily, none of them was hurt.

As the shooting intensified, air support was requested. Within a matter of minutes, four Apache helicopters started circling overhead. By then, all the shooting had stopped. The Taliban was afraid of aircraft, so much so that as soon as they heard or saw it, they immediately stopped fighting and retreated to their rat holes.

Envision if you can that our guys were in their military uniforms, walking in the wide-open field so they could be seen from all directions, while the Taliban, who never had uniforms so that we could distinguish them from civilians, could easily attack our soldiers. With the exception of a few, most of our soldiers considered everyone to be a civilian until proven otherwise, which obviously made it very difficult for our guys to fight back.

When we had finished this mission, through our platoon lieutenant, Thunder was told to ask if I would be able to go on another dismounted foot patrol, this time to the village of Yahya Khel, which was about five miles to the north of the district's center from where our compound was located. Of course, I accepted the offer and we were ready to go within a couple of days.

As noted earlier, since breakfast has always been my most important meal of the day, these days breakfast consisted primarily of a power bar, which kept me going. No lunch was provided at the compound, and dinner was usually a pork chop or pasta with sausage, neither of which I could eat. Care packages/boxes sent to the soldiers from the States were brought to me to go through. I found all kinds of canned goods, chips, and other food items, which the soldiers always shared with me; I was honored that they treated me like one of their older uncles. They told me I was different from the other linguists, who never sat to talk or hang out with any of the American soldiers. They chose, instead, to either hang out with other linguists or the ANA officers on the other side of the compound. The guys in my squad also loved the fact that the first thing I did when I arrived in Yahya Khel was to put up my American flag in the barracks above my bed. Most of the other linguists from the States didn't want to hang out with the American soldiers because they wanted to avoid being criticized or even seen by the other linguists with an American or the ANA or ANP soldiers. To them, doing so was considered a crime.

One morning, after I had poured my first cup of tea, I started hearing small-arm gun shots coming from the market area around the corner. The sound was rapidly getting closer and closer to the center of the district. As I looked to my left, I saw ANA officers, including their captain, on top of the roof where they usually hung out, but this time they were there to watch the fighting. Rather than fighting for their own country, watching a fight between the American and the Taliban was entertaining for the ANA and ANP. It is then fair to say not only that the Americans loved their country, but at the same time protected it. It must also be recognized and acknowledged that the Taliban sometimes fought us face to face, not to defend Afghanistan, but to defend Islam.

Within two minutes of when the first shots were fired, six guys from our squad were up on our roof, each taking security positions, one at each corner behind the sandbags. As the shooting intensified, more and more of our guys started shooting toward the many tree lines that surrounded the center of the district, which gave the Taliban the advantage of seeing us while hiding where we couldn't see them. As our guys continued shooting toward the tree lines, I heard the ANA captain and his soldiers shouting at me from their roof, "Hey interpreter, tell the Americans to shoot toward the other direction where the wall is. There are a couple of Taliban hiding there." That really pissed me off to the point where I got mad as hell. Not able to keep quiet about it, I told the ANA captain and his soldiers, "What the fuck is wrong with you guys? Since you know where they are, why don't you get the fuck out there and shoot the Taliban yourself? " The ANA captain responded, *"Ban key ya bokona, ya baray chea amadan inja"* ("What the hell are *they* here for? Let them do it!"). Not only had this become one of my least favorite phrases used by the ANAs, ANPs, and NDSs in the entire Afghan culture, but it also made my blood boil every time I heard it, which was much too often. Cowards that they were, I don't think that the ANA or ANP ever realized that they always took cover behind American soldiers.

While the shooting continued, I went to the barracks to get my video recorder. With the recorder in hand, I turned to return to the rooftop when Sergeant Patrick, who was on the radio monitoring communications, asked me where the fuck I thought I was going. When I told him I was going back to the rooftop to record what was going on, he said he thought that I was fucking crazy and he would not allow "crazies" access to the rooftop. Although surprised by his attitude, I pulled out my recorder and turned it to the left on a top of the bunk close to the window so I could record what was going on. Once the shooting stopped, I went back to the roof to get a better look at what was going on. Looking down to the dirt road, I saw several ANP officers carrying a couple of local militia fighters who had been wounded—based on the blood I could see, one was apparently hit in the stomach, while the other had been shot in his upper arm. They were both being rushed into our compound to our team medics to stop the bleeding and patch them up as best they could. Within 10 minutes after seeing our medics, an American medic evacuation helicopter arrived to pick them up and transport them to the nearest hospital in FOB Sharana.

As I stood on top of the roof to see who was doing what to whom, and how, the helicopter circled to land and pick up the wounded Afghan militia soldiers. Whenever the helicopter showed up, almost ever local from the bazaar would surround our compound to watch what was going on. Despite the fact that our guys didn't know the bad guys from the good, as brave as they were, they still walked out of the compound to hold security positions in the perimeter of the open field so the medic helicopter could land. In addition to the brave soldiers who held security positions, there were four other equally as brave American soldiers exiting our compound, carrying two wounded Afghan militia soldiers on stretchers. As they walked through the crowd of locals to get to the wide-open field where the helicopter was, it was again an emotional moment for me to see what Americans were really made of and what they were capable of doing in intense situations like this. Despite all the shooting just minutes earlier, and seeing everything from a rooftop, I was still trying to make sense of it all. Besides the four American soldiers who walked out of the compound carrying two Afghan militia fighters, there were six other American soldiers holding security positions so the bad guys couldn't attack them. At the same time, there were five to six other Americans overhead in two helicopters, circling in a hot zone that could shoot them down while trying to land to pick up the wounded Afghan soldiers.

Watching this half-hour drama unfold from the initial sounds of the small arms shootings to the helicopter pick-up of the wounded militia fighters as they disappeared into the blue sky over the mountain ranges of Paktika Province in eastern Afghanistan was truly an unforgettable sight to see. Unchecked tears ran down my cheeks. I repeatedly asked myself: *What motivated them to leave the safety and comfort of their homes in America, not only willingly putting themselves in harm's way, but also agreeing to give up their civil rights to be soldiers for America?* Seeing 15 to 16 young American soldiers risking their lives to save the lives of people with whom they have nothing in common is a visual memory I will never forget.

While all of this was going on in the air and on the ground, the ANA and ANP officers watched from their own rooftop how the Americans were risking their lives to save the lives of their fellow comrades of the Afghan militia described in my mind by four words: "Truly beyond my imagination." This all reminded me of the evacuation of Delta and the ANP officer who were shot on one of our combat missions in Ghazni a year ago. Unlike the evacuation in Ghazni, however, the only difference between the two was that in Ghazni, it was pitch black in the total darkness of the night, versus this one that was taking place in the bright daylight, which made it even more emotional to see as it unfolded before my eyes. In the course of one week, we had already been attacked twice, unlike when I was with Special Forces, where we would go out on dismounted missions to say hello to the bad guys—a much different scenario than that taking place in Yahya Khel. The bad guys knew we were in the middle of their village and would come and "visit us" by attacking our compound at least twice a week. Because our compound was considerably smaller than others, with not more than 70 soldiers, including the ANA, we were an easy target for the Taliban to attack. Additionally, our geographical location, surrounded by farmland with tall tree lines on the north, made it easy for the Taliban to take cover after they attacked us. From the south side of the compound, we were getting attacked because of the bazaar and all of the shops—another secure place for the Taliban to hide and take cover before and after they attacked us. Strategically speaking, our compound was located in a very hostile environment, which was probably the main reason why the Taliban could attack us as often as they did.

After the second attack, we were scheduled for our dismounted foot patrol mission the next day to the center of Yahya Khel village. As I had to volunteer to go out with the others, the lieutenant had plans to meet not only with the village elders, but with the district's school principal and its teachers. The platoon had a truck full of supplies that had been brought into the district center from Kabul a year ago to be distributed throughout the school by the sub-governor, who had been beheaded, so the distribution had never taken place. Before we left the compound, the lieutenant asked me to check with the ANA captain to find out if he could get one of his military trucks and load it with the school supplies of books, notebooks, and backpacks. The ANA captain responded that it wasn't possible for the lieutenant to take one of their our military trucks because the Taliban would attack. "Nas," the Lieutenant said, "ask the captain what he suggests we do to get these supplies to the school." When I did as the he requested, the captain shrugged his shoulders and asked, "What do you want *me* to do? *You* guys brought this stuff, and now you're asking *me* to take it to the village?" It was apparent that the captain was more concerned about his personal safety and that of one of the ANA's or ANP's half a dozen trucks parked around the compound than helping us get the supplies to the school.

In order for us to carry out our humanitarian mission, we had to ask one of the local interpreters if he would go into the market to find someone with a truck that we could use to transport the supplies. He was finally able to find a person with an unmarked pickup truck, which we loaded. Soon on our way, we then walked to the village located about five miles north of the compound. Before we left, we prepared ourselves for a possible attack by the Taliban. Fortunately, however, we reached the village without incident, and the lieutenant started giving out the supplies. I had a backpack of my own filled with pens and pencils that I had carried with me every time I went on dismounted missions. It was given to me by my buddy Oscar when we worked with Special Forces in Ghazni.

Believe it or not, most kids liked the pens more than the books and notebooks. I found it very funny when a 10-year-old boy rejected taking a book or notebook, telling me instead that he had no need for a book because he didn't go to school, which is why he'd prefer a pen instead. When I asked the boy why he wasn't going to school, before he could answer for himself, an older man standing behind the boy kept tapping him on the shoulder, telling him to take the book from me. The boy turned to look up at the man. "But I'm not going to school." In a more aggressive tone of voice, the man told the boy, *"Za wam zay, aow ta wayay chea na zam. Wakaha ketab zeney wakah."* ("I said you're going to school! Now stop arguing with me. Just take the damn book for now.") This was another perfect example in the Afghan culture for an older person to tell their youngsters not to argue with them, but simply do as they were told, even if it was a lie. Out of fear, the boy asked me for a book, notebook, and pen—most Afghans, young or old, do things because they have to, not because they want to.

As the boy was about to walk away, the man told him, *"Hagha the sawda khatczhona ham yaw dana deway zeni wakhla"* ("I want you to take a couple of those grocery bags as well"), referring to the backpacks for school supplies.

We left the south end of the village and moved into the center where the school, mosque, and madrasa (religious school) were located. The mosque and madrasa were on one side, adjacent to one another, next to a cemetery. The four-room mud hut that had served as a school building was now empty, had no window coverings, and also faced the cemetery on the opposite side of the mosque.

Upon our arrival at the center of the village, from the size of the crowd that had gathered, it was apparent that the villagers knew we were coming. Further into the outskirts of the village, directly across from the mosque and madrasa, we saw 20 to 30 people attending a burial ceremony for three of the dead Taliban who had been killed the day before while fighting with the local militia, which was confirmed by one of the school teachers standing in the crowd to receive school supplies for his students. One of a myriad of things I never understood was how we could fight this war on terror when we, the Afghan Security Forces, and the local villagers knew that the people in the cemetery were attending the funeral of their fighters who had been killed (or martyred, as the Taliban called it) the day before, but we couldn't do anything about it, because our guys were not allowed to attack them unless they were attacked first. Obviously, this scenario always give the Taliban the home-court advantage.

Well, one thing I do not personally support is being in war for political reasons. However, if war is necessary for the sake of saving society, then the rules should be equally applied. For example, let's say two fighters are put into the ring for one apparent reason—to fight. If only one of the fighters is allowed to follow the rules of the ring, while the second fighter can do whatever he wishes, without observing the rules of the ring, who'd win the fight? Of course, the answer is obvious.

I had witnessed precisely what we were fighting for in the Yahya Khel District, where our enemy knew exactly who and where we were and when to attack us. But when we knew from time-to-time exactly where they were, we weren't permitted to attack them because we weren't being attacked first. Where's the logic behind that way of thinking?

On a short-term basis, our mission to the village was somewhat of a success in that we had been able to distribute school supplies, including my personal backpack full of pens and pencils. How many of these supplies would be put to good use by the children would always be an unknown.

On our return to the compound, I interviewed numerous village elders that we passed on the path—mainly, to learn for myself what was on their minds regarding what was happening in the their district. Some of them were reluctant to talk with me, not because they didn't trust me, but usually because other villagers might overhear them if they complained about anything or anyone. Fortunately, depending on their age, and when others weren't around, many of the locals told me what was on their minds when I primarily asked them a variety of questions concerning their micro-situations, especially since most Afghans never think of anyone or anything other than themselves or their immediate surroundings. I always asked them what they thought about the Americans being in their district and how they were being treated by the Afghan Security Forces and government officials (e.g., like the sub-governor of Yahya Khel). A majority of the young people liked that the Americans were in their village, primarily because of the handouts, while most of the elders always complained—not because of the Americans, but because the Afghan officials were corrupt and physically abusive, which lead them to believe that the Americans were the reason the Afghan Security Forces were in their village in the first place. I could understand the corruptive aspects of the Afghan government officials, but when they told me about being physically abusive, I didn't understand why they would complain since most Afghans are physically abusive by nature. I also wondered why they would say Afghan government officials were being physically abusive when the Taliban used the same abusive, physical approach. To find out for myself, I asked one of the village elders if he could explain the difference between the physical abuse of the Afghan government and that of the Taliban. The elder gave me a very short and simple answer in Pashto (which I opted to immediately translate into English), "Physically being abused by the Taliban is the Islamic way. Physically being abused by the government is the infidels' way." Being younger than the village elder, not to be disrespectful, I knew there was no way for me to argue or try to convince him otherwise that physical abuse should never be allowed—whether to a human or an animal.

On another instance, I interviewed a villager and recorded our conversation. This particular villager liked the Americans but not the Afghan officials. I asked for specifics about what he didn't like, and he explained the ex-sub-governor had taken a parcel of his farmland adjacent to the center of the district, which had been used as a security parameter. At the time, the elder had complained to the sub-governor, who in turn asked the elder to file a complaint for a fee with the governor of the province if he wanted to reclaim his farmland. According to the elder, despite many attempts, he never heard anything from the governor's office in Sharana, the provincial capital, or anyone else in Yahya Khel for that matter. The elder asked me if I could do anything to help him. Most people in Afghanistan believe every interpreter who works for the Americans are also employees of the Afghan government—not the case, but applicable to most interpreters nonetheless.

I suggested that the elder file another complaint with the new sub-governor. When he said that he had already spoken with numerous other government officials in the district regarding his complaint that had been filed with the former sub-governor, he was told that his old complaint no longer existed and if he wanted to file a new complain he should do so with the new sub-governor—for yet another fee which, according to him, cost him 5,000 Afghanis every time he filed, with no guarantee that he would ever be compensated or get his land back.

The elder continued by explaining that the only reason he lost his land was because the Americans had brought back the Afghan officials and were supporting them, even though they aren't welcome in the district because they rob the villagers of their land, money, and anything else they may have of value. As you can see, here is an elder who, at the beginning of our conversation told me it had nothing to do with the Americans, but, by the end, blamed everything on the Americans because, in his mind, we brought the miseries they were experiencing because we were responsible for bringing the Afghan government back into their village. As Americans, despite what we do to give them freedom and protection, the local Afghan point of view changes in but a small, single paragraph because of the actions of their own government.

At 11:00 PM, we were being attacked for the third time in 10 days. This one differed from the others because it started with the usual small-arm firing in the distance but when it got closer to our compound, it became increasingly intense, much more so than the two prior attacks. After the small-arm firing had abated somewhat, they started using rockets, which came very close to hitting our compound, followed by such intense shooting we could actually hear the bad guys screaming and yelling in Pashto behind the walls of our compound. *"Allaho Akbar, wor walia por wolas wali!"* ("God is great, keep shooting at the center of the district!"). I couldn't help but wonder how they could be so close to our compound when our guys

were in the guard towers, apparently unaware of the attack. That didn't make sense to me at all.

Well, since our compound was attached to the main bazaar area on one side, there was absolutely no way for our guys to see anything from the guard towers during the day, much less at night when all of the shops in the market were closed. I turned my video recorder on, placing it by the window to record whatever might take place in this room so that our families would know what had happened to us during our last minutes in Yahya Khel District, Paktika Province, in eastern Afghanistan.

In prior fights, Patrick never showed any fear or panic, or at least that's how I viewed him. But this time was different, even for Patrick who was definitely showing fear. When the shooting started, our guys of the LLVI team never went to the roof to shoot back. I noticed that Thunder was moving around quickly to prepare his M249 Saw, a heavy machine-gun that shot 850 rounds per minute. Patrick did everything he could in an effort to stop Thunder from going to the rooftop with his weapon, but Thunder—who was so frustrated and mad, and despite being lower in ranks than Sergeant Patrick—told his superior that he didn't give a fuck about the rules right now. We were being attacked; him spending his time just sitting with a weapon full of 850 rounds would not do us any good, which is why he'd rather be on the rooftop so he could defend the DC (district center).

I believed Thunder might have been right about stating his argument, but wrong by not listening to his superior. Not knowing the military "policies and procedures," I wasn't sure who was right or wrong. From a moral standpoint, perhaps simply doing the right thing, even if it was not allowed for political reasons by your superior, made me realize that I would've done the same exact thing that Thunder ultimately ended up doing.

Within minutes, Thunder came down from the roof mad as hell because the lieutenant had ordered him to "get the fuck off the roof and back to your radio duty." I could not make sense of how the military worked and operated. Seeing and hearing live shooting where people were undoubtedly being killed, I couldn't understand why a soldier with an M249 would not be permitted to go to the rooftop in order to defend our compound before all of us got killed. Up to this point, I had never felt as trapped or helpless than I did at that moment when the enemy was so close, throwing grenade after grenade.

For the first time in my life, at one point I had given up on living because I didn't expect to come out of that attack alive. It's not that I was afraid of dying, but rather the fact that I wasn't able to say goodbye to my family that worried and saddened me the most. The more intense the fighting got, the more I wanted to make sure my camera was recording everything that was happening. At one point during the shooting and bombing, Patrick asked, "Hey, Nas, are you recording this shit?" I, of course, assured him that I was.

Every time an RPG or a hand grenade hit the DC, Patrick would say, "Goddammit, enough of this fucking shit! I had RPGs exploded many times in front of me in Iraq, but I can't take this shit anymore!" As Patrick got more panicky, I got more frightened, especially since I had no place to go or hide. At one point, I even left a few "last words" on the video recorder. "Well, this is it; see you guys on the other side."

After watching the video some time later, I realized that because of the way the RPGs were coming our way, I thought all of us were going to die in our room. I pulled out my helmet and body armor as a last resort and put them on. I asked Patrick to put on his helmet and body armor as well, but he refused, saying, "I'm all right, Nas." He asked me again if my video recorder was on. When I assured him that it was, he started to shout into the recorder a message for my family. "Welcome to Afghanistan, Nas' family." At one point at the end of the fighting, Patrick and I heard through our radio that our guys were talking about a medic evacuation, which meant someone had obviously been wounded. As we were hearing that medical evacuation was necessary—always bad news—we also heard over the radio that our guys were arguing about how low our supply of ammunition was, which was even more frightening. At the same time, seeing and hearing about the bravery of our young American soldiers, who were running outside of our compound, trying to chase the bad guys face on, was electrifying. "Come on you motherfuckers, you want to fight me? Then bring it on."

Our guys were the bravest and most heroic soldiers I have ever witnessed, by simply running out of the compound into the bad guys' territory in the middle of the night, not even knowing where they might be hiding. Every time our brave men and women walked out of the compound into the open field, they were fully aware that playing defensively was not the way to win the fight, especially knowing that's when the bad guys had returned to hiding in their holes like wolves. With our guys, the phrase, "The best defense is a good offense," worked every time.

The more I was in combat, the less I feared dying. It's like anything in life: the more you do it, the better you get at it. I'm not saying I was looking forward to dying, just that I was more and more prepared for it and not as fearful as I used to be. The kind of attacks we were under (e.g., being trapped in one spot, waiting for the Taliban to get lucky if one of their RPGs, grenades, or rockets hit us) was totally out of our control. I believed anything that was not in our control shouldn't be an issue. I learned that lesson at the very beginning of my deployment to Special Forces in Ghazni, when I asked my buddy Charlie if he was ever scared of flying on the Chinook. I will always remember Charlie's response that if it wasn't under his control, then he wasn't going to waste his time worrying about it. If his time was up, it was up—there would be nothing he could do to stop it from happening. What I have learned from guys in the military and applied to my own situations, has provided me with not only comfort, but courage as well. The only fear I couldn't change then, or now, was my fear of heights, especially in the open back of a Chinook, which I never liked, or flying on one of the many other [frightening] helicopters.

As noted earlier, our platoon's normal routine was to go out on a dismounted foot patrol mission after each attack. Therefore, the next day the lieutenant sent out half of the platoon on a foot patrol, just to be out there to get shot at by the bad guys, this time to walk around the market area from where we got attacked in the middle of the night before. If they really wanted to fight us, we were in their market area where they could attack us if they were brave enough to do so.

Before the mission, I asked Patrick if I could go, too. As in the past, Patrick told me I could only go out if Thunder or Hero accompanied me. Knowing that Thunder was tired from all the chaos the night before, I still asked if he would be willing to go. Being as tired as he was, psychologically he couldn't say no to me, so, we went on the mission together.

While walking the bazaar from one end to the other, we stopped by almost every shop to see if anyone was acting out of the ordinary, while, at the same time, fingerprinting most of the shopkeepers to see if they were in our data system. Gayle, who was in charge of our mission through my translation, asked the locals questions to see if anyone would tell us anything about the attack last night and if they had seen anyone wounded. As we walked and talked to each of the locals, as well as searching vehicles, I had my usual backpack full of pens and pencils, giving them out to children and adults alike.

As Thunder and I were passing by one of the shops, I noticed a string of pens hanging across the shop's window. I also noticed something even more familiar as we got closer: mostly blue pens made in Pakistan. But, at the very end of the string, I saw seven of the same brand of black pens, which I had given out to the children and adults in the village of Yahya Khel a week earlier. I called my buddy Thunder over, asking him to come and see the pens that I had distributed to the villagers, which were now hanging in this shop to be resold. Thunder was surprised by what he saw and said, "I would have never thought people would be reselling those pens in the market." I told Thunder that if anyone can make a buck in Afghanistan, almost anything is possible. I also told him that I wouldn't be surprised if we saw the books, notebooks, and backpacks that we had distributed to the villagers for sale in one of the other shops as well.

Just giving the Afghan villagers school supplies didn't mean that they would go to school, especially if there wasn't a school system in the first place. Because of the lack of funding and finding qualified teachers—much less the desire to learn—schools in remote villages were not easy to operate. For fear of their own safety from the Taliban, teachers are not motivated, since there is no protection from the Afghan government on the teachers' behalves. Seeing the reselling of the pens in the market reminded me of my own childhood back in the late 1960s or perhaps early 1970s when I was in elementary school.

My adoptive dad was the master teacher at the school in our village in Arghandab where I grew up. I recall one day when he took my older sister and me to a bazaar where the shopkeepers sold used textbooks. Those same books that Dad purchased from the shopkeepers might have been given to the schools in the city for learning purposes; however, instead, they were being sold to the shopkeepers who would then resell them to people [like my dad] who had a passion for teaching *and* reading. It was not only Dad's desire to educate the people in his village, but he would also pay for books with his own personal funding. I remember as a young boy, he pulled out a handful of red 100 Afghani bills and paid a shopkeeper for a myriad books that were all put on a donkey for transport to the school in our village where my dad taught. I compared these two scenarios where my adoptive dad was willing to pay his own hard-earned money for books for boys who wanted to go to school, while, at the same time, the Afghan government had absolutely no desire to do what my dad was doing as an individual. This was something that happened more than 40 years ago, but the memories are still with me as if it all happened just yesterday.

The school that my adoptive dad taught at happened to be a boys-only school in Arghandab. In Afghanistan, schools were categorized in two different ways: *Iftetadaya* (a starter school, from the 1st to the 8th grade) and *Laysa* (high school: grades 9 through 12). My dad taught at the *Iftetadaya* school. He and two of his cousins were also involved in running of the school.

Now, I have taken numerous risks just to be able to go out on dismounted missions to help Americans understand the Afghans, while at the same time providing the tools for the children to succeed in school. But when I saw the pens that I had given to the young kids in the Yahya Khel village not being used for that purpose, but instead being resold at the shop, it saddened me and reminded me of my past, which revealed a consistency in the Afghan predicament where the school supplies being provided were being sold.

As we continued walking through the bazaar, kids were following me, asking for pens over and over again. Once in a while, an adult would come along trying to keep the kids away from me by hitting them with sticks like they were animals, and then the adult would ask me for the pens as well. When I gave them one, they would ask me for five or six more by telling me that they had five to six more kids at home—all of whom were, of course going to school, too. Interestingly, the Yahya Khel village only had one four-room school, which we had already visited. Walking around the district, giving out more than 1,000 pens in the course of two weeks made it feel like the whole district was attending that one tiny school. Everyone wanted pens, whether they needed them or not, primarily because they could sell them back in the market for profit.

On one instance, I noticed that I was being followed by a man for almost the entire time we were walking around the market area. Obviously, I couldn't help but be curious, wondering if he was a bad guy or wanted to hurt me, or perhaps simply a poor man, hoping to pick my pockets (a common practice in Afghanistan). Noticing him, too, when Thunder cautioned me to be careful of the guy, I stopped walking and turned around to find the man standing directly behind me. "My friend, what do you want?" When he responded that he wanted a donation, I asked him, "A donation for what?" While showing me a five rupees note (Pakistani currency), he explained, *"Za ghareb yama, zakat ghwaram"* ("I am poor and am in need of charity"). The poor man was getting more and more frustrated that I wasn't giving him a donation while I was getting more and more frustrated that he was following and harassing me. By then, since I was essentially trapped with nowhere to go, a crowd of 20 to 30 adults and teens had gathered to see what I would do.

I noticed that Thunder, Gayle, and a majority of the other squad soldiers were increasingly concerned as to why this guy was yelling at me (yet another norm in the Afghan culture). Since my buddies didn't know the culture, they were concerned for my safety and kept asking me to keep moving rather than stopping in one spot. I was trying to keep moving forward, but villagers were surrounding me, which made me even more nervous because I had no way of knowing how many of them were Taliban. Most of my buddies got closer to me in an effort to ensure that the crowd would not lose control.

Meanwhile, by removing the Pakistani currency from the poor man's hand and pointing at it like he had done earlier, I continued to ask him, "What currency is this?" to which he responded, "It's Pakistani," which prompted me to ask, "Are we currently in Pakistan or Afghanistan?" When he said that we were in Afghanistan, I couldn't help but ask, "Well, if we're in Afghanistan, why the hell are you holding rupees in your hand?" His reply was, "Because Pakistani currency is the only thing in circulation here." I apologized when I said that I couldn't help him.

Another perfect example of how much Pakistan is trying to influence the Afghan society (or perhaps I should say how weak the Afghan government is): The Afghans themselves don't even carry their own national currency. Why aren't the Afghans capable of influencing their neighboring countries? Two reasons: (1) All of Afghanistan's neighbors have a strong sense of nationalism, which they are willing to defend at any cost. (2) Afghans, without a sense of nationalism, only associate with their own ethnicity.

Along the way, we continued to question the shopkeepers and fingerprinted those who looked out of the ordinary or suspicious. Before we reached the end of the bazaar, I was asked by the lieutenant to accompany him to talk with the bazaar's only doctor, whose clinic (which also provided a pharmacy, eyeglasses, dental care, skincare, pediatrics, etc.) was at the end of the road. The lieutenant had told me before that we wanted to talk with the doctor about the treatment of his recent patients (e.g., some of the people might have been wounded during the attack the night before). Walking toward the end of the road, we noticed a group of men sitting in front of his mud hut, "All in One Clinic."

After introductions, the doctor (who was holding one of his grandsons), offered us tea. The lieutenant thanked him for the offer, explaining that he came to the clinic to ask the doctor a couple of questions. When the doctor agreed, the lieutenant asked if he had treated anyone with gunshot wounds lately. The doctor responded that the only patient he had treated that week had been in that morning with tooth pain, so he ultimately had to extract the problematic tooth. As we were standing right in of the middle of the doctor's multitask clinic, the lieutenant couldn't help but see a trail of blood on the ground. When he asked the doctor who it was from, his reply was that it was the blood from the patient's tooth extraction.

Unfortunately, this is how things are done in the dentist offices in Afghanistan. By simply using the snap-on needle-type nose pliers, the extraction of a tooth is accomplished quickly. After a few more questions, we determined that there was nothing further the doctor could help us with, and whether he was lying to us about the trail of blood or telling us the truth would never be known. However, from the amount of blood on the ground, it didn't look like someone had only had a tooth extracted. We moved on to the next shopkeeper, who we learned was happy that the Americans had finally found a native Pashton interpreter, which I could immediately sense not only by his body language, but because he was so eager to talk with me. Without the shopkeeper knowing, I turned my recorder on. The shop was an Afghan version of an American convenience store that sold "everything," including condoms for the kids to play with as balloons.

In addition to the owner of the shop, two of his buddies were sitting outside by the front door. I greeted them in Pashto, *"Wrono Salamalykom!"* ("Greetings brothers!"). While his buddies looked on, the shopkeeper responded to my greeting, *"Walaykomo salam wrora"* ("Greetings to you, brother"). They were all happy that I spoke Pashto. When I asked the shopkeeper how his business was doing, he told me, *"Wala, bad na dey, makhsad gozara kawo."* ("It's all right, but we're just surviving"). I then wanted to know about the security situation, a question one of the shopkeeper's buddies answered by stating that the security situation is very unstable. As usual, by now, a crowd had gathered, so the shopkeeper was hesitant to answer any more questions, which was obvious because his answers became much more passive than direct. As our conversation continued, the crowd got larger, and the shopkeeper didn't want to talk with me any longer, so his second buddy started speaking for the shopkeeper. "He lied to you; business is shitty. He's afraid to speak out, to tell the truth." That made much more sense to me, especially since the shopkeeper had to make every effort to keep his shop open day after day, while his buddies didn't have that problem. When I asked "Who is he afraid of?" the buddy responded that the shopkeeper was afraid of everyone. Following this answer, because of the crowd that had gathered to listen, I couldn't help but notice that the shopkeeper's buddy was also afraid to mention names. I turned back to the shopkeeper in an effort to find out exactly what was meant when his buddy said he was scared of everyone. "Who are you guys afraid of the most: Americans, the Taliban, or the Afghan forces?" The shopkeeper scoffed when he said, "I'm not really afraid; they're all good people," which clearly indicated that he was still being very passive with his answers because he was, in fact, afraid. But I still wasn't ready to back off unless he either asked me to or if I was called by one of my commanders to help with something else.

Since I wanted more specifics regarding the shopkeeper's comments, I asked, "How is it possible for everyone to be good, especially with all the chaos going on in your district?" I noticed the second buddy looking around carefully to make sure that none of the ANA or ANP officers were around. After careful observation, and a nod from his buddy, he was willing to answer my question on behalf of the shopkeeper. "Well, I'll tell you. Business is bad, not because of the Americans or the Taliban, but because of the Afghan officials." At that point, I knew exactly what this villager's frustration was all about. Despite the nature of the Afghan government being bad to its own people, I wanted to hear it for myself while also recording what the villager was saying. So, I continued by asking the shopkeeper, "What is it that the Afghan officials have done to cause you such suffering?" The shopkeeper buddy, pointing to the bakery down the street, said, "Listen, do you see the bakery down there? Well, first, they never pay me for the bread they take from me, and second, every one of the locals who comes to the bazaar, either on their motorcycles or in their vehicles to shop, are stopped by the officials and asked for paperwork (i.e., vehicle registration). When the valid paperwork is provided, the officials tell them it's no longer valid. When the officials are told that the paperwork was just obtained three months ago, they are then told that the sub-governor has recently changed; therefore, the paperwork has to be changed as well. Needless to say, I could understand his frustration.

I thanked the shopkeeper and continued my conversation with the bakery owner regarding how he felt about the Americans being in his district. I felt the man answered honestly when he said, "The Americans are not bad people; unfortunately, they're not Muslims." This is how our guys are seen by both the civilians and the government. Civilians will say it as honestly as the baker did, but the government will never say it as long as they're in control and the Americans are supporting them. Once they lose their power, however, those with millions of American taxpayers dollars will move to Dubai, while those like Ansari will switch sides in order to be able to support their families; and, for the shopkeepers and local villagers, life will be peaceful from the harassment of the Afghan government.

I had witnessed it myself—Afghan government officials not paying for things they took from the shops in the bazaar. This was but one of the many instances I had seen over and over again where the Afghan government officials completely disrespected the locals with the blame always placed on the Americans.

On the way back to our compound, two of our local linguists who were considered by the locals as Afghan government workers, which meant that every shop we passed, they took something from the poor shopkeepers without paying for it. At one point, they even tried to jump on top of a shopkeeper's horse (without the owner's permission, of course) that was tethered in front of the shop. When the horse broke loose and suddenly moved away by running next door to a neighboring fruit stand, all the fruit and vegetables were knocked to the ground and ruined by the startled horse. The shopkeeper whose fruit stand was ruined demanded immediate payment for the damage. Of course, the linguists were not willing to pay for anything. When I intervened by asking the linguists to pay the poor man for the damages incurred because of their actions, one responded, "How could we have known that the fucking horse was wild? We only wanted to take a picture while sitting on his back." Persisting, I asked, "Well, why did you guys decide to get on the horse without asking for the owner's permission?" which made them laugh. "What in the hell are you talking about? No one asks for permission around here!" Sound familiar? (Remember the ANP officer and the apricots?) Sadly, the shopkeeper was never paid for the damage done to his fruit stand. With actions such as these, why would the locals even consider supporting people who hurt them both financially and physically?

It was a long day of walking and talking with numerous people in the bazaar, but there were no leads to any of the bad guys. Almost everyone in our platoon realized that the numerous local Afghans I had interviewed throughout the Yahya Khel District were all against the Afghan government. They thought their number one enemy was their own government because it took the poor men's property without their consent, which is one of the main reasons the locals sympathize with the Taliban.

During our downtime, another important observation I made while in the Yahya Khel District was that the ANA and ANP officers, on a daily basis, either slept most of the day or played volleyball to pass their time, while most of the American soldiers always kept busy by building things around the compound—not for themselves but for the ANA and ANP officers.

The news of our next mission was announced. It was going to be a high-value target mission somewhere on the border between Afghanistan and Pakistan. Our target location: the village of Spina. According to some, it was the village where Alexander the Great had once stayed. This would be an air-dropped mission where we would be flown over by a Chinook. Our major mission was scheduled for the following morning at 2:00. In order for us to be picked up by the Chinook, we were all going to have to walk about a mile or so, away from the compound since it was located in the middle of the district, which meant there was no place for the Chinook to land.

As we left the compound for the open field, I noticed Jimbo Junior (the name I gave him), the compound's puppy, was following us. Thunder, Hero, and I tried to stop him but he wouldn't turn back. He either didn't understand English or he *really* wanted to go with us. Well, poor Junior followed us all the way to the landing zone in the desert so when we all laid down flat on the ground so as not to get our heads chopped off by the Chinook, Junior was still with us.

Knowing how powerful the wind from the Chinook would be (sometimes it was known to knock down someone weighing 150 pounds), I was concerned about Junior—who never left our sides and, at best, weighed in at about five pounds. As the familiar *TaTaTa* sound of the Chinook got closer and closer, I tried to find Junior to see if I could hold onto him while the Chinook landed, but he was suddenly nowhere to be found. Somehow, he had wandered away. To makes things worse, for some reason, the wind from the Chinook was more powerful than prior landings. My guess for the change in wind was that we were probably on flat desert land where nothing could take away or absorb even part of the winds that were hitting us directly. Some who had been standing, waiting to getting on the Chinook, found themselves knocked to the ground.

Remembering the crash-landing from the last mission, I never got up after the one-minute preparation that was usually allowed by the crew prior to landing. Instead, I waited for the aircraft to touch the ground and then started moving toward the back of the aircraft, just to prevent myself from falling to the ground again. Not having an internal radio contact to listen to, I was kind of out of the loop about the conversation taking place as to why it was taking so long for the Chinook to land after the one-minute signal from the crew. Well, except for me, everyone was being informed through their internal radios that there was no place to land the Chinook, which means that everyone had to jump out of the aircraft. still not knowing what the hell was going on, suddenly, I heard Thunder shouting at me. "Hey, Nas. Get up. Let's go!" I stood, but still didn't feel the rough landing that usually occurred with the Chinook. The next thing I knew Thunder is again shouting in my ear. "Nas, you are going to have to fucking jump." Obviously, since I didn't know what the hell Thunder was talking about, I asked, "What do you mean I have to jump?" Then he told me, "Come on Nas, you need to jump; you're holding up everyone behind you, so let's go!" Since he was behind me, I asked him to get in front of me so he could jump first, which he promptly did. Of course, then I had no choice but to jump, too. Not knowing what the fuck I was jumping into, I again hesitated because I couldn't see anything below. Soon I heard Thunder again asking me to jump, that he would catch and hold onto me. When I looked up, all I could see were the sparks from the blades of the Chinook, which really freaked me out. When I looked down again, I still couldn't see shit while Thunder kept telling me to jump. Suddenly, I heard Hero, who was in line behind me, encouraging me to jump as he held me by my shoulders while Thunder pulled me by my boots. Meanwhile, I felt like a sack of potatoes being held from the four corners of my body so that Thunder and Hero could get me out of the damn helicopter. I was reluctant to jump because of my back pain, which was always bad, even if I did small jumps. I didn't want to be a burden on any one of our guys, ever, but most especially in the middle of a combat zone. This time I also packed a lot heavier than usual, with all the pens, pencils, water, and Gatorade, especially since we didn't know when we were going to complete this mission.

It was very dark; sunrise was about an hour away. I knew we were on a cliff that was very rocky. I had no clue how high up we were or where we were headed in the dark. It was comforting to be walking between two soldiers, one in front and the other behind. Then the next thing I heard was Thunder telling me that we were going downhill toward the village and to be careful not to slide on the sharp rocks. Since there was no flatland for the Chinook to land on, we were dropped at the foothills of the mountains and told by the commander of our squad to get some rest, because we would resume our walk once it was a little light.

First came the dark orange sky followed by the sun peeking through the mountains from Pakistan. All I could see were the tall dark mountains on the east and west. Surrounding the village with the only way in and out was a narrow pathway zigzagging through the village and then disappearing in the mountains into Pakistani territory. There were 16 of our guys, eight at each end of the village holding security positions to stop people from escaping, while the rest of our platoon was going through the village, house to house, searching for the bad guys. It seemed like people already knew we were in there since, once the sun was out, every villager had come out to see what was going on. Usually the noise from the aircraft got their attention, especially early in the morning. But, generally speaking, and having grown up in a village myself, the villagers always woke up before sunrise. Lots of children were showing up to see if there would be any kind of handouts, for which the Americans were famous. I gave out pens as usual, which I started giving out to two boys from the house across the dirt road from us; however, within an hour, kids from every house were crowded around me asking for pens, some as young as two or three—who weren't even wearing shoes, undoubtedly because neither had a pair. With a combination of sharp gravel and a multitude of other objects on the ground that could hurt their feet, it was a concern, especially because they were mostly barefoot.

We spent the day talking with the villagers, young and old alike. Unlike some villages where they would not want to open up to strangers, most of the kids were friendly. They were either hungry for handouts or were just simply being friendly to us. I had brought power bars and Gatorade with me for my breakfast, lunch, and dinner, while Thunder and Hero had their MREs with them. As I pulled one of the power bars from my pocket and started to eat it—a young boy wearing a knee-length traditional Afghan *kamis* (shirt; only used to cover most of his body) with no *partog* (pants), socks, or shoes—stood before me, his tiny eyes sparkling as the cold wind made it difficult for him to continue to stand in one place. As I looked at this little boy, I saw that the sparkle in his eyes was gradually turning into tears that were streaming down his dry, cracked, and dusty cheeks.

As I was about to open the wrapper and take a bite of the power bar, I couldn't do it. Instead, I changed my mind and gave it to the little boy who I'm sure needed it more than I did. Before I could even offer it to him, he asked, "Uncle, is it sweet? Does it taste good?" I told him, "Yes, it is sweet, and it fills you up!" Interest now more intense, he then asked, "Can you give me some?" Pointing to where Thunder and Hero were standing, I said, "Sure. Come with me, and I'll give you some." The boy (and the three or four other children who had gathered) followed me closely. Once I reached Thunder and Hero, I sat on a rock and picked the small boy up to sit on my lap. As he sat, I noticed his eyes continued to gaze hungrily at the power bar as he anxiously waited for me to open the wrapper and give it to him.

As I was feeding him my own breakfast, another small boy pointed to my pocket where he could see my lunch bar sticking out, and asked if he could have it. He also had his eye on the Gatorade, which was my drink to keep me hydrated for the day. Regrettably, I didn't had enough energy bars to feed every little kid, all just as poor, which is why I had no choice but to pull out not only my lunch bar, but my dinner energy bar as well, giving them to the other young boy and little girl, who were also barefoot.

While I was feeding the second young boy and girl, I heard Hero asking me, "Hey, Nas, do you see that little boy in the blue who is running around with no shoes on his feet?" When I looked to see who he was referring to, I saw that he was talking about the same boy I had given my breakfast to earlier. "Yes, I know, Hero. I gave him my breakfast bar and one of my Gatorades earlier. I figured that he could probably use it more than I could." As Hero looked around, noticing other children, he couldn't help but wonder aloud, "My God, I can't believe how they can even walk on this sharp gravel surface with all the other kinds of sharp objects on the ground without getting cut!" to which I responded, "Hey, buddy, welcome to the Afghan way of life—otherwise known as struggling to survive. Aren't you glad you're an American, and don't you appreciate life even more after seeing how hard kids in Afghanistan have to cope with the hardships they face every day?" Hero shook his head. "Hey, Nas, will you ask the older kids if there's a shoe store in the village so I can give them some money to buy those kids who are barefoot a pair of shoes?" I asked the older boys, who confirmed that there was a shoe store in the village. When Hero asked them if the shoe store would accept American currency, he was told that the store would only take *Kaldar* (Pakistani currency). Then Hero wanted to know how much a pair of shoes would cost, and one of the boys told him anywhere from 400 to 500 rupees, which would equal about $4.00 to $5.00 a pair in U.S. currency. "Nas, ask the older boy if he'd be willing to help buy the shoes if I give him twenty dollars." I asked the boy if he would do that, but he reminded us that the store would not take American money. Knowing that the ANA and ANP officers were with us on this mission, I thought they would probably have cash on them in either Afghan or Pakistani currency, but I didn't know where they were, which meant we'd have to wait until we were back together and buy the shoes just before we left to return to the compound. But Hero insisted that he was just going to give them $20.00 because he figured there had to be a way they could somehow use the money to buy the shoes.

I really wanted to tell Hero that he shouldn't even consider doing such a thing, because none of the children would get the shoes he wanted them to have. Someone was bound to take the $20.00 from the boys and no shoes would be provided to the poor children who needed them most. Nonetheless, Hero wanted to do it anyway and was trying to find his wallet when he suddenly remembered that he didn't bring it with him on missions. He asked me if I had my wallet with me, and I told him that I never carried my wallet with me on missions, either, because I never had a need for it. This was a heartbreaking situation, not only for Hero who was trying to buy the kids some much needed shoes and wasn't able to do so, but especially for the kids, because they thought they were getting the money to buy them. Their disappointment was sad to see.

I was emotional again at seeing the goodness of an American soldier, a young adolescent himself, with such a compassionate mindset, despite the fact that he was in a country where he had nothing in common with the young Afghan children, who all thought of Hero and Thunder as infidels. Being on this mission or any one of the other missions in Afghanistan, most of the men and women in the U.S. military never really saw the religious, ethnic, color, or gender aspects of the people they were trying to help. Nonetheless, I saw the *real* faces of caring American soldiers helping out the *real* faces of the Afghan people, fellow human beings, who needed help.

Throughout the day, the numbers of children had grown to about 50 or more, and they were all having fun with us. Thunder noticed that one of the kids had a very filthy bandage on his forehead and told me to ask the kid what had happened. When I asked the boy, he told me that someone had thrown a rock at him; unfortunately, yet another commonality in Afghanistan. After hearing his answer, I couldn't help but remember that while growing up in Afghanistan, I, too, had been hit on my head on more than one occasion. Unlike spoiled kids in America, who were so fortunate to have what they had, for fun, kids in Afghanistan, then and still today, throw rocks for fun to see who can throw the farthest. Kids in America are so preoccupied with their expensive toys, games, computers, iPods, and iPhones, they don't have time to communicate with their parents, much less go outside, like back in the "old" days. Not only are time and rocks the only things that kids in Afghanistan have plenty of it, they get it all for free. Aside from throwing rocks to pass their time, rock throwing also applies to the season for bird hunting, which starts in early spring and ends by early fall. Just like we in America would say, "Home of the brave, land of the free," Afghanistan should have something similar, except it would say, "Home of the rocks, land of the free time."

So, this was how and why this young man had been hit by a rock, and Thunder wanted to help him by changing his dirty bandage. Since we all have our own emergency first-aid medical supply kits, Thunder had opened his and started to pull the dirty bandage off so he could replace it with a clean one of his own.

Having removed the old bandage from the young man's forehead, we saw an infected cut that didn't look like he had been hit by a rock; instead, it looked more like a cut from a knife or something similar. Thunder cleaned the wound with sanitized gauze and wrapped the young man's forehead with new bandaging. Not long after the young man had left, more people started showing up with their own medical issues, ranging from tooth problems to ear infections, and eyes problems to stomach pains. Although none of us were doctors and, thus, couldn't prescribe anything medical, the villagers didn't know that. But, because Thunder, from the goodness of his heart, had changed one simple bandage on one young man's forehead, it triggered the presence of the most ill people in the village.

Thunder called our commanding officer, who was in the village with the rest of our guys, to ask if he could send one of the team medics to us for some medical care to the villagers. He was told that the medic would be sent to us within the next 30 minutes, news that we shared with the villagers. As promised, within half an hour, the medic arrived with his medical backpack full of first-aid supplies and prescription drugs. He started to prescribe medication to one of the village elders who had numbness in his legs and had been to Pakistan for treatment many times, but nothing worked for him, so he was hoping that this medication from the British (in his opinion) would work. Pointing to the American flag on my right shoulder, I told the elder, "We're not the British; we're Americans," to which the old man responded, *"Za Pashton yam, aow hitzh wakht ba na Afghan sam aow na Pakistani. Laka Angrayzai cheba hitzh wakht na Amrykayi sea aow na Rossian"* ("I am a Pashton, and I will never become an Afghan or a Pakistani, just like the British never become American or Russian"). I really didn't know what he meant, but told him nonetheless, "I didn't understand your point." He explained that, "Just like the British have changed the Pashton name to Afghan and Pakistani, they have done the same to change their British name to American." How did this old man know all of this in a place where kids still throw rocks as a way to pass time? This man, who had to be in his 90s at least, thought I was too young to know history and went on to tell that what he meant was that the British were still fighting the Pashtons under the banner of America, not to defeat the Afghans and Pakistanis, but the Pashtons. All of this leads me to believe that the only agenda the Taliban was using then was that all Afghans are not Pashtons and all Pashtons are not Afghans.

As we continued our humanitarian mission to care for the ill and poor villagers who needed and asked for our help, the more time I spent with all our compassionate American soldiers, the more I wanted to be with them. As our time to give as much medical care and attention as possible was coming to an end, the old man was not in the least ashamed when he accepted the free medicine from our medic.

Before we left the village to fly back to the compound, all the kids in the village said they wanted me to stay with them and spend the night. I told them that I regrettably had to go back to the compound because I was hungry and thirsty (which I really was). During that day, I not only didn't eat or drink anything, but I had talked for at least 12 hours, the entire time that we were there.

As we were preparing to leave, the old man asked me in Pashto, "You gave all of us medicine, and being my fellow Pashton, how about spending the night with us? I have a goat that I can slaughter for dinner." I thanked him sincerely for his warm hospitality, and, since he considered me a fellow Pashton, I told him, "The medication did not belong to me, nor did I give it to you. It belonged to the Americans, so it is they who have given it to you." The man insisted that "It was because you were here; Americans and other interpreters have been here in the past, and no one ever offered us any medication." How the locals saw Americans was very important to me, because the Americans that I knew and represented to the villagers were different than the Americans that most of the other linguists represented in the villagers' minds. I knew, too, that most of the Americans I represented were like Hero, who simply—out of the compassion and the goodness of his heart—was trying to buy the village's poor, young children the shoes they so desperately needed. And then there's Thunder, who had used his own personal first-aid kit to help the young man who had been struck on the forehead by a rock (or cut by something else), and the medic who had given all of his time and medication to help ease the villagers' various pains and medical issues. Most other linguists went on missions to stay out of sight so the Americans would not ask them to translate if they didn't have to, and they did this primarily for two reasons—either because they didn't know the language or for simply being too afraid of being out in the open in case things went bad.

Before leaving the village, I asked all the kids if they liked the Americans; of course, they all gave me a loud and resounding *yes*. I lined them up and turned on my video recorder while asking them to repeat after me, so I could record their voices. They agreed and I simply chanted, "USA, USA, USA", with all of the villagers gleefully shouting the same. I saw that Thunder, Hero, the medic, and three or four other soldiers were all laughing and one of them said, "Nas, you're awesome!"

Up to that point, that's exactly what I had lived for, risking my life to be on dismounted missions where I saw both my native Afghans and my fellow Americans together, in harmony. It was finally a moment where the two cultures could coexist in happiness on both sides, without any expense on either side.

As for the village elder who had taken our medicine and appreciated the generosity he had witnessed throughout the day, him saying "Pashton, and Pashton only" dates back to the early 1600s when Khushal Khan Khattak had united the Pashtons against the Mogual empire of India. With that said, the only way the Taliban can succeed in making people believe, and especially the Pashtons along the border between Afghanistan and Pakistan, is to be united as Pashtons in order to defend their territory. (I will explain more about the Pashtons and their history in the second part of this book.)

In any event, it appears that it's working to the Taliban's advantage for two reasons: (1) Most Pashtons, who are poor and mostly living in the remote villages, were (and still are) being abused by the government because of their support of the Taliban, primarily because they consider them as their own Pashtons, and (2) if the name Afghan includes the Tajiks, Hazaras, Uzbeks, and others, then the Pashtons don't want to associate themselves with Afghans. At least that's what I had sensed and felt throughout the villages of the Yahya Khel District and most of the other villages I had been to so far—and most especially the villages in the east of Afghanistan along the border with Pakistan.

Sometimes, being with the military can be very boring, so I would always find ways to keep occupied, either volunteering for other duties or playing with our four-legged friends who would show up at our compound gates. In this particular compound in Yahya Khel, we had three little puppies, one of which I named Jimbo Jr., who was never seen again after that night when we boarded the Chinook and who was introduced earlier—he was a cute little puppy who was always very hungry, much like we all were because of the lack of food. We all did everything we could to take care of the two dogs on our compound. All were quite afraid of the ANA officers, just like the Senior Jimbo had been in Ghazni. Not only did the ANA officers and the local linguists not give them any food, but they would either kick or throw rocks at them. And, by the way, this kind of rock throwing was not like the one kids did to pass their time. Rather, these were adults throwing rocks at the village dogs to keep them away because they were considered filthy animals.

So, the puppies were always hungry and would follow us around because, besides being hungry, we would always pick them up, then hug and bathe them—an example of how even those puppies knew who they should follow if they needed to be treated with respect. I would oftentimes look around the trashcans so I could pick up the leftover pork chops and bones that our soldiers would intentionally throw away specifically so they'd be given to the puppies. As an aside, the ANA and local linguists had plenty of food that they cooked only for themselves. Even though they were not worried about food shortages—and most of our guys wouldn't eat the food cooked by the ANA officers anyway, primarily because of the lack of running water and sanitation on the compound, which were the causes for numerous health concerns—being in Yahya Khel for about three weeks, most had lost at least 12 to 15 pounds and were just as desperate for food as the little puppies were.

It was already close to three weeks since we had last showered, so the smell in the room was getting worse and worse, especially when Private Eric fucked things up and Sergeant Gayle ordered him to do his pushups, which contributed to making the room smell even worse.

In order to make the situation more tolerable, our commanding lieutenant decided that one of our squads from the platoon should drive to

FOB Sharana to pick up as many food supplies as possible. At the same time, all of us who were going could take showers while we were there. The news was very gratefully received by everyone going on this mission, although we also all realized that it would be very dangerous because of all the IEDs on the road on which we would be traveling.

We left the compound at 6:00 in the morning. Since our drive was stop and go, we arrived in Sharana around noon. Compared to the compound in Yahya, Sharana was like a members-only club where you were privy to phones, computers, food, drinks, the gym, movies, ping pong, the PX store where you could buy almost anything you needed, and cold and hot showers. We were told that our time was limited to only three hours to do everything that had to be done. It felt more like one of those Black Friday events where people waited in lines to get into their favorite department store for Christmas to buy what's on sale. Well, that's how we felt by coming to Sharana after more than three weeks to shower and get some real food.

The first thing I did was take a nice, long, hot shower, and then walked to the DFAC to eat all I could. Please don't misunderstand: I'm not complaining. I'm happy to be with guys like Thunder, Hero, Sergeant Gayle, Eric, and Sergeant Patrick, who were all willing to do what they could by volunteering to be infantry soldiers—something other people would never even be willing to consider, much less actually accomplish. Their compassion and bravery gave me more of a perspective on appreciating life, especially for those of us who live in one of the greatest nations in the world, that provides men and women who serve in the U.S. Armed Forces.

We were all cleaned up, smelled damn good for a change, and were on our way back to the shithole of Yahya Khel District again. We had loaded the armored vehicles with what we wanted to eat and drink. During our 35-mile drive on this stretch of highway, usually used by pedestrians, motorcycles, bicycles, donkeys, horses, dogs, cats, the Taliban, ANA, ANP, whatever—you name it, we saw it. The soldier who was driving the vehicle in which Thunder and I were riding wasn't from our squad. I had seen him on the compound from time to time but didn't know him in person like I did all the other guys in the squad with whom we had all shared a room.

Thunder and I were both riding in the backseat while the two other soldiers—the driver and a gunner sitting in the passenger seat—seemingly chain-smoked cigarettes. Since Thunder and I weren't smokers, and both of the guys in the front seat were smoking (a lot!), the smoke from their cigarettes was floating into the backseat. Unfortunately, all the windows were closed for security reasons.

Since there was a NO SMOKING sign in the vehicle directly in front of him, I asked the driver to put out his cigarette, which he refused to do. Because of the horrific smell, when Thunder asked him to do so, the driver accommodated his request. Curious, I asked the soldier why he didn't put out his cigarette when I asked him to do it. He responded, "Who the fuck are you to tell me what to do? I don't even like you interpreters because while we try to defend your fucking country, you guys never do what we ask you to do." Sensing the soldier's frustration with all the interpreters that he had to deal with, I told him, "I don't blame you for not liking the interpreters, and I feel the same way." Surprised, the soldier turned around to look at me. "Really? You do, too?" When I nodded my head in response, he was obviously more comfortable to talk about what was on his mind (after he blessedly tossed his cigarette out the window!). He started talking shit about every local on the street that we had passed. Whether riding a bicycle, motorcycle, donkey, or even pedestrians on foot, this soldier cursed them all, blowing his horn to either scare them, or, if they looked at him, he would give them the finger and tell them, "Get the fuck out of my way before I kill you, you fucking Taliban." This ignorant soldier needed to be told how his perception of viewing every local on the road was wrong. For a while, I didn't say anything and thought to myself that the soldier might simply be too young and ignorant to comprehend, but when I listened to him when he started to curse every single person he passed, calling them, "You Afghan peace of shit, get the fuck out of my way," I realized just how much he was really getting on my nerves, which reminded me of an old saying:

"We're all born ignorant, but one must work very hard to remain stupid."
— BENJAMIN FRANKLIN

Seeing the stupidity in this 20-year-old soldier, I couldn't help but think to myself, *do I need to get involved in this or should I just shut up and enjoy the ride.* Well, as it turned out, I couldn't just sit there and listen to him going on and on. It was irritating. I didn't know what to make of his apparent ignorance and stupidity or how he managed to see and label every single local we passed. It's not like the locals could hear him, but he was getting on my nerves to the point where I decided to say something one more time. "Listen to me, Mr. Driver, since I don't know your name. Why are you doing this?" to which he arrogantly responded, "Hey, come on. Can't you see all of these fucking Taliban walking in the middle of the road?" Angered further, I asked, "Is that what you really believe? That everyone on the road you see is with the Taliban?" When he said, "Yes, they're all fucking related," I told him, "Sorry, dude, but you should *not* be in Afghanistan if you really think that everyone we drive by is with the Taliban. If you believe that to be the case simply because everyone in Afghanistan is dressed like someone involved with the Taliban, and they look like someone who you perceive *must* be involved with the Taliban, then, in your mind, they should all be treated like Taliban, right? If so, then is it safe to assume that Americans who look like Timothy McVeigh and Ted Kaczynski should be viewed as such, including you?"

Fortunately, the driver was quiet and didn't say anything until the soldier sitting in the passenger seat chastised him by saying, "Aowwww, Nas fucking nailed you! So what do you say to that, you dickhead?" Nonplussed, the driver responded with a big smile on his face. "I think Nas made a good fucking point here." I was happy to know that the soldier wasn't as stupid as I thought he was. He was ignorant, but at the same time open-minded with the wisdom to understand me. Fortunately, most of the soldiers I had worked with understood what I was telling them from time to time. The soldier who was driving told me that all the other linguists also got mad whenever he cursed at the locals, but they had never taken the time to explain anything to him the way I had so that he'd understand. I told the soldier that the reason I did things differently from most of the other linguists was because, as an American, I treated people as human beings. The driver understood my point and admitted to being ignorant about the Afghan society. Again, most American soldiers would admit to their wrongdoings and misunderstandings, and ultimately understand them when someone explained things in a more rational manner.

We finally arrived back at our smelly compound, which reeked even worse now than when we left, or, since we had all taken showers, maybe it only seemed that way. Since I had volunteered to be in Yahya Khel, my assignment here was only temporary and the company that I worked for was sending a permanent linguist, a Cat II who was currently on vacation, to the team to take my place, which meant I'd only be here for about one more week. I was then being sent back to the brigade in FOB Salerno. Until the transfer took place, I volunteered as much as I could to go out on dismounted missions, but sometimes it wasn't possible for me to do so since I could only go if one of my three man team members accompanied me.

Since the linguist who was supposed to be taking over for me was already in FOB Sharana, waiting to be picked up by one of our team members, it was finally time for me to go back to FOB Salerno. This time Patrick would go with me on the next convoy to FOB Sharana to drop me off and pick up the other linguist who would be waiting. I had spent close to five weeks in Yahya Khel, where, for food, I ate energy bars, potato chips, and beef jerky. I showered only once every five weeks, and went on seven dismounted missions. During those five weeks, our compound was attacked by the bad guys 11 times, and, by pure luck, three out of those 11 times I cheated death—or, as my buddy Charlie from Special Forces would say, "When your time is up, it's up," so I guess my time wasn't up in Yahya Khel and I had made it out of there alive, hungry, and tired.

On the roof top of our compound in Yahya Khel district.

The top bunk of our living quarter, where bullet marks are visible. April, 2010.

Valuable history lessons learned from this ninety-years-old elder, whom, like his ancestors, considered himself nothing but a Pashton who lived in Spena, Pashtonistan.

A compassionate American soldier, the true face of my adopted land, providing medical care to my native people.

My cute little friend Jimbo Junior from Yahya Khel.

CHAPTER NINE

May 14, 2010: FDS (Field Detention Site), FOB, Salerno, Khost Province, Afghanistan

A s soon as I arrived, I was picked up from the airfield by Wilder and taken back to my old room. He told me that the chief of the brigade wanted me to work at the FDS permanently, so, once I got settled in, Wilder was going to take me to the chief's office to discuss my assignment. Rather than unpacking everything, I just sat it all in the middle of my room so that Wilder and I could walk over to the brigade's headquarters and I could meet with the chief for the second time. Entering his office, we shook hands, said how nice it was to see each other again, and then he told me jokingly that since I would not be able to volunteer for dismounted missions any longer, the only place I could volunteer was at the FDS. I told him that I was fine with that. "Believe me, Nas, they can use you at the FDS; in fact, all of the interrogators are asking for you," he said, to which I responded, "Sir, I'm all yours; you can use me as much as you need." The chief walked with me back to the FDS and reintroduced me to Karr, telling him that this time I was staying at the FDS for good, which Karr was happy to hear, as were the other interrogators in the room.

Because of my skills and experience, the first thing Karr did was make me a Certified Interrogator. I was put back on the same schedule as before, from 8:00 AM to 2:00 PM, but that wasn't a set time, just one to get me started. Sometimes we had more guests to interrogate at The Taliban Motel, which would go on all day and perhaps even into late night, depending on how the detainees responded to our initial interrogation. I worked more hours than the other three to four Cat II linguists, who were also assigned to the FDS. Coming back, all the same interrogators were still at the FDS that were there when I left for Yahya Khel. Because the busy, summer fighting season was upon us, there was also an additional interrogator who had been added to the team while I was gone. The new interrogator was only at FOB Salerno on temporary duty, just like I had been when I went to the Marines in Helmand or the LLVI team in Yahya Khel.

His name was Allen, and he was stationed in Bagram where the main, central jail for all the hardcore detainees is located. After coming back from Yahya Khel, my first interrogation was with Allen, who told me that he had heard a lot of good things about me and my interrogation skills. I laughed. "Don't believe everything you hear!" After Allen was done with his first interrogation using me as his linguist, he came back and told the other team members in our room, "You guys were fucking right! He *is* good at his job!" I remember Karr telling Allen, "That's why the chief has assigned him to us for good." Pausing for a minute, Allen then said, "Hey, Nas, you seem like a smart man, so let me ask you a question so we can see if you know the answer: Detainees and interrogators have one thing in common. Do you know what it is?" I had no idea what Allen was talking about, but didn't want to simply say *no*, so since I had to come up with something, I said, "The detainees and interrogators all have beards?" Everyone in the room laughed uproariously. Although my answer was a guess, I was also guessing that everyone else in the room already knew the answer to Allen's question. Since I really didn't know if Allen's question referred to the detainees in Afghanistan or detainees in general, I was looking for someone to stop laughing long enough to tell me if I was wrong. As everyone continued to look at me and laugh, I suddenly realized that my answer was incorrect because we had a couple of women interrogators in our group who definitely didn't have beards.

I looked at Allen and asked, "Was my answer incorrect?" He laughed when he told me, "Yeah, afraid so, Nas. The answer I was looking for is that they both lie to each other." One of the female interrogators interrupted. "Well, I don't lie to the detainees, nor do I have a beard. But even if I were to lie, it'd be worth it, especially if it stops the bad guys from doing bad things. Under those circumstances, I wouldn't consider it a lie." Allen countered with, "But it's still a lie, whether you do it to stop the bad guys from doing bad things or otherwise—it's still intentional."

These were the kinds of conversations we would have on our free time while hanging out in the office and waiting for the next round of interrogations. During my interrogation at the FDS, the military oftentimes brought in Mr. Habibi, the Afghan prosecutor, who would observe a prisoner's interrogation, or he would interrogate some of the detainees himself. The first time that I met Mr. Habibi, he appeared to me to be an honorable man. In his late 60s, he spoke softly and wore clean, crisply ironed white Afghan clothes. He was also clean-cut with well-groomed silver hair and beard. After a couple of weeks of getting to know him and learning how he worked, I began to notice a few of his personal traits that indicated to me that he was not the person he presented himself to be.

One day all the linguists and Habibi were sitting outside in front of the office, when three, blindfolded detainees were brought in through the front gate by the military and then taken into the detainee building, while we all sat and watched.

Before we could even see the detainees' faces or talk with them, Habibi had already proclaimed that two of the detainees were guilty. On one hand, I hardly talked to any one of the other linguists, or even Habibi himself, unless something concerned work-related issues, while on the other hand they would always hang out together and talk about the detainees, the American soldiers who were guarding them, and primarily just so they could make fun of them all. While our medics were processing the detainees (e.g., physical exams, etc.), Habibi was telling all the other linguists in their native languages of either Farsi or Pashto that two of the detainees were absolutely 100 percent high-ranking Taliban commanders who needed to be turned over to Habibi's NDS custody once the Americans were done interrogating them. I could not help but ask Habibi how he had come to that conclusion before he even talked with the two detainees. "How can you tell if they're high-ranking Taliban, if no one has talked with them yet?" I asked. Habibi's answer? "I can tell just by looking at them and how they're dressed."

To me, the two detainees Habibi was referring to were wearing similar white, neatly-ironed clothes, and shiny shoes as Habibi himself was wearing. The two detainees looked more like wealthy Afghan government officials than Taliban. Most of the Taliban I had interrogated (who would admit to being Taliban) not only *never* wore white, neatly-ironed clothing, but they stank and most didn't even have shoes on their feet. I strongly believe Habibi wanted to take these detainees into custody so he could take bribes from them to be released. I am sure your remember the school principal in Ghazni for what he has gone through to get himself out of the NDS custody, not once but twice.

On another occasion, Hababi "showed his true colors" of not being an honorable prosecutor by disobeying the rules of the DFAC—in direct violation of the DFAC's signs, which were clearly posted on the front of every refrigerator—that no one was allowed to take more than two drinks of any kind (which mainly consisted of 12-ounce cans of soda or 8 oz. containers of milk). None of the linguists, including Habibi (an Afghan law enforcement official), paid even the slightest attention to the signs. In other words, as Afghan officials, in their minds they could all break the rules and not be held accountable for not following the rules and laws on a U.S. military base.

One night shortly before 9:00 when the DFAC was closing, Habibi entered, wearing an overcoat (during the month of July when the temperature in Khost Province was never less than 100 degrees). While I sat, enjoying my tea and dessert, I watched Habibi walk over to one of the refrigerators and then glance around to see if anyone was watching him. When he saw me, he waved his hand as a gesture of greeting and then, apparently thinking that I was one of his fellow Afghans, started stuffing the pockets of his overcoat with as many containers of milk as it could hold. Since I couldn't just sit there and watch, I got up, walked toward him, and jokingly asked in Farsi, *"Czharanwal Saheb, Shoma ba khyalam key mast mya may konin"* ("Mr. Prosecutor, you must be making yogurt out of all that milk you've been taking"). Habibi smiled and said, "Nope, it's for the local guys who go home at night. I usually give them some milk to take home with them." I shook my head. "Since you know we're only allowed to have two items per person, what you're actually doing is cheating—in other words, stealing."

From the look on his face, it was obvious that the prosecutor was not pleased with what I had just said, especially since he was an Afghan official who was taking more than his share from our soldiers, giving it, instead, to his local buddies. I never once saw an American soldier taking more than two containers of any of the drinks available to us. In fact, most of the soldiers would buy their own drinks from the PX. The prosecutor seldom, if ever, talked with me, because he (and the other linguists) considered me to be a traitor, someone not to be trusted by other Afghans. Regardless, he was right—I was (am) more American than Afghan.

Our work at the FDS was unpredictable. One week we would have a full house of guests at The Taliban Motel; the next week the motel would be empty, which allowed us the time to take advantage of the downtime. As mentioned earlier, I spent much of my free time in the library and gym from around 2:00 PM until 5:00 PM, when the gym was less crowded. I usually saw the same people every day during this timeframe. Then, I would go to my room, grab a towel and my shampoo, and walk over to the Connex, which was about a five-minute walk from my room, to take a shower.

On the way to the showers, I passed other barracks where soldiers were sitting outside their own rooms, socializing with their buddies. I also passed a couple of young, female soldiers who were smoking and socializing in front of their rooms. I saw one of them at the gym from time to time. As was my habit, as I passed them I would say, "Good evening, ladies," and they would smile and return the greeting. They were both in their late teens or perhaps early 20s at the most, both with the MP (Military Police) unit.

One day while en route to the showers, I saw that only one woman was standing with one of the young, local interpreters—who I had seen around the base on several occasions—that was in the same age range. When I got closer to them, the young man approached me and said in Pashto, *"Ustada, salamalykom!"* ("Greetings, Ustad!"). Then, the female MP joined us and said the same thing—*"Salam"*—in Farsi. After we had all greeted each other, the MP said, "I didn't realize that you're an Afghan!" to which I responded, "I am a native of Afghanistan, but I am here as an American." While the interpreter looked on, she told me what I had already been told a countless number of times, "You can *never* become an American! I am proud to be an Afghan, and so should you!" At first, thinking that I had perhaps misunderstood her, or maybe didn't hear her correctly, I asked, "Did you just say that you are honored and proud to be an Afghan?" With confidence in her voice, she responded, *"Balay, ma eftikhar my konom key Awghanistan watani ma ast."* ("Yes, I am honored to have a country such as Afghanistan.") I was so angered by her response that I didn't want to talk with her any longer. But before I walked away, I had to tell her one thing. "If you really mean what you just said, than I would strongly recommend that you take off that American Army uniform and wear an ANA uniform instead so that you can go outside the base and fight for Afghanistan's freedom." As I walked away, her last words to me were, "Wearing an American uniform doesn't make me an American."

I was so appalled that her allegiance was to Afghanistan rather than the United States, the next morning I couldn't help but share the details of my conversation with her with everyone in the office. Needless to say, as expected, they were all shocked. I also told them that for a minute, I thought she might be related to Major Nidal Hasan, who also wore a U.S. Army uniform.

For a while, The Taliban Motel was still empty and our downtime continued. One morning after breakfast, I went to the library and picked up the *Stars and Stripes* military newspaper first. As I started reading it, I saw a full-page article, half of which were pictures of my buddy, Fox, that I had worked with in Ghazni a year earlier. The other half of the page was an article under the picture of Fox surrounded by a group of local Afghan kids. The paper gave the location and date—"Eastern Afghanistan / May 2009—followed by a large headline that read: **Oh my God, I'm hit! Am I going to die?** Recognizing those exact words being said on a mission of which I had been a part, I continued reading the rest of the article. "When Sgt. 1st Class Sean Clifton kicked on the front door of a mud hut that Sunday afternoon last year in Afghanistan, more than 20 AK47s greeted him. 'Oh crap,' he thought. Within seconds, Clifton was hit at least four times, one bullet searing through his pelvis just below his body armor; another shattering his left forearm, causing him to drop his weapon. And again he thought: 'Oh crap.' He managed to stumble away from the door and toward his team's medics. He saw his friend a few feet away. 'His eyes were big, like saucers,' when he said, 'Save,' Sgt. 1st Class Mark Wanner recalled. 'I thought of his boys at that moment, and that I wasn't going to tell them their father had been killed.' Wanner and fellow medic SFC Matt Scheaffer worked to save their teammate, but it wouldn't be easy.

"'There was a volley of gunfire splashing around everybody,' Wanner said. He and Scheaffer dragged Clifton toward the side of the mud hut, thinking it would provide protection. It didn't. 'We were exposed the whole time,' Wanner said. The Green Berets were caught in the crossfire between suspected Taliban fighters and the 30 Afghan Security Forces embedded with the 12-member Special Forces team. While Scheaffer bound a tourniquet around Clifton's arm, Wanner tended to Clifton's abdominal wound. Clifton, meanwhile, wondered if he would die there in Afghanistan on Memorial Day weekend. 'Your mind processes a thousand things within those few seconds,' Clifton said. 'I was thinking everything from *Oh my God, I'm hit!* to *Am I going to bleed out? Am I going to die?* The shot to my arm was the most shocking. I could see my arm, my bones.... There was so much blood, and I remember thinking, *How many seconds of life do I have left before I bleed out?* And then I had visions of my boys running through my head. My wife. My family. I was thinking, *Who is going to contact them? How are they going to take the news?* While Clifton thought about his wife of seven years, about his sons who were ages 1 and 3, Wanner struggled to ensure that Clifton would see them again.

"'I am here today, alive, because of the heroic and competent action that Mark performed,' said Clifton, who turns 37 on June 19. For his effort, Wanner, 37, received the Silver Star. It is the first such award for an Ohio National Guard member since the Korean War. 'Oftentimes, it's easy to lose sight of what we have as a people," Ohio Gov. Ted Strickland said during a recent interview. 'Then we become aware of someone like this, this Sergeant first class—a real person with a charming personality, a beautiful wife, two children, in so many ways a regular guy. And we're appreciative that he chose to serve our country and chose to be a Green Beret and all that it involves.' The 20-year military veteran is a construction man who leaves his home in North Dakota at 6:30 AM for a job building custom homes and often puts in 12-hour plus days.

"He graduated from North Dakota State University with a degree in microbiology and a minor in chemistry and biotechnology, and he used to be a researcher at the University of Cincinnati College of Medicine, studying the impact of allergens on asthma patients. Though he and his wife liked Ohio, they longed for the quieter hamlets of North Dakota—and 'going from researcher to builder suited me fine,' he said. The simpler and quieter lifestyle offered by North Dakota provided the change of pace the family sought. Despite his schooling grounded in science, he opted for a career in construction, working for a childhood friend, and one that lets him work with his hands, get dirty, and relish the finished product, even if it means fewer Blue Moon beers with his friend Clifton. The round that penetrated Clifton's pelvis ripped through his abdominal cavity, hitting his small intestine, large intestine, bladder, urethra, the sciatic nerve, and caused extensive vascular damage. He was awarded the Purple Heart and a Bronze Star with a 'V' device. He's still not fully recovered. But he's alive."

Reading this article in the newspaper a year later was comforting news for me to know that Delta (a.k.a. Clifton) was doing well and that both Fox and Delta were awarded the medals that they deserved for protecting our nation. No other readers could possibly be able to relate to this newspaper article, than those of us who had been on that mission and seen everything that had happened from a 50-foot distance—I will never forget seeing such bravery firsthand.

Since there were still no detainees to interrogate, as you know by now, it was very easy for me to get bored with nothing to do, so this time I went directly to the chief and asked if he could find some translating work for me instead of me sitting around with idle time on my hands. Right after lunch that same day, I got a call from the chief asking me to stop by his office at 2:00.

When I arrived promptly at 2:00, he said that someone in his office needed help with translating the Khost Province NDS Chief, who would be visiting our base. With pleasure, I agreed to do so, and he took me to Bob's office for introductions. Bob commented that the chief always talked highly about my knowledge of the Pashton culture and their language. I thanked them both for their kind words but explained that I only understood the dialogue of Khosti Pashto about 50 to 70 percent. They both smiled as Bob said, "We'll gladly take your 50 to 70 percent understanding over all the other linguists' 26 percent any day of the week!"

I told Bob that I was there to help him in any way I could so that he would be able to understand the NDS Chief—whose name was Jan Mohammad—who was going to be visiting our base within the next few days. Bob gave me Chief Jan Mohammad's telephone number. Since most

Afghans only go by one name, from hereon I will refer to him as Jan to make it shorter and easier to pronounce.

Later, I called Jan and introduced myself, explaining that I was the new linguist who would be working with Bob. After the introductions, Jan told me he was glad to be talking with a fellow Pashton. Not knowing Jan, and since this was only my first time speaking with him on the phone, I didn't want to anger him by saying anything regarding his comment about ethnicity or nationality, even though it's the most important part of life when dealing with people in Afghanistan. Jan had invited Bob and me to visit him at his compound in downtown Khost City, which we had politely declined. Instead, I invited him to meet with us at FOB Salerno at 10:00 the following morning, which he accepted without hesitation. Bob asked me to tell Jan that when our meeting was over, we wanted to take him to lunch. Delighted by the invitation, Jan accepted.

After hanging up the phone with Jan, Bob and I went to the front gate. In order for Jan to get on base, Bob had to request a one-day visitor's pass in advance from the guards at the front gate so that those on duty would know that it was okay for Jan to be granted permission to come on the base the next day so that when he arrived, Bob and I would be able to go to the front gate to meet, welcome, and escort him around the base.

The following morning around 10:00 AM, I received a call from Jan apologizing that he was running late and advising that he should be at our front gate within the next 15 minutes, *"Inshallah"* ("God willing"). As soon as Jan had said, *Inshallah*, I knew that Jan wasn't going to arrive within the next 15 minutes. When I shared this news with Bob, he asked me what *Inshallah* meant. I explained by telling him that, in all actuality, Jan wasn't going to make it within 15 minutes but, instead, would arrive whenever he could. When Bob asked for further definition, I explained that Jan wasn't in control of his own schedule; it was up to God as to when he would show up. I also told Bob that when an Afghan tells you *Inshallah* at the end of a conversation, it means that he or she is not in charge of making the decisions where to meet and at what time. Afghans believe that the decision is up to God; therefore, in Jan's case today, we'd be lucky if he managed to arrive within an hour or two. "Nas, are you kidding me?" Bob asked incredulously. "Why would he do that?" I paused before answering. "Well, Sir, welcome to Afghanistan! That's how things work here when people are not in charge or control of making their own daily decisions." Bob shook his head. "Nas, this *Inshallah* thing sounds strange to me, especially if we're going to be waiting here not knowing when or if he's even going to show up—but since I have no other choice, I'll just take your word for it."

The next call I got from Jan was around 11:00. He didn't sound any different from the last time he had called, telling me that he'd be here within 15 minutes. *"Inshallah,"* he said again. After Jan hung up, Bob asked me, "Is he here?" *"Inshallah,"* I said with a smile and then told him, "He said he'd be here within the next fifteen minutes but don't believe it." Bob asked why Jan kept saying *Inshallah* when he obviously knew he wasn't telling us the truth. Otherwise, we wouldn't have to sit here and waste all of our time at the front gate." I nodded my head in understanding, but explained, "That's how business is done in Afghanistan, Bob. Unfortunately, there's no way around it." It was around 12:30 when Jan and one of his buddies finally showed up at the front gate—no big deal really because, after all, Jan was only two and a half hours late!

The guard at the front gate was not allowing Jan to come on base because we had only given the guards one person's name; he hadn't included his buddy's name. Why did he bring a friend with him in the first place? Another one of those cultural things: When you invite one person, that person will also invite one of his friends, just to be on the safe side, keeping the invitee company in case there's no one for the invited friend to socialize with. Anyone who doesn't know the Afghan culture should know [and be prepared for] two things when trying to set up a time to meet or invite them to a function of some sort: First, don't expect most of them to be on time, especially if they mention *Inshallah*. Second, have an extra chair and food ready for at least one of the invitee's friends. You have been forewarned!

To issue Jan's friend a temporary visitor's pass, Bob had to talk with the military officer who was in charge of the front gate, which was not an easy accomplishment. After all the hassle, we finally managed to get both Jan and his friend on the base, into our vehicle, and straight to the DFAC before it closed at 2:00. I talked with Jan and his friend and told them where everything was located. Bob and I got our lunch and found a table—and then we sat and waited [and waited] for Jan and his friend while they walked around armed with trays, one in each hand, to get all the food they could so that their trays were loaded with as much as they could possibly accommodate! Within another few minutes, they finally joined us, armed with far more food than they could ever hope to eat. They had each taken two cups—filled to the top—of ice-cream, which sat sitting next to them, melting, while they ate their lunch. I offered to put their ice-cream in the freezer but Jan declined. "No, but thanks. It's alright; we'll drink it if we have to." They only consumed about a third of the food they had taken; the rest was thrown in the trash.

Our 10:00 AM meeting regarding the security and stability of Khost City—for which Jan was the NDS Chief, in charge of the city's security—was now around 3:00 PM. Bob asked Jan how we could help him succeed in capturing the bad guys in his city and district. "My brother," Jan said, "I want you to assure Bob that for as long as you have Habibi working here, there will be no stability in Khost as far as the security situation is concerned." Bob interjected by asking Jan, "Why is that?" to which he responded, "I'll tell you why, but don't let Habibi know I did." Bob assured him that he wouldn't.

"The prosecutor is reporting on innocent people that you Americans are capturing, while the real criminals are still out there doing their thing," Jan explained. Then Bob asked Jan, "What would he do differently than the prosecutor to bring security to your district?"

Jan answered, "We need financial support for our security situation."

"As the Chief of the NDS," Bob queried, "isn't it your duty to bring security to Khost?"

"My twenty thousand Afghanis a month salary is only enough for me to feed my six children; I can't do anything else with it," Jan replied.

"Isn't the twenty thousand Afghanis a month salary for the work you're supposed to be doing to get the bad guys?" Bob asked.

With a disappointing look on his face, Jan said, "The prosecutor sits here on the base, eating free food while his family is safe and sound in Kabul. Not to mention that he gets paid more than one hundred thousand Afghanis a month!" It sounded like Jan and Habibi had their own little dilemmas going on. Jan continued, "I know there are a lot of Taliban in the area, but I don't have the men and financial power to do anything about it."

Now, here's Jan, who's the head of Security, getting paid 20,000 Afghanis a month for *not* doing his job. However, if he actually did his job, he'd probably report innocent Afghan civilians like the prosecutor does—just so he could get paid.

Our meeting with Jan wasn't successful. We primarily learned what various people were doing—*nothing*—just so they could get paid by the American taxpayers. For example, according to Jan, the prosecutor was paid well above 100,000 Afghanis ($2,000) a month, and the prosecutor would have undoubtedly said the same thing about Jan. This is nothing new in the Afghan government because they get paid for simply showing up, just like the older linguists in Helmand. Taking it a step further, perhaps even my own father-in-law would say how easy it was working for the government in Kabul, which might be in Afghanistan, but most people in Kabul don't know much about their own country.

The similarities between what Jan was telling us closely paralleled the same thing Habibi did: reporting innocent people, most of whom were wealthy enough to bribe their way out of jail. One particular detainee who was the only one out of four brothers who still lived in Afghanistan to care for his nephews and nieces, and his elderly parents was brought in as a detainee to our compound for interrogation. His three older brothers had moved to the United Arab Emirates so they would not be harassed by the Afghan government—that raid their homes in the middle of the night—anymore. During our interrogation, the detainee told us that the only reason he was in captivity and being interrogated was because his neighbor—who works for the Afghan government—had filed a report on him. So, in Afghanistan, if you work for the government, you screw the poor by bribing them to death. If you're a government employee, you leave the country (exiled) when it's in limbo, which Afghanistan has been ever since its birth.

One of our many interrogation stories was also somehow related to what Jan had said about the prosecutor or, truth be known, perhaps this example might be related to Jan. Anyhow, the detainees who were brought in for interrogation were three brothers; the older brother was a doctor who had a medical clinic in Khost, the younger brothers worked for the older brother at the clinic, and the middle brother was in the house visiting from Dubai when the house was raided.

After being in Afghanistan for just a little over a year, I had done close to 350 interrogations, which, according to Sergeant Karr, was over three times more than the other interrogators. I never assumed whether a detainee brought in for interrogation was innocent or guilty of anything until all of our questions were asked, and even then I would only give my opinion about the detainee's innocence or guilt when asked by the interrogators.

So, after the second round of questions to these three detainees, I decided that the brothers were innocent, but I didn't give my opinion until I was asked for it.

During our break, since the interrogator and I thought we were done with this detainee, the interrogator went to her office while I decided to opt for a short walk in the fresh air. After a few minutes, I thought that the interrogation should be done by now, so turned and went back to the interrogator's office to find her storming out of the office—by the look on her face—obviously mad as hell. "Nas, let's go in one more time." I didn't ask why or say anything else, but simply followed her into the interrogation room. As soon as we walked in, she started slamming her fist on the table and calling the doctor every curse word in the [proverbial] book. Even though the detainee spoke in broken English, he understood what she was saying because he had gone to medical school in India. He also didn't lose his temper or "blow his cool" even though he had to go through this third round of questioning.

Once she was done cursing, the detainee eliminated my translation and responded to her directly in English. "May I say something?" Ignoring his question, the interrogator said, "We know that you've been treating fucking wounded Taliban in your clinic," to which the detainee responded, "Madam, in my clinic, I do not question my patients about whether they're Taliban or not. As a medical doctor, I am required by the code of ethics to treat every patient who walks into my clinic." Even more frustrated now, I recommended that she take another break before we went on with the interrogation any further. She agreed by taking a walk in the fresh air while I went to Sergeant Karr's office to tell him I could not continue to help with this interrogation any longer. I did not want to be part of an interrogation that wasn't going anywhere. Karr said, "Not a problem, Nas." Then, he told me I could take the rest of the day off. Since she was being pressured by her superiors to produce bad guys out of good ones, all she wanted to do was score points just to prove that her interrogations were being productive. By trying to label every detainee as being with the Taliban, for the officials' own political or financial gain, it appeared to me that this particular interrogator was somehow related to Jay and Habibi.

One of my interrogations in Khost was similar to Abdul Bari in Ghazni where the detainee had admitted to the crime of which he was accused. This man was the oldest detainee that I had ever interrogated during my time in Afghanistan. According to him, he was probably close to 90 years old. Our initial interrogation didn't go smoothly. The detainee didn't want to talk to us and was constantly coughing so that we couldn't even get one word out of him. All he kept saying over and over again was that he needed to see a doctor. Once the detainee asked to see a doctor, we were not allowed to interrogate him until the doctor gave us the okay because the detainee was then considered fit for the interrogation to continue.

The following day, she started interrogating him again; he even cooperated with her by answering the questions she asked. Because he was the elder of his village, he explained why his house had been broken into and he had been detained. He had made a propaganda video that was used for recruiting young fighters willing to be suicide bombers or to take arms and carry a *jihad* (holy war against the infidels) against the Americans in the Khost District, his native land. First, I found it interesting that a man of his age could still make propaganda videos. Second, he referred to Khost Province as his homeland instead of the whole of Afghanistan; but then, it's common practice for local villagers to even refer to their village as their homeland.

Since in a tribal society such as Afghanistan every tribe protects their own community, the interrogator asked the old man if he was making the videos to promote violence against the government of Afghanistan and its international allies. When he first answered, he lied about doing that, but when he was shown a video in which he was clearly visible, he had no other choice but to admit that it was him. She again asked why he made the video, and also wanted to know who the other two people wearing masks were. "There were three people with me when we made the video," he said, "but you didn't see the third one because he was filming it." In the video, the old man and the other two were holding rifles and wearing suicide vests. The old man's face was not covered, but the other two men were wearing ski masks. When she persisted in again asking the old man why he was making the video to promote violence against his own countrymen, he finally responded that he did it because he wasn't scared of anyone—not the Taliban, not the Americans, and not the Afghan government. "I was born in this village," he said, "and I will die in this village protecting it from anyone who threatens to harm us."

He was asked what the Taliban had done to him, that he wouldn't allow them to be in his village. "When the Taliban comes to my village, you guys are going to come after them, and that's why I am not allowing anyone to come to my village, so that the people of my village don't go missing like the twelve people who have been missing from our village for many years, their families not knowing where they are, or, because they seemingly vanished, the families have not had anyone to provide for them; therefore, their farmland has dried out. I don't care who invades Afghanistan, but if anyone comes to my village, I will defend it with my blood, just like I did with the Soviets. When everyone left for Pakistan, I stayed in my village to protect it from the invaders. Now I am doing the exact same thing." She asked him who the other people in the video were. He responded that they worked for the Afghan government. "Since I am the village elder, they were just helping me make the video."

She asked how he knew that the other people in the video weren't going to use it for other reasons that could get him in trouble, just like he was right now. He responded that he trusted those people, and that he was never going to be in trouble. The only way he could be in trouble would be if he disobeyed God's will by not promoting jihad. Whatever he was doing, he knew that God was happy about it.

The next question asked was how he knew God was happy about what he was doing. "Everything is in the Quran," he responded. To the question about what he did for a living, he said that he'd been a farmer all his life. As though to prove his point, he showed me his hands, which looked like tree stumps.

When asked if he'd ever gone to school, he said, *"Yah, pa alip wo bay walaka pohazgem"* ("Nope, I can't tell an A from a B"). Asking if he spoke or understood a language other than Pashto, he shrugged his shoulders before responding. "I was born a Pashton and will die a Pashton, so what do I need another language for?" When asked, "If you don't know an A from a B, how can you read the Quran, which is in the Arabic language?" After pondering how to respond, he finally said, "Well, we're taught by our Mullah in our mosque what is in the Quran." Curious, he was then asked if he trusted his Mullah just as much as he did the two people in the video. "Yes, I trust our Mullah because he has studied Quran in Egypt." Since the old man had admitted that he was the person in the video and provided us with an explanation as to why he had made it, this part of the interrogation was finished.

So, deciding to take a brief break, the interrogator and I left the room, telling the old man she'd return shortly, all the while hoping that it had been made clear to the old man that what he was doing was wrong, that it was against all religions to kill innocent people.

Having changed my mind about not wanting to be involved with the interrogation any longer, I joined her after her brief break, and we walked back into the room. The interrogator handed the detainee a note. The old man opened the paper and looked at it, and threw it back on the table. When I asked him why he had done that, he reminded me that he had told me earlier that he didn't know an A from a B; therefore, he wondered why the interrogator handed him a note to read. I told him it was in English and asked if he'd like to know what was written on the paper.

The old man's face was grim. Had I been in his village, I had no doubt but that he would have beheaded me for disrespecting him: first, by giving him a note written in English, and second, because he had clearly told me that he couldn't read at all, so why were we asking him to read anything? Then, he started coughing again. When he had finished, I took the note from the table and asked him if I could read it to him. He shrugged his shoulders as affirmation. I was planning to read what was actually written on the paper, but decided to "read" something else (imaginary) with the hope he'd like me more and be on my side. He was still grinding his teeth, looking like he was going to bite me before I read the note to him. Fortunately, he didn't!

"Dear elder (since I didn't remember his name)," I began. "You are an honorable man, and we are very sorry for bringing you here. To atone for some of the pain we have caused you, we've decided to pay you for your trouble and release you very soon so you can go home to your family." The old man's face broke into a smile as he opened his arms in an effort to hug me. I stopped him before he got any closer so that he wouldn't actually touch me. He settled back on his chair, an obvious look of disappointment that I wouldn't allow him to thank me with a hug. When I told him that I was going to read what was actually written on the paper, I knew he was going to be very disappointed and angry.

"You are promoting violence against the Afghan government and the Afghan people. You will be locked up in jail for your actions until you die." As anticipated, he was mad as hell and started screaming at me for lying to him. Once he calmed down, I tried to explain that he could not understand or read Arabic or English, which was the cause for his corrupted behavior. As an example, I reminded him of how his Mullah repeatedly took advantage of him. The old man could not read Arabic, so he went to his Mullah who he trusted to communicate the words accurately from the Quran.

It was simple for me to miscommunicate and change the actual words on the note to a message of my own choice. Likewise, I believe it was just as easy for his "trusted" Mullah to miscommunicate the information from the Quran solely to benefit from and convince an old, trusting, and vulnerable man. His Mullah was taking advantage of him by promoting the recruitment of young men for suicide missions to kill innocent people. I asked him if he didn't think it was possible for the Mullah in his mosque to make up things as well and pointed out that if his Mullah was telling the truth that he should kill the Americans or the Afghan government officials, why didn't the Mullah not do it himself?

I could see and sense in the old man's facial expression that he had already started to doubt me because I was an infidel trying to tell him that his Mullah was betraying him. I had no idea what he had on his mind at that particular moment. I strongly believe every human has a conscience and most can think for themselves, much the same as this man had done by making a video promoting his ideology. His conscience was now probably also asking him whether his Mullah was telling him the truth about promoting violence against innocent people with whom he disagreed. Because of his condition, we could not interrogate him any further because, after being diagnosed with tuberculosis, he was being admitted to our military hospital.

The following day, the medic on base came over to the FDS to tell Karr that anyone who had been in contact with the old man was exposed to tuberculosis. There were six of us who needed to be put on a nine-month control program for tuberculosis detection.

A couple of days later, during lunch, my company site manager, who I respected very much, approached me. He told me that he had received an email from the company headquarters in Bagram; they were trying to relocate me for another assignment with the U.S. Navy who were in need of a Cat III linguist as soon as possible. I forewarned him that my POC, Karr, and the chief would not be happy that I would be leaving them again. "I'll tell them, but, since they already know that you're a Cat III linguist, they're aware that they can't keep you here forever." My manager called and talked with the chief, telling him that I was going to be leaving them very soon for another assignment.

As anticipated, the chief wasn't happy about it but knew that he had no choice but to let me go. Two days later my manager emailed me that I was leaving Khost for the assignment working with the Navy pilots on the aircraft out of Bagram Airfield. Before leaving, I went to say goodbye to the chief, Karr, and the interrogators with whom I had had the pleasure to work with for the past three months. None of them were happy that I was leaving, including the one I disagreed with for not doing what was right but opted to handle her interrogations in a way that was only good for her own personal gain.

CHAPTER TEN

August 4, 2010: Navy Cyber for Major Command CJTF-101, Bagram Airfield, Afghanistan

A RRIVING AT THE BAGRAM AIRFIELD was much more different than my arrival at FOB Salerno. The temperature was over 100 degrees and heavy clouds of dust were flying all over the base. Besides the transition tent being hot as hell, there was the addition of having to deal with the other linguists, while waiting to be permitted to live on the Navy compound until I was cleared by the medical staff after a complete physical by the Navy doctors. I was told the process usually took a week or so.

This was the longest I had been in a transition tent, primarily because of the necessity to wait for the Navy doctors to perform all of the required medical checkups in order to fly with the Navy pilots. Just to make sure I was fit enough to fly for five to six hours at a time, I had to go through a full physical (blood tests, heart checkup, and so forth). It took 11 days before I was approved to fly. As I was going through all of this, there was one other Cat III linguist who was also brought in for the same assignment. He did not spend more than one day in the transition tent before he was given his own room at the Navy compound. Since he lived on the Navy compound instead of being in the transition tent, his physical took more than two weeks before his results were in. I was curious why he was already living on the compound if he hadn't even as yet been cleared physically to fly for two weeks—my guess was there are just some people who always find ways to play the system.

In addition to the two of us being brought in, there was one other linguist who had been with the Navy for a long time—who, oddly enough, also happened to be the uncle of the linguist who had been brought in with me. I soon learned that both hated to be in transition tents more than I did (if that's possible!). The uncle had helped his nephew, before he could even pass his physical, by making it possible for him to live on the compound in order to avoid the transition tent. Both of my fellow linguists were ethnic Hazaras. The uncle and his nephew didn't like to be in the transition tent because most linguists there were either Pashtons and Tajiks, and the Pashtons and Tajiks combined didn't like the Hazaras or other foreigners, including Americans. It was all so mindboggling to me, I could have cared less whether they liked each other or not; yet they all were American citizens.

I met Ron, my new POC with the Navy, once I had been cleared by the Navy medical team. He introduced me to the rest of the flight crew I'd be flying with on our missions. I started working from 8:00 AM to 2:00 PM. My first day on the flight was very exciting. The pilots were all wearing their flight suits and boarding P3s (Maritime Surveillance Aircrafts). Since this was my first time working with Navy pilots, I found them all to be an awesome bunch of guys, just like everyone else in the military that I had worked with in the past, and was honored to be part of their team.

After boarding the aircraft, and before takeoff, I got the required, basic training from Ron regarding the aircraft and its operation. As a civilian, not knowing anything about aircraft, aside that one could fly from point A to point B and back, I was understandably overwhelmed by the information given to me in just that first day. I was amazed by the interior of the aircraft, primarily, I'm sure, merely because I had never seen one before. It was shaped more like a commercial aircraft but, once onboard, you could see everything inside out because it was all out in the open without anything covering the surface. It reminded me of the human body's nervous anatomy posters one might see in a neurologist's office. What amazed me further was that this aircraft was made by human beings who just so happened to be American.

It was my second week on the job when the other linguist finally passed his physical and was onboard with us on his first flight. Surprisingly, he had a very difficult time during the first hour and said he could no longer be on the aircraft and wanted to get off. Obviously, it wasn't possible for the pilots to cancel the mission because of one linguist who wanted to get off the aircraft. As the mission continued, the linguist was laying down in the back of the aircraft for the duration of the six-hour flight. I also got dizzy and nauseated from time to time, but not to the extent of the other linguist. In general, I really enjoyed working on the flight with all the pilots. What I liked even more about them was that their personalities were very similar to Detla2's, my buddy from Special Forces. The pilots would always ask me questions about the Afghans, their cultures, and the different ethnic groups. Despite being dizzy and nauseated, all the good things I felt being with the Navy guys on P3s, I really enjoyed everything the job entailed. After about a month, I was getting to the point that after four or five hours of flight time, I would get dizzy and get headaches to the point that I could not be productive for the overall mission. Not only that, but I couldn't fall asleep once I was back on the ground.

I did it for as long as six weeks before I could no longer handle the dizziness and lack of sleep, which were physically taking their toll on me. I didn't want to be on a mission if I couldn't contribute to it. Despite all the hardships of being dizzy, nauseated, and not being able to sleep, I would've worked with the Navy pilots in a heartbeat, if I could contribute to accomplishing their overall missions. Being on the P3 aircraft was an amazing and once-in-a-lifetime experience—to be up in the air for six weeks, flying over every corner of Afghanistan from above 33,000 feet, day and night, to see what Afghanistan really looks like. During our daytime missions, all one could see below was mostly rocky mountains and sandy deserts.

During nightly missions, all we could see was *nothing* but darkness. Afghanistan is probably one of the darkest corners of the world. Every time we flew over Afghanistan's airspace towards the south, if one would look toward the southwest, they could see the lights and brightness shooting up into the sky from all the countries around the Persian Gulf (United Arab Emirate, Qatar, Bahrain, and Kuwait). But coming back from the south of Afghanistan and returning to the Bagram Airfield in the north, all one could see was darkness and plenty of bright stars in the sky above. (As an aside, on a personal note, to most of my fellow native Afghans, who proudly admit Afghanistan's 5,000-year-old history, which they claim to be proud of, I merely wish to say that most Afghanistan still live in the 5,000-year-old historical times.)

Seeing everything from the Afghan airspace, the lightness of the Persian Gulf states, and the darkness of Afghanistan are all similar to the lightness of South Korea compared to the darkness of North Korea from the images of the satellite. To make my point further about my native Afghanistan, all the countries younger than 70-years-old, whose lights of the 21st century can be seen from Afghanistan's 5,000-year-old darkness are allies of the United States of America, my adopted country—America, a shiny city on top of the hill, will lead to a shiny world, whereas Afghanistan, a 5,000-year-old land of darkness, will only lead to more darkness. Flying over Afghanistan, one can see from a distance of 33,000 feet things like single light bulbs, some distance apart scattered throughout the country, most of which are American military bases that are lit up, especially when flying over Bagram, Kabul, and Kandahar Airfields.

My other darkest moment—and the scariest for me while working on the P3s with the Navy pilots occurred during my training on the first flight by Ron, my POC. I was told that I should be calm in case of an emergency where we might have to jump out of the aircraft using parachutes in order to ditch the aircraft, or if we had to make an emergency landing in enemy territory. One day after our official mission and right after leaving the station, we were headed from around the Kandahar area toward Bagram Airfield. I'd been on the Kandahar mission a couple of other times, but this time it was different.

When we went off the radio station, I would simply take off my headphones and start reading whatever book I had with me. Flight time from Kandahar to Bagram Airfield was about an hour and 15 minutes. It was a scorching hot, mid-August day, where one would think there shouldn't be any kind of winds that could cause the sudden turbulence that had just occurred. Anyone who feels like s/he is going to die will assume anything until the aircraft either hits the mountains or simply drops out of the sky. However, in our case, being in Afghanistan, after the first drop, the aircraft never found its balance when the second drop of about 200 feet took place. I thought maybe this was happening in order to avoid the wind. As I looked around, scared as hell, everyone else is just sitting around calmly doing other things. Since the aircraft only had a single row of seats facing the windows, I looked toward my left, which had me facing the back of the aircraft. As the aircraft rocked from side to side, I could see that no one was moving out of their seats yet.

Sitting one seat away from the cockpit door opening, which was covered by a half-closed curtain where I could see Captain Stan, one of the pilots was in the cockpit also sitting just like everyone else on the plane. Within 30 seconds of the first drop, there was another drop—this one even deeper and shakier than the last. Now I was really scared. I then saw the navigator coming out of the cockpit, pulling out the first parachute from above the top of the cockpit door. He put it on as quickly as he possibly could, while checking for leaks by four fingers on his right hand on the exposed wires, all the while holding his flashlight toward the emergency exit door. By now, I knew that something terrible had happened. Being a civilian, not trained for all of the flight procedures and not remembering anything Ron told me, except to be as calm as possible, I tried diligently to do just that. Seeing the Navy navigator, who was more freaked out than me by running around like a maniac from the front of the aircraft, putting his parachute on, checking every emergency exit, touching all the red lights on the wall that were flashing, *and* frequently looking out the window to see if we were going to hit the mountains, was definitely *not* the way for me to remain calm.

As I sat, scared and confused, trying to keep calm and carry on, wondering why everyone else wasn't getting up, I also wondered if I should just go ahead and get up, and start putting my parachute on so I'd be ready to jump as soon as the door opened. As sacred as I was, I remembered one other thing I needed to do besides keeping calm: I remembered when Ron told me that if we jumped out, I should not look down but, rather, I should look straight ahead, to the horizon. One thing I had realized was how good I was at following military orders. I continued to sit tight, not wanting to do anything until I was given the green light to do so. Meanwhile, I tried to get Ron's attention by waving my hand toward him. He was sitting three seats to the left of me, toward the back of the aircraft.

When I was finally able to get his attention, he signaled for me to put on my headphones so he could communicate with me that way. I immediately pulled my headphones from above, put them on, and turned the power on when Ron asked me, "Hey, Nas, can you hear me?" to which I responded, while looking at him as we talked, "Yes, Ron, but what the fuck is going on? Are we ditching the aircraft or what?" Ron laughed and told me, "No, Nas, why do you think that?" I told him my concern about the turbulence and the navigator running around from the cockpit to the back of the aircraft. Ron laughed again before he said, "Nas, don't worry, That was just a rehearsal, which we typically do just to be prepared in case of an emergency." I told Ron that I was freaking out and wanted to know why no one told me about what was going on. Ron told me that the pilot had announced it on the internal radio when I, of course, didn't have my headphones on because I would always take them off once we were off the station. If I'd been patient enough to keep them on for the duration of the flight, until we were landed, I would not have freaked out the way I did.

As much as I wanted to be with the Navy pilots and work with them on the aircraft, I found that I was practically having to drag myself to stay on the aircraft after the first four to five hours because I didn't want to be on an assignment where I wouldn't be able to perform completely, 100 percent—so I resigned. When I gave this news to Ron that I wasn't able to do the flying part of my job, I told him that if they needed me for any other linguistic assignments on the ground, I would be more than happy to do them. Ron told me there was nothing that he could offer me other than working with the pilots on their flying missions. Everyone on the team thanked me, and Ron told me that if there was anything he could do to keep me with his team, he'd welcome the opportunity to accommodate me. I told him that I had really pushed myself to be on the team, but, despite my best efforts, I just couldn't handle the six hours of flying. I was very disappointed with myself, and even though I had tried everything I could do to make it happen, it just wasn't happening for me because my ability to perform diminished, thanks to the dizziness I experienced during each flight and then because of my inability to sleep when we were finally back on the ground.

I was back to my company's office for reassignment. Since there were a limited number of positions for Cat III linguists at that time, outside of the Bagram Airfield, they tried to find a place that would be practical for me. I had asked the person in charge of our assignment in Bagram that if there was any way they could assign me to a unit in the Kandahar area, I would be more than happy to take it—especially because of the massive number of troops that had been moved into the Kandahar Province, primarily to the Arghandab District to root out the Taliban from their stronghold.

This was the time (2010) when almost 50 percent of the linguists were being sent to Kandahar because of the demand for the ongoing major mission in that Province, and I thought that there would be a greater opportunity for me to go to Kandahar while all the other linguists were doing everything they could to avoid going.

I waited two weeks in the [dreaded] transition tent before I could get an assignment. As everyone knew, I had always wanted to be assigned in the south of Afghanistan—especially Kandahar or Helmand Provinces where I could speak, read, write, and understand the language 100 percent. Despite the danger of fighting, I was ready for it and wanted to be there. By now, having already been in Afghanistan for more than 17 months, I had seen everything from IED explosions in front of me, numerous combat missions where I lost buddies during the fighting, been attacked 11 times from within a 500-foot range, jumped out of aircrafts, and interrogated hardcore Taliban who wanted to kill me. Despite all that, I lost my fear of dying, which was a good thing, especially if I wanted to be in the most challenging place in Afghanistan. Now, one challenge remained: how me going there could be coordinated with the military.

Then, the challenge I faced was the tuberculosis detection therapy that I had to continue for nine consecutive months, which started at the Bagram Medical Hospital on August 2, 2010. The doctor told me that I would only get a 30-day supply of the required medicine at a time, and at the end of every 30 days, I would need to have bloodwork done to make sure that every organ in my body was functioning as it should and there were no side effects from the medication, which meant that I had to be in Bagram at the end of 30 days. At the beginning of our deployment to Afghanistan, all linguists were provided with medical care by the military. Unfortunately, that medical coverage would expire at the end of the current year—while I was still in the middle of my treatment.

I was told by the physician who was treating me that he would do everything he could to provide the care I needed in order to finish my nine-month therapy trial, for which I thanked him most sincerely. Within a week, I was given a letter from the headquarters of the Department of the Air Force, 455th Air Expeditionary Wing of Bagram Airfield. It was under the command of Michael D. Stevens, Lieutenant Colonel, USAF, MC, Chief of the Medical Staff at the Craig Joint Theater Hospital, which authorized: "SUBJECT: Tuberculosis Therapy for Nasrat Kakar" (with my social security number). The letter stated that "Nasrat Kakar is currently obtaining tuberculosis therapy. He can continue to be seen in the Outpatient Clinic only for his INH therapy (to include labs, medication, and radiology studies) for the duration of his treatment, which is expected to be completed by May 2011." Because he was morally obligated, I was most appreciative of what Stevens had done to help me get the medication I needed.

Once out of the hospital, I walked into the company's offices that I was employed by and asked to see the deputy director of operations, who was in charge of my new assignment and would eventually help me get to Kandahar. He wasn't there because he was on PTO for the next couple of weeks. However, there was one other person who had worked with him who also knew that I had always wanted to go to Kandahar. Therefore, when I walked into the office, Dan was waiting for me so he could tell me that there were two places in the south that I could go to for a Cat III assignment. He gave me the choice between FOB Sharana in Paktika Province, where I had already been, or KAF (Kandahar Airfield).

I couldn't have asked for anything more and told Dan with a big smile on my face "I'll take KAF." Out of all the linguists, Dan told me I was the only one he had ever met who asked to go to Kandahar. I told Dan, "My friend, do you know how long I have waited for this? Seventeen fucking months to get to Kandahar, and it's finally happening." Dan asked me to sign on the dotted line and then I'd be on my way to my dream destination.

I really am amazed by the power of God's miracles, and how God makes things happen for you when you really want them from the heart. So far, I had been blessed every step of the way, not only for being deployed to Afghanistan, but for the many gifts God had given me, in general, throughout my lifetime—and I am humbled and most grateful for it all.

After receiving the good news about my new assignment, I believed in the old adage that "Good things happen to those who wait." more than ever. I realize that what's a good thing to one person, might not be to others (e.g., like the assignment to Kandahar). It was a good thing that I got that assignment but other linguists would disagree by telling you that I was crazy.

> *"It is better to be hated for what you are than to*
> *be loved for something you are not."*
> — ANDRE GIDE

CHAPTER ELEVEN

September 30, 2010: Major Command IJC (International Joint Command) Task Force: 525 BFSB (Battlefield Surveillance Brigade), Kandahar Airfield, Afghanistan

U PON MY ARRIVAL AT KAF, I couldn't help but notice that things were much different than the last time I was here, during my transition on my way to Helmand. It was then February, and the weather was a lot colder. Now it was the end of September, and the desert temperature was more than 100 degrees with not only dust blowing all around the base making it difficult to cope with, but the stench of the open sewer pond in the middle of the airfield only added to the misery. Unlike all the other military bases in Afghanistan that are controlled by the Americans, KAF is under the NATO command and ruled by the ISAF (International Security Assistance Force). Everyone who either works at KAF, or the unit they work for is stationed at KAF. A NATO identification card is required in order to be allowed to live on base.

As soon as I was picked up by our company movement people, I was given a 24-hour temporary transition card. After I was introduced to my unit (525 BFSB) by our company, I was then taken to the NATO command center by the lieutenant who was the POC in charge of my movement at KAF to get a permanent security card according to my company's site manager.

During my initial introduction by my site manager to the lieutenant in charge of my assigned unit, he was also informed by my company that I was on special medication that I needed at the Bagram Airfield at the end of each month for my prescription refills and blood tests. The lieutenant agreed to accommodate my needs and would have the refills flown to Bagram for my once-a-month medical treatment. Right after the lieutenant and I left so he could drop me off at the transition tent, he told me to be patient with him for a short while until he could send me to a unit where I was needed the most. For a second, I thought to myself, *Why am I even here if the lieutenant doesn't have an assignment for me?* I really didn't know how long I would have to wait in the transition tent before I could get out in the field and start working.

After a week at the transition tent, I still had not heard anything from the lieutenant. At the end of the week, I called to remind him that I was staying in the transition tent and waiting for my assignment. When I called him, at first he didn't know who I was, but soon after I mentioned my name, he apologized and said he had totally forgotten about me. After realizing that I was the new Cat III linguist on base, he said that he was still trying to find a place where Cat III linguists are required and then asked me to give him a couple more days. I acknowledged his request and hung up.

Well, by the fifth day, I was finally called and told by the lieutenant that he had two different locations in Kandahar Province where a Cat III linguist was required. He gave me a choice between the two available locations: (1) Spen Boldak in the eastern part of the Kandahar Province, or (2) Sarkari Bagh in the Arghandab District in northwestern Kandahar Province. As soon as the lieutenant said Sarkari Bagh in Arghandab, I was at first emotional, yet also excited—I don't recall experiencing such a moment before or since then. Despite being given a choice, I wasn't choosing between the two places—I was simply thinking, *Oh, my Great God, you are giving me something that I lost more than 40 years ago,* over and over again before I could even tell the lieutenant on the other end of the phone about my choice.

I could not stop the tears falling from my eyes, because I knew it was the goodness of God to return me to the place where I had learned many valuable lessons of life more than 40 years earlier—all of which I still carry with me because Sarkari Bagh is where I grew up (from six months to six

years) with my adoptive parents. As a grown man, I was shaking and crying just like I did when I was a young boy and would have to leave their
house after each visit to return to my biological family. This time I was
crying, not because I was hurt, mad, or sad like when I was a boy, but rather
because I was so grateful for what was happening to me, knowing that it
was possible for me to return to my childhood memories, to the village
where I had grown up. My mom and dad from the Arghandab District,
Sarkari Bagh, in particular, were the people who formed the foundation
for who I am today. I never dreamt that I would have this opportunity to
return again. After hearing my choice, the lieutenant said he would pick
me up the following day at 1:00 PM from the transition tent to take me to
the airfield so that I could catch a flight to Sarkari Bagh.

As promised, the lieutenant came over to the tent, helped me load
my gear into the vehicle, and we were on our way to the airfield. As we
drove across the base to the other side of the airfield, the lieutenant said,
"Mr. Kakar, you're the only linguist that I have found, not only willing to
go to a remote COP where there is fighting going on, but also not saying
something like, 'I don't speak Pashto.'" I told the lieutenant that I spoke
Pashto, Farsi, and English before I applied for the job to be a linguist in
Afghanistan, and at that point, I spoke it all better than I did when I was in
the States. The lieutenant laughed and said, "Why do you say that you speak
it better now?" I told him that it was because I had been in Afghanistan
for more than 18 months by now, and most linguists who applied for the
job in the States to be linguists in Afghanistan, spoke all three languages
while they were Stateside, just to get the job. A requirement was to know
all three languages to be able to get the job in the first place. However, once
the other linguists got the job and arrived in Afghanistan, they suddenly
forgot their native language—especially Pashton, which they seemed to
forget the most, especially when they were asked to go on missions.

The lieutenant agreed. "You're absolutely right, Nas. I usually ask them
if they speak any Pashto, before I even send them to any of the COPs in
remote locations." To the lieutenant's surprise, I was also the only linguist
who called to ask him why it was taking so long for me to be sent to my
unit, while he couldn't even find most of the other linguists when it was
time for them to go to their assignment.

The lieutenant dropped me off at the airfield, which was operated
by the Canadian military, where I would again be flying on a Chinook

that was going to be taking us to our destination. It was a full flight with four stops—all in the Arghandab District—along the way. I could hardly wait to get where I was going! As a young kid growing up in Kandahar City, I knew my way around very well. We had taken off from KAF and were headed northwest where the Arghandab District is located. Flying over the northeastern part of the city at a very low altitude, I couldn't help but notice that the city had doubled in size compared to when I had lived there 32 years ago. Everything remained simple and was mostly made of mud.

Remembering that the Arghandab District was separated from the city's center by a single ridge-line of mountains that ran from north to south, the only narrow dirt road that connected the city with Arghandab was a small strip of opening called *Baba Saheb Kotal*, a famous landmark referred to as the "Mountain overpass named after the founding father of that particular area."

As we flew over the city toward the countryside, I was very much interested in seeing *Baba Saheb Kotal* again. Seeing that narrow road, where I had traveled back and forth by foot on many occasions to visit my adoptive village, I became very emotional merely seeing that road that I didn't in my wildest dreams ever expect to see again. All of my childhood memories were coming back to me like it was just yesterday when I was walking that same road to visit my adoptive parents. One thing in particular that I was reminded of while flying over the overpass was that I cried just as I had as a young boy 40 years prior. Back then, as a young boy walking this same road to Arghandab, I was full of joy, going to be with people who not only loved and cared for me, but raised me—and I trusted them. Leaving my adoptive family to go back to the city was very difficult for me as we passed over *Baba Saheb Kotal*, which reminded me of when I would sit on top and cry for a while as I looked down at the Arghandab Valley to see everything, including our village in Sarkari Bagh from a distance for the last time, before I headed down to the city for my biological family's physical abuse and neglect.

Our first stop on the Chinook was Arghandab's District center located at the foot of the mountain overpass of *Baba Saheb Kotal* where I could discern the green, luscious valley of pomegranate tree orchards for as far as the eye could see. Our other two stops were on the west side of the Arghandab River, which runs from the north to the south, splitting the valley in half. Having now been on a Chinook more than 80 times, I had never experienced such a stress-inducing flight during which the aircraft was being flown at such a low altitude to the point where I felt we might hit the treetops. I assumed it was for security reasons since the valley was so densely covered with pomegranate trees to the point that would enable the enemy to easily hide and shoot at us if our altitude was high enough that they could see us, but we couldn't see them because of the trees.

Before we could get to the last stop where Sarkari Bagh was located, the aircraft circled for a little while at a higher altitude and more over to the mountainside away from the dense valley of trees. We finally made our approach into the landing zone right outside Sarkari Bagh, which enabled the enemy to shoot us down upon landing. Nonetheless, danger aside, after so many years, I was finally back in the village where I had grown up. Who would've thought that I—who had grown up here in the '60s and '70s and then immigrated to America—would be so blessed as to be back to see it again in 2010 as an American helping the natives of my village.

From the moment I arrived, despite the fact that this was the most dangerous part of Afghanistan, I decided to stay here for as long as I possibly could, working with the unit to which I was assigned. It was not going to get any better than this, where I could be helpful, not only to our soldiers, but to the villagers as well. I knew these villagers, their culture, their language, and perhaps some of their names if I was ever allowed to go outside the COP on dismounted missions.

Upon my arrival at the COP, no one knew who I was or why I was here. By asking everyone I came in contact with, I had to work my way around in order to find my POC. After asking many, I was finally introduced to my POC, Staff Sergeant Karen, who helped me take all of my gear to the tent where I would be staying. He told me that he hadn't been expecting a linguist to show up because no one had informed him that I would be coming. He also told me that while his team of three soldiers had been here since July, they were never able to find Cat III linguists who were willing to work under such harsh conditions. I assured him that I was in for the long haul, and that I had been born on that side of the mountains (pointing five miles to the east where downtown Kandahar City was). He was even more shocked when I pointed to my parents' house and told him I had been raised there.

There was one other thing I had to tell him concerning my medical issues, for which I needed to go to Bagram once a month, which he said would not be an issue. Since our compound was well beyond overcrowded, most of our gear had to be kept outside the tent. Living conditions were somewhat similar to the district center in Yahya Khel, except here we had limited running water so we were only able to shower every other day. The food situation was the same: scrambled eggs for breakfast; no lunch; and pork chops, spaghetti with meatballs, ham, and other canned vegetables for dinner, on a rotated basis. Unlike Yahya Khel, this COP was all tents, where in Yahya Khel it was an old district center built from concrete, which was much safer. If we were to be attacked the way we had been in Yahya Khel, I'm reasonably certain that no one would survive. Nonetheless, I loved this place/assignment more than any other I had been on since arriving in Afghanistan.

The next morning, I spent most of my day on top of our truck parked inside our compound (which was also our command center) where I could see my parents' house and orchard. Looking out from the inside of our compound, I couldn't wait to go outside and start talking with the locals just to see if I recognized anyone. My job did not require me to go outside the compound. One of the four soldiers from the team I was assigned to had gone home for R&R. Karen made a work schedule of two 12-hour shifts, the first from 7:00 AM to 7:00 PM, and vice versa, using me to cover 12-hour shifts, two people on each shift. I had the day shift with one other soldier, while Karen and the other soldier took the night shift. Because of our location, there was no work to be performed by any of us.

As mentioned on numerous other occasions in this book, I don't do well when I'm idle. The worst thing that can happen to me is to not be working or at least doing something, anything in my native village where I could communicate with the locals 100 percent better than any other linguist, anywhere. Knowing that my job required me to stay within the compound, and also knowing that there currently weren't any jobs within the compound, I decided to tell Karen that I would be happy to go out on dismounted missions if the company commander needed me to do so. To convince both, I asked Karen to tell the company commander that I was very familiar with the Arghandab District and its people. When the news of my willingness to go out on dismounted missions spread around the compound, I got numerous looks for being crazy from everyone on the compound, whether ANA, ANP, or the other linguists, but a thumb's up from each and every one of my fellow Americans—all of which made me even stronger as a person and braver as an American.

The following day, Karen told me he had talked with the captain, who was also our company commander, and told him that since there was nothing for me to do inside the compound, I was more than willing to go out on dismounted missions. The commander approved and told Karen that if any of his platoons needed a linguist for any of their dismounted missions, they were to let me know.

Meanwhile, as I waited, in order to pass my time I would walk around the compound, looking to see what was going on. One day I ran into First Sergeant Ray, who not only was a wonderful human being and a seemingly loving person, but he was also in command of the entire operation of the COP. Ray had kept the COP under control very well so everything was in excellent working order. He had also hired a number of local contractors to build a new dining facility inside the COP. When I arrived, the locals who worked to build the dining facility were almost done, with only the roof left to complete. In addition, just like in Ghazni, there were three other locals, who came early every morning to take out all the trash and clean the bathrooms. There was no Qasim here; instead, there was a much younger person—Mirwis, who was about 15 years old—whose job was to help the military cook prepare meals in the kitchen. Mirwis came to work at 8:00 AM every day.

All of the locals on the compound that I had been able to speak with told me in their native Pashto, *"Ah ows zamoge kar jor soo, chea yawczhok mo pa khabara poheyzge."* ("Now we're in business; someone can speak and understand our language.") Instead of calling me Ustad, like every other place that I had been stationed at while in Afghanistan, the locals started calling me "Mama," which to them meant uncle on mother's side, and was used more commonly in the Kandahari and Pashton cultures. When people younger than you call you Mama, it means they like, know, and trust you, which is why they are calling you one of their own.

Some of the locals may also call you "Kaka," which means uncle on the father's side. Since Kaka and Mama are both referred to as uncles, Kaka is oftentimes used by strangers who don't know you personally, or perhaps those who do know you but use either out of respect, which doesn't carry the intended heartfelt trust. In the Afghan culture, Mama, uncle on the mother's side is considered more trustworthy and kinder than Kaka, uncle on the father's side. In the English language, we only use "uncle" for both parents' brothers. I'm only going through this exercise in an effort to describe the importance of sensitive cultural barriers that exist in Afghanistan. In order for Americans/Westerners, in general, to understand the Afghan culture better, I think it's relevant for me to elaborate on issues such as the importance of small words (e.g., Mama and Kaka), which have a huge cultural impact.

Since the locals were now happy, comfortable, and trusted for giving me the Mama title, the first thing Mirwis asked me to do was help translate for him so he could talk with Ray about what was on Mirwis's mind. He had a long list of things but never had anyone who could understand his Kandahari dialogue. There were about a dozen other linguists on this COP. Only three of them, including me, were from the States, while the rest were local. The two Cat II linguists from the States were both Tajiks, they only knew a little Pashto. Most of the local linguists were Tajiks and Hazaras who spoke Farsi and were used for translation between the American forces and the ANA and ANP.

When we got to his office, Mirwis told Ray that he needed more hours of work to support his mom and seven siblings, all younger than him. Since his father had passed away, Mirwis also asked Ray if it was possible for him to get some financial help so he could put a roof on his family's three-bedroom house, which was currently covered with tarp. He was afraid the fast-approaching winter might leave his family out in the cold. As soon as Mirwis was finished with his request, Ray looked at me and said that a couple of months ago Mirwis had come to him with another interpreter, but Ray couldn't understand what Mirwis was asking for.

Ray knew something was wrong with Mirwis's house but didn't know exactly what it was, but now that he did, Mirwis was told that Ray would help him as much as he could. Needless to say, Mirwis left the office with a very big smile on his face!

As usual, breakfast at the compound was not a healthy meal for me. Mirwis became my go-to person for bringing me green tea from the market just like the local interpreter in Yahya Khel had done. However, unlike the interpreter in Yahya Khel—who charged $10 for a pound of loose green tea—it was much cheaper in Arghandab. Mirwis brought me a pound for 80 Afghani ($1.30), but refused to let me pay him for it.

When I insisted, he told me that if I paid him for the tea, he was going to pay me for translating what he had requested from Ray. I reminded Mirwis that I had already been paid for my translation by the Americans. "But you didn't translate for the Americans. You translated for me. Besides, all the other linguists charged me every time I asked them to translate for me." Here is why it's more important to be called Mama instead of Kaka. Not only did Mirwis refuse to take my money for the tea, but he also brought me quality Grade A tea (without the sand, dust, and donkey manure).

Local linguists got paid close to $1,000 a month by the American taxpayers, while Mirwis only got paid $120 a month for doing a lot more work. In addition to the green tea, he offered to bring me anything else from the market if I needed anything. Since breakfast and lunch at the compound were a no-go for me, I had to asked Mirwis to bring me one fresh baked flat bread from the bakery on his way to work every morning, which he did. He also brought me lunch as well, which, for the most part, would be pomegranates picked fresh from the orchard across from our compound. From September to mid-November was the peak season for pomegranates in the Arghandab Valley, which were known to be the best in Afghanistan. Mirwis brought me four whole pomegranates every day for lunch, for which he again refused the money I offered to pay him. After the first time he refused to take my money for the fruit, he explained that no one in Arghandab charges anything for pomegranates because no one (except me, in this case) ever buys them.

Back in the day, when I was growing up, I recalled that although everyone I knew in Arghandab either had a pomegranate orchard or worked as an orchard-keeper, no one actually paid for them. Curious, I asked Mirwis how much they cost in the store outside our compound. He told me that there was no store around the compound that sold them. However, the nearest store that sold them was located in Kandahar City. As I mulled over what Mirwis told me, I realized that Mirwis was right: Why would anyone sell pomegranates in his shop in the Arghandab District, where everyone either had their own orchard or could get them by working as an orchard-keeper?

As there was nothing for me to do work-wise, I spent the majority of my time talking with the locals who worked on our compound, including Mirwis, to find out what was going on in my adoptive village. Not only did

I want to know the situation in the village, but I also wanted to know the locals' mindset and find out how they felt toward the Americans being in their backyard. I sensed it in my heart that they would tell me everything I wanted to know.

One day, I had a conversation with Mirwis about his personal and family lives to see if it would somehow lead me to people I had known. I asked about his deceased father and how long he had lived in Sarkari Bagh. Mirwis told me that he, his father, grandfather, and great-grandfathers were all born in Arghandab. I also asked him what his father had done for a living when he was alive. Mirwis told me that his father was an orchard-keeper for "Doctor" who had purchased Haji Kaka's (title name in Pashto) orchard, which was a couple of orchards away from our compound. As soon as he mentioned Haji Kaka's name, I knew exactly who he was talking about because Haji Kaka was my adoptive uncle, who had also shared the same house where I had lived and grown up with my adoptive parents. My dad and Haji Kaka were first cousins whose relationship was so close, people in the village, including me, thought they were biological brothers. Haji Kaka was also a teacher at the same (and only) school in Arghandab where Dad taught in the '60s and '70s.

I asked Mirwis if Haji Kaka was still alive and, if so, where he was. Mirwis told me that Haji Kaka was getting old, and two of his older sons had both been killed during the Soviet invasion of Kandahar. Haji Kaka had moved to the city for his young sons' safety because they were frequently harassed by the Taliban on their way to and from school from Sarkari Bagh to the city. Haji Kaka sold his orchard and bought a house in the city so his sons could attend school without being harassed.

After listening to his answers to my questions, I told Mirwis that Haji Kaka was my uncle and asked him if he could find a way to let my uncle know I wanted him to visit me at the compound so I could talk with him again after 40 years. I wanted to see Haji Kaka again because I missed him, and knew, as did everyone else in the Arghandab District, that he was one of the most intelligent and well-informed person I could talk with regarding rebuilding a school in the village. Mirwis assured me that he would talk with his father and let me know if visiting arrangements could be made. I was shocked to hear him say he was going to talk with his father because, in a prior conversation he said his father was deceased, which left him as the only breadwinner for his family.

When I questioned Mirwis about his father being deceased, he explained that one day, as the American soldiers were out on foot patrol in the village, he had asked the local interpreter (who was working for the Americans) to ask if he could get a job at the compound. According to Mirwis, the local interpreter had promised him a job. For getting the job, he was told that he would have to pay the local interpreter kickbacks every month when he got paid. Mirwis accepted the linguist's offer and agreed to pay the kickbacks once the Americans hired him. Not only did he agree to pay the kickbacks, but he also realized that he was going against his parents' wishes because they would not be happy that their son would be working for the Americans. According to Mirwis, he desperately needed a job, so he accepted the offer, primarily because the Americans were paying 10 times more than if he had been paid for working in the city as a day laborer. Earlier that day, Mirwis told me that his parents were afraid for his safety because if the Taliban found out he was working for the Americans, they would probably behead him.

Well, feeling sorry for Mirwis, Ray—who was a compassionate man, just like most Americans were—hired him. In my personal opinion, because of safety reasons, not only for our soldiers but for everyone else in the compound, it could be dangerous to simply hire people off the street who were referred by other local linguists. The Americans' honesty and compassion could sometimes be used against them. It is well-known, worldwide, that Americans are the most trustworthy and compassionate people in the world in order for one to know that, one must be from that part of the world. It is always better for Americans to be cautious just like president Reagan had said to Mr. Gorbachev in Russian, *"Doveryai, no proveryai."* ("Trust, but verify.") Mirwis knew instantly that I was not happy with him for lying about his father being dead just to get the job. On the other hand, he did tell me everything else truthfully because he felt that he had some kind of bond with me more than with anyone else he knew on the compound. He also told me the reason why he lied was simply because the local interpreter told him to do so, primarily because Americans preferred lies to the truth. Mirwis was prepared for an interview by the local interpreter to meet with Ray, the commander of our compound. He was told to say three things that would guarantee him a job. First, his father was deceased, and he was the only person in the family to provide for his elder mother and his seven siblings. Second, he was to say that he and his family hated the Taliban, and third, that he and his family loved the Americans.

Of course, it's not really that the Americans liked lies better than the truth. It had more to do with the fact that the local Afghans who worked for them knew that the Americans trusted whatever they were told. For instance, how would the Americans—in this case, Ray—know that Mirwis was lying about his father being deceased? Ray thought that he was telling the truth and offered him the job. When I learned the truth, I asked Mirwis to come with me to tell Ray that he had lied about his father's demise. Mirwis started crying. "Mama, I am ashamed of myself and don't want to face the commander. I would like to go home and never come back to work here again. I lied to the commander. How can I ever face him again?" I sensed it in his voice that he was prepared to do just that.

Even thought he was a typical, young *Saraye* kid from Arghandab, much like I was at his age, I wanted to tell him something that I hoped he would remember for the rest of his life—that if he respected me as his Mama, then he was going to tell the commander what he had done. He had made a big mistake by lying to the commander to get the job. And now he had to go with me to apologize and tell Ray that he was sorry for lying.

"But, Mama, I am embarrassed and can't see the commander face-to-face." I told him that he should've been embarrassed when he lied to the commander in the first place. As I watched the expressions that crossed his face as he mulled over what I was asking him to do, with the hope that he would make the right decision, I noticed his tears were drying and the look on his face turned from one of shame to a slight smile as he made his decision. I could see that he was still hesitant to go, so I looked into his eyes, not as his Mama but more like an older brother and said, "It's easy to tell a lie, Mirwis, but only a real man with courage admits his mistakes and apologizes to the person he lied to." I suddenly walked away, as though I wasn't going to talk with him anymore, and went to get a bottle of water from the kitchen where I could still see him through the window. I waited inside while he carefully pondered what he should do. Within five or six minutes, he started walking toward the facility while I grabbed a can of Coke—which he loved—from the fridge for him, then I walked out of the kitchen so I could meet him halfway. As I walked toward him, his eyes were glazing more at the Coke than they were at me. The first words out of his mouth in Arghandab's Pashto were, *"Mama, Darza chea aos warso."* ("Uncle, let's go right now.") This was one of the fastest connections I ever made with an Afghan during my time in Afghanistan.

Walking to Ray's office, Mirwis followed me like a shy five year old, hiding behind my back all the way. When we reached the commander's office, I told Ray that Mirwis had something very important to say to him in English, which I had taught him (he was a fast learner). Ray glanced toward Mirwis and asked in his soft voice, "Yes, Mirwis, what would you like to tell me?"

Mirwis looked to me to start the sentences that we had rehearsed a few times before we got to Ray's office, but because he was nervous, he had forgotten them. He had never gone to school so didn't know how to write; all he knew was his native Pashto in thoughts and in sounds. When I was teaching him what to tell Ray, once we were in his office, Mirwis was good at pronouncing the words but was having a difficult time remembering them, which is why I had told him that once we reached Ray's office, he would repeat after me. As Mirwis and I stood there, both of us waiting for the other to start speaking, Ray was confused because he hadn't yet found out why we were there.

With the hope of speeding things along, I again told Ray that Mirwis wanted to tell him something in English. Ray was surprised but smiled his encouragement to Mirwis, as he said, "Wow! That's great, Mirwis! Please go ahead; I'm listening." I turned around to face Mirwis, translating what Ray had said to him. I then asked him to repeat after me, which he did word-for-word. "First Sergeant, I am very sorry for lying to you about my father being deceased. He is not, and I apologize." Ray stood, gave Mirwis a hug, and then told him, "Don't worry. If I'd been in your situation to get a job to earn money to support my family, I would've done the same thing."

When I translated what Ray had said to Mirwis, he smiled with gratitude. "Mirwis," Ray said, "I respect and trust you even more now than I did before, because you admitted your dishonesty, which is something a real man would do." Again, when I translated Ray's words, Mirwis's smile grew even bigger. While looking at me, he said in Pashto, *"Mama, hagha khabara chea ta wa mata wkra, kho komandan Saheb ham hagha khabara kawey"* ("Uncle, the commander is telling me the same thing you told me earlier"), to which I responded, "Yes, the commander and I both respect people who have the courage to tell the truth."

I knew all along that Mirwis was a good listener, but someone needed to take the time to realize that. Before he went home for the day, I told him, "People who lie can't even trust themselves, because all they're doing is lying to everyone, *especially* themselves. What difference does it make to tell other people a lie? After all, they don't know you lied, but in the end, *you* know that you lied, so, if you lie to yourself, then how can you expect other people to trust you?" I knew he'd be thinking about this for a while, but—for him *and* me—I had to tell him what I thought.

Before Mirwis walked away from me, he unexpectedly reached for my hand, trying to kiss it out of respect, but I wouldn't allow him to do so. Instead, I told him that the only person's hand he should be kissing was his wife and parents'. It was funny to him why I even mentioned kissing his wife's hand, which perhaps no one ever did in conservative Arghandab.

By now, everyone on the compound, Americans and locals alike, knew that I was born and raised right outside the compound, so I was not only familiar with the area geographically but also the local culture. I enjoyed helping everyone on the compound with translations because I could relate to the needs of the locals.

One night, a buddy soldier (with whom I had worked before) and I were sitting outside our tent about 20 feet from Ray's office. It was 7:30, right after dinner. It was dark where we were sitting; the only light in the whole compound was on the porch outside Ray's office. There were two couches where Ray met people whenever they wanted to talk with Ray or someone else in his office. I noticed that three ANP officers had shown up to talk with our commander and SFC Pat, regarding the upcoming dismounted mission. Apparently, Pat knew the officers from previous meetings—who were from a different ANP station somewhere within the Arghandab District and worked with us on the compound.

The only interpreter who could speak a very limited Pashto was a local named Ali, who was trying everything he could to translate between the ANP officers, Ray, and Pat. My buddy and I continued to sit and listen, trying to hear what they were talking about. All I could clearly hear from the three ANP officers telling one another was, *"Walaka me sar pa khalas sawey yee chea the oas czha wawayal"* ("I'm confused about what he just said"), referring to the local linguist. The miscommunication between the ANP officers, Ray, and Pat, continued for quite some time. (As an aside, this was the only time during my deployment to Afghanistan that I had witnessed and heard ANP officers, natives of Kandahar, who spoke and understood nothing but Pashto).

I asked my buddy if he thought I should go over and try to help. Before he answered, I thought to myself, *it might not be appropriate for me to get involved in their business.* However, the thought didn't prevent me from going there anyhow. I knew that if someone was misinterpreting, it might put our soldiers' or perhaps even civilians' lives in danger, which meant that I should get involved since my job was to translate, especially where I could completely understand the culture and language. I waited a few more minutes before I got involved.

As we continued to watch them sitting down under a single light bulb in the middle of darkness, we saw the captain leaving the porch. I didn't know whether the meeting was over, or if it was just too frustrating for him to stick around, especially since he couldn't understand what the interpreter was saying. Meanwhile, Pat stayed behind as one of the officers was now talking to the local linguist, asking him to tell the captain, once he returned, that the Americans are going to need an interpreter everyone could understand more clearly. I seriously doubted that the local linguist was going to tell the captain what the officer had just requested. Why would he do that, especially since the linguist had been faking that he knew Pashto, for only God knew how long?

The officer started to talk with the local interpreter in Pashto, fully aware that the linguist was a Farsi native who understood little to no Pashto. As I explained the situation to my buddy, he said, "If I were you, I would've gone over a long time ago to help with the translation," which helped me to decide to do so. The local linguist mumbled a few words to the officer next to him, which irritated the officer as he talked in Pashto in a raised and angry voice, *"Za sta pa khabara na pohazgham, aow ta zma pa khabara na pohazghey, da ba czhanga sey, da Amrikayan ba czhanga zma woa sta pa khabara pohsi?"* ("If I don't understand your language and you don't understand my language, how can the Americans understand any of us?") Even if I wanted to hold back a comment, I couldn't because it was my job to translate, especially in Kandahar so that I could help both the locals from my native land and the soldiers from my adoptive land to understand each other.

After walking over to where the meeting was taking place, out of respect, I greeted the officers in Pashto first, then greeted the Tajik interpreter in Farsi, and, last but not least, Pat, in English. Almost immediately after greeting them all, one of the officers suddenly stood, opened his arms, and was trying to hug me as he said, "The ground has cracked open and our own native Kandahari Pashton has come out just in time, and when we needed him the most. Where the heck have you been hiding while listening to our conversation but doing nothing to help?" he asked jovially. When the hugging finally came to an end, I told them that I had been sitting over there (pointing) with my buddy, watching and hearing what they were trying to talk about. Not able to listen any longer, I couldn't hold myself back so came over to see if I could of assistance. Everyone was happy to see me except the local linguist who realized that the Americans would soon find out that he was faking and couldn't speak Pashto at all.

If I ever thought that I was going to make a local linguist mad by doing something that was right, then I would've never done the job for which I was hired. I got involved to help the ANP and the American captain understand each other. They were coordinating an upcoming dismounted combat mission that both the Americans and ANPs were executing within the next couple of days. At the end of our meeting, the lead ANP officer (who was the first to hug me earlier) wanted to know where I was from. He said he thought I was a native of Kandahar, but wanted to confirm—again, it's an Afghanistan cultural thing for villagers to know who you really are and if you're a fellow Pashton. Everything leads to trust, so the closer you are to them, the closer the trust.

I told the officer I was from Sarkari Bagh right around the corner, and more specifically from Haji Toar Kaley. At first, he didn't believe me. He asked me for my father's name, and I gave him my adoptive dad's name. Because they now felt that I was just like one of them from Arghandab, all three of the ANP officers lined up immediately for a round of hugs, all far firmer than the last ones I had received.

Before they left the compound, the lead ANP officer turned to Pat and told him in Pashto, "We both need an interpreter like him," he said, his hand on my shoulder, "who can speak and understand us both." Pat smiled and then asked, "Nas, do you know these people?" Since it was my first time meeting them, I told Pat that he probably had seen them often prior to my arrival. Smiling, Pat said, "Well, I've never seen them reacting to other linguists the way they do to you." I told him that they reacted the way they did because not only was it a cultural thing, but once the locals realized I'm one of their own, they would treat me accordingly. I paused and then added that for the past 18 months, ever since my arrival in Afghanistan, I'd been trying to get assigned to Kandahar so I could be of more help, not only to our military, but the locals as well.

From that point on, everyone—locals and Americans alike—came to me for their translation needs, which more than made up for all those times when I had nothing to do. The commander asked Sergeant Karen to find out if I would be interested in going out on a dismounted mission with the platoon within the next day or so. When asked, I responded with an immediate, "Absolutely!"

The only thing our team of four soldiers had been doing was babysitting a multimillion dollar military truck—weighing in at 79,000 pounds—that had been parked in the same spot for five months, its engine running 24/7, using 55 gallons of fuel every 24 hours. If it was any other linguist but me, every one of them would've loved the idea of just sitting inside an air-conditioned truck in the 100+ degree summer heat, doing nothing but getting paid. Usually, I chose to be outside in the village-to-village dust.

Karen also said I was the only linguist they had received since they first arrived in Sarkari Bagh five months ago—a perfect example of how difficult it was to get linguists to fill the positions in the Arghandab District amidst the fighting in the summer of 2010.

During my conversation with the soldier who babysat the truck with me, he told me that he was just as frustrated as I was with the way things were going. For the five months he'd been here, he had done nothing as far as actual work was concerned. Like me, he wanted to go out on missions, but his on-the-compound jobs prevented him from leaving the compound. Once he found out that I was going on a mission, he told me how lucky I was and said he wished he was going, too.

The soldier also told me that the four men who worked on the truck were military linguists for languages other than Pashto. He added that the four were each fluent in different languages (e.g., much like the soldier who was trained in Arabic who was supposed to be sent to Iraq, but, at the last minute his deployment was changed to Afghanistan). According to the Arabic-speaking soldier, he had asked his commander before his deployment what good was he going to be able to accomplish in Afghanistan if he didn't speak the language. His commander told that he was going to Afghanistan to fill a vacant position—whether he could perform or not didn't really matter. The same was also the case with two other soldiers—one fluent in Mandarin, the other in Croatian—yet both were sent to Afghanistan nonetheless.

The following day I joined the platoons of American soldiers and ANA officers who were going on a house-to-house search for explosives in Sardey, which just so happened to be my adoptive mom's native village. Once we left the compound and headed toward the village, our drive was alongside *Low Wala* (Large Canal). It was one of those times where I again needed plenty of tissues to wipe the tears from my eyes as the old memories of walking alongside that some canal with my mom to visit her family came to the forefront of my childhood memories. The road and the canal between our village and my mom's native village, which used to be a dirt road in the middle of the desert, was now paved and the desert in between had been turned into mud homes and shops, which made it look like the two villages were merged into one. My eyes were glued to the outside from the little window of our military vehicle.

Although the people I saw were not the same ones I had left behind, those who were there now looked exactly the same. The village kids were running barefoot alongside our vehicles asking for things, anything that the American soldiers could throw their way, which also reminded me of my own childhood when I ran after foreigners who were visiting Afghanistan back in the early '70s, asking them for *Bakhshesh* (which meant "reward" in both Pashto and Farsi). Now, as a foreigner in my native land, I unfortunately didn't have anything to give them, especially since all of my goodies (e.g., pens and pencils) had been given out to all the kids while I was in the Ghazni, Khost, and Paktika Provinces. As I continued to look through the vehicle's small window, I couldn't help but be thankful that I wasn't one of the poor fathers, grandfathers, or uncles sitting on the side of the road with no sign of hope in any of their eyes as they watched the American convoy pass through their village. It was heartbreaking for me to see that people in my village were still living just as I had left them more than 40 years ago.

Once we were close to the area where we needed to be so we could start searching each home, I wanted to take the lead. But I knew I couldn't do that since none of the guys I was working for directly hadn't yet joined us. Since I was simply a volunteer, I was required to stay with the person I was assigned to in case he needed me for translation purposes. This mission was being carried out by the Afghan commandos. American soldiers weren't doing the actual search; they were just there to support and train the Afghans to take the lead and help them if things went wrong.

Upon arrival at the target area of the village, we were divided into four groups, each of which went into the village from each side, ultimately meeting at the center. While going from house to house, I saw Afghan forces in full force—doing what they do best, entering people's homes by breaking down their front doors without even knocking to see if anyone was home.

As poor as these villagers were, some didn't even have locks on their doors, so to see the Afghan commandos simply storm into their homes and break their doors down was unbearable for me. I asked my commander, whom I was following very closely, if we could do something about the way the Afghan Security Forces were breaking down the villagers' doors. It was the same situation that I had witnessed many times since my arrival in Afghanistan—reminiscent of the ANAs breaking into the poor man's shop to steal gasoline and his supply of firewood for the winter, when I had complained to Captain Alfa2. I had to wonder if I'd get a different response this time from my current commander. Although I didn't care about what kind of response I'd get, I was never hesitant of trying to stop harm from being directed toward poor people. Additionally, it wasn't a good thing to see Americans being a part of any abuse, which was my main concern about protecting the poor from being abused by the Afghan forces. The locals always saw what the Afghan forces were doing but never gave them the credit; instead, the Americans deserved all the credit for being behind the Afghan force's behavior since they never went out to search homes on their own. Yes, I am being sarcastic in this regard. Anyhow, when I asked, the commander agreed and told me to tell the Afghan commander to instruct his soldiers that they should be more protective of their own fellow Afghans, not invaders of their homes.

I believed that the commander made a very good point and told the Afghan Security Forces commander that I would be demonstrating how the Afghan forces should do it. I realized that no matter what I did to keep both the Afghan forces and the locals on the same page in respecting each other as fellow countrymen was going to be a huge challenge for me. To relay my message to the Afghan forces, I needed to take charge by setting a good example, while also risking my life to take the lead in many of our dismounted missions, to show how things should be done as far as respecting people as human beings, no matter what their ethnicity, religion, and nationality were, for which the Afghan Security Forces had no respect.

Before I took the lead to go ahead and be in front of the Afghan Security Forces, especially knowing the consequences of the danger involved, I told the Afghan commander that I was willing to take the risk. He told me in Farsi (he assumed that I was a fellow Tajik because I spoke Farsi fluently), "Ustad, all these fuckers are Taliban. If we give them enough time by not storming into their homes, they can be prepared to hit us before we can get inside." I told him if he assumed that everyone in this village or the next to be Taliban fuckers, he'll only succeed in not capturing members of the actual Taliban, which I could tell by the look on his face only seemed to confuse him.

I got straight to the point and asked him to let his soldiers follow me to the next house. He pointed out that I didn't even have a weapon to defend myself. I told him I was willing to take the risk. I asked my commander that if he would allow me, I was going to raid the next house for the Afghan commander and his forces so they could see how it should be done. He gave me his okay. Before I walked to the next house and knocked on the door, I was asked by my commander—who didn't even know my name, so he called me *Tarjuman* (Interpreter)—to be careful, especially since I wasn't carrying a weapon, to which I responded, "Sir, would you use a weapon if you were talking with people you know?"

He had a confused look on his face just like the Afghan commander did earlier. I wasn't sure if my commander understood me, but the important thing is that I understood myself because my point was that I knew these villagers, perhaps not personally, but through the bond of understanding each other culturally, which was far, far better and safer than carrying an AK47. My commander cautioned me to be careful, and I assured him that I'd try my best to do just that.

While walking through the narrow alleyways, the stench from the raw sewers running down the middle of them was overwhelming. I walked to the first house that we were going to search and knocked on the door loud enough to make sure someone could hear it clearly. After my initial knock, I waited about 30 seconds—all the while watching the Afghan and my commanders, who were standing about 10 feet behind, giving me a look implying that my way of doing this shit just wasn't working. After the first knock, I put my mouth close to the door and called out in Pashto as loud but also as gently as I could to make what I was about to say, sound more like I was asking rather than demanding, *"Ha wrora, ya Khori, za Afghani askar yam, tha darwaza ra khlasakey chea mozghe stasi the koar yawa khali talashe wakro?"* ("My brother or sister, I am an Afghan police officer. Can you open the door for a quick search of your house, please?") I had asked in a more civil way for them to respond without me sounding like an intruder on their privacy by breaking into their home without permission.

While looking into the house with one eye through the crack of the door, I saw only one brown curtain, which is usually put between the door and the main living quarters to avoid having strangers see through the door crack. I noticed a young boy, about eight or nine years of age, walking around the curtain toward the front door. Meanwhile, a woman I assumed was his mother responded to my question in Pashto as loud as she could from across the courtyard. *"Rasi wrora, wa gori, hagha zma the koar sary pa mazaka key dey, tha zama zoy be darwaza dar khlasakey."* ("Come inside, my brother, my husband is out in the field, but my son is on his way to open the door for you.")

The boy opened the door and said, *"Mama, rasee."* ("Uncle come on in.") I could not stop crying then, just as I cannot stop crying now as I write this, because it reminds me of the look and smile on the young boy's face. He hadn't been threatened by an AK47 held to his head by the Afghan Security Forces. These are the kinds of moments I will always remember of why I wanted to be in Kandahar, and these were the moments that made me enjoy my work more being outside in the villages of Afghanistan rather than on American military bases. My way of entering a villager's home versus the manner in which the Afghan forces terrorize their fellow Afghans once they break into their houses, is so much better than pushing them out of the way with their rifles or holding rifles to the heads of women and children while searching the house.

Was it dangerous for me to go into the house of the unknown without a weapon? In my opinion, you bet it was because gaining access my way was the safest way. I didn't assume that every house in Kandahar belonged to the Taliban; in fact, I thought every house we entered belonged to poor Afghans who were simply victims of circumstance. The Afghan forces could have performed a much better job and been much more productive had they treated every house and every person in Afghanistan more gently, without thinking everyone was with the Taliban, which was obviously not the case.

At the end of our mission, we had searched more than 20 houses that day, with only six to seven broken doors. Had it been up to the Afghan commandos, we would undoubtedly have had all 20 doors broken and hundreds of poor terrorized Afghans on our hands. None of the 20 houses we had searched had any evidence of anything out of the ordinary. Other than the six to seven broken doors, we found cooperative poor people who all lived in mud huts with four walls. Some of the villagers were so poor that the rooms in their houses didn't even have doors.

During many of my days, and while on a number of nightly missions, I video recorded things and people I saw when I had the chance or there was power in my camcorder. Since this was my very first mission going outside the compound in Arghandab, walking around brought back many of my childhood memories.

The following day the American soldiers on the compound were thanking me, and asking questions about how it felt to be back in my native village after 40 years. I had only this to say, "I thank God for choosing me to be an American, and I thank each and every one of you for making it possible for me to be out there helping my native people, who are all good and decent human beings."

Later in the day, Karen told me that the company commander wanted me to go out with Lieutenant Barron on another, unplanned, dismounted, humanitarian mission to the village of Ali Kaley, which was approximately a three- to four-mile walk south of our compound. I told Karen that I would welcome the opportunity to join Barron. But first, it was time for me to return to Bagram Airfield for my end-of-the-month blood test and prescription refill.

Following my arrival at KAF, I was picked up by the same lieutenant who had dropped me off and taken me to the transition tent. He told me that the company I worked for would make arrangements for my flight to Bagram and back. When I reported to my company's office and told them my situation, they asked me to be on alert for the next flight to Bagram.

During my time in KAF, I had another moment I never thought I'd experience. As I was sitting on one of the bunk beds, I saw someone with a shaved head who looked familiar and was walking toward me with a smile, his arms opened so he could give me a hug. As he got closer, I suddenly realized who he was: my brother-in-law from the States! It was shameful of him to be in Kandahar to work as an interpreter. For 30 years, I was the only true friend he had. Since we both lived in Flushing, New York, I worked locally while he worked in the upper eastside of Manhattan (Harlem). I had a car while he used the subway to go back and forth to work. When I had the time, I would sometimes offer him a ride in my car and even pick him up after work.

Well, one day when I went to pick him up from work, as I waited for him to finish I went to talk with one of my classmates from Kandahar, who also worked there. Since it was our native language, we always spoke in Pashto, especially since we didn't know that much Farsi. During our conversation, my brother-in-law (a friend at the time) approached us and said in Farsi, *"Bachem, chea dagha pagha ra andakhten, sayee insaney Farsi ghap bazanen?"* ("Hey, buddy, stop talking all this nonsense. Why don't you guys speak Farsi?") We reminded him that Pashto was our native tongue and that we couldn't speak to each other in other languages. *"Mara khoshem na myayad, az distey Pashto Afghanistana ela dadem."* ("I left Afghanistan because of Pashto; I don't like it!), said my brother-in-law.

Now that we were both in Kandahar, land of the Pashtons, I asked him where he learned the Pashto language that he didn't like and, in fact, left Afghanistan because of. How could he suddenly come all the way to Kandahar to be a Pashto linguist?

My brother-in-law had nothing to say to me at that moment, nor did he display any shame for faking it for the two years he had thus far spent in Kandahar. From time-to-time, I would see him working as a linguist in Afghanistan, and would always ask him how work was going for him. His response each time was that he loved his job as a linguist. When I'd ask what job that would be, he'd respond that it was the job far away from his family in the U.S. to the jobs in which he experienced the hardships of Afghanistan. When I asked if being a linguist in Afghanistan was the actual job he applied for, or was it being away from his family in the hardships of Afghanistan. He said that the Iranians and Pakistanis, who are not even Afghans, are working as linguists in Afghanistan, without any knowledge of the Pashto language at all. Since he's an Afghan, he asked why I thought he was doing something wrong.

I explained that just because some Iranians or Pakistanis he knew were doing it didn't make it right for him to do it as well. He argued that at least he's an Afghan, while they're Iranian and Pakistani. I asked him, "So you're not an American either, you're an Afghan?" to which he responded in the affirmative. Before I left him, I had one last thing for him to consider. "I thought we were all Americans and were hired as linguists to help our adopted country help our native land." Most Afghans will never admit their wrongdoings because they justify them based on other people's wrongdoings. My brother-in-law went on to tell me that he had already talked with the major, who was his POC in Kandahar, about not being able to speak or understand Pashto, and the major was okay with that, which left me thinking, *Why would a major in the U.S. military knowingly accept such a linguist for his unit? Wasn't it risky putting not only our soldiers' lives in danger, but the many others who were involved as well?*

I was back in Bagram. After my medical check before I left for Arghandab, I was told by one of the staff members of the company I worked for that I would not be going to my unit in Arghandab since the truck we would supposedly be working out of was no longer in Sarkari Bagh. Instead, I was going to be assigned to the AROCC unit in Bagram again. The reason why my company wanted me to stay was because the 525 BFSB (Battle Field Surveillance Brigade) unit, which required Cat III linguists, had no requirements at this time, and my medical issue that required that I travel back and forth would take 10–12 days every month I traveled from Arghandab to KAF and then Bagram. So the company decided to sign me up with the AROCC unit in Bagram, which is what I really did *not* want to do.

I told the office staff member that I could be much more helpful by being with the unit in Sarkari Bagh than I would in Bagram. Well, unfortunately, as it turned out, it wasn't up to me or those on the frontline who understood the need for linguists like me. Frankly, it was politics, as usual, rather than accomplishing a mission. I was told my medication was the main issue, which is why I had to be in Bagram. I had no choice but to sign my new assignment order. I was ordered by my company to go back to Kandahar then Sarkari Bagh to pick up my belongings.

As soon as I arrived in Sarkari Bagh, I told the commander of our compound (I had promised to go on a mission with his unit) that I was reassigned to another unit and was leaving on the next available flight out. He was shocked by what I had just told him, then he asked, "Do you know why they are taking you out of here?" I told him it was not clear to me, either, but perhaps it was because of my once-a-month medication issues, which were time-consuming according to my company—and with which I personally agreed. The captain asked me what my medication issue encompassed and said he was willing to accommodate me however he could in order to keep me in Sarkari Bagh. After I explained to him what my medical problems were all about, he immediately called his brigade colonel in the KAF to discuss what had to be done so I didn't have to fly to Bagram every month.

The captain recommended that I could just go to KAF for my medication once a month, traveling back and forth on the same day. I told the captain, "Sir, I would love to stay here with you, but you're really going to have to use your magic and power to keep me here." He agreed. "Yes, I know. To keep you here, I'll take it up with our one-star general if I have to." He asked me for my site manager's name, phone number, and email address, as well as what kind of medication I was taking to determine whether he could arrange for my treatment in KAF.

As I stood there while the captain spoke to his commander in KAF, he was finally able to get the okay from his commander that they would be willing to accommodate my medical requirements at KAF, which would be a single day of traveling time versus the 10–12 days to Bagram.

The captain had another, more important battle to fight by assigning me to his unit. He told me how bad he needed me on his COP. He said that while I was away in Bagram for my medication, locals from the villages around the compound had shown up at the front gate asking for me. Most of the villagers who knew me personally asked to talk with, "*Nasrat, Da Haji Malem Saheb ferzande Zoy.* ("Nasrat, Haji Malem (teacher), Saheb's adopted son.") As the captain was busy doing everything he could do to keep me there, meanwhile I did everything I could by volunteering for every dismounted mission that came up.

It was the beginning of November. A once-a-year Afghan religious holiday was coming up within 10 to 12 days. I asked the captain if it would be possible for us to go out on a humanitarian mission to my adopted village, which was less than a mile from our compound. The captain told me to ask Ray if he could set something up for a squad to go out with me. When I asked Ray about the mission and if we could go to my adopted village of Haji Toar Kaley, he was not only delighted, but assured me that it shouldn't be a problem. The upcoming holiday, which was called *Loay Akhtar* in Pashto, is a three-day, Muslim, religious holiday, especially for those who go to Mecca for a once-in-a-lifetime pilgrimage. During this particular holiday, people greet one another by visiting each other's homes. Usually, the older generation stays home while the younger generation visits them. Kids are all given cash money as holiday gifts.

As I was in Bagram for my medical requirements, I had converted $1,000 into Afghan currency (which was approximately 46,000 Afghanis). Not knowing where I'd be later, when I had converted the currency I figured that I was going to be stuck with pockets full of 46,000 Afghanis that I planned to give to a good cause, which led me to planning this humanitarian mission so I could give it to the kids as a gift for their *Loay Akhtar*. Fortunately, the mission was finally planned by Ray for November 14th, the first day of the three-day holiday. Ray was excited because he knew that I would be visiting my adopted village.

In the meantime, I kept my fingers crossed while still waiting for an answer from the captain regarding the status of whether I was staying or returning to Bagram. For a week, there was no news, so I opted to take no news as good news. While I waited, I helped the platoon on dismounted missions to the village of Ali Kaley. We were all going to walk through farms filled with orchards. It was not very safe walking in alleyways surrounded by dense pomegranate orchards, which would accommodate easy ambushes that the bad guys would be eagerly waiting to execute. Beforehand, we were told that Ali Kaley was one of the most densely populated Taliban villages in all of the Arghandab District. As one of the ANP officers had put it, "*Ustad, az Anar kada Taliba ziat ast.*" ("Ustad, there are more Taliban than there are pomegranates.")

As I was walking out of the compound toward my adoptive dad's orchard, it was all I could do not to cry. Old memories were hitting me hard again as I wondered what had happened to my dad, and how everything was ruined, not only for him and his family, but for me and Afghanistan, from which I had been fortunate enough to pull myself out. Unfortunately,

Afghanistan has a long way to go before its people realize the truth and pull themselves out as well. I still had a difficult time believing that one day I would return, and now that I had, after more than 40 years, here I was literally walking on the same, exact dirt alleyways. My heart was racing as I neared my dad's orchard, hoping and just imagining for a second that I would see him walking in the orchard, just like we once did; unfortunately, those thoughts were just 40-year-old memories that felt like they were lived yesterday. Obviously, I didn't see my dad nor could I thank him for choosing to raise me as his son—a son who could one day return and try to help his native land.

We were walking south on this narrow road, passing my dad's orchards on the west side of the road. There was also a narrow canal that was on the east side of the road, which provided water for all the orchards below. It seemed and felt like I was literally dreaming as we walked alongside the canal, seeing certain wide areas in it that my cousin, Zahir Shah, and I swam in during hot summer afternoons

Being here now, I realized one thing that I otherwise would have forgotten. The human brain is a miraculous organ because it's capable of storing memories that one forgets until you return to the same spot where the memory was first born. Approaching the wider area of the canal reminded me of Zahir and me climbing a tree branch, using it as a diving board that was right at the edge of the canal from which we could jump into the shallow water. At the moment, we were standing there, and I was looking at the tree that was still standing in a much larger form after the passage of time.

As we kept walking alongside the canal under the blue, crisp sky of early November, the trees all around us had changed into their seasonal colors throughout the scattered red of the pomegranate orchards. I couldn't help but notice that a majority of the trees were not as tall as they used to be, that the walls of the orchards were shorter and the canal narrower. Then, I recognized that nothing had really happened, at least to the walls—it was only because I had grown at least three feet, which is why the walls looked shorter.

As Lieutenant Barron and I continued walking side by side, I pointed out to him that I used to walk this same road with my dad, to the school where he taught, which still should be right around the corner where there should also be a bridge that crossed over the narrow canal. Once we turned the corner, Barron was astounded that I could still remember the bridge until we turned the corner and saw the same, exact one that I had crossed on many occasions 40 years ago, was still standing.

While the Afghan officers followed us, as dangerous as it was, every 19- to 23-year-old American soldier walking the zigzag alleyways was singing and smiling as though they were in Central Park in Manhattan. After walking through myriad orchards and climbing many walls, we reached Ali Kaley—fortunately, without incident. Young children started to follow us, asking for candy or anything else we might have to offer them. Knowing that it was a Taliban-friendly village, our mission was simply to walk around and talk with the locals about their safety and the overall security in the area. A village west of the Arghandab River, not too far from where we were, had been bombed earlier in the week by the Americans. Most of its inhabitants were Taliban.

At first, as we walked around and casually asked the villagers if they had any strangers in the village, I sensed their resistance to talking with us. Barron had once visited the village, but this was obviously his first time here, with me. He told me that the last time he had visited, not even one person in the entire village wanted to talk with him. This time, however, while people were talking, they were still holding back from saying anything that could hurt them later.

I kept talking with the villagers, sometimes telling jokes to the kids. As usual, everyone asked where I had learned to speak Kandahari Pashto. I told them that I was born in Kandahar and grew up in Arghandab. In disbelief, the children would ask me, *"Mama, no ta ham the Arghadaw yey?"* ("Uncle, you're a native of Arghandab?") I would nod my head that I was, and that simple acknowledgement brought them great joy, to the point that they would run all around so they could tell other kids. It was amazing to Barron and me how much people appreciated me for being in their village, talking and laughing with them, which gave them a sense of comfort knowing that they were talking to one of their own—unlike most other linguists or Afghan forces, who usually held an AK47 to their heads instead of telling them jokes with the hope of making them smile.

By the time we got to the center of the village where the large mosque was located, we had more than 40 kids running behind us—some holding my hands, as well as Lieutenant Barron's—and they were all asking us questions. It was unheard of for anyone to hold the hands of infidels in

Afghanistan, let alone in Taliban-friendly Ali Kaley, Arghandab, Kandahar Province. But these kids were young and innocent—three to 12 years of age—children who needed someone to love them with a smile, even if that someone happened to be Lieutenant Barron, an American.

We initially noticed resistance from the villagers: some would simply not talk with us; others said they were happier with the Taliban regime rather than the current Afghan government. Every time I received a negative response, I would try to somehow video record the conversation by covering the camcorder with a scarf so I could capture the looks on the kids' faces and record our conversation without them seeing me doing such a thing in conservative Arghandab.

Soon the whole village was informed that the Americans finally brought an interpreter from Arghandad who also spoke English. On many occasions, the villagers approached me and asked for all kinds of help: from needing food items, to medication, to everything else that came to mind. At one point, I had a middle-aged man approach me; he was wrapped up in his *Dobata,* which is a long, 3x7-foot piece of garment that Kandahari men usually carry on their shoulders, so it can be used as either a praying mat or, if the weather got cold, it could be wrapped around their shoulders or bodies to stay warm. So, the man followed me, asking in Pashto with a whispering tone to his voice so other villagers or the bad guys would not hear him, *"Ta gora, zama yawa dana hindara pakar da, dagha komak ba na rasara wakray?"* ("Hey, listen to me. I need a mirror; would you be able to help me with that?") When I asked him why he needed a mirror, he responded that he wanted to use it to run his sewing machine. Not too surprisingly, I was confused by his answer, so I asked him how he was able to run his sewing machine with a mirror. He invited me to his house so he could show me. Needless to say, I hesitated, thinking to myself, *This guy might kidnap or harm me in some way*, especially because of the way he was all wrapped up in his *Dobata.* Apprehensively, I told him that I wasn't able to go to his house. Nonetheless, he continued to follow me. He wouldn't let it go, and I didn't understand even my native from Arghandab who was speaking to me in Pashto. Since he wouldn't stop asking me to help him, I told him one more time that I didn't understand what a mirror and a sewing machine had to do with each other. I noticed that he was even more frustrated than I was when he said, "Okay, listen to me. My sewing machine uses a lot of batteries. If you can help me get a mirror, I could put it on top of my roof to run my sewing machine—then I would not need more batteries." Now I understood: that he was asking me if I could help him get a solar panel to put on top of his roof for electricity so he could operate his sewing machine.

To see and hear a man ask me for a solar panel in a village of nothing more than mud homes, their roofs covered with tree trunk/branches, raw sewage from the homes running through the village's center where the children played, was beyond my imagination. I would never have ever thought of anyone in the village knowing anything about a solar-power panel, especially in Arghandab. Well, my thoughts were once again proven to be wrong. My main point is that communicating with people is the key to our success, not only in Afghanistan but in any society, or for that matter, life in general, even if we spoke and understood the same language. If there had been any linguist other than me, a linguist native of Kandahar, I truly don't believe this villager would have approached him in the first place or even have bothered asking the question for help, let alone understand what the villager's needs were. The only reason the villager approached me was because he felt comfortable talking with me—knowing that he could communicate with me, whether we actually understood one another or not. Some would argue that these are small issues that would not affect the overall success of our mission in Afghanistan.

Well, respectfully to those "some," I say: It is extremely important when people are shooting at and trying to kill you on the frontline of the war on terror like all of the brave American soldiers that I was honored to serve with in the most dangerous places of the Taliban of Arghandab, Yahya Khel, Qarah Bagh, Merjah, and many other places throughout Afghanistan where a single missed translation could either save a life or take one. Someone sitting behind a desk in Kandahar, Kabul, or Washington, DC, cannot tell you what needs to be done to fix the ongoing conflict in Afghanistan.

Only guys like Alfa; Alfa2; Marine Captain Carter; the young lieutenant in Yahya Khel—and all their teams; Patrick, Thunder, Hero, Gayle, and his squad; the Captain here in Sarkari Bagh; Pat; Lieutenant Barron; and, last but not least, Ray and his company of soldiers—all brave Americans making lifesaving decisions while fighting on the frontline. These Americans are more than "qualified" to tell you how important it is to use the simple and small words of translation by communicating with the villagers, which could have such a huge impact on the overall accomplishments of the mission—to have the villagers understand and support you.

Most Afghan villagers are plain, down-to-earth people; they only understand simple words to communicate, and if one could understand their simplicity, and their needs, only then could the U.S. and our allies succeed in Afghanistan. I believe all decisions should be left to the people on the frontline. For me, as a linguist who is fluent in English, Pashto, Farsi, and some understanding of Hindi, every unit that I have worked with wanted me to stay with them because they knew the benefit of me being a part of their unit. Everyone in my current and previous units that I worked with realized how the locals were responding to me in a positive way, especially when we were, for the most part, in the middle of the Taliban hive of Arghandab.

As we walked around the village, little boys started asking Barron and me if we knew where Ali was. I didn't know Ali personally and asked Barron if he did. He told me that Ali usually hung out with the ANA guys. He never interacted with the locals or the Americans unless he was desperately needed. Barron also let me know that all of the other linguists never went out of their way to talk with any of the villagers. One of the boys who was holding my hand told me, "Uncle, I think Ali is mute. We never hear him talk. Every time we ask him where he's from, he either slaps or kick us."

Ali had his reasons for not being in contact with the locals. Had I been in Ali's shoes, not being able to speak the language, I would've played mute as well. In Afghanistan, most people don't respect kids, and some would even physically abuse them, just like what the little boy was telling us what Ali did to them if they asked even a simple question. Let's be clear on the subject of physical abuse in Afghanistan. The spanking kind of physical abuse that we in the West use on our kids from time to time is considered a slap on the wrist compared to the physical abuse used on children in Afghanistan. To even further support my point, I recorded one of the ANA officers carrying a stick to hit little boys with if they so much as got close to us. If the ANA, ANP, or any of the local linguists tried to hit or kick young children, why would the villagers like officials with the Afghan government? In addition to all the kicking and hitting, the officials also took personal possessions from their homes and bribes from their parents every time they attempted to settle a dispute of any kind.

For the villagers, the Afghan government was not their protectors—they were more a disruption in their daily lives.

After a long walk, Barron and I were sitting on the side of the creek that ran through the middle of the village. I started talking to young adults to get their opinions and could not believe what I was hearing. Since I am a realist, I didn't blame them for what they were telling with me about how they were treated by their government. One of the young men told me he liked the Taliban better than the Afghan government, as did most of the others who had gathered around us. I asked the young man, as they would do in Afghanistan by pointing my index finger, touching his chest, "Which government do you personally believe is beneficial to you—the current Karzai's government or the previous Taliban government?" Noticing that I had my video recorder on, the boy asked me to turn it off and then he would tell me. I assured him that whatever I was recording, it was for my own personal use, that I wasn't going to share it with anyone from the Afghan government. Since almost every villager thinks that Americans are also somehow part of the Afghan government, he still insisted that I turn it off.

I did everything I could to not piss him off and only recorded whenever I got the chance, which I was fortunately able to do from time to time when he and some of the other villagers talked about which government they preferred the most. One villager said to me, "Ever since the Taliban has been out of power and the Karzai government has taken over, more thieves have surfaced, especially in the government sector." Another man added, "During the Taliban times, you could've left a sack full of money on the street corner and no one would have even looked at it. But now, they're robbing our pockets."

They would rather have had one of the better of the two evils (i.e., the Taliban) who didn't steal from them like the Afghan government did. I asked the crowd a general question. "Don't you guys want us to build you schools, roads, and clinics?" They all answered almost simultaneously with the same answer, which surprised and, frankly, shocked me. "What do we need roads for? We don't even have cars or know how to drive one. What do we need schools for? They only corrupt our children, just like the Afghan government workers. What do we need clinics for, if we don't have doctors and can't afford to buy the medication?" Their thought that schooling would corrupt them was because, in their minds, they believed that every Afghan government worker had been to school, or at least that's what the government workers claimed, which is why they're all considered corrupt. How do we convince people like this? They really have to convince themselves or, even better, the government should stop stealing from them.

Barron told me to ask the villagers if they would like to work with us on a project that we were going to start to help the Afghan government renovate Sarkari Bagh. Anyone who wanted to work would be paid 500 Afghanis ($11) a day. No one in the village was interested in our offer because they were all afraid of the Taliban retaliation if they worked for either the Americans or the Afghan government. Knowing the people and their culture, particularly in Arghandab, I asked Barron if I could offer the villagers what I had in mind just to see their reaction, especially since they had already rejected his offer.

When I asked them if they would be willing to work on any kind of project that would benefit their village, their responses were nonverbal while the looks on their faces said, "Maybe." I updated Barron with what I had told the villagers, and he asked, "Sure, Nas, but what are you going to offer them?" I told him that I had two things in mind, even if they cost me personally, financially just to make my point—not only to the villagers but to our commander in Sarkari Bagh—to demonstrate how serious and willing I was to listen and understand the locals' needs from village to village. I apprised Barron that I was going to ask them if they would take a job in their own village, helping us build the canal that we sat beside while talking with some of the children. I didn't know if they would accept the offer, but I wanted to determine if they were interested in working on a project that would benefit their own village tremendously. By nature, because most Afghans are not interested in doing things if they don't benefit from them personally, I knew some of them would reject the idea. From a Western point of view, one might think that if we offered to help the locals build something in their own village (in this case, a canal) that would undoubtedly be a good thing that the whole village could benefit from, they'd jump at the opportunity to do so. Well, not even close. No one even cared about their village—but then, here again, that's not how things work in Afghanistan where the people are not even remotely interested in contributing to anything other than something that would apply to their personal interests. So, before I even told them what I wanted to do for the villager, I had a feeling they would reject my offer, but, I asked them anyway so Barron could see and come closer to understanding these people and their culture as well as which offer they would accept or reject.

So, there I was asking the question again whether anyone would work for us to rebuild the canal going through their village. I got the same exact answer that Captain Alfa and I received in the village of Dayak in Ghazni Province that early morning in front of the mosque when we offered to put the sewer underground. Their response in this village was that nothing was wrong with the canal; as long as the water flowed, that's all they needed. Even though the offer was rejected, I wasn't a person who gave up easily.

Since our ideas to convince the locals to work for us didn't work, Barron asked me to tell them that we would be returning on Friday, which was two days away, so that we could give out some humanitarian aid to the villagers. So, in other words, in a way we were going to try to bribe them, to get them on our side. Nonetheless, the offer was welcome news to the villagers. I had learned that giving humanitarian aid to the locals wasn't really a bad idea, but it was only a temporary solution to our problem of getting the locals on our side almost 90 percent of the time. Not only that, once the humanitarian aid was distributed, everything would go back to where Americans were infidels and the Afghan government—who stole from the locals—were supported by the infidels. It's like parents giving their children anything they ask for so that the parents could feel loved by their children, which in most cases, leads to the children's own destruction later because they had never known or learned the value of earning something for themselves. This is how we in the West are being portrayed: like parents who constantly give anything their children (Afghans) ask for. Here, too, things that are not earned will not be valued.

As we were leaving the village, I was approached by a couple of villagers who were interested in taking the $11 a day job offer. They explained that the reason they didn't ask me in the village center was because they didn't want the other villagers to know that they wanted to work for us. Their behavior told us that there were Taliban elements in this village, where people were afraid to speak out.

Before we went back to the zigzag alleyways between the orchards, at the very end of the village I was asked by a young villager, who was pointing to a small opening in the mud wall around the corner, "Uncle, can you help this lonely, elderly woman whose only son is currently associated with the Taliban in Peshawar (City in Pakistan)? He only visits his mother once or twice a year." I asked for Barron's permission to enter the mud house to find out what the young man was talking about.

As I walked toward the house, an elderly lady in her 90s (at least) was laying in the sun against the wall in front of the two-room mud hut. There were no doors or anything else that would make anyone believe that someone actually lived there. With that knowledge, there was no need for me to go any further into the house.

I attempted to get the poor lady's attention by saying hello to her. All I could hear in return in Pashto was, "My son, oh God, my son," over and over again. I asked her what she needed. She replied, "I want my son back." When I asked where her son was, she responded, "He's in Peshawar." I then asked her what her son was doing in Peshawar, and she pointed to one of the soldiers standing outside with a rifle in his hand before she said, *"Hagha ham dada pa rakam topak par ojha krey whyee chea jahad kawam."* ("He is like him, carrying a rifle on his shoulder, saying he is fighting a jihad.") She also complained of a headache. I told her that although we couldn't help her get her son back, we could help her with medication for her headache the next time we came to the village.

Since he had been here once before, according to Lieutenant Barron, the response from the villagers was somewhat positive. On the way back to the COP, Barron asked if I would come with him on the next mission on Friday to this same village. I told him I would. Barron reminded me that his next mission to the village would be humanitarian as he would be bringing supplies of rice, oil, sugar, and tea for the villagers' upcoming holiday. Like most of the other humanitarian missions by the American commanders, food items were purchased through the Afghan government officials, who would then charge the Americans 10 times more for what they could pay in the local market (e.g., the $1.80 tea that was sold to me for $10). This time, what Barron and our commander had decided was that before our mission, we would go to the local market right around the corner from our compound and buy all the supplies from the local shopkeepers. I thought it was a brilliant move by our commanders because it gave all the business directly to the local shopkeepers and we would undoubtedly save lots of money by not involving the local linguists or any of the Afghan officials.

As I waited in our compound to leave for our mission, the linguist who was supposed to be on the mission as well was sitting in front of his tent smoking and talking with one of his fellow linguists. We had a pit at one corner of our compound where we could burn all of our trash. Before it was time to do that, I saw a poor local man who came inside our base every single day, collecting paper and plastic bottles from the trash, which is how he made his living, by taking our trash and selling it in the city. The linguist, who never helped to translate for the poor Afghans, went out of his way to throw his cigarette on the poor man's pile of papers in the back of his donkey cart, setting them afire. Stunned by such an act of cruelty, I walked over to the donkey cart and doused the fire with the bottle of water I had in my hand. As soon as the linguist saw me, he went into his room to avoid a confrontation. I went after him nonetheless and asked why he had done that. His English was as weak as his Pashto, so he responded to me in Farsi, *"E mordagaw az tarafi roz kaghaz wo bottala jam maykonad, az tarafi shab Talib maybashad."* ("This motherfucker is a paper and plastic collector during the day, and Talib during the night.") I chose not to ask him anything further. Knowing that he didn't speak or understand Pashto or English, I couldn't help but be curious how he managed to get a job as a linguist, so I asked him. His response in Farsi was, "My brother paid a Pashton, who takes Pashto tests for a fee, for everyone who wants to be a linguist." Why was he telling me that he had cheated on the test just to get the job? Because it's only normal that a fellow Afghan would boast to his other fellow Afghans that he had cheated on the test. That is why only Afghans understand Afghans, and no other culture will ever understand how they work. In my case, this linguist and all the other linguists would tell me things that they would otherwise never tell to Americans, or anyone else for that matter, because they thought I was one of their fellow Afghans.

Before we went to stop at the market for the supplies, we needed a truck. Unfortunately, the ANA and ANP here were no different than those in Yahya Khel when we wanted to deliver school supplies. Out of the dozens of trucks parked in our compound for their personal use, they refused to allow us to use even one for the delivery of humanitarian supplies to the village of Ali Kaley. However, our commander was offered a privately-owned pickup truck by one of the ANP officers who had a brother-in-law who was going to help us load the supplies and take them to the village. But he was going to let us use his truck on one condition: if we would allow him to drive between our soldiers, since we were going to walk, so that he and his truck would be protected by the American soldiers from an attack by the bad guys.

The deal was made and we were on our way toward the village, the truck surrounded on all sides by American soldiers like a humanitarian motorcade. The only positive thing out of all of this humanitarian aid so far was that all the shopkeepers were very happy when we bought all of the supplies we needed from them directly, paying them cash right on the spot. Upon arrival of our motorcade at the village, I'm serious when I say that every kid in the village was running towards once we turned the corner, especially toward Lieutenant Barron and me, since we were the two who always talked with them and made them laugh. Some kids would rather gather around other American soldiers who gave them candy and made them laugh as well versus their own ANP or ANA officers, who, for the most part, hit them.

As the motorcade made its way to the open field in the center of the village, the driver of the pickup (the one with the frightening look on his face) wanted to dump the supplies as soon as possible and get the hell out of there. The thing that struck me the most was the fear on the faces of those who went on the mission with us in their own country.

Everything was dropped in the middle of an open field while a couple of American soldiers stood guard to protect it from looters. The village adults gathered in mass numbers, sitting in a circle around the sacks of rice, gallons of cooking oil, boxes of tea, and bags of sugar, while the kids all ran after Barron and me as we walked around the village to inform everyone to meet us in the center of the village at 3:00. In addition to the humanitarian aid being provided by our base commander, I also brought large 2,000-tablet bottles of Extra Strength Tylenol, which I carried throughout my deployment in Afghanistan, just in case someone needed it. Tylenol is the most common medication in Afghanistan that most people used for any kind of pain. Fortunately, my headaches, compared to every single Afghan I came across, were not as bad when compared to the locals. For them, just being in Afghanistan was a headache in and of itself—not to mention the headaches they faced when dealing with their own government, which Tylenol alone could not treat.

My first stop with the Tylenol was the elder lady's mud house, to see if I could at least ease her headache, at the least, or make it go away, if only for a short period of time. When I arrived, she was no longer there.

In fact, her place looked even emptier than it did when I had been here but two days before. I wanted to see if the next door neighbors would be kind enough to give it to her if I left it with them. I knocked on the neighbor's door. When a man answered, he look frightened and had a look of concern on his face seeing three American soldiers on his doorstep. He didn't realize that one of the three dressed in American military uniforms were natives of Kandahar, which most people don't expect—especially in Argahndab—until I opened my mouth to greet the man in Pashto. His concerned face suddenly smiled, although I could see that he was still somewhat curious why a native Kandahari like myself would show up at his door dressed in a U.S. Army uniform.

When I asked the man what his name was, he responded, *"Za Rahmatullah yam."* ("I am Rahmatullah.") I asked if he knew the elderly lady who lived next door and, if so, where she was. He told me that her relatives in the city had picked her up yesterday because she wasn't feeling well. I asked him if I left her some medication, if he would be kind enough to give it to her. He said, "Absolutely," so I gave him a small plastic bag of Tylenol to give to her if and when she came home again. Before I could invite him out to get some of the humanitarian items for himself, Rahmatullah offered us tea. I thanked him for his offer but told him that we were short on time, and then I asked him to join us in the center of the village.

Most of our soldiers held security positions around the villages—some protecting the aide, Barron, SFC, Pat, and me as we walked around the village talking with the villagers as well as asking them to join us at 3:00 at the open field to get some of the aid we brought with us. Some said they'd be there; others said they wouldn't. By the time we made the loop, the village seamed empty as most of the villagers were already sitting around in a circle waiting for the aid. It was around 2:00 when we returned to the middle of the village.

As we sat to take a rest after walking and talking for three to four hours, children gathered around us, still asking questions. Most of their questions concerned my personal life and why I had left Arghandab. I didn't have the time to explain to them why I left for the city of Kandahar and then for America. Even if I did have the time, they wouldn't have understood me anyway.

I watched the young American soldiers sitting on the side of the creek, looking around, each in their own way trying to entertain the

poor children of this village. I saw a 19-year-old American soldier surrounded by more than 20 kids, who were clapping, cheering, laughing
and asking the young soldier in Pashto, *"Eshala waka."* ("Dance for us.")
It was a great scene that reminded me of many other missions that I had
been on where the American soldiers would do everything they could
to give out candy, medical treatment, and school supplies to the Afghan
children, and when they ran out of everything they had brought, they
tried to entertain them to make them laugh, exactly like what I was
recording on this mission.

It brought tears to my eyes every time I saw young 19- to 20-year-
old American soldiers, who volunteered to be in the military to serve
their beloved country by not only fighting the enemies of Afghanistan
and America, but also being entertainers to the poor children of every
village we visited. I always wondered endlessly about the generosity of
the American soldiers and how it was possible for them to act in such a
compassionate way toward the local children that their own ANA and
ANP officers wouldn't do.

Before I continue, I would like to share an article with you that
relates and is germane to what I have just written about the American
soldiers. One day right after 9/11, I received an email that was sent out
by one of my coworkers at our office, which she distributed to everyone
in the office. Like me, she's a U.S. citizen by choice. Unlike me, who
was raised, for the most part, in one of the poorest of the nations in the
world, she was fortunate enough to be from one of the wealthiest nations
in Western Europe (Germany). Anyhow, in the email, she stated, "We
rarely get a chance to see another country's editorial about the U.S.
Read this excerpt from a Romanian newspaper, *Evenimentulzilei (The
Daily Event* or *News of the Day)*. The article was written by Mr. Cornel
Nistorescu and published under the title "C'ntarea Americii," meaning
"Ode To America."

"Why are Americans so United? They would not resemble one another
even if you painted them all in one color! They speak all the languages of
the world and form an astonishing mixture of civilizations and religious
beliefs. Still, the American tragedy turned 300 million people into hands
that they place over their hearts because of their love for their country.
Nobody rushed to accuse the White House, the Army, and the Secret
Service that they are only a bunch of losers. Nobody rushed to empty their

bank accounts. Nobody rushed out onto the streets nearby to gape about. The Americans volunteered to donate blood and lending a helping hand.

"After the first moments of panic, they raised their flag over the smoking ruins, putting on T-shirts, caps, and ties in the colors of their national flag, the latter of which they placed on buildings and cars as if in every place and on every car a government official or the president was passing. On every occasion, they started singing their traditional song: 'God Bless America!' I watched the live broadcast and rerun after rerun for hours, listening to the same story of the guy who went down 100 floors with a women in a wheelchair without knowing who she was, or of the California hockey player who gave his life fighting with the terrorists and prevented the plane from hitting a target that could have killed 100s or 1,000s of people.

"How on earth were they able to respond, united as one human being? Imperceptibly, with every word and musical note, the memory of some turned into a modern myth of tragic heroes. And with every phone call, millions and millions of dollars were put in a collection aimed at rewarding not a man or a family, but a spirit, which no money can buy. What on earth can unite the Americans in such a way? Their land? Their history? Their economic power? Money? I tried for hours to find an answer, humming songs and murmuring phrases with the risk of sounding commonplace. I thought things over, but I could reach only one conclusion: Only freedom can work such miracles!" (Well, Cornel sure hit the nail on the head with "freedom"—and only in America.)

I strongly agree with Mr. Nistorescu's perception of "Only freedom can work such miracles." And, at the same time, only those of us who have lived amongst the oppressed can really relate to what freedom really is; and, it's also because such freedom from the men and women of the U.S. military will protect and be passed on, not only to people like many natives of Afghanistan, but to all of society as well.

It was finally 3:00 and the crowd was larger than ever. The only time throughout my 18 months or so of being in Afghanistan up until that moment, was that this was the first time Afghans had ever made it on time to an event without using the word "Inshallah." Earlier in the day, during our walk through the village to invite everyone to get the aid we had brought for them, not once had I heard the word *Inshallah* (God willing or with God's will) from any of the villagers.

Before I started giving out the rations, I told Barron that I was going to give each adult their fair share so everyone there could be helped. Barron, not yet knowing the locals and their culture, wanted to give it to the village elder who could then divide it amongst the villagers himself. Again, I told Barron that giving everything to one person would not be good idea. Barron countered that he was not going to give it to just any person. His plan was to ask the locals to choose who their *Malak* (Village Elder) was. Once they had chosen that person, Barron would then hand over all the food rations, etc., to him so it could be split by the *Malak* amongst the villagers. Well, a *Malak* wasn't chosen by all the people who had been gathered there for hours. In fact, out of all the people there, with the support of a couple of the other villagers sitting next to him, only one elder claimed to be the *Malak*.

Before the distribution of the rations began, the first person who complained about the Afghan government was a villager by the name of Assadullah Aka, who seemed to be the only one who knew what was going on—politically, socially, and economically—not only in and around the village, but as well as within the District and Province. He was mostly concerned that the Americans would soon leave and then there would be chaos in Afghanistan again. He was not the only one was concerned about this. Others in the crowd were more worried about everyday events and more concerned, for selfish reasons, about things that only related to their own Pashton tribes, rather than Afghanistan as a whole. They thought they were being taken advantage of, even by their own Pashton leader, President Karzai.

Their main complaint about Karzai was that he had betrayed them because he never appointed people to a government post from the general population of Kandahar Province. Instead, he brought in buddies from America, Canada, and other Western countries and assigned them to posts in the governorship or mayoral positions within the city. I had no idea who the governor and mayor of Kandahar were. Since most people in Afghanistan generalize people or situations, I asked the man in the crowd if he could name those people specifically. While he was unable to answer, someone else in the crowd behind me said that the man in

Kandahar was not much of a governor by one man's account, and he, too, could not provide a name.

They all started talking in circles, no one really able to answer my question. Rather, all they managed to do was continue to express complaint after complaint, as if I was representing the president, governor, or the mayor. One man told me that all the governor did was take money from the Westerners (international donors, primarily from the U.S.) for the rebuilding projects in the suburb districts of Kandahar, but actually divided it amongst his own cronies without spending a dime on the projects themselves. The *Malak* was quiet for a while as he gathered his thoughts. Then, he told me that the only way things could be improved in Kandahar, or even perhaps throughout the entire province would be if Karzai would stop bringing in Afghans who lived in America to fill the government posts, because none of them were really interested in doing their jobs for the people of Kandahar—rather, they were only in Afghanistan for their own personal greed and power.

I asked the *Malak* if he knew anyone in Kandahar personally who would be able to run things in the city the way he wanted. I also asked: If there are such people, then why aren't they coming forward to take the posts as governor or mayor so that the local population can be satisfied? The *Malak* responded, in almost a single breath, with short pauses between sentences, "The local people, who should fill the positions, are not wealthy enough to bribe themselves into government posts. Just meeting with one of Karzai's government officials would cost a considerable amount of money, let alone actually getting the job. The only people who deserve to be in the government and can make things better in Kandahar would be those people who have lived all their lives in Kandahar and have fought for their *watan* (homeland). The only person who can be qualified to be mayor, governor, or any other available post in the government should be someone who has never left Kandahar. The cowards who exiled and escaped their land when the Soviets invaded have all returned, including Karzai and the members of his family, not because they love Kandahar as they claim—they're coming back because they like American dollars and the protection so they can abuse the poor. When Karzai brought Hamidi, one of his friends, over from America three years ago and appointed him mayor of Kandahar, none of the shopkeepers liked him or the way he treated them. Some even went so far as to attempt to kill him because he was bulldozing the poor villagers' shops. Those shopkeepers are the same poor people who fought the Soviets out of Kandahar. Now, the new mayor comes from America to tell the poor how and when they can do things to run the city, which neither the president nor the mayor ever tried to defend during times of war."

The *Malak* continued—once again in a tone like I was somehow related to all the people he was criticizing—that, "One of these days, the mayor is going to regret what he's doing to the poor people of Kandahar who have suffered for so long that the day will come when they won't take it anymore." By now, I could understand the *Malak's* frustration, particularly since everyone in every village that I had visited told me the same thing over and over again. As the *Malak* tried to defend the people of Kandahar, he said, "They don't need people who have exiled to the West to escape the hardships of war and are now back to dictate to them. They'd rather have dictators like the Taliban than the government. The people in the city claim that everything belongs to them, and those who came back try to implement Western-style rules over people who know no other rules but those of the Sharia Islamic law. If anyone tries to take that from them, they're willing to take that person's life, which the world has witnessed more recently because of the assassinations of government officials, not only in Kandahar but throughout Afghanistan."

I thought to myself that the *Malak* had gathered all of his thoughts as though they were written on a piece of paper, but that wasn't everything that came out of his mouthful of *Noswar* (dipping tobacco), as he would spit from time to time during his speech. Either he was with the Taliban himself, a loyal Taliban supporter, or just an elder who was sick and tired of the way Karzai was treating people in Kandahar. In my entire conversation with this elder, not once did I hear him mention Afghanistan. It had been proven to me time and time again, not only in Kandahar, but in every province that I had been to, locals only referred to their native province instead of Afghanistan as their country. Being in other provinces where people had complained about Karzai and his government officials' treatment of the locals would sometimes make me think and wonder if people in Kandahar would say bad things about Karzai and his government as well. When I heard them complain in the Khost, Ghazni, Paktika, Paktia, Uruzgan, and Wardak Provinces about Karzai and his government, I could understand their point because Karzai was a Pashton from Kandahar. In the heart of Kandahar Province, I heard far more criticism of Karzai than in all the other provinces combined.

As you can undoubtedly sense, blood relations are more important in the Afghan society than is nationalism. I asked a general question of the crowd—including the *Malak*, knowing that he lived in the city—if anyone complained to any of the government officials in Kandahar regarding their social, cultural, and economic issues. Again, the *Malak* answered the question by confirming that he lives in the city and knows exactly what's going on and who is doing what, but he doesn't have the willpower to take a stand alone against anyone or anything. He said that all he could do was observe things for himself, and not talk about it for the sake of his own personal security. In addition to everything else that the *Malak* had said thus far, he added that someone from his village contacted him yesterday and asked him to come over [to the village] because the Americans were coming with a native from Arghandab (i.e., me) as their interpreter. According to the *Malak*, that was the only reason he made the trip to the village so that he could talk with me so I could tell the Americans how bad the Karzai government was.

As an aside, I must point out that although the villagers liked the *Malak*, he was difficult to trust, because it was an unknown as to whose side he was on. I remember at one point during our conversation, when I translated between Barron and the *Malak*, Barron told the *Malak* that the Americans don't make decisions for Karzai's government nor do the Americans tell them what to do. Well, no matter what we told the locals in every village, most of them didn't believe us, preferring to be left alone. The *Malak* got angry about what we told him and made it clear that he didn't believe Barron. Angering the *Malak* was the last thing we wanted to do. Since most of Karzai's friends had returned from the West to hold government posts, especially most of those in Kandahar, Americans were immediately blamed for everything that went wrong.

The elder wanted to know, "Why is Karzai, as a Pashton himself, sending Hazara and Tajik soldiers and police into the homes of Pashtons in the middle of the night to terrorize or kill innocent villagers—all the while being supported by the American soldiers?" he asked this while pointing to the Afghan soldiers who were with us on this mission. "None of these Hazaras or Tajiks would ever have the courage to come to Kandahar without the Americans' support for Karzai's government." It was difficult for Barron and me to simply sit and listen, not being able to reason with the elder. This experience brought to mind another time when I had seen an elder, who was about 80 years old, being frustrated to the extent that his voice was shaking while he was demanding answers, much like the 90-year-old detainee with tuberculosis in Khost who was making a propaganda video.

Before we concluded the meeting, I asked a general question of the crowd regarding what the elder had said. They were all in support of him and demanded the same answers. During most of our meetings when the locals would talk, they always talked directly to me and then I, in turn, would tell my commander (or whoever else might be in charge on a particular mission). At one point during our conversation, the elder, in a voice combined with excitement and frustration, turned directly toward Barron, shaking his head as he said in Pashto, *"Awal, Tasi Amrikayan bayed daghasi tarjomanan rawaley laka dey, chea ham zamoj pa khabara poh she aow ham sta pa khabara poh she. Aow dawaham, da the pashtano pa koro wornanawatal mo dear ghalat kar dey."* Not knowing if the *Malak* was happy or mad by talking to him directly in Pashto, Barron obviously wanted to know what the elder had said to him. I told him the he had said, "First, you Americans should bring interpreters like him (pointing to me) who can understand both of us. Second, invading the Pashtons' homes is a very bad thing for you guys to be doing." Barron told me to tell him that he had no control over which linguist he could bring with him. Second, Barron wasn't in Afghanistan to invade Afghan villagers' homes.

As anticipated, the elder really didn't want to hear what Barron told him, nor did he want to believe it, so he just got up and left, cane in hand. Out of respect, Barron and I stopped him, asking him to stay so he could equally distribute the rations to the villagers. He handpicked four people he could trust out of the group who then divided everything into fourths. Once the four villagers started carrying the bags of rice on their backs, everyone else jumped up and start taking all that remained: oil, sugar, and tea. It had all disappeared within a matter of a minutes. Actually, it looked more like the villagers were looting, especially several who had taken more than others. It was an out-of-control situation to step in and even try to stop the crowd from what they were doing. Most of the sugar and tea bags were ripped open in the dirt because everyone was snatching both items from one another. What I had witnessed there will be witnessed by the world because everything the international community had built in Afghanistan up to that point had been looted and destroyed, not just in Kandahar, but in all of the other villages where we had provided humanitarian aid. Again, if you don't earn it, you don't value it.

A week had passed and there still was no news whether I'd be staying in Sarkari Bagh or going back to Bagram. Figuring that no news was good news, I remained patient. Ray told me he had arranged a personal mission so I could visit my adoptive village to give out *Akhtar Mobarakeys* (monetary gifts) to the villagers. I wasn't sure if doing so was selfish on my part by going to my adoptive village, putting everyone else going with us at risk of being attacked by the Taliban. I asked Ray for reassurance one more time before we left the compound, if I was in any way putting anyone in danger by going on this mission. His response was, "Nas, you're not putting anyone in any danger. Everyone in this COP under my command loves to go outside the compound to help the local villagers—besides, that's what they were trained for and that's what they're all here to do." His response brought my emotional side to the surface, even though I still feel guilty within my heart and soul as I thought, *What if any one of these young soldiers got attacked going on this mission? Will I blame myself for risking their lives?* Since I had lived most of my life already, I wasn't scared for me, but I was worried that the platoon of soldiers going with me might be risking their lives. Even Ray, who never went on any of our other missions, was going on this one, his gear ready and even a backpack full of candy for the villagers.

Ray also asked Sergeant Peter to join us; he, too, was going to be carrying a large backpack filled with candy. I was grateful and honored to be with these great guys who would risk their lives to do good not only for the poor Afghan people of Haji Toar Kaley, my adoptive village, but most especially for me. Once we were on our way, I became very emotional walking toward the village, seeing that nothing had changed physically. It was only me who had changed after 40 years, the last time I had walked these same alleyways.

For security reasons, in order for us to avoid being attacked, we walked through the orchards. As we walked to the end of one of them, I saw an open door connecting the orchard to the main house. I knew it would not be a good idea if a couple of the soldiers who were way ahead of me, walked into the main house. I hurried to stop them from entering without first alerting the owner of our presence. I managed to take the lead so that I could pull every one of our soldiers out of that orchard and into the house by first asking for the villager's permission. I didn't want us to storm the house like most of the ANA and ANP officers did, who, gratefully, weren't with us on this mission—only Americans were allowed!

Since most villagers would not expect anyone who came to visit the house via the orchard (unless, of course, it was one of their own family members), I knocked on the door, especially since most of the doors in the back of the house provided access to the orchards for the owner's use only.

After a soft knock on the door, I said in Pashto, "Hey, brother or sister, is there anyone at home?" As usual, one never saw a female answer the door. Instead, a young, shy boy come to the door and simply stood there. I asked, "Is this your house?" He nodded his head that it was. I then asked if he could show us the way to the front of his house, to which the boy responded, "Come with me, Uncle."

We all followed the young boy through his house into the front, which faced the small rocky hills alongside the Arghandab River. Today was the first day of *Akhtar*, (a Pashton religious holiday; just like Christmas in Christianity) so this little boy was the first villager to receive his gift. When I asked him if he had brothers or sisters in the house, he replied that he had two little sisters, so I gave 100 Afghanis to him and for each of his sisters, instructing him to be sure to tell his parents what the Americans had given him and his sisters.

Once we were out of the house, the soldiers told the boy how much they appreciated his help, which I translated so he understood what they were telling him. I remember one of our soldiers, who was 19, telling me, "Sir, for the past six months that I have been here in Sarkari Bagh, this is the first time that a young villager didn't run away from us; instead, he was willing to help us, all the while with a smile on his face." I told this young soldier that most people in the villages are innocent; if you speak their language and respect their culture, they will do likewise. When we went on missions, on more than one occasion, I told the ANP and ANA officers to respect the villagers. But the officers never saw things the way I did by respecting people, no matter what their ethnicity might be. Since I only worked with the American military, I can proudly say that despite the Americans supposedly being the infidels, they were more respected by most of the villagers than their own fellow Muslims of the ANA and ANP officers.

As I was handing the boy the money, one of the young soldiers asked me if I would give him one of the Afghan currency notes. I gave him 50 Afghani notes. He was delighted as he admitted, "Sir, it's not like I'm going to use it to buy anything here; I just want to keep it with me as a souvenir from Afghanistan."

Once out of the house, we climbed the rocky hill from where you could see the entire Arghandab Valley, from north to south, east to west, divided by the partially-dry Arghandab River that ran through the lush green pomegranate orchards on both sides. As a child growing up here, the top of this rocky hill behind our house occupied much of my cousin Zahir's and my time throwing rocks into the river down below.

While Ray and Peter were busy coordinating our guys into security positions before we walked into the village, I sat and looked around. All I could see was simplicity of a quiet and remote area. Everything looked as though it were frozen in time because it all appeared the same for decades, including the trees—the only exception was the river, now a bit narrower and partially dry.

As I continued to sit on the rock, in the back of my mind were a myriad of old memories returning to the forefront of my mind, much like a projector running in my head with round tapes of film showing me the black and white movie of my childhood from the late '60s and early '70s in which Zahir and I ran around, full of joy, until one or the other of our mothers would call us down from the rooftop of our house when it was time for us to go home. Being there 40 years later, I asked myself, *Why am I not feeling like I used to, being in Arghandab, despite the trees, river, mountains, and mud homes having changed?* To answer my own question, I realized that it was none of those things that made me love Arghandab—instead, it was the people who loved, cared for, and raised me that made Arghandab so special for me. Of course, those people were no longer there, but just by coming back here again, I had discovered and brought that wonderful black and white film—that I never knew existed—to mind.

Ray had sent Peter up to ask if we were ready to go into the village to see if I could find anyone from the old days who would still live in the village and recognize me, and vice versa. Along the way, I greeted everyone who could afford to do so on the first day of the holiday, wearing their new clothes. It's only twice a year that the villagers bought clothes: once for the *Khochiny Akhtar* holiday at the end of the month for the Ramadan celebration, and for the *Louy Akhtar* celebration, which were 70 days apart, each year. I handed out 100 Afghanis to every child and 200 to every adult.

At one point, Ray asked me what I was saying to the villagers because everyone was smiling at me, even before I pulled out the money. I told him it was simply a holiday greetings similar to the way one would greet someone in America by saying "Merry Christmas" during Christmastime, while handing them $20. Ray asked me to teach him so he could start greeting the villagers the same way, even though he would not be able to hand them money like I was. Besides being a compassionate and brave soldier, Ray was also a fast learner, because in no time, he was saying in Pashto, *"Da Akhtar dey Mubarak sa"* ("I wish you a happy holiday") very quickly. I soon realized that Ray taught the greeting to three of our young soldiers who were following us so that they could greet the villagers in the same way, too. People were so happy and cheerful that one of the villagers approached and complimented me by saying, *"Yar dawa dey sa, da kaferano ta dey la da Akhtar Mobarakey waor zada karey da."* ("I salute you for teaching the infidels (referring to my American buddies, of course) how to say it").

As we walked the narrow alleyway, getting closer and closer to my adoptive parents' house, mere words could not express my emotional excitement. Only Ray could relate to my joy of being in the village where I had grown up. So, that was the moment when I, as a grown man, walked with tears of joy streaming down my then (and now) wrinkly cheeks, rather than my boyhood tears of sadness when I left on this same alleyway, but in the opposite direction to return to the city that I loathed. Today, I was fortunate to be back alive and able to see it all again—everything memories until that day—that I thought I would never see again. As an Afghanistan native of these dusty alleyways and mud homes, wearing an American military uniform while walking through the village, I couldn't help but wonder what my father would have thought of me that day had he been alive to see me. I have no answer to that question, but do believe that he is with me at all times, watching over me, and sharing in both my sadness and my joy.

News of my arrival had spread through the village rapidly. It felt like every kid in the village was following me to my parents' house as if it were their own. (Or, I'd probably be more correct by saying they were following Santa Claus who was handing out money!)

The closer I got to the front of the house, the slower I progressed because I was surrounded by kids asking for money, some even for the second and third time, even though they were watching me cry and smile at the same time, never once understanding or wondering why. It was such a blessing to see the front door of the house, which was in the same place as it was when I left the village. I was so overwhelmed with joy at not only seeing the house, but by the smiles on all of the children's faces. At one point, I felt like the statue at Rome's famous Trevi Fountain where my tears were streaming out of my eyes as kids and adults gathered, asking me for money instead of throwing coins into the fountain.

Before I entered the house, I asked the adults if they knew whose house it was. Out of all the people gathered, only two adults—both in their late 20s—knew whose house it used to be. When asked, they both said, "*Haji Malem Saheb's*" ("Dear Teacher's"), referring to my adoptive dad. I told the villagers that I was his adopted son, *Malem*. Of course, since none of them was older than 30, they hadn't known me.

I knocked on the door but no one answered, so one of the kids who knew the people who lived in the house now, went inside to see if anyone was home. He came back with two other kids and said they lived in the house with their parents. I asked them if they could go back inside to ask their parents if it was possible for me to go inside the house just to see it, since I had lived in it in the past. In most of the villages we went to, the villagers always thought we were there to search their houses, which in a way was true. In fact, this was the only house so far that only Americans were going into, and not because we had to so we could get the bad guys but, in this case, because I wanted to capture my childhood memories from 40 years ago.

The kids who lived in the house now told me that their father wasn't home and his older brother was sleeping. While I was talking to them at the front door, a woman approached and was trying to go inside the house when one of the kids told her that I wanted to see it and why. The woman, covered from head to toe, looked at me through a small hole in her long and heavy *Porany* (a scarf that covered her head), standing quietly for at least five seconds, undoubtedly thinking to herself, *Why are four American soldiers standing at my front door so they can enter only because they want to see what the house looks like?* To stop her from walking away, I started to talk with her in Pashto. I could see that she was confused even more by someone talking to her in Pashto, dressed in a U.S. military uniform. I could also sense from her shaky voice that she was afraid of talking to a stranger, especially when she told me that her husband had gone to the city and then asked what I wanted from them. Culturally, she should not have been talking to me at all, unless I was one of her blood relatives. Regrettably, that's how women are treated in Afghanistan.

Once I introduced myself to her and told her that my name was Nasrat, the adopted son of Haji Malem Saheb, she immediately recognized me. For her to make sure I knew that she knew exactly who I was, she started telling me the names of my mother, sister, uncle, grandmother, and everyone else who have lived with us in this house, 40 years ago. Now that she felt more comfortable with me because she had proven that she knew who I was, I asked her who she and her husband were, knowing all the while that men usually don't ask women personal questions—but, hey, she started it by remembering the names of my adoptive family. Dressed in military uniform and sunglasses, I continued my conversation with the veiled women as Ray, Peter, and everyone from the village, who had gathered in front the house, watched.

A young man in his 20s came out of the house looking like he had just gotten out of bed. At first, I thought he was probably the woman's husband, despite her mentioning that he wasn't home. Also, he looked much younger than the women did. It's usually the other way around in Afghanistan where a woman, or perhaps I should say a girl in her teens, marries an older man as much as two to three times older than she is.

The woman said the young man was her oldest son, and her husband's name was Mohammad Hashim, who had gone to the city for *Edgah* (the first festival day of the three-day holiday), which is held in downtown Kandahar. When she mentioned his name, I knew exactly who her husband was. Since I knew him personally, I asked her to confirm if she was referring to the same person who was the son of our Aunt Mamey. "Yes, brother, exactly," she said. "Mamey is deceased and may God bless her soul with all the others, like your parents, sister, grandmother, and your cousin Zahir." While I was talking with this woman who knew so much about me and my family, I wanted to ask her who she was and find out more about her family but before I did that, I chose to update Ray and the rest of the guys who were all standing around looking at me, not knowing what I was talking about with this woman behind the veil.

I told Ray everything the woman had told me thus far. I also asked him if it was possible for me to stay here for a few more minutes to take some pictures of the house, including the inside if the woman would grant me permission to do so. Being the kind, compassionate, and honorable soldier that Ray was—who not only risked his own life by accompanying me on this mission, but also the lives of the other soldiers under his command—he, of course, said, "Absolutely, Nas, that's what we're here for, so take your time." I will never forget the sacrifice Ray and his entire platoon made for me. You may have heard it said to never forget three types of people in your life: (1) those who helped you through difficult times, (2) those who left you in your difficult times, and (3) those who put you in difficult times. Well, I will *never* forget the people who lived in this house 40 years ago, and each and every one of the guys in the platoon under Ray's command who brought me here 40 years later…definite memories to last a lifetime.

Before asking the woman for her permission to enter the house, Ray asked me to give him my camera so he could take my picture, an offer I promptly accepted. I handed my camera to Ray and he took my picture standing in front of my childhood home, and then I asked the woman who she was, to which she replied that she was Mamey's niece. I couldn't recall her from my childhood, primarily because boys and girls were never allowed to play together while growing up. She knew all of my family, which was enough for me to know about her, and when I requested her permission to enter the house, it was graciously granted. "Why not, my brother? You're more than welcome to do so—it is your house, after all," she said.

I literally started running through the house like a child walking into Toys R Us, not knowing what toys to pick first, but in my case, I was crying as I tried to decide which room I was going to look at first. After going from room to room and then into the kitchen, the basement, and the barn, my mind was filled with a flashback of so many wonderful memories: when I was three or four years old, holding my mom's hand when she milked the cow every morning before sunrise so my sister and I had fresh milk every day. It was very emotional for me to stand in the middle of the courtyard where my dad, Haji Kaka and his son, my cousin Zahir Shah, and I would sit in the middle of the courtyard during the warm summer months, while listening to the news on the only AM radio in the house or perhaps the entire village.

Before leaving the house, I gave the woman and her children their holiday gifts, and then noticed that there were many people in front of the house, waiting to receive their gifts as well. As children clustered around Ray and Peter, who both were giving out candy from their backpacks, it was obvious that they were all grateful for the Americans' generosity.

As I watched them, I couldn't help but remember from back in the day that our village was very small and secluded, where everyone knew everyone. There weren't as many children then. My dad and Uncle Haji Kaka, both teachers, were the only two intellectuals in the village. I recalled how the other villagers used to come to our house and ask my dad and uncle for their advice before doing anything that their intellect required. Immediately after the Soviet invasion of Afghanistan, the only person who had been removed from our village was my dad. Until this very day, no one has ever heard what happened to him after the government officials, armed with AK47s, arrived on his doorstep in 1980.

As I walked around the village, from one corner to the next, as though it were only yesterday, I vividly remembered holding my dad's hand as people in the village stopped him to ask questions while we all stood, leaning against the wall in the narrow alleyway where oftentimes a shepherd rode by on his donkey under a cloud of dust, following his sheep, goats, and even cattle to the river for water. Not only could I still envision my walks with my dad, but I could still hear his words as he told me to be respectful to others, if I wanted to be respected; not to cheat others, if I didn't want to be cheated; work hard; help those in need; and, most importantly, be a good husband to my wife and a good father to my children, which he said repeatedly. I still carry that advice with me every day. Visiting my childhood village again was like seeing a movie with me playing the leading role. Some might argue that because I was so young, I would remember little to nothing about being raised in this village—but they would be wrong.

As time went by, more and more villagers, especially the elders, would remember me and offer me hugs. All of the villagers turned out to be very friendly as well, as demonstrated by the elders who were pushing the children, who were following me too closely, in an effort to keep them from bothering me.

Reaching the center of the village to the main and only mosque, more and more of the villagers were gathering, asking questions, particularly where I'd been for the past 40 years. They were all happy to see me, and I didn't really care if it was because of me personally (especially the younger villagers) or simply because I was giving them holiday gifts. Either way, I was happier than them all, just for being able to be there, which I considered a miracle from God.

As we were exiting from the south end of the village, before saying goodbye to everyone, a man approached me from behind and asked in Pashto, *"Ta Nasrat naya?"* ("Nasrat, is that you?"). I turned around and studied the man's face before I responded. *Woa, za Nasrat yam"* ("Yes, I am Nasrat"). As I looked at the man's face more closely and heard his voice, he was very familiar. But I couldn't recall his name. As I continued to stare at him closely, trying to remember his very familiar face and voice, which somehow resembled my dad's, he was still looking at me with a huge smile on his face, waiting for me to tell him if I could remember who he was. However, no matter how hard I tried, my mind was filled with all of the old memories that had come back to me during the day, and I was just unable to recognize this villager. As I diligently continued trying to remember, the man again asked, more emotionally this time, *"Nasrata, za dey payad yam?"* ("Nasrat, you can't remember me?"). I could sense and see it in his tearful eyes that he was very happy to see me again.

Needless to say, I was anxious to know who he was, so I told him, "Okay, I give up. Your voice and face are very familiar to me, but I can't recall who you are. Please tell me your name." Opening his arms as wide as he could, he stepped forward for a hug. "My name is Malem. I am Abba's (my dad's nickname) nephew, your cousin." *Of course,* I thought. With a cry of joy to see each other still alive, we hugged amidst all the children and adults who still surrounded us. After we had embraced, Malem asked everyone to back away from us, as he again opened his arms for a second hug. Malem told me he didn't believe it when one of the villagers had told him a couple days ago that I was with the Americans on the base in Sarkari Bagh. He was also told that I had gone on a dismounted mission to the village of Ali Kaley a couple of days ago.

Finding Malem well and alive was like winning the lottery. I knew I could talk and trust him, and that he could help me with something I had in mind to do since my first day back in Afghanistan. Following our long greetings and hugging, Malem invited Ray, his soldiers, and me to come over to his house for tea and pastries. I was going to accept his invitation, but first I had to ask Ray something before I said anything to Malem about it. As though sensing that I wanted to talk with him about something, Ray approached and asked me, "Nas, who is this? It definitely appears as though you two know each other very well!" I smiled and told him, "Yes, Sir, this is my long-lost cousin, Malem. We haven't seen each other for more than forty years. If you hadn't agreed to bring me here, I wouldn't have found him. Thank you and your brave soldiers for making this all possible," I said emotionally.

I could see the emotion and joy in Ray's eyes and hear it in his voice how happy he was that Malem and I were reunited after so many years. I relayed Malem's offer of tea and pastries for all of us. He told me to tell Malem that he and I would be happy to accept his offer, but his soldiers would not be able to do so because of security concerns. When I told Malem what Ray had said regarding security, he smiled and told me to tell Ray, *"Zama wa kaley ta pa da dersho kalo key cha doghoundi ghayrat payda na krey che rasy, aos ba czhanga rasi. Razey, razey wa farmyast danana rasi."* ("In the past thirty years, no one has been brave enough to come to my village. I can't help but wonder how anyone could come today. Please, follow me inside.") After accepting Malem's offer, he immediately asked his oldest son, who was in the crowd, to keep his eyes and ears open while we were inside the house. He also told one of his grandsons to run to the house to tell his mother to start making the tea right away, as they were having visitors. Meanwhile, Ray was also telling Peter and three other soldiers to stay alert while we were inside; he was also contacting the rest of the soldiers to hold their security positions around the village. Then, Malem took us to his *saracha* (guesthouse), which was in front of the main house.

Once we were inside the guesthouse, Ray asked Malem if our being in his home would cause him any harm from the Taliban. Malem responded that, "In my sixty years of life, I have not left my village, and will not allow anyone to make me leave it, nor will I allow anyone to destroy my village!" I could see Ray's reaction to what Malem had said. "Nas, why don't we have more people like Malem who would take a stand to protect their village the way he does?" I told Malem what Ray had said and was told, "Just last week, the Taliban came to our village and shot at my elder son, but God saved him." Ray asked Malem if he was afraid for his family's safety. Before responding, Malem pointed his index finger to the ground and then toward the only exit door from the room. "This is my home and this is my village. I will destroy anyone who tries to destroy either. In the past fifty years, I have not supported any government or the Taliban, and that's why every government no longer really exists but my house and village are still here." Ray and I were honored to find such a brave man who would protect his home and village, despite the negative factors that surrounded them both—that is, his home and village—on a day-to-day basis.

The tea and pastries brought in by Malem's grandson were enough to feed the whole platoon. Malem encouraged us to eat (it's a cultural thing if you *don't* eat because, otherwise, Afghans will load your plate with an assortment of foods that you *must* eat or you would be considered disrespectful)! Just like the old adage, "It's going to happen whether you like it or not." So, we, of course, were going to eat whatever was put on our plates, whether we liked it or not! (Oh, and by the way—just a tip: Once you have finished eating whatever they loaded on your plate, be aware that even though you may not have liked it [in fact, you may have even hated it], you are still "required and expected" to say that you absolutely loved it! And, I kid you not: If you asked for the recipes, thus pretending that you loved it very much, even if you found it difficult to swallow, you would be respected for eating what they made you eat. In the Afghan culture, they do the same to one another, too.)

Ray asked Malem if he would be kind enough to accept our invitation to come to our compound to talk with our captain, the commander of our compound, Lieutenant Barron, and SFC Pat. Malem accepted. Ray's intention for inviting him, of course, was to see what we could do to help his village, specifically regarding education and the school. Malem grew up with teachers, like my dad and uncle, and had worked in the school in the past.

Ray asked me, "Is this a commitment on Malem's part, or what?" As mentioned before, a person who grew up around teachers would always like to teach, no matter the consequences, and Malem was just proving that point to us. I looked forward to finding more people like Malem. If we can understand the Afghan culture and be able to connect with people like Malem and others to help us to help them help their village, or perhaps the whole district by educating their young boys and girls, the objective could then be implemented throughout Kandahar Province and, hopefully, all of Afghanistan. The task would not be easy but it would be doable.

If one tenth of the money we had spent in Afghanistan since the war began, had been spent in the villages where people like Malem existed—Malem, who was willing to help us to help him—we would see tremendously different results than what we have seen to date. I strongly believe that we should help and support people like Malem first, who is not afraid of the Taliban. Malem is committed to help his people versus those who are doing it for political reasons only.

Meeting and talking with Malem was inspiring for every one of our team members who met him. His encouraging words and strong commitment to help build the school was welcoming news, not only to me, but to the rest of the commanders on our compound, especially the captain who was trying very diligently to do everything he could to keep me with his battalion.

Once we had returned to our compound, I thanked each and every one of the soldiers who volunteered for the mission of taking me to my village. Needless to say, I was emotionally touched by a comment one of the young soldiers I was thanking said, "Oh no, Sir, you don't need to thank me. I love helping those who need it." I don't know about you, but I don't know many 19-year-olds who would tell you that he loves going on missions to help people, even if those same people might be shooting at him in a war zone 9,000 miles away. Not very many, I would assume. One can never relate to what our young soldiers go through unless one physically goes out there and puts on the uniform in an effort to stop the bad guys.

Barron asked me if I would like to join him again to visit Ali Kaley. I told him I was ready for as long as I was still here, so he didn't need to ask—all he needed to do was tell me the time and I'd be ready. During that particular time, being in Arghandab, the risk of dying as an American soldier was very high. Because of the IEDs and the unknown ambushes by the Taliban, most of our soldiers died just by being out on routine patrol. However, the fear of dying never stopped American soldiers from going outside the compound. It was the motivation of helping people that sent us out on missions. Once we were in the village, I asked Barron for his permission to visit the main mosques to see if they needed any refurbishing help. I had already been to the village twice and sensed that Ali Kaley was nowhere near the condition of my adoptive village where Malem lived. People in Ali Kaley were very poor and Taliban-friendly compared to my village. As I had already told Barron, our strategy of helping the villagers should be different. Since the strategy of building a school in Haji Toar Kaley was logical, we also needed to apply logic to Ali Kaley that would be accepted by its people. Knowing the culture and the people, I had to inform my fellow Americans who wanted to help, but didn't know where to start. By visiting a village once, I could immediately come away with a different approach to the needs of that particular village. First, I wanted the people of Ali Kaley to be on our side. However, most of the people there were not willing to work for us in Sarkari Bagh or even in their own village to build the canal. My only other alternative was to offer them help by building their village's mosque, which was the only project I knew that they would value the most.

Barron, knowing his previous tactics didn't work, not only allowed me to visit the mosque, but he was very happy that I brought up the idea and wanted as well to see if it would work. I knew in my heart that it would work, even if I had to come up with my own personal funding just to make my commander believe and see a village the size of Ali Kaley, with more than 100 homes, be on our side once I proposed my idea to the local villagers. My strategy was simple: In order for us to get the Taliban out of Ali Kaley, we would have to do something for the villagers that would be more acceptable to them. Knowing that Ali Kaley was strictly ruled by the Taliban's version of Sharia Islamic law, in order to be better than the Taliban, sometimes you had to fight them by showing the villagers that our Sharia was considerably more beneficial to their village than the Taliban's—in other words, you fight fire with fire. I wholeheartedly believed the only way to change Ali Kaley was to do something for the villagers that they valued more than what we had thus far offered them. Our previous three offers to the villagers were of no benefit or value. Not only that, but it would undoubtedly be dangerous for the villagers if the Taliban found out that they were working for the Americans and Afghan government. I did my homework during the time I'd been on the compound. I spoke with the local contractors who were building a DFAC and were now busy building a gym facility as well.

They were all non-governmental, local contractors who were considered to be very good at what they did. The owner of one of the contracting companies was a local guy from the Arghandab District. Just to get an idea, I asked him one day how much it would cost to build something similar to the DFAC that they built on our compound. The contractor told me it would cost anywhere between 400,000 to 500,000 Afghanis, which would be less than $10,000. So, I had my idea, I had my funding, and, most importantly, I had my contractor who was ready to start work whenever I asked him to do so. All the contractor needed was my word, and where and when to start the work. The contractor had also given me a timeframe that the project would take three to six months to complete. Knowing the people of Kandahar, and Arghandab particularly, I strongly believed that my strategy would work perfectly, which is why I was willing to risk my own personal funding.

After the positive response following my visit to my village, Barron had randomly planned a mission to Ali Kaley. Despite the villagers not knowing that we were coming, upon our arrival word spread quickly. Everyone came out of their homes, including the village elder, Assadullah Aka. Barron, Pat, all of our soldiers, the ANP officers, and I walked to the southern end of the village where the main mosque was located. Once we got there, we found that the mosque door was locked and there was no one to show us the inside. Right around the corner from the mosque, we stopped at the village's only convenience store to talk with the shopkeeper to see if he knew who the person in charge of the mosque was. The shopkeeper, an elderly man, told us the mosque had been closed for the past couple of days because of the Akhtar Holiday. Since he served us tea, we spoke with the shopkeeper for a bit longer because we wanted to get a general idea about what his thoughts and opinions were regarding the security situation of his village, which unfortunately were not very good. "Well, what can I tell you? Every time you guys come here and bring the ANA and ANP with you, they then return the very next day to see who you guys have talked with or given anything to." When I asked the shopkeeper who "they" were, he responded, "Well, I want you to figure that one out for yourselves." It was obvious to us that "they" were the Taliban. We were always followed by a crowd of people throughout every village we visited, so it was difficult who was in the crowd listening to what people were telling the Americans. I could understand the shopkeeper's fears for holding his tongue by not articulating his thoughts. Even though the shopkeeper could not say their names, his point was clear. He then told us that we would be better off with our security situation if neither one of us came to his village. Well, I couldn't argue with the shopkeeper's statement because he and the other villagers just wanted to be left alone.

Since we weren't successful at the mosque at the southern end of the village, I was told by the crowd that there were a total of three mosques in the village. So we returned to the center of the village where the second mosque was located. Before I entered, we found that Assadullah Aka was out in the open field waiting to talk with us. Like the Malak from our last visit, Assadullah Aka also had his own agenda. Once we reached him, he already knew the purpose of our mission and had his own recommendations by telling me the only mosque that really could use help was the one that belonged to his father, who he pointed out as one of the men sitting in the crowd, which was the largest ever. As I had noticed from my previous meeting with Assadullah Aka, he was knowledgeable and his recommendations usually saved me a tremendous amount of hassle.

I told Barron I was going to walk over to the mosque at the north end of the village. I asked the man who was referred by Assadullah Aka as being in charge of the mosque if it was possible to accompany me to where its location. He agreed to take me there in person by taking the lead so that I could simply follow him. Of course, there were more than 20 kids who followed us as well.

During our walk, not knowing the condition of the mosque, I asked the man what it needed done the most. The man said that his father was the person who made all the decisions when it came to the issue of the mosque's requirements. He said that he was only the Talib for the mosque, while his father took the lead role of being the Mullah, although he shared that the mosque didn't have anything besides two old runners used as prayer mats. Before I could even tell him my plan, he already had the idea of reconstructing the entire two-room mud hut. I had the thought that he probably sensed that I was trying to help; otherwise, why would I be going to see the structure if that wasn't my plan?

Three of the kids who were following us closely overheard our conversation and were squabbling about who would hold my left hand just because I wanted to help them with their mosque. I was holding my video recorder in my right hand as I recorded our walk, and even then, there were other kids holding onto my right elbow, all between the ages of four and seven, and I couldn't help but be impressed with their interest in the mosque.

Once we had entered the hut, it didn't even come close to looking anything like any other mosque I had ever seen. As mentioned earlier, it was a simple, two-room mud hut; only one of the rooms was used for praying, while the second room (which was called the *Ojera*, or multipurpose room) was currently full of trash and human waste. The owner told me that people sometimes came to sleep in the multipurpose room overnight, which is why it was such a mess. Hmm, guess who sleeps there at night? The Taliban, of course. The whole purpose of Ojera is for the Taliban to sleep and study. But the room before me definitely was not the norm for an Ojera, especially the one I had been to when I was a young boy living in Afghanistan. This Ojera resembled a dumpsite much more than it did a multipurpose room!

After seeing the mosque and taking pictures and a video to show the contractor on our compound, we returned to the center of the village for our talk with Assadullah Aka, Barron, Pat, and any other villagers who were waiting. This time, I wanted to be the one to talk with the villagers. Since my commander, the young 25-year-old Lieutenant Barron, knew what I was going to say, he gave me the thumbs up that I was good to go. (As an aside, the American thumbs up in the Afghan culture, and most especially in Kandahar, is the same as their thumbs down.)

I started by offering two things to everyone who was sitting in the dusty field. Since we always had our medic with us when we went on missions, I first asked the crowd if any one of them—or anyone else they might know—had any medical issues and, if so, would they please come forward so our medic could help by giving them any medical attention they might require or prescribe medication, if necessary. Surprisingly, no one stepped forward in this village where the life expectancy was only 47 years of age. Despite how poor they were, needless to say, I was surprised and astounded that everyone in Ali Kaley was so healthy, especially since I sensed that was not the case, and regretted that no one would accept our offer or help.

Typically, on all of my other dismounted missions, someone would ask us for medication. In this case, the villagers were either very healthy or very afraid to take anything from us. Well, since I couldn't force them to take our medication if they really didn't need or want it, I shifted gears and went straight to my second question, which I said louder than my first one, in case some of the older villagers hadn't heard me. I guessed that the answer would be 99 percent positive for what I was about to ask. "Who's willing to help me build that mosque while earning three hundred Afghanis a day?" Not a single hand in the crowd wasn't raised! Most of the people in the crowd shouted, "We're willing to help rebuild the mosque for free." Now, if I really wanted to turn this village, or any other village in Afghanistan, into a coalition-friendly village, not too much was required in this case. None of these people would be supporting the Taliban once their mosque was built. When Barron asked these same villagers just a couple of days ago the question about refurbishing Sarkari Bagh or fixing the canal in their village, none of these same people had agreed to help. Even if they had, the money would've been wasted, because the Taliban would come back to kill one of the villagers so that no one would work for us or the corrupt Afghan government.

By offering them a job in their own village (for which they were willing to work for free), it was also obvious that there would be no Taliban to stop them from building their mosque, and even if the Taliban did try to stop them from doing so, what would happen then? Well, the whole village would be against the Taliban, then our soldiers wouldn't have to die to defeat an enemy that 99.9 percent of the time we couldn't even see, even when they were shooting at us. In the saddest villages of Afghanistan, there was not one person in the crowd who wasn't smiling at me when I told them what I planned to do for their village; plus, one of the villagers approached and whispered in my ear that his father had heart problems and he wanted to know if the medic had any medication for that. When I called the medic over to ask if he had such medication, he told me that unless the father had a prescription he could see, he could not prescribe anything if he didn't even know what the patient's illness really was, because "heart problems" could mean any number of things. I related what the medic had said to the villager. Most people in Afghanistan associate any pain in their body to somehow be associated with a heart condition. The villager told me that his father had a prescription at home from a doctor in Pakistan, and wanted to know if he brought that to the medic, would he then be able to get the medication his father needed? The medic confirmed that he would be able to do so.

Once I had made known my offer to build the mosque, the villagers started opening up to us and even taking medicine from the American infidels.

While waiting for the villager to return with his father's prescription, Assadullah Aka asked me if our medic would be able to remove a couple of bullets from one of the villagers. The medic and I were shocked by the question. When I asked what he was talking about, he turned and told a villager, "Hey, you, son-of-a-bitch, come over here and take off your shirt so this son-of-a-gun can examine you." (That's how people in Kandahar talk to each other.) The villager did as he was told. When he removed his shirt, none of us could believe what we saw. We learned that the man had been shot three or four times in his left shoulder, right arm, and upper right chest by the Soviets back in the early '80s. He was a teenager then, running toward one of their tanks when he was shot. He not only survived the shooting, but two of the bullets were still in his body at this writing (mid-November 2010).

I immediately pulled out my video recorder and started recording what I was seeing. This time I had my video recorder uncovered, so it was right in the open, recording without objection from any of the villagers. Obviously, it was all about trust the people had put in us because of my offer to rebuild their mosque.

The villager expected our medic to cut into his body right there, in the middle of his village, to remove the bullets. When I asked why he thought that was going to happen and explained why it wasn't possible for the medic to operate on him in the village, he responded that he thought we were Americans doctors and that we probably knew a trick or two so the bullets could be removed. Obviously, he was disappointed when he learned that was not the case.

By then, the villager with the prescription for his father had finally returned. When he handed the prescription to me, at first I thought he was handing me pages from a newspaper. But when I looked at it more closely, it was actually more than 10 to 15 pages of prescriptions, each on an 8x12 piece of paper. When I looked at them, the only thing English I could see was the name and specialty of the health provider—Pediatric Clinic. I asked the villager why his father's prescriptions were from a children's doctor, and he responded, "Well, dear interpreter, because he's a very good doctor, which is why adults and children go to him for treatment." In Afghanistan and rural Pakistan, there is no shortage of "supposed" pediatricians or dermatologists, who also claim to be cardiologists, practice internal medicine, and any/every other specialty imaginable. Most of these so-called doctors only prescribed aspirin to their patients, some of whom they saw on a daily basis.

While I was busy trying to go through the villager's prescriptions to explain to the medic what each was for (because they were all in Pashto and Urdu), the villager still had his shirt off so he could continue to show us the bullet that remained in his arm. At one point, he was literally moving one of the bullets under his skin up and down on his arm, from around the elbow area to the top of his shoulder. Understandably, our medic wanted to know why the villager hadn't had the bullets removed sooner. He responded that he had pulled one of the bullets out, but he had to go all the way to Pakistan to have it done, which cost him 35,000 Pakistani rupees. He didn't have the money to pull out the remaining two bullets. Rare it is that can one be shot three times and still live to talk about it while moving one of the remaining bullets under his skin. The only thing that we could recommend was that he go over to the hospital at Kandahar Airfield, which was run by the American military, where they would undoubtedly be able to remove the bullets. To this, the villager responded that he feared if he went to the hospital at Kandahar Airfield, he might be accused of being a Talib and put in jail.

The medic and I told him that the scars on his body were far too old for anyone to think he had been shot recently, and we didn't think that he would be accused of being a Talib—unless, of course, he was a Talib or one of their supporters. Despite our best to encourage him to go to the hospital in Kandahar, the villager still refused to do so, saying he would rather live with bullets in his body than be put in jail. When I asked the villager why he hadn't been afraid to tell us about the bullets in his body, he quickly reminded me that he hadn't planned to say anything about it—"It was Assadullah Aka who told you guys."

Before we left the village, Assadullah Aka had approached me to say, "You're just as brave as your dad was." When I asked him, "How so?" he responded, "I have been watching during your last three visits to the village. You just go freely anywhere you want, without fear, just like you went to the other end of the village with the local villagers to see the mosque. All the other interpreters are too scared to leave the American soldiers' shadows." Was it dangerous for me to walk over to the other end of the village to see the mosque without any protection? Probably. Was it foolish of me to do such a thing? Undoubtedly. But the villagers and I shared mutual trust, which is without a doubt why I came out of there alive, not to mention coming out alive after a 33-month deployment to Afghanistan. Whether luck or not, above all else it was also God's protection, for which I am very grateful.

As we left the village, people came out of their homes to say goodbye as well as to tell me things that they otherwise couldn't have told me, for fear of retribution, while we were in the middle of the village. This one poor villager had approached me to tell me that his half of the village hadn't received any rice, cooking oil, sugar, or tea that we had brought for them just a couple of days ago. When I asked him why, he told me the Malak, who lives in the city, took most of the rations for himself, and gave some to his friends, but the poor didn't receive anything. Within minutes, everyone else at this side of the village were walking toward Barron and me with similar complaints. When I told Barron what these people were complaining about, he admitted that giving the elder all the rations was obviously a huge mistake. He said to tell the villagers that the reason he gave everything to the elder was because he was the one who the villagers had chosen.

Almost everyone in this crowd argued that they had never chosen him to be their village's elder because he didn't even live in the village—he lived with the rest of his cronies in the city; furthermore, they insisted, he was chosen by only a few of the villagers. As Barron and I listened to the crowd, two of the ANP officers, a captain and his son who were both natives of Kandahar, agreed with what the villagers were telling us. I had always wanted to record a conversation of the locals when they started complaining about the Afghan government, especially those government officials like the ANP officer and his son, who were both working for the same government about which they were also complaining. None of the Afghan officials liked to be recorded, but I did it anyway, primarily because it was humorous to hear them "telling the truth" while they were talking with others who they considered to be Afghans, such as me. They only told me what they wanted to tell me, and they either wanted me to feel sorry for them, or they were really telling me the truth about their own government.

Since I was considered as one of their own, the ANP captain and his son were both talking to me regarding how things were so messed up within their own government. The ANP captain started by referring to the villagers who were complaining about their village elder. I asked him why the villagers hadn't said anything about this sooner, especially if the man they chose wasn't really their elder, when we specifically asked them to choose one. His response was that he and I both knew why the villagers did what they did because: (1) most of the villagers are so poor and uneducated, they don't even allow themselves to talk in public, let alone voice their opinions, and (2), others only kept their mouths shut because they weren't allowed to say anything when an elder took the lead. Since the man they chose was once the elder of the village a long time ago, he was considered qualified to be so now, even if he didn't live in the village any longer. When I asked the captain why he hadn't told us that the person claiming to be the village's elder wasn't actually one so that Barron and I would have been able to stop him from taking the food from the poor villagers, the captain responded that it was none of his business about what went on between the villagers and their elder, because it wasn't his village and, therefore, not his problem.

I asked the captain that if he was wearing the uniform of a police officer, wasn't it his job to protect the poor from being cheated by the elder? He told me that he didn't want nor did he like to be involved in the villagers' internal problems. He also told me that oftentimes he and his son simply worked for free because no one wanted to pay them their salary. He shared a story when he had recently gone on a particularly long mission (i.e., a 21-day combat mission in 110-degree weather with no food or water being provided). The captain said his commander not only didn't provide what he was supposed to, but instead told his men that the Americans would provide the food and water needed by the ANPs. The captain acknowledged that he knew it wasn't the Americans' responsibility to provide them with food or water, so they had no other choice but to either steal from the Americans or the village shops and even the villagers' homes in order to feed themselves. When the ANP officers returned from their 21-day mission of fighting the bad guys, upon entering the police station, he and his son saw the rest of the officers having a feast—food meant for a king—while the captain, his son, and all of his squad officers were literally dying of hunger and thirst, despite the fact that they had either been stealing from the Americans or had to steal grapes and other fruits and vegetables from the locals' orchards in an effort to keep themselves alive. I realized that hearing recants like this while walking the dusty alleyways of Arghandab and other villages were the stories that were never told so that others could realize who the real victims were.

The following day after our mission to Ali Kaley, Pat asked if I could help translate for him as three ANP officers had shown up at our compound and wanted to talk. As we walked to the front gate to meet the officers, we saw that one of them knew the man who transported the humanitarian aid to the village using his own private pickup truck. After the exchange of greetings, I asked them the reason for their visit to our compound. One of the three responded that they were there to collect the rent for the use of the pickup truck. "What are you talking about?" Pat demanded. "We weren't going to pay extra money for your truck. It was the ANP's job to help us transport the humanitarian aid to the village."

Pat continued by telling them that they could've used one of their police trucks, and if they hadn't wanted to do that because they were afraid of being attacked by the Taliban, then they—not us—should be responsible to pay for the use of the truck. The lead officer said that they had paid the friend for the use of his truck already and were now here for reimbursement. Pat and I were fully aware that they didn't plan to leave until they got the money they thought was due them. When asked how much they had paid their buddy for the truck, they were too quick to say $1,200. The amount was outrageous, especially when we had only used the truck for two hours! I was so angry I was shaking. Knowing that they were fucking around with us, I asked the officer in Pashto, *"Da reshtya wayast, ka poskhand wahey?"* ("Are you serious, or are you just fucking with us?") Even though they were fully aware that they were taking advantage of us, they nonetheless were clearly surprised to see the anger on my face; therefore, to intimidate me even further because I was taking the side of the Americans, the officer said in an even more serious tone, *"Yah wrora mozgh tha poskhand da para nayo raghaley."* ("Nope, my brother. We're not fucking with you; we're serious.") I wasn't there as the decision-maker, but had that been the case, I would simply have said a resounding *no* to the fuckers for trying to rip us off. I then turned to Pat and told him that they wanted a $1,200 fee for the use of the pickup truck.

Pat's response was, "First, you guys must be out of your fucking minds! Second, you never told us beforehand that it would cost us anything, much less $1,200, for the use of the truck." I knew we weren't going to get anywhere with this conversation, and could sense from Pat's body language that he was going to pay them. They knew it as well; otherwise, they would not have allowed us to use the truck in the first place. Since the majority of Americans didn't understand them, they simply paid the Afghan government officials for either personal or moral reasons, or just to "keep the peace" so the Afghan officials were appeased and satisfied. Simply put, the phrase that we were "fighting fire with fire" applied in this instance, too. Sometimes you fight Afghans with other Afghans in order to win a fight, because they—and only they—understand one another, with one exception. The Afghan on your side must believe you are valuable and willing to make whatever sacrifices are necessary to protect that value in order for you to be considered as the winner of the fight.

As I pointed out earlier, the ANP and ANA officers on our compound had more than a dozen new Ford Ranger pickup trucks (all paid for by the American taxpayers, of course). Yet, they didn't want to use those trucks, and had they done so, they couldn't charge us a rental fee but could for a friend's pickup truck that wasn't even worth $50 at best. I knew I was not going to be able to convince the officer otherwise but told him anyhow, that if I wanted to rent a U-Haul truck in the U.S. for a couple of hours, it would not only cost me only about $50 for two hours, but it would be four times the size of their piece of trash. Knowing that I wasn't the one to make the final decision regarding their demands, they were standing firm. Furthermore, because they know that money is no object to Americans, especially since we tend to handle almost every problem we face with it, Afghan government officials went out of their way to create problems, which they did over and over again so they could get paid—and they did this because we allowed them to do so.

Of course, the company commander paid the ANP officers the $1,200 they were demanding for the rental of the truck. This is just one of the many incidents that follows the chain of command in the Afghan government—the higher the rank, the higher the $$.

The next day I got an email from my site manager asking why it was taking so long for me to get to KAF and then to Bagram for my assignment at the AROCC. I emailed the site manager back, telling him that, according to the unit commander, I was supposed to be staying in Sarkari Bagh as part of the unit with which I was currently working. He emailed me back, making it plain and simple by telling me to get on the next flight. Well, needless to say, when I told the commander and everyone else in the unit that I had been ordered to leave on the next flight out, it was bad news for us all, including me. It was not only bad news to be leaving Sarkari Bagh but even worse because I would be breaking my commitment to the villagers of Ali to rebuild their mosque. However, the most important commitment I'd be breaking was the one I made to Malem to help him build a school.

The military units that I worked with—whether here in Sarkari Bagh, or anywhere else in Afghanistan—simply did not understand why things worked the way it did, why the military pulled the right people/person (i.e., in this instance, me) from a place where I could be more productive, not only to the unit as a while, but to the Afghan villagers. Although I was officially ordered to leave, I was still waiting for my adoptive cousin Malem to visit our compound as he had promised. The purpose for Malem's visit was, of course, to get together with our commander regarding the strategy for building the school, with our commander's support to Malem, who would take the lead. I had one more day before I could catch the next flight out of Sarkari Bagh, and was hoping that Malem would show up in the meantime—not only so we could say goodbye and thank him, but I wanted him to know how much I admired him for his bravery and fight to protect his home and village, and the courage to do what was right by helping to educate the future generations of Afghanistan. I knew if I didn't get a chance to say goodbye, he would be disappointed that I had departed Sarkari Bagh without seeing me first. Unfortunately, leaving was something that I couldn't control; in fact, frankly, had it been up to me, I would've stayed in Sarkari Bagh for good.

The only way for me to stay with the battalion would be to involve someone higher in the military, in this case the captain who had promised me he would do anything he could to bring me back, even if I had to leave the next day, which I was not looking forward to doing, especially because I could see positive results from the local villagers just in the short six weeks that I had spent in Sarkari Bagh. Besides, others on our compound told me they could understand the villagers better when I was with them on dismounted missions. At the request of our commander, I attempted to delay my departure from Sarkari Bagh as much as I could. He told me if I got in trouble with my site manager, I could blame him for it because he was going to keep me in Sarkari Bagh longer. While I wanted Malem to meet the captain, even if I left Sarkari Bagh, they could still stay in touch with each other so the captain could help Malem build the school. Yet, I couldn't also help but worry about how the understanding and translation between the commander and Malem could move forward. I waited for my flight, which sometimes could take days, and Malem to show up at the compound as promised.

One day, as I waited for my flight and Malem to show up before I departed Sarkari Bagh, I ran into a local barber who came to the compound once a month to give our soldiers a haircut, for which he charged $5 each, which was paid by Ray from his budget. He worked from 8:00 AM to 4:00 PM, doing as many haircuts as he possibly could, most requiring a simple shave of the soldier's head. Ray provided the barber with a log-in sheet on which the soldier would sign his name after he had gotten his haircut from the barber, who would then turn in the log-sheet to Ray at the end of the day so he could get paid.

As usual, for me, sitting at the compound doing nothing, was as boring as watching grass grow. So, I decided that day to go and sit where the barber was doing his thing. There were about five or six soldiers standing in line to get a haircut. It was around 4:00 PM, and the barber was about to close his station and leave for the day. He had a nine-year-old boy with him who helped sweep up the hair after every cut. I asked the barber who the young boy was and was told that he was the barber's younger brother and a trainee.

Curious, I asked the younger brother if he was going to school, and he told me, although shyly but with pride in his voice as well, *"Ya, Ah"* ("Nope"), like going to school was a bad thing. When I asked him why not, the boy pointed to his older brother and said, *"Da da czakha poshtana wakra"* ("Ask him"). I casually asked the barber why his younger brother wasn't going to school and was told that there was no need for his brother to go to school, because he had already been enrolled into a madrasa (religious school). According to the barber, the madrasa would help the boy more than anything he might possibly learn in a normal school. I told him that there was nothing wrong with his brother going to school after the madrasa. The barber told me that it was his duty, as the older brother, to send him to a madrasa so he would know and understand his religion better. As though I was the one who was misinformed, the barber then asked, "What good would school do for him, other than make him corrupt just like everyone else who had ever attended one?"

This is a perfect example of the normal mentality of most people in the villages of Afghanistan, which Western society not only doesn't understand, let alone even know that it exists. The barber was from Sha Bazar (the heart of Kandahar city), not one of the conservative villages.

As I sat chatting with the barber and his brother, while soldiers came and went, I observed how the barber operated his business, and when I asked him how it was going, he handed me the log-sheet with all the signatures. So far, he had done 68 haircuts times $5, which totaled $340, not including tips. Almost every soldier gave him a minimum of a $1 tip every time they got their hair cut. So, quickly equating that in my head, I determined that he was earning more than $400 a day, including tips. I was always cautious learning things of this nature—whether I was just being nosy or really interested in knowing all the facts before I came to any conclusion. As the barber continued to do his thing, I left to find Mirwis so I could ask him what it would cost for a haircut outside the compound.

When I finally found him, he looked at my shaved head and smiled, I'm sure wondering why I would ask that question, since I really didn't need a haircut. But he answered anyway by telling me that it cost any-where from 35 to 50 Afghanis (or about $1, max). With this information in mind, I returned to the barber as casually as I could and watched him again before returning to the conversation we were having when I left. I asked how much money he would earn if he worked the same hours off base. The barber didn't answer the question directly; instead, he told me that most of the money he earned from the military haircuts was going to someone else who had given him permission to be on the base. Then, I asked him what his share of the $5 was, and he told me that he got $1 for each haircut, plus whatever tips he could make. Curiosity compelled me to ask what happened to the other $4; he said if he told me, he would lose his job for coming to the base.

I left it at that because by now I knew that there had to be an Afghan government official or local interpreter involved in such a contract. Before I walked away from him, he offered me a haircut knowing my head had already been shaved. Even though I told him he already knew I didn't need a haircut, he insisted I get one anyway and reminded me to just sign the sheet like most of the other fellow Afghan linguists did. I had to ask why he thought I would do such a thing, and his response was, "For the signature." When I refused to sign the sheet, he angrily asked, *"No tha ham the Amrykayano pa gata kar kaway, no tha khpalo Kandaryano?"* ("So you are for the interests of the Americans, rather than for the benefits of your fellow Kandaharis?") I told him that it had nothing to do with what he'd just said. It was simply the act, based on facts, of doing the right thing. He should be ashamed of himself, not only for what he was doing by cheating the same Americans who had given him the job on the base, but for doing it while his younger brother was with him so he could learn the dishonesty of everything he, his older brother, did.

It was obvious that the barber wasn't one of the Afghan government officials. But, by his own confession, he had been brought in by a government official to whom he was paying $4 (80 percent) of each haircut. I again recommended that the barber send his younger brother to school so he could learn something rather than just sitting and watching his older, corrupt brother cheat the Americans. The barber just so happened to be from the secular part of the Afghan society—which I had personally observed and experienced by living life in villages compared to what life was all about in the cities, like Kandahar and Kabul, for example. One must be truthful, first to himself, and then to society, and have lived and experienced both ways of life—village versus city—to be able to differentiate between the secular society in the city from the conservative society of the villages throughout Afghanistan. The barber is a primary example of the secular existence of the Afghan societies in most major cities of Afghanistan, which is the primary reason igniting the local, conservative villagers to support the Taliban, at least in most of the cases I had witnessed, occurred. Again, that is not to say that the people in the villages are happy with the Taliban; they just prefer the Taliban over their fellow seculars from the city.

To make my point even more strongly, the barber took the time off from his work to pray—not only in the middle of a soldier's haircut, but while others waited in line. I had no way of knowing whether he was serving his God by not missing a prayer or if he was simply trying to be a role model to his younger brother, who prayed with him as well. In any case, prayers aside, asking me to sign the sheet was a clearer example of his character, or lack thereof. If I were to question the barber further, my first question would be, how can a person pray to God one minute, and then forget God the next by stealing $5 from the infidels. Once they were done praying, the barber continued the haircuts for the soldiers who were still in line, patiently waiting.

The next morning, Mirwis brought me my usual fresh bread from the local bakery for breakfast. He also told me that Malem was at the front gate asking for me. I immediately went to the front gate so I could escort him into the compound. I then notified Ray, Barron, and the captain that Malem was here for our talk. I escorted him to our DFAC where we settled down to discuss the plan for the new school, when a soldier from the front gate interrupted to tell us that there were two local villagers asking for me. I excused myself so that I could go with the guard. Once outside, I realized that I had seen the two villagers once before sitting against the wall by the front gate of our compound when we left for a mission. As soon as they saw me, they apparently recognized me immediately, too, even though I wasn't dressed in my usual military gear. They both opened their arms to hug me as they told me that although they had been sitting in front of the front gate for many days, they had not seen me leave the compound. I told them that was undoubtedly because I was dressed in a military uniform complete with helmet and dark glasses, in which case I sometimes couldn't even recognize myself.

While I still didn't know who they were, the elder of the two immediately explained, "Nasrat, we have been coming here for the past two weeks. We can't communicate with the guards, so we just sat here hoping you would come out so we could see and talk with you." Unfortunately, while that still didn't help me identify them, in Afghan culture it's normal that complaining or complimenting starts first before anyone introduces themselves to you. From some of the things they said, it sounded as if they knew everything about me. Meanwhile, I was thinking to myself, *I have Malem sitting in the DFAC with three other Americans, waiting for me to return, while two guys outside the compound are playing a "guess who we are" game, for which I neither have the time nor patience.*

Wanting to cut to the chase so they'd tell me their names, I asked the eldest of the two, *"Wrora nome dey rata wawaya."* ("Brother, tell me your names.") His disappointment apparent, he told me, *"Yara, tha ka moghe year karey you, kho hagha jala khabara da, aow zamoghe hitz wakht na hareyjhe. Za Abdul Razik yam, aow da me mashar zoy dey."* ("Well, you probably forgot about us, but we never forgot you. I am Abdul Razik and he is my oldest son.") I apologized and told him that he was correct that I had forgotten them and, actually, with my short-term memory, many other people I had met. Fortunately, shortly after telling me their names, I remembered that I did, indeed, know them and, in fact, had just left them yesterday, not 40 years ago.

I remembered the oldest very well, because my dad would always say good things about him, like being a very hard worker and one of the most polite kids in the entire village that I was allowed to play with. As I recalled, Abdul Razik always stopped me and Zahir from throwing rocks because he thought it was dangerous and that we might hit someone, which we vehemently disagreed with because we were throwing rocks into the river.

Meanwhile, Abdul Razik was now before me again; he was apparently married to one of my cousins, Haji Kak's oldest daughter. Now that I remembered, I was so amazed to see him, I invited him and his son to come inside the compound. I took them immediately into the DFAC where Malem and everyone else had been patiently waiting for my return so we could continue our conversation regarding the school. Before continuing our meeting, I introduced Abdul and his son to Ray, Barron, the Captain, and Pat. Again, Ray, as always, was pleased that I had found another one of my childhood friends. I told everyone that not only was Abdul a childhood friend, but he was now married to one of my cousins. To make it even more interesting, he was in charge of most of the village in Sarkari Bagh, while Malem was in charge of Haji Toar Kaley, our home village.

Whatever the circumstances, finding these two—who had survived more than 30 years of conflict in Afghanistan—was a milestone, not only for me, but for our military unit who was there to help and were grateful that Malem and Abdul Razik had been willing to risk their lives to help the Americans succeed by promoting the education of young boys and girls in the religiously conservative Arghandab District, which otherwise would not be possible without their assistance. Malem and Abdul Razik, both of whom I grew up with and trusted with all my heart, would've done everything and anything I would have asked of them if I was given the opportunity to stay with our battalion captain and his team to help everyone on the path of assisting village children succeed in their education.

My time with Malem and Abdul Razik was rapidly coming to an end because it was almost time for me to board my flight. I was still given some hope by the commander in Sarkari Bagh, who was trying everything he could to get me back here so we could continue our work. Ray and Barron told me to tell Malem and Abdul Razik that whenever and whatever they needed from the Americans, we would be glad to help them as much as possible—all they had to do was ask by coming to the compound just like they did today. Abdul Razik already had something on his mind: "The only way you Americans can help us is by not allowing the ANA and ANP to get involved in our community, because no one likes them." From what I had seen thus far, I could relate to Abdul Razik's frustration, as did every other American regarding the ANA and ANP's treatment of the locals. Despite the Americans' knowledge of the Afghan Security Forces' treatment of the locals, it was not possible for the U.S. military to follow every ANA and ANP officer to see what they were doing and why.

Knowing and understanding both the American and Afghan cultures, I sensed in both cultures that the set strategy for our commitment did not really exist. When Barron asked Abdul what the ANA and ANP officers had done that he didn't like, the first thing he told us was that the ANA compound right across the road from ours was once his brother's home. The ANA had forcefully—without even asking for permission—taken it away by throwing his brother out of his own house and turning it into their compound. Additionally, according to Abdul Razik, they just came over with their tank, knocked off the main wall of the house, and then took it over.

Barron asked if his brother had complained to the Afghan government officials. Abdul said that he had, more than five times. Every time his brother went to the city to talk with someone so he could complain, he was at first told that they couldn't find anyone for him to complain to, and then when they did, he had to pay a fee to do so. Ultimately, the only answer he got from them was that the ANA were told by the Americans which house they could take. Additionally, Abdul and his brother were told by the city officials that if they needed to get paid for the house, they should talk with the Americans in Sarkari Bagh. When Barron wanted to know if Abdul had ever contacted anyone in this compound regarding this situation, Abdul told him that his brother had talked with the previous commander, but he never got a clear answer from him, either. He added that he didn't trust the linguist who was translating his problems regarding his house to the previous American commander. This was yet another case where miscommunication was the culprit and reason why Abdul and his brother had given up pursuing their case against the ANA.

After saying what he needed to say, Barron looked at me and said, "Nas, I think Abdul has a legitimate argument. Please tell him that I will personally look into this matter myself." As I told Abdul what Barron had said, he wasn't convinced, saying that the Americans were not at fault; it was the fault of the officials of the Afghan government, who simply blame and use the Americans as an excuse for their own corruption just to get the poor villagers off their backs. I told Barron what Abdul had just said; since he had been in Afghanistan for a little over two months, he was familiar with the Afghan culture nonetheless.

While Abdul was making his case in front of our commanders, Malem merely sat, observing everything that was taking place. Once Abdul was done, Malem immediately asked me to tell the commanders, who were all present, that whatever money the Americans were spending in the Arghandab District was being wasted. Since none of the commanders knew what Malem was talking about, Ray told me to ask Malem to explain what he meant. "In my opinion," Malem said, "you Americans are spending way too much money that is all being wasted. Spending more money is not going to make the local villagers happier." As Malem pointed his hand in the direction of the river, he said, "A very good example will be the bridge that you guys have started to build over the Argahndab River, right behind my house. I was told that it was a six million dollar project. Well, first, the bridge was only half built three years ago; no one has worked on it since the Taliban attacked the workers. We have a six million dollar bridge that is only half built, and even if it were completely built, who would drive over it? People in Arghandab don't need a six million dollar bridge for their donkeys—they need food, and in order for them to earn the money needed to provide for their families, they also need to be able to get an education so that they, too, can one day build their own bridge when there is a need for it."

I thought Malem was done, but not yet, because he went on to say, "I am a teacher and so is Abdul. If we get the opportunity to build the facility required and the tools to educate the children in our village, I would start first by enrolling my own sons and daughters." To everyone in the room, including me, Malem's idea was well received.

Since I was leaving that same morning, I looked at every one of my commanders and told them, "I hope you guys try very hard to get me back here, so that Malem and I can start building the school and set an example for every other village in the Arghandab District." My heart was aching as I prayed to God to bring me back to the Arghandab District as soon as He could. Before leaving, I also told my commanders that if they could get me back in Sarkari Bagh, not only would we succeed in building the school, but I would also be able to fulfill my personal commitment and the promise I made to build the mosque in Ali Kaley.

Unfortunately, my time was running out in Sarkari Bagh. It was around 11:30 AM when we all heard the familiar *TaTaTaTaTa* sound of the Chinook coming from a distance. "Nas, buddy," Ray said, "I think that's your ride. Here, let me help you move your stuff to the landing zone."

It was difficult for me to say goodbye to any unit I worked for; however, in this case, it was even harder because of the special circumstance of Sarkari Bagh, for which I could never thank everyone enough—men like Ray and his soldiers, who had arranged everything for my visit to my parent's house. I knew that one question would always linger in my mind: *Why didn't the U.S. send linguists like me to places where we were more useful to the commanders on the ground, like those of Sarkari Bagh, who tried everything they could to keep me with the unit?* I hoped to get an answer to that question one day, which will probably be that America should have a well-planned strategy if they ever really want to succeed in Afghanistan.

Rather than doing it right, why do anything just for the sake of doing it? It was mindboggling for me to see American military linguists, fluent in Arabic, Mandarin, and Croatian, sitting in the middle of Pashto-speaking Arghandab for four months during one of the busiest fighting seasons of the war in Afganistan!

My visit with Malim, whom I consider one of the many brave native villagers I met.

On our visit to Ali Kaley, one of the Taliban's strongholds in
Arghandab District, Kandahar Province. November, 2010.

Our humanitarian missions to the village of Ali Kaley.

The end of our non-productive conversation with the villagers of Ali Kaley.
from left to right. Barron, Assadullah Aka, myself, and the elder Malak.

Inside of the mud hut mosque I was allowed to visit by my
commander Barron, to ask what would it cost to build.

The children of Ali Kaley who were very happy to hear
I was going to build their village mosque.

Standing in front of the room in the court yard of my adoptive mom and dad's house
where I had grown up from age six months to six years. November 15, 2010.

CHAPTER TWELVE

November 23, 2010: Major Command USFOR-A Task Force: AROCC, Bagram Airfield, Afghanistan

Although I was assigned to the AROCC unit before I had even returned to Bagram Airfield, I could not go directly to the unit until I was issued a badge to be on the compound. The process took three to four days, so I had to spend that time in the transition tent [again] until my badge was issued. As you now well know, I was no stranger to the transition tent and, while I didn't think it possible, this time was the worst of all. Since it was a very cold night when I arrived at the tent, I walked around it to look for a warm spot, which was usually at the end of the tent where the heaters were located. But I had no luck finding anything there this time, and even if I had, I didn't want to be there anyway since it was already extremely noisy.

I finally found a spot at the opposite end of the tent near the main exit. As I settled in at the bottom of a bunk bed, a young man in his mid-20s was on his cell, talking quite loudly to whoever was on the other end, an example of how most of the linguists in this tent had no respect for the rules or others while in the tent. As I looked around, I noticed a man who was trying to sleep on one of the top bunks by the exit door, but was twisting and turning more than he was sleeping. After a couple of minutes had passed, he ultimately asked the young linguist on the phone to please take his phone conversation outside so he could go to sleep. Instead of the linguist doing as he was asked, he told the man to shut up and stop interrupting him while he was on the phone. The man in the bunk sat up, trying to get the linguist's attention by asking him again, "Excuse me, brother; all I'm asking is that you please take your conversation outside so I can get some sleep." Again, the linguist refused to do so. Instead, he told the man, "If you're man enough, come down and make me go outside, you fucking American. Remember, you're in *my* country." I didn't think that was called for at all, and besides that, he said it as loud as he could, thus waking up others who were trying to rest and sleep as well. I could only assume that he did it to gather support by making sure everyone else in the tent heard him and came to his rescue, just in case the man on the top bunk came down and tried to kick his ass, which is exactly what ultimately happened.

The linguist on the phone was a native Afghan American; the man in the top bunk was an American Caucasian—and he did come down from the bunk so he could say to the linguist, softly, but loud enough for the linguist to hear, "I don't care who or where the fuck you are; again, all I'm asking is that you take your phone conversation outside the tent so others will not be bothered." By now, there were 15 to 20 other linguists, some who were just there to see a fight, others, to support their fellow native Afghan.

When the linguist saw that others had gathered to support him, despite his misconduct and lack of respect for the rules of the tent, he jumped on the man, pushing him to the ground. Before I knew what was happening, four or five other linguists jumped on the man as well and started to kick him while shouting and yelling, "You fucking American. You're in Afghanistan now, so don't think you can try to fuck with us because we'll have no hesitation in killing you, if necessary." I couldn't help but notice and hear that most of the other linguists who were standing around watching what they considered to be entertainment, and to support the thugs who continued to kick and stomp on the man on the ground, were offering their words of encouragement in Farsi, *"Bazanen e mordagawa, zorey Awghwana ne deda"* ("Kick the motherfucker! Show him the power of the Afghans!").

Physically, I could not defend one man being attacked by five to six guys, but I could take a verbal stand by saying something. As soon as I opened my mouth, a couple of other linguists who didn't want to get involved suddenly wanted to support me. First, not wanting to actually touch any of them, I tried to verbally separate them by just saying a couple of simple words to get their attention. I said them loud and clear, in English, so that everyone could hear me. "If any one of you thinks that because you're in Afghanistan, you should consider yourself an Afghan, you're wrong. First, we're all Americans, on an American military base, which belongs to the U.S. and the American taxpayers. Second, if any of you guys really consider yourselves to be an Afghan, then I recommend you leave this military base and put on an ANA or ANP uniform so you can fight for the country you claim to love so much. I don't think any one of you has the courage to do what the Americans have done for you and Afghanistan, in general, as a country."

After my verbal reprimand, a number of the linguists backed off, while others still tried to cause the man on the ground as much damage as they possibly could—now, by trying to destroy all of his belongings. More and more of the linguists were returning to their bunks. When everything finally quieted down, I helped the man up from the ground so we could gather all of his belongings, which were scattered throughout the tent. After gathering most of his things, the man discovered that his military ID card was missing, along with a couple of other items as well. The MPs were called in, and the tent was emptied so they could search for the man's missing items. The linguist who started the fight and another linguist who had been more physically involved in the fight were taken into custody. (As I pointed out earlier, this is the main reason why I didn't like to be around most of the other linguists: because they like to fight good people rather than going off base to fight the bad guys.)

I learned that my assignment at the AROCC was going to be dealing with more than 90 other linguists that I would be working with at the same compound, in the same office building. After four days in the transition tent, I was finally taken by my company's movement person to the AROCC compound and issued a badge by the security personnel at the front gate. One of the soldiers from the unit I was assigned to was called away from the front gate so that he could escort me to the office for the required check-in to the compound. I had been with most of the other military units in Afghanistan—the majority of whom had to live in tents in small, remote COPs, some without running water. But, for me, the AROCC didn't even come close to the living conditions I had experienced with other military units. Frankly, in my opinion, going to the AROCC compound was like going to a timeshare or a members-only club, or perhaps it was like the military's own Ritz-Carlton, as my first roommate would describe it.

The process was like checking into a hotel. I filled out some paperwork with my personal contact information in case of an emergency; then, all of the rules about what I could and could not do were explained by the member of personnel who was checking me in. I was given the key to my room so that a soldier could help me with my duffle bags and any other personal belongings, and then escort me to my room. Before the young soldier could take me to my "suite," I was approached by one of the linguists who had worked at the AROCC and known me since the early '80s when I lived in New York.

Every time I visited Bagram Airfield during my numerous transitions from one military base to another, he would always ask me to come and work at the AROCC at Bagram, wanting to know why I chose to go to units that always went out on combat missions—which, of course, had convinced him that I was crazy. He would try his hardest to talk me out of volunteering for combat missions, because, as he put it, they were dangerous *and* I never got paid anything extra, so why did I do it? His idea was for me to stay in Bagram—not because he was concerned for my safety or well-being, but because he could then choose me as his roommate (for whatever reason, he apparently had never gotten along with any of his previous roommates).

Although I had already been assigned a room, I stood dumbfounded when the linguist proceeded to tell the soldier that since he had known me for more than 30 years, he wanted me to be his roommate. At the time, I didn't know whether to accept his offer or not—nor did the soldier. Before the soldier or I could make a decision about which room I should be in, the linguist was already pulling one of my boxes, filled with some of my personal belongings, to his room. I remember the soldier telling me, "I guess you don't have a choice; he obviously wants you to be his roommate much more than you want to be." Overhearing the soldier's comment, the linguist told him, yet again, "Well, we've known each other for at least 30 years," which I promptly corrected by saying, "We saw each other briefly thirty years ago; we have not *known* each other for thirty years." To him, they both meant the same thing. Before I could add anything further, the soldier did it for me. "He's right. Knowing someone for thirty years is *not* the same as seeing each other briefly thirty years ago," after which I thought it important to add, "The only person I have known for thirty years is my wife." In any event, we ended up as roommates.

Upon our arrival at the room, the linguist welcomed me by saying, "Welcome to my room, the luxury suite of the AROCC." After only a few minutes with him, I figured that this "30-year-friend" of mine probably offended every other linguist he had had as a roommate prior to my arrival just by making off-the-wall comments like welcoming me to "his room," to which I responded, "It's really the U.S. taxpayers' room, or, in other words, it's *our* room." He immediately caught on to where I stood on such issues and knew that he would not be able to push me around but, rather, we would have to learn to respect each other.

The room had its own bathroom, fridge, flat-screen TV, and DVD player. The linguist was right about luxury at the AROCC. Unfortunately, as a roommate, he acted like a 12-year-old, ignorant, selfish kid within a 55-year-old body. In other words, he presented as more of a "mamma's boy" who was never happy about anything going on in his life. Just as he hated Afghanistan and the locals, he had lived in and hated America for more than 35 years. I'm a strong believer in the fact that everyone is entitled to their own opinion and freewill of whether they like America or any other country. In this instance, I personally could have cared less whether he liked America or not; that was his choice. But one of the things that bothered me about him was that when he came to the room from work every night, the first thing he would say to me (just to irritate me, I know), was how stupid the Americans and Afghans were that he worked with.

Within the first couple of weeks, I was sick and tired of his nonsense— and, most especially, him! To hell with him and his luxury Ritz-Carlton suite—I wanted to live with my buddies at the Motel 6 in Sarkari Bagh!

Just as he did on prior occasions when I transitioned through Bagram, he once again asked me why I wanted to volunteer to go out on combat missions, especially knowing that it was dangerous and I wasn't going to get paid anything extra. I explained to him, yet again, my reasons why. "First, when I came to Afghanistan, I wanted to be with the brave American soldiers who went out and fought the bad guys. Second, I wanted to be out there in the villages where I could help the U.S. military and the poor Afghan villagers understand each other. Third, I want to be away from guys like you at the AROCC," to which he smiled and asked, while pointing at the flat-screen TV, DVD, fridge, air-conditioner and heating units, *and*, of course, the indoor bathroom, "So, you don't like all of this luxury that we have here at the AROCC, plus the fact that we don't have to work very much?" I told him that's exactly why I didn't want to be at the AROCC. I added, "I have all of this luxury at home. If I wanted it, then I should've stayed at home with my wife and children." Americans, Pashtons, Hazaras, Pakistanis, Iranians, Arabs—whatever the nationality, he hated them all. He was only obsessed with himself and his own needs.

Our room was a Connex, just like the one I had lived in when I was with Special Forces in Ghazni. It was during a very cold winter when I moved in with him. The weather was in the freezing digits. The room's heater was directly above my head (I slept on the top bunk) and would only heat the upper half of the room, so he would turn the heater up to the max of 85 degrees, which only made the upper-half of the room hotter, making it difficult for me to sleep. So, one day, since he was cold most of the time and complained that the room was cold, I asked him if he would switch beds with me. Well, of course, he didn't want to do that because he'd have to climb a small ladder to get to his. He wanted the 85-degree temperature in the bottom bed, which was never going to happen. Even though I told him he couldn't have it both ways, he just didn't get it! So, I continued to put up with everything the way he wanted it, but would not tolerate the way he badmouthed everyone who worked on the AROCC compound. I told him on more than one occasion not to tell me anything bad about anyone; that if he had issues with anyone, he should be man enough to tell the person directly to their face.

Those same "bad" people that he complained about all the time would, of course, become his best friends once he was working in the office with them. In addition to complaining about his coworkers, when he bashed America one day, we had our first really serious argument during which I told him, "If you don't like the U.S. or Americans, and you don't like the local Afghans or anyone who calls themselves an Afghan with American citizenship, and you don't like anyone in between, then who or even what do you like?" When he didn't answer, I asked him the same question phrased differently. "When you're with the American soldiers, you try to fit in like they're your best buddies, which, according to you, they're not. Then, when you're with the local Afghans, you act like *they're* your native countrymen and friends and say you can feel their pain, which you don't even care about. When you're with other native Afghan linguists who are American citizens, you act like you're one of them by hating the Americans and the locals. With that said, who and, frankly, what are you—really, after all is said and done?" My roommate didn't like what I was asking him, because he didn't know who he really was, either. I told him he needed to find an identity for himself before he could even consider hating others.

I wanted so badly to move out of the room and find another roommate. Unfortunately, those I wanted to share a room with already had roommates, and the roommate I had was the only roommate no one else wanted to live with because of his selfishness, amongst other things.

During my initial meeting with Staff Sergeant Jay, my shift leader, I told him if he ever needed anyone to work extra hours at any hour of the day or night, I would be more than happy to volunteer to do so. I realized the work that I had done before coming to the AROCC was a lot more difficult and rewarding for me than working at this office eight hours a day, six days a week. There were more than 90 linguists in this office, divided into three groups, simply known as A, B, and C. The work schedule was also divided into three eight-hours shifts with 30 linguists on each shift. Fifteen minutes before the start of every shift, each and every day, we had to be where information was passed on to all 30 linguists by the military personnel, but also for any comments or concerns (of which there were many—mostly complaints) that the linguists might have to share with the military. Everyone was asked to be present at no later than 11:45 PM for the midnight shift, which happened to be my A group of linguists.

Out of the 30 linguists, most of them never made it to the briefings on time—not even once!—even though our living quarters were only 200 feet away from our office. During our "pass-ons," when our shift leader would tell us the tasks at hand for that particular day, everyone would interpret them as being orders handed down to them by the military. At the end of our pass-on, the shift leader would then invite questions, comments, or concerns that anyone might have. Rarely did a linguist not raise their hand to ask a question, make a comment, or express a concern. In fact, the questions and comments were never about their performance at work, or what to do to make their work more efficient; rather, they were always about how bad their living conditions were and how badly they were being treated by military personnel. The most common complaints were: "My roommate sucks"; "My military personnel shift leader is a racist"; "My company manager is not allowing me to go on vacation"; "I don't like my work schedule"; and last, but not least (and my all-time favorite), "I work too many hours."

There was not one linguist on my shift who had anything positive to say, not to mention that 80 percent of them never left the compound to go on dismounted missions. Therefore, they really didn't have hardships to face at all. The 20 percent of those who had been on dismounted missions and knew that the AROCC was the Ritz-Carlton of the military, complained the loudest. Most who were at the AROCC faked it (e.g., either they didn't speak Pashto or simply weren't physically capable), so they were pulled out of dismounted missions and put to work at the AROCC office.

So, during the "questions, comments, and concerns" part of our meetings, I would just listen and shake my head at most of the ridiculous things that were being said. In addition to everything else they complained about, they didn't like the requirement that they must follow the professional dress code by wearing a military uniform (or business casual). This rule was ignored by at least 80 percent of the linguists who worked in the building, and in some cases, many of the linguists would come to work in their slippers, pajamas, and robes straight from their beds. If the shift leader asked them to go back to their rooms to change, they would call the shift leader a racist motherfucker—not in English, but in Pashto or Farsi, when they would all gather in groups to socialize (i.e., mock others).

For the first 15 to 20 minutes at the start of our shift, greetings were exchanged between the groups as one departed and the other arrived. Once those greetings were over, it was then time to make tea and exchange greetings for the next 20 minutes amongst themselves. Once work had started, it was the normal Afghan hospitality way of doing things to start walking from station to station, passing out pastries, candy, and/or dried fruit and nuts. In the first hour and a half, they actually spent their time doing absolutely nothing that was work related. By the time the other linguists had finally made their tea and gotten their greetings and gossiping out of the way, I had already completed more work than any of them would accomplish during their 8-hour shift.

Two linguists had once come over to my desk and asked me not to work as much as I did. When I asked them what difference it made to them whether I worked more or less, they responded that if I worked more than they did, I'd be making them look bad and the military would expect them to do as much work as I did so that they then wouldn't have as much free time to socialize (mock) for the majority of their shift.

I explained that I really wasn't there to hang out and socialize with them, especially since the U.S. was paying me to do the work they had sent me here to do. I also told them that I would like very much to socialize with them after we got off, not during the time we were supposed to be working.

It was my sixth week on the job at the AROCC; no one had been hired after me, so I was still the rookie. There were other linguists who had worked there from five to seven years. The first week that I started working at the AROCC, there were other American civilians who also worked with us in the same building, but they weren't linguists. These other Americans would come to my desk to thank me not only for my work but also for the amount of work I was performing compared to all the other linguists.

One morning during our pass-on briefings, our shift leader told us that visitors were coming to the compound within the next day or so, time unknown. One of those visitors would be General David Petraeus, the commander of U.S. forces in Afghanistan. The following day I was working at my station as usual, when Sergeant First Class Patricia, who was our shift leader that day, came over to my station to ask, "Mr. Kakar, will you please come with me? The chief would like to talk with you." The chief was the commander in charge of all the linguists in the language branch of the AROCC. I had only met him once, very briefly when I joined the team six weeks earlier for my initial introduction, at which time he had welcomed me to the AROCC.

At the request of Patricia, I accompanied her to where the chief was waiting to talk with me. He opened the conversation by telling me that I was going to be working in a different building for a couple of hours until General Petraeus' visit was over. The chief and Patricia took me inside a building that I had never been in before. When we were completely inside, Patricia asked me to take a seat at the station where another linguist was already sitting. Patricia asked the other linguist to take a break for a of couple hours so I could use his station. The linguist, knowing that General Petraeus was coming to the building, refused Patricia's request. Patricia had no choice but to order the linguists to let me use his station for a couple of hours. As the linguist was walking away from his station, he asked Patricia why she was letting me use his station. Patricia explained to him that the chief specifically requested that I be at that station during the general's visit. It was my first time meeting this particular linguist, who was not happy that I was there. I had no control over where I was assigned; if I had, I would rather have been in Sarkari Bagh. Although I was simply following my commander's orders, the linguist's attitude toward me was anything but pleasant when he said to me in Farsi as he was walking away, *"Toara braye chea inja aworda, e kho jaye ma bod?"* ("What the hell did they bring you here for; this is my station"). I responded, *"Aowra ma ham na my fahmom, khodi cheefa porsan ko"* ("I don't know either; why don't you ask the chief yourself?") Once I got settled into the station, I resumed my work and soon after, the chief walked over to thank me for being where he wanted and needed me the most.

He informed me that the General would be visiting this particular section where my station was. Since there were more than 90 other linguists who had been working at the AROCC compound, I had no idea why the chief had chosen me for this particular station. Did it matter which linguists had worked the longest, or was it important which linguist was most knowledgeable of all three languages involved? I didn't ask.

Within half an hour General Petraeus had arrived, and our building was indeed the first he visited. We had a brief conversation, he thanked the soldier who was next to me and then me, shaking both our hands before he left. Since cameras were not allowed in the building, I didn't have a chance to take any pictures. Once the general was out of our building, the chief thanked me and said that if I wanted to be in a group picture with the General, I could wait outside the building where more than 50 other civilians and military personnel would be gathered for the picture to be taken.

The chief also mentioned that the group picture would only be taken if the general had time. I asked the chief if it would be possible for me to get my own, personal camera from my room so that I could have a picture of my own with the general. The chief said he would allow me to do so and told me to hurry to get my camera because he didn't want me to miss the general's departure, which he planned to do soon. I went to my room and got my camera just in time for when the general walked out of the building. As he was walked toward the exit where his motorcade was parked, one of his staff members told him that all the people to his right were waiting for a group picture. The general looked to his right and then walked over to stand in front of the group so the military photographer could take the group picture. Since I had my own camera so I could have a personal picture taken with the general, I realized that I was going to have to ask him if had the time to do so. Fortunately, one thing I'm good at is never being afraid to ask for things that I want, so I made a split-second decision that while I was shaking the general's hand, I was going to ask him directly about having his picture taken with me.

But first I needed someone to take the picture and looked around to see who I could entrust my camera to. My eyes settled on Jay, our shift leader, who was also the closest person to me. As I gave him my camera and told him I was going to ask the general about having our picture taken together, Jay balked and immediately said, "No, Nas, don't do that; you can't ask the general for something like that." I asked him to just take the picture for me, while Jay asked me again not to ask because I'd be making a fool of myself. I insisted that all Jay had to do was simply take the picture, I'd do the rest by asking the general and shaking his hand whether I'd be making a fool of myself or not.

Just before the general walked out of the compound gate, I ran up to him and asked, "Sir, may I please shake your hand and have a personal photo taken with you?" The general looked at me while I waited to hear his decision, as Jay whispered in my ear, "Oh my God, no, Nas." Meanwhile, the general said with the smile, "If you're brave enough to ask, why not? Come on over here and let's hurry it up." Dumbfounded, Jay muttered so that only I could hear, "I can't believe you just did that." I whispered back, "Please be sure to take a nice picture, okay?" I ran over toward the general and shook his hand while Jay took that historic picture. "Now, see how easy that was?" I asked Jay. By the look on his face, he was apparently still shocked that I'd actually pulled the whole thing off!

The general's visit made things more difficult for me since I had not been welcomed by most of the linguists at the AROCC compound because they knew that Jay undoubtedly told the general that I volunteered for every linguistic duty and worked endlessly and tirelessly, which made them look lazy; and, as an American, I did what was asked of me by the military personnel without question. After being picked by the chief for knowing all three languages well enough to be qualified to be at the station the general was attending, the linguists displayed even more hostility toward me, and I was constantly being mocked more and more, especially after the general's visit to the compound.

In addition to the 60x35-inch American flag that I put up in my room everywhere I went in Afghanistan, I also had an American flag that I carried with me with a pocket-size portrait of my family throughout my deployment. The pocket-size family picture and small American flag were carried in the left arm pocket of my uniform every time I went on dismounted combat missions. Since I was not going on dismounted missions anymore while at the AROCC, I put my family's portrait on my desk and the small flag on the wall at my work station.

I also had some sticker flags, one of which I put on the overhead cabinet door to mark my cabinet. While I was never criticized by any of the linguists directly for putting up the American flags at my station, one morning when I came to work, someone have peeled the sticker flag off the top of my overhead cabinet. I had no way of knowing whether the individual(s) who ripped the flag off was against my country's flag or me personally. Since I never plan to run out of American flags, all I did was simply put another sticker on the cabinet door, but this time I pressed on it even harder to make sure it could not be as easily removed as the last one.

Needless to say, within a couple of weeks someone tried again to peel it off, but they couldn't do it this time—at least not all the way as only half the sticker was ripped off. This behavior worried me, and I couldn't help but wonder why we even had individuals in this building who didn't like the flag of a country of which they were citizens. Since no one in command was really interested in doing anything about it, I tried with all due diligence to find the enemy within our compound, but, as expected, never succeeded.

One day, one of the linguists came over to me, introduced himself, and proceeded to compliment me for putting up my American flags. "I'm just like you," he said. "I love America and the democracy that it represents. But most linguists who work here don't like you because you put them up in your room, too." I couldn't help but wonder how he knew about the flags in my room, especially since I'd never met the man before, so he'd never been in my room at all. Therefore, curiosity compelled me to ask him, "Who told you they don't like me, and how do they or you know I put the American flag up in my room, particularly since I've never had any of you in my room except my roommate?" He responded, "Dear Mr. Kakar, certainly you know very well that the Afghans are not capable of doing anything for themselves, so when they see someone else doing something productive, they will do everything they possibly can to destroy them." I had to agree that was indeed the Afghan way of doing things; however, I still continued to worry.

When I asked the linguist again who had been talking about the flag in my room and why people were talking bad about me, he wouldn't answer the questions directly but did say, "Let's forget about it. Don't worry about them; they can't do anything," which did little to make me feel better about the situation. My concern grew and was really bothering me until one day my new roommate, who I respected far more than my previous roommate because of his character and for being somewhat patriotic toward America than most other linguists, told me he had overheard other linguists talking about me, not only because I was an American, but for offending them because, to their way of cultural thinking, I was actually an Afghan. I handpicked him as my roommate for his American patriotism, not for his knowledge of speaking or even understanding Pashto, which was at about the same level as my previous roommate or perhaps at that of most of the other linguists. In Farsi, he told me, *"Aghaye Kakar, ma besyar ba shoma ehteyram darom, wa may khowastom yak cheezi bogoyometan."* ("Mr. Kakar, because I have a lot of respect for you, I would like to tell you something.") I told him, *"Chora nay, hazar dafah"* ("Absolutely, please do"), at which point he proceeded to tell me something similar to what the other linguist had told me a couple of days ago "Most of these linguists are talking bad behind your back to the point that I'm afraid they might do something to harm you. I'm just warning you to be careful."

I thanked my roommate for his candor and for sharing his concerns, but told him my life had been threatened before by another local linguist and even a number of ANP officers in Ghazni Province when I was with Special Forces. If I wasn't worried about that linguist or the ANP officers who wanted to kill me simply for doing my job to stop them from stealing from the villagers and local Afghans, I wasn't going to worry about this, either. I wasn't going to change who I was because other people didn't like me for doing my job as an American. I was more concerned about America's enemy within and wanted to talk about it all with my POC, which I did by reporting everything that had been going on to the captain in charge of all the linguists.

Most of the linguists who worked at the AROCC needed to be babysat by either our company site manager or the military POC, who would constantly remind them on a daily basis what they could and couldn't do while on the compound. Most had lived in the U.S. for more than 30 years among more than 300 million Americans, but still would not display an ability to follow the rules of the compound. Oftentimes, I wondered how it could be possible for Americans and our allies to think that roughly 150,000 Western troops could implement the rules or laws on more than 50 million Afghans in the course of a couple decades. I don't believe the job of the military is, or should be, to discipline other cultures. I thought military personnel were trained how to fight the bad guys rather than fixing cultural issues for which they have had no training whatsoever. I sometimes felt sorry for my site manager, who would go through the hassle of babysitting more than 90 linguists like a kindergarten teacher because she had to discipline them constantly to not do a myriad of things they had repeatedly been told were not permissible; for example, like taking other people's belongings without their permission; smoking in areas designated as non-smoking; cooking in their rooms, which was a definite no-no; or putting their trash in front of the doors to their rooms, expecting the military personnel to clean up after them instead of putting their own trash in the bin where it belonged.

And, by the way, these weren't "ordinary" people; they were people who had top secret clearances, all of whom considered themselves as being the elite Afghans because at one time, they had worked in all the ministries of Afghanistan and run the government before the Soviet invasion.

One day, my shift leader asked me if I would like to attend a meeting that would be attended by numerous military officials who were coming to the compound to talk with the most experienced linguists; they wanted to ask them for their opinions and get feedback on how to make things work better, not only for the linguists but for the military personnel as well. When I showed up for the meeting, there were four high-ranking officials—three of them military (a colonel, major, and captain) and then the TLM (Theater Linguist Manager).

Out of the 90+ linguists, eight of us attended the meeting during which the colonel asked for our opinions to see what the military could do to make things better for all linguists, for the most part because they complained the most. They knew that the more they complained, the more the military would do for them. The military was simply spoiling the linguists by catering to their every whim—and the more the military did so, the more the linguists complained, not to mention how much less they performed or accomplished in their jobs.

After explaining the purpose of the meeting, the colonel asked us to briefly introduce ourselves and our experience as interpreters in Afghanistan, following which we were all given an opportunity to express our opinions about the military unit itself. This was all followed by a question and answer period. It's interesting to interject at this point that out of eight linguists, only two of us—a fellow linguist and I—were the only ones who didn't complain throughout the hour-long meeting. Every other linguist in the room did exactly what they were accustomed to doing all the time: complaining to our shift leaders and each other about how badly they were treated every day, not only by the military personnel, but the company they worked for as well.

Not once did they said anything positive about anything. Their main complaints were more about their work schedules, which was always surprising to me particularly since the majority of them had never really worked for a living a day in their lives until they were hired to fill jobs at the AROCC. Their other concerns were the living conditions, and above all, their own cultural issues amongst the linguists themselves, with which, as noted earlier, the military had no clue how to handle. Most Westerners who had been to Afghanistan undoubtedly would know by now that after more than a decade of being in Afghanistan, if you attempt to negotiate with two Afghans in the same room, you'd be sure to get three different opinions, making any negotiations impossible to achieve.

When it was my turn to say something, unlike most of the other linguists who looked for support from their fellow linguists in order to make their cases stronger, I simply said directly to the colonel—perhaps in a challenging way now that I think back to that day—"Sir, despite the 24 hours of the luxury living conditions here at the AROCC, I was brought here a couple of months ago from Kandahar Province, not only against my will, but against the will of the commander of the COP where I was working. I would like to return there to live in a tent with the soldiers, where my knowledge of the American/Afghan culture can be very helpful, not only to the military but the local Afghans as well. I am asking and challenging you, Sir, to send me back to that unit, which has tried everything in its power to keep me there, but I guess politics sometimes get in the way of doing the right thing," I concluded, shrugging my shoulders. Well, needless to say, everyone in the room, including the colonel, was shocked by what I was asking of him.

However, I wasn't done, so continued by saying, "Despite the hardships and hazards, which some of my fellow linguists in this room will never know, I was much, much happier and would rather be with those combat soldiers who are out there, not only fighting the bad guys, but doing good things for a lot of good people who needed help. Being here now, listening to all of the complaints and whining from most of my fellow linguists, serves to not only distract me from my work but from accomplishing our overall mission. With the exception of one, the other linguists in this room have only worked at the AROCC; since they have never left the base, they haven't got a clue how their fellow Afghans make a living." The colonel told me he would look into the matter and if there was anything he could do to accommodate my request, he would do so and let me know one way or another. Of course, just like I did with everyone else in the military, I took the colonel seriously, as did a couple of other linguists who later asked me why I would possibly want to return to Sarkari Bagh, a place other linguists did everything they could to avoid. Meanwhile, the colonel said, "I think you've done more than your fair share of combat fighting for the past eighteen months or more, and you're not as young as the nineteen-year-old infantry soldiers anymore, either. At this point in your life, you should be working behind a desk." I couldn't help but respond, "Sir, I might be close to forty-eight years of age, but I can still go out there and be with those young nineteen- to twenty-three-year-old brave soldiers who are doing all the dirty work, and I would like to be a part of their team." The colonel assured me again that he'd check into the matter to see what could be done, to which I simply responded, "Thank you, sir."

Not too surprisingly, days, weeks, and months passed, and nothing had happened. I was still stuck with the linguists whose characters I did not respect because, frankly, they had absolutely no identity. As noted earlier in this book, all of them were American citizens, and most of them couldn't even describe what it meant to be an American or perhaps even an Afghan, for that matter, which is what they claimed to be. I simply chose to call them people with no identity. Here's a good example of what I mean about people with no identity, which is the story of a fellow linguist, who not only didn't have an identity of her own, but had the audacity of labeling me as a traitor. She undoubtedly didn't even know what the word "traitor" meant, and, if she did, she would have been better served had she labeled *herself* as a traitor, not only to her beloved Afghanistan but to America as well—therefore, my idea of a person without an identity.

One day, a couple of American soldiers made a legitimate argument concerning this particular linguist. The soldiers didn't directly complain to me, but wished someone could point out to her that she was using excessive perfume when she showed up for work. Why would the soldiers themselves not tell her directly, but instead ask me to do so? Well, military personnel were not supposed to complain about the linguists; instead, they were told to cater to them and their complaints. Her perfume bothered not only the soldiers, but everyone else in the office with whom she worked. Knowing who she was, I wanted to confront her myself before the soldiers even brought up the subject. Since I only saw her from time to time, for the sake of the soldiers who sat next to her for eight hour a day, I was going to find an opportunity when I could tell her that she wore way too much perfume in the workplace. When I was finally able to confront her and try to relay the message that people in the office, including me, were overwhelmed by the excessive amount of perfume she used, I politely asked her if she could in any way consider using less of it.

Most of the other linguists talked about the problem behind her back but had never had the nerve to address the problem with her directly. So, even though I asked her politely, she was overly offended because she thought I was making the whole thing up just to mock her, which was certainly not my intent. Instead of taking my comment and considering it first—even for a few seconds—in a very confrontational way, she asked me to tell her the names of those people who were complaining. I told her that I was one of them, and then gave her the names of the other two soldiers who had first brought it up. Unfortunately, she was enraged as she explained that she was in the mid-70s, and from a cultural standpoint, it's permissible that she be allowed to wear perfume if she wanted to do so. In fact, culturally speaking, no one can tell an elder what they can or cannot do, even if they only mean to point out something they're doing wrong—it's simply disrespectful. But then again, I saw respect from a different perspective. Her rage ever increasing, she said, "How dare *you* take sides with the American soldiers! As a fellow Kandahari, you should've been there for me when the American soldiers complained. You should've stopped them right there and protected me, but instead, you joined forces with them to complain about me!" Consider for a moment how this much rage can cause people to simply blast you with so much hate for the Americans that they don't even realize their own wrongdoings! Most people do not listen with the intent to understand; rather, they listen with the intent to reply. In any event, I simply went on to tell her that I thought we were all Americans working here. It's not whose side I'm going to choose to be on, it's about right and wrong, and if she didn't even realize that her perfume bothered so many other people, then the matter, in this case, should be brought to her attention. She seemed to be a tad bit less enraged when she responded with, "Well, you're different from all of us other Afghans. Unlike yourself, I will always protect my fellow Kandahari, and then, my fellow Muslims." When I asked her what she meant by that, she said, "What I meant is that you have taken sides with the infidel Americans to criticize your fellow Kandahari Muslim," to which I responded, "Yes, it is true that I am a native of Kandahar, but that has nothing to do with who I am today and what I want to do as an American. I had done more for the people of Afghanistan as an American than you can ever hope to be able to do as an Afghan, or perhaps even as a Kandahari, which you claim to be, while holding American citizenship. As far as I know, everyone that works in this building is considered an American and should be acting as such by respecting other people, regardless of who they are."

A couple of days after our talk, I was told by both of the soldiers that she had stopped using perfume and had also apologized to them both for her excessive usage. She had also come up to me to further explain that the reason she used so much perfume was because she was a heavy smoker, so after every cigarette, she would use perfume to cover the smell of the cigarette smoke.

Before the end of our work shift, most of the linguists usually stopped working about 45 minutes before their shift was over. They would start going from station to station, socializing to kill the time and to relief some of their stress from having worked so tirelessly. Well, not only was it distracting to my work, but also quite annoying with the same repeated complaint about their work, military POCs, their company site manager, living conditions, and so on and so forth. I wished they could say something productive—just once—so that I could learn something from them. But, no, unfortunately it was the usual complaints, which is why most of them were never happy, despite the money they were paid for doing little to no work to earn it.

Since lack of gratitude always made them believe that society "owed them," one day two linguists were standing by my station, talking in Pashto as they complained about one of the POCs who had recently left for the States. Their conversation distracted me from doing my work. Also, knowing the POC about whom they were talking, I got angry when I heard these two guys saying stuff about the POC that just wasn't true, and that really bothered me. I thought to myself, *I must ask them to stop or, at the very least, take their conversation elsewhere.* So, I asked them in English (specifically, so that my other fellow Americans who were working could hear and understand me as I spoke), "Hey, would you guys have said what you're saying now about the POC in front her if she was here right now?" One of the two, who always thought I was taking sides with the American soldiers and never liked me, backed off and returned to his station across the aisle from me. The other went on to say, "Yes, I would've done it again even if she'd been here right now." I asked him if he had already done that, what was the point in talking about it to the point that I was distracted from doing my work? The linguist said, "Well, it seems to me that you liked her more than your fellow Afghans, so that's why you're taking her side." I retaliated with, "I've only known her for as long as I have known you, which is only a couple of months, and if someone else was talking behind your back right now, right here, I would tell them what I am telling you—not to talk about someone who is not here to defend themselves," to which the linguist responded, "You can act like an American all you want, but you will always be a Pashton and an Afghan in my eyes." I told him that I respected his opinion, but would appreciate him letting me get back to my work without any further interruptions like bad-mouthing people that weren't present to defend themselves.

This was the struggle I had to deal with while working with 90 other linguists, particularly on the AROCC compound. Seeing their laziness and hearing their constant whining motivated me to work even harder. I told my POC I would be coming to work every day with no days off. As usual, my seven-day work schedules were not welcome news for the other linguists. At our meeting with the colonel a couple days prior, most linguists asked to have two days a week off, and work 10 hours a day (time they would *never* even remotely consider dedicating to their jobs) the remaining five days. They hardly worked when they were on an eight-hour shift, so how could they do it if the military had asked them to work 10 hours a day? Simply put, their focus was simply to work less and have more days off.

I was once approached during lunchtime at the DFAC by one of the two linguists whose eyes only saw me as a Pashton Afghan. He asked if it was okay for him to join me for lunch. I told him he was more than welcome to do so. During our conversation, his first question asked was what had been triggered in my mind to become an American, because, according to him I would never be an American in his eyes nor in the eyes of other Americans. He was not only speaking for himself but talking for other Americans as well as far as what they thought of me. I told him why I chose and wanted to be an American more than anything else in the world. Secondly, since I couldn't determine why others thought I wasn't an American, especially in the eyes of the Americans, his point was lost to me. He said he thought that all Americans were very racist, which was one of the reasons why he didn't want to become one. I knew at that point that if I tried to continue my conversation with this person, he would never understand me. His ignorant comments changed the features of my face, which I could see he had noticed as well. Fortunately, he sensed that I wasn't even remotely interested in anything he had to say, especially when he started asking me more questions about racism in America. He wasn't very well informed about America at all, so it was not wise for me to continue talking with him about the subject at hand. When it came to the issue of race, I wanted him to focus on Afghanistan. I told him that the only place where I had experienced racism being a major issue, was in our native land. Furthermore, in my opinion, the reason why we both left Afghanistan was probably because of race, but now we were both not only citizens of one of the world's less racist country (America), which was probably also the farthest away from Afghanistan.

No matter what I did, I could not convince him otherwise. However, in a last-ditch effort to make my point to him, and try to make him understand what I was trying to tell him, since he initially brought it up, I focused back on the race issues in America. I told him that if he didn't believe that America was the least racist country, then he should simply look at the results of the 2008 U.S. presidential election. In a country with less than a 13 percent African American population, Americans had elected their first president who was not Caucasian. I could sense he got my point, but he wasn't a person one could make a legitimate argument with, nor would he simply say that he would agree with what I had just told him because it was the truth. Another thing about most Afghans and their culture is that they're not accustomed to agreeing with the person to whom they have to defer.

I went back and forth with him, example after example, to compare and see where he would be more comfortable with the truth. I went back to his own country of Afghanistan, which he claims it was, even though he was an American citizen and chose to live in America, the country he considered to be the most racist of all. I asked him, "As an ethnic Pashton, would you ever accept or vote for a Tajik, Hazara, or Uzbek to be the president of Afghanistan if you ever had to vote in the Afghan election?" He smirked but did not answer the question directly. I knew by now that I had made my point with him, and something had clicked in his head when it came to the subject of race. I also told my fellow linguist that the difference between America and Afghanistan was like day and night when it came to the issues of race.

After my conversation with the linguist, surprisingly, I was approached by one of the DFAC workers—yes, the same one I had argued with the first day I arrived in Bagram regarding the way he was being treated by the Americans, who made him work harder for less money. In fact, I saw him from time to time whenever I transitioned through Bagram, where, despite our argument, I would say hello to him. By now he had worked 33 more months from the time I first met him, but he was still as poor as he was at the beginning according to him. He would also occasionally ask me for money, either for his wife or kids' prescriptions that were much too expensive for him to afford himself. I once gave him a $20 bill, but stopped doing so when I had been told by another linguist, who had worked in Bagram, that the local worker had been doing the prescription scam on everyone new to the base. During my time there, he made it a point to become friendly with me and, from time to time, he would come to my table and offer to bring me some meat (a.k.a. a luxury item from all the other food items in Afghanistan) from the buffet table, which I could've done on my own, had I wanted to do so. Since I primarily eat fruit and vegetables, he would laugh at me and tell me that vegetables were cow and sheep food—men should eat meat.

I asked him one day what his name was, how many children he had, and wanted to know their ages. He said his name was Taza Gulm, which in Farsi translates to Fresh Flower, and he had one wife and six children, whose ages he didn't provide. Curious as to why he had only one wife, he smiled and said, "If I were rich like you guys from America, I would have more than one wife and many more children." When he asked me about my family, I told him, "Like you, I have one wife and two children, 18 and 24 years of age." He smiled, not because I said one wife, but because he was surprised that I knew the ages of my children. I again asked him how old his children were, to which he laughed as he responded, *"Ma az omrey khod khabar nadarom, to az awlada ra porsan maykoni!"* ("I don't know my own age, so I certainly can't remember how old my kids are!"), which was a typical local response.

When I told him that I was going home for good next month, he asked me if I would consider giving him my jacket. I looked at him incredulously. "It's snowing outside; how can I go back to my room if I give you my jacket?" He told me with a smile, "I ride my bike to work in the same snow every day, without a jacket, and you can't even walk to your room once without wearing one?" Hearing that he rode to work on a bike without benefit of a jacket, I started to cry and then removed my jacket and gave it to him. Surprised by my tears, he said, *"Eqadar chezey bad kho na goftom key shom da gerya shoden!"* ("I didn't say anything that bad to make you cry!"). Even if I had tried to explain it to him, he wouldn't have understood that my crying wasn't because of anything he had but for how he loved his life, being born in the same country as I was, and how fortunate I had been to be able to leave and return to give him my jacket so that he'd be warmer when he rode his bike to and from work. His last words to me were, *"Amadom key bogoyomet, e nafar key hamrayet shishta bod azo Pashtonaye beysyar mordagowy adamkhor ast. Tajikara beysyar bad may bena."* ("I came here to tell you, the person who was sitting with you is one of the motherfucker Pashtons who hates the Tajiks.") I was surprised to learn that even Taza Gul, whom I considered to be an Afghan, turned out to be a Tajik, which he, of course, had every right to be, just like I have every right to be an American.

The AROCC wasn't a place for me to be working with more than 90 linguists, most of whom didn't have a real identity as to who they were or why some of them were even here in the first place. I was ready to leave and had, in fact, turned in my resignation to the company 60 days prior so I could go home to my family. When my military POC gave me a special assignment to monitor the work of all the other linguists at the compound,

I was tired even then of being amongst linguists who didn't like the U.S. military. I never said no to whatever the military needed me to do. It was discouraging for me to be in Afghanistan to see that there was absolutely no strategy on our part to take the time to understand the Afghan people. As I have written throughout my book, only Afghans can understand Afghans. The message of America to the two thirds of Afghanistan's Pashtons, Tajiks, Hazaras, Uzbeks, and other minorities had been stonewalled by the one-third of the other Afghans (a.k.a.: people without identities, which consisted primarily of most linguists and government officials).

I will briefly address the overall history of these Afghans and their conflict with one another in the second part of this book. To close this first part, I must say that after many years away and then returning to my native land, even I, as a native, was blindsided to learn that there was really no such place called *Afghanistan*—it's a myth. Therefore, as a society, we shouldn't then be calling it Afghanistan if it doesn't exist. Afghanistan as a state is as George Orwell had once said, *"There are some ideas so wrong that only a very intelligent person could believe in them."*

General David Petraeus and myself on his visit to our compound. Bagram Afghanistan. January 8, 2011.

4343 Easton Commons
Suite 100
Columbus, OH 43219
T 1 614 416 2345
F 1 614 416 2346

MISSION ESSENTIAL
P E R S O N N E L

2011 ANNUAL ASSESSMENT - OCONUS
Linguist

This form is used to assess each linguist's performance during 2011 and to identify opportunities to further develop and utilize their skills. The results will be used to help determine salary action and potential career paths.

Summary Information

Employee Name: KAKAR, Nsrat   Review Period: 1/1/2011 - 12/31/2011

Position: Linguist   Location: AROCC / Bagram Air Field

Employee ID: 3607   Evaluator: Amanda Thomas   Relation to Employee: Site Manager

Sources of Feedback: POC/SLCO, Military Team Leads and Officer In Charge (OIC), Production Statistics
(customers, colleagues, metrics)

Performance Ratings: *Please put an X in the appropriate box, in each row*

COMPETENCY	Outstanding	Exceeds	Meets	Meets Minimum Requirement	Unsatisfactory
Compliance: Follows policies, procedures and workplace practices	X				
Cooperation: Supports customer, other managers, and teammates	X				
Customer Satisfaction: Meeting unit POC's expectations and requirements	X				
Dependability: Conscientiously completing tasking with little supervision	X				
Initiative and Creativity: Ability to proactively design, begin, execute and improve tasking	X				
Job Knowledge: Understanding mission, their role, and how to be an effective linguist	X				
Judgment: Choices made (decisions, opinions) in various environments	X				
Mission Readiness: Ability to show up on time and remain engaged in mission/unit tasks	X				
Quality of Work: Producing complete and accurate translations and/or interpretations	X				
Quantity of Work: Volume of work and sustainment of OPTEMPO	X				
Timeliness of Work: Ability to deliver expected work products/results on time	X				
Overall Performance	x				

Outstanding: Consistently exceeds all job competencies and requirements
Exceeds Requirement: Always meets, and frequently exceeds all job competencies and requirements
Meets: Generally meets all job competencies and requirements
Meets Minimum Requirement: Meets only minimum job competencies and requirements; does not meet all requirements
Unsatisfactory: Does not meet minimum job competencies and requirements

Fully Exhibits Core Values and Guiding Principles (Y or N): Y	Completed All Required Training (Y or N): Y

If either of these values is No (N), please provide an explanation on the next page.

My 2011 two page military performance evaluation as a
linguist/culture adviser at the AROCC compound at Bagram Afghanistan.

Additional Information and Next Steps *(please also attach any available supporting documentation from Military POC)*

Employee Name: KAKAR, Nsrat   Employee ID: 3607

Recognition/Rewards (i.e., from client or MEP): Coin from departing AROCC POC
Certificate of Excellence and Achievement

Comments Regarding Performance Ratings: Specifically selected for special project based on linguistic (Pashto and English) skills. Able to recognize problems and identify mistakes. Knows what he is talking about. Outstanding work ethic; can be left alone to perform mission as needed. Closest to mentality of a military linguists at the AROCC.

Recommended Development Action/Next Steps: While it is obvious mission related training/development is not needed, everyone always has room for improvement. Work with 1st Lt Fletcher and/or her replacement to learn something new.

Employee Comments:

Evaluated By (Supervisor's Signature)	Date 12/13/2011
Reviewed By (Manager's Signature)	Date
Employee's Signature	Date: 12/13/2011

My signature only acknowledges that I have received, read and understand the contents of this Performance Evaluation. It does not necessarily mean I agree with its contents.

PART 2

Ansari and Zuhair's Own Words to Me: *"Ustad, Kodam Awghanistan?"* ("Ustad, Which Afghanistan?")

I CHERISH THE EXPERIENCE OF spending time with all the different groups: Pashtons, Tajiks, Hazaras, and Uzbeks within the ANA, ANP, NDS, local linguists, linguists from the States, high-ranking Afghan government officials (governors, sub-governors, prosecutors, and NDS chiefs), but most importantly, the local villagers that I admire the most for being real with their identity in that they themselves are not admitting to being Afghans. Each group associated themselves with their deep-rooted tribal ethnicity rather than their Afghan nationalism. Local villagers make up two thirds of the population; therefore, they should rightfully be given credit for being real about their identity, whether it be Pashton, Tajik, Hazara, or Uzbek.

If we in the West are giving a mythological nationality to a country where its inhabitants (e.g., Ansari, Zuhair, Taza Gul, Abdul Bari, the elder detainee with tuberculosis, and the elder in Paktika Province who didn't believe in either Afghanistan or Pakistan, plus the two thirds of the others that I visited in their villages) do not believe in it, then it's time to change courses for everyone, not just for the sake of the people in a particular part of the country. Afghanistan, per se, is a misnomer. Instead, there are four main tribes that should be recognized as being radically different, both in ethnicity and the language they speak, with little in common, each equally dysfunctional with each other in a multitude of ways. Apart, they are unworldly; together, they're a disaster. The history on each of the four main tribes, who for centuries have been in an ongoing conflict with one another, is discussed in the remainder of this book. A foreign power in Afghanistan only makes things worse, especially for the combat troops patrolling the various villages.

After hearing and seeing things for myself during my 33 months of deployment to Afghanistan, I had come to the point of asking myself a question that I believe every other American and Western society whose focus is to help Afghanistan should perhaps be asking themselves.

After reading this book, I hope you can ask yourself, "Is there really a place called Afghanistan that we Americans and everyone else in the West are trying to help democratize and free from the oppression of the Taliban, which most of the local Afghan villagers are in support off, and, if so, why?"

I have diligently attempted to help my fellow Americans as well as the rest of the world distinguish between the true Afghans and the so-called Afghans, who are simply giving themselves a false title and identity just to be able to claim financial support from the international community for purposes of their own personal greed—especially most of those who associate themselves with the Afghan government. Every government throughout the history of the world has had (and always will have) flaws of some sort so as to be able to take advantage of its citizens. The Afghan government, however, happens to be the mother of all flaws. In the remainder of this book, I will explain whether or not the U.S. or any of its allies should ever be involved in aid/combat/conflict in the concept of a place called Afghanistan, before fully understanding the people.

The West only looks at Afghanistan from their perspective, without knowing who the Afghans really are. In some cases, it is simply people not even trying to take the time out to really find out for themselves what is going on, and the dynamics of the Afghan culture to separate some from the others, like Afghans (i.e., Pashtons, Tajiks, Hazaras, and Uzbeks) from those who pretend to be (e.g., those who work in the Afghan government). The biggest problem underlying all of this lack of knowledge is something that is uncontrollable. It is not the Americans' or any other nation's "fault" for not understanding; it is simply a Western complex that is inevitable. I didn't plan on writing this book; however, throughout my deployment to Afghanistan, it's only because of my dual knowledge of both the Afghan and Western cultures that I have decided to do so now—collecting the thoughts of everyone I had met, foreigners and "Afghans" alike, who did not know much about each other's cultures but were there to help those who so badly needed it.

I want to share my thoughts, not only because I have a perspective of both sides, but because—for the sake of the West, to understand the people I grew up and lived with, just as I am able to understand the Americans that I then chose to live and integrate with. Mixing both of these perspectives allows me to explain why the U.S.'s involvement in Afghanistan is futile with the current strategy in place and being used, if we even have one. It is not just the Americans who are confused; the same is true for the *real* two thirds of the Afghans who are "experiencing" Westerners (a.k.a.: infidels) and are equally as confused. In their minds, why are the infidels in their conservative Muslim villages attempting to help them build roads, schools, clinics, and bridges? They *must* be taking something in return, which is the message that only the Taliban can sell to the villagers rather than the Afghan government can, especially since they've already been labeled as being supported by the West.

The message Western society is trying to get to the remote villages of Afghanistan has been lost, mostly in the translation (or lack thereof) between the West and the two thirds of the Afghan population that need help the most, which, because of this perspective predicament, I personally (nor should the remaining one third of the remaining so-called Afghans) shouldn't blame any other country for the problems in Afghanistan when they themselves are responsible. Let me be clear about this: When I say the Afghans themselves, I am referring to those one third who are mostly involved in the Afghan government, which the West unfortunately supports. In addition, for as long as the people of Afghanistan call themselves Pashtons, Tajiks, Hazaras, and Uzbeks, they will always be influenced by foreign powers, whether those powers are their next door neighbors: Pakistan, Iran, and Tajikistan, or Britain, Russia, America, and soon China. To make a simple point clearer, following is an example of a most recent incident that occurred not long ago.

Certainly, we all remember a country that was once called Yugoslavia, an entity of different ethnic groups of people which, for almost half a century, were being influenced by Germany, Italy, and the Soviets. The goal to achieve their (German, Italian, and Soviets') objectives by influencing different ethnic groups of people in this entity known as Yugoslavia, was short-lived. The breakaway of Yugoslavia into five different countries, living side by side, each with their own single ethnic groups, has been peaceful. Prior to the breakaway, however, and despite the fact that the country was known as Yugoslavia, people didn't associate themselves as Yugoslavians, per se; instead, they each fought as individual ethnic groups for their own independence. Is the same scenario possible for Afghanistan? When it came to fighting, yes—the Pashtons will fight because that's all they primarily know how to do. But as a breakaway? Well, I am going to predict whether it is a good thing or not—and will go so far as to say it's not going to happen if peace ever achieves itself democratically. If they want to live in peace as a true nation, the decision will have to be made by the Afghans themselves. According to the villagers, we have already experienced a peaceful Afghanistan under the Taliban. Are we willing to take that risk again? I hope not.

Realistically, there are only two choices: (1) Afghanistan (with one border, one national language, and one culture) is one unto itself, and (2) breakaway countries side by side (Pashtonistan, Kabulistan, and Hazarajat). Before I go forward to briefly describe each of the ethnic tribes, I will also add one other fact to the breakaway scenario: In accordance with an 1893 agreement between India and Afghanistan, when Pakistan did not exist, since there are twice as many Pashtons in Pakistan than there are in Afghanistan, Pakistan must be willing to give the land west of the Durand line (referred to as the Hindu River) back to the Pashtons.

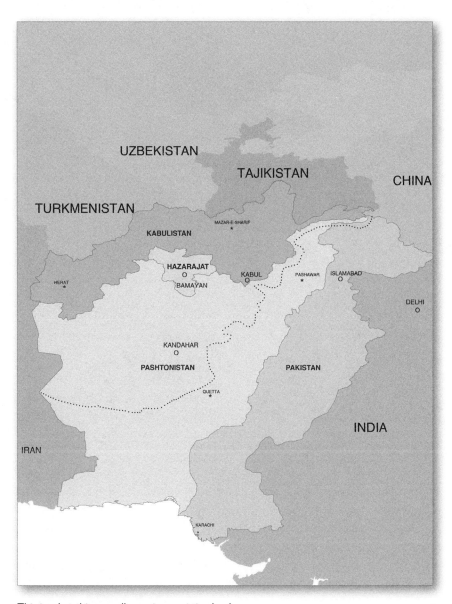

This is what things really are in my native land.

Pashtons = 50 Percent of the Population in Afghanistan

THE ROOTS OF THE PASHTON TRIBES (a.k.a.: *Yusufazai)* and their native Pashto language was originated in Kandahar. The tribe was mentioned as *Isapzais* by Alexander the Great in 330 BC. By 1585, their numbers reached in excess of 100,000 households, and—from the mid-1600s to the mid-1700s—their population had spread as far as New Delhi, India, to the northeast and Isfahan, Iran, to the west, which today accounts for an estimated 100 million Pashtons, mostly residing in current-day Pakistan. Pashtons consist of two main sub-tribes: the Ghilzai natives of Kandahar in the south and the Abdali natives of Herat in western Afghanistan. Although both sub-tribes have more than 100 clans scattered throughout Afghanistan and Pakistan, for now, we'll simply stay with the "trees of citrus (Pashtons), limes (Ghilzai), and lemons (Abdali)," instead of its branches (i.e., hundreds of clans).

First, Ghilzai—two prominent figures in this tribe that come to mind are Khushal Khan Khattak (hereafter, KKK), and Mirwis Khan Hotaki (hereafter, MKH), both of which are considered as the George Washington and Thomas Jefferson of the Pashtons and their land.

KKK (1613–1689) lived a life of misery and conflict, but never bowed to the invaders (Mughals). Educated at home, some consider his poetry to be the greatest ever written, while others consider him to be the greatest warrior and still others consider him to be the greatest philosopher, statesman, preacher, and lover of humanity. He also spoke in soft Kandahari Pashto. Besides defeating the Mughal troops of India in many engagements, he was the only ideological and intellectual leader of the Pashton tribes who had spent most of his old age preoccupied with the idea of the unification of the Pashtons. KKK had never used his religious beliefs while fighting to defend his territory from the Mughals, especially since they were also Muslims of the same sect (Sunni). KKK gradually struggled for peace and changes in national integrity for his region, free from Mughal emperors. In one of his couplets, he wrote, "If I have girded up my sword against the Mughals, I have revealed all the Pashtons to the world." This couplet makes it clear that KKK's wars were not based on his personal greed or enmity.

MKH (1673–1715), born in Kandahar, was from a well-known politically wealthy family involved in social and community service around Kandahar. MKH only became a warrior and a true fighter against the governor of Kandahar, Gurgin Khan (a.k.a.: George XI), who put MKH in prison for taking a stand against George of the Safavid Persian empire. George XI was sent to Kandahar to convert Sunnis to Shia, unlike KKK, who never took others' territory nor allowed others to take the Pashtons' territory. MKH fought to protect not only his people from being converted— but after the killing of George and the conquer of Persia (Iran)—the result was the defeat of the 220-year-old Safavid Persian empire. KKK always fought Mughal to keep his Pashton land free from the invaders, while MKH fought the Persians from invading Kandahar.

Two of the most important dates in Ghalzais Pashton's history to remember are: First, after the death of KKK in 1689, the Mughals of India invaded Kandahar in 1707 to fight the Safavid Persian empire (turned Kandahar) to a state of chaos that led to the rise of MKH and his dynasty, which brought peace and stability to Kandahar and its region. More than well over two centuries later, after the Soviet withdrawal from Afghanistan in 1989, all of the different ethnic groups of warlords fought over Kabul, which turned into another state of chaos that lead to the killings of many, poor Tajiks, which then lead to the increased power of Mullah Omar (leader of the Taliban).

In 1707, fighting to defend the Pashtons' land, MKH fought not only the Persian's Shia from the west to protect Sunni Islam in Kandahar but the Mughals Sunni from India. In 1992–1996 Mullah Omar (Taliban) fought the Tajiks over Kabul to take back the land that was once taken by their ancestors, KKK and MKH, 248 years prior.

Second, the Abdali: Unlike the Ghilzai, who were leaders, the Abdalis never led Afghanistan; with the support of Nader Shah of Iran, they only struggled to rule it. The founder of Afghanistan, Ahmad Shah Abdali, born in Herat in western Afghanistan, not only changed his name from Abdali to Durrani, but he also named the Pashtons' land Afghanistan in 1747 to rule the people in the region under a different identity, just like he did, only to fool himself for not being who he really was. Abdali, being the elite of the Pashton tribes because their connections were influenced by the Persians, knew that the only way for them to take over the territories from the Mughals' Suni Muslims of India would be to use the Ghilzais to fight, especially since they were warriors like KKK and MKH. Ahmad Shah Abdali after taking the name Durrani had invaded India on many occasions for their own personal desires and for the benefit of taking over various territories from the Mughals with the help of Persians. This repeated tactic by the Durranis upon the Mughal would convince the Ghilzais that their fight was not because the Durranis wanted to capture territories from the Mughal empire plus taking all of their treasure, but to tell the Ghalzai that Durranis were doing their duty of spreading Islam towards the east on the Indian subcontinent—a well-planned tactic by Nader Shah of Iran to make the Durranis fight for him while the same Durrani Pashtons took advantage of their own Ghilzai sub-tribes.

Since the Ghilzais were more conservative Muslims and, thus, willing to do anything for Islam to please Allah, the tactic of the Durranis using the Ghilzais to spread Islam had worked for the many times since the Durranis had invaded India. The Abdali rulers were all brutal, even to their own Pashtons, from Ahmad Shah Durrani (1747) to Zahir Shah Telai (1973). They never did anything for their people or the land; it was all for treasure, whether that treasure was the gold for breaking of temples in India, a Persian Riyal, a British pound, Soviet rubbles, or American dollars. (On a personal note, during my time in Kandahar attending school, in our history book we had a poem in Pashto about Ahmad Shah Durrani. Every time we started our history class, we would read it aloud for the whole class, which everyone, including me, loved, even if we didn't know whether it was true or not—but then again, in Afghanistan you don't question, you simply nod.)

As a naïve 13-year-old at the time, I memorized it so accurately, not only because I loved the poem, but because I hoped one day I'd become a man. Here is how the poem for Ahmad Shah Durrani was read, *"Ahmad shah Baba Ghazi / Khodie de wey lada razi / diy rahey so pa saman / warsarawa sardaran / pa hindwano ya malk or kiy / Islam ya halta khpoar kiy."* ("Ahmad Shah, the elder as well as the destroyer of the nonbeliever [Hindus], may God bless him; with his well-coordinated effort to attack with the help of his fellow tribal chiefs, he has turned the Hindus land into a burning hell to convert them to Islam.") Now, until this day, more than 40 years later, I can still remember that same exact poem as though it were only yesterday. (**Note**: Ahmad Shah Durrani didn't fight the Hindus in India as much as he did the Mughals, who were enemies of the Persians.)

After the many invasions by the Afghan warlord rulers of the Durrani tribes, it was in 1893 that the Durand line—referred to as the porous international border between India and Afghanistan—was established by a representative, Mortimer Durand, of the colonial British India. The Durand line (a.k.a.: The Indus River Agreement) was created between the then ruler of Mohammadzai clan under Amir Abdur Rahman Khan, simply for the purpose of stopping the Afghans from invading India. During the course of the Durrani invasion of India, with the help of Ghilzai's Pashton army, both Durrani and Ghalzai stayed in the present-day Pakistan for implementing their religious roots, and never came back to Kandahar.

The two thirds of the Pashton population still lives on the west side of the Durand line, or perhaps most Pashtons in Pakistan would call it "Pashtonistan," which is the western half of Pakistan that borders Afghanistan—another interesting fact I discovered during my time with Special Forces in Ghazni Province. Hearing, seeing, and discovering hard facts make me believe in *Mythological Afghanistan*.

On one of our missions to a village in Gardez, Paktia Province, east of Ghazni and south of Kabul, the capital, during one of our foot patrols, we ran into an old abandoned school—probably built in the mid-1980s during the Soviet invasion in the regime of Babrak Karmal, an ethnic Tajik with an ideologue of the Parchami (in Farsi, known as the people of the flag), supported by the Soviet communist ideology that had been ruined by Mujahedeen.

Walking through the rundown school building, one could see signs of atrocity. It must have been an attack on the school by the Mujahedeen, and everyone was probably murdered in that school as could be surmised by the bullet holes and stains all over the walls throughout the school. While walking to one of the classrooms, I discovered a textbook containing four subjects: math, history, geography, and (since part of the book was missing) some Physics. As I opened the book, I saw that it was written in Farsi, so I took it with me to read. Going through the book section by section, I had noticed in its history/geography section, in its written content and its map, it didn't show Pakistan as being Afghanistan's eastern neighbor. Instead, it had been replaced with "Pashtonistan," referred to as being Afghanistan's neighbor to the east, whose native language was Pashto. Was the idea of the Parchami to influence the locals in their books that Pashtons were from the neighbor country to the east of Afghanistan? Probably. As Ahmad Shah Durrani had changed the name of the Pashton land to Afghanistan to give it an identity of its (his) own, it was obvious to me that the Parchamis were now physically stripping Pashtons out of their land.

Within the Abdali tribe, just like with Ghilzai, there are hundreds of other tribes, two of which particularly come to mind because they benefited from the name Afghanistan while every other poor village in that section of land had been victimized and suffered considerably because of the foreign invaders. First, the Mohammadzai and Telai tribes from 1826 to 1973 kept the land called Afghanistan in the dark just like the Taliban did from 1996 to 2001. The only difference was (and some will argue otherwise, even though facts always speak for themselves), from 1772 to 1973 all the Durranis did was to move its capital from Kandahar, the land of Ghilzais, to Kabul simply to get away from the Ghilzais and make that one city their country. They did anything they could to keep everything in that city they referred to as Afghanistan, while the rest of the country had no idea what was taking place. The Taliban, on the other hand, when they claimed Afghanistan in 1996, what did they do first? They, of course, took Kabul back and turned it into their land of darkness like the rest of the land that was kept in the dark by the Abdalis. If the Abdalis Pashtons would've shared the wealth they were getting from the outside world, just like they're getting it today from America, with their fellow countrymen who they always kept in the dark, Afghanistan would not be as dark as it is today.

Just as Karzai, a Popalzai sub-tribe of the Abdali Pashton, was also put into power in Kabul immediately after the Taliban's defeat in October 2001 by the CIA who never served in the Afghan National Amry. Most Abdalis never served in the Afghan National Army either, and who were also put into power by foreign power. All of that responsibility was put primarily on the shoulders of the poor Hazaras, Tajiks, and Ghilzai Pashtons. Karzai, ever since taking power as ruler of Afghanistan, just like every other ruler from the Abdalis tribes, had done very little for his natives. Just as every other Abdali Pashton either died while in power or exiled, Karzai will also go either way. Staying in Afghanistan that they themselves have just created to fulfill their own personal greed would be a foolish thing to do. Karzai has also assigned most of its government posts to the inner circles of family members and friends. Most of those people were also in exile while Afghanistan went through the war with the Soviets in the 1980s and, likewise, its civil war in the 1990s over Kabul between the Tajiks, Pashtons, and Uzbeks.

Since you now know the difference between the two Pashton tribes (i.e., Abdalis and Ghilzas), also be aware that the Durrani, Mohammadzai, and Telai branches of Abdali would do everything possible to take everything of value that Afghanistan had been given, even if their lives were at risk (although some might get lucky by exiling). Second, the Ghilzai would also do everything they could to stand their ground and fight, and die if necessary, for not only Islam but also for their Pashton ethnicity. Therefore, my questions would then be, why and whom are we fighting today? Are we, as a society, ever going to win the battle against the Pashtons?

Just to go one step further about the numbers of Pashtons in the region, which could be wrong from what I had personally witnessed, the actual number could be more than three times the population, which has been approximated by the U.N. and the World Bank. The precise number of Pashtons will never be known. I have been to the most remote villages of Afghanistan where no one had ever been before. I had seen and spoken with many people on numerous occasions regarding the number of people in their families and homes in their villages, which none of them had ever been asked before. If the locals had never even been asked how many people were in their families, then how can anyone predict or correctly estimate the population of Afghanistan? To be more clear and accurate in my analogy, let me start with myself. When I lived in my village back in the '60s and '70s, the estimated population of Afghanistan was 12 million to 14 million. Today's World Bank numbers (as of this writing in 2012) estimated 34 million. How can either number be accurate, since no one has ever traveled to the remote villages in Afghanistan where 80 percent of the population in every village is under the age of 15? Again, I am still on the subject of the Pashton population now since 99 percent of my missions were to Pashton villages. Having seen so many things firsthand, my own estimate would be that the population should be more than double the current estimate of 34 million. I can comfortably say that in every village I visited, I saw many households, each with more than six to seven young children between the ages of three to 15, in some cases even 10 to 14 children per family. If the population of Afghanistan was 12 million to 14 million back in the 1970s, when in our village at the time, there were no more than 10 children my age versus going back to the same village now to find more than 100 children, how can the U.N. and World Bank continue to approximate that the population is still estimated to be 34 million? If most families have 10 to 15 people per household, with 80 percent of those under the age of 15, doesn't that tell us that the population has more than tripled just in the past few decades, let alone in four decades? Knowing that life expectancy is very low in Afghanistan, where some estimates show that one in five children dies before the age of five, my argument here is not meant to even attempt to correct the population number of Afghanistan—all I'm trying to point out is the truth.

But there are more important issues that need immediate attention other than guessing at the number of inhabitants. For these purposes and the sake of argument, I'll stay with the current estimated number of more than 40 million combined Pashtons between Afghanistan and Pakistan. It is also important for one to remember that of the more than 40 million (estimated) Pashtons, only one third live in Afghanistan, and the other two thirds in Pakistan. Almost every Pashton I have spoken with or known on a personal level has claimed the title to the land called Afghanistan, including one of our high-ranking detainees named Abdul Bari, a name you may recall. The conflicts even within the Pashton tribes between the Abdalis and the Ghilzais have not been settled for centuries, especially after the territory was first called Afghanistan by Ahmad Shah Durrani; or, on the other hand, perhaps it might have been the cause of the conflicts today. As you now know a bit more about the Pashton tribes and their history, I will explain more in the remaining sections of this book regarding their conflict with the Tajiks, Hazaras, and Uzbeks. To start, I'll briefly describe the Tajiks.

Tajiks = 27 Percent of the Population in Afghanistan

TAJIKS ALL SPEAK FARSI and live predominantly in the northeast and western parts of the country. Tajiks are also known as Sarts (a.k.a.: Margilan of current day Uzbekistan) which has had shifting meanings over the centuries. They do not have any particular ethnic identification and were usually town-dwellers. They are also referred to as a synonym for the Persian language. They make up the bulk of Afghanistan's educated elite; they possess considerable wealth (a.k.a.: foreign donations, which have been sent to Afghanistan for the rebuilding of the country's infrastructure). Instead, it has been shared between the Tajiks and Abdalis (e.g., Durrani, Mohammadzai, Popalzai, and Telai) mostly diverted for their personal infrastructure in the United Arab Emirates and other western nations. Tajiks are Afghanistan's second largest ethnic group; they have significant political influence and power control that lies predominantly within the government ministries, public services, and trade bodies. In the past three centuries, the Tajiks have not ruled Afghanistan as a country, but only Kabul once, for a very brief period of time, by Habibullah Klakani (1929). The second time (1980–1986), it was ruled by Babrak Karmal with Soviet support, and the last time by Burhanuddin Rabbani (1992–1996); therefore, it's quite obvious that the Tajiks, Mohammadzai, and Telai Pashtons were only interested in Kabul, and their rules never extended beyond the city.

Most wealthy Tajiks live in the major cites of Afghanistan. The Tajiks of Kabul get along well with the Mohammadzai and Telai Pashtons, who were in power, which is the main reason both are more secular than the

Tajiks outside of Kabul and the Ghilazis of conservative Kandahar, which makes me wonder why the original capital of the Pashtons was moved to Kabul. Unlike the Pashtons, the Tajiks have no sub-tribes and are more focused on the city they are living in (e.g., Kabuli Tajiks, Panjsheri Tajiks, Badakhshani Tajiks, etc.) and associate themselves accordingly. Being married to a Tajik from Kabul, I can only speak for the Tajiks of Kabul, who are only focused on one city, and one city only—Kabul. It's normal in every society for people to be attached to their native city or state, just like in the U.S.—for example, New Yorkers who love New York, Californians who love California, Texans who love Texas, or Floridians who love Florida, etc., and so forth. However, unlike the U.S., everyone stands united as Americans first; New Yorkers, Californians, Texans, and Floridians, etc. second—which the world witnessed on 9/11. Well, it's different in Afghanistan because if Kabul was attacked, all those who work for the government would care less. They would simply loot the ministries and exile to the West knowing that the city doesn't belong to them physically, only its liquid assets, which they can take with them.

A prime example of this is the Soviet invasion of Afghanistan, where most of the wealthy Tajiks of Kabul and the Mohammadzai and Telai sub-tribes of Abdali exiled to the west. Most "worked" in government ministries, or as my father-in-law would say, "[They] hang out at the office to socialize and drink tea." Instead of defending their beloved Kabul Jan (dear Kabul), they left the city behind to their fellow majority—mostly the poor Tajiks who had nowhere to go, except to be tortured by the Ghalzai for a decade once the Soviets left.

Habibullah Kalakani, a poor Tajik of Kabul, had met King Shah Amanullah of the Mohammadzai's Pashtons, who was not only wealthy but had a strong army that claimed to have defeated the British in 1919 for Afghanistan's independence. Amanullah also probably claimed to have defeated the British, just like Babarak Karmal, who claimed to be Ghilzai Pashton but was proven to be otherwise. If Amanullah couldn't stop a poor Tajik Habibullah Kalakani on horseback from overthrowing him with all his wealth and an army by chasing him out of Kabul in the middle of the night in his Rolls Royce as he raced to Kandahar and then to Switzerland, how could he claim to have defeated the British? Upon Amanullah's escape from Kabul, Habibullah Kalakani had discovered more than 750,000 British pounds (cash), which he then divided amongst Amanullah's soldiers, who, not having been paid for months, were probably happy hearing that Amanullah had been overthrown. Habibullah Kalakani's nine months of strict, Sharia Islamic rules over Kabul were overturned by another secular Telai ruler, Nadir Shah, who ruled from 1929–1933 and was assassinated by an ethnic Hazara high school student in Kabul. Nadir Shah's son, Zahir Telai, took the throne as King of Afghanistan, not only with the help of his uncle but every secular Tajik in Kabul. Most governmental posts were either assigned to his four uncles and family members or the Tajiks who had influenced the young king, only in his teens, who didn't know much about being a king. He was so influenced by the Tajiks of Kabul, he had turned his back on his fellow Pashtons to the south and east, to the point that most of them denounced him, especially those of Pashtonistan (current day Pakistan).

In order for Zahir Telai to stay alive, he had to throw some sort of support to the Tajiks of Kabul for protecting him from the Ghilzai Pashtons who were now supported by the newly-carved country of Pakistan from half of Afghanistan's territory; however, Zahir Telai did nothing. Zahir Telai has not only given Pakistan half of the Pashtons' land in 1947, but literally converted to becoming a Tajik of Kabul. In 1963, he gave the Farsi-speaking Tajiks a new identity by changing the name of the Farsi language to Dari. Simply changing the name of a language doesn't actually change the language; it only creates more confusion. Or, changing the Pashton land's name to Afghanistan doesn't actually change Pashtons to become Afghans, does it? Well, again, in Afghanistan people constantly change things, making it very difficult for the rest of the world to understand them. That's why they use the word *Inshalah* so often so as to give them the leverage of change that they're so accustomed to. Remember Jan in Khost? No matter how hard the Tajiks of Kabul tried to protect Zahir Telai or turn him into a Tajik, it also didn't work; he had finally escaped to Rome, Italy, in order to stay alive while most of Afghanistan (the fake name that his ancestor had created) had suffered because he was a fake Pashton, Tajik, Afghan and, most importantly, a fake human being.

During Babrak Karmal's rule from 1980–1986, Kabul's mostly poor Tajiks and Hazaras fought in Karmal's small army to protect their city while the wealthy Tajiks, who were in charge of Kabul's government before the Soviet invasion, enjoyed life in the West with their Telai friends, praying every day that someone would free Kabul from the Parchami communists who were supported by the Soviets. Well, thanks to the Ghilzai Pashtons, with help from the U.S., specifically the CIA, Kabul was finally freed from the Soviets a decade later. But not only did no one return to Kabul, every Parchami Tajik who worked for the communist government left Kabul after the Soviets did. Now, I ask you: Who became victims of circumstance? Again, the poor Tajiks of Kabul Jan, who suffered the most at the hands of the same people who claimed to have fought the Soviets, and were now fighting for greed and power while killing their own people. The basic ideology of Parchami was one of a gradual move toward socialism in Afghanistan. The Parchami fiction supported this idea because it was felt that Afghanistan was not industrial enough to undergo a true proletarian revolution called for in a communist manifesto. The Parchami fiction had more urban-based members who belonged to the middle- and upper-middle classes, mainly Farsi-speaking Tajiks, an educated urban dominant group. Under a lot of pressure from the Pashtons and to prove, in 1986, its ruler, Babarak Karmal, asserted that he was a Farsi-speaking Pashton from his mother's Ghilzai tribe, but that turned out to be fictional as many claimed him to be Tajik since his family integrated into the community.

By the early '90s, Kabul was now abounded by both groups of Tajiks—the group who associated themselves with the Telai and Mohammadzai Pashtons, who were overthrown by the Soviet invasion—and the Parchami group, who were put in power by the Soviets and overthrown by the Ghalzai Pashtons after the Soviet withdrawal. By 1992, Kabul was emptied, not only of all the Tajiks in power who once called it Kabul Jan, but as well as everything else that Kabul had. The only people left in Kabul were the poorest of the poor Tajiks, now ruled by one of their own, Burhanuddin Rabbani with the help of Panjshiri Tajik name Ahmad Shah Masood (1992–1996). It was hell for all of the different groups of so-called Mujahedeen who were trained by the CIA, had fought the Soviets for 10 years, and were now starting to fight for control of power in Kabul.

Kabul had been turned into ruins within the first couple of years of the early '90s—not by the Soviets or by the poor and hopeless Tajiks of Kabul—but by the Ghilzai Pashton's leader, primarily Gulbadin Hekmatyar, and his loyalists who were firing rockets from the southeast toward Kabul to defeat the Tajiks of Panjshir under the command of Masoud and his loyalists in the northeast who were in control of Kabul, while Rabbani sat as a lame-duck in the presidential palace. In the process, they killed more than 50,000 inhabitants of the city, who were mostly the poor Kabuli

Tajiks who, once again, had nowhere to go. With no end in sight, the struggle for Kabul went on between the different groups of Mujahedeen. Most of the poor Tajiks in Kabul regretted the Soviet withdrawal. This was the darkest time for the people in the city, who were trapped between a rock (Warlord Masoud, a Panjshiri Tajik) and a hard place (Warlord Hekmatyar, a Pashton) or actually, they were trapped between rockets/ bullets and their mud huts. Since most civilians, whether the poor Tajiks or Pashtons of Kabul, were affected by the warlords of the Mujahedeen fighting amongst themselves, killing innocent Pashtons and Tajiks in the crossfire. They desperately needed peace and stability in their city, even if that peace and stability were brought to them by the Taliban. The Tajiks and the Abdali Pashtons are much alike because they like money and will always be supported by either the West or the Persians and Russians. While the Ghilzais will fight for free, first for Islam and then for the Pashtons' land if supported by the CIA and ISI (like in the 1980s) and were, once again by the ISI in the 1990s.

On a personal note, I remember Laila once telling me that her family left Kabul in the early 1980s, not because of the Soviet invasion of Kabul (since most Tajiks in Kabul had no interest in the rest of the country), but, according to her father, because of the fear of Mujahedeen returning one day to take over Kabul. My point here is that most Tajiks of Kabul who exiled to the West only loved Kabul during times of peace. They had no desire to defend Kabul. Masoud and Rabbani were prime examples because they were sent back to the mountains of Panjshir where they belonged, according to prisoner Abdul Bari. Masoud was later assassinated by Al Qaeda, only days before September 11, 2001. Rabbani was assassinated by the Taliban a decade later on September 20, 2011.

Hazaras = 9 Percent of the Population in Afghanistan

THE HAZARAS ARE OVERWHELMINGLY Shia Muslims whose native language is Farsi. They comprise the third largest ethnic group in Afghanistan. They are also divided into eight different sub-tribes. Babur, the founder of the Mughal reign in India, used the name Hazara for the first time in his records during the early 16th century. The word Hazara most likely was derived from the Persian word for thousand. It may also be the translation of the Mongol word *ming*, used for a military unit of 1,000 soldiers at the time of Genghis Khan, who invaded the region from 1206 to 1279. The Hazaras have catered to the wealthy Tajiks of Kabul and have also been persecuted by both the Abdali and Ghalzai Pashtons. During the 21-year ruling of Amir Abdur Rahman Khan's regime from 1880 to 1901, most of his Mohammadzai tribes were sent to northern Afghanistan for more tribal influence on the Uzbek, Tajik, and Hazara tribes in the region. Amir Abdur Rahman Khan massacred 62 percent of the Hazara population, but was never questioned about his brutality. This forced the majority of the Hazaras to flee Afghanistan to the neighboring countries of Russia, Iran, and western India (the present day Pakistan).

It seems to me that Amir Abdur Rahman Khan was probably related by blood to Saddam Hussain, or perhaps, because of the way they both massacred other human beings, he might have been the great-grandfather of Saddam. I'm not saying that they literally were blood related—my point here is to say their idea for being brutal dictators to people who either were of a different race or different religion were very similar. I personally found the Hazaras to be the hardest working class of people, not only in Afghanistan but in society elsewhere as well, which is probably the reason they have survived every time they have immigrated to other neighboring countries. The Hazaras were once again persecuted during the Taliban ruling from 1996–2001; this time, however, most fled to Iran because of their religious affiliation with the majority Shia population there.

Being involved in their training during my time with Special Forces, every one of the ANP officers, who happened to be Hazara, told me during their job application screening that they lived in Iran during the Taliban era. Whether the Hazaras liked the Tajiks more than they liked the Pashtons, I don't know. During my time with their training or when we went out on dismounted missions together, one thing was certain: They were always involved in many petty thefts, either from the homes or shops of the Pashtons we raided. Whether they did it out of revenge or because they were now in power, at least for the moment, or were simply stealing because of the opportunity, is unknown, but I think they did it for both reasons because they were being cheated by their superior, just like Afzali had once complained for not being paid for his monthly rations, or like the young boy inside the still-standing mud hut after the bombing, who was not only being stolen from but beaten as well.

The Hazaras were also the only tribes, that I had personally known, who didn't claim to use the word Afghanistan. I might be wrong, but that's what I was told not only by Ansari and Zuhair, but by everyone else in their platoon that I had worked with for close to eight months. With the exception of Afzali and Ramazan, who claimed to be Afghans, if all of the remaining 33 were, then that would make me believe that the overwhelming majority of Hazaras in Afghanistan refer to themselves as being just that, Hazaras. They even have their own enclave within central Afghanistan called Hazarajat.

They're being dictated to by both the Pashtons and Tajiks—more so by the Pashtons for not only being Hazara, but also for speaking Shia Farsi (Persian). I personally don't like dictatorships, especially when innocent people are being dictated to; however, at the same time, dictatorship can *sometimes* be beneficial to society. You might be asking yourself right now: What has he been smoking while writing this? Actually, nothing. In fact, the last time I had a cigarette was in 1990. But let me get back to trying to make my point as to why I believe dictators or a dictatorship can be beneficial.

I am not a physician nor am I trying to be one by writing this scenario, which is simply for the sake of making my point here. I refer to dictators the same way I refer to cholesterol because both are silent killers. Our body needs both good and bad cholesterol to survive. The world as a whole also has both good and bad dictators.

Addressing cholesterol first, just as our body always produces more bad cholesterol than good, it also produces good cholesterol, which requires the body to do certain things stringently (e.g., sometimes physical activity, medication, and/or proper diet are required in order for your body to produce enough good cholesterol to constantly fight with the bad so that your body remains as healthy as possible. However, if one is not willing to be physically active, pay for the medication required, and/or change their eating habits to support the good cholesterol, the bad will take over so that the body eventually dies.

As for dictators or dictatorships, as with cholesterol, the world has bad dictators who harm the world by killing innocent people for their own personal ideology, and the world is also required to have a number of good dictators in order to prevent the bad from growing stronger, which would eventually destroy society without society even noticing it—just like the body will never feel the pain of cholesterol taking over, until a massive heart attack or stroke occurs, which obviously dysfunctions the body, eventually leading to death.

Not to be off the subject about the Hazara tribes, and before going to the next section about the Uzbek tribes, I want to provide you with a good example in order to make my point about dictators.

In most of the recent history regarding the world, let me first point out, at least in my opinion, the good dictators: (1) Both father and son with the same names, Reza Shah, of Iran (1925–1979): They accomplished greater good for not only Iran, but for the region as well. On the other hand, in the rules of their dictatorship, they had obviously also killed people to stay in power, even though the rules of their dictatorship also contributed to saving millions of lives that would otherwise not have been possible. (2) Other good dictators are both Egyptians. First, Anwar Sadat (1970–1981). Second, Hosni Mubarak (1981–2011). Both of their dictatorships contributed to society in the same way of those of the Shahs of Iran. History has shown us what the world looked like during their times as dictators—well, let's just give them the credit they deserve and call them what they really were—good dictators—the kind the world needs to survive.

The actions of other bad dictators (e.g., Hitler of Germany, Mussolini of Italy, and Hirohito of Japan), during World War II alone, contributed to more than 60 million deaths. Frankly, in my mind, the word *dictatorship* is not the proper title for them; more appropriate would be the title of *totalitarianism*, which fits the atrocities they committed against innocent people.

In the recent past, the world has also seen other bad dictators like Stalin, Saddam, Assad, Kim, and Amin, whose actions also led to millions of innocent people's deaths. The force that eventually stopped totalitarianism from society's further distraction came from the goodness of the U.S. military, who fought the war on three deferent fronts at the same time, where close to half a million brave Americans have made the ultimate sacrifice. Today, America's closest friends and allies are Germany, Japan, and South Korea, who all being bombed by America, but love America even more than some of my fellow Americans because only people from those countries can tell you what it's really like to live life under totalitarianism—just like the Hazaras can tell you what it is to live life under the Pashton and Tajik dictatorships.

Uzbeks = 9 Percent of the Population in Afghanistan

T HE UZBEKS ARE MOSTLY IN the northern part of Afghanistan. In addition to their native language (i.e., Uzbeki), they're also fluent in Farsi. Most Uzbeks get along easily with all of the other tribes of Afghanistan. Their part of Afghanistan happens to be the most peaceful during any conflict Afghanistan goes through from time to time, or should I say, most of the time, the only exception being the Taliban years, during which they also suffered.

The Uzbeks are not known for their resistance to either the Soviets or any other regimes that have been in power in Kabul, except for their minor resistance to the Taliban. They're more like an "out of sight, out of mind" type of people, who primarily associate themselves more with the Tajiks of Kabul than with the Pashtons, Hazaras, and Tajiks of Panjshir. As a matter of fact, one of the Uzbek leader's. Abdul Rashid Dostum, who was a strong supporter of the Kabuli Tajik leader, Babrak Karmal, a Parchami who invited the Soviets to Afghanistan in late 1979 with Dostum's help. The Uzbek warlord Dostum also had a rivalry going on with the Tajik leader, Masod a Panjshiri, just as he did with the Ghalzai Pashtons from the east and south.

Others = 5 Percent of the Population in Afghanistan

THE OTHER FIVE GROUPS CONSIST OF the Turkmen and Aimak, who primarily live in the northwest region of Afghanistan near the Turkmenistan border; the Pashai and Nuristani, both in northeastern Afghanistan along the Pakistan border; and, the Baloch, who are mainly located in the deep south of Afghanistan, around Kandahar and Helmand Provinces, in particular. They are so commonly unheard from, most people in the world don't even know they exist. Since they all live in very remote regions of Afghanistan, they have never been ruled by foreign invaders or any government, including the current one in Afghanistan. Governments in Afghanistan have no rules of law outside the major cities of Kabul, Kandahar, Mazar-e-Sharif, Jalalabad, and Herat. Most of these cities are not even under the control of the central government in Kabul.

These other 5 percent of the population would only fight if their territory was invaded. An invader could be anyone other than the ethnic groups. In addition to the others, Afghanistan also has a very small minority Hindu population, who have lived in Afghanistan for as long as Hinduism has existed. However, during the Taliban regime, Hindus were forced to wear yellow badges in public to identify themselves as non-Muslims so they would not be punished for not going to the mosques during prayer time. The Hindus still live in conservative Muslim Afghanistan because the Afghans were aware that the Hindus were honest contributors to the Afghan society, more so than the Afghans themselves, which is the primary reason they trust and will always call Afghanistan their homeland.

Most of the Hindus are wealthy and are engaged in the business of trade and money exchange. They're also very professional in their business dealings, and—because of their trustworthiness—even all of the Afghans would rather deal with the Hindus than the Pashtons or Tajiks. The Hindu population is mostly in Kabul and Kandahar. Even the Hindus of Afghanistan don't have a nationalistic allegiance to Afghanistan, but, rather, tend to be more like the Pashtons and Tajiks—who only consider themselves as a Kandahari if they are a native of Kandahar, or a Kabuli if they are a native of Kabul—in order to avoid persecution. During my deployment to Afghanistan, I had witnessed it myself: where a Kandahari Hindu would associate himself with Kandahari, and a Kabuli Hindu would associate himself with Kabuli.

Mythological Afghanistan

N ow that you know the different tribes who live in *Mythological Afghanistan*, I'd like to shed some light on the people who are behind *Mythological Afghanistan*, who also carry the name "Afghan." In reality, the only things that we're born with are our race and ethnicity, which cannot be changed by applying any other names to them, but we can chose everything else on our own. For political reasons, through the Western perspective, we can only see the physical shape of a map of Afghanistan and can also consider that everyone who lives either within the boundaries of that map or those who live outside of that map, are Afghans. The one third of the population, who have ruled Kabul for the past two-and-a-half centuries, combined of the Abdali Pashton tribes and the Tajiks of Kabul, acknowledge the ignorance of the West and play along with the game of representing themselves as Afghans, while taking advantage of the other two thirds of the population that only associate themselves with their ethnicity of Pashton, Tajik, Hazara and Uzbek. If the Abdalis and Tajiks of Kabul were really the Afghans that we in the West think they are, then why did Afghanistan continue to be broken up, tribe by tribe and village by village, more than a decade after the fall of the Taliban and while the fight for control of different parts of Afghanistan still continues?

Some reports have indicated that by September 10, 2011, Congress estimates the U.S. alone has spent $450 billion waging war there—for which every Afghan man, woman, and child could have been handed $15,000, or 10 years' earnings for an average Afghan. The rivers of cash that have flooded through Afghanistan have left many wondering why they still live in one of the poorest countries in the world, and questioning where it went. During my time there, I saw many multimillion dollar unfinished projects throughout Afghanistan, being paid for by the U.S. On the other hand, during my half dozen visits to the United Arab Emirates (UAE), all the other multibillion dollar projects had been completely finished for the Afghan government officials' lavish lifestyle, with funds diverted from the funds that had been given to the Afghan people by the international community. The day the Americans leave Afghanistan, most of the Afghan government officials will be in Dubai on the next flights out of Kabul and Kandahar. If anyone in Afghanistan deserves that $450 billion "invested" by the U.S., it's the two thirds of the Afghan population. Americans have rushed into Afghanistan with cash, forces, and talented ignorant officials, but years of relative neglect meant they lacked one critical ingredient to the mix: understanding the complexities of all the different tribes that live in Afghanistan who hate each other and whose only goal is to destroy each other in any way possible, even if it means the loss of lives of their own people. Most of all that cash donated to the Afghan people went to the ministries in Kabul, which are mostly in control of the Tajiks and Hamid Karzai's own cronies who have been appointed to high-ranking positions. Instead of funding growth, much of the money has been diverted into the pockets of both the elite in Kabul, Kandahar, and other major cities, which is helping to fuel a culture of rampant corruption.

Everything that revolves around the Afghan government, from justice to reconstruction projects, is tangled up in demand for bribes throughout the major cities. Throughout my deployment, I had sensed that there is a common perception that Western forces are seeking quick results. The Afghan commanders were settling personal scores by giving false tips to informers seeking payment, which I had seen on numerous occasions—particularly, Jan Mohammad, the NDS Chief, and Mr. Habibi, the prosecutor in Khost Province, who arbitrarily sent our soldiers to kill and be killed where success was measured in terms of enemy body counts. We don't even know who our real enemy is in *Mythological Afghanistan*: whether it's those we support or those we want to kill. This is only accomplishing the diminishment of American prestige and leadership not only in Afghanistan, but in the region as a whole. I would have believed Karzai, just as the people in charge did, by putting him in power in October 2001. But today, according to most people I met in the south and east of Afghanistan, Karzai is not the same person he was then, and the people in Kandahar, civilians and government officials alike, have told me that, ever since Karzai went to Kabul, he has turned his back on his own people.

On every occasion, I asked many of those same people what had changed that made them think that Karzai was neglecting them? In return, one of the village elders in Arghandab asked me, "Listen, my brother, I don't understand why it is, but I want you to tell me, what is there in the cities of Kabul and Kandahar that makes people who go there to become thieves?" Seeing everything for myself while in Afghanistan, I could feel the frustration in the villager's voice as well as see it in his face. But all I could say to the villager, as well as others sitting and listening nearby, was a simple example (which would only imply if Karzai was as innocent as these poor villagers thought he was before going to Kabul). Since most people in Arghandab were owners of fruit orchards, the example I wanted to tell them was one they could relate to and understand. I started by saying, "I want to ask all of you this question, to which you should already know the answer. If any one of you took one good apple and put it in a box of rotten apples and let it sit there, would any of you expect the good apple to turn the box of bad apples into good apples? Or would the chances be that the single good apple would become a rotten apple with the passage of time?" Everyone understood and agreed with me; some even said that this had happened not only in Karzai, but to anyone else who went to the city and worked for the government, whether the city was Kabul or Kandahar.

Since the group around me really wanted to find a solution to the problem of corruption that was going on amongst the government officials, several people in the crowd asked me if I had one. But there were others who were pointing fingers of blame at our U.S. military officials for their support of a government like Karzai's, one that not only cannot protect its population, but that steals from it. I agree almost 100 percent with the villagers regarding the Afghan government stealing from them. I was told by another villager in Arghandab about the ballot stuffing in the presidential election of August 2009—how the voter fraud scheme had worked. Within the hierarchical structure of Afghanistan, key local leaders, for example, like the Malak in Ali Kaley who had simply shown up to get all the humanitarian aid from the poor villagers during our visit, can do the same thing when it comes to ballot stuffing during an election. People like the elders of the villages have the ability to persuade large numbers of people, whether they want or don't want to vote for one candidate or another. The village elders are usually approached by teams from the contenders of the presidential election with monetary bribes (e.g., if one candidate gives $5,000, and another gives $10,000, and a third offers even more). It has become such a lucrative and competitive business, "I don't know where they get their money from," said one elder.

The elder went on to say, "I knew where Karzai and his cronies got their money—from an international community donating to the Afghan people or taking bribes from the Chinese firms who signed contracts with the Afghan government without even putting anything out for bid, supposedly for the sake the country." As noted earlier, Assadullah Aka was very knowledgeable, not only about things around his village, but about the country as well. Is it ever possible for a free and fair election to ever be held under the Afghan constitution in a society where a tribal elder can make a decision for the more than 500 people in his village, like in the case of Ali Kaley, for example, where the elder usually made all of the decisions? Well, if Karzai has the power to buy the elder, then the elder has the power to buy the votes of at least 400 people in his village from the highest bidder. Just like Lord Acton once said,

> *"Power tends to corrupt, and absolute power corrupts absolutely."*
> — LORD ACTON

People in Afghanistan as well as our government officials in Washington, D.C., believed that Karzai wasn't corrupt; however, once he got to Kabul and began to possess more and more power, the more corrupt he became. I was once told by a very frustrated villager that, "For the past nine years, our own government forces have broken into our homes to steal from us." In their minds, the difference was clear between the Taliban, who protected them, and their own government, who stole from them.

I had another villager tell me that during the Taliban regime, if anyone in the village had a feud or a dispute with any other villager, all they needed to do was inform the Taliban representative, who would come once a week to the village mosque for *Juma's* (Friday's) prayer. Once the complaint was presented to the Taliban representative, he would then call out both of those people from the audience who had issues with each other, and they would be questioned by the representative in front of everyone else regarding what their feud was about so everyone else would know as well. If one was found to be at fault, the representative simply pulled out a complaint form, wrote down the complaint and the defendant and plaintiff's names, and asked both to put their right thumbprint on the paper (since at least 90 percent of the villagers couldn't read or write). They were then told that if it happened again, the next time there would be no fingerprinting on the paper; instead, the same thumb used this time would be cut off. Cruel? Yes, I certainly think so, but it was easy for the villagers to understand not to break any of the rules under the Sharia law that the Taliban was enforcing.

Each person would then be given their copy and the dispute would be settled right there. No trial lawyers, no bribes taken or given, and last but not least, no appeals to the supreme leader, Mullah Omar. All of this was done in front of everyone else in the village so that they could see what would happen and/or not steal or harm any of their fellow villagers. The fee for this service was just the cost of the paper on which the rules were written in the same ink used for the fingerprint, that only cost 50 Afghanis ($1). Not only was the process of filing the complaint so simple, but the local villagers didn't even have to go to the district center or the city because it was a service delivered by the Taliban at the village mosque under Sharia Islamic Law. With all of our technology here in the States, sometimes I can't even login in to a website fast enough, let alone file a dispute.

The villager went on to tell me that with the new government, the poor villagers had to pay for a ride to go to the city every time they had issues. Once in the city, they had to pay a fee (a.k.a.: bribe) just to get into the government office to see and talk with anyone. It also doesn't help their case since all the complaints these days are against the government officials themselves—similar to the same case scenario as that of the villager in the Yahya Khel District when I had asked him how the security situation was where he lived, and he said that security could not be the main issue because they were far more concerned with the harassment they were facing from the government officials. The problem in Yahya Khel was so preposterous, it was chasing people away from even coming to the market to buy food and other items, or those whose land has been taken by the government. Will the West ever succeed in a land where we can't even identify the real Afghans that we want to help? How can we in the West define success if we can't even find our target? If we can't identify the problems in Afghanistan, then I don't believe we can ever succeed in Afghanistan, and if we can't succeed, why should we be there in the first place? Some would argue that promoting democracy in Afghanistan or protecting human and women's rights, in particular, would be a good enough reason for us to be in Afghanistan. What do you think?

Personally, I am not all for it, but I went to Afghanistan so I could be part of the mission regarding both issues. After witnessing all that I did while there, my thoughts quickly dissolved as to how things are done, and now I have to wonder if our "method" will not only lead those of us in the West to want to achieve, but also make it worse for more people than the few that we're trying to help now.

Upon arriving in Afghanistan, I was more determined than ever about defeating the terrorists who attacked us on 9/11. But throughout my entire experience there, while talking to the real victims face to face, and getting much-needed answers from the villagers, I have come to realize that it is not possible for Americans or the international community to ever succeed in Afghanistan with the strategy that asks: Who are we trying to help, or perhaps even better stated, aren't we hurting those same people we're trying to help?

Our main objective of going into Afghanistan in the first place, with which I agree, is because of the actions of 19 Arabs, Al-Qaeda terrorists supported by the Taliban, who attacked us. Fifteen of those terrorists were from Saudi Arabia, two from the United Arab Emirates, one from Lebanon, and one from Egypt. That leaves us with zilch from Afghanistan; however, since the Taliban had given the terrorists sanctuary in Afghanistan to train for and coordinate their attack on American soil, I believe that the Taliban was just as responsible for the attack on America as were the 19 terrorists who were physically involved in the actual attack. But that doesn't make every civilian in Afghanistan a Talib. With that said, I'm also taking this opportunity to remind my readers that during the Taliban regime of 1996 to September 11, 2001, Pakistan, Saudi Arabia, and the United Arab Emirates were the only three countries who recognized and supported the Taliban in their Sharia law rulings of Afghanistan—not to mention that the Al-Qaeda terrorist leader, Osama Bin Laden, lived and was protected by the Inter-Services Intelligence (ISI), which was not too far away from the Pakistani military base in Islamabad. As Pakistan and Bin Laden did what they were doing behind the military base, Americans' taxpayer dollars went into that same Pakistani government ISI agency for their support of helping us in the war on terror and the capturing of Osama Bin Laden, who was found sitting in the Pakistani military's backyard.

America urged Pakistan to do more by not allowing the Taliban to coordinate their attacks on the Afghans and the American forces, but it wasn't possible for Pakistan to do what we needed them to do for us: help defeat the Taliban, because there are more Taliban and Pashtons living in Pakistan than there are in Afghanistan.

At this writing, according to a website article I recently read, while they had Osama Bin Laden, the U.S. had provided $20.7 billion in aid to Pakistan since 2002. Just to be fair, my question is this: Did America give $20.7 billion in aid to support the Taliban regime from 1996–2001 when they had Osama Bin Laden in Afghanistan, while 99 percent of the poor villagers there didn't even know who Bin Laden was?

Pakistan, the "bad boy" in the neighborhood, should be responsible for all four unfortunate situations—first, for the deaths of not only all the brave American soldiers and civilians who died in Afghanistan, and for the innocent and poor and hopeless victims who live there; second, for the hundreds of billions of dollars from the American taxpayers; and third, for allowing the Taliban to move freely to coordinate their attacks.

We realized Pakistan was holding the biggest terrorist fish in the pond—Osama Bin Laden—which we also knew from the days when the Tora Bora disappeared. Knowing the Afghan society and culture, especially those of the Pashtons, Osama Bin Laden had no chance of hiding in Afghanistan. I experienced that for myself on every mission we went on and to every village we went to, that even I, a native Pashton, could not find a place to hide, let alone a more than 6-foot-tall Arab being chased by the American Special Forces.

Afghanistan is a very secretive society. If you're one of them, you'll be protected and no one will ever find you, but if you're even from a different village, let alone from a different province, different tribes, or perhaps from a different country, you're out of luck.

I'm going to take a couple of steps back to address the main reasons why we went to Afghanistan.

1. To topple the Taliban regime, who was supporting and harboring Osama Bin Laden.

2. To promote civil rights and introduce democracy and freedom so Afghanistan would not become a training camp for the Al-Qaeda to attack us again.

If it truly is human/women's rights that we are trying to promote in Afghanistan, then why don't we try to do the same thing in Pakistan and Saudi Arabia, where there are no civil rights in existence? If it's democracy we're trying to introduce, then how can we even touch the subject in the most conservative Islamic country in the world, where democracy is against the Sharia Islamic law?

For five years, the Taliban-ruled Afghanistan imposed the strict Sharia Islamic law as two thirds of the local population who lived in the villages were happy with the Taliban rules then, and still are today, but no Afghan government officials would ever consider telling us that because they don't represent the two thirds. The people in the villages must want democracy in their nation more than we want to give it to them. If democracy is somehow interfering with their strict interpretations of the Islamic Sharia Law, then our efforts to promote democracy is not going to work in Afghanistan, certainly not overnight; in fact, it will only impose on the people's freewill. I'm not saying that it won't work—I'm saying it could work with a much better and well-thought-out, long-term strategy, which we currently (and have on many other occasions emphasized) don't have. The only strategy that will work in Afghanistan is that we first need to identify the problem. Once we have done that, the strategy can then be implemented and applied, working with the passage of time. Our current strategy of supporting the corrupt Afghan government will not help us succeed in Afghanistan. The militarist Americans fail to understand that the Pashton (KKK's) patriots naturally despise foreign armies of occupation and puppet governments, and it will end with even bigger problems in the future. I believe that the British and the Soviets failed in Afghanistan because they could not figure out how the Pashton culture really worked. We, as Americans, will also fail if we don't find out who the Afghans are that we're trying to help.

I can think of an example using three different analogies for the current *Mythological Afghanistan*. Let's consider Afghanistan as being part of the world, which is like diagnosing someone with Stage III cancer, and then let's take it one step further by considering that cancer as being the

Taliban. Is it fair to say that if not cared for, it will undoubtedly grow and spread even more aggressively to other parts of the world? And, let's also say that Afghanistan, the infected part of the body, has already had other surgeries in the past by other surgeons from Alexander the Great to the Soviets, which all ended up with complications causing the cancer to return because the previous surgeons never took the time to fully understand not only the kind of cancer involved, but the cancer had now become aggressive because there was no long-term chemotherapy after performing the surgeries to remove the cancer to ensure that it never returned.

Now, consider whether it would be possible for the current surgeon (America) to succeed in curing the cancer by following the same procedures all the previous surgeons tried but failed? Before the surgery, it would also be wise for the surgeon to know the patient's medical and family histories or perhaps even allergies that the patient might have. Yet, even if the current surgeon is financially capable of caring for the ill patient longer than all the other surgeons, especially if the patient did not tell the surgeon the truth about his allergies, family and medical history, then, is it the surgeon's fault that the patient is not getting better, or is it the patient's fault for not telling the surgeon the truth? One would say both, but only if the doctor and patient had the same goal to merely perform the surgery without all the other necessary steps that needed to be taken to prevent the cancer from returning. But if they both want to succeed, each needs to be totally committed: (1) by the patient telling the surgeon the truth (if the patient really wants to be cancer-free), and (2) by the surgeon being committed by knowing all the facts about the patient's allergies, family, and medical history so he can properly treat the patient.

To provide you with an analogy of my personal family life in comparison to the situation of Afghanistan being a family of four (Pashton, Tajik, Hazara, and Uzbek), as you are aware, I am a native Pashton, my wife is a native Tajik, and my two children are "natives" of America. However, since Afghanistan consists of four different ethnicities, for the sake of argument, I'll be even more precise in my analogy. For example, for purposes of ethnicity my son chose California, and my daughter, New York. If the four of us are living in the same household with me always dictating to my wife and two children, then Pashto should be the language of our house, and both of our children should be raised as Pashtons. While my wife, on the other hand, argues that Farsi should be the language of the house, in which case both of our children should be raised as Tajiks. As the man of the house, especially in the Afghan culture where men dictate to enforce their rules, while the wife can only argue to some extent, two kids watch their parents, day in and day out, always arguing about whose culture or language should be implemented in our household. At the same time, while mom and dad are both asking their children to speak each of their individual languages, the kids understandably become confused as to which language and what ethnicity they should choose; then, throw into the mix the fact that everyone outside of our home, including those in school, speaks English—the direct opposite of what their parents want them to speak.

If the four of us in our family did things in our own individual ways, our family and home wouldn't survive. Would it be better off for our family if my wife and I opted not to speak our native languages but, rather, chose the language of America, the land of which we chose to be citizens? Furthermore, it would be beneficial for all four of us to communicate better in one common language (English), not only with one another but with other people in our community and country. I strongly believed and chose the path I did, not only for me and Laila, but more importantly for the sake of our children and our country. Having then chosen the U.S., I was, and still am, obligated, for the sake of my country and my family, to want all of us to choose nationalism rather than our ethnicity in order for all of us to be a successful American family.

If this strategy were implemented in my household, and it worked for the four of us as a native Pashton and Tajik (with American children), to choose one language, one nationality, and one culture in order to succeed, I have no doubt but that it would work in any household or perhaps in any country, even if that country happened to be *Mythological Afghanistan*. Again, strong leadership and sacrifice are required in order to achieve what needs to be done. In my case, I have been very focused all of my life, and knew I needed to make some tough choices, not only for my family, but for us to be a united and successful family. I know that life is tough, but somehow it was a bit tougher for me growing up, moving from my village to the city, then from the city to a country with which I had nothing in common, not to mention marrying a Tajik whose language I could not speak. I am sure there are others who probably had it a lot tougher than I did, but, for me, and hopefully some of you, it made me stronger as a person to take the lead for all of the difficult decisions that have had to be made throughout my life.

Instead of inflicting mine on them, the love of my wife and my country made me learn both of their languages. The love of my children made me take responsibility to be a good father so I could provide for their needs—all of this because I chose for my house not to be divided like in Afghanistan but united like in America. Abraham Lincoln once said, *"A house divided against itself cannot stand."* I agree with our beloved President Lincoln 100 percent, when he made this statement during his speech on June 16, 1858, in Springfield, Illinois.

Afghanistan is in desperate need of one common language, border, and culture, as do family members and relatives, and friends who are natives of Afghanistan, living their lives either in the United States or other Western countries. Unfortunately, it never crosses those minds. To keep the trend alive, most native Afghans are forcing their native American- or other Western-born children to be Afghans with their primary language being Pashto (if Pashtons) and Farsi (if Tajiks). If that should be the case, then my simple question has always been to those fellow natives of Afghanistan who consider themselves as Afghans while living in the West, "What is the definition of the word Afghan?" So far, I have not heard a satisfactory answer when I have posed the question to many of my fellow Afghans. If a word cannot be defined, then how can it be associated with anything?

My third and last analogy is that I consider Afghanistan to be a bad marriage, one where divorce is not an option. How could that even be possible? Well, it could be, but only in Afghanistan. But, that's what today's *Mythological Afghanistan* is like, with its neighbors on the east and west, while the "marriage counselor" today is America.

Pakistan's Self-interests in Afghanistan

Pakistan always interfered with Afghanistan's internal affairs, even before its creation in 1947. Before their independence from the British Raj of India in 1947, the Sunni Muslims fought under the banner of the Mughal Empire ever since the 1500s, with both the Hindus of India and the Shias of Persia. KKK and MKH were the only Pashton warriors who stopped the Mughals and Persians from invading their territories of Pashtonistan at the time before Pakistan's independence. When the British allowed for Pakistan to be its own state for the sake of keeping peace, the Pashtons didn't have a leader at the time to protect the territories, which resulted in Pakistan taking more than half of the Pashtons' land west of the Durand line. As noted earlier, in order for Pashtonistan to exist, Pakistan would be required to give up the land that is mostly occupied by the Pashtons in their present day Pakistan. The border area of Pakistan and Afghanistan is the largest tribal society in the world, where not only the border is nonexistent but the Pashtons are not associating themselves with either Pakistan or Afghanistan. Since twice as many Pashtons live in Pakistan than in Afghanistan, Pakistan will always do everything to keep their side of the Pashtons to focus on the Tajiks and Hazaras in Afghanistan, rather than the Pashtons taking a stand against Pakistan in order to reclaim their land.

In the summer of 1976, the Pashtons in Pakistan raised the issue of independence for Pashtonistan by marching in protest, which was quickly responded to by the then dictator of Pakistan, Zulfikar Ali Bhutto, by killing thousands of Pashtons. The only leader of the Pashtons after KKK and MHK, Daoud Khan—who I remember visited Kandahar when I was a kid—had taken a stand in support of the Pashtons against the Pakistani dictator for killing thousands of innocent Pashton protesters in Pakistan that summer. In addition, in 1977 President Daoud Khan also signed a formal agreement with Zulfikar Ali Bhutto to recognize the 1893 Durand line treaty to take back the Pashtons' land. Before the agreement was ratified, Zulfikar Ali Bhutto invited Burhanuddin Rabani, Ahmad Shah Massoud, and Gulbadin Hekmatyar to Peshawer, Pakistan, to prepare for Daoud Khan's assassination, which occurred a year later during the spring of 1978. Those same three people who had planned Khan's assassination, become Mujahedeen warlords for the CIA, and were supported by the ISI to fight the Soviets in the 1980s while the focus of the Pashtons was then turned away from the issues of Pashtonistan to fighting against the Soviets.

After the Soviets withdrew from Afghanistan, the Tajiks took control of Kabul, which the ISI was against. Again, the only way to divert the attention of the Pashtons from the issues of Pashtonistan and the Durand line border was for the ISI to get involved by coming up with the idea of a new movement to train the Ghilzia Pashtons how to fight the Tajiks in Kabul under the banner called the Taliban. Pakistan will always want to do what they know best—playing both sides of the coin.

Money Will Never Solve the Problem; Perhaps It Will [Only] Make It Worse

BESIDES TIME, ASIDE FROM ROCKS, sand, and opium (the only items the Afghans really have to sell), throughout history Afghanistan has always had the most corrupt government. Unfortunately, in recent years, it has been worse because we in the West have permitted it to happen. According to the local population, corruption was down to zero under the Taliban's rule. Imagine how much the British might have spent from the 1800s to the early 1900s; the Soviets in the late 1900s kept buying time but never stayed in Afghanistan. Is the U.S. going to do the same?

Our money-giving strategy to fix the problem in Afghanistan will not succeed this time around, either. I am in no way saying we can achieve any/everything without money. The amount of money the West puts into Afghanistan trying to build its infrastructure left Afghanistan long before our troops started leaving—just like every leader of Afghanistan who, with the West's support, was lucky enough to escape. In other words, none of the Afghan leaders stayed in Afghanistan once they no longer had power. The only reason they were in power to begin with was the *time* the West paid for, of which Afghanistan took full advantage. Those who followed their money and made it out of Afghanistan alive, were considered the lucky ones; while all the others, who could not make it out alive, were assassinated right after, or immediately afterward, they no longer had their power.

If there ever is a higher learning institution to teach corruption, it will be the University of the Afghanistan Presidential Palace (ARG), which will issue their masters' degrees in corruption. If only one third of the 34 million approximated population of Afghanistan lives in major cities like Kabul, Kandahar, Mazar, and Herat, who would benefit from international donations for their personal Western lavish lifestyle at the expense of the other two thirds who are still living in 14th century mud huts? How can we in the West say that we're helping the Afghans, when we're really not?

The higher the rank in the Afghan government, the larger the amount that is stolen from the Afghan population. Kabul Bank became a symbol of the country's deep-rooted corruption when $1 billion went missing during a 2010 investigation. Established in 2004, the Kabul Bank is a commercial bank in Afghanistan, with its main branch located in Kabul's capital. It is also the main bank used to pay the salaries of the Afghan Army and Security Forces. The bank is under the supervision of Da Afghanistan Bank, which is the central bank of Afghanistan, involved in a major financial scandal in 2010 when its chairman, Sher Khan Farnood, and others were spending the bank's $1 billion for their own personal, lavish lifestyles, as well as lending (as loans) money under the table to relatives and friends.

In September 2010, one of the principal owners of the bank said that depositors had withdrawn $180 million in two days, and he predicted a "revolution" in the country's financial system, unless the United States and the Afghan government moved quickly to stabilize the bank. Apparently, Mr. Farnood had been to the school of cronyism and knew how to play the game.

Farnood, an Ethnic Uzbek, who was the chairman of Kabul Bank, also owned one of Afghanistan's private airlines (Pamir Airway), in partnership with Kahlilullah Fruzi and Mohammed Fahim, the latter of whom was also the vice president of Afghanistan. As you may recall, before becoming the vice president of Afghanistan, Mr. Fahim spent most of his adult life in the mountains of Pajshir under the command of the Tajik leader, Ahmad Shah Masoud, shooting rockets toward Kabul, killing his fellow Tajiks who were too poor to leave Kabul but simply wanted to survive their day-to-day lives. Fahim is not in power because of his intellectual knowledge of anything; he is in power because of his all-Tajik militia fighters controlling Kabul, all of whom are afraid of Karzai. Both Karzai and Fahim would steal from those same people that they and every other government official call "Fellow Afghans"; but they're not Afghans—they're poor Pashtons, Tajiks, Hazaras, and Uzbeks. Karzai, Fahim, and everyone else in the government are Afghans who keep everything to and for themselves.

By November 2010, the Afghanistan bank removed Farnood and Fruzi, and in 2011 both were effectively under house arrest (which prevented them from stealing at least until the dust settled). As far as their educational backgrounds are concerned, Farnood received his education and started a business in Moscow, Russia. During the 1980s and 1990s, he ran a *hawala* (an informal money transfer) organization in Moscow. The hawala was reportedly transferred to Tajikistan and Afghanistan by heroin and opium smugglers. In 1998, Russian authorities closed down the hawala because of money laundering and its role in the transfer of drug money. Farnood, who had left Russia shortly beforehand, escaped arrest. He operated in Russia under the name of "Sherhan Mohammad Morad," and became a prominent poker player, taking part in the 2008 World Series of Poker Europe (WSOPE). He also owned a number of villas under his name on Palm Jumeirah in Dubai, UAE, just like Jabar did—and you remember Jabar, right?

In early 2010, the Kabul Bank, with its ties to the Karzai family and questionable practices, played a part in the enriched politically and connected insiders, dismaying the Afghan population during the process. Despite the billions of American taxpayer dollars given to the Afghan government (which was unaccounted for), we are still turning blind eyes to this ongoing problem of the Kabul Bank's crisis that has jeopardized up to $1.8 billion in foreign aid earmarked for Afghanistan. The bank's reserves were even being looted, with officials recovering less than 10 percent of nearly $1 billion that went missing.

Another one of the Afghan government officials' corruption cases involved missing medicine from the Afghanistan Defense Ministry, who said they would be investigating the missing medicines and pharmaceutical supplies that had been donated by the U.S. for its Army and police. The Ministry said they would assess and investigate how much was missing from the $42 million worth of medical supplies that the U.S. had donated. According to the Afghan Defense Minister, General Abdul Rahim Wardak, an investigation into the issue had been launched, and Surgeon General Ahmad Zia Yaftali had been removed from his post as part of the inquiry. Wardak also said that three officials from the country's top medical facility, Dawood National Military Hospital in Kabul, had been fired. They're probably in Dubai.

It's unclear just how much has disappeared from the medical goods the U.S. has donated. U.S. officials say they do not account for the supplies after delivering them to the Afghans. The Americans have repeatedly urged Karzai to root out government corruption to show that his administration can be a true partner in reestablishing control over the country's assets. Karzai was asked by the Americans to root out corruption; however, many anticorruption campaigns have stalled, and Karzai has also blocked an investigation into high-level aids supposedly accepting bribes. No kidding; is that right? It is not clear whether Yaftali was involved in misappropriating medicines, Wardak said. "Once the investigation is finalized, we will know." Yaftali denied the accusations of corruption, saying medicines disappeared before making it to his department and had shown up in pharmacies. Doesn't that tell us that the person lower in rank than Mr. Wardak has beat him into it? He suggested contractors providing the supplies could be to blame, along with the U.S. advisers he said entered into the contract. Yaftali indicated that he was possibly removed because of ethnic issues (i.e., he's an ethnic Tajik). He did not provide any details on why that would be an issue. He claimed he was the eighth ethnic Tajik general who had been removed from his position in the past three months, and that none of the others had received a new post.

In another corruption case, a road that was paid for was never built. I have seen this road and driven on it during my time in Ghazni Province. Sometimes, it's very difficult for people to believe what they read, but when you've been there and then you read about it, it's enough to make you believe that the truth is being told about the story from the frontline.

It was like reading the newspaper story about my buddies Sean, Mark, and Matt during our combat fight during which Sean and the ANP officers were both wounded in Ghazni. Following is how U.S. Navy Commander Tristan Rizzi told the story:

"Heading back from a remote section of Ghazni Province, Rizzi radioed his base in eastern Afghanistan and said he wanted to take a slight detour. He had his Chinook helicopter fly over the site of the long-stalled, U.S.-financed road project on which the Afghan contractor had pledged repeatedly to resume work. From the air, Rizzi saw a vacant site and no sign of the contractors. Once on the ground, he dialed one of them from a cellphone and asked where they were. The contactor said they were working on the road. Rizzi replied, 'No, you're not.'"

Two weeks later, alleging corruption and theft, U.S. officials in Ghazni terminated the $10 million road contract, putting themselves at odds with powerful governors whose coalition forces had hoped would be a key ally. Well, this is another example of our government's neglect of not knowing who our allies really are; treating every Afghan official as our ally can be destructive, especially while they are stealing from us under our very noses. We really do not have any allies in Afghanistan—except for money, which is the only thing allies (i.e., the so-called Afghans) understand.

From 2008 to 2010, the U.S. government paid $4 million to RWA—a [implied] consortium of corrupt Afghan contractors—only to see it pave less than two thirds of a mile on a road that was supposed to stretch 17.5 miles. The contractor said the area had become too violent, but U.S. and Afghan provincial officials think two of the principals fled with much of the cash to New Zealand or the Netherlands.

At first, I was confused by how U.S. officials described the Ghazni affair in positive terms, but I guess when the Afghan contractors steal $4 million of the American taxpayers' money, it's probably a good thing compared to the billions that have been stolen and mostly invested in Dubai. Americans were happy that they saved the $6 million that remained on the contract for other projects, terminated RWA's existing contract, and blackballed it from future work. They say they're now ready to cooperate with Afghan investigators, if they decide to pursue legal action against RWA. My question to those who are seeking legal action against any government officials in Afghanistan is: What does "legal action" really mean? House arrests in Dubai?

As far as I know, I can say that there is no other legal action besides bribing the Afghan officials, because that's the only law they understand, and even then, we'll be throwing good money after bad (which is already missing). Even before the failed road project, RWA was notorious in Ghazni because one of its principals, Ghulam Seddiq Rassuli, served jail time approximately three years prior. According to Afghan intelligence officials, the Taliban ambushed one of Rassuli's construction teams, and his security guards fired back indiscriminately, killing at least one civilian. U.S. officials, who have awarded Rassuli multiple construction contracts, apparently were unaware of his legal difficulties. As the U.S. led military coalition plans to directly control the nation's security to Afghan forces by the end of 2014, American diplomats and military officials say they're trying to clean up a contracting system in which hundreds of millions of dollars meant for reconstruction were misspent or given to unsavory characters. U.S. government funding for at least 15 large-scale Afghan programs and projects ballooned from more than $1 billion to nearly $3 billion, despite questions about their effectiveness or cost.

If the Afghans who were hired to help the Americans understood the Afghan culture and told nothing but lies or sold every piece of fabricated information just to get paid, then how could the Americans or the West in general really understand the Afghan culture?

Here is what General McChrystal, a one-time leading commander in Afghanistan said regarding Afghanistan (a statement that I wholeheartedly support). "We didn't know enough, and we still don't know enough. Most of us, me included, had a very superficial understanding of the situation and history, and we had a frightening simplistic view of recent history the last 50 years." U.S. Forces did not know the country's languages and didn't make 'an effective effort to learn them.'" The General hit the nail right on its proverbial head! In addition to my agreement with him, I also believe everything in society is about directly communicating with people you want to understand and vice versa. In Afghanistan, it is more difficult for the Pashtons, Tajiks, Hazaras, and Uzbeks to understand and get along with each other, let alone understand the Westerners who have been running through their villages for the past decade, which is why violence has continued to increase.

Another one of Karzai's inner circles of cronies that led to a major investigation into an influential Afghan governor accused of taking bribes, has been shut down and its top prosecutor transferred to a unit that doesn't handle corruption cases. With the closing of the investigation into the former Governor of Kapisa Province, Ghulam Qawis Abu Bakr, substantive corruption prosecutions were taking place in Afghanistan, despite President Hamid Karzai's pledge to root out graft. How can it be possible for Karzai to root himself out of power to save the country when he doesn't even love or care about its growth and prosperity? Abu Bakr's instigation raises the troubling question yet again about how much of the U.S. taxpayers' money is lining the pockets of powerful Afghan officials. It also raises the question of whether the U.S. is doing all it can to persuade

Karzai to crack down on corruption and suggests that the lax prosecution of corruption has pervaded all levels of government. The Americans had hoped that the case would be the first conviction of a relatively significant person in the Afghan government. While most of Abu Bakr's influences are in Kapisa Province, he is also connected to the Hizb-e-Islami political party, which the government has been trying to court with the hope of getting the group to cut its ties with militants.

Nothing changes; only the fee for bribes goes higher by 20 to 40 percent for the government officials to stay out of prison and be kept under house arrest, and those fees are passed along to the poor villagers. Since the U.S. and our allies want to understand Karzai's government better, they shouldn't pay anymore of our taxpayer dollars to Karzai's government. There are approximately 2,000 cases under investigation by the anticorruption unit since its birth in 2009 which have been stalled, and the 28 convictions so far have all been minor players. This might have been because the 28 were convicted just to show the donor countries some kind of system for political reasons, and to the U.S. officials that there is some progress; the convicted criminals are probably out of prison through the backdoor for a much lower bribe to the guards. Most of those convicted and released are already bidding on other governmental contracts for road, clinic, or bridge projects, under another one of their fake names that are funded by U.S. aid. From top to bottom, the people who are involved are ranging from lawmakers to warlords, who are systematically blocking cases. They have infiltrated the attorney general's office—but, remind me again, who does the attorney general work for? The answer, of course, is obvious.

Every time Karzai makes a promise to the American taxpayers, just like every other promise he has made, little has come of them, especially after the fraud that marred the 2009 election during which he rooted our graft as one of his priorities. In fact, a corruption scandal in the interim involving the country's largest private bank has incriminated a number of Karzai allies, including relatives.

The first evidence that corruption was not being taken seriously in the attorney general's office came in the summer of 2010, when a Karzai aide was arrested on charges of accepting a car in exchange for his help in thwarting off a corruption case. Karzai ordered the release of the aide, Mohammad Zia Salehi. Because of the onslaught of negative publicity, Attorney General Mohammad Ishaq Aloko ordered his prosecutors not to discuss details of their cases with U.S. officials who were advising them, saying that if they did, they would be considered U.S. spies—this from an Afghan official who worked in the anticorruption unit.

The case against Abu Bakr's allegations surfaced when he received a $200,000 bribe in exchange for the contract to build a cell tower. Abu Bakr lives in a large house in Mahmud-I-Raqi, the capital of Kapisa Province. He has three other houses in Kabul, all built, according to the original witness statements, with stone and gravel paid for by foreign donations intended for roads, schools, and clinics. These people in the Afghan government who we Americans support have no shame whatsoever. One person who works for the Afghan government is capable of buying four houses with the money donated, while two thirds of the Afghans go to bed hungry. How can humans be so cruel to other humans, perhaps even their own fellow countrymen. Well, the answer is very simple in the case of those who claim to be Afghans. There is a difference between being one and claiming to be one. To be an American or an Afghan, one must be born a naturalized citizen, speak the language of the land, and live physically within the borders of that land. Likewise, the same is true for any other country and its citizens. Most foreigners I know personally, and especially the Afghan community in America, do not consider themselves Americans. They hold American citizenship and take advantage of all the benefits America has to offer, but consider themselves to be whatever country they came from, much like that young MP woman I met in Khost who was wearing a U.S. Military uniform, even though her allegiance was to Afghanistan.

My father-in-law has lived in the United States for more than 25 years. Every time I see him, the most common thing to come out of his mouth, in Farsi, is, *"Hitch cheazze inja ba watan na may rasa."* ("Nothing here can be as good as those of our homeland.") What he means is that everything here in America is not as good as it was in his homeland. Remember my fellow linguist I had a conversation with regarding fruit upon our arrival in Afghanistan? Well, it's a pattern with all those who claim to be Afghans.

Just like the linguist, one day I had no choice but to confront my father-in-law and tell him that he should go back to Afghanistan if he likes it there so much. (That was when my mother-in-law was still alive.) His excuse then was that he didn't want to leave her behind, and I could understand that, but I also knew in my heart that he would never, ever trade America to go back and live in Afghanistan. Well, my mother-in-law passed away in 2009, but he is still here in the U.S. and considers himself an Afghan and that his beloved Afghanistan is the best place on the face of the earth, while he has never contributed even one iota to the well-being of his native land. Nor did he make the journey to go back to his homeland that he says he loves so much. I consider him to be one of those men who has no identity, while living in one country where he can use every benefit that country has to offer and yet still consider himself a citizen of his native land where he doesn't like to live.

Corruption will *always* exist in Afghanistan. Of course, corruption can and does exist everywhere; it is not exclusive to Afghanistan. Some face more corruption than others, but in the case of Afghanistan, the U.S.'s money is corrupting them even more. Just to add to the circles of Karzai's cronies, as I was told by many villagers in Arghandab during one of my visits there, Assadullah Aka specifically told me that the people of Kandahar City were sick and tired of the treatment they were receiving, not only from the mayor of the city but the governor of the province as well. Both were handpicked by Karzai and brought in from America. I vividly recall what Assadullah Aka told me, as he held my chin with his thumb and folded index finger as if I had a beard, which in the Kandahari culture is a guarantee of whatever comment he was going to make would happen. He told me that either the mayor or the governor would be killed if they kept treating the poor shopkeepers in the city of Kanadahar the way they were. When I asked him why he was making such a prediction, he responded that the governor, mayor, and the president's brother would eventually be killed if they didn't stop harassing the people in the city by taking away their land and selling it to developers who are all somehow related to Karzai's inner-circle of cronies. As noted earlier, most of the Durrani tribes would try to take away all the rights to the useable land from the poor Ghalzis in and around Kandahar City and Province. It has been done for centuries, which is exactly what Assadullah Aka's argument was during our meeting in the village of Ali Kaley.

Since becoming president in 2001, Hamid Karzai tried in vain to lure his old friends to Afghanistan for political positions. One of those friends, Mr. Hamidi, happened to be the mayor of Kandahar City. He was a naturalized U.S. citizen who had come to Afghanistan at the request of Karzai to take a post as the Mayor of Kandahar. According to the *Stars and Stripes*, in late July of 2011 a suicide bomber killed Mr. Hamidi.

The extent that Assadullah Aka knew about the politics of Kandahar City was unknown to me at that time, but as time passed I realized that because of the unhappiness of most Afghan villagers, our cause in Afghanistan had become a tremendous struggle. The report in *Stars and Stripes* also read that Mr. Hamidi had brought a "reformer's zeal" to the job. He demanded payment of delinquent taxes from storeowners; if they rebuffed him, he ordered that their shops be razed. He required developers to make space for parking and bathrooms in their building plans and ousted tribal leaders who illegally occupied public lands. His call to modernize the city spurred the building of schools, roads, and sidewalks.

I would have agreed with the mayor for his vision of bringing modernization to the city of Kandahar, and especially schools which I am a huge supporter of; unfortunately, one thing he skipped was doing his homework about the land that he was taking away from the shopkeepers who had worked in that city all their lives and had gone through wars, including the Soviet invasion, and many other hardships too numerous to mention. It didn't make any sense why their land would be taken by those who are not even considered to be Afghans when they had left Afghanistan during its hardships (e.g., like the Soviet's invasion).

To those who left Afghanistan because of the Soviet invasion, and those like myself who left Afghanistan a year before the invasion occurred, what gives us the right to go back to our native land and dictate anything to its people? I didn't leave Afghanistan because of the hardship of war, but rather because of my biological family's history of immigrating to the United States and England in the late '50s, '60s, and '70s when Afghanistan was the most prosperous and peaceful according to all Afghans who worked for the government and all who exiled to the West to simply ignore the problem of Afghanistan that they didn't want to deal with while being invaded by the Soviets. And, to my knowledge—at least as far back as I can remember—none of my uncles or my biological father had ever worked for the Afghan government.

The *Stars and Stripes* further reported that Mr. Hamidi's ties to the Karzai family, including Ahmad Wali Karzai, the president's half-brother and powerful provincial chairman of Kandahar, sparked accusations of influence peddling. Criticism about Hamidi's role in transferring public lands to Mahmoud Karzai, another of the president's brothers, and private developers close to the family, reached a crescendo during the first half of the year (2011). Tensions climaxed on July 12, 2011, when a member of Hamidi's security detail gunned down Ahmad Wali Karzai.

Because of their loss, I can personally feel the pain and frustration that Hamidi's family went through. At the same time, I also felt the pain of those poor shopkeepers who were out there trying to provide for their families in every bazar in Ghazni, Paktika, and Kandahar, where none of them had anything positive to say about any of Afghanistan's government officials.

What right do we American Afghans have to tell them how they should be running their daily lives? Answer: none. For example, just like the shopkeepers who had been harassed either by the new rules of the mayor in Kandahar City regarding the modernization of the city by bulldozing their shacks on the side of the streets or any other shopkeepers I have met throughout Afghanistan who are being harassed by the Afghan government officials. If the only thing those shopkeepers knew was that no one ever collected taxes from them before, what would make us think that a mayor who had just arrived from America was trying to implement the rules for modernization in a city where there are no rules?

If the city officials are trying to enforce their rules over the poor shopkeepers, wouldn't the shopkeepers have the right to expect some sort of security from those same people who are collecting taxes? Answer: of course. But, instead, the government officials steal from them by way of bribes or taking their land and selling it to the developer who happens to be the president's brother.

The reason why the rules of law would not work in Afghanistan overnight, especially using the manner in which the mayor of Kandahar was enforcing it, will only work with the passage of time. For example, what if a blind person who has never seen the light of day regained his eyesight for the first time? Wouldn't it be better for that blind person to open his eyes gradually so that his eyesight would not be blinded by the light that he has never seen before and, therefore, to which his eyes are unaccustomed? Well, obviously. So, by the same token, shouldn't the strategy of making people pay real estate taxes, whether that person is a shopkeeper or any other citizen who has never paid taxes in the past, be enforced gradually, with the understanding of what benefit it will provide for the shopkeepers and the citizens of a state with a new government that is attempting to impose new rules?

I have another corruption case to mention, this time in Washington D.C. According to the Justice Department, a federal grand jury has indicted two men for allegedly trying to bribe a U.S. Army contracting official with $1 million to win a road construction project in Afghanistan,. Rohullah Farooqi Lodin of Irvine, California, and Hashmatullah Farooqi of New York City, New York, are each charged with one count of conspiracy to defraud and commit an offense against the U.S. and one count of attempting to bribe a public official. The indictment, filed in federal court in Virginia, alleges that the men offered $1 million in bribes to an Army captain, who is not named in the court documents. In exchange, the officer was to help disqualify lower bidders to build a road in Logar Province and award the project to two general contracting firms in Afghanistan. Lodin and Farooqi allegedly claimed to represent the companies, so each submitted $18 million bids for the work. The road contract was to be paid for out of an account called the Commander's Emergency Response Program (CERP) that has been vulnerable to waste and fraud. The investigation was handled by the FBI, the U.S. Army Criminal Investigation Division, the Special Inspector General for Afghanistan reconstruction, and the Defense Criminal Investigation Service (DCIS).

Corruption is not the only factor that is derailing our efforts to succeed in Afghanistan, which is contributing to the world's other major problems that Afghanistan has been contributing to for decades: the opium that Afghanistan is producing. According to the U.N., revenue from opium production soared by 133 percent in 2011 to about $1.4 billion or approximately one-tenth of the country's GDP. Since definitive statistics are difficult to obtain in Afghanistan, just like the population numbers are not accurate, it might be more, both in the case of opium and the population. But opium is a significant part of the Afghan economy and provides not only considerable funding to terrorism, but it also fuels corruption. Income from opium finances weapons and equipment purchases for the Taliban. Afghanistan provides around 90 percent of the world's opium, the raw ingredient for heroin. Most of the opium from land-locked Afghanistan is shipped through Iran and Pakistan.

Since the whole world certainly is aware that Afghanistan is providing 90 percent of the world's opium, I have a question for the U.N. officials: Instead of the U.N. reminding us over and over again about something we already know, why doesn't it do something about the problem, instead of calling for a stronger commitment from the Afghan government and international partners? In my opinion, in 1979 Dubai had learned a valuable lesson from the Iranian revolution and the Soviet invasion of Afghanistan; but, trouble has its bright side for some at the expense of others. In this particular case, the poor Pashtons, Tajiks, Hazaras, and Uzbeks, who are being victims of the Afghans and those who support them, must wait.

Frightened by the chaos in their own countries, Iranian and Afghan traders moved to Dubai, taking with them their businesses, thereby bolstering the local economy. Since there was neither income nor sales tax, Dubai steadily developed a reputation as being a safe place in the Middle East to keep your money. Since 1979, Dubai has always prospered during a regional crisis (one country's sufferings become another country's prosperity). Isn't that what the Afghan government is doing today when taking all the donated money that was intended for all of Afghanistan, not just the one third's lavish lifestyle in Dubai? To make matters even worse, since 2001 when the war in Afghanistan started, the city of Dubai expanded to double its size during the prior decade, which is exactly when, during the decade of the 1980 cultivation of the opium poppy, it had skyrocketed by more than 1,000 percent within the first year of Afghanistan's occupation. It was not long before the Taliban was rearming itself by taxing the opium harvest. Attempts by Western governments and agencies to limit the poppy harvests continue to be an abysmal failure.

Afghanistan's Mines Minister, Mohammad Ibrahim Adel, whose name, in both Pashto and Farsi, means "honest." Nonetheless, he took an estimated $30 million in bribes to award the development of the Aynak copper reserves to a Chinese firm. The state-owned China Metallurgical Group received a contract for a U.S. $2.9 billion project to mine copper from the Aynak project. The bribes were paid to Adel in Dubai, so he could keep the cash there.

Speaking of Dubai, for the Afghans, it's always happy hour there when Afghanistan's natural resources have been sold by the Afghan government officials' personal greed to another corrupt government official of the Chinese. Why did Adel sign a contract with the Chinese in Dubai? Well, aside from happy hours, he could: (1) keep the $30 million in bribes he received from the Chinese in his bank account in Dubai, and (2) he didn't want to put the contracts out for bids for other Western countries who probably would have paid more for the contracts. I'm guessing, too, that Adel would probably not have received the $30 million that he wanted if he'd put the contract out for bids, and at the same time he probably sold the contract to the Chinese because he didn't put it out for bids from the remaining Western nations. Obviously, Adel was not looking out for the benefits of the two thirds' ordinary people in Afghanistan. He was only looking out for his own self-interests and those of Karzai, his boss. (As an aside, why would the Chinese government get away with such a corrupt business "transaction"? And how many Chinese soldiers have sacrificed their lives for the freedom of the people of Afghanistan?)

Just like the Afghan government, Chinese companies might not be subject to a Chinese version of the U.S. foreign corruption practices. China is in a position to dominate the future development of the Afghan mining and natural resources sector. Their firms can package their tenders to include what Western countries refer to as "foreign aid." The Chinese way of doing business is the same as the Afghan way. Why would one even think otherwise? I don't believe that the Chinese support the kind of open and transparent democratic capitalism that the international community would agree is essential to building Afghanistan, or even to engage the support of the people. Most of this corruption has occurred when Karzai's Western allies, including the Obama Administration, pressed Karzai to root out corruption. It was Karzai's second term for his reelection campaign in August of 2009 when he was indeed reelected for a second term. But, ever since, corruption has continued and, not too surprisingly, has even become more deeply widespread and deeply rooted in his administration.

Karzai talks through both sides of his mouth at the same time, depending on who he's meeting with and how much money is involved comes first before he says anything. If he is angry about the Americans because his last paycheck had too many deductions, he would simply tell the Pakistanis that he is their brother, and if America ever went to war with Pakistan, he would defend Pakistan. Likewise, if he were to be angry with the Pakistanis because they didn't deliver on their promise to send the Taliban to attack American bases to "stir things up" so that both Pakistan and Karzai would benefit from it while innocent Americans died, he would be very displeased and angry. Now, if Karzai is angry with America and Pakistan at the same time, he would then sign all the natural resources contracts with China. How can one be trusted if he caters to everyone around him in a form other than that in which he believes? For example, in one of Karzai's many debriefings to ask the U.S. and the international community for more funding for his corrupt government, he said, "The ten-year occupation by the U.S.-led international coalition forces has brought 'political stability to Afghanistan.'" He went on to say that the U.S.-led occupation and the Afghan government had failed to "provide the Afghan people with their own individual and personal security." What does he mean by that? I don't know, either, but I will ask this: Who was proving his own personal security to bring him to where he is today? The only failure the U.S. coalition has done is supporting Karzai's government, and as long as the U.S. and its allies support his government, the security of the Afghan people will always be in jeopardy.

In one of his interviews in October of 2011, on the Pakistani GEO television network, Karzai said, "God forbid, if ever there is a war between Pakistan and the U.S., Afghanistan will side with Pakistan." He went on to say, "If Pakistan is attacked by either the U.S. or India, and if the people of Pakistan need Afghanistan's help, as a brother, Afghanistan will be there to help them."

I have so many questions for Karzai, most of which are primarily from the poor villagers that Karzai could not care less about, let alone consider helping them. If I ever got the chance to ask him just one question, it would be: How can you support Pakistan if you can't even support yourself without the help of the U.S and its allies?

Not too long after pledging his allegiance to Pakistan, Karzai changed his position. I have to wonder if Karzai or anyone in his administration is aware that two thirds of the Afghan population use Pakistani currency because they value it more than their own Afghan currency. During my time in Afghanistan, of the people we detained, almost 80 percent carried Pakistani currency. Likewise, every shopkeeper in Yah Khel and most people in Ghazni used Pakistani currency for their purchase of goods.

Karzai and the majority of his government officials can say anything they want regarding Pakistan, but reality will never change Pakistan's influence over the Afghan population, and it also proves that Karzai and his administration are out-of-touch with their own people. Most Afghans will tell you that Afghanistan has such a rich history dating back 5,000 years. I would agree with them, but only as far as the two thirds of the Afghan population I've met throughout the remote villages of Afghanistan are concerned.

Another question I would have for the Afghan government is: If Pakistan, as a nation, has less than 70 years of history, and most of the people in Afghanistan are using Pakistani currency, then what benefit is there for the 5,000-year-old, rich history that Afghanistan claims to have, besides fighting amongst themselves? To my knowledge, no one in Afghanistan has used Afghanistan's other neighbors' (e.g., Iran, Uzbekistan, Tajikistan, Turkmenistan, and China's) currency. Afghanistan can be as old as the Afghans claim it to be, but what benefit is there to society or the Afghans themselves from an aging Afghanistan? Furthermore, it's not the actual physical location of a land that's important—it's the people of that land who make that location valuable. Physically and geographically, I believe the world is created by one God. It's important to know that the people of one particular part of the world represent their part of the world for what it is.

Karzai's February 16–17, 2012, visit to Islamabad, Pakistan, wasn't a very pleasant one because the president confronted the Pakistani leadership, demanding that it produce the Taliban officials to partake in peace talks and come to an understanding about the distrust between Kabul and Islamabad that stood in the way of a deal to end the decade-long Afghan conflict. Karzai's frustration boiled over with Pakistan when it was accused of harboring the Taliban. His language and tone of voice flared so much, the Pakistani prime minister paused the meeting. After a break, top officials, including Karzai, reconvened for a smaller meeting after a rocky start to his two-day visit to Islamabad. Just like a vegetarian would order a salad, or a meat lover would order steak, peace talks depend on the neighbors being able to cooperate, but Karzai long demanded that Pakistan bring the leadership of the Taliban to the table, including their chief, Mullah Omar, to negotiate with him, a stance that shocked the Pakistanis.

This is what I meant when I said earlier that Karzai would talk from both sides of his mouth, even in a single conversation. At one point, apparently directing his remarks to foreign Minister Hina Rabbani Khar, Karzai asked, "Would you be willing to stop girls studying in schools and universities in Pakistan?" Does anyone take Karzai serious? I don't, but I can understand him. All I need to do is take the words coming out of his mouth at any given time and apply the opposite meaning to them. For substantiation, I'll use one of the Afghans' own phrases that is common: If Karzai said milk is white, you must know that milk is black. One has to wonder why Karzai would go to Pakistan, trying to convince them to be the mediator in the negotiations between Karzai and the Taliban, especially if Karzai doesn't even like the way the Taliban has taken Afghanistan back to the Dark Ages by stopping girls from attending schools and banning women from working.

In this meeting, Karzai wasn't an ally to anybody; he was simply a master of his bad habits involving corruption, which he will continue to do as long as he remains president. While Karzai is talking from both sides of his mouth, there are American and coalition soldiers contributing and dying as they try to protect Afghanistan's prosperity. As of today (at this writing: July 11, 2012), there have been 2,041 American casualties and 1,034 of our allies' casualties. At the same time, Karzai's government had signed a deal with China's state-owned National Petroleum Corporation (NPC), allowing it to become the first foreign company to exploit the country's oil and natural gas reserves.

Maybe our leaders in Washington don't get the concept of the Chinese involvement in Afghanistan, but I can tell you that even the Taliban knows that the next battle of fighting for their children and grandchildren will be with the Chinese, according to one of the detainees I had interrogated. But that would be a huge mistake on the part of Afghanistan for two reasons: (1) the Chinese would not be as nice as the Americans, and (2) since the Chinese are right next door with a population of more than 1.3 billion, they can simply walk over Afghanistan without difficulty—just like the Mongols did eight centuries ago.

America's Sacrifices, Not Only to My Native People, But All Other Human Races As Well

IN ADDITION TO ALL OF THE courageous, compassionate, and brave soldiers I had the honor and opportunity to work with, there were countless others whose stories will always bring tears to my eyes as I read about them in the military newspapers at the DFAC. Americans of all walks of life have left their families and jobs to serve their country, while trying to help my native people at the same time—selfless men and women in our military, just like the story of Chief Warrant Officer 3 Jason LaCrosse, in the *Stars and Stripes*' December 14, 2010, article; or the story of others who were recognized with Silver Stars for their bravery in the December 7, 2011 edition.

It was the worst battle for the German forces since World War II: Eight German soldiers were severely injured in an ambush by an estimated 200 Taliban forces on April 2, 2010, outside the city of Kunduz in northern Afghanistan. Three of the men later died because of their wounds. But the death toll could have been even higher had it not been for a group of U.S. soldiers, who were part of an Army Medical Evacuation Unit, being in the area: Eight of them from the 5th Battalion, 158th Aviation Regiment, were recognized for their effort at a ceremony in Katterbach, Germany; one man, Chief Warrant Officer 3 Jason LaCrosse, received a Silver Star for his bravery, and seven others were awarded the Distinguished Flying Cross. As indicated, LaCrosse was awarded the Silver Star—the U.S. military's third-highest medal for combat heroism. The fellow members of his unit honored during the ceremony were Captain Robert McDonough, Chief Warrant Officer 3 Nelson Visaya, Chief Warrant Officer 2 Jason Brown, Staff Sergeant Travis Brown, Sergeant Steven Shumaker, and Sergeant Antonio Gattis, all of whom were awarded the Distinguished Flying Cross, which is given to service members who have distinguished themselves by heroism or by an extraordinary achievement while participating in an aerial fight. Earlier that year, Spc. Matthew Baker and Spc. Gregory Martinez were awarded the German Gold Cross of Honor by the German government. The award is Germany's highest for valor; and, it was the first time foreign troops were so honored.

The ambush took place when the Taliban opened fire on the German soldiers, who were on a mission to clear a roadside bomb in the Chahar Darah District, southwest of Kunduz. The fighting raged for hours, and LaCrosse and his men were called on to evacuate the wounded. I'm guessing that this must have been the same kind of situation when Captain Alfa called for medics to evacuate Delta and the wounded ANP officer that Sunday night on Memorial Day weekend in the Qarah Bagh District of Ghazni Province.

The report went on to claim that Master Sergeant Patrick Bonneik, a German joint terminal attack controller, called for assistance. He recalled after the medal ceremony that he was worried that the landing zone was too hot for the U.S. medical evacuation crew. The first time the rescue helicopters came in for a landing, the area came under immediate, intense fire. "I thought [the pilot] was going to fly away," Bonneik said. "But he sat the chopper down on the hot landing zone with bullets ricocheting off the helicopter from every direction. By flying in, he saved at least three more of his comrades."

On the second landing, the pilots were given the option of an alternate landing zone that was farther from the wounded but under less enemy fire. The pilots didn't want to waste any time, however. "As I told him that I had an alternate landing zone," Bonneik said, remembering his conversation with the U.S. pilots, "his response was, 'You know what, buddy? The first landing zone was cold enough for me.'" This is what America is all about! The pilot was, of course, talking with LaCrosse when he continued. "Allied troops on the ground are injured, and if we don't get them to a hospital, they're going to die, and I'm not going to allow that to happen."

As I am writing this book, just as I had seen it on the battlefield, the emotion is overwhelming as the tears stream down my cheeks, dropping inches away from my computer's keyboard—all the while also giving me chills and the joy for being so lucky and fortunate to be an American.

Since I am very familiar with the stories when it comes to courage, compassion, and bravery, a similar story about the Special Forces was written a year later. The report stated that when Captain David Fox regained consciousness, shortly after a massive roadside bomb had been detonated nearby, the only words his comrades down the mountainside could understand on the radio were: "Urgent...surgical!" That was enough. After hearing their commander's muffled radio message and seeing a plume of black smoke billowing high above the ridgeline in Kapisa Province, Fox's men sprang into action. Under heavy enemy fire, Sergeant 1st Class McKenna Miller, Staff Sergeant Matthew Gassman, and another of their members, Miller, began a desperate climb up the mountain. According to their medal citations, they then made the harrowing journey back down, one carrying an injured Afghan soldier, another a dead French trooper, and the third providing cover for them all the way.

Fox, Gassman, and Miller, all of the 1st Battalion, 10th Special Forces Group in Stuttgart, were pinned with Silver Stars during a ceremony at the U.S. European Command headquarters, Patch Barracks. "These are not obscure actions and dusty stories in a book somewhere," said Major General Michael Repass, Commander of the Special Forces Operations Command, Europe. "These are real-life friends, neighbors, teammates, people that we know." This is exactly what I had experienced during my time with Special Forces, when I was told that all 18 of them would die first before I did. Needless to say, I took that to heart because it made me stronger as a person and a patriot of America.

The report further stated that two other soldiers were honored: According to his medal citation, Staff Sergeant Jeffery Musgrave received a Bronze Star Medal with a "V" for valor for his actions during deployment in Wardak Province in 2010. Musgrave, despite being wounded three times in the arm, repeatedly left the safety of covered positions to fire on the enemy and ensure that his team gained the upper-hand in the fight. Spc. Willie Smith was honored for bravery while in a garrison. Smith, an administrator assigned to the 1–10, received the Soldier's Medal for helping rescue an elderly couple from a burning building earlier that year in

Boblingen, Germany. "They are casual heroes who walk humbly among us," Repass said. "We have the opportunity to recognize their actions publicly, because the truth is—and we all know this—they would never tell this story. So we'll tell it for them."

It had been nearly one year since the December 17, 2010, battle for which Fox, Miller, and Gassman were recognized by receiving Silver Stars. During the nearly three-hour battle, the Green Berets (a.k.a.: Special Forces) repeatedly exposed themselves to enemy fire. Not only were they fighting for each other, but they were also protecting their French and Afghan comrades. "Anybody we go on missions with is going to come back," Fox said. "It's not an option to leave someone out there." In an interview, the men recalled the chaos and danger. "You're just going on instinct and detaching yourself from what's going on around you," Fox said. "You go into autopilot," Gassman added. After the mountaintop IED blast, which killed the French trooper, critically injured an Afghan commander, and knocked Fox unconscious, enemy fire poured in all around the men, who were scouting potential checkpoint locations in the remote Tagab District. From the start of the operation, the men had been under heavy enemy and sniper fire. However, "the number of fighters the team faced eventually grew from 10 to more than 70," Fox said. "We were essentially surrounded," he added.

When the explosion occurred, Gassman knew Fox and his comrades were in trouble and began the nearly vertical climb, scaling hand over foot several hundred feet of mountain as enemy rounds landed all around him, he said. Once he reached the top, Gassman realized he was too far south, so he raced back down the mountain and climbed up again. Reaching the team, he began to administer first-aid to the injured Afghan commander. "Once you get up there, you just get to work," Gassman said. During the descent, Gassman carried the Afghan through enemy fire to a landing zone, but it was too dangerous for the incoming helicopter to land. Gassman, now covered in the Afghan's blood, moved the man to a safer landing zone 1,000 meters to the west. Meanwhile, Fox and Miller, who had also made the dangerous climb, were working their way down the mountain. According to the commendation, while Miller carried the body of the 200-pound Frenchman, Fox laid down gunfire to protect his team's sergeant. Struggling under the Frenchman's weight, Miller fell repeatedly, but picked the Frenchman up again and moved forward.

"In risking his own life to recover the fallen French officer, Sergeant Miller demonstrated the resolve and fortitude that exemplifies the spirit of the U.S. Special Forces," his medal citation read. "Throughout their perilous descent, Captain Fox again and again placed himself between his team sergeant and the threat of the voluminous enemy fire." The battle pushed the men to their physical limits, Fox said. "You realize that when you think you're exhausted, you still have a lot more in you," he continued. "You can take your body to greater limits than you think."

I agree with this brave soldier, because even at my age, when I was working with Special Forces, I sometimes dragged myself the best I could, and never knew my own limits as to how far I was going to make it, especially on one of our longest walking missions in the mountains of Ghazni, Urozgan, and Dey Kondi Provinces, where we had to rescue four of our soldiers on the ATVs, which were stuck in the middle of an open field, allowing for an easy ambush. The article also revealed that Admiral James Stavridis, the head of the U.S. European Command (EUCOM), noted during closing remarks at the ceremony, that during the war in Afghanistan some 200,000 medals have been given out. Of those, only about 200 have been Silver Stars. "You saw three Silver Star medals at a single ceremony," Stavridis said. "Those are three out of one-in-a-thousand young men. It's about bringing order out of chaos," Stavridis continued. "It's about saving your comrades and, above all, standing for something larger than yourself."

Afghanistan is a theocratic nation. Whenever anyone tries to solve problems in "theocracy," they wind up with even bigger problems. A good example would be the two most recent incidents that happened that cost the U.S. the lives of our bravest of the brave. The first incident happened on December 30, 2009, in Khost Province when, at the time I was stationed at Camp Clark not too far away from where eight American CIA agents were killed by a Jordanian doctor-turned-suicide bomber who killed seven CIA employees at a base in Afghanistan. According to his wife, he is, of course, regarded by his family as a martyr in the holy war against the United States.

I asked the local Afghans and also those whom we interrogated on numerous occasions while in Afghanistan, why one would become a suicide bomber? Oftentimes, I was told that it's because they're poor and uneducated, so life becomes meaningless to the point that they are willing to die for their cause. Well, my argument would go both ways, especially in the cases regarding the Jordanian doctor, most of the 19 of those who had flown aircrafts into the buildings, and perhaps the next story of Ahmad Gul, an Afghan pilot—all of whom were educated. But even an educated life had no meaning for them; life was only meaningful by becoming a suicide bomber. Well, whether educated or not, it's well beyond my ability to understand how one can become a suicide bomber so they can kill innocent people. My take is that at least the uneducated ones are anxious to blow themselves up to meet the 72 virgins that they have been promised. But why would an educated Jordanian doctor or the Afghan pilot who were married do such a thing? Again, the answer is well above my level of understanding.

Ahmad Gul, the Afghan military pilot, acted alone when he killed eight U.S. airmen and a civilian contractor at the Kabul International Airport in 2011. The Taliban claimed responsibility for the April 27, 2011, shooting by Colonel Ahmad Gul, who died during the attack that also wounded several Afghans. Gul's relative told the media he had been depressed but was not affiliated with terrorists, and coworkers told investigators they didn't believe he had been a religious radical. At least one person interviewed, however, told investigators that Gul had begun to follow the teachings of the Taliban in the 1990s, and he later said that he "wanted to kill Americans." When a crazy person says crazy things like that, they must be taken at face value. In this case, however, Gul ultimately opened fire with his pistol during a morning meeting at the Afghan Air Force Headquarters, shooting each American victim a multiple number of times.

Gul was then shot by "first responders" soon after the attack began. Wounded, he wrote messages in Farsi, including, "God is one," with blood on the walls of the HQ building. He then climbed to a higher floor of the building and killed himself with two gunshots to his torso. Killed in the attack were Major Philip D. Ambard, of Edmonds, Washington; Major Jeffery O. Ausborn, of Gadsden, Alabama; Major David L. Brodeur, of Auburn, Massachusetts; Master Sergeant Tara R. Brown, of Daytona, Florida; Lieutenant Colonel Frank D. Bryant, Jr., of Knoxville, Tennessee; Major Raymond G. Estelle II, of New Haven, Connecticut; Captain Nathan J. Nylander, of Hockley, Texas; Major Charles A. Ransom, of Midlothian,

Virginia; and, James McLaughlin, Jr., of Santa Rosa, California, a retired U.S. Army lieutenant colonel working as a civilian contractor. "These airmen paid the ultimate sacrifice while serving our nation in a combat zone," Air Force Chief of Staff General Norton Schwartz said in a statement accompanying the investigation, "Each of these airmen bravely and purposely performed their duties, and their selfless sacrifices leave behind an honorable legacy that we continue to see in the commitment of airmen who serve as air advisers today."

All of these stories are similar to that of my dear friend, Sergeant First Class Delta2, a medic and ex-Marine who made the ultimate sacrifice; or Sergeant First Class Delta, who was shot five times; and because of the brave and selfless acts of his fellow teammates, Fox and Damon, who saved Delta's life; plus, the thousands of others who have served and protected our nation by not giving up on my native people for their chance for freedom and prosperity, that the Afghan government officials won't even do for their own people.

Each story of the American soldiers had affected me the same way, whether I knew them personally or read about them, because I knew it was all true, just like the Medevac, who are knowingly flying into a hot zone where the enemy can shoot them down, and yet they still risk their lives in order to save the lives of others they don't even know—to me, the most courageous act on the part of our brave soldiers.

The story of Sergeant Nathaniel Dabney is yet another story of bravery. His story reads that, *"No one dies in my aircraft."* One morning, Dabney's crew was first in line to go out on missions. The first call came at 9:15 and was listed as top priority. The patient was a British soldier who had been hit by a concussion grenade. He was loaded onto the aircraft in just his underwear and boots. He has no visible injuries, but he was clearly in pain and scared. Dabney put an oxygen mask over the soldier's face, and then started him on an IV drip. He leaned in close, rubbed the soldier's forehead and told him he'd be okay. The soldier's eyes were shut tight as he motioned for someone to hold his hand, which he wouldn't let go of until the Black Hawk got to Camp Bastion, the main British base in Helmand, about 30 minutes later.

The next "nine-line" message comes in at just after 9:00 PM. Two Afghan soldiers had been wounded in a bomb blast. One of them is dead. U.S. troops have him in a body bag on the darkened helicopter. The surviving soldier has a possible fracture near one of his eyes. Dabney cut open the Afghan's shirt, looking for further wounds, but found none. The soldier's vital signs were stable. Dabney again leaned over, rubbed the soldier's forehead and spoke a few words of comfort, even though the Afghan probably had no idea what he was saying. The soldier laid there calmly, his face etched in pain. Later, when the flight was over, Danbey explained that before he joined the Army four years prior, he spent 12 years working as a paramedic. One of the most important things he learned was that the human touch goes a long way in helping to keep a patient calm—and it can become a source of vulnerability. "Blood and guts don't affect me," he said. "It's the personal bond that you establish with your patient—that's what gets to you." Dabney said he had one rule: *No one dies in my aircraft,* which bears repeating. "So far," he said, "it hasn't happened—but it's probably only a matter of time. It has nothing to do with my skills," he added. "I've just been lucky. I don't know how I'd handle that yet."

Generally speaking, as humans, there is a reason for whatever you want to do in life, and you get to choose how you want to do it. Some of us want to bury our heads in the sand while others (like the United States Armed Forces) move forward and create something special by sacrificing everything they have to make things better for others, just like the next story of a 4-year-old Afghan girl named Azerha whose life was saved by our brave Marines.

Azerha was hit by shrapnel and her brother Qasim did the only thing he could think of—approaching a group of armed Marines miles away and asking for medical assistance. He drove his sister east from near the city of Marjah toward an intersection known as "Five Point," a key intersection of roads connecting northern Marjah with the eastern areas of Helmand Province. Marines and Sailors of Company C, 1st Battalion, 3rd Marine Regiment, seized the Five Point area the day prior, during a helicopter assault. Azerha had been struck in the chest by a fragment of metal from an improvised explosive device (IED) using 82 mm mortar rounds, which detonated near her home.

The wound had caused bleeding and breathing problems for Azerha by the time Navy corpsmen arrived. They examined and began to stabilize her for evacuation to a medical trauma facility. "When the car came and I approached the vehicle, I saw the blood coming from her chest," said Petty Officer 1st Class Eric E. Casasflores, an independent duty corpsman assigned to Company C, 1st Battalion, 3rd Marine Regiment. "I could see there was a small wound where something had penetrated. Once we put the dressing on, she began having more trouble breathing and I determined we needed to do a medical evacuation for her."

While waiting inside the walls of a farming compound for a helicopter to arrive, corpsmen treating Azerha found her lung was beginning to collapse. Between the time her flight was scheduled to arrive and her worsening symptoms, Casasflores, the senior corpsman on the scene, decided they had to act quickly to stabilize their patient. "Her vitals began to drop while we were waiting for the medevac, and we had to do a needle decompression," said Casasflores. "She wasn't bleeding very badly, but with almost any trauma to the chest, you have to do a needle decompression (to allow the lung to expand again). She took it extremely well for a small child," said Petty Officer 3rd Class Adam E. Neep, a field hospital corpsman with Weapons Company, 1st Battalion, 3rd Marine Regiment. "For taking a big needle through her chest, she barely fussed." Once the needle was in, Azerha began to breathe easier, and she and her brother seemed to relax. As Azerha began to stabilize in the open field, the corpsmen decided to move her back into their compound's aid station and redress her wound. They wrapped her in emergency blankets to keep her warm and Neep talked to her through an interpreter to keep her awake and alert to help ward off shock. Only minutes before the helicopter's arrival, Azerha's vitals began to wane again, and Casasflores decided to perform a second decompression. Azerha winced at the momentary pain of the needle but quickly calmed as her vital signs stabilized.

As soon as the helicopter touched down, corpsmen rushed to get Azerha evacuated. Qasim joined his sister on the flight and remained with her throughout her treatment. "The quick reaction from the Marines and corpsmen by getting her the medical evacuation required was what made a huge difference for her," said Casasflores after the helicopter lifted off. "I foresee a good prognosis for her coming back and playing with her brother at home again." For Neep, treating Azerha struck a personal chord with him after she departed. He said seeing the older brother with blood on his clothes, helping his injured sister, made him think of his own sister back home, who was 10 years younger than he. "I'm glad we were here to save her life," said Neep. "If she didn't get the proper medical attention, she would have died. It's that simple." Casasflores credits the success to the

Marines and his corpsmen at the scene. "Our corpsmen did well treating her," said Casasflores. "Everyone stayed calm and things moved smoothly. That's exactly what you want in a trauma situation." Navy medical officers report they performed surgery on Azerha upon her arrival and removed a piece of shrapnel close to her heart. At the time, they expected her to make a full recovery.

Will Democracy and Women's Rights that Our Brave Soldiers Have Sacrificed for in Afghanistan Ever Work?

O NLY IF WE KNOW WHAT WE'RE dealing with. Again, the physician must know the patient's symptoms and family and medical history before treatment. They both should be cooperative with one another, as one without the other would be a loss to both. So far, the Afghan government has taken us into this dark, one-way tunnel and would like to keep us there for as long as they possibly can, especially when it comes to democracy and women's rights. We need to back out of this dark tunnel *(Mythological Afghanistan)* and then find out if there is even a light at the other end. Otherwise, we'll be stuck in this tunnel until we're completely broke and the tunnel collapses so that we all die.

So far, none of the democracy or women's rights' implementations have worked. First, the democracy that we in the West refer to is not suitable for a tribal society like Afghanistan. Furthermore, that tribal men dominate society also does not allow for women's rights since women aren't equal to men not only in the Afghan culture, but as well as the region. Both of these issues are religious in nature, which are against Sharia Islamic Law; at least, that's how this more than 1,000-year-old tribal society seems to be. Whether they're Pashtons, Tajiks, Hazaras, Uzbeks, or any of the other minorities, the majority supports the Taliban for their interpretation of Sharia law, rather than the Afghan government, because of the democracy and human rights' issues. The Taliban are groups of patchwork held together by common religious beliefs, social objectives, and most importantly, an opposition to foreign "occupation" in both Afghanistan and Pakistan.

Most of my natives in the villages are very simple and plain, decent people just like the Americans or other people on earth are. All they know is how to provide for their families by simply farming, most of them just enough to survive, which is the way they have lived their entire lives for centuries. How can we all of a sudden change that, for them to become free from the Taliban oppression and live under the new constitution of the Afghan government, when the government officials don't apply it to their own behavior?

The last time I checked, Afghanistan's elites and students at Kabul University were shouting during a protest against the U.S., NATO, and the Afghan government parliament: "Down with America!" and "Death to the infidels!" and "No democracy; we just want Islam!" This is all going on because of Karzai's own lack of leadership, by following his own administration's newly established constitution. When negotiations in the constitutionalism of the parliament fail, Karzai will then form Loys Jirga (the gathering of tribal elders) to overturn any decision made by parliament. Again, this all takes me back to my milk example. Karzai wants to cater to everyone around him, whether it's the Tajiks, Hazaras, or Uzbeks within his own administration, or the outside powers like the U.S., Pakistan, or today, China. I believe he is probably one of the best "flip-floppers" of our time, and everyone he's fooling is merely going along for the ride. When the world (America, China, Pakistan, European Union) comes to the heels of the Afghan government, it will become a very unstable place.

The constitution of Afghanistan has failed for many reasons, and one concern is the most important: human and women's rights. The law meant to protect Afghan women from a host of abusive practices—including rape, forced marriage, and the trading of women to settle disputes—is being undermined and unenforced. Afghanistan's Law on the Elimination of Violence Against Women was passed in August 2009, raising hope among women's rights' activists that Afghan women would get to fight back against abuses that had been ignored under Taliban rule. The law criminalized many abuses for the first time, including domestic violence, child marriages, driving a woman to resort to suicide, and the trafficking of women.

But who is enforcing that law? Answer: the same people who are breaking it, of course. Well, the Afghan government only pursued a small percentage of reported crimes against women. Between March 2010 and March 2011, the first full Afghan year the law was in effect, prosecutors opened 594 investigations involving crimes that fell under the law. That's only 26 percent of the 2,299 incidents registered by the Afghan Human Rights Commission! And prosecutors went on to file indictments in only 155 cases, or 7 percent of the total number of crimes reported. I'm guessing that it's probably because money has changed hands in a patriarchal Afghan society where women would be punished no matter who was actually guilty of the crime. Sometimes victims were pressured to withdraw their complaints or to settle for mediation by traditional councils. They, of course, want to go to a traditional council, and who makes up the traditional council? The same people who wrote the law, but now they are met so they can be paid for the crime in a different room called the *Reshwat Khana* (the room to pay).

Sometimes prosecutors didn't proceed with mandatory investigations for violent acts like rape or prostitution. Other times, police simply ignored complaints. In one instance in Kandahar in March 2011, a woman reported that her daughter got married, an in-law used the young woman as an unpaid servant, and forced her into having sex with visiting men. She committed suicide by setting herself on fire in her room, and her mother brought the case to the police. The U.N. report indicates that the police recorded the mother's complaint but made no attempt to investigate, even though the law specifies that all cases where a woman is suspected of being driven to kill herself, such as self-immolation, are required to be investigated, even without a complaint.

Before I left Afghanistan, there was the case of a 15-year-old girl from Baghlan province north of Kabul who was being tortured. Sahar Gul had been severely tortured for months by her in-laws in an attempt to force her into prostitution. Her mother- and sisters-in-law were arrested, and her husband of seven months was being sought, revealed Interior Ministry spokesman Sediq Sediqi. The case shocked Afghanistan, though rights' activists say serious abuse against women and girls in the conservative society are common. Karzai also said that whoever used violence against Gul would be punished. Which side of your mouth are you talking out of, Mr. President?

According to officials in northeastern Baghlan Province, Gul was kept in a basement for six months, where her fingernails had been ripped out, she was tortured with hot irons, and her fingers were broken. She was freed from the basement after her uncle called the local police. Her mother-in-law and other members of the family were reportedly involved in what had been described as "criminal activities," which included selling alcohol and prostitution. Despite pressure from the West and human rights' groups in their efforts to convince the Afghan government to do more by rooting out corruption and protecting women's rights, the Afghan government has done little to nothing to enforce this change. Since the fall of the Taliban, billions of dollars, more than 3,000 American/ally troop casualties, and more than a decade later, nothing has been changed.

There is only one way to get rid of some of the problems in my native land, but it sure isn't using the way of this dark tunnel that the West has been taken into by the current Afghan government. If anyone had asked me back in 2009 if the Taliban should ever be given the chance to be involved in the politics of Afghanistan, I would've said, "absolutely not!" But, after spending 33 months there, going from village to village, tribe to tribe, province to province, Pashtons to Tajiks to Hazaras to Uzbeks, and even the only two tribes of Hindus, one Kandahari and the other Kabuli, I have come to the conclusion that the way for the U.S. and the international community to succeed is not by putting our troops on the ground in Afghanistan, hunting for the Taliban (who we will never find). And, before you think that I might be out of my mind for suggesting or even thinking of involving the Taliban (who I personally label as terrorists) back in the government of Afghanistan, especially when not knowing how to separate the minority Taliban terrorists supported by Pakistan from the majority of the Taliban who are the poorest of the poor—most from the Ghilzi Pashton tribes, who simply want to honor God first and then their Pashton tribes because of two of their ancestors: one MKH, who protected his people from being converted from their religion by the Persians, while KKK protected his Pashton land from the Mughal empire of India (current day Pakistan).

Everyone in Afghanistan who lives in the major cities loves us on the surface—remember, after all, we're infidels. For certain, they do love our dollars, but our dollar lovers are not doing us any good, and we need to be loved by those who really need our help so we can get their support. As pointed out earlier in this book, most of the Taliban are Ghilzai, scattered throughout the east, south, and southeast in the villages of Afghanistan alongside the border of Pakistan. Not only do they not wear a uniform to fight us, but their cause to fight is not about defending Afghanistan. Their loyalty to the homeland is displayed through their willingness to defend tribal and personal territory, property, and individuals, just like their ancestors, KKK and MKH, did close to 400 years ago.

A good example would be the detainee with tuberculosis who simply wanted to defend his village by recording propaganda videos to recruit young fighters for his cause. That was the only way he knew how to fight the Americans because they were in his village. Malem in Arghandab is another example of someone who had been willing to defend his home first, his village second, and his District last. How can it be possible to fight people who are willing to die for their cause, doing it for the will of Allah, for which, in return, they will be rewarded in paradise for the rest of their eternal lives. No army in the world (except the Taliban army) would give you this kind of retirement, pension, 401k plan, or whatever else you might want to call it, for your eternal life. Consider, too, that every soldier who fights for this army is doing it for no monetary gain, like the Afghan government does. Since we're in two fights—with the Taliban and the Afghan government in *Mythological Afghanistan*, how is it possible to win the fight? Let's start winning the fight that is in our control, by topping the monetary battle to defeat the Afghan government first, which will then lead us to a much easier fight with the Taliban—or perhaps there'd be no fight at all.

President Karzai's brother was gunned down in Kandahar by another Pashton. It all has to do with money, and as long as money flows into the Afghan government directly, there will be killing amongst the Afghans. But foreigners are involved by running through the villages of Afghanistan; the Afghans will fight them first, then, once the foreign invaders withdraw, we're back to square one: the Ghilzais fighting the Abdalis and Tajiks to reclaim their land, all with the support of the neighborhood's bad boys where the Taliban will rule again on their own, which will stop the fighting and corruption. Fighting is the only game the Ghilzais can play well, and they are known for not being defeated. Abdul Bari told me, just as KKK told the Mughals, and MKH the Persians more than 400 years ago. Anyone with doubt can review the history of Alexander the Great and the Mongols, Persians, Mughals (Pakistan), Soviets (Russians), Ottomans (Turkey), and the British. Corruption, on the other hand, is the only game that the Afghan government (Tajiks and Abdali) plays that no one other than the Ghilzais would understand or know how to fight. So, then, why are we spending all this money and losing 99.999 percent of innocent human lives to play a game that no one has ever succeeded in playing except Pakistan, who fights it not only free of charge, but gets paid at the same time.

Being in the neighborhood for more than 500 years, the Mughals (today's Pakistan) know how to use the Ghilzais for their fighting skills just like the Abdali rulers have used them for more than 200 years. It doesn't get any better than having skilled and committed fighters for free. Why are we in the West too naïve to understand something so simple? Are we so over-educated that our minds don't understand the simple uneducated people like the Ghilzais? As a young boy growing up in Kandahar, I saw not only people fighting amongst themselves, but putting dogs out to fight other dogs, merely for the "entertainment." However, such entertainment wasn't exclusive to dogs; they even had chickens fight chickens, goats fight goats, donkeys fight donkeys, and birds fight birds. Even flying kites were used primarily for the sake of competition, to see who won and who lost. Just as fighting was a passion, it was also a hobby.

Hearts and minds of the local villagers are more important to win than the hearts and minds of the Afghan government, which doesn't possess minds, only hearts, but their hearts are also with the money. The example and strategy I had applied to my very last missions in Arghandab District during our campaign of 2010 to root out the Taliban from their stronghold was not only a welcome strategy from every villager in Ali Kaley, but for our commanders who desperately wanted me to stay with them. They had realized the impact of my understanding of the local population, and the abundance of positive responses we received from the locals. There are two reasons why people responded to me in a positive way, and why my commander and Lieutenant Barron wanted me to stay with them in Sarkari Bagh: (1) understanding the people and (2) understanding what they wanted, not what we wanted for them. On my first visit to Ali Kaley, people realized that they could now talk to someone who could understand them in their native language and they were not only willing to talk and listen, but to trust.

What is it that the Taliban is doing to get the support of the villagers, that we aren't? The reasons for this are simple: (1) the Taliban are not breaking into their homes and stealing from them in the middle of the night, and (2) the Taliban are considered as not only their fellow Pashtons, but fellow Muslims as well. Why would the locals be supporting the Afghan government, who breaks into their homes/shops and steals from them, while the blame is passed on to the Americans? My personal strategy was hitting the Taliban where it hurt the most, for the villagers to not support them, by offering them my own plan to help in the rebuilding of their mosques. As soon as I broke the news to them, Lieutenant Barron and I could see the immediate impact of our proposal. They wanted to work for me, and the majority of the villagers were willing to do the labor for nothing, because it was an honor for them to work on a project associated with their religion. There was so much joy amongst the villagers, Barron couldn't believe that they were willing to work for free, as they had rejected his cash offer. Well, I could understand Barron's reaction. Again, only a native who has no personal self-interest could understand both the Americans and local villagers for the sake of helping both.

I recalled one of the villagers in Ghazni once telling me that one of his fellow villagers asked one of the Taliban representatives during their Juma's prayer, why didn't the Taliban allow the Americans to build schools, clinics, and roads? The representative's response was that the Americans weren't building schools, clinics, and roads to benefit the Pashtons; they were building them to make the villagers' children go to school to get corrupted like everyone else in the city. He said, "Your women go to the clinics so they can be treated by infidels, and the roads are built only so they can drive their tanks on them, so eventually one day the Muslim land can become an infidel country, God forbid." This is how we have been portrayed to the villagers by the Taliban. If the Taliban's message was the same in Ghazni, it was the same in Ali Kaley and every other village throughout Afghanistan. I was proving to the villagers that by rebuilding their mosques, the Americans weren't in their country to convert them from their religious beliefs. Well, none of what I had planned to do in Ali Kaley was ever implemented because I wasn't allowed to stay in Sarkari Bagh.

Not only has my plan for Ali Kaley left a false-promise image of me in the villagers' minds, but I also wasn't able to help Malem build the school for his village, where he wanted to teach. Sometimes decisions are made not by people who are in the field seeing things firsthand like I and our commanders who saw a positive response from the local villagers. But with people not being on the ground to see things firsthand, who are only concerned with the politics in Karzai's government (like our high-ranking officials who have no idea what really goes on in the field), both of the options that the West is pursuing in Afghanistan, staying to fight or pack and leave, will not only fail miserably, but could also be disastrous and result in a civil war once the withdrawal of U.S. forces from Afghanistan in 2014 occurs.

We trained three different security forces in Afghanistan: the ANA, ANP, and NDS—agencies that hate each other, just like all the tribes do in Afghanistan. Every time we went on a mission, and if we had both the ANP and ANA with us on the same mission, half of the time Americans would focus on them more they did on the bad guys to stop them from killing each other or stealing from the locals. In addition to the three security forces, who are directly working under the command of the Afghan Defense Ministry, there's a fourth group of fighters called the *Arbakayian* (local militias), who are supplied and armed by the U.S. and fight independently from the Afghan Defense Ministry to protect their own village and territory. Depending on the situation, they can switch their pledge of allegiance to either the government or the Taliban in a matter of hours.

Most of the local militias can also be the Taliban. However they're referred to—for instance, Taliban, Mujahedeen, terrorists, insurgents, ISI, or any other name that could apply—they will always be mostly Ghilzais and will fight to their death like Abdul Bari, if need be—not for Afghanistan, but for their faith and individual freedom. The West is constantly in conflict with each other as well but, because of their education, their fight is at the ballot box. People in Afghanistan will always fight with their boxes of bullets, whether those bullets come from the ISI, KGB, CIA, or soon, the Chinese. Who fights over Afghanistan is not the question at hand. My question is: Why is it fair to the two thirds of the population (who are victims of circumstance and have done nothing wrong? Is it wise to fight people (Taliban) who we can't even identify but who will eventually win because time is on their side? Or, is it wise to take the time and think about what's in the best interests of not only the region, but society as a whole. It's better to bring them to join in on our democracy than to go back to their darkness, as we have already witnessed. Remember who supported the Taliban, our allies: Saudi Arabia and Pakistan, which do not represent either democracy or women's rights.

What and Who Are the Taliban?

ELL, THE ANSWER TO THE above question is simple, albeit very complicated, not only for our military personnel who serve our great nation, but also for every American in the U.S. as well as the rest of the world. (1) *Talib* is singular and refers to a student. (2) *Taliban* is plural and refers to students. Everyone, either in the military or civilians, Americans, or any other nationality that I met or worked with during my time in Afghanistan, refers to (2) as the Taliban (or Talib), whether one or more people, which is incorrect, especially with the locals when Americans refer to them as being Taliban. On one occasion, one of our detainees, who couldn't even speak or understand English, got very offended for being called a member of the Taliban rather than a Talib. Now that I have described what the word Talib and Taliban means, let's go a little farther to explain who they really are.

For many centuries, since intellectual education was nonexistent in Afghanistan, or perhaps even until the 1940s or 1950s—and in most cases, even today—in Afghanistan and the eastern tribal areas of Pakistan, most people still don't send their children to schools, but, then, if there aren't any what other choice do they have? I realize [now] that everyone is not like my adoptive father who valued education so much he homeschooled, or my cousin Malem, who was willing to teach at a school. Most people sent their children to the village mosque to be taught and fulfill their religious obligation to be true Muslims just like the cheater barber and his younger brother. There were two types of people who sent their children to the mosques. Those who were wealthy enough (Abdalis) to put food on the table, sent their children to the mosque to avoid being criticized by their tribal society. The poor (Ghilzai) sent their children, not only to learn about their religion, but as well as to provide a single meal for their family by permanently becoming a Talib in the mosque under the supervision of the Mullah where, just like in any other profession, the Talib will eventually become a Mullah himself one day.

What's required for one to become a Talib? Well, the poorer you are, the more committed you are to move into the mosque, not only by helping the Mullah teach the children, but also taking care of the mosque as the House of God by doing anything and everything to keep it all in order. The larger the village, the larger the congregation—the larger the overhead for the Mullah to run the mosque, which required more Taliban. Since most people were poor, the only thing they could do to help the Mullah and the Taliban was to donate food to the mosque. To collect the food items, the Mullah would send a couple of the Taliban late in the afternoon to different parts of the village or city, since dinner was the only meal that most Afghans from the various homes ate. The food items consisted of mostly one or two flat Afghan bread or equaled value in cash, depending on the household's generosity. The more children who became Taliban so they could take the lead to teach newcomers and collect more items from homes, the less work for the Mullah.

During my time growing up in Kandahar City, our neighborhood mosque was very large with more than one Mullah to lead every prayer, and many more members of the Taliban compared to the mosque in Arghandab. Daily, I would see a couple of our mosque's Taliban selling the bread (collecting from the homes the night before), standing on street corners to get as much cash as they could to use for their other expenses, like buying clothes for the Taliban for the once or twice a year religious holiday, or for helping homeless people (who showed up on the steps of the mosque) with food or the medications they needed. Aside from everything they did for the mosque—from running its daily operation to teaching the children—they (the Mullah and the Taliban) would oftentimes settle civil disputes between the villagers for free instead of the villagers having to go to the government. This, of course, all changed after the Soviet invasion, when all of the wealthy Abdalis and Tajiks from the cities were exiled; plus, most of the Mullahs left for Pakistan to escape being killed by the Godless Soviets. The only people left were the poor Ghilzais, Tajiks, and Hazaras, who were slaughtered by the Soviets from time to time.

As the war with the Soviets intensified, with the help of the CIA and ISI, most of the Mullahs who moved from Afghanistan to Pakistan were convinced to fight the Godless Soviets to protect not Afghanistan, but Islam, which would make the fight and argument stronger for the ISI and CIA to get as much help not only from every mosque in Afghanistan to send every Talib to the fight (Jihad) for Allah, but from the Arab world as well. Most who fought the Soviets were Ghilzai Pashtons from both sides of the border between Afghanistan and Pakistan, while they were all camped out in western Pakistan on Pashton land. The movement that fought the Soviets was called *Mujahedeen* (protectors of Islam), no matter their ethnicity or nationality. This movement created many different warlords amongst the ethnic groups from Afghanistan. Each fought their own battles and gathered their own tribes, for the single purpose of defending Islam. Since money was no object for the CIA, the different groups of Afghan warlords controlled their own militias on all different fronts and every Ghilzai Pashton fought the war for Allah, not for the multitudes, while their leaders (Rabbani, Hekmatyar, Masoud, Abdulhaq, and the Palestinian Arab Yusuf Azzam, who also recruited Osama Bin Laden to join the fight) kept all the money for themselves. As money was raised and fighters were recruited from all the Arab gulf states, a rich, tall Arab man by the name of Osama Bin Laden had shown up to fight the Jihad.

Fortunately, the war was won and the Soviets were gone; so, since Afghan society doesn't allow foreigners, Bin Laden and the Arabs returned either to their homeland or countries in East Africa that were ruled by dictators who would allow Bin Laden to stay. However, on the border of Afghanistan and Pakistan, guess who was still there? Yes—the ISI and Ghilzai Pashtons. The ISI didn't do anything for a couple of years after the Soviets' withdrawal from Afghanistan until the Tajik rulers, Rabani and Masoud, took control of Kabul, as the warlords fought over Kabul for power, killing more than 50 thousand people, mostly the innocent Tajiks. Now, a whole new game was being coordinated by the same experienced coach (ISI) and quality players.

Since most people, not only in Kabul but throughout Afghanistan, were sick and tired that their own people (the former mujahedeen) were now killing them in mass numbers greater than the Soviets had done, they were simply asking for peace from bombs being dropped on them on a daily basis, even if that peace was brought to them by the Mullah Omar himself. He, being a Mujahedeen, left for his home village in Kandahar to be what he had a passion to be—a Mullah to his Taliban. Since Mullah Omar simply fought jihad and didn't have an interest in power like all of the other warlords, the ISI knew if the Tajiks were to take charge of "Kabul Jan," chances were that the Ghilzai Pashtons might be preceded by the Tajiks to bring up the issues of Pshtonistan (land of the Pashtons), which was two thirds occupied by Pakistan. With the support of Saudi Arabia, UAE and Pakistan, Mullah Omar had taken the banner of the Taliban to defeat all the other groups who fought for the power of money; however, Mullah Omar and his Taliban soldiers (40 thousand) took control of 90 percent of Afghanistan with little to no major resistance. Furthermore, ISI did not spend any money to pay the Ghilzais Pashtons to fight. All they had to do was convince the Ghilzais that the Tajiks were not entitled to their land, and the Ghilzais fought barefooted, with only bread and water to sustain them, just like their ancestors KKK and MKH did. So, whether you call them Mujahedeen or Taliban, it will only confuse you more. If you call them Ghilzai Pashtons, chances are you would understand them—I'm not saying literally understanding them (i.e., their mindsets) as they speak Pashto with you. For that, you might need my help to translate, which I would be more than honored to do!

One last question that I don't even have the answer for: Are the Taliban Muslims by the book? Well, as I said, I don't know the answer to that question but *can* say that they were supported by both of our allies, Saudi Arabia and Pakistan. I can understand why Pakistan supported them, but why did Saudi Arabia do so as well? One other important point in regards to whether the Taliban are Muslims by the book or not. One thing I learned during my time interrogating them. In their mind, you're either Muslim by the book like they're, or not Muslim at all.

My work as a translator, interpreter, linguist, culture adviser, or whatever else one may prefer to call it, was very eye-opening for me. I preferred to be called Nas because all of my buddies in Special Forces called me that, which brings back memories to last a lifetime. There were good days during my work, where people were compassionate towards one another, whether they were my fellow Americans or my fellow natives, which would make me cry from the joy of it all, But then, of course, there were other days where people would make me sad for doing things for their own personal self-interests with no concern for others, whether they were my fellow Americans or my fellow natives (which also made me very angry). Additionally, there were also days that made me laugh at the expense of other linguists for their misinterpretations so (they thought) Americans would appear as being honorable to the local villagers.

For example: An American Army Captain had once left his remote COP to visit with a village elder to see what kind of help their village needed. He had a local Afghan interpreter with him. As is the norm in Afghanistan, the elder offered the captain and his soldiers tea, an offer that the captain accepted. At the end of their meeting, the captain, through his local interpreter, thanked the village elder and expressed his appreciation for the elder's hospitality. However, the linguist (who only spoke and understood very limited, broken English) translated the captain's words to the villager elder. When the Captain and the interpreter left, the village elder as well as the other villagers who had gathered around, had big smiles on their faces as the elder thanked the captain once again for his visit. Having been so warmly welcomed, the captain left, very happy by how the villagers had received him with such warm enthusiasm.

Well, a while back, a newly arrived lieutenant wanted to visit that same village to see if he could win the hearts and minds of the locals, much the same as what I did in Argahandab. This time, the linguist was a bit better with his English translation abilities than the last linguist who had visited the village with the Captain.

Upon their arrival at the village, no one wanted to talk with them. Well, they finally found the village elder, and as soon as he approached, the lieutenant attempted to extend his hand so he could shake the elder's hand in greeting. But the elder opened his mouth and spoke with rage in his voice, telling the lieutenant, "You lying Americans are not welcome in my village." As the interpreter translated the elder's words to the lieutenant, he was shocked to hear the elder making such a comment with so much venom in his voice, and said, "I've never been here before and not even had the chance to offer you anything as yet." The elder told the lieutenant that an American had come to the village a while back and promised to build a hospital. He made it perfectly clear to the lieutenant that he didn't want to listen to what he had to say and/or offer.

Well, my dear readers, it was very important to me personally to be as accurate as much as I possibly could when writing this book, because I know how critically important it can be to mistranslate a simple word of gratitude from the American captain to a once-in-a-lifetime dream come true for the elder because of the Cedar Sanai Hospital that was built in his villa.

~ The End ~

References

Articles used with permission:

Stars and Stripes © (2009–2014)

- July 25, 2009

- June 14, 2010

- December 14, 2010

- October 11, 2011

- December 7, 2011

- January 18, 2012

Wikipedia (www.wikipedia.org) throughout the book

Glossary

****:	Team numbers, which I am not authorized to publish
ANA:	Afghan National Army
ANP:	Afghan National Police
AROCC:	Afghanistan Remote Operation Cryptologic Center
ASF:	Afghan Security Forces (includes ANA, ANP, NDS)
COP:	Command Outpost
DFAC:	Dining Facility
FDS:	Field Detention Site
FOB:	Forward Operation Base
ISAF:	International Security Assistance Force (NATO)
ISI:	Inter-Services Intelligence (Pakistan)
JTAC:	Joint Tactical Air Controller
LLVI:	Lower Level Voice Interception
MWR:	Morale Welfare Recreation
NDS:	National Defense Services (Afghan)
ODA:	Operational Detachment Alpha (Standard Special Forces 12-Man Team)
POC:	Point of Contact
PRT:	Provincial Reconstruction Team
PTO:	Personal Time Off
SFC:	Sergeant First Class
TDY:	Temporary Duty